Communications
in Computer and Information Science 90

Natarajan Meghanathan   Selma Boumerdassi
Nabendu Chaki   Dhinaharan Nagamalai (Eds.)

Recent Trends
in Networks
and Communications

International Conferences
NeCoM 2010, WiMoN 2010, WeST 2010
Chennai, India, July 23-25, 2010
Proceedings

 Springer

Volume Editors

Natarajan Meghanathan
Jackson State University, Jackson, MS, USA
E-mail: nmeghanathan@jsums.edu

Selma Boumerdassi
CNAM / CEDRIC, Paris, France
E-mail: selma.boumerdassi@cedric.fr

Nabendu Chaki
University of Calcutta, India
E-mail: nchaki@gmail.com

Dhinaharan Nagamalai
Wireilla Net Solutions PTY Ltd, Australia
E-mail: dhinthia@yahoo.com

Library of Congress Control Number: 2010930431

CR Subject Classification (1998): C.2, H.4, H.3, D.2, H.5, I.2

ISSN	1865-0929
ISBN-10	3-642-14492-6 Springer Berlin Heidelberg New York
ISBN-13	978-3-642-14492-9 Springer Berlin Heidelberg New York

springer.com

© Springer-Verlag Berlin Heidelberg 2010
Printed in Germany

Typesetting: Camera-ready by author, data conversion by Scientific Publishing Services, Chennai, India
Printed on acid-free paper   06/3180   5 4 3 2 1 0

Preface

The Second International Conference on Networks and Communications (NeCoM 2010), the Second International Conference on Wireless and Mobile Networks (WiMoN 2010), and the Second International Conference on Web and Semantic Technology (WeST 2010) were held in Chennai, India, during July 23–25, 2010. They attracted many local and international delegates, presenting a balanced mixture of intellects from the East and from the West.

The goal of these conferences is to bring together researchers and practitioners from academia and industry to focus on understanding computer networks, wireless networks, mobile networks and the Web, semantic technologies and to establish new collaborations in these areas. Authors are invited to contribute to the conference by submitting articles that illustrate research results, projects, survey work and industrial experiences describing significant advances in the areas of all computer networks and Semantic Web technologies.

The NeCoM 2010, WiMoN 2010 and WeST 2010 committees rigorously invited submissions for many months from researchers, scientists, engineers, students and practitioners related to the relevant themes and tracks of the workshop. This effort guaranteed submissions from an unparalleled number of internationally recognized top-level researchers. All the submissions underwent a strenuous peer-review process which comprised expert reviewers. These reviewers were selected from a talented pool of Technical Committee members and external reviewers on the basis of their expertise. The papers were then reviewed based on their contributions, technical content, originality and clarity. The entire process, which includes the submission, review and acceptance processes, was done electronically. All these efforts undertaken by the Organizing and Technical Committees led to an exciting, rich and a high-quality technical conference program, which featured high-impact presentations for all attendees to enjoy, appreciate and expand their expertise in the latest developments in computer network and communications research.

The book is organized as a collection of papers from the NeCoM 2010 WiMoN 2010 and WeST 2010 conferences, the First International Workshop on Ad Hoc, Sensor and Ubiquitous Computing (ASUC 2010) and The First International Workshop on VLSI (VLSI 2010).

In closing, NeCoM 2010, WiMoN 2010 and WeST 2010 brought together researchers, scientists, engineers, students and practitioners to exchange and share their experiences, new ideas and research results in all aspects of the main workshop themes and tracks, and to discuss the practical challenges encountered and the solutions adopted. We would like to thank the General and Program Chairs, organization staff, the members of the Technical Program Committees and external reviewers for their excellent and tireless work. We also want to thank Springer for the strong support and the authors who contributed to the success of the conference. We also sincerely wish that all attendees benefited scientifically from the conference and wish them every success in their research.

It is the humble wish of the conference organizers that the professional dialogue among the researchers, scientists, engineers, students and educators continues beyond the event and that the friendships and collaborations forged will linger and prosper for many years to come.

Natarajan Meghanathan
Nabendu Chaki
Selma Boumerdassi
Dhinaharan Nagamalai

Organization

General Chairs

Jan Zizka	SoNet/DI FBE, Mendel University in Brno, Czech Republic
Hwangjun Song	Pohang University of Science and Technology, South Korea
S.K. Ghosh	Indian Institute of Technology, Kharagpur, India
David C. Wyld	Southeastern Louisiana University, USA
Selwyn Piramuthu	University of Florida, USA

Steering Committee

Jacques Demerjian	CS, Homeland Security, France
Sriman Narayana Iyengar	VIT University, India
Doina Bein	The Pennsylvania State University, USA
A.P. Sathish Kumar	PSG Institute of Advanced Studies, India
Shamala Subramaniam	Universiti Putra Malaysia (UPM), Malaysia

Program Committee Members (NeCoM 2010)

Augusto Neto	Telecommunication Institute (IT) of Aveiro, Portugal
Doina Bein	The Pennsylvania State University, USA
Xiliang Zhong	Mircrosoft Corp, USA
Wang Wei,	Beijing University of Posts and Telecommunications, China
Qin Xin	Simula Research Laboratory, Norway
Ma Maode	Nayang Technical University, Singapore
Natarajan Meghanathan	Jackson State University, USA
Jae Kwang Lee	Hannam University, South Korea
Jung-Gil Song	Hannam University, South Korea
Jungwook Song	Konkuk University, South Korea
SunYoung Han	Konkuk University, South Korea
Paul D. Manuel	Kuwait University, Kuwait
Dhinaharan Nagamalai	The American University, Cyprus
Abdul Kadhir Ozcan	The American University, Cyprus
Nabendu Chaki	University of Calcutta, India
Robert C. Hsu	Chung Hua University, Taiwan
Yeong Deok Kim	Woosong University, South Korea
Balasubramanian Karuppiah	MGR University, India

N. Krishnan	Manonmaniam Sundaranar University, India
Dhinaharan	Wireilla Net Solutions Inc., India
Jose Enrique Armendïriz-Inigo	Universidad Publica de Navarra, Spain
David W Deeds	Shingu College, South Korea
Henrique Joïo Lopes Domingos	University of Lisbon, Portugal
Jung-Gil Song	Hannam University, South Korea
Jungwook Song	Konkuk University, South Korea
SunYoung Han	Konkuk University, South Korea
Andy Seddon	Asia Pacific Institute of Information Technology, Malaysia
Bong-Han, Kim	Chongju University, South Korea
Cho Han Jin	Far East University, South Korea
Ramayah Thurasamy	Universiti Sains Malaysia, Malaysia
Ponpit Wongthongtham	Curtin University of Technology, Australia
Prabu Dorairaj	Wipro Technologies, India
Yannick Le Moullec	Aalborg University, Denmark
Hwangjun Song	Pohang University of Science and Technology, South Korea
Sarmistha Neogy	Jadavpur University, India
Marco Roccetti	Universty of Bologna, Italy
Jan Zizka	SoNet/DI, FBE, Mendel University in Brno, Czech Republic
Phan Cong Vinh	London South Bank University, UK
Jacques Demerjian	Communication & Systems, France
Doina Bein	The Pennsylvania State University, USA
Sattar B. Sadkhan	University of Babylon, Iraq
Jabber selman Aziz	University of AlNahrain, Iraq
Hikmat N. Abdullah	AlMustansyria University, Iraq
Sabu M. Thampi	Rajagiri School of Engineering and Technology, India

Program Committee Members (WiMoN 2010)

A. Arokiasamy	Eastern Mediterranean University, Cyprus
Rajesh Kumar P.	The Best International, Australia
Jeong-Hyun Park	Electronics Telecommunication Research Institute, South Korea
H.V. Ramakrishnan	MGR University, India
Balasubramanian K.	Lefke European University, Cyprus
Paul D. Manuel	Kuwait University, Kuwait
Nabendu Chaki	University of Calcutta, India
Yeong Deok Kim	Woosong University, South Korea
Yun Ji Na	AICIT, Dongkuk University, South Korea
Franz Ko	Dongkuk University, South Korea
Dhinaharan Nagamalai	The American University, Cyprus
Abdul Kadir Ozcan	The American University, Cyprus

Andy Seddon	Asia Pacific Institute of Information Technology, Malaysia
Bong-Han, Kim	Chongju University, South Korea
Cho Han Jin	Far East University, South Korea
David W. Deeds	Shingu College, South Korea
Farhat Anwar	International Islamic University, Malaysia
Girija Chetty	University of Canberra, Australia
Natarajan Meghanathan	Jackson State University, USA
Paul D. Manuel	Kuwait University, Kuwait
Phan Cong Vinh	London South Bank University, UK
Rakhesh Singh Kshetrimayum	Indian Institute of Technology, Guwahati, India
Ramayah Thurasamy	Universiti Sains Malaysia, Malaysia
Sarmistha Neogy	Jadavpur University, India
Sudha N.	SKR Engineering College, India
SunYoung Han	Konkuk University, South Korea
Thandeeswaran R.	VIT University, India
Yannick Le Moullec	Aalborg University, Denmark
Yeong Deok Kim	Woosong University, South Korea
Boo-Hyung Lee	KongJu National University, South Korea
Yun Ji Na	AICIT, Dongkuk University, South Korea
Franz Ko	Dongkuk University, South Korea
Cynthia Dhinakaran	Hannam University, South Korea
Ho Dac Tu	Waseda University, Japan
John Karamitsos	University of the Aegean, Greece
Johnson Kuruvila	Dalhousie University, Canada
Jose Enrique Armendariz-Inigo	Universidad Publica de Navarra, Spain
Johann Groschdl	University of Bristol, UK
Ford Lumban Gaol	University of Indonesia
Susana Sargento	University of Aveiro, Portugal
Khoa N. Le	Griffith School of Engineering, Australia
Geuk Lee	Hannam University, South Korea
Chih-Lin Hu	National Central University, Taiwan
Solange Rito Lima	University of Minho, Portugal
Debasis Giri	Haldia Institute of Technology, India
Shubhalaxmi Kher	Arkansas State University, USA

Program Committee Members (WeST 2010)

Robert C. Hsu	Chung Hua University, Taiwan
Abdul Kadir Ozcan	The American University, Cyprus
A. Arokiasamy	Eastern Mediterranean University, Cyprus
Andy Seddon	Asia Pacific Institute of Information Technology, Malaysia
Balasubramanian K.	Lefke European University, Cyprus
Balasubramanian Karuppiah	MGR University, India

Athanasios Vasilakos	University of Western Macedonia, Greece
Yuh-Shyan Chen	National Taipei University, Taiwan
Chih-Lin Hu	National Central University, Taiwan
Hanh H. Hoang	Hue University, Vietnam
Lei (Leon) Shu	National University of Ireland, Ireland
Chih-Lin Hu	National Central University, Taiwan
Serguei Mokhov	Concordia University, Canada
Chih-Lin Hu	National Central University, Taiwan
Seungmin Rho	Carnegie Mellon University, USA
Emmanuel Bouix	iKlax Media, France

Organized By

ACADEMY & INDUSTRY RESEARCH COLLABORATION CENTER (AIRCC)

Table of Contents

The Second International Conference on Networks and Communications (NeCoM 2010)

Second International Conference on Wireless and Mobile Networks (WiMoN 2010)

Second International Conference on Web and Semantic Technology (WeST 2010)

First International Workshop on Ad Hoc, Sensor and Ubiquitous Computing (ASUC 2010)

First International Workshop on VLSI (VLSI 2010)

Improving TCP Performance over Wireless Networks Using Cross Layer

Sathya Priya S. and Murugan K.

Ramanujan Computing Centre, Anna University Chennai
Chennai, Tamil Nadu, India
sathyapriya80@yahoo.co.in, murugan@annauniv.edu

Abstract. The rapidly increasing importance of wireless communications together with the rapid growth of high speed networks, pose new challenges to transmission control protocol (TCP). To overcome them, a wide variety of TCP enhancements has been presented in the literature with different purposes and capabilities. Cross-layering represents a perspective design principle for adapting natively wired protocols to the wireless scenario and for improving their performance. In this paper, a novel cross-layer approach (Link Layer CLAMP –TCP [L^2CLAMP-TCP]) designed for performance enhancement of TCP over a large variety of wireless networks is proposed. L^2CLAMP-TCP avoids TCP Acknowledgement (ACK) packet transmission over the wireless channel, thereby saving time, which can be utilized by the nodes for data packet delivery. The TCP Acknowledgement is generated at the base station itself. The congestion measure is also calculated at the base station based on which the receiver advertised window is calculated. The protocol performance is compared with existing TCP New Reno and TCP New Reno with CLAMP.

Keywords: Advertised Window, Automatic Repeat Request, Congestion Control, Cross-layering, Performance Enhancement.

1 Introduction

TCP is a connection oriented byte stream transport protocol. The problem of TCP over wireless networks is that wireless links have different characteristics with respect to wired ones, in terms of less reliability, fading / shadowing problems, node mobility, handoffs, limited available bandwidth and large Round Trip Time (RTTs).

In wireless networks, TCP reaction to frequent packet losses severely limits the congestion window and thus underestimates the capacity of the networks. To prevent congestion loss, an active queue management is required to avoid buffer overflow and also a fair scheduling is necessary to allocate bandwidth. The latest trend is having scheduled service at the Base Station (BS) / Access Point (AP) i.e., the traditional first come first served (FCFS) is replaced by a set of queues with a scheduler allocating the capacity between different streams.

This paper presents a novel cross-layer approach, called Link Layer Clamp- TCP (L^2 CLAMP-TCP), where the acknowledgement at the receiver is suppressed and is generated at the base station. The congestion measure is also calculated at the base station and is attached with the acknowledgement.

N. Meghanathan et al. (Eds.): NeCoM, WiMoN, and WeST 2010, CCIS 90, pp. 1–10, 2010.

2   Related Work

A useful survey of TCP enhancements for wireless networks is provided in [3]. Most work on TCP over wireless channels had focused on the issue of packet loss, its detrimental effect on TCP [4], [5], and the mechanisms at layers 1 and 2 to reduce packet loss rates [6], [7], [8], [9], [10], [11]. Retransmissions can also be handled at layer 4 [12].TCP ACK transmission over the wireless link can be avoided through local generation of ACKs at the sender node or at the base station, thus improving throughput. [1] A protocol CLAMP was suggested [2] on the receiver side and provides a separate queue at the AP. The CLAMP protocol removes the window fluctuations and achieves much better fairness than TCP New Reno.

3   TCP New Reno and CLAMP

TCP New Reno is able to detect multiple packet losses and thus is more efficient than Reno in the event of multiple packet losses. New-Reno enters into fast-retransmit when it receives multiple duplicate packets, but it differs from Reno in that it doesn't exit fast-recovery until all the data which was out standing at the time it entered fast recovery is acknowledged.

CLAMP algorithm controls the receiver Advertised Window (AWND) based on feedback from the access point. This algorithm runs at the mobile device and ACKs are sent back to the sender containing the new values of AWND as calculated by CLAMP. Since all versions of TCP interpret the AWND as an upper limit on the allowable window size, which is a mechanism to avoid an overflow of the receiver buffer, this provides an effective method of control provided that the AWND value is smaller than the CWND value calculated by the sender.

4   The Proposed Protocol (L^2 CLAMP- TCP)

4.1 L^2CLAMP Architecture

The proposed scheme enhances the protocol stacks of the wireless sender (or a base station /Access Point) and the receiver with L^2CLAMP agents which support ACK suppression. The network scenario taken is infra-structure based with four different senders S1, S2, S3and S4 and three mobile nodes MN1, MN2 and MN3.

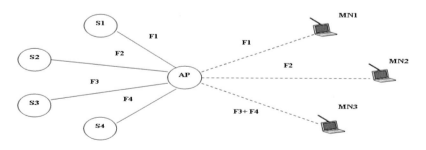

Fig. 1. Infrastructure WLAN Model

Figure 1 shows four different flows F1, F2, F3 and F4. The flow F1is between S1 and MN1 and F2 is between S2 and MN2. F3 and F4 start from sources S3 and S4 respectively and reaches the same mobile node MN3 (shared flow).

The L²CLAMP agent suppresses the outgoing L²CLAMP -TCP ACKs at the receiver side and generates them locally at the sender or base station. The basic idea behind approach is to shift TCP ACK generation point from mobile receiver to the base station. L²CLAMP -TCP requires implementation of a software module, called L²CLAMP agent, inside BS / AP protocol stack above the link layer. The L²CLAMP agent sniffs the ingress traffic from the fixed network assuming to have access to the network and transport layer headers. Whenever a TCP data packet is detected, the L²CLAMP Agent in the BA / AP, performs service rate, congestion measurement, received rate and calculates the AWND value, stores flow-related information such as flow sequence number carried by the packet, port numbers, ACK flag and ACK sequence number, along with the AWND value. L²CLAMP agent calculates the desired size of the AWND window based on the values of congestion measure, received rate and RTT. To calculate congestion measure, a separate Sync packet is sent from the base station to the receiver and the acknowledgement for the Sync is received back by the sender, based on which the transmission time for each packet is calculated. This is done before actual TCP packet transmission. The parameters used for calculation of congestion measure is b, q,α μ_c

$$p(q) = (bq - \alpha) / \mu_c \qquad (1)$$

where b = 1 for safer purpose. τ is the parameter (fixed size in bytes) used to calculate the value of AWND and α is used to calculate the congestion price signal. Similarly α is free to be chosen by the AP, but is fixed once chosen.

On the receiver side, module referred as L²CLAMP client in Figure 2 silently drops all standalone non-duplicate TCP ACK packets. The generated TCP ACK packet is then forwarded to the sender. The AP maintains a separate queue for each receiver and acts as a router, routing the packets to the destined MN. The TCP flows destined for the respective MN are put into the same queue.

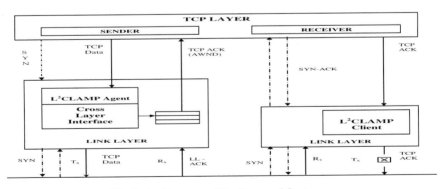

Fig. 2. Architecture of the Proposed System

In the scenario taken, a separate queue is maintained for flows F1 and F2 as they are destined to different mobile nodes MN1 and MN2. The flows F3 and F4 share a same queue as they are destined to the same mobile receiver MN3. A scheduler incorporated in the access point takes care of scheduling the two flows. The scheduler is based on the principle of multi-user diversity. At each slot, a new scheduling decision is made, and the general preference is for scheduling a mobile that is in a good channel state. At each slot, the scheduler picks the queue i with the largest utility that has data to send in this slot. The utility U_i is calculated as

$$U_i = \mu_i / r_i \tag{2}$$

μ_i is the current rate for the mobile 'i' at the beginning of the slot and r_i is the exponential moving average of the rate obtained by mobile- i with an averaging time constant of 100 ms.

4.2 Algorithm

Receive New Data Packet from Network
If (Data Packet == TCP) then
    Generate a TCP Acknowledgement with the respective fields.
    Store it in the buffer.
    Calculate the Congestion measure.
    $p_s(q)= \max((q-a)/\mu_c , 0)$ (3)
    Calculate the AWND window size

$$\mu^*(t_k) = \frac{\sum_{i=k=\alpha}^{k} S_i}{\left(t_k - t_{k-1}\right)} \tag{4}$$

$$\Delta w(t_k) = \frac{r - p(q(t_k))\mu^*(t_k)}{d^*(t_k)}\left(t_k - t_{k-1}\right) \tag{5}$$

    if $(\Delta w(t_k) < 0)$ or (3 Duplicate ACK's)

        Stop Slow start

        Set w $(t_k +1) = w (t_k) / 2$

    endif

    AWND $(t_k) \cong \min (w (t_k), AWND)$ (6)
    Add the information to the Stored ACK Buffer.
    Forward the TCP Data Packet for Transmission
    Wait for Link Layer Acknowledgement
    if (LL-ACK received==yes) then
        Pop the generated ACK from the buffer and transmit to the sender
    else
        Drop the ACK generated stored in the buffer.
    end if
else
    Forward the packet to the wireless node.
end if

where q is the current value of moving average, t_k is time instant of kth packet when received by MN, $\Delta w(t_k)$ is the change in window size, α, β are smoothing factors, AWND (t_k) is the actual Window size, d^* is the RTT of the flow in seconds(propagation delay + queuing delay), μ_c is the service rate of a queue, d is the propagation delay and q(t) is calculated as τ / b (amount of flow in bytes).

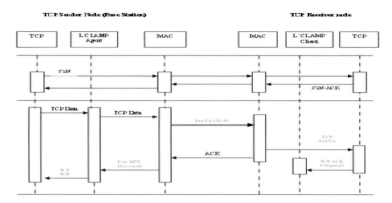

Fig. 3. Sequence of Process for Packet Delivery

5   Performance Evaluation

To observe how TCP performance is influenced by our L^2CLAMP approach, it is compared with existing TCP New Reno and TCP New Reno with CLAMP. The simulation is carried out with Network Simulator (ns-2) with a transmission range of 75 m, packet size of 250 to 1250 bytes, queue delay of 100 to 150ms, simulation time of 50 to 200s, bandwidth of 0.5Mbytes/s and a propagation delay of 20ms.

5.1   Analysis by Varying Queue Delay

Figure 4. shows that the queue delay is varied between 100ms and 150ms with a packet size of 1250 bytes and a simulation time of 200 secs.

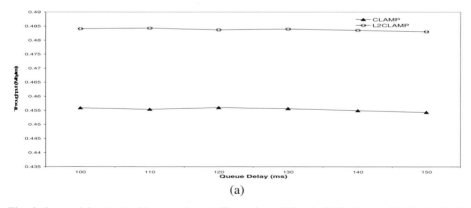

(a)

Fig. 4. Queue delay (ms) with respect to (a) Throughput (Mbps), (b) End-to-end Delay (ms), (c) Throughput per flow (Mbps), (d) Throughput (shared)

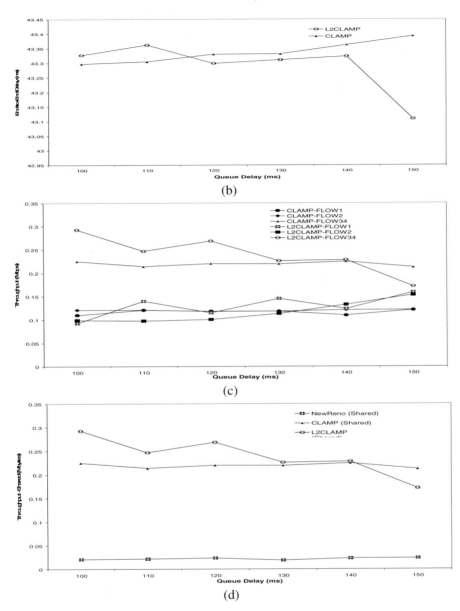

Fig. 4. (*continued*)

The inference made from Figure 4 is that throughput of L^2CLAMP is approximately 6% higher than that of CLAMP. The end-to-end delay of L^2CLAMP is very less when compared to that of CLAMP. The throughput for individual flows F1 and F2 as well as the combined flow F3+F4 of L^2CLAMP shows considerable improvement in performance when compared to that of CLAMP. The throughput of shared flow for CLAMP is approximately 8 times higher when compared to that of New Reno and performance of L^2CLAMP is nearly twice better than that of CLAMP.

5.2   Throughput Analysis by Varying Packet Size

Figure 5 shows that the packet size is varied between 250 bytes and 1250 bytes with a
Queue delay of 150 ms and a simulation time of 200 sec.

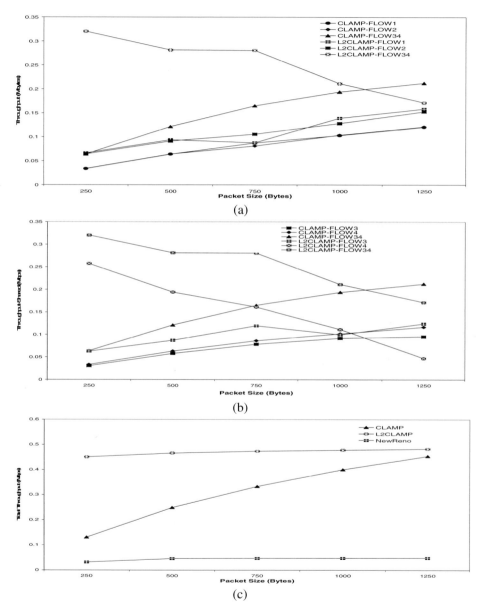

Fig. 5. Packet Size with respect to (a) Throughput per flow (Mbps), (b) Throughput (shared),
(c) Throughput (Mbps)

It can be observed from Figure 5 that the throughput of CLAMP is approximately twice higher than New Reno and that of L^2CLAMP is nearly 3.5 times higher than CLAMP as we vary the size of the packet. The throughputs in case of individual flows as well as the shared flows of L^2CLAMP show considerable performance improvement when compared to CLAMP.

5.3 Analysis by Varying Simulation Time

Figure 6 shows that the duration of simulation is varied between 50 secs and 200 secs with a Queue delay of 150 ms and packet size of 1250 bytes.

From figure 6, it can be noted that the throughput of L^2CLAMP is nearly 8 to 9 times higher when compared to that of New Reno and is approximately twice higher than that of the CLAMP. The end-to-end delay of L^2CLAMP is nearly half that of New Reno. The queue performance is also studied for all the three different protocols with varying simulation time.

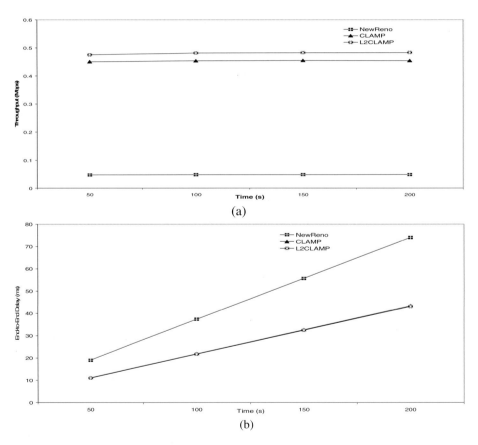

Fig. 6. Simulation time with respect to (a) Throughput (Mbps), (b) End-to-end delay (ms) (c) Queue (Kbytes), (d) Window size (Kbytes)

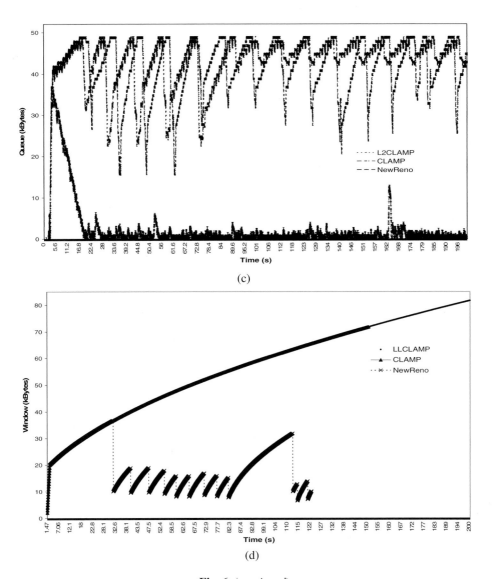

Fig. 6. (*continued*)

6 Conclusions and Future Work

This paper presented a novel yet generic approach for performance enhancement of TCP over wireless networks. Performance improvement comes from cross-layer optimization. The proposed solution, L^{2}CLAMP, avoids TCP ACK transmission over the wireless link through local generation of ACKs at the sender node or at the base station. The congestion measure is also calculated at the base station based from which the receiver advertised window is calculated. The protocol performance is compared with existing TCP New Reno and TCP New Reno with CLAMP. The performance of L^2CLAMP is better than the CLAMP whose performance is observed to be much better than the TCP New Reno.

A dynamic switch-over of the modules on-demand can be provided depending on the traffic load of the Access Point. The performance of the protocols can also be studied in an error-prone environment by the introduction of error models.

References

1. Kliazovich, D., Granelli, F., Gerla, M.: Performance improvement in wireless networks using cross-layer ARQ. Computer Networks 51, 4396–4411 (2008)
2. Andrew, L.L.H., Hanly, S.V., Mukhtar, R.G.: Active Queue Management for Fair Resource Allocation in Wireless Networks. IEEE transactions on Mobile Computing 7(2), 231–246 (2008)
3. Andrew, L.L.H., Hanly, S.V., Mukhtar, R.G.: CLAMP: Maximizing the Performance of TCP over Low Bandwidth Variable Rate Access Links. Technical report, Univ. of Melbourne (2004)
4. Eryilmaz, A., Srikant, R.: Fair Resource Allocation in Wireless Networks Using Queue-Length-Based Scheduling. In: Proc. IEEE INFOCOM, vol. 3, pp. 1794–1803 (March 2005)
5. Andrew, L.L.H., Hanly, S.V., Mukhtar, R.: CLAMP: A System to Enhance the Performance of Wireless Access Networks. In: Proc. IEEE Global Telecomm. Conf. (GLOBECOM 2003), vol. 7, pp. 4142–4147 (December 2003)
6. Andrew, L.L.H., Hanly, S.V., Mukhtar, R.G.: CLAMP: Differentiated Capacity Allocation in Access Networks. In: Proc. 22nd IEEE Int'l. Performance Computing and Comm. Conf. (IPCCC 2003), April 2003, pp. 451–458 (2003)
7. Xu, S., Saadawi, T.: Does the IEEE 802.11 MAC protocol work well in multihop wireless ad hoc networks? IEEE Communications Magazine 39, 130–137 (2001)
8. NS-2 simulator tool home page, http://www.isi.edu/nsnam/ns
9. Kliazovich, D., Granelli, F.: Cross-layer Congestion Control in ad hoc Wireless Networks. Journal on Ad Hoc Networks, 687–708 (August 2005)
10. Sardar, B., Saha, D.: A Survey of TCP Enhancements for Last- Hop Wireless Networks. IEEE Comm. Surveys 8, 20–34 (2006)
11. Chen, X., et al.: A Survey on Improving TCP Performance over Wireless Networks. Network Theory and Applications 16 (July 2006)
12. Lakshman, T., Madhow, U.: The Performance of TCP/IP for Networks with High Bandwidth-Delay Products and Random Loss. IEEE/ACM Trans. Networking 5, 336–350 (1997)

Improving Tracking Performance of FxLMS Algorithm Based Active Noise Control Systems

P. Babu[1] and A. Krishnan[2]

[1] Assistant Professor, ECE, K.S.Rangasamy College of Technology,
Tiruchengode, Tamilnadu, India
babuoag@gmail.com
[2] Professor, Dean, K.S.R. College of Engineering, Tiruchengode,
Tamilnadu, India
a_krishnan26@hotmail.com

Abstract. Several approaches have been introduced in literature for active noise control (ANC) systems. Since FxLMS algorithm appears to be the best choice as a controller filter, researchers tend to improve performance of ANC systems by enhancing and modifying this algorithm. In this paper, the existing FxLMS algorithm is modified which provides a new structure for improving the tracking performance and convergence rate. The secondary signal y (n) is thresholded by Wavelet transform to improve tracking. The convergence rate is improved dynamically by varying the step size of the error signal.

Keywords: active noise control, FxLMS algorithm, wavelet transform, soft threshold, dynamic step size.

1 Introduction

Acoustic noise problems become more and more evident as increased numbers of industrial equipment such as engines, blowers, fans, transformers, and compressors are in use. The traditional approach to acoustic noise control uses passive techniques such as enclosures, barriers, and silencers to attenuate the undesired noise [1],[2]. These passive silencers are valued for their high attenuation over a broad frequency range; however, they are relatively large, costly, and ineffective at low frequencies. Mechanical vibration is another related type of noise that commonly creates problems in all areas of transportation and manufacturing, as well as with many household appliances. Active noise control (ANC) [3]–[4] involves an electro acoustic or electromechanical system that cancels the primary (unwanted) noise based on the principle of superposition; specifically, an anti-noise of equal amplitude and the primary (unwanted) noise based on the principle of superposition; opposite phase is generated and combined with the primary noise, thus resulting in the cancellation of both opposite phase is generated and combined with the primary noise, thus resulting in the cancellation of both noises.

The most popular adaptation algorithm used for ANC applications is the FxLMS algorithm, which is a modified version of the LMS algorithm [5]. The schematic diagram

N. Meghanathan et al. (Eds.): NeCoM, WiMoN, and WeST 2010, CCIS 90, pp. 11–20, 2010.

for a single-channel feed forward ANC system using the FxLMS algorithm is shown in figure.1.Here, P(z) is primary acoustic path between the reference noise source and the error microphone and S (z) is the secondary path following the ANC (adaptive) filter W (z). The reference signal x (n) is filtered through S (z), and appears as anti- noise signal y' (n) at the error microphone. This anti-noise signal combines with the primary noise signal d (n) to create a zone of silence in the vicinity of the error microphone. The error microphone measures the residual noise e (n), which is used by W (z) for its adaptation to minimize the sound pressure at error microphone. Here $\hat{S}(z)$ account for the model of the secondary path S(z) between the output of the controller and the output of the error microphone. The filtering of the reference signals x(n) through the secondary-path model $\hat{S}(z)$ is demanded by the fact that the output y(n) of the adaptive controller w(z) is filtered through the secondary path S (z). [7].

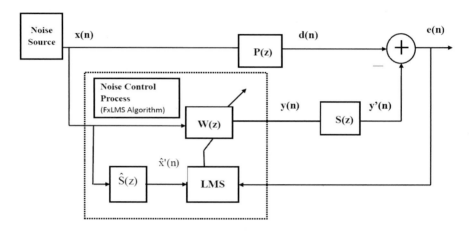

Fig. 1. Blockdiagram of FxLMS based feed forward ANC system

The main idea in this paper is to further increase the performance of FxLMS algorithm in terms of Signal to noise ratio. In modified FxLMS, secondary signal y'(n) is soft threshold by wavelet transform to improve the tracking performance. The step size is varied dynamically with respect to the error signal. Since error at the beginning is large, the step size of the algorithm is also large. This in turn increases convergence rate. As the iteration progresses, the error will simultaneously decrease. Finally, the original step size will be retained. The organization of this paper is as follows. Section 2 describes the Secondary path effects. Section 3 describes FxLMS algorithm. Section 4 introduces Wavelet transform. Section 5 describes the proposed method. Section 6 describes the simulation results and Section 7 gives the conclusion.

2 Secondary Path Effects

In ANC system, the primary noise is combined with the output of the adaptive filter. Therefore, it is necessary to compensate $\hat{S}(z)$ for the secondary-path transfer from

$y(n)$ to $e(n)$, which includes the digital-to-analog (D/A) converter, reconstruction filter, power amplifier, loudspeaker, acoustic path from loudspeaker to error microphone, error microphone, preamplifier, anti-aliasing filter, and analog-to digital (A/D) converter. The schematic diagram for a simplified ANC system is shown in figure2.

From Figure 2. , the -transform of the error signal is

$$E(z) = [P(z) - S(z)W(z)]X(z) \qquad (1)$$

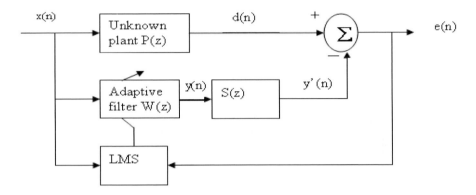

Fig. 2. Blockdiagram of simplified ANC system

We shall make the simplifying assumption here that after convergence of the adaptive filter, the residual error is ideally zero i.e., E (z) =0. This requires $W(z)$ realizing the optimal transfer function.

$$W^{\circ}(z) = \frac{P(z)}{S(z)} \qquad (2)$$

In other words, the adaptive filter has to simultaneously Model $P(z)$ and inversely model $S(z)$. A key advantage of this approach is that with a proper model of the plant, the system can respond instantaneously to changes in the input signal caused by changes in the noise sources. However, the performance of an ANC system depends largely upon the transfer function of the secondary path. By introducing an equalizer, a more uniform secondary path frequency response is achieved. In this way, the amount of noise reduction can often be increased significantly [8]. In addition, a sufficiently high-order adaptive FIR filter is required to approximate a rational function $1/S(z)$ shown in (2). It is impossible to compensate for the inherent delay due to if the primary path does not contain a delay of at least equal length.

3   FxLMS Algorithm

The FxLMS algorithm can be applied to both feedback and feed forward structures. Block diagram of a feed forward FxLMS ANC system of Figure 1.Here P (z) accounts for primary acoustic path between reference noise source and error microphone. $\hat{S}(z)$ is obtained offline and kept fixed during the online operation of ANC. The expression for the residual error e (n) is given as

$$e(n) = d(n) - y'(n) \tag{3}$$

Where y' (n) is the controller output y(n) filtered through the secondary path S(z). y'(n) and y(n) computed as

$$y'(n) = s^T(n)y(n) \tag{4}$$

$$y(n) = w^T(n) x(n) \tag{5}$$

Where w (n) = $[w0 (n) \; w_1 (n) \; .....w_{L-1}(n)]^T$ is tap weight vector, x(n)= [x(n) x(n-1).... ....x(n-L+1) $]^T$ is the reference signal picked by the reference microphone and s(n) is impulse response of secondary path S(z). It is assumed that there is no acoustic feedback from secondary loudspeaker to reference microphone. The FxLMS update equation for the coefficients of W (z) is given as:

$$w(n+1) = w(n) + \mu e(n)x'(n) \tag{6}$$

Where $x'(n)$ is reference signal x (n) filtered through secondary path model $\hat{S}(z)$

$$x'(n) = \hat{s}^T(n) x(n) \tag{7}$$

For a deep study on feed forward FxLMS algorithm the reader may refer to [7].

4   Wavelet Thresholding

The principle under which the wavelet thresholding operates is similar to the subspace concept, which relies on the fact that for many real life signals, a limited number of wavelet coefficients in the lower bands are sufficient to reconstruct a good estimate of the original signal. Usually wavelet coefficients are relatively large compared to other coefficients or to any other signal (especially noise) that has its energy spread over a large number of coefficients. Therefore, by shrinking coefficients smaller than a specific value, called threshold, we can nearly eliminate noise while preserving the important information of the original signal.

The proposed denoising algorithm is summarized as follow:

i)   Compute the discrete wavelet transform for noisy signal.
ii) Based on an algorithm, called thresholding algorithm and a threshold value, shrink some detail wavelet coefficients.
iii) Compute the inverse discrete wavelet transform.

Figure.4. shows the block diagram of the basic wavelet thresholding for signal denoising. Wave shrink, which is the basic method for denoising by wavelet thresholding, shrinks the detail coefficients because these coefficients represent the high frequency components of the signal and it supposes that the most important parts of signal information reside at low frequencies. Therefore, the assumption is that in high frequencies the noise can have a bigger effect than the signal. Denoising by wavelet is performed by a thresholding algorithm, in which the wavelet coefficients smaller than a specific value, or threshold, will be shrunk or scaled [9] and [10].

The standard thresholding functions used in the wavelet based enhancement systems are hard and soft thresholding functions [11], which we review before introducing a new thresholding algorithm that offers improved performance for signal. In these algorithms, λ is the threshold value and δ is the thresholding algorithm.

4.1 Hard Thresholding Algorithm

Hard thresholding is similar to setting the components of the noise subspace to zero. The hard threshold algorithm is defined as

$$\delta_\lambda^H = \begin{cases} 0 & |y| \leq \lambda \\ y & |y| > \lambda \end{cases} \tag{8}$$

In this hard thresholding algorithm, the wavelet coefficients less than the threshold λ will are replaced with zero which is represented in fig. 3-(a).

4.2 Soft Thresholding Algorithm

In soft thresholding, the thresholding algorithm is defined as follow: (see Figure 3-(b)).

$$\delta_\lambda^S = \begin{cases} 0 & |y| \leq \lambda \\ \text{sign}(y)(|y| - \lambda) & |y| > \lambda \end{cases} \tag{9}$$

Soft thresholding goes one step further and decreases the magnitude of the remaining coefficients by the threshold value. Hard thresholding maintains the scale of the signal but introduces ringing and artifacts after reconstruction due to a discontinuity in the wavelet coefficients. Soft thresholding eliminates this discontinuity resulting in smoother signals but slightly decreases the magnitude of the reconstructed signal.

5 Proposed Method

In the proposed method $y'(n)$ is the secondary signal of FxLMS is denoising by wavelet is performed by a thresholding algorithm, in which the wavelet coefficients smaller than a specific value, or threshold, will be shrunk or scaled. The signal $y'(n)$ can be soft thresholding because of eliminates the discontinuity and resulting in smoother signal such that λ is the threshold value and δ is the thresholding algorithm in order to improving the tracking performance of FxLMS algorithm.

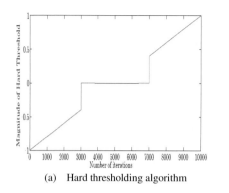

(a)   Hard thresholding algorithm

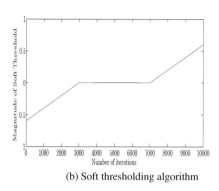

(b) Soft thresholding algorithm

Fig. 3. Thresholding algorithms (a) Hard. (b) Soft

The wavelet transform using fixed soft thresholding algorithm for signal $y'(n)$ is defined as follow:

$$\delta_\lambda^S = \begin{cases} 0 & |s^T y| \le \lambda \\ \text{sign}(s^T y)(|s^T y| - \lambda) & |s^T y| > \lambda \end{cases} \tag{10}$$

The wavelet transform using fixed soft thresholding will improve the tracking property when compared with traditional FxLMS algorithm based on active noise control systems. The threshold value used in fixed soft thresholding algorithm is $\lambda_0 = 0.45$, since the amplitude of the noise signal is small. The performance of the system can be further increased by using fixed threshold function with dynamic step size rather than the FxLMS and FxLMS with fixed soft threshold function based on the error signal $e(n)$.

In modified FxLMS, the step size is varied   dynamically with respect to the error signal. Since error at the beginning is large, the step size of the algorithm is also large. This in turn increases convergence rate. As the iteration progresses, the error will simultaneously decreases. Finally, the original step size will be retained. Figure.5 shows the block diagram for purposed method. Thus the convergence rate of the FxLMS algorithm is improved by varying the step-size as well as wavelet threshold value with respect to error signal. From the Figure 5, the expression for the residual error e(n) is given as

$$e(n) = d(n) - s^T y \tag{11}$$

Initially the error in the system is very high and so very large step size is selected. Hence the convergence rate is also very high .Then the step size is varied for the instant and the previous value of the error signal e (n). Finally the error is reduced greatly by the implementation of the dynamic step size algorithm.

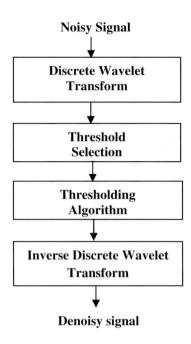

Fig. 4. Denoising by wavelet thresholding block diagram

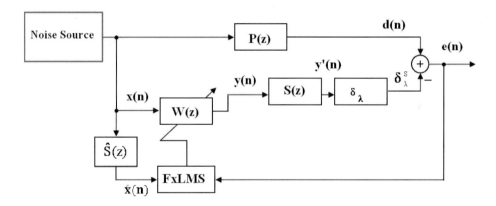

Fig. 5. Block diagram for purposed Method

This idea of dynamic step size calculation is represented in (12) and (13).

$$w(n+1) = w(n) + \mu(n)e(n)x'(n) \tag{12}$$

Where,

$$\mu(n) = \frac{\mu_0(n)}{1 - \mathrm{abs}(e(n))} \tag{13}$$

Thus the (13) is called as modified FxLMS algorithm for improving the performance of existing algorithm.

6   Simulation Results

In this section the performance of the proposed modified FxLMS algorithm with wavelet thresholding is demonstrated using computer simulation. The performance of the fixed wavelet thresholding dynamic step size algorithm is compared with FxLMS algorithm and wavelet thresholding algorithm on the basis of noise reduction R (dB) and convergence rate is given in (14) and (15).

$$R(dB) = -10\log\left(\frac{\sum e^2(n)}{\sum d^2(n)}\right) \tag{14}$$

$$\text{Convergence   Rate} = 20\log 10\{abs(e)\} \tag{15}$$

The large positive value of R indicates that more noise reduction is achieved at the error microphone. The computer simulation for modified FxLMS algorithm is illustrated in Fig.6.and Fig.7. Figure.6 shows the characteristics of Noise reduction versus number of iteration times. It has been seen that the modified FxLMS with fixed soft thresholding having dynamic step-size produce better noise reduction when compared to FxLMS and FxLMS with fixed soft thresholding.

Fig.7. shows the characteristics of convergence rate in dB with respect to number of iterations. It has been seen that the convergence rate of modified FxLMS with fixed soft thresholding having dynamic step-size increases by reducing the number of iterations when compared to FxLMS and FxLMS with fixed soft thresholding.

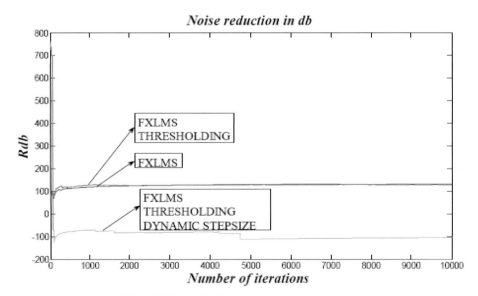

Fig. 6. Noise reduction versus iteration time *(n)*

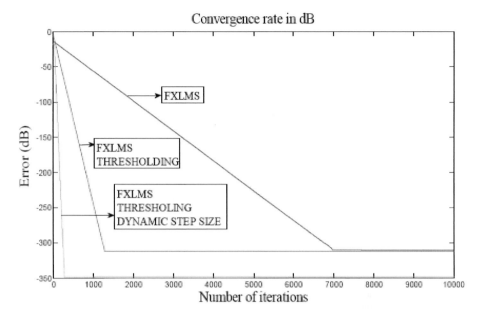

Fig. 7. Characteristics of convergence rate

7   Conclusions

Here a modified FxLMS structure for ANC system is proposed. This structure combines the concept of wavelet fixed soft thresholding with the dynamic variable step size. It shows better tracking performance and convergence rate than the conventional FxLMS algorithm and FxLMS wavelet soft threshold algorithm. Thus this method achieves an improved performance than the existing methods.

Acknowledgement

The authors would like to thank the reviewers for their many insightful comments and useful suggestions. The authors also would like to express their gratitude to our beloved chairman Lion Dr.K.S.Rangasamy and our principal Dr.K.Thagarajah for supporting this research.

References

1. Harris, M.: Handbook of Acoustical Measurements and Noise Control, 3rd edn. McGraw-Hill, New York (1991)
2. Beranek, L.L., Ver, I.L.: Noise and Vibration Control Engineering: Principles and Applications. Wiley, New York (1992)
3. Nelson, P.A., Elliott, S.J.: Active Control of Sound. Academic, San Diego (1992)
4. Hansen, C.H., Snyder, S.D.: Active Control of Noise and Vibration. E&FN Spon, London (1997)

5. Kuo, S.M., Morgan, D.R.: Active Noise control systems, algorithms and DSP implementation functions. Wiley, New York (1996)
6. Kuo, S.M., Morgan, D.R.: Active noise control: a tutorial review. Proc. IEEE 8(6), 943–973 (1999)
7. Davari, P., Hassanpour, H.: Designing a new robust on-line secondary path modeling technique for feed forward active noise control systems. Elsevier Journal of signal Processing (2009)
8. Kuo, S.M., Tsai, J.: Acoustical mechanisms and Performance of various active duct noise control systems. Appl. Acoust. 41(1), 81–91 (1994)
9. Donoho, D.L.: Denoising by Soft thresholding. IEEE Trans. on Information Theory 41(3), 613–627 (1995)
10. Jansen, M.: Noise Reduction by Wavelet Thresholding. Springer, New York (2001)
11. Ghanbari, Y., Karami, M.R.: A new approach for Speech enhancement based on the adaptive thresholding of the wavelet packets. Speech Communication (2006)
12. Widrow, Stearns, S.D.: Adaptive Signal processing. Prentice Hall, New Jersey (1985)
13. Kuo, S.M., Vijayan, D.: A Secondary path Modeling technique for Active Noise Control Systems. IEEE Transactions on Speech And Audio Processing (July 1997)
14. Akhtar, M.T., Abe, M., Kawamata, M.: Modified-filtered-xLMS algorithm based active noise control system with improved online secondary path modeling. In: Proc. IEEE 2004 Int. Mid. Symp. Circuits Systems (MWSCAS 2004), Hiroshima, Japan, pp. I-13–I-16 (2004)
15. Akhtar, M.T., Abe, M., Kawamata, M.: A method for online secondary path modeling in active noise control systems. In: Proc. IEEE 2005 Int. Symp. Circuits Systems (ISCAS 2005), May 23-26, pp. I-264–I-267 (2005)
16. Hu, A.Q., Hu, X., Cheng, S.: A robust secondary path modeling technique for narrowband active noise control systems. In: Proc. IEEE Conf. on Neural Networks and Signal Processing, December 2003, vol. 1, pp. 818–821 (2003)
17. Babu, P., Krishnan, A.: Modified FxAFA algorithm using dynamic step size for Active Noise Control Systems. International Journal of Recent Trends in Engineering 2(1-6), 37–39 (2009)

Source and System Features for Text Independent Speaker Recognition Using GMM Speaker Models

A. Revathi[1] and Y. Venkataramani[2]

[1] Professor, Dept. of ECE, Saranathan College of Engineering, Trichy
revathidhanabal@rediffmail.com
[2] Director, Saranathan College of Engineering, Trichy
principal@saranathan.ac.in

Abstract. The main objective of this paper is to explore the effectiveness of perceptual features combined with pitch for text independent speaker recognition. In this algorithm, these features are captured and Gaussian mixture models are developed representing L feature vectors of speech for every speaker. Speakers are identified based on first finding posteriori probability density function between mixtures of speaker models and test speech vectors. Speakers are classified based on maximum probability density function which corresponds to a speaker model. This algorithm gives the good overall accuracy of 98% for mel frequency perceptual linear predictive cepstrum combined with pitch for identifying speaker among 8 speakers chosen randomly from 8 different dialect regions in "TIMIT" database by considering GMM speaker models of 12 mixtures. It also gives the better average accuracy of 95.75% for the same feature with respect to 8 speakers chosen randomly from the same dialect region for12 mixtures GMM speaker models. Mel frequency linear predictive cepstrum gives the better accuracy of 96.75% and 96.125% for GMM speaker models of 16 mixtures by considering speakers from different dialect regions and from same dialect region respectively. This algorithm is also evaluated for 4, 8 and 32 mixtures GMM speaker models. 12 mixtures GMM speaker models are tested for population of 20 speakers and the accuracy is found to be slightly less as compared to that for the the speaker population of 8 speakers. The noteworthy feature of speaker identification algorithm is to evaluate the testing procedure on identical messages for all the speakers. This work is extended to speaker verification whose performance is measured in terms of % False rejection rate, % False acceptance rate and % Equal error rate. % False acceptance rate and % Equal error rate are found to be less for mel frequency perceptual linear predictive cepstrum with pitch and % false rejection rate is less for mel frequency linear predictive cepstrum. In this work, F-ratio is computed as a theoretical measure on the features of the training speeches to validate the experimental results for perceptual features with pitch. χ^2 distribution tool is used to perform the statistical justification of good experimental results for all the features with respect to both speaker identification and verification.

Keywords: Gaussian mixture models, Frequency response, Noise, Speech recognition, Speaker recognition, Spectral analysis, Speech analysis, Speech processing.

N. Meghanathan et al. (Eds.): NeCoM, WiMoN, and WeST 2010, CCIS 90, pp. 21–30, 2010.
© Springer-Verlag Berlin Heidelberg 2010

1 Introduction

Speech signal carries information about speech message, speaker and channel/environment of recording. For speaker recognition speech data is collected and is used to develop a clustering model for capturing speaker specific information. In speaker identification, speaker is identified as one associated with claimant model which has maximum posteriori probability density function computed by taking features of the test utterance and mixtures. Variations in shape of the vocal tract are characterized by resonances and anti resonances and spectral roll-off features. It is very difficult to characterize the suprasegmental features such as intonation, duration, stress and co-articulation. Proposed features extracted from short-segments of speech signal provide a compromise between source and system features. There are many features depicting the characteristics of the vocal tract such as LPCC, MFCC, DCTC, LSF, PLP and their use in speaker identification/speaker verification task has been discussed in [1,5,6,7 & 8]. This paper [10] mainly deals with use of prosodic and acoustic features and GMM-UBM recognizer for improving the performance of speaker identification. Linear predictive cepstrum and LP residuals are used as system and source features and AANN models as training models for speaker recognition [11]. Speaker identification is done [12] using mel frequency cepstrum and inverted mel frequency cepstrum as combined features and GMM for developing training models. This paper [13] deals with the use of spectral features and mel frequency cepstrum for enhancing the performance of speaker recognition. The experimental results based on our algorithm give the comparative analysis of system features and combination of source and system features in identifying / verifying speakers.

2 Feature Based on Cepstrum

The short-time speech spectrum for voiced speech sound has two components: 1) harmonic peaks due to the periodicity of voiced speech 2) glottal pulse shape. The excitation source decides the periodicity of voiced speech. It reflects the characteristics of speaker. The spectral envelope is shaped by formants which reflect the resonances of vocal tract. The variations among speakers are indicated by formant locations and bandwidth.

2.1 PLP, MF-PLP and Pitch Extraction

PLP (perceptual linear predictive cepstrum) speech analysis method [2-4] models the speech auditory spectrum by the spectrum of low order all pole model. The detailed procedure for PLP (Perceptual linear predictive cepstrum) and MF-PLP (Mel frequency perceptual linear predictive cepstrum) extraction is given below. The block diagram for PLP and MF-PLP extraction is shown in Fig.1.

1. Compute power spectrum of windowed speech.
2. Perform grouping to 21 critical bands in bark scale or 47 critical bands in mel scale for the sampling frequency of 16 kHz.
3. Perform loudness equalization and cube root compression to simulate the power law of hearing.

4. Perform IFFT
5. Perform LP analysis by Levinson -Durbin procedure.
6. Convert LP coefficients into cepstral coefficients.

The relationship between frequency in Bark and frequency in Hz is specified as in (1)

$$f(bark) = 6 * arcsinh(f(Hz)/600)$$ (1)

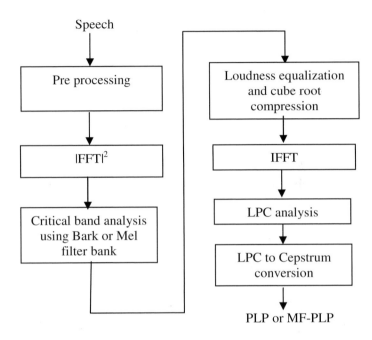

Fig. 1. Block diagram of PLP (MF-PLP) extraction

Pitch frequency is extracted by using pitch determination algorithm which works on the principle of finding sub harmonic to harmonic ratio. Pitch frequencies are normally in the range of 50 to 250 Hz and 120 to 400 Hz for male and female speakers respectively.

3 Development of GMM Training Models

The speaker classifier models the distribution of features from a person's speech by a Gaussian mixture density. For a feature vector denoted as $\vec{x}_i$, the mixture density for speaker S is defined as in (2)

$$p(\vec{x}_t / \lambda_s) = \sum_{i=1}^{M} b_i^*(\vec{x}_t)$$ (2)

The density is the linear combination of M component Gaussian densities $b_i^*(\vec{x}_i)$. Collectively, the parameter of a speaker's density model is denoted as λ_s.

Given a sequence of feature vectors extracted from person's training speech, maximum likelihood parameters such as mean vector and covariance matrices corresponding to the number of mixture components have been derived by expectation maximization algorithm. Speaker is classified by computing log likelihood value as in equation (3)

$$\hat{S} = \arg\max \sum_{t=1}^{T} \log p(\vec{x}_t / \lambda_k)$$
$$1 \le k \le S$$

(3)

For classifying a test speech corresponding to a particular model, 100 test vectors have been taken for each test speech segment of each speaker. The speaker whose model produces the largest log likelihood value been then determined to be the identified speaker.

4   Speaker Identification Based on Proposed Features

The identification system involves extraction of features from the training and testing data, building GMM models for all enrolled speakers and testing each utterance against a certain number of claimant models to detect the identity of the speaker of that utterance from among the claimants. TIMIT speech database is used in this work. The identification system involves extraction of features from the training data formed by combining TI random contextual variant sentences and MIT phonetically compact sentences and features from the test data formed by combining SRI dialect calibration sentences. Present study uses the training speech of 20 seconds and test data of 7 seconds duration. Feature vectors of test speech of nearly 1.6 seconds duration are considered. Each speaker has been tested on an average of 75 test speech segments and the speeches are sampled at 16 kHz. For creating a training model, speech signal is pre-emphasized using a difference operator. Hamming window is applied on differenced speech frames of 16 msecs duration with overlapping of 8 msecs. Then the features such as PLP and MF-PLP are obtained. Pitch is extracted by finding sub harmonic to harmonic ratio on the clean training speech. Perceptual features are concatenated with pitch and the combined features are applied to develop the training models. For each speaker, GMM model is developed based on expectation maximization algorithm to generate mean vectors and 'full' co-variance matrices with respect to the number of mixtures corresponding to the speaker model. In this algorithm there is a mapping from L training vectors into M mixtures. Each block is normalized to unit magnitude before giving as input to the model. One model is created for each speaker.

For testing, speech signal is obtained by considering the speeches of SR1 dialect calibration sentences. The features PLP and MF-PLP are extracted for the test speech. Pitch is also extracted for the test speech by using sub harmonic to harmonic ratio principle. To evaluate different test utterance lengths, the sequence of feature vectors was divided into overlapping segments of 100 feature vectors in each segment. The combined perceptual features with pitch are applied to all the enrolled training models. Then the posteriori probability density function is found between each test vector and mixtures of GMM speaker models. The log likelihood is found for test segments with mixtures for all speaker models. The test utterance best matches with a speaker model which has maximum log likelihood value. System evaluation is extended to the variations in number of mixtures. The performance measure is then computed as a ratio of correctly identified number of test segments to the total number of test segments considered for each speaker.

For speaker modeling, the objective is to choose number of components necessary to adequately model a speaker for obtaining good accuracy. Choosing too few mixture components can produce a speaker model which does not sufficiently describe the distinguishing characteristics of a speaker's distribution. Choosing too many components can reduce the performance when there are a large number of model parameters relative to the available training data and can also result in excessive computational complexity for training and testing.

5 Results and Discussion

The performance of speaker identification system based on the feature is evaluated by finding log likelihood value between test vectors and all speaker models described with mean vectors and covariance matrices. The discriminative potential of statistical parameters is commonly evaluated by F- ratio (Fisher's ratio), which is calculated as ratio of between-speech variance of parameter value means to mean within-speech variance of the same parameter values. For normal variables, the probability of misclassifying a speaker i to speaker j is a monotonically decreasing function of F-ratio. Fig. 2 indicates the intra speaker feature variation of one speaker for MF-PLP + PITCH. Fig. 3 depicts the pitch frequency distribution of one female speaker and one male speaker chosen from the group of speakers in 8 different dialect regions. Pitch frequency is between 50 Hz and 250 Hz for male speakers and it is between 120 Hz and 400 Hz for female speakers. This is evident from plot shown in Fig.3 Frequency response plot shown in Fig. 4 indicates spectral variation in two speeches of one speaker.

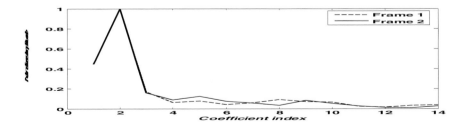

Fig. 2. Intra speaker feature variation of MF-PLP + PITCH

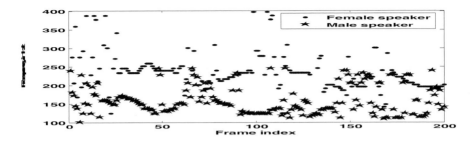

Fig. 3. Pitch frequency distribution

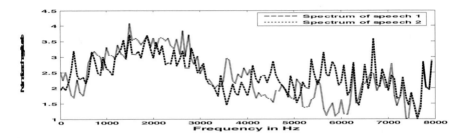

Fig. 4. Frequency response of different speeches of same speaker

Fig. 5 shows the comparison between the perceptual features and perceptual features combined with pitch for speakers chosen from 8 different dialect regions There is 100% as individual accuracy for 5 speakers and 4 speakers for MF-PLP+PITCH and PLP+PITCH respectively for the GMM speaker model of 12 mixtures.

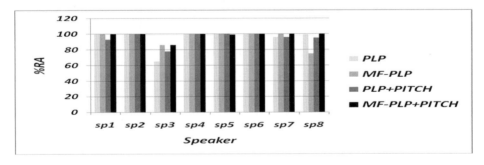

Fig. 5. Comparison chart - individual accuracy of features for 12 mixtures (8 speakers from 8 different dialect regions)

Speaker identification system is evaluated for GMM models of 4, 8, 12, 16 and 32 mixture components and it is found that accuracy is better for 12 mixtures model. Accuracy of MF-PLP+PITCH is better than PLP+PITCH for 12 mixtures GMM speaker model by considering speakers from same dialect region with respect to variations in taking no. of test speech segments into consideration. Average accuracy of combined features is better for the speakers chosen from different dialect region compared to the case of speakers chosen from the same dialect region. Reason is quite obvious that speaking style, accent and pronunciation of words by speakers in the same dialect region may be same. Speaking style normally differs for the speakers from the different dialect regions. So, accuracy is obviously better for the speakers from the different dialect regions. Since 12 mixtures GMM performs in better manner for all the features, it is extended to evaluate the performance for the speaker population to 20 speakers.

Table 1 indicates the performance of speaker identification for the combination of source and system features with F-Ratio. F- ratio (Fisher's ratio) calculated on the training data is useful to decide the selection of features before the application of testing to all the speaker models. From Table 1, it is clear that accuracy is monotonically increasing function of F-ratio. Table 2 indicates the overall average accuracy of perceptual features and perceptual features combined with pitch for 12 and 16 mixtures. Table 3 indicates performance measure for speakers chosen from same dialect region. Since, 12 mixtures GMM model performs better, its analysis is extended to the speaker population of 20 speakers chosen randomly from different dialect regions. Comparative analysis between the features with respect to speaker population is shown in Table 4. Performance is found to be equally good for considering 20 speakers as compared to the case of considering 8 speakers from 8 different dialect regions.

Table 1. Overall accuracy of speaker identification for the combined features with F-ratio

Feature	%Recognition accuracy	F-Ratio
PLP + PITCH	95.25	0.0096
MF-PLP + PITCH	98	0.0113

Table 2. Overall accuracy for features for speakers from different dialect regions

Feature	%RA/No. of mixtures	
	12 Mixtures	16 Mixtures
PLP	95	94.25
MF-PLP	95.125	96.75
PLP+PITCH	95.25	93.125.
MF-PLP+PITCH	98	95.125

Table 3. Overall accuracy for features for speakers from same dialect region

No. of Mixtures	%RA/Features			
	PLP	MF-PLP	PLP+PITCH	MF-PLP+PITCH
4	89.5	90.125	88.5	94.5
8	90.625	96.5	90.5	94.75
12	89	93.5	89.875	95.75
16	90.875	96.125	90.125	93
32	87.2	91.75	81.25	92.25

Table 4. Overall accuracy for features for 12 mixtures GMM speaker models

Feature	%RA /Speaker population		
	8 speakers from different dialect regions	8 speakers from same dialect region	20 speakers from different dialect regions
PLP	95	89	90
MF-PLP	95.125	93.5	91.65
PLP+PITCH	95.25	89.875	90.9
MF-PLP+PITCH	98	95.75	91.05

Testing of algorithm is also extended to evaluating the features for speaker verification system and Table 5 indicates the performance of the speaker verification system measured in terms of average %FAR, average %FRR and %ERR.

Table 5. Performance of speaker verification system for 20 speakers

Features	%FAR	%FRR	%EER
PLP	7.655	10.07	3.9
MF-PLP	6.65	8.565	6.2
PLP+PITCH	7.15	9.23	4.6
MF-PLP+PITCH	6.315	9.56	2.4

6 Statistical Analysis on Features

Weighted average accuracy for features is obtained as greater than or equal to 90%. Accuracy obtained for all the features is analyzed using χ^2 distribution. On an average of 60 test speech segments taken for all the speakers is referred to as expected frequency. The number of correctly identified test speech segments is referred as observed frequency. The set of 20 speakers has been taken as 20 attributes. Since the sample size is greater than 50, χ^2 distribution is applied to test the level of significance of the feature.

On the basis of the average, correctly identified test speech segments for most of the speakers are more than 90%. Hence, hypothesis is set as under:

H_o : Average accuracy is equal to or greater than 95%
H_1 : Average accuracy is less than 95%

χ^2 test is applied at 5% level of significance. $\chi^2_{calculated}$ values for PLP, MF-PLP, PLP+PITCH and MF-PLP+PITCH are 23.87, 19.3, 28.4 and 29.9 respectively. $\chi^2_{0.05}$ value from the table is 30.144. Since calculated values are less than the table value, null hypothesis is accepted. Thus, average accuracy of text independent speaker recognition for all the features is statistically justified to be more than 95%.

7 Conclusions

This paper proposes robust perceptual features combined with pitch for improving the performance of speaker identification system. GMM speaker models of 4, 8, 12, 16 and 32 mixtures are formed to represent the L vectors of training data, thus achieving the reduction in the size of the data to be used subsequently while evaluating the test data in recognizing speaker. It is found that MF-PLP+PITCH has performed better than PLP, MF-PLP and PLP+PITCH by considering the cases of speakers chosen randomly from 8 different dialect regions and from same dialect region for GMM speaker models of 12 mixtures which is verified theoretically by using F-ratio on training data. So, the combination of source and system features for 12 mixtures speaker model provide consistently good performance for considering speakers from different dialect regions and from same dialect region Performance of the algorithm is also extended to speaker verification system and it is measured in terms of %FAR, %FRR and %ERR. MF-PLP and MF-PLP+PITCH give better results than PLP and PLP+PITCH both speaker identification and verification.

References

[1] Revathi, A., Chinnadurai, R., Venkataramani, Y.: T-LPCC and T-LSF in twins identification based on speaker clustering. In: Proceedings of IEEE INDICON, IEEE Bangalore section, September 2007, pp. 25–26 (2007)

[2] Hermansky, H., Tsuga, K., Makino, S., Wakita, H.: Perceptually based processing in automatic speech recognition. In: Proceedings of IEEE international conference on Acoustics, speech and signal processing, Tokyo, April 1986, vol. 11, pp. 1971–1974 (1986)

[3] Hermansky, H., Margon, N., Bayya, A., Kohn, P.: The challenge of Inverse E: The RASTA PLP method. In: Proceedings of twenty fifth IEEE Asilomar conference on signals, systems and computers, Pacific Grove, CA, USA, November 1991, vol. 2, pp. 800–804 (1991)

[4] Hermansky, H., Morgan, N.: RASTA processing of speech. IEEE transactions on speech and audio processing 2(4), 578–589 (1994)

[5] Revathi, A., Venkataramani, Y.: Text independent speaker identification/verification using multiple features. In: International conference on computer science and information engineering, Los Angeles, USA (April 2009)

[6] Revathi, A., Venkataramani, Y.: Iterative clustering approach for text independent speaker identification using multiple features. In: Proceedings of International conference on signal processing and communication systems, Gold coast, Australia (December 2008)

[7] Revathi, A., Venkataramani, Y.: Use of perceptual features in iterative clustering based twins identification system. In: Proceedings of International conference on computing, communication and networking, India (December 2008)

[8] Revathi, A., Chinnadurai, R., Venkataramani, Y.: Effectiveness of LP derived features and DCTC in twins identification-Iterative speaker clustering approach. In: Proceedings of IEEE ICCIMA, December 2007, vol. 1, pp. 535–539 (2007)

[9] Rabiner, L., Juang, B.H.: Fundamentals of speech recognition. Prentice Hall, NJ (1993)

[10] Zheng, R., Zhang, S., Xu, B.: Improvement of speaker identification by combining prosodic features with acoustic features. In: Li, S.Z., Lai, J.-H., Tan, T., Feng, G.-C., Wang, Y. (eds.) SINOBIOMETRICS 2004. LNCS, vol. 3338, pp. 569–576. Springer, Heidelberg (2004)

[11] Yegnanarayana, B., Sharat Reddy, K., Kishore, K.P.: Source and system features for speaker recognition using AANN models. In: Proceedings of IEEE International Conference on ASSP, pp. 409–412 (2001)

[12] Chakraborthy, S., Saha, G.: Improved text independent speaker identification using fused MFCC and IMFCC feature sets based on Gaussian filters. International journal of signal processing (2009)

[13] Hossienzadeh, Krishnan: Combining vocal source and MFCC features for enhanced speaker recognition performance using GMMs. In: Proceedings of IEEE 9th workshop on Multimedia Signal processing, October 2007, pp. 365–368 (2007)

Optimization of ASIC Design Cycle Time

Vrushank Shah[1], Nirav Parmar[2], and Rahul Shah[3]

[1] L.D.College of Engineering, Ahmedabad
Vrushank_2005@yahoo.co.in
[2] Nirma Institute of Technology, Ahmedabad
nirav.parmar@einfochips.com
[3] eInfochips, Ahmedabad
rahulv.shah@einfochips.com

Abstract. Due to the high complexity of modern circuit designs, verification has become the major bottleneck of entire design process. Common industry estimates are that functional verification constitutes near 70% of the total effort on any ASIC project. In this paper, we have tried to describe various ways to optimize verification time, comparing their effect on verification time and complete design cycle, with the conclusion of selecting modeling as better mechanism. The present paper has proved modeling as the best approach for optimizing ASIC design cycle with the experimentation taking a case-study.

Keywords: ASIC, TLM, Modeling, Verification.

1 Introduction

The ultimate goal of ASIC verification is to obtain the highest possible level of confidence in the correctness of a design. But the complexity of ASICs is growing exponentially along with the market pressuring design cycle times to decrease as well. This dual challenge of increasing complexity and decreasing time is creating an urgent need for the application of advanced verification methods. Register transfer level test benches have become too complex to manage and slow to execute. New methods and verification techniques began to emerge over the past few years. In this paper we have divided the various methods which optimizes ASIC verification into Hardware Based Method giving review about Emulation and FPGA prototyping, Reusability Method that deals with verification environment reuse, Abstraction based Method by making a level above RTL called transaction level, Assertion Based Method, Co verification based method by creating parallel hardware & software execution environment and finally, the Model Based Methods which deals with creation of models of important system components.

The remainder of the paper is organized as follows. Section II describes various ways which optimizes ASIC design cycle timings, Section III describes how model based design is best in optimizing ASIC design cycle time. Section IV introduces you with the case-study, Section V and Section VI shows Implementation of verification environment, Results and Conclusion for a given case study.

N. Meghanathan et al. (Eds.): NeCoM, WiMoN, and WeST 2010, CCIS 90, pp. 31–40, 2010.

2 Methods of Optimization

2.1 Hardware- Based Method

The first approach to control the verification bottleneck is to go for Hardware based methods. The three main options are simulation, emulation, and FPGA based prototyping. Software based simulation is widely used, but even when running on a really high end (and correspondingly expensive) computer platform, it runs six to ten orders of magnitude slower than the actual ASIC hardware, which makes it an extremely time consuming and inefficient technique.

Hardware based emulation is another alternative, but it is still at least three orders of magnitude slower than the actual ASIC hardware, because the massive amounts of multiplexing involved slows the verification speed down to only 500 KHz to 2 MHz [1]. Furthermore, this approach is extremely expensive, both in terms of budget and resources.

The third method of ASIC design verification is FPGA based prototyping. It is possible to use increased capacity of FPGAs and readily available off-the-shelf prototyping boards to prototype a multi-million gate ASIC by mapping the original RTL code to several FPGAs on a board. So we are checking the functionality directly on silicon, which reduces lots of verification effort[1,2].

2.2 Re-usability Method

Verification reuse offers great opportunity to improve verification time. Reuse can be done as below [3]:

1. Verification Components Reuse
2. Verification Plan and Environment Reuse

The verification components are as shown in figure, which together makes compete verification environment.

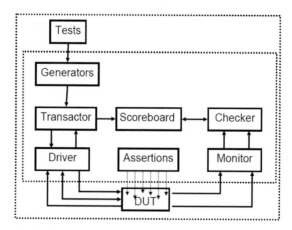

Fig. 1. Simple Verification Environment. This figure shows various components of verification Environment.

The three major parts of a verification environment are the DUT, the test bench (the inner box above), and the test which controls the test bench. Inside the test bench are the following parts [4,5]:

Driver controls the signals into the DUT. It executes single commands such as a bus read or write, or driving a cell/packet / frame into the DUT. Monitor- bundles signal changes from the DUT into transactions. Assertions- constantly check the DUT for correctness. These look at external and internal signals. The test bench uses the results of these assertions to see if the DUT responded correctly. Transactor- takes high level transactions such as a burst read into individual read commands, or a single USB transaction into multiple USB packet TX/RX commands. Scoreboard- stores the transactions from the transactor for later comparison. Checker- compares the output of the DUT, as seen by the Monitor, to the Scoreboard, using a predictor or reference model. Generator- generates transactions, either individually or in streams.

Now we can reuse these components of verification environment or whole environment in two ways, either horizontally and vertically. Horizontal reuse means to one or more components can be reuse in another application. Vertical reuse means one or more components can be reuse at different abstraction level. The main advantage of reusability is it reduces cost and labour, which ultimately adds in optimizing ASIC design cycle Time.

2.3 Abstraction-Based Method

While today's RTL design and verification flows are a step up from the gate level flows of two decades ago, RTL flows are straining to meet the demands of most product teams. When designs are sourced and verified at the register transfer level, IP reuse is difficult, functional verification is lengthy and cumbersome, and architectural decisions cannot be confirmed prior to RTL verification. So here idea is to move to next level of abstraction above RTL to get a much needed boost in design productivity.

That next level of abstraction is based on transaction level modeling (TLM). By creating TLM IP as their golden source, design teams can ease IP creation and reuse, spend less time and effort in functional verification, and introduce fewer bugs. Design iterations are reduced because TLM verification is much faster than RTL verification, and architectural choices can be verified well before RTL verification [6]. Further, transaction level models can be used for hardware/software co-verification, and can be part of a virtual platform for early software development. The net result of all these advantages will be much higher designer productivity.

Transaction level modeling uses function calls, rather than signals or wires, for inter module communications [6]. It lets users analyze transactions such as reads or writes rather than worrying about the underlying logic implementation and timing. As said the advantage of transaction-level modeling is that it makes IP creation reuse easy. However, additional effort increases to built TLM.

2.4 Assertion-Based Method

Assertion based Verification can also be used to achieve the goal of reduction in verification cycle time. Assertions are design checks that continuously get evaluated in form of an expression [7],[8]. When any expression does not hold true, an assertion flag is raised. This allows the verification engineer to directly go to the problem instead of tedious back tracing of waveforms. Assertions can be utilized in various ways. They can be included directly within the hardware description language (HDL) code that comprises the register transfer level (RTL) description of the design [7] or, they can be applied from outside in the form of test benches, or collections of test vectors, to check the response of the design to stimulus, or to control a stimulus generator or model checker.

Assertion based verification benefits users by simplifying the diagnosis and detecting bugs by localizing the occurrence of a suspected bug [8]. It thereby reduces simulation debug time significantly. Secondly, self checking code helps a lot in reuse of design and Interface assertions help find the interface issues early on. Using assertions to specify interfaces is far superior to natural language and waveforms because assertions are unambiguous and executable. The clarity of assertions comes from having well defined syntax and semantics. Assertion languages enable us to clearly specify any interface, but often require significant coding to describe complex interfaces and RTL components. However, present day Assertion based method requires intelligent debug systems which understand and analyze assertion.

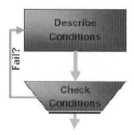

Failures indicate improper operation localized to an operation or set of signals

Fig. 2. Assertion- Based Verification. This figure shows when the specified assertion goes wrong. It raises assertion flag or indicates improper operation to localized a bug.

2.5   Co-verification-Based Method

In present day traditional design cycle, hardware and software are often developed separately, then integrated after the hardware has been built. Not surprisingly, often the hardware and software do not work correctly together the first time. In many cases, the real software and integration debugging begin only after the hardware has been built.

Hardware/software co-verification is one of the techniques that can be used to begin the debugging process sooner, [1] before physical prototypes are available. This Method will explain what hardware/software co-verification is and how it helps in verification bottleneck. Co-verification systems are comprised of a hardware and software execution environment [9],[10]. There is some mechanism to pass events, commands and control between these environments. There will be some type of debug and control interface for the hardware and software.

As said debugging has started earlier by using this method whereas traditionally software designers have to wait until hardware becomes available before starting the debug process. Using co-verification gives the design team the ability to improve the overall design of the system [10].

2.6 Modeling or Model-Based Design

The Final approach to significantly reduce system verification time and perform system verification earlier in the design process is to use model based design. Model based design is a method that emulates system [11] behavior using modeling and simulation. In other words, a virtual abstraction level is created. This abstraction level provides valuable insight into the hardware and software design.

Generally in traditional approach textual specification is directly connected to RTL implementation, this leads to the misinterpretation. Model based design creates algorithm model in terms of executable specification. So misinterpretation is not possible here.

For algorithm-intensive signal processing in communications, electronics, semi-conductor, imaging, medical, and aerospace applications, verification time and costs are escalating, we have to spend 50% or more of their time writing verification code. To alleviate the problem, Modeling helps us to turn to multi domain system verification, integrating Matlab, C/C++, and HDL (hardware description-language) IP into Simulink. Models. Designers can develop a golden reference model in Matlab, develop a test bench in Matlab or Simulink, and perform co simulation with embedded IDEs (integrated development environments), HDL simulators, or analog simulators, leading to a DSP or an FPGA prototype without requiring low-level programming. Next section will compare all the methods and shows how modeling is better than other approaches.

3 Why Modeling or Model-Based Design?

On the Basis of survey carried out, for above described methods, we have derived certain results in terms of design, verification effort and percentage time reduction. The complete survey results are mentioned in table 1.

As seen from survey data model-based design or modeling is found to be the best approach to optimize maximum verification time for ASIC design. The percentage mentioned is derived based on certain concrete implementation. Section 5 show implementation for traditional, transaction level modeling and Modeling approach.

The major advantages provided by Model-based design are: 1) In traditional verification approach we have to depend on textual specification, these may lead to to mis-interpretation at various abstraction level. While model based design convert textual specification into executable specification (Algorithm level) and so we can reuse it through out the development process. 2) Modelling provides readily available data generator, reference Model and data analyzer, so our major effort of development of verification environment reduces. 3) Major Advantage provided by model based is reduce total development time and complexity of verification environment. Also, we have golden reference model from modelling tools which eases difficulty of traditional approach. (bcoz real life applications can be easily created using prevalidates matlab modules which is highly difficult for traditional environment)[11].

Table 1. Survey results of various ways of optimizing ASIC verification time. This table compare various ways and shows result in terms of design and verification effort[1,3,4,7,11].

Methods/ Metrics		Design effort	Verification effort	Verification time Improvement	Level of Verification
Hardware based Methods	FPGA Prototyping	****	Medium	30.0%	****
	Emulation based		Medium	20.0-25.0%	****
Re-usability		High	Low	Upto 20.0 %	At RTL
Abstraction-based Method		High	Low	15.30 %	Above RTL
Assertion-based Method		Low	Medium	50.00%	Only RTL
Co-verification Method		High	Medium	20.0-30.0 %	At Each Level(application based)
Modeling or Model-based design		Medium	Low	55.3- 70.0%	Any Level

4   Case-Study

Filters are used for a variety of applications in Digital Signal Processing. The main task of any filter is to attenuate signals in a certain range of frequencies. Digital Filters are implemented based on the transformations in the s-domain representation of filter equation and sampling frequency, analog pass-band frequencies and stop band frequencies. There are 2 possible Digital Filters:

1. Finite Impulse Response (FIR).
2. Infinite Impulse Response (IIR).

FIR is non-causal, Linear Time Invariant (LTI) so it is unconditionally stable whereas IIR is causal LTI system so it is conditionally stable. The filter used here as case study here is stable as it's poles are within the unit circle in z-plane and it shows constant attenuation after 0.06pi digital frequency which at 8kHz sampling frequency is 240Hz. It is direct form 2(DF2) implementation of the equation.

$$H(z) = \frac{[3+(6z^{-1})+(3z^{-2})]}{[512-(936z^{-1})+(436z^{-2})]}$$

Here we have used fixed point implementation. Such implementation of fixed point filter is a challenging task as there need to be multiple numbers of adders and multipliers of different word length and fraction length. The design of the Device or the RTL (Register Transfer Logic) needs to be synthesizable. So use of floating point numbers and arithmetic operators is not possible. Next Section will discussed the implementation of verification environment for presented case-study.

5   Implementation and Results

Implementation is done in three different verification environment.

1. Traditional Verification environment using System verilog
2. Transaction-level Modeling using VMM-1.2
3. Modeling using System Verilog and Matlab

5.1   Traditional Verification Environment Using System Verilog

System Verilog is hardware verification language which is presently used by industry for verification environment of ASIC. The three major parts of a verification environment are the DUT, the test bench (the inner box above), and the test which controls the test bench.

System Verilog based environment is a transactions based environment. Transaction based verification raises the level of abstraction from signals to transactions, thus easing the development of reusable test benches. The test bench is separated into two modules: the test program and the Interface (transactor). The test program is written at a higher level of abstraction than the DUV and the Interface is the mechanism that translates the test from transactions to signals activity. A Interface is defined a high-level data transfer characterized by its begin time, end time. These data represent the parameters of the transaction. As an example, in Driver class has a task Dri_2_intf which include "in" bit data as the transaction's parameter. This example represents a relatively simple transaction. However, a more complex transaction format will be used to describe a complete communication channel structure[12].

The whole verification environment for traditional approach is created in System Verilog.

5.2   Transaction-Level Modeling Using VMM-1.2

Transaction-level modeling (TLM) is a high-level approach to modeling digital systems where details of communication among modules are separated from the details of the implementation of functional units or of the communication architecture. Transaction requests take place by calling interface functions of these channel models, which encapsulate low-level details of the information exchange. At the transaction level, the emphasis is more on the functionality of the data transfers - what data are transferred to and from what locations - and less on their actual implementation that is, on the actual protocol used for data transfer. This approach makes it easier for the system-level designer to experiment.

The VMM 1.2 supports the TLM concept and further VMM for System Verilog describes a flexible, scalable verification methodology for System Verilog users. It is possible to use concepts from the VMM methodology both in small ad-hoc testbenches for module testing and in the creation of large, complex high-grade verification environments by specialized verification engineers.

In VMM-compliant test-bench, the transactors that drive the DUT form a protocol stack, with the simplest transactions (signal transitions) at the lowest level of DUT interface, and the most complex (scenarios) coming from the generator at the top. We show one level of functional-level transactor, but there could be more if required.

Similarly, the monitoring transactors form a protocol stack. Connection to the DUT is implemented in a standardized way using the System-Verilog interface construct. The architecture of VMM is same as in system verilog for my case study of Fixed point IIR Filter. But communication is simple and easy. because VMM provides TLM based analysis ports so, here no special callback class and function are needed[6].

5.3   Modeling Using System Verilog and Matlab

Here the verification environment is created using a combination of tools such and Matlab and system verilog.

The complex task such as data generation and reference model are created in maltab while remaining components of environment are in System Verilog.

The advantage of this platform compared to other verification solutions, is the possibility to reuse the high level algorithmic model to assist the verification environment.

Table 2. Implementation results of verification environment in three different approaches. This table compare three ways of verification environment and shows improvement of one over another.

Parameters		Traditional Verification (System Verilog)	Transaction Level Modeling (VMM 1.2)	Model based Design (Matlab +SV)
Arch. Of Verification (in man hrs)		5	3	3
Design Time for verification Blocks (in man hrs)	Transactions	3	1	0
	Generators	3	0	1
	Driver	6	3	3
	Monitor	5	3	3
	Ref. Model	7	7	0
	Scoreboard	4	4	4
	Total Time	28	18	11
Debug Time for verification (time to Solve bugs of verification Environment)	Transactions	1	0.5	0
	Generators	1	0	1
	Driver	9	8	8
	Monitor			
	Ref. Model	10	10	1
	Scoreboard	2	2	1
	Total Time	23	20.5	11
Total Development Time		56	41.5	25
Development Time w.r.t Traditional Enviornment (%)		100	74.1	44.56
Improvement (%)		0	25.9	55.44
Improvement w.r.t. (36%)		0	9.32	19.96

The development time of the verification environment using traditional Approach (in System Verilog) took approximately 56 man hours in my project. The transaction level using VMM based verification environment time tooks around 40.5 man hours. Using the algorithmic level Matlab model of Fixed Point IIR Filter as Reference Model in System Verilog environment, where the development time of verification environment took around 25 man hours.

As the design is being redefined at the system level and the RTL level, the verification platform efficiency begins to pay off. As we know that the verification effort is represents 70% of total design time using traditional design flow. Where the RTL level verification time takes around 35%-36% time in total verification efforts.

So, Using this data in our Case Study of Fixed Point IIR filter, The traditional design flow, where the verification effort represents 35% of the total design time. The Transaction level Modeling design flow, where the verification efforts represents of 27.79 % of the total design time. This represents a productivity gain of around 7.20% over a traditional design flow that has limited test bench components reuse and software interoperability. And Same way using Matlab Reference Model in System verilog verification efforts represent 17.15% of total design time. This represents a productivity gain of around 17.84% over a traditional design flow. So, improvement around 55.44%. The design can be simulated quickly with real world test scenarios; compared to other verification methods that required some time to create the test bench environment and test cases. Combining System verilog verification library and Matlab we created a unified verification framework that cuts verification time and increases the quality of functional verification.

6 Conclusion

With today's complex designs, the verification task has become the primary bottleneck in the design flow. Manually coding all possible verification scenarios quickly becomes a fastidious and error prone task. Our approach is to reduce development time of ASIC and to start the verification early in the design flow. The surveyed results shows that maximum optimization in verification time can be achieved using modeling or model-based design. Implementation of the case-study shows that almost 56% of RTL level verification time gets reduced using modelling. Here we have used DSP based application; however, the application domain of our platform is not restricted to only DSP circuits. It can be used by all kind of complex ASICs that are represented at multiple abstraction level.

Acknowledgments. The authors would like to thank EInfochips, India for their financial support. Special thanks to Ms. Ekata Mehul for their support and encouragement through out the project work. Her advice and precious suggestions helped steer this work in right direction.

References

1. Gallagher, J.: Verification techniques:going beyond simulation. Synplicity (2004)
2. Mudigoudar, B.: FPGA Prototyping for fast and efficient verification of ASIC H.264 decoder, The University of Texas, Arlington (May 2006)

3. Abbe, J.: Verification Reuse Methodology, white paper (April 2002), `http://www.verisity.com`
4. Bergeron, J.: Writing Testbenches using SystemVerilog. Springer, Heidelberg (2006)
5. Santarini, M.: Cadence moves toward intelligent testbench. EE Times (June 1999)
6. Brown, S.: TLM Driven Design and Verification, white paper (June 2009), `http://www.cadence.com`
7. Einfochips, `http://www.einfochips.com/download/Tech_June04.pdf`
8. Mcmillan, K.: Assertion-Based Verification, Cadence Berkeley Labs (2005)
9. Bailey, B.: Co-Verification: From Tool to Methodology, white paper (June 2002), `http://www.mentor.com`
10. Klein, R.: Solving problems early on using co-verification. SoC Verification Business Unit Mentor Graphics Corp. (November 2004)
11. Advantages of Model-based design, `http://www.xilinx.com`
12. Lam, W.K.: Hardware design verification. Pearson Education, London (2005)

Optimal Solution for RFID Load Balancing

Vijayakumar G. Dhas, Ramanathan Muthukaruppan, Konguvel Balakrishnan, and Rajarajan Ganesan

Department of Information Technology,
Anna University, Chennai
vgdhas@annauniv.edu, mraman2006@gmail.com, konguvel31@gmail.com,
rajarajan248@gmail.com

Abstract. Radio Frequency Identification (RFID) comprises of uniquely identifiable, less expensive tags and readers that monitor these tags through Radio Frequency signals. The information in the tags will be collected with the help of the readers. The load for any reader is the number of tags that the reader has to monitor. For the effectiveness of the RFID system several algorithms like Load Balancing algorithm and Redundant Reader Elimination algorithm were proposed. In these existing schemes the former concentrates on the load of the reader while the latter concentrates on reducing the power consumption by the RFID system. Here in Optimal Solution for RFID load balancing, a solution for optimizing the effectiveness of the RFID system by focusing on two parameters is provided. Load of the reader and Power consumption by the RFID readers are the parameters considered. Here the maximum number of readers that can be switched off without leaving any of the readers overloaded is found out. And also the relocation of the tags from the reader which got overloaded to the least loaded reader in the RFID system increases the overall performance of the RFID system for the same power consumption. A mobile agent, RFID Mobile Agent (RMA) is implemented to collect workload information, from RFID middleware embedded in each RFID reader and execute load balancing strategy for RFID middleware.

Keywords: Load Value, Load balancing, Mobile Agent, Redundant Reader.

1 Introduction

Radio Frequency Identification (RFID) system consists of Tags and Readers. Tags are uniquely identifiable. Tags can be associated with an object in order to identify the object. Tags can be active or passive. Passive tags do not have any power source. They generate power from the signal sent by the Reader. Active tags have their own power source.

Each tag has memory to store a small amount of data in it. Reader can issue a write signal to store the data in the tag. Reader can monitor the tags that are present in its reading range. Reader periodically reads tags in its vicinity. If there is more number of tags present in its vicinity, then energy of that reader will be depleted more. Also, there is a less probability to monitor all the tags in its vicinity, within the next period. Hence, it becomes necessary to balance the load on each reader.

N. Meghanathan et al. (Eds.): NeCoM, WiMoN, and WeST 2010, CCIS 90, pp. 41–49, 2010.

In the Load balancing scheme in large-scale RFID systems proposed by Q.Dong et. al [3], the tags are allocated to the readers in a fair manner such that no reader in the entire system is allocated to more number of tags. When a set of tags are within the range of each reader, which of these tags should each reader monitor, such that the cost of monitoring tags across the different readers is balanced. Each tag is monitored by at least one reader. They have proposed the localized probabilistic assignment (LPA) scheme, for finding a tag-driven probabilistic assignment of tags to readers. In this scheme, each tag knows which readers are in its vicinity and what the load on the readers is and each reader only knows which tags are in its vicinity and its load. In order to achieve a more load balanced assignment, each tag should decide its probability of reporting to some reader based on the load. If a reader in its vicinity has a relatively high load (compared with other readers in its vicinity), the tag should report to it with a relatively low probability. Subsequently, in the LPA scheme, each tag will only consider reporting to its candidate readers instead of all readers that can cover it with maximum transmission range. The candidate readers of a tag are the readers that can reach that tag at the minimum transmission power level.

After each round of data retrieval, each reader and tag automatically obtains up-to-date knowledge about its vicinity. If a reader or tag leaves the system, it will be automatically detected at least after the next round of data retrieval. Therefore, no additional processing is needed to handle reader/tag leaves.

In this scheme, the load gets distributed evenly. There is a possibility for readers to get assigned only one tag each. This leads to more amount of energy depletion. If there are redundant readers, then energy can be saved by switching off redundant readers. Load balancing in large scale RFID systems, follows a tag driven probabilistic assignment of tags to readers. Tag should decide the probability with which to report to the reader. It reports with a low probability to highly loaded reader and with high probability to lightly loaded reader. Tag driven approach leaves more processing on the tag.

The Redundant Reader Elimination in RFID Systems proposed by B.Carbunar et. al [2] addresses the energy conservation by putting redundant readers to sleep state. Redundant readers cover a set of RFID tags which are also in the reading range of other RFID readers. In order to maximize the number of RFID readers that can be simultaneously deactivated, the minimum number of readers that cover all RFID tags needs to be discovered. Redundant Reader Elimination (RRE) consists of two steps. In the first step, each RFID reader attempts to write its tag count (number of covered tags) to all its covered RFID tags. An RFID tag stores the highest value seen and the identity of the corresponding reader. In the second step, an RFID reader queries each of its covered RFID tags and reads the identity of the tag's holder. A reader that locked at least one tag is responsible for monitoring the tag and will have to remain active. However, a reader that has locked no tag can be safely turned off. This is because all the tags covered by that reader are already covered by other readers that will stay active. Each tag is locked by the reader in its vicinity that covers most tags. A reader that locks at least one tag is required to remain active.

There is a possibility for a single reader to get overloaded and all other readers having no load. This results in poor performance. As the tags move in a random manner, the topology of the network changes frequently. When a tag moves from one reader's vicinity to another, then the tag has to be disassociated from the previous reader and it has to be associated with the new reader. In RRE scheme, a tag is allocated to the reader only if the reader has a load value higher than the one that is already in the tag's memory. When a tag moves from a reader's vicinity whose load is 5 to a new reader's vicinity whose load is 3, the new reader will compare its load value with the value in tag which is 5. So, it does not monitor the tag, even though the tag is not monitored by the old reader. Hence, there is a possibility for a tag to go blind.

2 Proposal

The tags considered for optimal solution are Passive tags. Passive tags have no processing power, i.e. they have no external power source. They generate power from the signal sent by the reader. The tag then sends the information present in its memory. Since the tag is much less expensive and requires no external power source, the tag finds extensive applications. Readers retrieve the information from the tag and decide whether to monitor the tag or not.

The tags are allocated to the readers based on the algorithm described in section 4.1. The tags are allocated such that no reader gets overloaded. Tags are initially assigned to the reader which sends the signal first. When a new reader's signal reaches the tag, which is already allocated to a reader, the new reader decides whether to monitor the tag or not based on the algorithm. When a reader decides not to monitor the tag, then the number of tags in its vicinity is reduced by one. When a reader decides to monitor the tag, then it updates the reader id, load value and timestamp values in the tag. Reader updates the entry when the number of tags in its vicinity is more than the load value in the tag and it is lesser than the threshold value. This ensures that a reader does not monitor the tag, which is monitored by another reader, if it is going to be overloaded by monitoring this tag.

The optimal solution finds out the effective solution by identifying maximum number of readers that can be switched off in order to save the power consumption by the RFID readers to some considerable level based on the algorithm described in section 4.2. Each tag will contain the load of the reader that monitors it and the reader ID. Every reader checks the tags in its vicinity to identify the tags allocated to it. If no tags are allocated to it, then Reader is switched off. This leads to conservation of energy. Redundant readers that are turned off can be turned on, when a reader in the system gets overloaded in order to share the load of the overloaded reader. In the optimal solution for the RFID load balancing scheme when a tag moves from one reader's vicinity to another then the information in the tag will not be considered because it is written by the reader to which it was connected before. Timestamps are used to find out whether the tag has been probed within a certain time period. This ensures that each tag is monitored by at least one reader and prevents the tag from going blind.

Middleware in RFID collects the tags' data from the reader and passes only relevant information to the RFID system. Applications make use of the filtered information to perform business processing. Middleware can be any of three types: they can be at the lower level of application, or they can be implemented as third party software or they can be embedded in reader itself. Here we consider embedding the middleware in RFID reader. When there is more number of tags present in exclusive range of a reader, then the reader will be overloaded. Exclusive range of a reader here means the tags are present only in that reader's range. In this case the middleware in RFID reader gets overloaded. This can be avoided using the mobile agent which is explained in the following section.

3 Agent Based Approach for RFID Middleware

RFID mobile agent (RMA) performs the collection of the load status of each middleware and updates it in the global middleware table and in the local middleware table. RMA moves across middleware and collects details about the status of middleware.

RFID system finds whether the middleware is overloaded or not. System then finds out the middleware that is lightly loaded and transfers a set of tags from that middleware to the lightly loaded middleware.

RMA moves to each middleware and collects the current load status and updates each time. If a middleware is overloaded, system finds out the tags to be relocated. Then the target middleware is chosen to which the tags have to be moved. Then, the tags to be relocated are noted and they are moved to the new middleware. And it finds out the appropriate middleware which is lightly loaded, so as to move the tags to that middleware. Finally the tags are relocated. Now, the middleware in each RFID reader is balanced.

4 Algorithm

4.1 Algorithm for Allocation of Tags

Threshold value= NT/NR + NR/2;   (1)

```
For each reader in the system

{

Find out the number of tags in the reader's
vicinity(NOTV)

For each tag in the vicinity

{

Check the timestamp of tag.

If timestamp=NULL then

        Create an entry in the tag's memory with the
        current reader's NOTV value, id, and timestamp

Else if timestamp not old then

        LV=Load value in the entry of the tag

        If LV > Threshold Value and NOTV < Threshold
        value then
```

```
              Update the tag's entry with current
              reader's NOTV value, id and update the
              timestamp

        Else if LV < Threshold value and NOTV <
        Threshold then

        value and NOTV> LV)

                Update the tag's table entry with
                current reader's NOTV value, id and
                update the timestamp

        Else

                Don't update

                Reduce the NOTV of current reader by one.

        End if

  Else

          Update the tag's entry with current reader's value
} //for each tag in the vicinity

}
```

The number of readers and the number of tags that is present in the RFID system are noted.

Threshold value is calculated as,

Threshold value = (Number of tags / Number of readers) + (Number of readers / 2)

Each reader finds out the number of tags that are present in its vicinity, which will be denoted as NOTV. Readers send signal to tags in its vicinity. Reader checks the timestamp present in the tag. If the timestamp is null, then the tag is yet to be probed by the reader. Hence, the reader issues a write command to the tag to store its identity and NOTV. Similarly, for all the yet to be probed tags present in its vicinity the reader issues a write command.

When the timestamp is not null, the reader checks the whether the tag has been probed before within a certain period. If it has been probed within the certain time interval, then the reader decides whether to monitor the tag or not based on three criteria.

Criteria 1:
When the load value present in the tag, i.e. the NOTV value written by the reader which previously monitored it, is greater than the Threshold value calculated as above and the NOTV value of current reader is lesser than the Threshold value, then the current reader will monitor it.

Criteria 2:
When the load value present in the tag is lesser than the Threshold value and the NOTV value of the current reader is lesser than the threshold value and NOTV value

of the current reader is greater than the Load value of the tag, then the current reader will monitor the tag.

Criteria 3:
If the above two criteria's are not satisfied then, reduce the NOTV value of the reader by one and tag will be monitored by the previous reader itself.

When the tag has not been probed for a specified time interval, then the tag is no longer in the range of the previous reader. Hence, the new reader monitors the tag. After the first period, the readers that are in on state, share the load of other readers if there are tags present in the intermittent range. This enhances balancing of the load among readers.

4.2 Algorithm for Turning off Redundant Readers

```
For each reader in the system
{
Initialize Flag for Sleep = 0;
Find out the number of tags in the reader's vicinity (NOTV)
For each tag in the vicinity
{
Read the reader name in the entry of the tag (RN)
If RN=current Reader then
            Flag for Sleep =1
            Monitor the tag
            Update the Server table (i.e., increment the
            number of tags monitored by the corresponding
            reader)
Else
            Continue to check other tags
End if
} // for each tag in the vicinity
If Flag for sleep = 0 then
            Put the reader into sleep state
            Update the Number of tags monitored column in
            server table for that reader to 0.
End if
} //for each reader in the system
```

During the next cycle, the reader checks whether any of the tags in its vicinity has its id stored in it. If no tag has its id stored, then the reader has no tags to monitor. Hence, the reader can be turned off. In this way, energy can be conserved by turning off redundant readers.

4.3 Wake-Up Criteria

If during next cycle, new tags are introduced, then there is a possibility for readers to get overloaded. During that time, the redundant readers which were put to sleep are turned on. Overloaded reader creates a trigger that enables the redundant readers to be turned on. If the overloaded reader has tags that are also in the reading range of redundant readers, then the redundant reader shares the load of the overloaded reader.

5 Evaluation and Results

Consider the scenario as given in Fig 1.

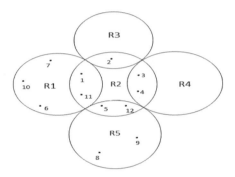

Fig. 1. Scenario containing 5 readers and 12 tags

As per the optimal solution, threshold value is calculated as 4. There are totally 12 tags and 5 readers in the system. Reader R1 monitors 3 tags, R2 monitors 3 tags, Reader 4 monitors 2 tags and R5 monitors 4 tags. R3 is turned off, since it is a redundant reader, i.e. tags in its vicinity are monitored already by another reader. Thus tags are equally distributed among the readers, with no reader overloaded.

For the scenario in Fig 1, as per the load balancing scheme the tags will be allocated as follows: R1 monitors tag t1, t6, t7, t10, t11. R2 monitors t5, t12. R3 monitors tag t2 and R4 monitors t3, t4. R5 monitors t8, t9.

In RRE scheme the readers R3 and R4 are found as redundant readers since R2 is found as the minimum set of reader that can monitor all the tags (t1–t5, t11, t12) in the scenario given in Fig 1. R1 monitors t6, t7, t10. R5 monitors t8, t9.

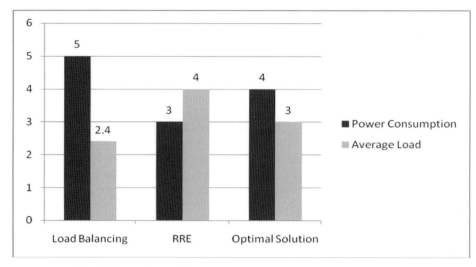

Fig. 2. Comparison of three schemes for the scenario shown in Fig 1

For the scenario as shown in fig 1, the performance of Load Balancing, RRE and optimal solution is compared in fig 2. As the figure shows, optimal solution allocates tags to readers such that threshold value is not exceeded.

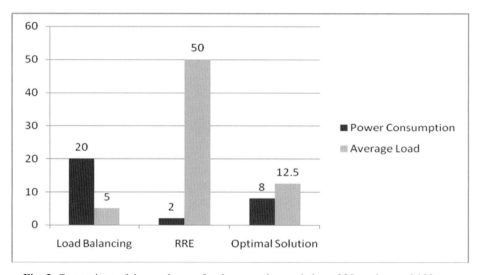

Fig. 3. Comparison of three schemes for the scenario consisting of 20 readers and 100 tags

The performance of the three schemes for complex RFID system consisting of 20 readers and 100 tags is shown in the fig 3. It is observed from the figure that RRE scheme is having the least power consumption, but the average of the readers get increased to a large extent. Optimal solution yields good result when compared to load balancing and RRE schemes.

6 Conclusion

In this paper, balancing tags among the readers, switching off the redundant readers, and agent based approach for rfid middleware load balancing are addressed. Optimal Solution performs effectively better. Maximum number of readers that can be switched off are found out and turned off. This reduces the power consumption. Tags in the intersection range of two or more readers are balanced among readers using algorithm proposed in section 4.1. If there is more number of tags concentrated in the exclusive range of an rfid reader, then the middleware in RFID reader gets overloaded which is prevented by implementing the RFID mobile agent based approach. RMA effectively balances the load among the RFID. Results demonstrate that this scheme can perform effectively even in highly dynamic RFID systems. When a reader fails or does not function, then the tags may not get monitored. Our future work concentrates on overcoming this problem with the help of RFID Mobile agent.

References

[1] Bejerano, Y., Han, S.-J., Li, L.E.: Fairness and load balancing in wireless lans using association control. In: ACM MobiCom (2004)

[2] Carbunar, B., Ramanathan, M.K., Koyuturk, M., Hoffmann, C., Grama, A.: Redundant-reader elimination in rfid systems. In: IEEE SECON (2005)

[3] Dong, Q., Shukla, A., Shrivastava, V., Agrawal, D., Banerjee, S., Kar, K.: Load balancing in large-scale rfid systems. In: INFOCOM (2007)

[4] Engels, D.W., Sarma, S.E., Weis, S.A.: RFID systems and security and privacy implications. In: Kaliski Jr., B.S., Koç, Ç.K., Paar, C. (eds.) CHES 2002. LNCS, vol. 2523, pp. 454–469. Springer, Heidelberg (2003)

[5] Floerkemeier, C., Wille, M.: Comparison of Transmission Schemes for Framed ALOHA based RFID Protocols. In: Workshop on RFID and Extended Network Deployment of Technologies and Applications, Phoenix, AZ (January 2006)

[6] Cui, J.F., Chae, H.S.: Mobile Agent based Load Balancing for RFID Middlewares. In: ICACT 2007 (Feburary 2007)

[7] Kobayashi, M., Zhen, B., Shimizu, M.: To read transmitter-only RFID tags with confidence. IEEE (2004)

[8] Jurdak, R., Ruzzelli, A.G., O'Hare, G.M.P.: On the RFID wake-up impulse for multihop sensor networks

[9] Zheng, R., Hou, J.C., Sha, L.: Asynchronous wakeup for ad hoc networks. In: MobiHoc 2003: Proceedings of the 4th ACM international symposium on Mobile ad hoc networking & computing, pp. 35–45. ACM Press, New York (2003)

[10] Jain, S., Das, S.R.: Collision Avoidance in a Dense RFID Network. In: WiNTECH 2006 (September 2006)

[11] Kim, S., Lee, S., Sunshin: An Reader Collision Avoidance Mechanism in Ubiquitous Sensor and RFID Networks. In: WiNTECH 2006, Los Angeles, California, USA, September 29, 2006. ACM, New York (2006) 1-59593-538-X/06/0009

[12] Zhou, F., Chen, C., Jin, D., Huang, C., Min, H.: Evaluating and optimizing power consumption of anti-collision protocols for applications in RFID systems. In: ACM ISLPED 2004 (August 2004)

Fault Management in Grid Using Multi-agents

S. Thamarai Selvi, C. Valliyammai, G. Subbiah, S. Parthi Kumar, and S. Siva Samraj

Department of Information Technology,
Anna University Chennai, Chennai-600044
stselvi@mitindia.edu, cva@annauniv.edu, subaibrettmit@gmail.com
parthi.mit@gmail.com, samraj.mit55@gmail.com

Abstract. Network faults are mutative in nature; it could not be ignored due to its vital importance irrespective of grid type and setup. Hence managing those faults is not an easy task to be carried out, it requires complete knowledge regarding the entire grid workflow. An agent based sensor network sensing the workflow for grid network fault management is proposed in this paper. The agents are trained to regularize the flow of activities within the network. As the grid is highly distributed and large, a cluster based approach is carried out. Working nodes are allowed to concentrate more on the job assigned to them rather in management activity which is carried out by the proxies created. As the proxies are configured based on the individual links, they provide quick consensus time in detection. At the same time, the failure detection is also made at a linear time and minimum bandwidth utilization. The relationship between inter and intra cluster timings are found out through the timer agents. This analysis ensures more reliability into the detection. An agent repository is created which can be used as a sensor system for any kind of grid supporting scalability and distributiveness.

Keywords: Grid, Multi-agents, Agent Repository, False positive, False negative, Event correlation.

1 Introduction

The grid will act as the tool for intensive computing and storage space as the internet had become the tool of mass communication. More and more grid related projects are coming up making the need for automation of the component management in the systems. These require complex fault identification and management systems. Fault management in networks can be done through monitoring and setting up traps in the network. These steps should make a good deal between the root cause identification and the overload induced for the detection. Therefore, event correlation and filtering should be done to bring about the source of the fault. One such event in networks is the node failure which forms the root cause of many faults. Failures in networks are unavoidable but earlier detection and classification of their source is essential. The taxonomy of faults [2] occurring in grid covers all the resources which directly or indirectly affects its working. The work done in this paper mainly deals with the node

N. Meghanathan et al. (Eds.): NeCoM, WiMoN, and WeST 2010, CCIS 90, pp. 50–59, 2010.

failure detection among the network faults in the worker node, cluster head and network. Once the network changes its state, the node that identifies the change, disseminate the state through agents. The fault management system uses the state change for event correlation function. Agents are implemented at the application level and therefore, they can cover all activities needed to make the fault tolerance process efficient and manageable. It also provides a freedom to select any node in the network to handle the fault tolerance at any stage which makes the system flexible for managing. This will also provide the facility of monitoring, studying the network by the schedulers and meta- schedulers distinctly before scheduling a job. Grid Information Service (GIS) can also make use of the agent system for querying the resources of the clusters. The error once caused by the fault will make the management to restart the job at a new location or select the suitable redundant system for job completion. There will be a switch delay in each of these two techniques. The normal approaches need complex interactions to make the transition to happen increasing the switch delay. But the agent based system handling the fault will transfer the information to the new node through data agents reducing the switch delay involved. Defining separate strategies for each combination of faults is a tedious and difficult job. Hence, classify the faults, handle them, and correct them. Hence, the node failure which is one of the root causes for many faults should be handled in an extensible and flexible manner.

2   Related Work

The membership management technique and heart-beat messaging discussed in [1] form the base for the detection process and provide the strategies for the partitioning and backup node designating. It also proposes an algorithm for membership management for the dynamic nature of grid. They make the grid to be viewed as a group of networks each headed by a node whose position may be replaced by a backup and the member nodes. It helps to identify all type of failures such as single node failure, a group failure etc. Research on fault-tolerant grid and high performance computing has traditionally focused on recovery strategies implemented principally through checkpointing and job migration applied to local networks of computing hosts under a centralized management [11]. The checkpointing and job migration techniques are part of any fault-tolerant grid management framework, but more emphasis needs to for monitoring, detection, and prediction of faults with preventive approaches addressing the challenges in grid computing environment. This is particularly important since preventive maintenance measures would diminish the need for frequent check pointing and complex recovery procedures which may involve rescheduling jobs on different execution environments [7].A fault-tolerance framework that provides the necessary models to manage the local faulty behavior associated with the operation of hosted services is proposed in [4]. The framework includes a quantification mechanism of the fault vulnerability of grid nodes and their hosted services. The resulting measures of fault vulnerability are globally disseminated to enable the synthesis of decentralized fault- tolerant decision making strategies. Good fault tolerance mechanisms can ensure the reliable execution of Grid workflow applications, which is a critical issue in grid computing. Fault detection is the starting point of any fault tolerance. On the one hand, early fault prediction and detection is able to enhance the reliability and eliminate considerably amount of overheads from belated fault handling [8, 9]. Human-assisted computer discovery techniques and computer-assisted human discovery techniques are discussed in [26]. In this paper we have proposed a model which can bring transparency in the fault management system. The working nodes are managed through their proxy agents working in the cluster head. This makes the system a failure detector of minimal false findings and reaching earlier consensus time compared with the traditional approach of direct management of the working nodes. The vital modification from the architecture discussed in [1] is the introduction of proxy agents for the working members at the cluster head site. The waiting time defined inside the proxy reflects the network parameters such as roundtrip time and delay for the link between cluster head and the respective working member.

3   Architecture and Design

The architecture of the nodes participating and the agent environment is shown in Figure 1. The agent system surrounding the component nodes of each sub-cluster is also shown in Figure1. The head agents of each sub-cluster interact to form the virtual cluster. The distinction of the nodes involved in grid as head, backup, member makes the agents functionalities to depend on the type of node on which it is working. This proxy binds the working member and the head. The component agents are:

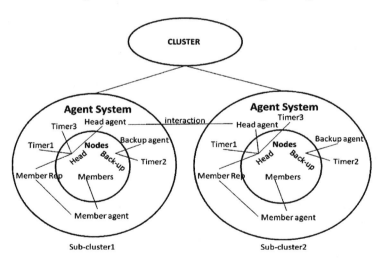

Fig. 1. Overall Architecture of the Grid setup

3.1   Head Agent

It is a stationary agent working on the head node. It functions as the controlling agent for the network. It communicates with the member nodes through the member representative agents present within the head node. The return of the message from the member node is handed over by the representative agents to the head agent. It also messages the back-up node to ensure its presence. Head agents from different networks manage to form a group and represent their group through messaging the group. Head agents work based on two timer agents (timer1, timer3) that are discussed below and their interrelationship with head agent forms the significant part to manage the delay in node failure detection.

3.2 Back-Up Agent

It is a stationary agent working over the back-up node. It is mainly used for the substitution of the head node when the head fails. All the members are made to contact the back-up agent when the current head fails. A new back-up agent is created by the new head agent from the member agents through algorithm. The communication between the head and back-up agent can be done efficiently if the selected back-up is based on nearest neighbor or the strongest link. Back-up node depends on a timer agent (timer2) to arrive at the head node failure which is based on the link between the two agents.

3.3 Member Agent

It is a stationary agent working at each member node. The functionalities of the agent are low as to reply its presence to the head agent whenever the head asks for it though the member representative present in the head node. They are made minimum so that more amount of resources can be allocated to the job rather than wasting the resources in fault tolerance activity.

3.4 Proxy or Member Representative Agent

It is a mobile agent made to move from the respective member node to the head node by the member agent. It is like a proxy agent for the member agent present in the head node. Once a new head node is created and the old representative agents will be inactive. New representative agents will be created and sent to the new head node by the respective member agents. The member representative agents will be made to wait for the reply from the member agent based on the link between the head and the respective member. Thus, the head node communicates with the member nodes based on the different link properties, which is expensive without the use of proxy agents at the application level. This will help to reduce the false positive and false negative findings about each member node.

3.5 Timer1 Agent

It is a stationary agent and also a control agent present in the head node and created by head agent used for the time between the regular heartbeat messages between the head and members. The timer alerts the head agent to broadcast the message to the proxy agents present locally. It controls the intra-cluster communication.

3.6 Timer2 Agent

It is a stationary and control agent in the back-up node and created by the back-up. It is based on the link between the head and the back-up nodes. Efficient back-up selection will help us to low this time which will decrease the failure detection time. It is helpful in finding the head failure.

3.7 Timer3 Agent

It is a stationary and control agent present in the head node created on the whole for the entire system and cloned for each sub-cluster network. The head nodes of each sub-cluster communicate with each other based on this timer. It controls inter-cluster communication.

3.8 Ping Agent

This mobile agent knows the reliable path to each working member and updated whenever new node joins. Whenever the waiting member representative agent did not receive any reply from the member agent it complaints the head agent about the abnormality. In turn the head creates the ping agent to check and it takes the original reliable path. If it is unreachable, then the node is declared failed.

3.9 Agent Repository

This represents the database for the agents. It can be made available to all the nodes by distributing the codes to all the nodes believing that each node can take the role of different types. A data agent can also be used to transfer the code to the node which is about to take a different role. This helps to avoid the exhaustive changes to the repository when a particular functionality changes.

4 Implementation

Agent environment is created through IBM aglets. Message passing interface provided by them is used for the inter-communication of agents. The sequence diagram in Fig 2 depicts the working of the agent system in detecting the node failure. Initially when the working node joins the cluster, a proxy agent representing the member is sent to the cluster head. Timer 1 agent induces the head agent to broadcast a message which reaches member through proxy. Proxy waits for the time defined in it. If there is no reply from the member agent, head agent creates the ping agent. The ping agent routes the working node through the reliable path and gets the status.

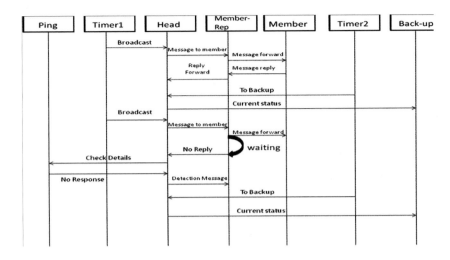

Fig. 2. Working of Agent system in detecting Node failure

where the subscript *i* stands for a parameter out of the of n chosen parameters and the subscript *j* stands for the set of values existing in the traffic for the parameter *i*. S_{ij} is the value j of the parameter *i*. Then the time series is smoothened using moving average [3], with α=0.3, in order to avoid false alarms. This smoothened time series is taken as the input for wavelet analysis. The wavelet analysis procedure involves the use of the abstract wavelet function, called mother wavelet. Here the initial analysis is performed on the mother wavelet function, while further analysis is performed with a wavelet obtained with a scaled and translated version of the same wavelet. As the original signal or function can be represented in terms of a wavelet coefficient, any further operations can be performed using wavelet coefficients itself.

Since the network traffic is continuous, it is better to choose the wavelet corresponding to continuous wavelet transform. Some of the continuous wavelets are Morlet, Gaussian, Mexican hat, etc. The energy distribution variance in traffic behaviour under DoS attack changes markedly and this change in distribution is used to detect the attacks. The energy values generated using different wavelets are compared and the properties of wavelets are anlysed to identify the most efficient one for attack detection.

5   Results and Discussions

Let a node 'i' fails after successfully replying to the head. Consider the total nodes be divided into 'm' groups of average working nodes 'n'. Let T1 be the timer1 agent value, T2 be the timer2 agent value and T3 be the timer3 agent value. Let us consider the processing of messages at each node takes a constant time and also the ping agent is designed to take constant time for routing as it searches within the sub-cluster. The consensus time 'C' required for the failure detection can be discussed as:

Head agent comes to know at H_t , then

$$H_t = T_1 + RT_{hi} + P_t \tag{1}$$

where, RT_{hi} is the round trip time between head and the failed node.

P_t is the time taken by the ping agent to test the status of the node which is linear. Other members come to know at O_t

$$O_t = T_1 + RT_{hj}/2 \tag{2}$$

where, RT_{hj} is the average round trip time between head and jth node.

Back-up agent comes to know at B_t, then

$$B_t = T_2 + RT_{hb}/2 \tag{3}$$

where, RT_{hb} is the average round trip time between head and back-up nodes. Other group heads come to know at G_t, then

$$G_t = T_3 + \sum_{a=1}^{m-1} RT_{ha}/2 \tag{4}$$

where, RT_{ha} is the average round trip time between head nodes.

$$C = (H_t + O_t + B_t) + G_t + (n-1)(O_t + B_t)$$
$$C = H_t + G_t + n(O_t + B_t) \tag{5}$$

Equation (5) forms a linear time of order (m). Thus, the consensus time is linear which is verified from the graph which is shown in Fig 3. It also signifies the importance of proxy agent which reduces the consensus time.

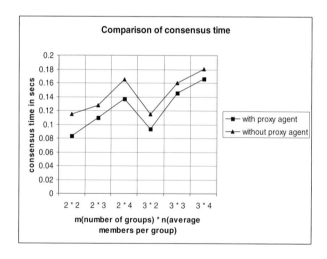

Fig. 3. Consensus time with proxy agents

A study for suitable timer values is shown in fig.4 which is given by

$$Timer_3 = L(Timer_1 + Timer_2) \qquad (6)$$

where, L is an integer constant. It shows that L value between 1.5 and 2 reduces false findings which ensure reliability.

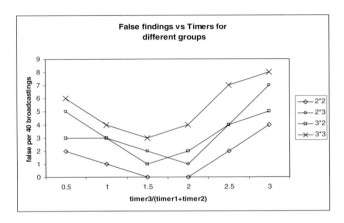

Fig. 4. False Findings

6   Conclusion

Thus the proxy agents bring out earlier detection of node failure which helps the event correlation to avoid extensive analysis of events for node failure detection as it is made explicit. The scalability and the network bandwidth usage remain unaffected with the use of the multi-agents. The minimum false findings from the proxy agent system give a clear picture of the reliability when the agent system provides the detection of failures and faults. Amid all these advantages, a location transparency exists when abstracts the individual clusters as grid.

7   Future Works

Future work may include handling more faults like messaging faults, service faults with the introduction of new agents and rule sets to handle them. Also, the relationships between the more commonly occurring faults can be established which helps to improve the fault handling time. Artificial Intelligence can be made into the system making the agents more intelligent. A replication based fault resistant system can be built through the agents. The replica is easily made through the cloning of the agents and can be made to carry out the functions in parallel. The mobile grid coming up in future will be highly benefited by the concept of proxy agents. The location transparency of the system makes the application layer working unaware of the working member location. This will help in building grid portals for submitting jobs over the internet. Head agents as the controller of the sub-cluster can monitor it, with security policies. Rules for fault management regarding inter-cluster interactions can be implemented at the intelligent head agents, intra-cluster interactions being controlled by the member agents. The rule set defined for the various types of faults which can be extended further based on the application specifications. This will lead to a global set of rules defined for grid community in fault management domain. New artificial intelligence techniques can also be applied to the fault detection and identification process which helps in studying the suitable technique for the specific application.

References

[1] Jain, A., Shyamasundar, R.K.: Failure Detection and Membership Management in Grid Environments. In: Proceedings of the Fifth IEEE/ACM International Workshop on Grid Computing, GRID 2004 (2004)

[2] Hofer, J., Fahringer, T.: A Multi- Perspective Taxonomy for Systematic Classification of Grid Faults. In: Proceedings in: 16th Euromicro Conference on Parallel, Distributed and Network- Based Processing (2008)

[3] Derbal, Y.: A new fault-tolerance framework for grid computing, Multiagent and Grid Systems. An International Journal 2, 115–133 (2006)

[4] Waheed, A., Smith, W., George, J., Yan, J.: An Infrastructure for Monitoring and Management in Computational Grids. In: Computer Sciences Corp., offett Field. NASA Ames Research Center, CA 94035-1000

[5] Chao, C.-S., Yang, D.-L., Liu, A.-C.: A LAN Fault Diagnosis Systems. Computer Communications 24, 1439–1451 (2001)

[6] Ekaette, E.U., Far, B.H.: A Framework For Distributed Fault Management Using Intelligent Software Agents. In: CCECE 2003, Montréal (May 2003)

[7] Wrzesinska, G., Van Nieuwpoort, R.V., Maassen, J., Bal, H.E.: Fault-tolerance, malleability and migration for divideand- conquer applications on the grid. In: Proceedings – 19th IEEE International Parallel and Distributed Processing Symposium, Piscataway, NJ, vol. 13a, Institute of Electrical and Electronics Engineers Computer Society, United States (2005) 08855-1331

[8] Lee, H.M., Chin, S.H., Lee, J.H., Lee, D.W., Chung, K.S., Jung, S.Y., Yu, H.C.: A Resource Manager for Optimal Resource Selection and Fault Tolerance Service in Grids. In: Proceedings in: IEEE International Symposium on Cluster Computing and the Grid (2004)

[9] Gorde, N.B., Aggarwal, S.K.: A Fault Tolerance Scheme for Hierarchical Dynamic Schedulers in Grids. In: Proceedings IEEE International Conference on Parallel Processing (2008)

[10] Medeiros, R., Cirne, W., Brasileiro, F., Sauvé, J.: Faults in Grids: Why are they so bad and What can be done about it? In: Proceedings in: IEEE Fourth International Workshop on Grid Computing, GRID 2003 (2003)

[11] Wang, L., Pattabiraman, K., Kalbarczyk, Z., Iyer, R.K., Votta, L., Vick, C., Wood, A.: Modeling coordinated checkpointing for large-scale supercomputers. In: Proceedings of the International Conference on Dependable Systems and Networks, Piscataway, NJ, pp. 812–821. Institute of Electrical and Electronics Engineers Computer Society, United States (2005) 08855-1331

[12] Dabrowski, C.: Reliability in Grid Computing Systems, http://www.ogf.org/OGF_Special_Issue/GridReliabilityDabrowski.pdf

[13] Duan, R., Prodan, R., Fahringer, T.: Data Mining-based Fault Prediction and Detection on the Grid. IEEE, Los Alamitos (2007)
[14] Scalzo, R.C., Roth, H.: A Meta-Model for Fault Management. In: Proceedings in Conference on Object-Oriented Real-Time Dependable Systems, pp. 135–144 (1994)
[15] Baras, J.S., Ball, M., Gupta, S., Viswanathan, P., Shah, P.: Automated Fault Management. IEEE, 1244–1250 (1997)
[16] Burgess, J.: Guillermo. Raising. Network Fault Management Intelligence. In: Proceedings in:Network Operations and Management Symposium IEEE/IFIP, pp. 861–874 (2000)

Minimizing Response Time in an Autonomic Computing System Using Proportional Control

Harish S. Venkatarama[1] and Kandasamy Chandra Sekaran[2]

[1] Reader, Computer Science & Engg. Dept.,
Manipal Institute of Technology, Manipal, India
`harish.sv@manipal.edu`
[2] Professor, Dept. of Computer Engg.,
National Institute of Technology Karnataka, India
`kch@nitk.ac.in`

Abstract. Ecommerce is an area where an Autonomic Computing system could be very effectively deployed. Ecommerce has created demand for high quality information technology services and businesses are seeking quality of service guarantees from their service providers. These guarantees are expressed as part of service level agreements. Properly adjusting tuning parameters for enforcement of the service level agreement is time-consuming and skills-intensive. Moreover, in case of changes to the workload, the setting of the parameters may no longer be optimum. In an ecommerce system, where the workload changes frequently, there is a need to update the parameters at regular intervals. This paper describes an approach to automate the tuning of MaxClients parameter of Apache web server using a proportional controller based on the required response time and the current workload. This is an illustration of the self-optimizing characteristic of an autonomic computing system.

Keywords: autonomic computing, ecommerce, proportional control.

1 Introduction

The advent and evolution of networks and Internet, which has delivered ubiquitous service with extensive scalability and flexibility, continues to make computing environments more complex [1]. Along with this, systems are becoming much more software-intensive, adding to the complexity. There is the complexity of business domains to be analyzed, and the complexity of designing, implementing, maintaining and managing the target system. I/T organizations face severe challenges in managing complexity due to cost, time and relying on human experts.

All these issues have necessitated the investigation of a new paradigm, Autonomic computing [1], to design, develop, deploy and manage systems by taking inspiration from strategies used by biological systems. Ecommerce is one area where an Autonomic Computing system could be very effectively deployed. Ecommerce has created demand for high quality information technology (IT) services and businesses are seeking quality of service (QoS) guarantees from their service providers (SPs). These

N. Meghanathan et al. (Eds.): NeCoM, WiMoN, and WeST 2010, CCIS 90, pp. 60–67, 2010.
© Springer-Verlag Berlin Heidelberg 2010

guarantees are expressed as part of service level agreements (SLAs). As an example, performance of an Apache web server [16] is heavily influenced by the MaxClients parameter, but the optimum value of the parameter depends on system capacity, workload and the SLA. Properly adjusting tuning parameters for enforcement of the SLA is time-consuming and skills-intensive. Moreover, in case of changes to the workload, the setting of the parameters may no longer be optimum. In an ecommerce system, where the workload changes frequently, there is a need to update the parameters at regular intervals.

The simplified architecture for autonomic computing is shown in fig. 1. Adding an autonomic manager makes the resource self-managing [2]. The manager gets required data through the sensors and regulates the behavior of the resource through effectors. This shows how self-managing systems are developed using feedback control loops. This observation suggests that control theory will be of help in the construction of autonomic managers.

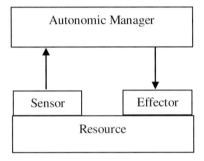

Fig. 1. Autonomic computing architecture

Control theory has been applied to many computing systems, such as networks, operating systems, database management systems, etc. The authors in [3] propose to control web server load via content adaptation. The authors in [5] extend the scheme in [3] to provide performance isolation, service differentiation, excess capability sharing and QoS guarantees. In [4][8] the authors propose a relative differentiated caching services model that achieves differentiation of cache hit rates between different classes. The same objective is achieved in [6], which demonstrates an adaptive control methodology for constructing a QoS-aware proxy cache. The authors in [7] present the design and implementation of an adaptive architecture to provide relative delay guarantees for different service classes on web servers.

Real-time scheduling theory makes response-time guarantees possible, if server utilization is maintained below a pre-computed bound. Feedback control is used in [9] to maintain the utilization around the bound. The authors in [10][11] demonstrate the power of a control theoretic analysis on a controller for doing admission control of a Lotus Notes workgroup server.

MIMO techniques are used in [12][13] to control the CPU and memory utilization in web servers. Queuing theory is used in [14] for computing the service rate necessary to achieve a specified average delay given the currently observed average request arrival rate. Same approach is used to solve the problem of meeting relative delay guarantees in [15].

This paper describes an approach to automate the tuning of MaxClients parameter of Apache web server using a proportional controller. The controller maximizes the number of users allowed to connect to the system subject to the response time constraint as given in the SLA. This is an illustration of the self-optimizing characteristic of an autonomic computing system.

2 System Background

The system studied here is the Apache web server. In Apache version 2.2 (configured to use Multi-Processing Module prefork), there are a number of worker processes monitored and controlled by a master process [16]. The worker processes are responsible for handling the communications with the web clients. A worker process handles at most one connection at a time, and it continues to handle only that connection until the connection is terminated. Thus the worker is idle between consecutive requests from its connected client.

A parameter termed MaxClients limits the size of this worker pool, thereby providing a kind of admission control in which pending requests are kept in the queue. MaxClients should be large enough so that more clients can be served simultaneously, but not so large that response time constraints are violated. If MaxClients is too small, there is a long delay due to waits in the queue. If it is too large resources become over utilized which degrades performance as well. The optimal value depends on server capacity, nature of the workload and the SLA.

3 Modeling and System Identification

Fig. 2 shows the scheme used for system identification. The simulation environment consists of a workload generator which generates requests and a server program which services the requests.

In this model, parameter max-requests is varied from 200 in steps of 10 and the corresponding response time values are noted. A first order ARX model is used to describe the relationship between inputs and outputs.

$$y(k+1) = a*y(k) + b*u(k) \tag{1}$$

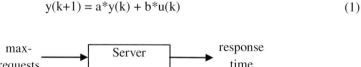

Fig. 2. Modelling the system

Here, u is the input or actuating signal, y is the output signal and a and b are scalars. Since a discrete signal has value only at specific instants of time, an integer k is used to index these instants. Using least squares regression, values for a and b are estimated as a = 0.1 and b = -0.36. That is, we arrive at the model

$$y(k+1) = 0.1*y(k) - 0.36*u(k) \qquad (2)$$

4 Controller Design

We use the proportional control law.

$$u(k) = K_P*e(k) \qquad (3)$$

Here K_P is a constant called gain of the controller. The actuating signal is proportional to the present error signal. It is not dependent on the past values of the error. Taking Z transform of equation (2) and manipulating, we get the open loop transfer function.

$$G(z) = Y(z) / U(z) = -0.36 / (z-0.1) \qquad (4)$$

Closed loop transfer function is as follows.

$$F_R(z) = Y(z) / R(z) = K_P*G(z) / (1+K_P*G(z))$$

Solution of the characteristic equation, $1+K_P*G(z) = 0$ gives the poles. For the system in question, there is only 1 closed loop pole, given by the following equation.

$$p1 = 0.1 + 0.36*K_P$$

For stability, we need to have,

$$| 0.1 + 0.36*K_P | < 1 \text{ or } -3.1 < K_P < 2.5$$

5 Implementation

Fig 3 shows the system for proportional control which is used for the implementation. In terms of fig. 1, server is the resource and controller is the autonomic manager. Response time is converted to error signal, which corresponds to input to the manager from the sensor. Just as the behavior of the resource is influenced by the effector, the server is influenced by max-requests.

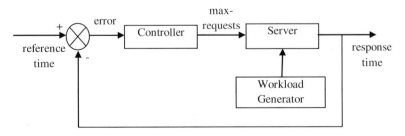

Fig. 3. System for Proportional control

The incoming request from the workload generator is first put into a queue in the server. When the server becomes free, the first request in the queue is dequeued. The time spent by the request in the queue is called the response time. The workload generator generates requests such that the time between generations of consecutive requests is exponentially distributed. Also, the time taken by the server to process each request is exponentially distributed. Thus, the client server architecture is simulated here as an M/M/1 queue.

Workload generator is set to generate requests such that the time between arrivals of consecutive requests on an average (mean interarrival) is 0.2 second. That is 300 requests per minute on an average. Mean service time is set to 60 seconds. Readings are noted every 3 minutes. To ensure that transients do not affect the readings, readings are taken for the last 1 minute of the 3 minute interval. Response time values of the requests which entered service in the last 1 minute are noted and the average is calculated. In this simulation, MaxClients is simulated by max-requests.

The controller tries to drive the error signal to 0 by adjusting the value of max-requests at regular intervals. That is, it tries to make the response time equal to the reference time.

The simulation is carried out using C-based simulation language "simlib" [17]. The experiment was repeated for different values of reference times and different values of gains. Each simulation was run for 60 minutes.

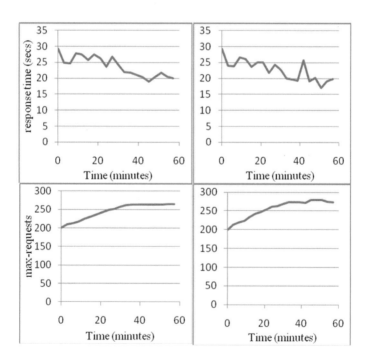

Fig. 4. With reference time = 20 secs, K_P = -1.0 (left hand side) and K_P = -1.5 (right hand side)

6   Results

Fig. 4 shows the results for reference time = 20 seconds with gain values equal to -1.0 (top and bottom figures on left hand side) and -1.5 (top and bottom figures on right hand side) respectively. The plots at the top of the figure show the variation of response time, while the plots at the bottom show the variation in max-requests. It is seen that when the gain is larger, the controller tries to correct the error more aggressively, but it results in undershoot. There is very little undershoot when the gain is less. Fig. 5 shows the results for reference time = 25 seconds with gain values equal to -1.0 (left hand side) and -1.5 (right hand side) respectively. Here also, undershoot is observed in case of larger gain.

For verifying the stability of the system, the simulation was run for durations upto 18,000 seconds (5 hours). For gain values shown above, the system was stable for the entire duration. However, for larger values of the gain, it was observed that the system was becoming increasingly unstable. Hence, results shown are only for those values of gains for which the system was stable.

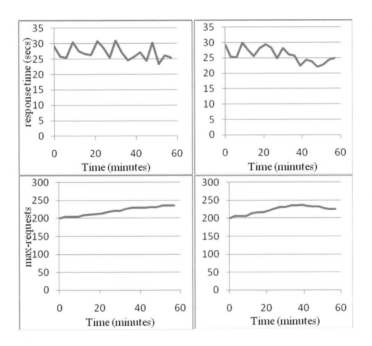

Fig. 5. With reference time = 25 secs, K_P = -1.0 (left hand side) and K_P = -1.5 (right hand side)

7   Conclusions

This paper describes an approach to minimize response time in an ecommerce system using proportional control. This is an illustration of the self-optimizing characteristic of an autonomic computing system. Specifically, the system studied here is tuning of MaxClients parameter of the Apache web server to satisfy the parameters mentioned in the SLA. The workload and server are simulated as an M/M/1 queue. The controller attempts to maximize max-requests, which is equivalent to MaxClients. It is easily seen from the results, that a single fixed value of max-requests will not be optimum for all cases. Since workload of a server can change rapidly, it is of immense benefit to have a controller which updates the value of MaxClients at regular intervals.

Though the controller is properly able to adjust value of max-requests, it takes some time for it to converge to the optimum value. Increasing the gain led to stability problems. Thus, as part of future work, it is intended to find ways to speed up the working of the system. It is also intended to test the functioning of the controller under different simulation environments like having an arbitrary (general) distribution for the service time, i.e., simulating the workload and server as an M/G/1 queue.

References

1. Salehie, M., Tahvildari, L.: Autonomic Computing: Emerging trends and open problems. In: Proc. of the Workshop on the Design and Evolution of Autonomic Application Software (2005)
2. Diao, Y., Hellerstein, J.L., Parekh, S., Griffith, R., Kaiser, G.E., Phung, D.: A control theory foundation for self-managing computing systems. IEEE J. on Selected Areas in Communications 23(12) (December 2005)
3. Abdelzaher, T.F., Bhatti, N.: Web server Quality of Service management by adaptive content delivery. In: Intl. Workshop on Quality of Service (June 1999)
4. Lu, Y., Saxena, A., Abdelzaher, T.F.: Differentiated caching services - A control-theoretical approach. In: Proc. of the International Conference on Distributed Computing Systems (April 2001)
5. Abdelzaher, T.F., Shin, K.G., Bhatti, N.: Performance guarantees for web server end-systems: A control-theoretical approach. IEEE Trans. on Parallel and Distributed Systems 13(1) (January 2002)
6. Lu, Y., Abdelzaher, T.F., Lu, C., Tao, G.: An adaptive control framework for QoS guarantees and it's application to differentiated caching services. In: Proc. of the Intl. Conference on Quality of Service (May 2002)
7. Lu, C., Abdelzaher, T.F., Stankovic, J.A., Son, S.H.: A feedback control approach for guaranteeing relative delays in web servers. In: Proc. of the IEEE Real-Time Technology and Applications Symposium (June 2001)
8. Lu, Y., Abdelzaher, T.F., Saxena, A.: Design, implementation and evaluation of differentiated caching services. IEEE Transactions on Parallel and Distributed Systems 15(5) (May 2004)
9. Abdelzaher, T.F., Lu, C.: Modeling and performance control of internet servers. In: IEEE Conf. on Decision and Control (December 2000)
10. Parekh, S., Gandhi, N., Hellerstein, J., Tilbury, D., Jayram, T., Bigus, J.: Using control theory to achieve service level objectives in performance management. In: IFIP/IEEE Intl. Symposium on Integrated Network Management (May 2001)
11. Gandhi, N., Tilbury, D.M., Parekh, S., Hellerstein, J.: Feedback control of a lotus notes server: Modeling and control design. In: Proc. of the American Control Conference (June 2001)
12. Diao, Y., Gandhi, N., Hellerstein, J.L., Parekh, S., Tilbury, D.M.: Using MIMO feedback control to enforce policies for interrelated metrics with application to the Apache web server. In: Proc. of the IEEE/IFIP Network Operations and Management (April 2002)

13. Gandhi, N., Tilbury, D.M., Diao, Y., Hellerstein, J., Parekh, S.: MIMO control of an Apache web server: Modeling and controller design. In: Proc. of the American Control Conference (May 2002)
14. Sha, L., Liu, X., Lu, Y., Abdelzaher, T.F.: Queuing model based network server performance control. In: Proc. of the IEEE Real-Time Systems Symposium (2002)
15. Lu, Y., Abdelzaher, T.F., Lu, C., Sha, L., Liu, X.: Feedback control with queuing-theoretic prediction for relative delay guarantees in web servers. In: Proc. of the 9th IEEE Real-Time and Embedded Technology and Applications Symposium (2003)
16. Apache Software Foundation, http://www.apache.org
17. Law, A.M.: Simulation Modeling and Analysis. Tata McGraw Hill Publishing Company Ltd., New Delhi (2008)

Elucidation of Upcoming Traffic Problems
in Cloud Computing

Mohit Mathur

Sr. Lecturer, Department of IT &CS
Jagan Institute of Management Studies (Affiliated to GGSIP University, New Delhi),
Rohini, Delhi, India
mohitmathur19@yahoo.co.in

Abstract. Cloud computing is generally believed to the most gifted technological revolution in computing and it will soon become an industry standard. It is believed that cloud will replace the traditional office setup. However a big question mark exists over the network performance when the cloud traffic explodes. We call it "explosion" as in future we know that various cloud services replacing desktop computing will be accessed via cloud and the traffic increases exponentially. This paper aims at addressing some of these doubts better called "dangers" about the network performance, when cloud becomes a standard globally. Our study concentrates on, that despite of offering better round-trip times and throughputs, cloud appears to consistently lose large amounts of the data that it is required to send to the clients. In this paper, we first give a concise survey on the research efforts in this area. Our survey findings show that the networking research community has converged to the common understanding that a measurement infrastructure is insufficient for the optimal operation and future growth of the cloud. Despite many proposals on building an network measurement infrastructure from the research community, we believe that it will not be in the near future for such an infrastructure to be fully deployed and operational, due to both the scale and the complexity of the network. We explore this problem, and offer deduction that might explain this erratic behavior. We also suggest a set of technologies to identify and manage cloud traffic using IP header DS field, QoS protocols and some high speed edge routers. Our solutions assume that cloud is being assessed via basic public network.

Keywords: Cloud computing, traffic, Round trip time, Throughput, IP, DS field, MPLS, RSVP, Sampling.

1 Introduction

Akin to how very few people today prefer to build a house on their own, but rather prefer to rent one, in the next generation of computing, people may prefer to opt for renting a scalable and reliable provider for their computing needs. This will actually minimize risks while induction a new application, rather than build an entire new enterprise for the purpose of launching products. Cloud computing is such one of the hottest topics in information technology today. This is the outsourcing of data center

N. Meghanathan et al. (Eds.): NeCoM, WiMoN, and WeST 2010, CCIS 90, pp. 68–79, 2010.

functionality and resources to a third party via a network connection. Companies use IT for highly distributed activities including transaction processing, Web retail and customer support, data analysis and mining and regulatory reporting. If these applications are hosted via cloud computing, it will be necessary to link cloud resources to a company's own data center resources for data access, and it will also be necessary to provide user access to the applications in the cloud.

Though there is much talk about the rewards of using the cloud, there is no existing measurement study to validate the claims. Also no clear comparisons have been made between the performance of a cloud computing service and that of an established web hosting service. With relation to Cloud Computing, we can classify measurement studies into two broad categories: computation-based measurements and network-based measurements. The computation-based measurements include Storage, Process cycles, and language engine performance. These measurements can only be made at the server level and hence are taken by the service providers themselves or by authorized third parties. The network based measurement is a quantities and qualitative metrics that may include throughput, round trip time, data loss and other QoS (Quality of Service). The main attention of our work is on network-based measurements of the Cloud Computing service.

1.1   The Network Based Measurement

The three important metrics that we shall be analyzing for the cloud network measurement are Network Throughput, Roundtrip time (RTT), and Data Loss, using the measurement tool. A brief description of each of these metrics is provided below:

i) Network Throughput: The average rate of successful data transfer through a network connection is known as network throughput. It is important to differentiate this term from network bandwidth, which is the capacity for a given system to transfer data over a connection. Though providers base their billing on bandwidth and not throughput, throughput is more important from a client's perspective as it decides the data rate they receives for there request.

ii) Round-trip Time (RTT): RTT is defined as the time elapsed from the propagation of a message to a remote place and to its arrival back at the source. The choice of this metric is obvious it provides the exact amount of time that a client accessing a web application would experience as delay in receiving the output of her query from the time of her input.

iii) Packet/Data loss: Packet loss occurs when one or more packets of data traveling across a computer network fail to reach their destination. This metric is important as it places a quantitative test on the data that a client actually received from the server. Loss can be measured either as loss rate – which detects the amount of data in bytes or as packets lost per unit of time - or simply as loss - the amount of data in bytes that were lost during transfer. It is important to note that none of these metrics can alone provide a general picture of the performance of the cloud computing service.

The various dimensions by which network will get affected with cloud data can describe as:

I. Cloud data storage: The network will be affected by data needed in applications running in the cloud When there are large quantities of data involved (a large database or several large databases) in an application, access to the data must be fast and reliable or the application's runtime will be excessive. That means either data should be stored in the cloud (which may present cost and privacy concerns) or have a very fast network with very high QoS to support cloud connections.

II. Cloud Data updates and backup: If the source data for the application is highly dynamic, the link between the cloud data resources and enterprise data resources will need to be very efficient. But if the data is more static, network requirements for maintaining the data will be less important and there may be little impact on a company's network. The most difficult application class to support efficiently in cloud computing outsourcing is simple "overflow" or backup applications where traditional enterprise applications are run in the cloud instead. This class of application can create enormous data access requirements unless the entire enterprise database is hosted in the cloud, something few organizations would consider. If this application of cloud computing is supported, the only effective strategy will be to create a high-speed connection between the cloud computing data center and the enterprise data center, so that traffic can then jump to the normal enterprise network.

III. Cloud data access. If the application is to be accessed from many locations in many countries, the access must be secure, fast and reliable. If access is primarily from a company's own facilities, then it may be necessary to connect the cloud computing resource to the company's own network. Where a cloud application is highly incorporated with a company's own data center resources for any reason, the performance of that connection is absolutely critical. If it fails, not only is there a risk that the application will fail, there is a risk that data between the cloud and the enterprises own storage resources will lose synchronization, requiring a complex and expensive restructuring. Thus, this kind of cloud application should probably be supported with a private data link to the cloud computing resource. Tense integration between cloud computing information resources and the data center may also increase requirements on the data center network and on any trunk connections between the data center and other primary or regional headquarters locations.

2   Current State of Cloud Computing Services

The problem Definition: There are a number of cloud computing services in the market today, each offering a variety of services ranging from powerful tools like Google App Engine offers to the complete server solution that Amazon EC2 offers. According to the Network Performance Frustration Research Report by Dimension Data, IT users lose a monthly average of 35 minutes on network log-in delay and 25 minutes on e-mail processing activities such as downloading of mail from a server. File transfers take up an average 23 minutes per month. According to the report, shorter delays were associated with applications such as VoIP (voice over Internet Protocol) and video, but such applications have low tolerance for delays that any time lapse might render them unusable. The survey also found that 30 percent of end users including decision makers--reported frequent computer crashes and slow running applications. On the other hand, about 30 percent of IT departments have well-defined processes for handling network performance issues. In addition, fewer than 40 percent of IT departments have complete capability to monitor network performance, and even smaller groups have access to a "rough view" of network traffic. Lack of visibility could result in either unnecessary over-investment, or conversely too little investment, and may lead to unnecessary costs and performance implications.

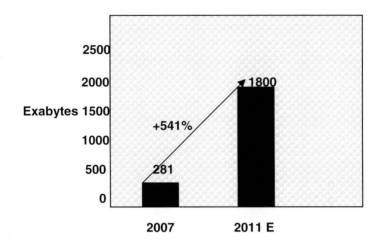

Fig. 1. Worldwide growth of digital Information

Studies indicate that cloud engines perform exceedingly poorly under heavy loads, opposite to claims made by the cloud companies. What actually is the scenario in most cloud is, at zero load, App Engine will not dedicate much server resource to an application, letting a single server monitor the application. When this server is subjected to an extremely heavy load, the single App Engine server appears to make connection and service every request that arrives to an application at least partially, regardless of the number and size. In the meantime, it appears to be calling for assistance from the other servers in the cluster in order to distribute the load efficiently. This would probably result in a delay in servicing a request for the client. With a more robust client like a browser, a slightly longer delay is permissible. According to a study, The Internet traffic that includes cloud services of 2015 will be at least 50 times larger than it was in 2006.Thus the network growth at these levels will require a dramatic expansion of bandwidth, storage, and traffic management capabilities in core, edge, metro, and access networks.

2.1 Networking Vendors Are Forced to Change Their Equipments: The Efforts Going On .....

When a company builds a web site in the real world, they assemble servers, routers, switches, load balancers and firewalls, wire them up, configure them and go live. But when that application moves into a cloud environment, things change. In a cloud model, the customer isn't dealing with physical equipment. Many operational clouds still require their customers to accumulate their own machines, however virtual. To build an application, the operator still needs to do what they do in the real world — assemble servers, routers and switches to make a data center — only this time; they're configuring virtual servers instead of real ones. All this means a big transition for the makers of traditional networking equipment. The company's like Cisco, Juniper Networks and many more are adding some new piece of telecommunication equipments. Cisco will give its customers like cable and mobile phone companies and Internet service providers six times the capacity of products from competitors. The change is desperately needed because the rapid explosion of data and movies distributed on the Web will mean a doubling of Internet traffic by 2010 and again by 2012. Edge routers will play a crucial role in determining whether that future consumer experience will be a pleasant one, or simply another excuse to keep your cable company's customer service division on speed-dial. Unlike core routers, which send data packets within a network, edge routers are the traffic cops for data that travels between local area networks (LANs). They sit on the boundaries, of service areas and are that much closer to the actual users. They are expected to handle a lot of the diverse media now heading to homes and cell phones. In future, routers might function via load balancing over passive optics, with packets distributed randomly across the lines. A passive optical switch, which consumes no power itself, will regulate data flow, eliminating the need for arbiters (directional data packet buffers), and increase performance. Flow by flow load-balancing will enable the building of a mesh network, which will operate over a logical mesh of optical circuits, support all traffic patterns, will be resilient against failure, demonstrate simple routing and cost less to run. Presently, no network provider makes a profit from generating a public internet service, which has to be subsidised by Voice (especially mobile) and VPN activities. Ultimately this lack of profiteering will lead to the consolidation of the number of network providers, which will inevitably converge into one monopoly provider. Potentially optical dynamic circuit switches will be used. These are well suited to optics, are simple, have high capacities to unit volume and wattage, low cost, no queues and no delay variation.

3   Existing Solutions and Associated Problems

3.1   VPN (Virtual Private Network)

The easiest application of cloud computing to support the enterprise network is one where access to the application is via the Internet/VPN, where the cloud computing host can be joined to the VPN, and where little synchronization of data is needed between the cloud host and the enterprise data center. In this case, there will be little traffic impact on the enterprise network, but the support of a cloud resource as a member of the VPN will cause security considerations that will have to be resolved both in a technical sense and through a contract with the cloud computing provider. However the cloud computing providers may incur significant network bandwidth charges as their business grows. These charges can result from traffic to and from customers and traffic between provider's sites. Moreover to implement private tunnels service providers can use there own WAN with multiple peering points with all major ISP's, however small cloud vendors lack the resources to implement it.

3.2 Use of Geographical Distribution Services

With the increase of cloud traffic, some cloud support service providers give network and system administrators a DNS based alternative to costly hardware based global server load balancing systems. They direct their client's traffic to the geographically closest available servers. It gives an ability to route, load balance and control cloud traffic to the applications running on the dedicated servers that they provide. This solution may have to deal with all the problems related to geographical distribution like replication of data, fragmentation, updating etc. Moreover it is difficult and inefficient for a cloud vendor to keep servers globally.

4 Differential Services(DS), QoS Protocols(MPLS, RSVP), Sampling Packets and High Speed Edge Routers — A Proposed Solution to Traffic Problems

We know that the telecommunication companies are making efforts to develop new high speed telecommunication devices like high speed routers and putting fiber optics path against traffic demands of cloud. But this will not be going to happen globally in near future since replacement of these technologies will cost high and cannot be employed globally in one day. Therefore with a little support of these paths and routers, we propose a solution to traffic problems just described above. The solution involves marking cloud traffic with the use of IP Header DS (Differential Services) to identify cloud vendors traffic and providing QoS protocols (RSVP, MPLS) to satisfy the traffic demands along with high speed Edge routers. Because these high speed routers/ routers identifying QoS protocols will be very few, they use tunneling approach to forward packets to each other and identify cloud traffic using DS field. In this paper we suggest a solution that involves use of following technologies:

4.1 Use of IP header DS field to identify cloud traffic.
4.2 Use of QoS (Quality of Service) protocols such as RSVP to reserve resources, MPLS to label such packet for forwarding and providing required services.
4.3 Use of high capacity edge routers.
4.4 Use of sampled packets to monitor cloud traffic

The overall procedure and use of these techniques to provide QoS and to monitor cloud network are as follows: As traffic increases need for a guaranteed quality of service (QoS) for network communication grows for cloud systems. The Internet Engineering Task Force (IETF) has proposed many service models and solutions to meet the demand for QoS. Cloud systems should provide some communication capability that is service oriented, configurable, schedulable, predictable, and reliable. In our paper we are suggesting to use RSVP and MPLS protocols to achieve QoS. RSVP is signaling protocols for setting up paths and reserving resources and MPLS is a forwarding scheme that labels the packet and then forward those packets based on the label.

4.1 Use of Differential Services

We suggest Differential service field of IP header to be used to classify and recognize cloud network traffic. Differential services categorize the packets at the edge of the network by setting the DS field of the packets according to their DS value. In the middle of the network packets are buffered and scheduled in accordance to their DS field. MPLS Label Switching Routers (LSR) provides fast packet forwarding compared to routers, with lower price and higher performance. They also offer traffic engineering, which results in better utilization of network resources such as link capacity as well as the ability to become accustomed to node and link failures. According to RFC 2474 six bits of the DS field are used as a code point (DSCP) to select the PHB a packet experiences at each node. A two-bit currently unused(Fig 2).

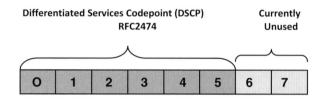

Fig. 2. Differentiated Services Field

Since we want to differentiate usual internet traffic and cloud traffic we can use one LSB's i.e last bit(8th Bit) which is unused by internet, to identify cloud traffic(Fig. 3). If the 8th bit is set it identifies packet as cloud packet, in this case the 6 MSB's contain 101110 which is suggested for Expedited forwarding in internet and having highest priority over all the traffic. Expedited Forwarding minimizes delay and jitters and provides the highest level of aggregate quality of service. But if 8th bit is not set it will be identified as internet traffic and the router can then check for the 6 MSB's to serve internet traffic as defined in IETF standard.

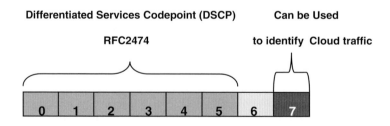

Fig. 3. Suggested classification for cloud traffic

4.2 Use of Qos Protocols

4.2.1 Use of MPLS

MPLS is an advanced forwarding scheme. It extends routing with respect to packet forwarding and path controlling. Each MPLS packet has a header. MPLS capable

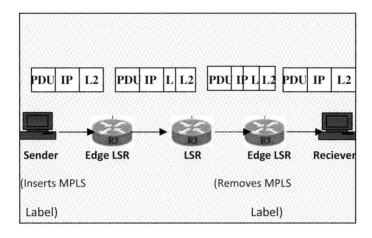

Fig. 4. MPLS

routers, termed Label Switching Router (LSR), examine the label and forward the packet. In MPLS domain IP packets are categorize and routed based on information carried in the IP header DS field of the packets. An MPLS header is then inserted for each packet. Within an MPLS proficient domain, an LSR will use the label as the index to look up the forwarding table of the LSR. The packet is processed as specified by the forwarding table entry. The incoming label is replaced by the outgoing label and the packet is switched to the next LSR. Before a packet leaves a MPLS domain, its MPLS header is removed. This whole process is showed in Fig. 4. The paths between the ingress LSRs and the egress LSRs are called Label Switched Paths (LSPs). MPLS uses some signaling protocol like RSVP to set up LSPs. In order to control the path of LSPs efficiently, each LSP can be assigned one or more attributes. These attributes will be considered in computing the path for the LSP. When we use Differentiated Service filed to identify cloud traffic, packets are classified at the edge of the network. The Differentiated Services-fields (DS-fields) of the packets are set accordingly. In the middle of the network, packets are buffered and scheduled in accordance to their DS-fields. With MPLS, QoS is provided in a slightly different way. Packets still have their DS-fields set at the edge of the network. In addition, the experimental fields in the MPLS headers are set at the ingress LSRs. In the middle of an LSP, packets are buffered and scheduled in accordance to the experimental fields. Whether MPLS is involved or not in providing QoS is transparent to end users. Sometimes it is advantageous to use different LSPs for different classes of traffic. The effect is that the physical network is divided into many virtual networks, one per class. These virtual networks may have different topology and resources. Cloud traffic can use more resources than best effort traffic. Cloud traffic will also have higher priority in getting the backup resources in the case of link or router failure. LSP's will be treated as a link in building the LSPs for VPN. Only the endpoints of LSPs will be involved in the signaling process of building new LSPs for VPN. LSPs are therefore stacked.

4.2.2 Use of RSVP

RSVP is protocol for resource reservation in network nodes along traffic's path. To achieve it the sender sends a PATH Message to the receiver specifying the characteristics of the traffic. We are assuming that DS field is used to identify cloud traffic. RSVP enables routers to schedule and prioritize cloud packets to fulfill the QoS demands. Every middle router along the path forwards the PATH Message to the next hop determined by the routing protocol. Upon receiving a PATH Message, the receiver responds with a RESV Message to request resources for the flow. Every intermediate router along the path can reject or accept the request of the RESV Message. If the request is rejected, the router will send an error message to the receiver, and the signaling process will terminate. If the request is accepted, link bandwidth and buffer space are allocated for the flow and the related flow state information will be put in the router.

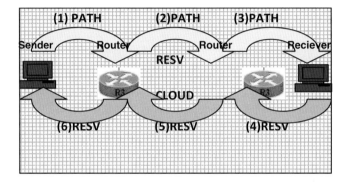

Fig. 5. RSVP Signaling

4.3 Use of High Speed Edge Routers

Another requirement for traffic problem elimination is installing high-performance, carrier-class, intelligent routers at the edge of the network, through which operators can efficiently manage bandwidth while delivering cloud services over cable infrastructure. Cloud networks require carrier-class edge routers with high levels of cleverness so that all traffic flows can be efficiently classified and treated according to network policies. The key feature of this position in the network is that the edge router is the first trusted device in the network and must therefore have the intelligence to implement traffic classification, management and policing. Edge routers focus on processing large numbers of cloud packets with simplified per packet logic.

The routers at the edge of the network recognize and classify traffic flows and need to provide per-flow dealing according to network policies. After dealing with the flows, the router must proficiently forward the traffic to the appropriate destination. Traffic treatments include applying the suitable Quality of Service (QoS) controls as well as implementing Admission Control and other traditional router services. To be effective edge routers also need to offer support advanced-load balancing to guarantee the optimization of network infrastructure assets. The packets are processed by Edge routers in the following way: The most basic function of packet processing is the classification function, which performs packet differentiation and understanding based on the packets' header information.

To achieve both high-speed packet processing and complex processing with flexibility, the packet engine is constructed from multiple programmable processing units (PU's) arranged in a pipeline-manner as shown in Figure. Each processing unit is specialized for table lookup operation and packet header processing. These processing units are controlled by micro-code processing units are controlled by micro-code which can be programmed to meet the customers requirements. Implementing multiple processing units may increase the circuit-size; but given the recent advances in LSI technology, this will not be a significant issue. The packet access registers in the processing units that the packets go through. These packet access registers form a cascaded packet transmission route The incoming packets are forwarded in synchronization with clocks with no additional buffering delay time. The processing units can perform operations on the packets only when they are passing through their packet access registers. The processing is distributed among multiple processing units.

It provides 1) high-speed processing, 2) the packet classification function essential for QoS processing, and 3) the ability to flexibly define these functions. QoS performs 1) flow detection, which maps each packet into an associated QoS by classifying them according to the DS field information, and 2) QoS management, which measures and polices the flow quality (bandwidth, delay, jitter, etc.) and manages the packet sending order by scheduling.

After marking the packets according to their QoS requirements, the packet has to be transmitted within the network according to a routing scheme, which searches a table to find a routing. Then, the packet headers must be modified in accordance with the routing.

4.4 Sampling Cloud Data

To make the cloud traffic smooth and to minimize traffic problems we can use techniques for monitoring cloud networks. The monitoring techniques describe a mechanism to capture traffic data in switched or routed networks. It uses a sampling technology to collect statistics from the device and is, for this reason; applicable to high speed networks (at gigabit speeds or higher). An agent is the implementation of the sampling mechanism on the hardware (for example a switch). The collector is a central server which collects the data grams from all agents to store or (later) analyze them. The agent uses two forms of operation: statistical packet-based sampling of switched or routed packets, and time-based sampling of interface counters.

Based on a defined sampling rate, either for the complete agent or for a single interface, 1 out of N packets is captured and sent to a collector server. This type of sampling does not provide a 100% accurate result in the analysis but it does provide a result with quantifiable accuracy.

5 Conclusion

Cloud computing is a relatively new concept, and the current services are emerging. As a result, a very limited amount of literature is available in the area. Furthermore, no clear standards exist in this industry, and hence each service provider has its own definitions for resource usage. The upcoming near danger of traffic explosion is really a challenge for the cloud services. Though a lot of telecommunication companies get involved to solve the problem, yet a lot of efforts need to be done. Traffic shaping, load balancing, traffic monitoring, adding new high capacity routers, adding high bandwidth fiber optic networks and many more keywords like these need to be considered for the success of next generation computing- Cloud Computing. That's a big challenge for the IT service vendors. Nobody should jump into cloud computing on a massive scale; it must be managed as a careful transition. A smart enterprise will trial out applications of cloud computing where network impact is minimal and gradually increase commitments to the cloud as experience develops. That way, network costs and computing savings can both be projected accurately.

Acknowledgements

First of all I would like to acknowledge Goddess Saraswati for making me capable of writing this research paper. This work would not be possible without support of my respected parents. Further, I would like to thank everyone at my workplace and anonymous reviewers for their useful comments and suggestions.

References

[1] Beard, H.: Cloud Computing Best Practices for Managing and Measuring Processes for On-Demand Computing. Applications and Data Centers in the Cloud with S LA's. Amazon.com: Emereo (2008)
[2] LaMonica, M.: Amazon storage 'cloud' service goes dark, ruffles Web 2.0 feathers I Webware - CNET (2008)
[3] Weiss, A.: Computing in the clouds. netWorker 11(4) (2007)
[4] Buyya, R., Yeo, C.S., Venugopal, S.: Market Oriented Cloud Computing: Vision, Hype and Reality for delivering IT Services as Computing Utilities
[5] Brodkin, J.: Loss of customer data spurs closure of online storage service. The Linkup. Network World (August 2008)
[6] Bechtolsheim, A.: Cloud Computing and Cloud Networking talk at UC Berkeley (December 2008)
[7] Mccalpin, J.: Memory bandwidth and machine balance in current high performance computers. In: IEEE Technical Committee on Computer Architecture Newsletter, pp. 19–25 (1995)
[8] Rangan, K.: The Cloud Wars: $100+ billion at stake. Tech. rep., Merrill Lynch (May 2008)
[9] Network-based Measurements on Cloud Computing Services-Vinod Venkataraman Ankit Shah Department of Computer Sciences, The University of Texas at Austin, Austin, TX 78712-0233 Yin Zhang
[10] Davie, B., Rekhter, Y.: MPLS Technology and Applications. Morgan Kaufmann, San Francisco (2000)
[11] Black, U.: MPLS and Label Switching Networks. Prentice-Hall, Englewood Cliffs (2001)
[12] Armitage, G.: Quality of Service in IP Networks. Morgan Kaufmann, San Francisco (2000)

[13] Rosen, E., Viswanathan, A., Callon, R.: Multiprotocol Label Switching Architecture. Internet Drafts<draft-ietf-mpls–arch-06.txt> (August 1999)
[14] Braden, Ed, R., Zhang, L., Berson, S., Herzog, S., Jamin, S.: Resource ReSerVation Protocol (RSVP) – Version 1 Functional Specification. In: RFC 2205 (September 1997)
[15] Li, T., Rekhter, Y.: A Provider Architecture for Differentiated Services and Traffic Engineering (PASTE). RFC 2430 (1998)
[16] Nichols, K., Blake, S., Baker, F., Black, D.: Definition of the Differentiated Services Field (DS Field) in the IPv4 and IPv6 Headers. In: McKeown, N., Izzard, M., Mekkittikul, A. (eds.) RFC 2474 (December 1998)
[17] Xiao, X., Ni, L.M.: White Paper: Internet QoS: A Big Picture Department of Computer Science, 3115 Engineering Building, Michigan State University, East Lansing, MI 48824-1226
[18] Sawant, A.R., Qaddour, J.: White Paper: MPLS DiffServ: A Combined Approach Applied Computer Science,Illinois State University
[19] Black, U.: MPLS and label Switching Networks. Prentice Hall, Upper Saddle River (2002)
[20] Blake, S.: An Architecture for Differentiated Services. RFC 2475 (December 1998)
[21] Cisco Systems, Diffserv–The Scalable End-to-End QoS Model, http://www.cisco.com/warp/public/cc/pd/iosw/ioft/iofwft/prodlit/difse_wp.htm
[22] White Paper Quality of Service and MPLS Methodologies by ipinfusion Inc.
[23] CESNET technical report number 14/2004 Notes to Flow-Based Traffic Analysis System Design Tom Kosnar 7.12 (2004)
[24] White paper: Managing Incoming Traffic Ashok Singh Sairam Supervisor: Gautam Barua Dept. of CSE, IIT Guwahati, India
[25] Mathur, M., Saraswat, N.: Can we Afford a Cloud? published in ICACCT, APIIT Panipat, India (2008)
[26] Mathur, M., Saraswat, N.: Assessment of Strong User Authentication Techniques in cloud based Computing. In: IACC 2009, Thapar University, Patiala
[27] Internet Traffic Explosion by 2015 - Next Phase is Rich Media for Infrastructure 2.0 February 2, Posted by John Furrier in Technology (2009)

Scenario Based Analysis of Localization of Sensor Nodes Using HMM

Arthi R. and Murugan K.

Ramanujan Computing Centre, Anna University,Chennai,
Chennai - 25, Tamilnadu, India
darthi73@gmail.com, murugan@annauniv.edu

Abstract. The Sensor Network Localization problem deals with estimating the geographical location of all nodes in Wireless Sensor Network. The focus is on those node sensors to be equipped with GPS, but it is often too expensive to include GPS receiver in all sensor nodes. In the proposed localization method, sensor networks with non-GPS nodes derive their location from limited number of GPS nodes. The nodes are capable of measuring received signal strength and the need for a framework that could benefit from the interactions of nodes with mixed types of sensors for WSN.In this paper, localization is achieved by incorporating Mobility Models with Hidden Markov Model (HMM). Scenario based mobility models like Random walk, Random Waypoint, Reference Point Group mobility (RPGM)and Semi-Markov Smooth mobility (SMS) model are used with Hidden Markov Model to estimate error, energy, control overhead, with respect to node density, time and transmission range.

Keywords: Localization, Hidden Markov Model, Mobility Model, Estimation error, Energy, Control overhead, Node density, Time and Transmission range.

1 Introduction

Sensor networks are composed of large numbers of sensors that are equipped with a processor, memory, wireless communication capabilities, sensing capabilities and a power source (battery) on-board. A fundamental problem in wireless sensor networks is localization – the determination of the geographical locations of sensors. While in most existing sensor networks sensors are static, some modern applications involve sensors that are mobile. A more reasonable [4] solution to the localization problem is to allow some nodes to have their location information at all times and allow other nodes to infer their locations by exchanging information with nodes. Range-based localization uses Received Signal Strength Indicator (RSSI), Time of Arrival (TOA), or Time Difference of Arrival (TDOA) to estimate the distance between the nodes that needs to discover its location and each reachable anchor that estimates the node's location based on these distances and the anchors' locations.

This paper presents a Localization algorithm to estimate the location of sensors. The main advantage of choosing this HMM is the use of hidden (or unobservable) states makes the model generic enough to handle a variety of complex real-world time

N. Meghanathan et al. (Eds.): NeCoM, WiMoN, and WeST 2010, CCIS 90, pp. 80–89, 2010.

series, while the relatively simple prior dependence structure (the "Markov" bit) still allows for the use of efficient computational procedures. However, there is an exception in cases when only RSSI sensors are used and the coverage is high. With the help of ns-2, the estimation error, energy, control overhead, with respect to node density, time and transmission range, the mobility model is used to learn the path of the hidden nodes that needs to be localized.

In this paper, section 2 investigates related researches. The Hidden Markov Model Algorithm is discussed in section 3.Section 4 presents the performance metrics.5 presents the simulation results. Finally section 6 concludes the paper.

2 Related Work

In [1] the approach is based on Markov localization and provides rational criteria for setting the robot's motion direction (exploration), and determining the pointing direction of the sensors so as to most efficiently localize the robot. In [2] numerical results show that the HMM method improves the accuracy of localization with respect to conventional ranging methods, especially in mixed LOS/NLOS indoor environments. In [3] the author has attempted to illustrate some applications of the theory of HMMs to simple problems in speech recognition, and pointed out how the techniques could be (and have been) applied to more advanced speech recognition problems.

3 Contributed Work

This section deals with Hidden Markov Model algorithm to localize the sensor nodes based on various Mobility Model.

3.1 Hidden Markov Model

A Hidden Markov Model (HMM) [5] consists of a set of N states, each of which is associated with a set of M possible observations. The parameters of the HMM include:
An initial matrix of state probabilities is known by assumption

$$\Pi = [P_1, P_2, \ldots P_N]^T \tag{1}$$

whose elements P_i, $i \in [1, N]$, describe the position distribution probabilities of the node over the initial state set at the beginning $t = 1$.The Transition Probability is the matrix A that depends on the speed distribution of the node, on the geographical feature of the area and on the allowed transition. The Probability distribution from the observed signals is the matrix B.

The Fig.1. shows the value of the hidden variable x (t) at time t only depends on the value of hidden variable x (t-1). The value of the observed variable y (t) [11] only depends on the value   of the hidden variable x (t).

Finally, the HMM parameter set is denoted by $\lambda = (A, B, \pi)$. As usual, the HMM have three problems [5]: First is the Evaluating problem, what is the probability of the observation O, given the model λ, i.e. $P(O/\lambda)$? => Solution: Forward or Backward algorithm. The effectiveness in forward and backward procedures is almost identical. The result $P(O/\lambda)$ is mainly used for criterion of training model.

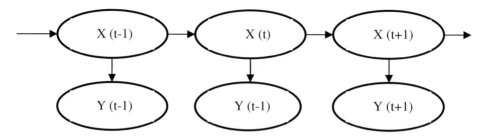

Fig. 1. Model of HMM

For the decoding problem, the solution for the most likely state sequence given the observation O is i.e. $\arg_s$ [max (P(S, O/λ)], the solution is Viterbi algorithm.

$$\delta_t(i) = \max_{q_1,q_2...q_{t-1}} P(q_{1,}q_{2...}q_{t-1}, q_t = S_i, O_1, O_2...O_t/\lambda) \qquad (2)$$

$\delta_t(i)$ is the highest probability along a single path at time t, which accounts for the first t observations and ends in state S_i.

By induction, we have $\delta_{t+1}(j) \left[\max_i \delta_t(i)a_{ij} \right] b_j(O_{t+1})$ \qquad (3)

The study shows that Viterbi algorithm creates a better trajectory than the traditional algorithm because Viterbi algorithm decides the real states depended on all states. The final one is the most likelihood states.

For Estimating problem, the estimate parameters given for the training observation sequences, λ * = arg $_\lambda$ [max P O/ λ], the solution is Baum-Welch algorithm.

We define: $$\xi_k(i, j) = \frac{\alpha_k(i)a_{ij}b_j(O_{k+1})\beta_{k+1}(j)}{P(O/\lambda)} \qquad (4)$$

In which $$\beta_{k+1}(i) = \sum \beta_{k+2}(j)a_{ij}b_j(O_{k+1}); \beta_k(i) = 1 \qquad (5)$$

and we have: $$\gamma_k(i) = \sum_{j-1}^{N} \xi_k(i, j) = \frac{\alpha_k(i)\beta_{k+1}(i)}{P(O/\lambda)} \qquad (6)$$

$$a_{ij}' = \sum_{k-1}^{K-1} \xi_k(i, j) \Big/ \sum_{k-1}^{K-1} \gamma_k(j) \qquad (7)$$

The result: $$b_j'(O_{k=i}) = \sum_{k-1}^{K-1} \gamma_k(j) \Big/ \sum_{k-1}^{K} \gamma_k(j) \qquad (8)$$

$$\pi_i'(k = 1) = \gamma_i(i) \qquad (9)$$

Equation (7) (8) (9) produces a new set of training parameters of HMM system. The trained model $\lambda' = (A', B', \pi')$ has a property: $P(O/\lambda') \geq P(O/\lambda)$. This means that the trained model parameters are more suitable to observations than the former model. Furthermore, we can learn model parameters from K observation sequences in [5]. It is proven that the model λ' is becoming the real one when a range of K observation sequences is used.

3.2 Random Walk Mobility

In this mobility model [7], a Mobile Node moves from its current location to a new location by randomly choosing a direction and speed in which to travel. The new speed and direction are both chosen from pre-defined ranges, [speedmin, speedmax] and [0, 2π] respectively. Each movement in the Random Walk Mobility Model occurs in either a constant time interval t or a constant distance traveled d, at the end of which a new direction and speed are calculated. If a node which moves according to this model reaches a simulation boundary, it "bounces" off the simulation border with an angle determined by the incoming direction. The mobile node then continues along this new path.

3.3 Random Waypoint Mobility

The Random Waypoint Mobility Model (RWP) includes pause times between changes in direction and/or speed. A Mobile node begins by staying in one location for a certain period of time (i.e., a pause time). Once this time expires, the mobile node chooses a random destination in the simulation area and a speed that is uniformly distributed between [minspeed, maxspeed]. The node then travels toward the newly chosen destination at the selected speed. Upon arrival, the node pauses for a specified time period before starting the process again. It is noted that the movement pattern of an MN using the Random Waypoint Mobility Model is similar to the Random Walk Mobility Model if pause time is zero and [minspeed, maxspeed] = [speedmin, speedmax].

3.4 Reference Point Group Mobility

The movement of the group leader [7] determines the mobility behavior of the entire group. Each node has a speed and direction randomly deviating from that of the group leader. The movement in the group mobility can be characterized as follows

$$\left|\vec{v}_{member}(t)\right| = \left|\vec{v}_{leader}(t)\right| + random() \times SDR \times \max\_speed \tag{10}$$

$$\theta_{member}(t0 = \theta_{leader}(t) + random() \times ADR \times \max\_angle \tag{11}$$

SDR is the speed Deviation Ration and ADR is the Angle Deviation Ratio. SDR and ADR is used to control the deviation of the velocity of group members from that of member.

3.5 Semi-markov Smooth Mobility

Each SMS [9] movement, a node will randomly select a target direction φ_α and a target speed V_α. Each SMS movement contains three consecutive moving phases: Speed Up phase for even speed acceleration from 0 m/s to the target speed V_α; Middle Smooth phase for maintaining stable velocities which respectively fluctuate around V_α and φ_α in each time step; and Slow Down phase for even speed deceleration to 0 m/s. The node experiences a random pause time after each SMS movement.

4 Performance Metrics

In this section, the performance of HMM with various mobility models via simulation is evaluated. The key metric [6] for evaluating localization schemes is the location estimation error. Since the objective of localization schemes is to obtain higher localization accuracy using fewer controls overhead, the evaluation of control overhead is used as a secondary metric. Third Metric is the Energy. The definitions of these metrics are as:

Location Estimation error: The average distance between the estimated location $x_{n_{est}}$ and the actual location x_n of all sensor nodes. The location error is scaled as the percentage of transmission range r.

$$\text{Location Estimation error} = \left(\sum_{n=1}^{N} \| x_{n_{est}} - x_n \| / N \right) / r \qquad (12)$$

Control Overhead: The total number of control packets transmitted by the anchors to localize an unknown node in each localization process. Assume to localize a node n, B_n control packets should be transmitted by A_n packets. The control overhead for an unknown node is

$$\text{Control Overhead} = \sum_{n=1}^{N} \left(B_n / A_n \right) \qquad (13)$$

Energy: Total Energy consumption of the sensor nodes during localization, which is measured in joules.

5 Performance Evaluation

In this section, we have conducted a simulation experiments to validate the effective of our solution using ns-2.The proposed work was implemented using ns-2, in order to evaluate and validate the performance of the HMM based localization. The network area has been set to   1000m X 1000m .The network area consists of 250 nodes and 5% of the total nodes are considered as a anchor nodes which know their position. All the nodes in the network have transmission range of 250m.Initally the energy level of each node is set to 5.1 joules. The transmission rate is 500Kb/sec of control packet size 512 bytes. The simulation was conducted for various mobility models such as Random walk Mobility, Random Waypoint Mobility, Reference point Group Mobility, Semi Markov Smooth Mobility with speed of 5m/sec.

The effect of node density on the estimation error is shown in Fig.2. The error estimate of RPGM proves to be a better. The reason is that, in RPGM each node move near each other as a group with almost similar speed and direction angle this mobility model has very high degree of spatial dependence because there is high similarity in motion of nodes in a group. But in comparison with other mobility models it has lowest relative speed because each of the nodes in a group chooses a random speed and direction according to the speed and direction of the group leader. For realizing group mobility in tactical scenarios, the RPGM model seems to be the better approach, as with an appropriate choice of parameters relative positions of nodes inside the groups can be modeled explicitly.

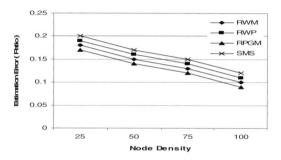

Fig. 2. Impact of network size over Estimation Error

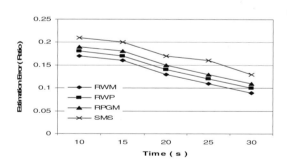

Fig. 3. Impact of Time over Estimation Error

The impact of time on estimation error is shown in Fig.3.As the time increases the estimation error decreases because more anchors get localized that results in faster convergence. As the increase in the time leads to decrease in Estimation error, the reason is that due to the increase of reference nodes.The random walk model shows better estimate because there is no pause time.However Random waypoint uses pause time, part of the time is spent for pause state.In all cases, the estimation error is low due to recursive back tracking of most likelihood of location estimates using Baum Welch algorithm.

The effect of transmission range on the estimation error is shown in Fig.4. The result shows that the error is low in random waypoint model. The reason is that as the simulation starts, each node randomly selects one location in the simulation field as the destination. It then travels towards this destination with constant velocity chosen uniformly and randomly from $[0, V_{Max}]$. Upon reaching the destination, the node stops for a defined by the 'pause time' parameter. If $T_{Pause} = 0$, this leads to continuous mobility. After this duration, it again chooses another random destination. During pause time, the node localization is better. The effect of coverage becomes high when the network is sparse, i.e., increase in transmission range. The estimation error increases due to increase in the transmission range.

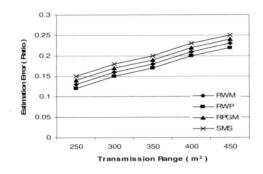

Fig. 4. Impact of Transmission Range over Estimation Error

The Fig.5. shows the performance of Node density over Control Overhead .With the node density growing, the control overhead decreases gradually. More denser the nodes, the anchor node becomes closer to the unknown nodes. Localization is achieved with minimum control overhead. In the case of RWP and RPGM there are slight variations. Comparing all four mobility models, the overhead is low in the case of RPGM. This effect is due to exchange of control packets only depends on the group leader.

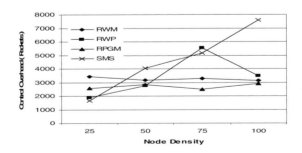

Fig. 5. Impact of network size over Control Overhead

Control overhead gradually increases as shown in Fig.6 and gets consistent with increase in time due to the earlier Localization. As the simulation time increases the reference nodes also increases, the algorithm uses only the control packets from first hop neighborhood. Hence the control overhead rises to certain level and goes to consistent. The overhead is more in the case of SMS Mobility model.

The control overhead packets get increased as shown in Fig.7 due to sparse node availability with increase in Transmission Range. As the transmission range increases the overhead increases in RWM. In the case of RWP, RPGM the overhead is consistent. RPGM mobility minimizes the overall control overhead during localization due to its implicit characteristics. In SMS mobility, there is more variation in the control overhead.

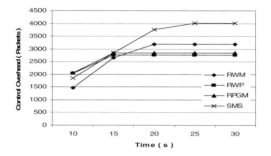

Fig. 6. Impact of Time over control overhead

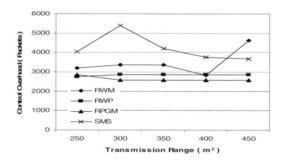

Fig. 7. Impact of Transmission Range over control overhead

Energy over the node density is shown in Fig.8. This shows energy consumption gets varied due to increase in the node density. The average energy dissipated during localization gets increased as the node density increases in RWP and RWM, SMS and slight variation in RPGM model then its goes to consistent state. However, the energy spent during in movement is more, but the energy spent in localization process is low. Hence the average energy spent by each node shows moderate variation.

The energy consumption in Fig.9 decreases and becomes consistent as there is increase in time because the node gets localized very fast in the initial stage. The energy

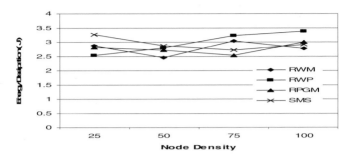

Fig. 8. Impact of network size over Energy

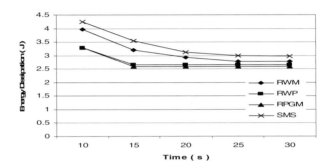

Fig. 9. Impact of Time over Energy

dissipation slightly decreases as the time increases and then it goes to consistent. This effect is due to the increase in the more no. of localized nodes called anchors.

In Fig.10 the energy consumption in HMM shows as the transmission range becomes more the energy gradually decreases due to sparse connectivity of the sensor nodes. Although the network becomes sparse as the sensor range increases, the energy spent in localization is low due to fast prediction of HMM method by exchange of location estimates with its single hop neighbor.

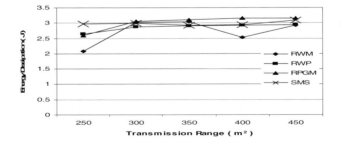

Fig. 10. Impact of Transmission Range over Energy

6   Conclusions

Our analysis and simulation studies validate the effectiveness of combining sensor capacities of RSSI with learning movement model using HMM.The movement of nodes can be predicted fast with exchange of location estimates in multihop way using HMM .Furthermore, our analysis shows that employing RSSI sensors can achieve better localization using HMM in wireless sensor networks. This model could be further improved for AoA sensor capacity. More importantly, this framework allows the networks consisting of nodes with different sensor types to collaborate in the Localization process.

References

1. Fox, D., Burgard, W., Thrun, S.: Active Markov Localization for Mobile Robots. Robotics and Autonomous Systems 25, 195–207 (1998)
2. Morelli, C., Nicoli, M.(Member, IEEE), Rampa, V.,Spagnolini, U. (Senior Member, IEEE): Hidden Markov Models for Radio Localization in MixedLos/NlosConditions. IEEE Transactions on Signal Processing 55(4), 1525–1541 (2007)
3. Rabiner, L.R. (Fellow, IEEE): A Tutorial on Hidden Markov Models and Selected Applications in Speech Recognition. Proceedings of the IEEE 77(2), 257–286 (1989)
4. Bouukerche, A., Oliveira, H.A.B.F., Nakamura, E.F., Antonio, F., Loureiro, A.F.: Localization Systems for Wireless Sensor Networks. IEEE Wireless Communications 14, 6–12 (2007)
5. Hieu, H.Q., Thanh, V.D.: Ground Mobile Target Tracking By Hidden Markov Model. Science & Technology Development 9(12), 6–12 (2006)
6. Wang, W., Zhu, Q.: Sequential Monte Carlo Localization in Mobile Sensor Networks. In: LLC 2007, WirelessNetworks. Springer Science+Business Media (2007) doi:10.1007/S11276-007-0064-3
7. Camp, T., Boleng, J., Davies, V.: A Survey of Mobility Models for Ad Hoc Network Research. Wireless Communication & Mobile Computing 2(5), 483–502 (2002)
8. Aycard, O., Charpillet, F., Fohr, D., Mari, J.-F.: Path Learning and Recognition using Hidden Markov Models. In: Proc. IROS 1997 0-7803-4119-8/97/$1001997, pp. 1741–1746. IEEE, Los Alamitos (1997)
9. Zha0, M., Wang, W.: Design and Applications of a Smooth Mobility Model for Mobile Ad-hoc Networks. In: MILCOM 2006, pp. 1–7 (2006)

Network Security and Networking Protocols

Arvind Kumar Sharma [1] and Chattar Singh Lamba [2]

[1] Research Scholar
arvind_vyas07@yahoo.co.in
[2] Research Guide
kunjean_lamba@yahoo.com

Abstract. In the field of networking, the specialist area of **Network Security** consists of the provisions made in an underlying computer network infrastructure, policies adopted by the network administrator to protect the network and the network-accessible resources from unauthorized access, and consistent and continuous monitoring and measurement of its effectiveness (or lack) combined together.

The terms Network Security and Information Security are often used interchangeably. Network Security is generally taken as providing protection at the boundaries of an organization by keeping out intruders (hackers). Information Security, however, explicitly focuses on protecting data resources from malware attack or simple mistakes by people within an organization by use of Data Loss Prevention (DLP) techniques. One of these techniques is to compartmentalize large networks with internal boundaries. Employees have to cross these boundaries and be authenticated when attempting to access protected information.

1 Introduction

In the field of networking, the specialist area of **Network Security** consists of the provisions made in an underlying computer network infrastructure, policies adopted by the network administrator to protect the network and the network-accessible resources from unauthorized access, and consistent and continuous monitoring and measurement of its effectiveness (or lack) combined together.

The terms Network Security and Information Security are often used interchangeably. Network Security is generally taken as providing protection at the boundaries of an organization by keeping out intruders (hackers). Information Security, however, explicitly focuses on protecting data resources from malware attack or simple mistakes by people within an organization by use of Data Loss Prevention (DLP) techniques. One of these techniques is to compartmentalize large networks with internal boundaries. Employees have to cross these boundaries and be authenticated when attempting to access protected information.

Network security starts from authenticating the user, commonly with a username and a password. Since this requires just one thing besides the user name, i.e. the password which is something you 'know', this is sometimes termed one factor authentication. With two factor authentication something you 'have' is also used (e.g. a security token or 'dongle', an ATM card, or your mobile phone), or with three factor authentication something you 'are' is also used (e.g. a fingerprint or retinal scan).

N. Meghanathan et al. (Eds.): NeCoM, WiMoN, and WeST 2010, CCIS 90, pp. 90–97, 2010.
© Springer-Verlag Berlin Heidelberg 2010

Once authenticated, a firewall enforces access policies such as what services are allowed to be accessed by the network users. Though effective to prevent unauthorized access, this component may fail to check potentially harmful content such as computer worms or Trojans being transmitted over the network. Anti-virus software or an intrusion prevention system (IPS) help detect and inhibit the action of such malware. An anomaly-based intrusion detection system may also monitor the network and traffic for unexpected (i.e. suspicious) content or behavior and other anomalies to protect resources, e.g. from denial of service attacks or an employee accessing files at strange times. Individual events occurring on the network may be logged for audit purposes and for later high level analysis.

1.1 Introduction to Networking

A basic understanding of computer networks is requisite in order to understand the principles of network security. In this section, we'll cover some of the foundations of computer networking, then move on to an overview of some popular networks. Following that, we'll take a more in-depth look at TCP/IP, the network protocol suite that is used to run the Internet and many intranets.

A "network" has been defined as any set of interlinking lines resembling a net, *a network of roads* an interconnected system, *a network of alliances*." This definition suits our purpose well: a computer network is simply a system of interconnected computers. *How* they're connected is irrelevant, and as we'll soon see, there are a number of ways to do this.

1.2 Network Security, Modern Network Security Threats

Router Based Network Security is a process, not a product. Network security encompasses those steps that are taken to ensure the confidentiality, integrity, and availability of data or resources. Network security is the protection of information and systems and hardware that use, store, and transmit that information.

Network security is now an integral part of computer networking. Network security involves protocols, technologies, devices, tools, and techniques to secure data and mitigate threats. Network security solutions emerged in the 1960s but did not mature into a comprehensive set of solutions for modern networks until the 2000s. When the first viruses were unleashed and the first DoS attack occurred, the world began to change for networking professionals. To meet the needs of users, network professionals learned techniques to secure networks. The primary focus of many network professionals evolved from designing, building, and growing networks to securing existing networks.

1.3 Risk Management – A Game of Security

It is very important to understand that in security, one simply cannot say ``what's the best firewall?'' There are two extremes: absolute security and absolute access. The closest we can get to an absolutely secure machine is one unplugged from the network, power supply, locked in a safe, and thrown at the bottom of the ocean. Unfortunately, it isn't terribly useful in this state. A machine with absolute access is extremely convenient to use: it's simply there, and will do whatever you tell it, without questions, authorization, passwords, or any other mechanism. Unfortunately, this isn't terribly practical, either: the Internet is a bad neighborhood now, and it isn't long before some bonehead will tell the computer to do something like self-destruct, after which, it isn't terribly useful to you.

1.4 Securing Networking Devices

Securing outgoing network traffic and scrutinizing incoming traffic are critical aspects of network security. Securing the edge router, which connects to the outside network, is an important first step in securing the network.

Device hardening is an essential task that must never be overlooked. It involves implementing proven methods for physically securing the router and protecting the router's administrative access using the command-line interface (CLI) as well as the Router and Security Device Manager (SDM). Some of these methods involve securing administrative access, including maintaining passwords, configuring enhanced virtual login features, and implementing Secure Shell (SSH). Because not all information technology personnel should have the same level of access to the infrastructure devices, defining administrative roles in terms of access is another important aspect of securing infrastructure devices.

1.5 Authentication, Authorization and Accounting

AAA (Authentication, Authorization and Accounting) is a way to securing Routers in networks. AAA Plays different rolls in the network Security, Like Authentication tell you that who are you, Authorization tells you that what you can do and Accounting tell you that what you did.

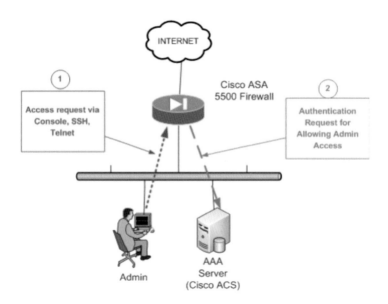

1.6   Implementing Firewall Technologies

A firewall is a secure and trusted machine that sits between a private network and a public network. The firewall machine is configured with a set of rules that determine which network traffic will be allowed to pass and which will be blocked or refused. In some large organizations, you may even find a firewall located inside their corporate network to segregate sensitive areas of the organization from other employees. Many cases of computer crime occur from within an organization, not just from outside.

1.7   Implementing Intrusion Prevention System

Intrusion prevention is a preemptive approach to network security used to identify potential threats and respond to them swiftly. Like an intrusion detection system (IDS), an intrusion prevention system (IPS) monitors network traffic. However, because an exploit may be carried out very quickly after the attacker gains access, intrusion prevention systems also have the ability to take immediate action, based on a set of rules established by the network administrator. For example, an IPS might drop a packet that it determines to be malicious and block all further traffic from that IP address or port. Legitimate traffic, meanwhile, should be forwarded to the recipient with no apparent disruption or delay of service.

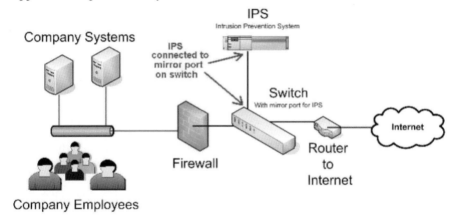

1.8   Securing Local Area Networks

In the Local Area Networks, There are so many types of internal threats regarding break you network. We can stop these type activities by the End Point Security, VLAN's, NAC Devices, Port Security, and your date by the SAN Security.

1.9   Implementing Virtual Area Networks

A virtual private network (VPN) is a network that uses a public telecommunication infrastructure, such as the Internet, to provide remote offices or individual users with secure access to their organization's network. A virtual private network can be contrasted with an expensive system of owned or leased lines that can only be used by one organization. The goal of a VPN is to provide the organization with the same capabilities, but at a much lower cost.

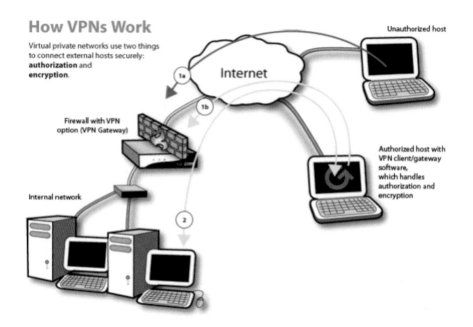

How VPNs Work

Virtual private networks use two things
to connect external hosts securely:
authorization and
encryption.

Internet

Unauthorized host

Firewall with VPN
option (VPN Gateway)

Authorized host with
VPN client/gateway
software,
which handles
authorization and
encryption

Internal network

2 Network Protocols

Network protocols define a language of rules and conventions for communication
between network devices.

2.1 Definition

A **network protocol** defines rules and conventions for communication between network devices. Protocols for computer networking all generally use packet switching
techniques to send and receive messages in the form of *packets*.

Network protocols include mechanisms for devices to identify and make connections with each other, as well as formatting rules that specify how data is packaged
into messages sent and received. Some protocols also support message acknowledgement and data compression designed for reliable and/or high-performance network
communication. Hundreds of different computer network protocols have been developed each designed for specific purposes and environments.

2.2 Internet Protocols

The Internet Protocol family contains a set of related (and among the most widely
used network protocols. Besides Internet Protocol (IP) itself, higher-level protocols
like TCP, UDP, HTTP, and FTP all integrate with IP to provide additional capabilities. Similarly, lower-level Internet Protocols like ARP and ICMP also co-exist with
IP. These higher level protocols interact more closely with applications like Web
browsers while lower-level protocols interact with network adapters and other computer hardware.

2.3   Routing Protocols

Routing protocols are special-purpose protocols designed specifically for use by net-work routers on the Internet. Common routing protocols include EIGRP, OSPF and BGP.

2.4   How Network Protocols Are Implemented

Modern operating systems like Microsoft Windows contain built-in services or dae-mons that implement support for some network protocols. Applications like Web browsers contain software libraries that support the high level protocols necessary for that application to function. For some lower level TCP/IP and routing protocols, sup-port is implemented in directly hardware (silicon chipsets) for improved performance.

2.5   OSI Layers and Their Protocols

2.5.1   Layer 1 Protocols (Physical Layer)

ADSL Asymmetric digital subscriber line, ISDN Integrated Services Digital Network, T-carrier (T1, T3, etc.),E-carrier (E1, E3, etc.), RS-232 (a serial line interface origi-nally developed to connect modems and computer terminals).

2.5.2   Layer 1+2 Protocols

Ethernet, OTN ITU-T G.709 Optical Transport Network also called Optical Channel Wrapper or Digital Wrapper Technology.

2.5.3   Layer 2 Protocols (Data Link Layer)

ARCnet   Attached Resource Computer Network, CDP Cisco Discovery Protocol, DCAP Data Link Switching Client Access Protocol, Dynamic Trunking Protocol, FDDI Fiber Distributed Data Interface, Frame Relay, ITU-T G.hn Data Link Layer, HDLC High Level Data Link Control, IEEE 802.11 WiFi, IEEE 802.16 WiMAX, LocalTalk, L2F Layer 2 Forwarding Protocol, L2TP Layer 2 Tunneling Protocol, PPP Point-to-Point Protocol, PPTP Point-to-Point Tunneling Protocol, NDP Neighbor Discovery Protocol, SLIP Serial Line Internet Protocol (obsolete), STP Spanning Tree Protocol, Token ring, VTP VLAN Trunking Protocol, Layer 2+3 protocols, ATM Asynchronous Transfer Mode, Frame relay, a simplified version of X.25, MPLS Multi-protocol label switching, X.25, ARP Address Resolution Protocol, RARP Re-verse Address Resolution Protocol.

2.5.4   Layer 1+2+3 Protocols

MTP Message Transfer Part, NSP Network Service Part, Layer 3 protocols (Network Layer), EGP Exterior Gateway Protocol, EIGRP Enhanced Interior Gateway Routing Protocol, ICMP Internet Control Message Protocol, IGMP Internet Group Manage-ment Protocol, IGRP Interior Gateway Routing Protocol, IPv4 Internet Protocol ver-sion 4, IPv6 Internet Protocol version 6, IPSec Internet Protocol Security, IPX Inter-network Packet Exchange.

2.5.5   Layer 3 Protocols (Network Layer Management)

IS-IS Intermediate system to intermediate system, OSPF Open Shortest Path First, BGP Border Gateway Protocol, RIP Routing Information Protocol, ICMP Router Discovery Protocol, Gateway Discovery Protocol.

2.5.6   Layer 3.5 Protocols

Layer 3+4 protocol suites, Xerox Network Systems, Layer 4 protocols (Transport Layer), AHAH Authentication Header over IP or IPSec, ESPESP Encapsulating Security Payload over IP or IPSec, GRE Generic Routing Encapsulation for tunneling, IL Originally developed as transport layer for 9P, SCTP Stream Control Transmission Protocol, Sinec H1 for telecontrol, SPX Sequenced Packet Exchange, TCP Transmission Control Protocol, UDP User Datagram Protocol, Layer 5 protocols (Session Layer), 9P Distributed file system protocol developed originally as part of Plan 9, NCP NetWare Core Protocol, NFS Network File System, SMB Server Message Block, SOCKS "SOCKetS".

2.5.7   Layer 7 Protocols (Application Layer)

BitTorrent, A peer-to-peer file sharing protocol, BOOTP, Bootstrap Protocol, Diameter, an authentication, authorization and accounting protocol, DNS Domain Name System, DHCP, Dynamic Host Configuration Protocol, ED2K, A peer-to-peer file sharing protocol, FTP, File Transfer Protocol, Finger, which gives user profile information, Gnutella, a peer-to-peer file-swapping protocol, Gopher, a hierarchical hyperlinkable protocol, HTTP, HyperText Transfer Protocol, IMAP, Internet Message Access Protocol, Internet Relay Chat (IRC), LDAP Lightweight Directory Access Protocol, MIME, Multipurpose Internet Mail Extensions, MSNP, Microsoft Notification Protocol (used by Windows Live Messenger), MAP, Mobile Application Part, NetBIOS, File Sharing and Name Resolution protocol - the basis of file sharing with Windows, NNTP, News Network Transfer Protocol, NTP, Network Time Protocol, NTCIP, National Transportation Communications for Intelligent Transportation System Protocol, POP3 Post Office Protocol Version 3, RADIUS, an authentication, authorization and accounting protocol, Rlogin, a UNIX remote login protocol, rsync, a file transfer protocol for backups, copying and mirroring, RTP, Real-time Transport Protocol, RTSP, Real-time Transport Streaming Protocol, SSH, Secure Shell, SISNAPI, Siebel Internet Session Network API, SIP, Session Initiation Protocol, a signaling protocol, SMTP, Simple Mail Transfer Protocol, SNMP, Simple Network Management Protocol, SOAP, Simple Object Access Protocol, STUN, Session Traversal Utilities for NAT, TUP, Telephone User Part, Telnet, a remote terminal access protocol, TCAP, Transaction Capabilities Application Part, TFTP, Trivial File Transfer Protocol, a simple file transfer protocol, WebDAV, Web Dist Authoring and Versioning.

3   Conclusions

Security is a very difficult topic. Everyone has a different idea of what ``security" is, and what levels of risk are acceptable. The key for building a secure network is to *define what security means to your organization*. Once that has been defined, everything that goes on with the network can be evaluated with respect to that policy. Projects and systems can then be broken down into their components, and it becomes much simpler to decide whether what is proposed will conflict with your security policies and practices.

Many people pay great amounts of lip service to security, but do not want to be bothered with it when it gets in their way. It's important to build systems and networks in such a way that the user is not constantly reminded of the security system around him. Users who find security policies and systems too restrictive will find ways around them. It's important to get their feedback to understand what can be improved, and it's important to let them know *why* what have been done has been, the sorts of risks that are deemed unacceptable, and what has been done to minimize the organization's exposure to them.

References

1. Watkins, M., Wallace, K.: CCNA Security: Official Exam Certification Guide. Pearson Education, London
2. Lammle, T.: CCNA: Cisco Certified Network Study Guide. Sybex
3. Odom, W.: CCNA Exam Certification Guide. Cisco Press,
4. Lowe, D.: Networking: All-in-one Desk reference for Dummies. Wiley, Chichester
5. Stewart, B.D., Gough, C.: CCNP BSCI Official Exam Certification Guide. Cisco Press,
6. Hucaby, D.: CCNP BCMSN Official Exam Certification Guide. Cisco Press
7. Tanenbaum, A.S.: Computer Networks. Pearson Education, London
8. Morgan, B., Lovering, N.: CCNP ISCW Offical Exam Certification Guide. Cisco Press
9. Bastien, G., Degu, C.: CCSP Cisco Pix Firewall Advance Exam Certification Guide. Cisco Press
10. Hall, E.: Internet Core Protocols, The Definitive Guide. O'Reilly, Sebastopol

A Dynamic Grid Based Route-Driven ECDH Scheme for Heterogeneous Sensor Networks

S. Pradheepkumar, R. Fareedha, M. Jenieferkavetha,
A. Geanremona, and R. Juliajoyce

Christ College of Engineering and Technology, Pondicherry, India-605014
{spradheepkumar,fareedha1990,jeniferkavetha}@gmail.com
{geanremona,juliajoyce.b.tech}@gmail.com

Abstract. Ongoing research work shows that homogeneous sensor networks have poor security, connectivity, performance and scalability. Heterogeneous sensor network (HSN) consists of physically different types of sensor nodes. The feasibility of implementing Elliptic Curve Diffe-Helmen (ECC) in HSN is simulated in this approach. Under dynamic condition of sensor node, implementation of grid-based coordinate route driven scheme has been proposed. This route driven scheme is highly adaptable for public key management scheme for HSN. It also compares the energy and throughput efficiency for dynamic position of sensor nodes. The proposed method is compared with the existing routing techniques like AODV and DSR. The proposed method dramatically increases network lifetime based on the elected coordinator nodes and the size of the grid area.

Keywords: Heterogeneous Sensor Network (HSN), Key Management, Elliptic Curve Cryptography (ECC), Elliptic Curve Diffie-Hellman (ECDH).

1 Introduction

Wireless Sensor Networks (WSN) has recently focused a lot of interest in the research community due to their wide range of attractive applications and its important position is promoted rapidly. Each sensor node contains a battery-powered embedded processor and a radio, which enables the nodes to self-organize into a network, communicate with each other and exchange data through wireless network links. HSN are a result of the combination of advances made in the field of analog and digital circuitry, wireless communications and sensor technology.

HSN deployments increasingly employ in-network processing to achieve scalability, integrity, energy-efficiency and timeliness. HSN are commonly used in ubiquitous and pervasive applications such as military, homeland security, health-care, and industry automation [1]. An important area of research interest is a general architecture for wide area wireless sensor networks that seamlessly integrates homogeneous sensor network and HSN. HSN have different types of sensors, with a large number of ordinary sensors in addition to a few potent sensors. The main goal of key management in HSN is the establishment of secure links between neighbour

N. Meghanathan et al. (Eds.): NeCoM, WiMoN, and WeST 2010, CCIS 90, pp. 98–106, 2010.

sensors at network formation phase. In order to provide secret communication in a sensor network, shared secret keys are used between communicating nodes to encrypt data. Key establishment protocols are used to set up the shared secrets, but the problem is complicated by the sensor nodes' limited computational capabilities, battery energy, and available memory. The proposed key management scheme is resilient against collusion attack. The rest of the whole paper is designed as follows. In Section II and III discuss about the proposed scheme in detail. Section IV discusses the matrices, simulation results and outputs. Finally Section V concludes the proposed method.

2   The ECDH Based Key Management Scheme

One possible key management scheme is to permit every LN-sensor (lower end sensor node) set up shared keys with each of its neighbours by using the ECDH key exchange scheme. In many existing reliable sensor networks, nodes are obtusely deployed in the field. One sensor node could have as many as 40 or more neighbours in the network. Although ECC public-key cryptography is executable for small sensor nodes, a 160-bit [2] ECC point multiplication still takes about less than one second. It would need too much computational time and energy for LN-sensor to run ECC with each of its 30 neighbours. In this section, an efficient key distribution management scheme requires only a small number of ECC computations in each LN-sensor. A server node [3] is used to generate pairs of ECC public and private keys, one pair for each LN-sensor and HN-sensor (Higher end sensor node). The server node selects a new elliptic curve EC over a large Prime field F and a point P on that curve. Each LN-sensor (say x) is pre-loaded with the private key (say $SK^y_x = I_x$). A HN-sensor has large storage space and is pre-loaded with public keys of all the LN-sensor (ex: $SK^x_x = I_x P$, etc).Each HN-sensor also stores the association between each LN-sensor and its private key. Each HN-sensor is pre-loaded with a pair of ECC public key and private key. The public keys[4] of HN-sensor are also loaded in each LN-sensor and the keys are used to authenticate broadcasts from HN-sensor.

The ECDH algorithm is used for authenticating broadcasts from   HN-sensor. Each LN-sensor can verify the digital signature by using HN's public key and thus authenticate the broadcast. In addition, each HN-sensor is pre-loaded with a special key SK_H, which is used by a symmetric cryptography algorithm for verifying newly deployed sensors and for secure communications among HN-sensors. Even if an adversary captures a HN-sensor, she could not obtain the key materials. Given the protection from the tamper-resistant hardware, the same pair of ECC public/private keys may be used by all HN-sensor and this can reduce the storage overheads. Assume [5] each LN-sensor can determine its location by using some secure location services, such as the scheme. After selecting a cluster head HN, each LN-sensor x sends to HN a clear *key-request* message, which includes the LN-sensor ID_i and i's location. A proposed scheme may be used to forward the *Key-request* message to HN [6]. Fig.1 shows the basic example of ECDH secret key exchange.

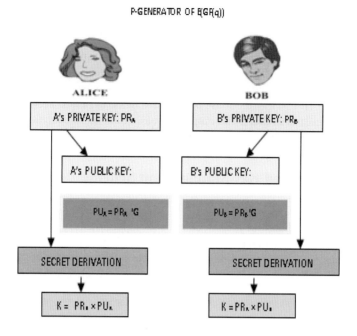

Fig. 1. ECDH secret key exchange

3 Dynamic Grid Based Coordinate Route Driven Scheme

Here, the key management scheme [7] is highly depend on mobility of sensor node (i.e.) dynamic grid-based coordinate route driven scheme [8], which assume the deployment knowledge for HSN. In dynamic grid-based coordinate route driven scheme, the sensor nodes are assumed as dynamic after deployment. The distribution of nodes can be predicted from deployment model in fig. 2 and fig. 3 that shows how sensor nodes are deployed. The main focus of dynamic grid-based coordinate route driven scheme is on dividing the network into square shaped grids to extend network lifetime. The entire network is partition into equally shaped grids, and in each grid a non-stationary nodes, the coordinator is elected, like in the span algorithm. The implicit routing algorithm used in dynamic grid-based coordinate route driven scheme is similar to level flooding. In dynamic grid-based coordinate route driven scheme, messages reaches only selected nodes in the field instead of all the nodes in the network.

The main idea of partitioning the network into grids is to make only one node dynamic-alive for each grid, while the rest of the nodes in that grid are sleep mode so as to conserve their battery-energy life. In each square grid, the coordinator participates in routing as long as the amount of energy level in that coordinator is above a certain threshold value. When the energy level drops below the threshold, a new coordinator is elected for that grid. The source node transmits information to the sink node through the active coordinators node, and the sink node traces a route back to the source. The process of flooding algorithm continues till the nodes participating in the routing run out of energy level, when new coordinators are elected and a new route back to the source node from the sink node is calculated. The source node starts flooding algorithm by sending a query information message to all the neighbour coordinators nodes, which flood other coordinators node in the network till the query information message reaches the sink node. For example, each square grid of side of a fixed length, 200 m. Connectivity level in the network depends on the square grid size, coverage transmission range and the sensitivity of all the nodes. When square grid coordinators are elected, care should be taken such that the coordinators node must still be able to connect to neighbouring grid coordinators node. Therefore, square grid size is very important to maintain connectivity level throughout the network as too large a grid size will result in loss of connectivity level of the nodes in the network.

In [9], dynamic grid-based coordinate route driven scheme places an upper bound on the square grid size and determines the conditions to maintain connectivity level throughout the network depending on the grid size and the transmission range of the nodes. It also maintains load balancing as does Geographic Adaptive Fidelity (GAF). The function of the coordinator node is distributed amongst the nodes in the network based on the ranking of the nodes in each grid. It observes the effects of transmit power, receiver sensitivity and grid size on network lifetime, and determines that decreasing the transmit power increases network lifetime. The idea of a virtual square grid over the network field was proposed in the   GAF algorithm. Dividing the entire network into equal sized grids, and electing nodes in each grid to participate in routing while other nodes were put to sleep was introduced in dynamic grid based coordinate route driven scheme. Two types of grid based coordinate route driven scheme have been seen in proposed system. They are; uniform grid-based coordinate route driven scheme for dynamic sensor nodes and non-uniform grid-based coordinate route driven scheme for dynamic sensor nodes. Uniform grid-based coordinate route driven scheme is more efficient when the distribution of the sensor nodes in the sensor field is uniform. Varying the square grid sizes in the network extends the lifetime of the network.

In [10], the relation between optimal radio range and traffic is used to define in both uniform and non-uniform grid for the GAF protocol. In this proposed scheme, the non-uniform grid size for the dynamic grid-based coordinate route driven scheme is implemented and the results were analyzed. The underlying route algorithm of non-uniform grid-based coordinate route driven scheme is the same as the grid-based coordinate route driven scheme. The entire sensor surveillance field is divided into non-uniform sized grids. For adopting these route driven techniques, partition the network into small grid size. And calculate the best suite grid structure with the help of collision rate in the network with respect to grid structure and result the life time of the network. When considering the grid size of 50 units, the number of sensor node deployed in the 50 unit grid size will be very less. So obviously wastage of resource will be highly seen in HSN. But the collision rate will be less. When considering the grid size of 100 units, an average number of sensor nodes can be adopted by the 100 unit grid size, so that the collision will be at normal rate. When considering the grid size of 200, and an average-limit numbers of sensor nodes were adopted by the 200 unit grid size, so the collision rate will be slightly above the normal rate. Collision rate for 200 unit grid size will be more than 100 unit grid size.

So, by keep on increasing the unit of grid size, more number of sensors will be adopted according to the respective grid size, so the collision rate is highly seen. Hence by the simulation result, the grid size for 100 units and 200 units is suited for the network partition. To maintain the life time of the HSN, energy level is maintained at very low threshold level and throughput is highly maintained. By using the metrics like energy efficiency and throughput, the life time of the sensor network can be calculated. And by comparing the network life time of the proposed technique with respect to Ad Hoc On-Demand Distance Vector Routing (AODV) and Dynamic Source Routing (DSR) in terms of energy spent by the sensor node in the sensor network and by throughput efficiency of the sensor node in the HSN. All the simulation results are done using GLOMOSIM simulator and shown in fig.4-8.

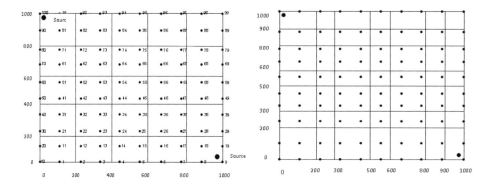

Fig. 2. Uniform grid based coordinate route driven scheme for dynamic nodes

Fig. 3. Non-uniform grid based coordinate route driven scheme for dynamic nodes

4   Performance Metrics

4.1   Energy Comparison of Uniform Grid-Based Coordinate Route Driven Scheme for Dynamic Sensor Nodes

Fig. 4 shows the simulation results of energy comparison for different routing technique like uniform grid-based coordinate route driven scheme, AODV and DSR. Under dynamic condition of sensor nodes, uniform grid based coordinate route driven scheme consumed less energy when compare to AODV and DSR.

4.2   Energy Comparison of Non-uniform Grid-Based Coordinate Route Driven Scheme for Dynamic Sensor Nodes

Here the non-uniform grid-based coordinate route driven scheme had consumed less energy when compare to AODV and DSR with respect to dynamic condition of sensor nodes. Fig. 5 shows the simulation result of energy comparison for different

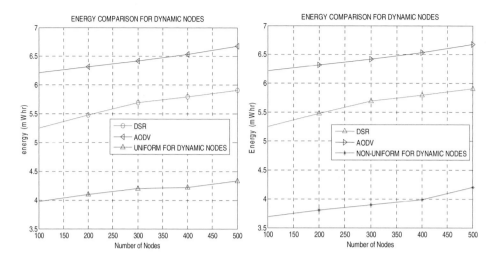

Fig. 4. Energy comparison for Uniform grid-based coordinate route driven scheme for dynamic nodes

Fig. 5. Energy comparison for Non-uniform grid-based coordinate route driven scheme for dynamic nodes

routing techniques like non-uniform grid-based coordinate route driven scheme, AODV and DSR. When comparing with uniform grid-based coordinate route driven scheme, the energy consumption is very less in non-uniform grid-based coordinate route driven scheme.

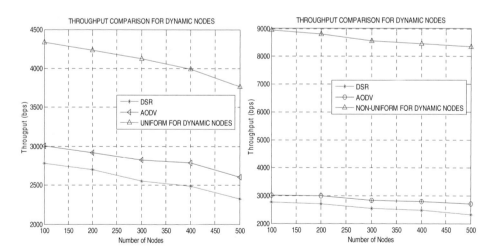

Fig. 6. Throughput comparison for Uniform grid-based coordinate route driven scheme for dyanmic nodes

Fig. 7. Throughput comparison for Non-uniform grid-based coordinate route driven scheme for dyanmic nodes

4.3 Throughput Comparison Uniform Grid-Based Coordinate Route Driven Scheme for Dynamic Sensor Nodes

Fig. 6 shows the comparison of throughput between DSR, AODV and uniform grid-based coordinate route driven scheme. Here the uniform grid-based coordinate route driven scheme has higher throughput when compare to AODV and DSR.

4.4 Throughput Comparison for Non-uniform Grid-Based Coordinate Route Driven Scheme for Dynamic Sensor Nodes

For Dynamic condition of sensor nodes, the non-uniform grid-based coordinate route driven scheme has higher throughput when compare to AODV and DSR. Fig. 7 shows the simulation result of throughput comparison for different routing. When comparing with previous results (i.e.) fig.6, the throughput is very high in non-uniform grid-based coordinate route driven scheme when compare to uniform grid-based coordinate route driven scheme.

4.5 Network Life Time for Different Routing Techniques

Fig.8 shows the simulation result of network life time for different routing techniques for mobile sensor nodes. Here, it compare the network life time for non-uniform based coordinate route driven scheme, uniform based coordinate route driven scheme, DSR and AODV. Network life time is referred as the total number of days survived by sensor node in the network. Here the comparison demonstrates that non-uniform grid-based coordinate route driven scheme has more number of days count to live. Here the life time is calculated for the sensor node by the mean of energy consumed by the sensor nodes in the portioned network.

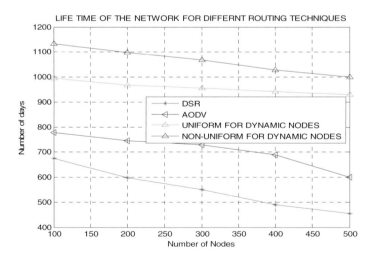

Fig. 8. Network life time for different routing techniques

When comparing network life time with different routing techniques, non-uniform grid-based coordinate route driven scheme has more number of days to live.

5 Conclusion

The proposed key distribution scheme describes a dynamic grid based route driven ECDH scheme for HSN. This proposed scheme utilizes the fact that a sensor only communicates with a small portion of its neighbours and thus greatly reduces communication and computation overheads of key setup. Simulation results show various attributes for densely random and uniform deployed sensor networks. The proposed route driven scheme is tested for scalability by varying the node density from 100 nodes in the network to 1000 nodes in the network. The performance shows that the lifetime network of the sensor network increases by using the non-uniform grid-based coordinate route driven scheme. The results are compared and contrasted to non-uniform grid-based coordinate route driven scheme, uniform grid-based coordinate route driven scheme and the existing routing techniques. By using the non-uniform grid-based coordinate route driven scheme, the sensor network can achieves goals for their survival. Hence non-uniform grid-based coordinate route driven scheme plays a major role in routing the information from source to destination. And they can be easily applicable and adaptable for any type of real time application for HSN.

References

1. Brown, J., Dug, X., Nygard, K.: An efficient public - key base heterogeneous sensor network key distribution scheme. In: Proceedings of IEEE Telecommunication conference, Washington, DC, pp. 991–995 (2007)
2. Duarte-Melo, E., Liu, M.: Analysis of energy consumption and lifetime of heterogeneous sensor network. In: Proceedings of Global Telecommunications Conference, GLOBECOM, pp. 23–35 (2002)
3. Chan, H., Perrig, A., Son, D.: Random – key pre-distribution scheme for Sensor network. In: Proceedings of IEEE Symposium on the Security and Privacy, USA, pp. 197–213 (2003)
4. Du, X., Yang, X., Song, C., Guizani, M., Chen, H.: A routing-key management scheme for heterogeneous sensor network. In: Proceedings of IEEE Global Conference, Scotland, pp. 3407–3412 (2007)
5. Mhatre, V.P., Rosenberg, C., Kofman, D., Mazumdar, R., Shroff, N.: A minimum cost heterogeneous sensor network with a lifetime constraint. IEEE Transactions on Mobile Computing, USA, 4–15 (2005)
6. Du, X., Yang, X., Guizani, M., Chen, H.: A Pseudo - random function based key Management scheme for heterogeneous sensor network. In: Proceedings of Global IEEE Telecommunication Conference, Washington, DC, pp. 5138–5142 (2007)
7. Kim, J.M., Cho, J.S., Jung, S.M., Chung, T.M.: An Energy-Efficient Dynamic Key Management in Wireless Sensor Networks. In: 9th International Conference on Advanced Communication Technology, Gangwon-Do, pp. 2148–2153 (2007)

8. Wen, Y., Shiang, C.: Integrated design of grid - based routing in heterogeneous sensor network. In: IEEE International Conference on Advanced Information Networking and Applications, Niagara Falls, ON, pp. 625–631 (2007)
9. Baoxian, Z., Mouftah, H.T.: Efficient grid – based routing in heterogeneous multihop networks. In: Proceedings of 10th IEEE Symposium on the Computers and Communications, Spain, pp. 367–372 (2005)
10. Akl, R., Kadiyala, P., Haidar, M.: Non-uniform grid - based coordinated routing in wireless sensor network. Journal of Sensors (2009)

Novel Resource Allocation Strategy Using Network Metrics in GRID

C. Valliyammai, S. Thamarai Selvi, R. Satheesh Kumar, E. Pradeep, and K. Naveen

Department of Information Technology, Anna University, Chennai
{cva,stselvi}@annauniv.edu,
{satheesh.ravindranath,pradeepfree4u,naveen19892000}@gmail.com

Abstract. Grid monitoring involves the monitoring of the available resources and the network. Monitoring the resource metrics helps the grid middleware to decide which job to be submitted to which resource. The resource metrics is not enough for deciding a job to be submitted in a resource. A study and analysis of the network metrics also do equally contribute to the decision making while submitting a job.

Keywords: Grid Monitoring; Network metrics; Resource metrics; Resource Selection.

1 Introduction

A Grid platform is an extended distributed environment wherein it is composed of loosely coupled computers acting in concert to perform very large tasks. The computers in the grid network may have different operating systems or hardware, which results in being a heterogeneous environment and are often in a decentralized network, rather than contained in a single location. Grid computing arena involves large amount of academic research projects and has proved to be a collaborative method of solving a given problem using the shared high-end computational computers.

2 Need for Grid Monitoring

The high-level computing jobs can be efficiently performed by analyzing various parameters that impact the process of computing. This process of analyzing the various parameters of the grid setup is known as monitoring [11]. Satoshi describes the need for maintaining the level of quality of the grid setup [26]. There are various factors affecting the quality such as network faults, component interdependencies etc. The quality of the grid setup can be maintained by regularly monitoring the activities within the grid setup, through the process of grid monitoring. This process of monitoring gives the details of the current execution scenario and can also help in predicting the future performance of the setup which will be useful to estimate the time required for completion of jobs as specified in [31]. After the submission of jobs

N. Meghanathan et al. (Eds.): NeCoM, WiMoN, and WeST 2010, CCIS 90, pp. 107–113, 2010.

to the grid setup, users often experience delay in job completion. This can be reduced to a great extent if the grid setup is monitored regularly and the performance problems [2] detected are rectified soon. The purpose of grid monitoring extends its concept leading to performance prediction and performance tuning of grid setup. In the grid setup there are various issues arising during the job execution. These issues namely the delayed job execution, blockage of the job may be due to the resource metrics or the network metrics. These issues should be identified by the process of monitoring, and should be corrected by the process of tuning. The process of identifying and tuning of grid performance is robust since the resources are distributed at different geological location and are connected together by network links [3]. Wu-Chun Chunga and Ruay-Shiung Chang have proposed an efficient protocol called the Grid Resource Information Retrieving (GRIR) protocol [10], which is based on the push data delivery model to obtain the accurate network status.

A monitoring and information system (MIS) is a key component of a distributed system or Grid, which provides information about the available resource metrics and their status. MIS can be used in a variety of ways: a resource broker may query the MIS to locate computing elements for the CPU and memory requirements according to a job submitted by the end-users; a program may collect a stream of data generated by MIS to direct an application or to a system administrator to send a notification when system load or disk space availability changes while identifying the possible performance anomalies [4].

There are two types of monitoring.

i.   Active monitoring - Few test packets are injected in the original data channel and the performance is monitored. This measures the behavior of the packets on the network.
ii. Passive monitoring – Some observation posts are formed to monitor the flow of data packets without disturbing the actual flow of the data packets. This measures the behavior of the application while using the network.

3 Network Monitoring

Albert describes the use of networked computational resources for the implementation of high sensor applications [28]. These high sensor applications required parallel computing in which the network performance is vital and needs to be monitored regularly. The process of network monitoring involves the evaluation of network performance of the links between the clients and head node of the grid setup. Some of the common metrics identified for network monitoring [6] viz., latency, jitter, packet loss, throughput, link utilization, availability and reliability. *Latency* in a network may vary because of the congestion in the channel, router, load of the end – end hosts and also the path followed by the packet during it's to and fro travel. *Jitter* generally means short-term variations. Jitter is a delay that varies over time. Jitter is also known as variation latency. *Packet loss* may take place due to hardware fault, congestion in the channel, corruption in the data packet sent. *Throughput* is constituted by several parameters namely, packet loss ratio, latency, jitter, delay, round trip time and available bandwidth. *Link utilization* can be calculated from the above throughput divided by the access rate and expressed in percentage. For some types of link, the service provider may give Committed Information Rate (CIR). *Availability* refers to the channel availability for a particular application to use at certain point of time. *Reliability* is related with the packet loss ratio and availability. This also involves the retransmission rate. The system administrators and application developers need variety of monitoring tools to analyze various network metrics such as round trip time, packet loss, bandwidth, jitter, latency, throughput etc. Various network-monitoring tools are available which helps in the efficient monitoring of the network [20]. In [32], various network metrics are considered for monitoring and are also tuned for the better performance of the grid setup. The network metrics and the cost function that are used in [32] shall be useful in estimating the overall performance of the grid setup.

4 Resource Monitoring

By maintaining the resource status constantly, the necessary information can be quickly provided as requested. However, the maintenance cost of resource status is heavily related to the total number of resources and number of times the status is updated. Therefore, trade-off between maintenance cost and data accuracy should be considered. Resource monitoring involves monitoring the available resources whenever a job is submitted to the grid middleware. A submitted job is often executed whenever sufficient amount of resources are freed by other jobs. Rajkumar enumerates various issues in Grid Resource Management [27]. The resources are geographically distributed and have their own scheduling mechanisms, prices, access permissions. All these factors need to be managed properly to provide better system performance and user satisfaction. Fufang describes the agent based resource management system [29] where the agents are designed to locate the largest available computation power within the grid setup and provide proper load balance. Junwei also describes the advantages of Agent-Based Resource Management Infrastructure [30], which reduces two major challenges of *adaptability* and *scalability* in grid environment.

In [10], Wu-Chun has introduced a Grid Resource Information Monitoring (GRIM) prototype. To take into account the dynamicity of the changing resources in grid, a push based data delivery protocol called Grid Resource Information Retrieving (GRIR) is used. Resource information is updated completely based on its availability and the requirement of sufficient resource metrics. One of the prominent techniques for resource monitoring is Grid Monitoring Architecture (GMA). Resources available in grid network are present in Producer or product Service. Monitoring of the resources in grid is done by the Consumer Service. Director Service is one, which makes the bridge between the consumers and the producers [22].

Resource monitoring will identify the bottlenecks among the available resources in the grid network. Globus Alliance developed the Globus toolkit, in which the *Monitoring and Discovery System (MDS)* is the most prominent monitoring software. The status of the resources is gathered by the Information provider [23]. Swift Scheduler allocates jobs in Computational Grid by considering the length of the jobs, processing time, jobs' memory, and CPU requirements with respect to the priority of resources [23].

5 Resource Monitoring vs Network Monitoring

In general, the node selection procedure for the job execution is done based on the resource parameters such as computational speed, CPU usage, memory etc. These parameters decide which node has the capability of performing the computation efficiently. In some cases the selection of nodes is done by also considering the network performance between the links to the nodes. Though the nodes may have high resource availability, it may delay the execution of the job due to network performance degradation. To reduce this kind of issues, the network parameters are also to be considered along with the resource parameters during node selection. Job submission is based on both CPU loads among the servers and latencies available in the network [24].

Though the resource parameters may be monitored well, the network parameters may have a role in effective transfer of data between the compute and head nodes. The need for network monitoring in grid is mainly when the parallel jobs are submitted to compute nodes with equal resource performance. In this case though the resource performances of the compute nodes are equal, the response from both the nodes may not be received in the same time. This effect is due to the variation in network performance between the links of the computational nodes. The purpose of network performance monitoring becomes crucial as the network size of the grid setup increases. This involves monitoring of more number of links on the network and estimates its network performance and support fault detection [6]. Collecting, relating and analyzing of network information are one of the important aspects of effective grid application and services. GMMPro, grid network and monitoring system provides the basic support for monitoring the grid network and has SNMP as its lower layer protocol [5].

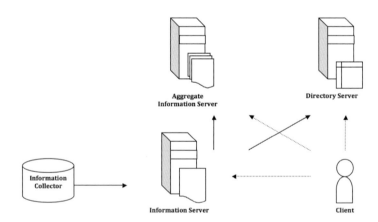

Fig. 1. General Model of monitoring system

Figure 1 shows a general model of a monitoring system. The client queries and gets the information from all the servers. Different monitoring systems implement each block in their own way as compared in Table 1.

Table 1. Comparison of Existing monitoring systems

	MDS-2	**R-GMA**	**Hawkeye**
Information Collector	Information Provider	Producer	Module
Information Server	GRIS	Producer Servlet	Agent
Aggregate Information Server	GIIS	Producer and Consumer	Manager
Directory Server	GIIS	Registry	Manager
Use Case	Single Query	Streaming Network Data	Single Query
Push/Pull model	Pull	Push and Pull	Triggers and Push

GRIS - Grid Resource Information Service
GIIS - Grid Index Information Service

6   Research Issues

There are various research issues in improving the efficiency of grid setup. Though the resource metrics contribute to the decision making of the resource selection, network metrics do play a significant role in deciding the hosts for job execution. The network metrics gives more detailed information regarding the quality and the performance of the hosts. Resource metrics gives information of the local system's efficiency only in terms of CPU utilization, concurrent processing, and memory utilization. There is a need of overlooking the degradation due to network metrics while considering the resource metrics too. Hence, analysis of the network metrics along with the resource metrics for the selection of the compute nodes during job submission is essential. The strategy for resource allocation can be designed in the form of an algorithm. The algorithm can be optimized to handle both the resource metrics as well as the network metrics.

One of the key issues is to consider the network metrics for monitoring and prediction of the grid setup apart from the regular resource metrics used. The efficiency of a grid setup can be estimated more accurately considering the network metrics. The existing resource selection and job scheduling algorithms can be altered by including the network metrics to improve the efficiency. Such improved version of algorithms will also consider the dynamic change in network load and other bottleneck situations. Another research issue is to optimize the dynamically varying network load by the process of tuning. The impact of network monitoring and tuning has to be optimized such that it doesn't source the bottleneck situation while monitoring and as well as in tuning.

References

1. Coviello, T., Ferrari, T., Kavoussanakis, K., Kudarimoti, L., Leese, M., Phipps, A., Swany, M., Trew, A.S.: Bridging Network Monitoring and the Grid. In: CESNET 2006, Conference on Advanced Communications and Grids (2006)
2. Gunter, D., Tierney, B., Jackson, K., Lee, J., Stoufer, M.: Dynamic Monitoring of High-Performance Distributed Applications. In: 11th IEEE International Symposium on High Performance Distributed Computing 2002, p. 163 (2002)
3. Millar, A.P.: Grid monitoring: a holistic approach. Grid PP UK Computing for Particle Physics (2006)
4. Zhang, X., Freschl, J.L., Schopf, J.M.: Scalability analysis of three monitoring and information systems: MDS2, R-GMA, and Hawkeye. Journal of Parallel and Distributed Computing 67(8) (2007)
5. Wang J., Zhou M., Zhou H.: Providing Network Monitoring Service for Grid Computing. In: Proceedings of the 10th IEEE International Workshop on Future Trends of Distributed Computing Systems, FTDCS 2004 (2004)
6. Leese, M., Tyer, R., Tasker, R.: Network Performance Monitoring for the Grid. In: UK e-Science 2005, All Hands Meeting (2005), http://gridmon.dl.ac.uk/
7. UDPmon webpage, http://www.hep.man.ac.uk/u/rich/net/index.html
8. TCPmon webpage,
   http://www.hep.man.ac.uk/u/rich/Tools_Software/tcpmon.html
9. Hughes-Jones, R.E.: Writeup for UDPmon: A Network Diagnostic Program (2004)
10. Chunga, W.-C., Chang, R.-S.: A new mechanism for resource monitoring in Grid computing (2008)
11. Zanikolas, S., Sakellariou, R.: A taxonomy of grid monitoring systems. Future Generation Computer Systems 21, 163–188 (2005)
12. Davenhall, A.C., Leese, M.J.: An Introduction to Computer Network Monitoring and Performance (2005)
13. Pinger webpage, http://www-iepm.slac.stanford.edu/pinger/
14. Medinets, D., Cafaro, D.A.: Monitoring and scheduling. IBM (2007)
15. Jacobson, V.: Traceroute: A tool for printing the route packets take to a network host, ftp://ftp.ee.lbl.gov/nrg.html
16. Jacobson, V., Leres, C., McCanne, S.: tcpdump, ftp://ftp.ee.lbl.gov/tcpdump.tar.Z
17. Mah, B.: pchar: A tool for measuring Internet path characteristics, http://www.employees.org/bmah/Software/pchar/
18. Goujun, J.: Methods for Network Analysis and Troubleshooting, http://www-didc.lbl.gov/~jin/network/net-tools.html
19. IPerf: http://openmaniak.Com/iperf.php
20. Hacker, T.J., Athey, B.D., Sommerfield, J., Pittsburgh, Walker, D.S.: Experiences Using Web100 for End-to-End Network Performance Tuning for Visible Human Testbeds
21. List of network measurement tools, http://ncne.nlanr.net/software/tools/
22. Tierney, B., Aydt, R., Gunter, D., Smith, W., Swany, M., Taylor, V., Wolski, R.: A grid monitoring architecture. In: The Global Grid Forum Draft Recommendation (GWD-Perf-16-3) (August 2002)
23. Monitoring and discovery system, http://www.globus.org/toolkit/mds/

24. Somasundaram, K., Radhakrishnan, S.: Task Resource Allocation in Grid using Swift Scheduler. Int. J. of Computers, Communications & Control, IEEE Transactions on Parallel and distributed Systems IV(2), 158–166 (2009) ISSN 1841-9836, E-ISSN 1841-9844
25. Ranjan, S., Knightly, E.: High Performance Resource Allocation and Request Redirection Algorithms for Web Clusters
26. Shirose, K., Matsuoka, S.: Autonomous Configuration of Grid Monitoring Systems. In: Proceedings of the 2004 International Symposium on Applications and the Internet Workshops, SAINTW 2004 (2004)
27. Buyya, R., Abramson, D., Giddy, J., Stockinger, H.: Grid Resource Management, Scheduling and Computational Economy. In: Proceedings of the 2nd International Workshop on Global and Cluster Computing, WGCC 2000 (2000)
28. Reuther, A., Goodman, J.: Dynamic Resource Management for a Sensor-Fusion Application via Distributed Parallel Grid Computing
29. Li, F., Qi, D., Zhang, L., Zhang, X., Zhang, Z.: Research on Novel Dynamic Resource Management and Job Scheduling in Grid Computing. In: Proceedings of the First International Multi-Symposiums on Computer and Computational Sciences, IMSCCS 2006 (2006)
30. Cao, J., Kerbyson, D.J., Nudd, G.R.: Performance Evaluation of an Agent-Based Resource Management Infrastructure for Grid Computing
31. Valliyammai, C., Thamarai Selvi, S., Santhana Kumar, M., Sathish Kumar, S., Suresh Kumar, R.: Network Performance monitoring using mobile agents in grid. In: 2009 IEEE International Advance Computing Conference (2009)
32. Valliyammai, C., Thamarai Selvi, S., Satheesh Kumar, R., Pradeep, E., Naveen, K.: Multi-agent Based Network Performance Tuning in Grid. In: BAIP 2010. Information Processing and Management, LNCS, vol. 70, pp. 297–304 (2010)

Energy Efficient Routing Protocol for Wireless Sensor and Actor Networks

Srinivasara Rao Dh[2], Ramesh Babu Battula[1], Srikanth Vemuru[1],
Rajasekhara rao Kurra[1], Pavan Kumar Tummala[1], and S.V. Rao[2]

[1] K L University, School of Computing
Vijayawada, Andhra Pradesh, India
[2] Indian Institute of Technology,
Guwahati, India
d.rao@alumni.iitg.ernet.in, battula@alumni.iitg.ernet.in,
srikanth_ist@klce.ac.in, rajasekhar.kurra@klce.ac.in,
pavankumar_ist@klce.ac.in, svrao@iitg.ernet.in
http://www.kluniversity.in, http://www.iitg.ac.in

Abstract. Wireless Sensor and Actor Networks (WSANs) are composed
of heterogeneous nodes referred to as sensors and actors. Sensors are low-
cost, low-power, multi-functional devices that communicate untethered
in short distances. Actors collect and process sensor data and perform
appropriate actions on the environment. Hence,actors are resource-rich
devices equipped with higher processing and transmission capabilities,
and longer battery life.In WSANs, the collaborative operation of the
sensors enables the distributed sensing of a physical phenomenon. After
sensors detect an event in the deployment field, the event data is distribu-
tively processed and transmitted to the actors, which gather, process, and
eventually reconstruct the event data. WSANs can be considered a distributed control system designed to react to sensor information with an
effective and timely action. For this reason, in WSANs it is important to
provide real-time coordination and communication to guarantee timely
execution of the right actions and energy efficiency of the networking
protocols is also a major concern, since sensors are resource-constrained
devices. We propose an energy efficient routing protocol for wireless sensor and actor networks to cope with these challenges keeping in mind the
resource constraints of the network and the early response by the actor
nodes for delay sensitive applications with number of transmissions as
less as possible. Our protocol is based on clustering (virtual grid) and
Voronoi region concept.

Keywords: Sensor, Actor, Voronoi diagram, Virtual Grid.

1 Introduction

A Wireless Sensor and Actor Network(WSAN)[2] can be considered as a specialized WSN with the addition of resource-rich actor nodes that have better
processing capabilities, higher transmission power, and longer battery life. Since

N. Meghanathan et al. (Eds.): NeCoM, WiMoN, and WeST 2010, CCIS 90, pp. 114–123, 2010.

actors have higher capabilities and can action large areas, they are fewer in number compared to the number of sensor nodes in an environment. The actor is present in the network to take action based on the sensed information received from the sensor nodes. WSANs will be an integral part of systems such as battlefield surveillance, nuclear, biological or chemical attack detection, home automation, and environmental monitoring[7]. Figure - 1 represents a simple WSAN with a sink that is present to take care of overall communication and coordination.

Fig. 1. Wireless Sensor and Actor Networks Architecture

One of the major challenges of WSAN for efficient communication is the coordination among sensor and actor nodes. Sensor-Actor coordination is for quick event reporting to appropriate actor node. Actor-actor coordination is to avoid redundant action in overlapped action area and a reliable action.

2   Realted Work

2.1   Static Actors in WSAN Area

A Distributed Coordination Framework for WSAN. A coordination protocol framework for WSAN is addressed with a proposed sensor-actor coordination model based on event driven clustering paradigm, where cluster formation is triggered by an event so that clusters are created on the fly to optimally react to the event and to provides reliability with minimum energy consumption[5]. This way, only the event area is clustered,and each cluster consists of those sensor nodes that send their data to the same actor. **A Coordination Protocol for WSAN** - A sensor-sensor coordination protocol for WSAN based on clustering and Voronoi region concept is proposed in [6]. This protocol creates clusters consisting of sensors detecting the same event and forwards to the nearest actor. **ELRS: An Energy-Efficient Layered Routing Scheme for WSAN** An energy efficient layered routing scheme is described in[9] for semiautomated architecture, where the network field is divided into different sized (overlapped) actor fields, which covers all the sensor nodes. **Delay-Energy Aware Routing Protocol for Sensor and Actor Networks** - Delay energy aware routing protocol(DEAP)[10] mainly consists of two components- Routing based on Forwarding Sets and the Random wakeup Scheme. **Resource-Aware and Link Quality Based Routing Metric for WSAN** - This paper presents a resource-aware and link quality based(RLQ)[11] routing metric to address energy limitations, link quality variations, and node heterogeneity in WSAN.

2.2   Mobile Actors in WSAN Area

A Communication Architecture for Mobile WSAN. The coordination and communication problem has been studied and a hybrid location management scheme has been proposed to handle the mobility of actors along with a geographical routing algorithm for sensor-actor communication [7]. The sensor-actor communication uses forwarding rules based on geographical position in the presence of Rayleigh fading channels. **Real-time Coordination and Routing in Wireless Sensor and Actor Networks** Mobile actors proposes a real-time coordination and routing framework for sensor-actor coordination to achieve energy-efficient and reliable communication [12]. **Intelligent actor mobility in wireless sensor and actor networks** - A inherent clustering algorithm is introduced to connect sensor nodes and cluster's are formed by using the sensor node locations, sensor nodes transmission range. Sensor node locations can be obtained using localization techniques such as angle-of-arrival measurements, distance related measurements, and received signal strength profiling techniques [21]. The main goal is to develop intelligent mobility models for an actor node in a wireless sensor and actor network to maximize timely detection of events. Random mobility models are unsuitable for sparsely connected networks[22], 100% event detection by single actor is possible. These mobility models are not studied for fully connected network and actor mobility cost is not considered. This mobility models good for the applications where the actor collect event inform from sparsely connected network. **A Real-time Communication Framework for Wireless Sensor-Actuator Networks** - This paper[23] main objective is to provide a low latency event reporting algorithm for sensor-to-actor communication and an effective coordination algorithm among the actors.

2.3   System Model and Assumptions

This protocol considers few assumptions for simplicity in building system model:

a) The network is composed of N_s sensors and N_a actors, and they are deployed uniformly in the network area with high density of sensor nodes and low density of actor nodes i.e, $N_s >> N_a$. Every sensor node associates itself to one of the actor nodes to which it is nearest, which leads to the construction of Voronoi regions around actor nodes. It is also assumed that all the nodes (both sensor and actor) are equipped with GPS enabled devices and hence each node is aware of its own location information.

b) Sensors are homogeneous and wireless channels are bi-directional, symmetric and error-free and equipped with a low data rate radio interface. This interface is used to communicate with other sensor(s) and actor(s) if they are in the communication range of sensor.

c) Sensors nodes are assumed to be immobile. Data transmission and reception are major energy consuming activities. Each sensor node sends the information about events in multi-hop communication to actor.

d) Actor nodes are mobile, and these are equipped with two radio transmitters, i.e., a low data rate transmitter to communicate with the sensors, and a high rate wireless interface for actor actor communication. From the perspective of sensors, actors are equivalent recipients of information.

e) Actor nodes have much more efficiency in terms of energy level and transmission power compared to sensor nodes. Sensor nodes communicate with the actors by sending data via multiple hops and actor to actor communication is through actors.

2.4   Voronoi Diagram

Voronoi diagram is a most fundamental data structure in computational geometry [25]. Voronoi diagram can be used in finding a partition of the given set of points into subsets whose members are similar. Let S be the set of N nodes on a plane. For two nodes P and Q of S the dominance of P over Q is defined as the subset of the nodes being at least as close to P as to Q. Dominance of P and Q is a closed half plane bounded by the perpendicular bisector of P and Q. The bisector separates all nodes of the plane closer to P from those closer to Q and will be termed as the separator of P and Q. The region of a node P is the portion of the plane lying on all the dominance of P over the remaining nodes in S. They form a polygonal partition of the plane. These partitions are called Voronoi regions and combination of such regions for a plane is referred as Voronoi diagram. As we know that the set $A=\{a_1, a_2, a_3, ...a_n\}$ of actor nodes are sparsely deployed. It is advisable for each sensor node to report sensed events to the closest actor node in order to reduce latency and communication cost. All the sensors which are closer to an actor a_i than any other actor in the region called Voronoi region at a_i, denoted by $V(a_i)$. The Voronoi region $V(a_i)$ is a set of points closer to a_i than any other actor a_j, where $i \neq j$. Union of all Voronoi regions of A is called Voronoi diagram. In other words Voronoi diagram of a set of actors is a partitioning the plane into regions such that each actor node is associated to a region in which all points of that region is closest to it than any other actor node. Formal definition of Voronoi diagram of a set $A = \{a_1, a_2, a_3, ...a_n\}$ of actors is defined as follows: We denote the set of points closer to a site a_i than the site a_j is denoted by $B(a_i, a_j)$. Voronoi region $V(a_i)$ of a site a_i is

$$\cap_{i=1,j\neq1}^{n} = B(a_i, a_j) \tag{1}$$

Voronoi diagram of the set of points

$$\cup_{i=1}^{n} V(a_i) \tag{2}$$

3   The Procedure

The protocol has three different phases. Before we discuss details of the procedure we will take a look at overview of procedure

3.1 Initialization Phase

Sensor and actor nodes are deployed uniformly throughout the network area under consideration. Each node uses location and grid size to determine the grid ID. The estimation of Grid size is also important for reliable connectivity and we have to ensure that the active member in adjacent grids are within transmission range. Active member in adjacent grids must communicate with each other provided they are within their transmission range. If the grid size is too large some active member in adjacent grids may be out of transmission range. This must be avoided so as not to experience early network partition. The upper bound for a square grid with width r is calculated as follows:

$$r \leq \frac{R_c}{2\sqrt{2}} \tag{3}$$

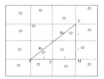

Fig. 2. Grid size computation

This Figure - 2 shows that if the grid size is less than or equal to r, where R_c is the maximum transmit distance, the active member in adjacent grids are within their transmission ranges. **Node Scheduling** - Sensor nodes within a grid coordinate and the node having highest energy level becomes active. Each sensor node calculates an expected life time considering maximum utilization of its energy level. After some predefined time interval, every other sensor node of that grid wakes up to receive a message broadcasted by current active sensor node. The broadcasted message contains the nodes remaining life and the next wakeup time for other sensor nodes of that grid. At this moment, if the current active sensor node expected life value is less than a threshold value, the awake sensor nodes remain awake until the next sensor node having highest energy level becomes active and broadcasts its expected life along with the next wake-up time for other sensor nodes. **Neighbor Discovery** - Once node scheduling is formed among grid members, the active member in the grid sends HELLO message to one-hop grid neighbors. This hello message including location id, grid-id, rate of energy consumption, fraction of energy consumption. The last two parameters are useful in selecting next hop neighbors while forwarding data to actor. **Actors Association** - Each actor node periodically broadcast it's location id, actor-id within it's communication range.

3.2 Event Detection and Reporting Phase

When an event occurs it is detected by the active sensor node inside the grid(s) and forwards towards nearest actors by energy-aware greedy forwarding. If the

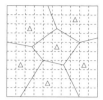

Fig. 3. Network area divided into grids and Voronoi regions

Actor is in communication range of the sensor then directly forwards to actor. If it is not in the communication range, the sensor node selects the next hop grid active member based on the cost computing parameter. Each sensor node periodically broadcast it's hello message to one hop neighbor, it contains rate of energy consumption and fraction of energy consumption. **Rate of Energy Consumption** - Rate of energy consumption is the energy consumption per unit time. It is calculated after each hello period, H_p. Each grid active node keeps the track of number of hello periods occurred. We now calculate the rate of energy consumption of a node at the start of nth periodic interval. Let E_{in} be the energy at the start of the nth periodic interval and E_{i0} be the initial energy of the node i. Energy consumption of the node i till the start of n_{th} periodic interval is given by (E_{i0} - E_{in}). Number of periodic intervals that elapsed till the start of n_{th} periodic interval is (n-1). Therefore, total time elapsed is (n-1) $\times$ H_p. Thus, the rate of energy consumption after n^{th} periodic interval, R_{in}, is given by

$$R_{in} = \frac{E_{i0} - E_{in}}{(n-1) \times H_p}. \tag{4}$$

Fraction of Energy Consumption: Fraction of energy consumption is defined as the total energy consumption per unit initial energy of node. Like rate of energy consumption, fraction of energy consumption is also calculated after each H_p. It is assumed in the proposed scheme that for n_{th} periodic interval, value of fraction of energy consumed is F_{in} till the start of $(n+1)^{th}$ periodic interval. Fraction of energy consumption of node i, F_{in}, is calculated using below equation

$$F_{in} = \frac{E_{i0} - E_{in}}{F_{i0}} \tag{5}$$

Cost Computation Parameter: When sensor node A needs to forward the packet to actor node B, and the distance of sensor node A to actor node B is D and distance of its neighbors (which are in the radio range of A) to B is d_1, d_2, d_3, . . . , d_k, then reasonable fairness of energy at nodes can be achieved if the packet is forwarded to the node, which has least fraction of energy consumption (F_{in}). Further, reasonable fairness of number of hops traveled can also be achieved if the packet is forwarded to the node which is at the minimum distance from the destination. We aim at a scheme so that a packet should be forwarded to

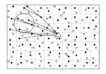

Fig. 4. Data aggregation along forwarding path within a Voronoi region

a Actor which also has minimum rate of energy consumption. We propose the cost metric as

$$C_{in} = R_{in} \times \left(\frac{d_i}{D} + F_{in} \right) \tag{6}$$

3.3 Actor Coordination and Reaction

The objective of this phase is to select best actor(s) to form the actor team, and to control their motion toward the action area. The position of the sensors that generate readings defines event area. The action area represents the area where the actors should act, and is identified by processing the event data. In general, the event area and the action areas may be different, although they may coincide in several applications.

4   Simulation and Results

4.1   Performance Metrics

We use the following performance metrics to analyze the performance of our protocol in terms of throughput, packet delivery ratio, average delay and normalized routing overhead. *Throughput:* Throughput is considered as one of the significant performance metric for any routing protocol. It is computed as the amount of data transferred (in bits) divided by the simulated data transfer time (the time interval from sending the first CBR packet to receiving the last CBR packet). *Packet Delivery Ratio:* It is measured as the ratio of the number of packets delivered to destination and the number of packets sent by source. *Average Delay:* Average delay is the ratio of sum total of delay for each packet and the total number of received packets. *Average Energy Consumption:*The metric is measured as the percent of energy consumed by a node with respect to its initial energy.

4.2   Simulation Environment

We simulate our idea in NS-2 with simulation parameters as shown in the table 1.

The topology of the network is generated by dividing the network area into square size grids of fifteen meters length and placing two nodes in each grid randomly.

Table 1. Simulation parameters

1	Simulator	NS-2
2	Simulation time	200sec
3	Simulation Area	200×200
4.	Number of Nodes	200
4	Transmission Range	50 meters/sec
5	Grid size	15 meters
6	Traffic Type	CBR
7	Data Payload	128 bytes
8	Mac Layer	802.11
9	Propagation Model	Two-RayGround
10	Antenna	Omni-directional

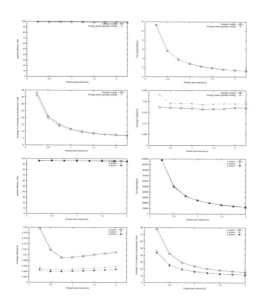

Fig. 5. Simulation Results

4.3   Results and Analysis

During the simulation process we have closely observed the different performance metrics for various CBR intervals ranging from 0.25 seconds up to 2.0 seconds with a step of 0.25 seconds. This is basically the variation of traffic load in the network. Graphs for CBR intervals (traffic load) against all the performance metrics(as mentioned in the above section) were constructed which clearly depicts that our protocol outperforms in all respects. First four graphs are comparing the greedy forwarding vs energy aware greedy forwarding against all performance metrics. Rest graphs are comparing all performance metrics by considering two actors, three actors, four actors. For the all simulation results are taken with initial energy of each sensor node is considered as 25 units and transmission power is 0.6w, receiving power is 0.3w.

5   Conclusion

The protocol emphasizes on coordination among sensor and actor nodes for WSAN based on Voronoi region and virtual grid and reduce congestion and redundancy in the network. The protocol divides the network area into grids and in each grid only one sensor node remains active. Sensor nodes gather event information and send it to nearest actor node based on Voronoi region. The important characteristics like real-time requirements and efficient utilization of available node energy are also taken into consideration. The advantage is that as for each sensor node there is only one closest actor node based on the Voronoi region, there will be no problem of deciding the actor node to which data needs to be transmitted upon detecting an event which is a major challenge in WSAN.

References

1. Akyildiz, I.F., Su, W., Sankarasubramaniam, Y., Cayirci, E.: Wireless sensor networks: A survey. Computer Networks 38, 392–422 (2002)
2. Akyildiz, I.F., Kasimoglu, I.H.: Wireless sensor and actor networks:Research challenges. In: Ad Hoc Networks, October 2004, vol. 2, pp. 351–367. Elsevier, Amsterdam (2004)
3. Heinzelman, W.R., Chandrakasan, A., Balakrishnan, H.: Energyefficient communication protocol for wireless microsensor networks(leach). In: Proceedings of 33rd Hawaii International Conference on System Sciences (2000)
4. Intanagonwiwat, C., Govindan, R., Estrin, D.: Directed diffusion: a scalable and robust communication paradigm for sensor networks. In: Proceedings of the sixth annual international conference on Mobile computing and networking, Boston, MA USA, pp. 56–67 (2000)
5. Melodia, T., Pompili, D., Gungor, V.C., Akyildiz, I.F.: A Distributed Coordination Framework for Wireless Sensor and Actor Networks. In: Proceedings of 6th ACM international Symposium on Mobile Ad-hoc Networking and Computing (May 2005)
6. Bouhafs, F., Merabti, M., Mokhtar, H.: A Coordination Protocol for Wireless Sensor and Actor Networks, PGP Net (2006)
7. Melodia, T., Pompili, D., Akyildiz, I.F.: A Communication Architecture for Mobile Wireless Sensor and Actor Networks. In: Proceedings of IEEE SECON (2006)
8. Yuan, H., Ma, H., Liao, H.: Coordination Mechanism in Wireless Sensor and Actor Networks. In: Proceedings of the First International Multi-Symposiums on Computational Sciences, IMSCCS 2006 (2006)
9. Peng, H., Huafeng, W., Dilin, M., Chuanshan, G.: Elrs:An Energyefficient Layered Routing Scheme for Wireless Sensor and Actor Networks. In: Procedings of the 20th IEEE International Conference on Advanced Information Networking and Applications, AINA 2006 (2006)
10. Durresi, A., Paruchuri, V., Barolli, L.: Delay-Energy Aware Routing Protocol for Sensor and Actor Networks. In: Proceedings of the 11th International Conference on parallel and Distributed Systems, ICPDDS 2005 (2005)

11. Cargi Gungor, V., Sastry, C., Song, Z., Integlia, R.: Resource-Aware and Link-Quality-Based Routing in Wireless Sensor and Actor Networks. In: Proceedings of IEEE ICC (June 2007)
12. Shah, G.A., Bozyigit, M., Akan, O.B., Baykal, B.: Real-time Coordination and Routing in Wireless Sensor and Actor Networks. In: 6th International Conference, NEW2AN 2006, St. Petersburg, Russia (2006)
13. Xu, Y., Heidermann, J., Estrin, D.: Geography-Informed Energy Conservation for Ad-hoc Routing(GAF). In: Proceedings of 7th annual ACM International conference on Mobile Computing and Networking (July 2001)
14. Mitton, N., Busson, A., Fleury, E.: Self-Organization in Large Scale Ad-Hoc Networks. In: The Third Annual MED-HOC-NET Workshop (June 2004)
15. Wang, Y.C.R.P.X., Xing, G., Gill, C.: Integrated Coverage and Connectivity Cconfiguration in Wireless Sensor Networks. In: Proceedings of Sen-Sys 2003, Los Angeles, USA, pp. 7–14 (2003)
16. Aurenhammer, F.: Voronoi diagrams: A Survey of a Fundamental Geometric Data Structure. ACM 23, 345–405 (1991)
17. Bouhafs, F., Merabti, M., Mokhtar, H.: A Semantic Clustering Routing Protocol for Wireless Sensor Networks. In: Proceedings of IEEE CCNC (2006)
18. Heinzelman, W.R., Chandrakasan, A., Balakrishnan, H.: Energyefficient Communication Protocol for Wireless Microsensor Networks (LEACH). In: Proceedings of 33rd Hawaii International Conference on System Sciences (2000)
19. Bouhafs, F., Merabti, M., Mokhtar, H.: A Semantic Clustering Routing Protocol for Wireless Sensor Networks. In: Proceedings of IEEE CCNC (2006)
20. Yu, Y., Govindan, R., Estrin, D.: Geographical and Energy Aware Routing: A Recursive Data Dissemination Protocol for Wireless Sensor Networks (2001)
21. Mao, G., Fidan, B., Anderson, B.D.O.: Wireless Sensor Network Localization Techniques. Comput. Netw. 51(10), 2529–2553 (2007),
    http://dx.doi.org/10.1016/j.comnet.2006.11.018 Issn - 1389-1286
22. Camp, T., Boleng, J., Davies, V.: A Survey of Mobility Models for Ad Hoc Network Research. Wireless Communications and Mobile Computing (WCMC): Special issue on Mobile Ad Hoc Networking: Research, Trends and Applications 2, 483–502 (2002)
23. Ngai, E.C.-H., Lyu, M.R., Liu, J.: A Real-time Communication Framework for Wireless Sensor-Actuator Networks. In: IEEE Aerospace Conference (2004)
24. Mc Neff, J.G.: The global positioning system. IEEE Transactions on Microwave Theory and Techniques 50, 645–652 (2002)
25. Aurenhammer, F.: Voronoi Diagrams: A Survey of a Fundamental Geometric Data Structure. ACM 23, 345–405 (1991)

A Novel Visual Cryptographic Technique through Grey Level Inversion (VCTGLI)

Jayanta Kumar Pal[1], J.K. Mandal[2], and Kousik Dasgupta[1]

[1] Computer Science and Engineering, Kalyani Government Engineering College,
Kalyani- 741235, West Bengal, India
jkp_it08@yahoo.com
kousik.dasgupta@gmail.com
[2] Computer Science and Engineering, University of Kalyani,
Kalyani- 741235, West Bengal, India
jkm.cse@gmail.com

Abstract. In this paper a new (2, 2) visual cryptographic technique has been proposed, where the aspect ratio and the dimension of the secrete image/share with respect to source image remains constant during the process. In the VCTGLI technique grey level of some pixels of the input image has been inverted using random function to generate shares, instead of generating new pixels for shares. The scheme may be more secured and easy to implement like other techniques of visual cryptography.

To expound the effectiveness of the technique the obtained results are compared with the technique of Naor and Shamir [1], Yue and Chiang [2] and Jena and Jena [3] where it has been shown that VCTGLI gives better performance.

Keywords: Visual Cryptographic Technique through Grey Level Inversion (VCTGLI), (2, 2) visual cryptography, grey level inversion.

1 Introduction

Visual Cryptography is a new type of cryptographic scheme, where decryption is done directly through the human visual systems, instead of any cryptographic computation. Using the visual cryptographic technique, any text or image to be encrypted is fed as an image (as the input) in the system to generate 'n' number of (where n is a positive integer greater than or equal to 2) different output images (called shares). A share looks like an image of some random noises. For the decryption the recipient has to stack a minimum number of shares (printed in transparencies) in an arbitrary manner with the proper alignment.

There are two types of visual cryptography, viz. (n, n) visual cryptography and (k, n) visual cryptography. They are defined in section 1.1 and 1.2 respectively.

1.1 (n, n) Visual Cryptography

In this type of visual cryptography, n numbers of shares are generated from the source image, and all shares are needed to reveal the secret image. Here $n \geq 2$, where 'n' is an integer.

N. Meghanathan et al. (Eds.): NeCoM, WiMoN, and WeST 2010, CCIS 90, pp. 124–133, 2010.
© Springer-Verlag Berlin Heidelberg 2010

1.2 (k, n) Visual Cryptography

In this technique n numbers of shares are generated but 'k' out of 'n' number of shares are needed to reveal a secret image, where $2 \leq k \leq n$, and k and n both are integers.

The remaining portion of this paper is organized as follows. Section 2 presents a brief overview of the related works. Section 3 describes the proposed technique. An example of the share generation process of the proposed technique is presented in the Section 4. Analysis of the performance of the proposed technique is presented in the Section 5. Section 6 draws the conclusions and future scope of work.

2 Related Works

Visual Cryptography was first developed by Moni Naor and Adi Shamir [1], in 1994. In this technique, shares are generated based on two matrices, C_0 and C_1. The elements of the matrices represent the grey levels value for the pixel. The matrices C_0 and C_1 are used for the input of a white and a black pixel respectively. Shares are generated by permuting the columns of the two matrices. The technique is given in Fig. 1.

In the picture (Fig. 1) a white box and a black box represents a white and a black pixel respectively and in the share, combination of four b/w pixels are generated with three different options for each.

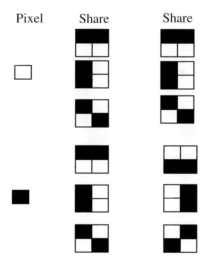

Pixel   Share   Share

Fig. 1. Share generation technique in Naor and Shamir [1] for (2, 2) visual cryptography

In year 2000 a neural network based approach for visual cryptography has been proposed by Tai-Wen Yue and Suchen Chiang [2]. The share generation method used for (2, 2) visual cryptography in this technique is given in the Fig. 2. In this technique combination of two b/w pixels are generated with two different options for each pixel with equal probability.

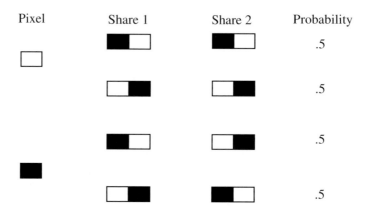

Fig. 2. Share generation in Tai-Wen Yue and Suchen Chiang [2] for (2, 2) visual cryptography

Jena and Jena [3] devised a technique for (2, 2) visual cryptography in 2008 where a single pixel generates either two pixels or four pixels in each share. The pictorial representation of the share is given in the Fig. 3

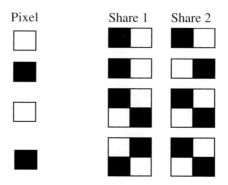

Fig. 3. Share generation in Jena and Jena [3] for (2, 2) visual cryptography

Various other algorithms [4, 5, 6, 7, 8] are available for different visual cryptographic schemes, where efforts have been made to enhance the security. From the literature it can also be traced that efforts has also been made to increase the ease of use of the visual cryptography. For example Wei-Qi [9] developed a scheme for proper alignment of the shares.

All the share generation techniques described above, generates more output pixels than the input pixels in each share. As a result the dimension or the aspect ratio of the decrypted image does not remain constant. In this paper a new share generation technique has been proposed where both the aspect ratio and dimension of the decrypted image remains constant.

3   The Technique

The proposed technique is a (2, 2) visual cryptographic scheme, which means that two shares are generated from the input image. During decryption, shares are stacked in an arbitrary order but with the proper alignment.

To generate shares, two consecutive pixels of the input image are taken together as input. Pixels of both the shares are generated from it. The share generation technique is applicable to all pixels of the input image. Since two consecutive pixels are taken as the input at a time, therefore during share generation process four cases may occur. They are, either both adjacent pixels may be black or both may be white or combination of white and alack and vice versa.

If two adjacent black pixels are taken as input, there are two possibilities of generating two shares taking two adjacent pixels together, out of which one set may be alternately black and white or vice versa and other set will be just reverse of the previous set and the probability of occurring each set is random and equal to .5. In case of two adjacent white pixels one set of share may be consisting of black pixel followed by white pixel where as the other set will be just reverse i.e. white pixel followed by black pixel and the probabilities of occurrence of each set is .5. In other two cases i.e. for input black followed by white pixel and vice versa the two adjacent pixels of each share will remain same. Pictorial representation of share generation technique for the proposed technique is given in Fig. 4

The pixel generation technique for the VCTGLI is given in the Fig. 4

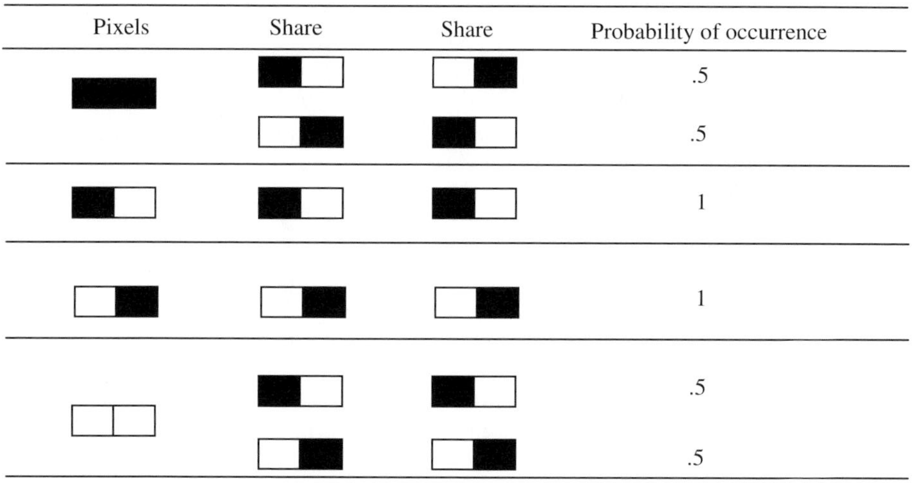

Pixels	Share	Share	Probability of occurrence
■■	■□	□■	.5
	□■	■□	.5
■□	■□	■□	1
□■	□■	□■	1
□□	■□	■□	.5
	□■	□■	.5

Fig. 4. Share generation technique by the VCTGLI

There may be the case where input image contains odd numbers of pixels, if it is so then the last single pixel is kept as it is in both the shares.

The VCTGLI technique, depicted pictorially in the Fig 4, can also be represented through matrix representation. Let us consider four matrices C_0, C_1, C_2, and C_3, for input pixels black-black, black-white, white-black and white-white respectively. It has been considered that '1' and '0' represents a single black and white pixel respectively. All pixels of the shares can be generated by permuting the columns of the appropriate matrix. The matrices can be represented as follows:

$$C_0 = \begin{bmatrix} 1 & 1 & 0 & 0 \\ 0 & 0 & 1 & 1 \end{bmatrix}$$

To generate output pixels of the shares, for two black pixels, C_0 matrix is used and any two sets of different columns are to be selected from the matrix in random order.

$$C_1 = \begin{bmatrix} 1 & 0 \\ 1 & 0 \end{bmatrix}$$

For the case of one black and one white pixel, two out of two columns from the C_1 matrix to be selected.

$$C_2 = \begin{bmatrix} 0 & 1 \\ 0 & 1 \end{bmatrix}$$

For the case of one white and one black pixel, two out of two columns from the C_2 matrix should be selected.

$$C_3 = \begin{bmatrix} 1 & 1 & 0 & 0 \\ 1 & 1 & 0 & 0 \end{bmatrix}$$

For the last case where the input is two white pixels, two sets of different columns form the matrix C_3 are selected in random order (with probability .5).

3.1 Proof of Decoding

If a transparencies printed by black colour is superimposed with a blank transparencies then black colour will be seen as the resultant colour. This logic has been used for developing this technique. Here '0' and '1' represent one white and one black pixel respectively. In the stacked shares two black pixels will be visible as two black pixels and others should be visible as one black and one white pixel.

The relation between the pixel in the shares and the stacked shares can be represented by the logical 'OR' operation. In this paper stacked pixels are given the name as ORed pixels and if Hamming Weight [10] of the ORed pixel is 2, then the corresponding input pixels will be both black and 1 otherwise. So, the relations between the pixels in the shares and the stacked shares can be represented as follows:

H (S_1 OR S_2) = 2, if both the input pixels are black.
       = 1, otherwise.

Here S_1 and S_2 represent the pixels in each of the share respectively, (S_1 OR S_2) represents the ORed pixel and H (S_1 OR S_2) represents the Hamming Weight of the ORed pixel.

4   Illustrative Example

The image given in Fig. 5 is used for simulation of the proposed VCTGLI and corresponding generated shares are shown in the Fig. 6 and 7. If we stack the shares of the images of Fig. 6 and 7 the decoded image will be generated as given in Fig. 8.

Fig. 5. Input Image

The Fig. 9 and 10 represent the two shares respectively.

Fig. 6. Share 1 of input image (Fig. 8)   **Fig. 7.** Share 2 of input image (Fig. 8)

Fig. 8. Decoded image generated in stacked shares

5 Performance Analysis

There are many algorithms in the field of visual cryptography. All of them have their own merits and demerits, which conforms the analysis of the performance of a newly developed algorithm compared to other existing algorithms.

Here the proposed algorithm has been compared with three existing algorithms viz. Naor and Shamir [1], Wen Yue and Chiang [2], Jena and Jena [3].

Consider the algorithm of Naor and Shamir [1], where four output pixels are generated in each share from a single pixel of the input image as a result the dimension of the each share becomes four times of the input image. In case of Yue and Chiang [2] two output pixels are generated in each share for a single pixel of the input image hence the dimension of the shares are doubled the size of input image. Again in case of the algorithm of Jena and Jena [3] variable size shares may be generated where the dimension of the shares is at least doubled or almost four times of the input image. But for the proposed VCTGLI technique two output pixels are generated for each share for two input pixels, which means that the dimension of shares remain same as input image. Hence there is no storage overhead in the proposed technique.

Table 1. Comparison of space requirement in the case of (2, 2) Visual Cryptography

Algorithms	No. of input pixels	No. of output pixels
Naor and Shamir [1]	1	4
Yue and Chiang [2]	1	2
Jena and Jena [3]	1	2 or 4
VCTGLI (Proposed)	2	2

The graphical representation of the overheads as given in Table 1 are shown in Fig. 9 in worst case and that of Fig. 13 for the best case.

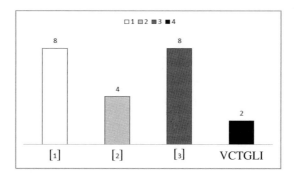

Fig. 9. Graphical presentation of number of pixel generated in each share in worst case out of two pixels for various techniques

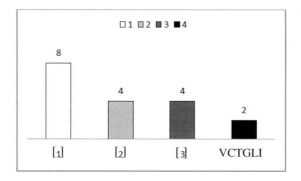

Fig. 10. Graphical representation of no. of pixel generated in each share in best case out of two pixels for various techniques.

It is clear that algorithm of Jena and Jena [3] and Naor and Shamir [1] produces eight pixels in each share out of two pixel from the input image in worst case (Fig. 11). In case of Yue and Chiang [2] four pixels are generated in each share for two input pixel. Again in best situation the the algorithm of Naor and Shamir [1] and Yue and Chiang [2] generates shame overheads that of worst case, where as algorithm of Jena and Jena [3] produces share images which is two times of the original images.

Table 2 outlines a comparetive accounts of aspect ratio and image dimensions where it conforms that except proposed VCTGLI and Naor and Shamir [1] algorithm aspect ratios are changing in all other cases but regarding the dimension of images except the proposed technique in each cases dimensions are increasing in shares/outputs. Whereas proposed VCTGLI dimension remains constant.

From the Table 2 it is clear that the generated shares using the proposed technique is capable of reconstructing more perfect image (in dimension and aspect ratio) compared to the other algorithms.

Table 2. Comparison of image dimension and aspect ratio (in (2,2) visual cryptography) after stacking the shares

Serial No.	Algorithms	Aspect Ratio	Image Dimension
1	Visual Cryptography by Moni Naor and Adi Shamir [1]	Constant	Increasing
2	A Neural Network Approach for Visual Cryptography by Tai- Wen Yue and Suchen Chiang [2]	Increasing	Increasing
3	A Novel Visual Cryptography Scheme by Debasish Jena, Sanjay Kumar Jena [3]	Constant/Increasing	Increasing
4	VCTGLI (The proposed technique)	Constant	Constant

6   Conclusion

In this paper a novel visul (2, 2) visual cryptogtaphic technique has been proposed which is easy to implement and generates less space overheads than existing techniques. One most important feature in the proposed algorithm is the aspect ratio and dimension of the input image remains constant. So, after revealing the image by stacking the shares the recepient can get the image with its original aspect ratio and dimension, where the fidelits of the stacked image may be improved. The techmique may be applied to generate (n, n) and (k, n) visual cryptography.

Acknowledgments. The authors are thankful to the anonymous referees and the Organizing Chairperson (NeCom-2010) for their helpful suggestions and comments which have led to improve the quality of presentation of the paper.

References

1. Naor, M., Shamir, A.: Visual Cryptography. In: De Santis, A. (ed.) EUROCRYPT 1994. LNCS, vol. 950, pp. 1–12. Springer, Heidelberg (1995)
2. Yue, T.W., Chiang, S.: A Neural Network Approach for Visual Cryptography. In: IEEE-INNS-ENNS International Joint Conference on Neural Networks, vol. 5, pp. 494–499 (2000)
3. Jena, D., Jena, S.K.: A Novel Visual Cryptography Scheme. In: The 2009 International Conference on Advanced Computer Control, pp. 207–211 (2009)
4. Hegde, C., Manu, S., Shenoy, P.D., Venugopal, K.R., Patnaik, L.M.: Secure Authentication using Image Processing and Visual Cryptography for Banking Applications. In: 16th International Conference on Advanced Computing and Communication (ADCOM 2008), MIT Campus, Anna University, Chennai, India, pp. 433–439 (2008)

5. Heidarinejad, M., Yazdi, A.A., Plataniotis, K.N.: Algebraic Visual Cryptography Scheme for Color Images. In: IEEE International Conference on Acoustics, Speech and Signal Processing, pp. 1761–1764 (2008)
6. Arce, Z.Z., Di Crescenzo, G.R., Halftone, G.: Visual Cryptography. IEEE Transactions on Image Processing 15(8), 2441–2453 (2006)
7. Houmansadr, A., Ghaemmaghami, S.: A Novel Video Watermarking Method Using Visual Cryptography. In: IEEE International Conference on Engineering of Intelligent Systems, Islamabad, Pakistan, pp. 1–5 (2006)
8. Geum-Dal, P., Eun-Jun, Y., Kee-Young, Y.: A New Copyright Protection Scheme with Visual Cryptography. In: Second International Conference on Future Generation Communication and Networking Symposia, pp. 60–63 (2008)
9. Wei-Qi, Y., Duo, J., Kankanhalli, M.S.: Visual Cryptography for Print and Scan Applications. In: International Symposium on Circuits and Systems, pp. 572–575 (2004)
10. Gravano, S.: Introduction to Error Control Codes. Oxford University Press, USA (2001)

A Frequency Spectral Feature Modeling for Hidden Markov Model Based Automated Speech Recognition

Ibrahim Patel[1] and Y. Srinivas Rao[2]

[1] Assoc. Prof., Department of BME, Padmasri.Dr.B.V.Raju Institute of Technology,
Narsapur Medak (Dist), A.P.
[2] Assoc. Prof., Department of Instrument Technology, Andhra University, Vizag, A.P.
Ptlibrahim@gmail.com, srinniwasarau@gmail.com

Abstract. This paper presents an approach to the recognition of speech signal using frequency spectral information with Mel frequency for the improvement of speech feature representation in a HMM based recognition approach. A frequency spectral information is incorporated to the conventional Mel spectrum base speech recognition approach. The Mel frequency approach exploits the frequency observation for speech signal in a given resolution which results in resolution feature overlapping resulting in recognition limit. Resolution decomposition with separating frequency is mapping approach for a HMM based speech recognition system. The Simulation results show a improvement in the quality metrics of speech recognition with respect to computational time, learning accuracy for a speech recognition system.

Keywords: speech-recognition, Mel-frequencies, DCT, frequency decomposition, Mapping Approach, HMM.

1 Introduction

Speech recognition is a process used to recognize speech uttered by a speaker and has been in the field of research for more than five decades since 1950s [1]. Voice communication is the most effective mode of communication used by humans. Speech recognition is an important and emerging technology with great potential. The significance of speech recognition lies in its simplicity. This simplicity together with the ease of operating a device using speech has lots of advantages. It can be used in many applications like, security devices, household appliances, cellular phones, ATM machines and computers.

With the advancement of automated system the complexity for integration & recognition problem is increasing. The problem is found more complex when processing on randomly varying analog signals such as speech signals. Although various methods are proposed for efficient extraction of speech parameter for recognition, the MFCC method with advanced recognition method such as HMM is more dominant used. This system found to be more accurate under low varying environment but fails to recognition speech under highly varying environment. This needs to the development of a efficient recognition system which can provide is efficient varying system.

N. Meghanathan et al. (Eds.): NeCoM, WiMoN, and WeST 2010, CCIS 90, pp. 134–143, 2010.

Research and development on speaker recognition method and technique has been undertaken for well over four decade and it continues to be an active area. Approaches have spanned from human auditory [2] and spectrogram comparisons [2], to simple template matching, to dynamic time-warping approaches, to more modern statistical pattern recognition [3], such as neural networks and Hidden Markov Model (HMM's) [4].

It is observed that, to extract and recognize different information from a speech signal at variable environment, many algorithms for efficient speech recognition is proposed in past. Masakiyo Fujimoto and Yasuo Ariki in their paper "Robust Speech Recognition in Additive and channel noise environments using GMM and EM Algorithm" [5] evaluate the speech recognition in real driving car environments by using a GMM based speech estimation method [6] and an EM algorithm based channel noise estimation method.

A Gaussian mixture model (GMM) based speech estimation method proposed in J.C.Segura et al [6] estimates the expectation of the mismatch factor between clean speech and noisy speech at each frame by using GMM of clean speech and mean vector of noise. This approach shows a significant improvement in recognition accuracy. However, the Segura's method considered only the additive noise environments and it did not consider about the channel noise problem such as an acoustic transfer function, a microphone characteristic etc.

A Parallel model combination (PMC) method [7] has been proposed by M.J.F Gales, and S.J.Young adapts the speech recognition system to any kinds of noises. However, PMC has a problem, of taking huge quantity of computation to recognize the speech signal. Another method for speech recognition called "spectral subtraction" (SS) is also proposed as a conventional noise reduction method [3]. However, using spectral subtraction method degrades the recognition rate due to spectral distortion caused by over or under subtraction. Additionally, spectral subtraction method does not consider the time varying property of noise spectra, because it estimates the noise spectra as mean spectra within the time section assumed to be noise.

Hidden Markov Model (HMM) [4] is a natural and highly robust statistical methodology for automatic speech recognition. It was tested and proved considerably in a wide range of applications. The model parameters of the HMM are essence in describing the behavior of the utterance of the speech segments. Many successful heuristic algorithms are developed to optimize the model parameters in order to best describe the trained observation sequences. The objective of this paper is to develop an efficient speech recognition algorithm with the existing system following HMM algorithm. The paper integrates the frequency isolation concept celled as sub band decomposition to the existing MFCC approach for extraction of speech feature. The additional feature concept of provides the information of varying speech coefficient at multiple band level this feature could enhancement the recognition approach then the existing one.

2   Hidden Markov Modeling

A Hidden Markov Model is a statistical model for an ordered sequence of variables, which can be well characterized as a parametric random process. It is assumed that the speech signal can be well characterized as a parametric random process and the parameters of the stochastic process can be determined in a precise, well-defined manner. Therefore, signal characteristics of a word will change to another basic speech unit as time increase, and it indicates a transition to another state with certain transition probability as defined by HMM. This observed sequence of observation vectors O can be denoted by

$$O = (o\,(1),\,o(2),......o(T))$$

Where each observation of ('t') is an m-dimensional vector, extracted at time 't' with

$$O(t)=[0_1(t),0_2(t),.....,o_m(t)]^T$$

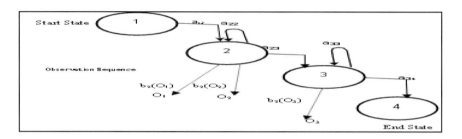

Fig. 1. A typical left-right HMM (a_{ij} is the station transition probability from state i to state j)

Figure.9 A typical left-right HMM (a_{ij} is the station transition probability from state i to state j; O_t is the observation vector at time t and $bi(O_t)$ is the probability that O_t is generated by state i).

The HMMs is used to solve three main problems. These problems are described as following:

1: Given the model $\lambda = \{A,B, \prod\}$ and the observation sequence, how to efficiently compute $P(O|\lambda)$, the probability of occurrence of the observation sequence in the given model.

Problem 2: Given the model $\lambda=\{A,B, \prod\}$ and the observation sequence, how to choose a optimal corresponding state sequence.

Problem 3: How to adjust the model parameters $\lambda= \{A,B,\prod\}$ so that $P(O|\lambda)$ is maximized.

Problem 1 and Problem 2 are analysis problems while problem 3 is a synthesis or model-training problem. To solve these three problems, some basic assumptions are being made in HMM.

a. The output independence assumption: The observation vectors are conditionally independent of the previously observed vectors.

b. The stationary assumption: It is assumed that state transition probabilities are independent of the actual time at which the transition takes place. It can be formulated mathematically as,

$$P[q_{t1+1}=j\,|\,q_{t1} = i] = P[q_{t2+1}=j\,|\,q_{t2} = i] \quad \text{for any } t_1 \text{ and } t_2.$$

The determination of the optimal set ω of parameters in correspondence to a given utterance can be undertaken by relying on a simple property of the quantities to be maximized in both the two cases (MLE, MAP). Both the quantity to be maximized and the parameters we are looking for are probabilities, i.e. nonnegative quantities is smaller than 1. Their variations during the optimization process from the starting values to the final optimized ones are very small. As a consequence, all these variations can be considered as differentials. If Q is the quantity to be maximized and its starting and final value, after maximization, are respectively Q_{start} and Q_{opt}, we can write

$$Q_{opt} - Q_{start} = Dq$$

Similarly, the variations of the parameters of the model, from the starting values to the final optimized ones, can be considered as differentials: d, π_i, da_{ij}, $db_i(Y_t)$, i = 1,...,N, J=1,...N, t =1,..., T.

q being a parameter, q' denoting its optimal value and q_{start} the initial value from which we start the maximization. Consequently, the determination of the optimal values of e can be simply undertaken by maximizing above equation with respect to ω' and therefore neglecting in above equation the initial values ω_{start}. The coefficients multiplying logarithms of the parameters are determined on the basis of Y_T and ω_{start}. The maximization procedure initially requires modeling densities $b_i(y)$. Among the several possible solutions, the most used is based on mixtures of Gaussian functions and the $b_i(y)$ is themselves constrained to,

$$\int b_i(Y) \, dy = 1 \; ; \; \int b_{ik}(Y) \, dy = 1$$

The above model is reasonable on the basis of the regularization theory applied to the approximation of unknown mappings, as is the case in the present situation. The consequence of this model on function a (ω, ω') is that of modifying the term where the output probabilities appear.

3 Mel Spectrum Approach

Thus for each tone with an actual frequency, f, measured in Hz, a subjective pitch is measured on a scale called the 'mel' scale. The mel-frequency scale is linear frequency spacing below 1000 Hz and a logarithmic spacing above 1000 Hz. As a reference point, the pitch of a 1 kHz tone, 40 dB above the perceptual hearing threshold, is defined as 1000 mels. Therefore we can use the following approximate formula to compute the mels for a given frequency 'f' in Hz;

$$mel(f) = 2595 * \log_{10}(1 + f / 700)$$

One approach to simulating the subjective spectrum is to use a filter bank, spaced uniformly on the mel scale where the filter bank has a triangular band pass frequency response, and the spacing as well as the bandwidth is determined by a constant mel frequency interval. The modified spectrum of $S(\omega)$ thus consists of the output power of these filters when $S(\omega)$ is the input. The number of Mel spectrum coefficients, K, is typically chosen as 20.

Note that this filter bank is applied in the frequency domain; therefore it simply amounts to taking those triangle-shape windows in the Figure 1 on the spectrum. A useful way of thinking about this Mel-wrapping filter bank is to view each filter as an histogram bin (where bins have overlap) in the frequency domain.

The log Mel spectrum is converted back to time. The result is called the Mel frequency cepstrum coefficients (MFCC). The cepstral representation of the speech spectrum provides a good representation of the local spectral properties of the signal for the given frame analysis. Because the Mel spectrum coefficients (and so their logarithm) are real numbers, we can convert them to the $\tilde{S}_k, k=1,2,...,K$ time domain using the Discrete Cosine Transform (DCT). Therefore if we denote those Mel power spectrum coefficients that are the result of the last step are we can calculate the MFCC's, $\tilde{c}_n$, as the first component,

$$\tilde{c}_n = \sum_{k=1}^{K} (\log \tilde{S}_k) \cos\left[n\left(k - \frac{1}{2}\right)\frac{\pi}{K} \right], n = 1,2,3...K$$

$\tilde{c}_0$, from the DCT since it represents the mean value of the input signal, which carried little speaker specific information. As shown in the figure 3.

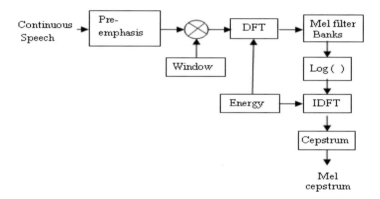

Fig. 2. Speech process models

By applying the procedure described above, for each speech frame of around 30msec with overlap, a set of mel-frequency cepstrum coefficients is computed. These are result of a cosine transform of the logarithm of the short-term power spectrum expressed on a mel-frequency scale. This set of coefficients is called an acoustic vector. Therefore each input utterance is transformed into a sequence of acoustic vectors. As these vectors are evaluated using a distinct filter spectrum the feature information obtained is limited to certain frequency resolution information only and needs to be improved. In the following section a frequency decomposition method incorporated with existing architecture is suggested for HMM training and recognition. These mel spectrum is used a recognition information in conventional speech recognition system. The spectrum doesn't exploit the variations in fundamental resolution & hence is lower in accuracy to improve the accuracy of operation a spectral decomposition approach is respected.

4   Spectral Decomposition Approach

Filter bank can be regarded as wavelet transform in multi resolution band. Wavelet transform of a signal is passing the signal through this filter bank. The outputs of the different filter stages are the wavelet and scaling function transform coefficients. Analyzing a signal by passing it through a filter bank is not a new idea and has been around for many years under the name sub band coding. It is used for instance in computer vision applications.

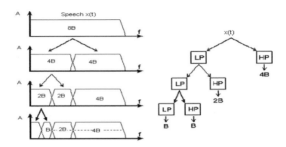

Fig. 3. Splitting the signal spectrum with an iterated filter bank

The filter bank needed in sub band coding can be built in several ways. One way is to build many band pass filters to split the spectrum into frequency bands. The advantage is that the width of every band can be chosen freely, in such a way that the spectrum of the signal to analyze is covered in the places of interest The disadvantage is that it is necessary to design every filter separately and this can be a time consuming process. Another way is to split the signal spectrum in two equal parts, a low pass and a high-pass part. The high-pass part contains the smallest details importance that is to be considered here. The low-pass part still contains some details and therefore it can be split again. And again, until desired number of bands are created. In this way an iterated filter bank is created.

Usually the number of bands is limited by for instance the amount of data or computation power available. The process of splitting the spectrum is graphically displayed in figure 4. The spectral decomposition obtained coefficient could be observed as,

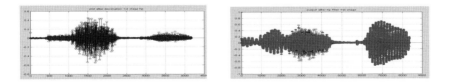

Fig. 4. Output after 1st stage decomposition for a given speech signal

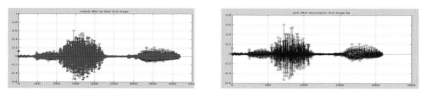

Fig. 5. Plot after 2nd stage decomposition

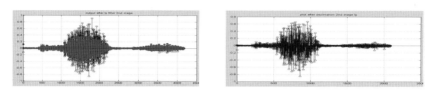

Fig. 6. Output after 3rd Stage decomposition

The advantage of this scheme is that it is necessary to design only two filters; the disadvantage is that the signal spectrum coverage is fixed.

Looking at figure 3 it is observed that it is left with lower spectrum, after the repeated spectrum splitting is a series of band-pass bands with doubling bandwidth and one low-pass band. The first split gave a high-pass band and a low-pass band; in reality the high-pass band is a band-pass band due to the limited bandwidth of the signal. In other words, the same sub band analysis can be performed by feeding the signal into a bank of band-pass filters of which each filter has a band width twice as wide as its left neighbor and a low-pass filter. The wavelets give us the band-pass bands with doubling bandwidth and the scaling function provides with the low-pass band. From this it can be concluded that a wavelet transform is the same thing as a sub band coding scheme using a constant-Q filter bank. It can be summarized, as in implementation of the wavelet transform as an iterated filter bank, it is not necessary

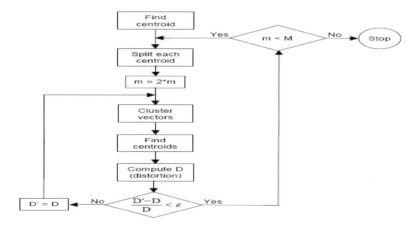

Fig. 7. Flow diagram of the LBG algorithm

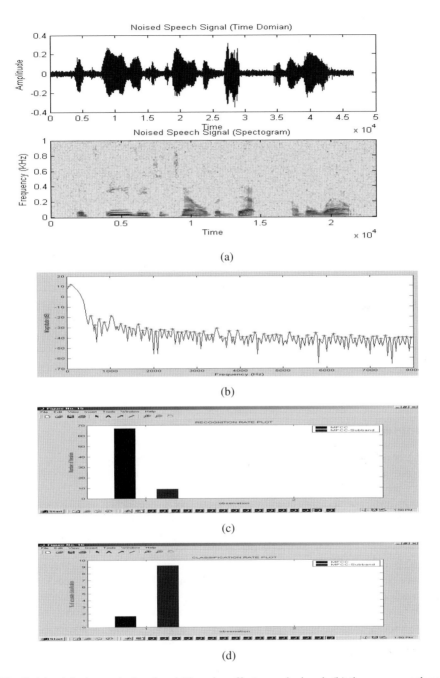

Fig. 8. (a) original speech signal and it's noise effect speech signal, (b) the energy peak points picked for training, (c) the recognition computation time for the MFCC based and the modified MFCC system, (d) the observed correct classified symbols for the two method, (e) the estimation error for the two methods wrt. Iteration, (f) the likelihood variation wrt iteration for the two methods.

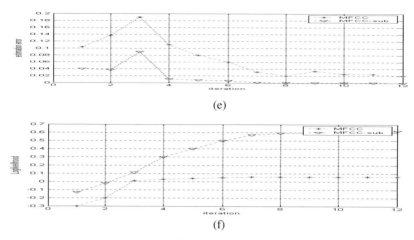

Fig. 8. (*continued*)

to specify the wavelets explicitly The actual lengths of the detail and approximation coefficient vectors are slightly more than half the length of the original signal. This has to do with the filtering process, which is implemented by convolving the signal with a filter. The spectral decomposition reveals the accuracy of individual resolution which was not explored in mel spectrum. This approach is developed with a mapping concept for speech recognition as outlined between evaluation of the suggested system for a simulation of the purposed system is carried out on mat lab tool & the resolution obtained are as outlined below.

5 Mapping Approach

After the enrolment session, the acoustic vectors extracted from input speech of a speaker provide a set of training vectors. A set of 'L' training vectors from the frequency information is derived using well-known LBG algorithm [4]. The algorithm is formally implemented by the following recursive procedure. The LBG algorithm designs an M-vector codebook in stages. It starts first by designing a 1-vector codebook, then uses a splitting technique on the codewords to initialize the search for a 2-vector codebook, and continues the splitting process until the desired M-vector codebook is obtained. Figure 7 shows, in a flow diagram, the detailed steps of the LBG algorithm. "Cluster vectors" is the nearest-neighbor search procedure, which assigns each training vector to a cluster associated with the closest codeword. "Find centroids" is the centroid update procedure. "Compute D (distortion)" sums the distances of all training vectors in the nearest-neighbor search so as to determine whether the procedure has converged. A general operational flow diagram of the suggested LBG mapping approach is shown in fig.7.

6 Simulation Observation

For the training of HMM network for the recognition of speech a vocabulary consist of collection words are maintained. The vocabulary consists of words given as,

"DISCRETE", "FOURIER", "TRANSFORM", "WISY", "EASY", "TELL", "FELL", "THE", "DEPTH", "WELL", "CELL", "FIVE", each word in the vocabulary is stored in correspondence to a feature define as a knowledge to each speech word during training of HMM network. The features are extracted on only voice sample for the corresponding word.

The test speech utterance: used for testing given as "its easy to tell the depth of a well", at 16KHz sampling.

7 Conclusion

A speech recognition system for robust to noise effect is developed. The MFCC conventional approach & extracting the feature of speech signal at lower frequency & is modified in this paper. An efficient speech recognition system with the integration of MFCC feature with frequency sub band decomposition using subband coding is proposed. The two features passed to the HMM network result in better recognition compared to existing MFCC method. From the observation made for the implemented system it is observed to have better efficiency for accurate classification & recognition compared to the existing system.

References

1. Varga, A.P., Moore, R.K.: Hidden Markov Model decomposition of speech and noise. In: Proc. IEEE Intl. Conf. on Acoustics, Speech and Signal Processing, pp. 845–848 (1990)
2. Allen, J.B.: How do humans process and recognize speech. IEEE Trans. on Speech and Audio Processing 2(4), 567–577 (1994)
3. Kim, W., Kang, S., Ko, H.: Spectral subtraction based on phonetic dependency and masking effects. IEEE Proc.- Vision, Image and Signal Processing 147(5), 423–427 (2000)
4. Elliott, R.J., Aggoun, L., Allen, J.B.: Moore Hidden Markov Models: Estimation and Control. Springer, Heidelberg (1995)
5. Fujimoto, M., Riki, Y.A.: Robust speech recognition in additive and channel noise environments using GMM and EM algorithm. In: Proceedings of IEEE International Conference Acoustics, Speech, and Signal Processing ICASSP 2004, May 17-21, vol. 1 (2004)
6. Segura, J.C., de la Torre, A., Benitez, M.C., Peinado, A.M.: Model Based Compensation of the Additive Noise for Continuous Speech Recognition. In: Experiments Using AURORA II Database and Tasks, EuroSpeech 2001, vol. I, pp. I–941–944 (2001)
7. Gales, M.J.F., Young, S.J.: Robust Continuous Speech Recognition Using Parallel Model Combination. IEEE Trans. Speech and Audio Processing 4(5), 352–359 (1996)
8. Renals, S., Morgan, N., Bourlard, H., Cohen, M., Franco, H.: Connectionist Probability Estimators in HMM Speech Recognition. IEEE Trans. on Speech and Audio Processing 2(1), 161–174 (1994)
9. Neto, J., Martins, C., Almeida, L.: Speaker-Adaptation in a Hybrid HMM-MLP Recognizer. In: Proceedings ICASSP 1996, Atlanta, vol. 6, pp. 3383–3386 (1996)
10. Furui, S.: Digital speech processing, synthesis and recognition, 2nd edn. (2001)

A Novel Trust Management Scheme Using Fuzzy Logic for a Pervasive Environment

V. Rhymend Uthariaraj, J. Valarmathi, G. Arjun Kumar,
Praveen Subramanian, and R. Karthick

Ramanujan Computing Center, Anna University, Chennai, India
valar.sakthi@gmail.com

Abstract. One of the most critical issues in distributed system is security. The ideal solution to this concern is to have an environment that is fully trusted by all its entities. Our proposed approach is truly unique and fully comprehensive incorporating fuzzy logic for subjective concepts and integrating various trust related characteristics. The trust values(TV) calculated between the entities are stored in a global data store. This TV can be used as a basis for future transactions of the entity concerned. Since the global data store contains the trust value of all the users of the environment, these trust values are more accurate than that which has been calculated through recommendations. This also obviates the necessity for entities to know each other beforehand, which is a prerequisite in the case of recommendations. Also the security issues related with the global trust scheme is analyzed and an efficient solution to it using fuzzy logic has been proposed.

Keywords: Trust, Global Trust Model, Pervasive Environment, Fuzzy Logic.

1 Introduction

In pervasive environments the nodes are highly mobile. So we can not implement formal cryptographic methods of security. And also formal methods of security implementation are highly processor intensive which is not a desirable feature in pervasive devices which are characterized by their low computing power. So trustworthy computation of security could be used as it is less processor intensive and provides better solutions overcoming the problems in the formal method.

The trust value of an environment gives the quantitative measure of how much that environment is dependable. This trust can be calculated based on the interactions with the environment directly and also from the result of the interaction with other users. This information from other users have been so far calculated based on recommendations from these users directly. But this would result in the loss of some valuable information. So in our proposed scheme we are moving towards a global data store which contains the trust information obtained from cumulative user interactions about the various environments and also the users of this environments.

And also there is a constraint that we should have prior knowledge about atleast a few nodes in the new environment. This has a very low probability when we are in a new environment. Some of the Security issues which are associated with the global

N. Meghanathan et al. (Eds.): NeCoM, WiMoN, and WeST 2010, CCIS 90, pp. 144–152, 2010.
© Springer-Verlag Berlin Heidelberg 2010

trust model should be found out and an efficient method to overcome these problems should be given.

The paper is organized as follows. Section 2 consists of related works in the areas of trust and pervasive computing, section 3 explains about the proposed work, section 4 shows our model implementation in a hospital scenario, section 5 discusses about the performance evaluation as compared with the deterministic model and finally section 6 consists about the conclusion and future works.

2   Related Works

The development of pervasive computing from isolated "smart spaces" to generic ubiquitous systems has heralded a new era in the development and sophistication of humans. We follow the definition of trust as in [2], that "Trust is the subjective probability by which an individual, A, expects that another individual, B, to perform a given action the way it wants on which its welfare depends". The importance of trust in pervasive computing is underscored by the low processor intensity and the unpredictability of the new devices that enter a pervasive environment. . This has led to trust being used as a basis for providing security and as as mentioned in [1], "a trustable entity is believed to to secure". In [3], trust was quantified to be between -1 to +1, which we have retained in our paper. The proposed negotiation scheme that was suggested in [6] is found to be wanting in situations where in the users of a systems cannot identify new entrants, in which case , a global trust storage and retrieval mechanism is found to be more useful. Also in [6], a global trust model in a peer to peer network was demonstrated that has the potential to be extended to a pervasive environment.

Trust is not a concept unique to pervasive computing; it has been widely used in many other disciplines. Work [4] builds a trust model to improve mobile ad hoc networks' collaborations based on a Bayesian network.

In paper [15] use of fuzzy logic in a wireless sensor network has been described. And also in paper [16] the various use of fuzzy logic in trust calculation of a pervasive environment has been described. In that paper use fuzzy logic in the decision making for access control has also been discussed.

3   Proposed Work

In the traditional trust value computation, the trust value is computed by using recommendation from neighbor nodes. In our method we are trying to store the calculated trust value in a global data store which can then be the basis for future transactions.

3.1 Global Data Store

The trust values will be stored in a global data store which contains information about all the environments and users, and they should be made available anywhere, anytime on request. This could be achieved by accessing these data through the various wireless communications available everywhere.

The data value of each tuple contains <T,N,E,t> where, T → Average trust value of the environment will be between -1 to +1, where -1 implies complete mistrust, 0 implies no trust and +1 implies complete trust, N → Number of previous users of the environment, E → Type of the environment, t → Time of update of trust value.

3.2 Local Data Store

The local data store is specific to each environment or user and it is used to store information about the recent users of that environment or entity. This data value can be used as a basis because an entity can be assumed to retain its behavior in the same environment. This data is stored in the local machine for the fast retrieval of trust value. It gives better result than global data store because each user-environment relationship will be distinct.

Each tuple in the local data store is represented as <T,E,t> where, T → Trust value of the environment, E → Type of environment, t → Time of update of data.

3.3 Credential Matching

When a new device is detected in the environment, the environment must try to establish communication with the device. For this the environment first transfers some of its credentials to the device. If the device finds the credential satisfying its requirements, then the device would in turn send its own credentials to the environment. The environment also checks them with its requirements. Then both the device and the environment uses the credentials obtained to look up the trust values of each other in the data store.

3.4 Trust Negotiation

The trust value of the environment or the user must be calculated for establishing connection with them. This trust value could be obtained from the local data store if it is available and from the global data store. The following algorithm would gives the details about calculation of the initial trust for a new user.

```
INPUT       :   New user enters the environment

OUTPUT      :   NONE

ALGORITHM  :

   Step 1 :  Get the trust value of the user , T₀(U) and
             time t₀ from database

   Step 2 :  If information about the user is already
             available  with the environment get it as
             T_E(U) and the time of interaction t_E

   Step 3 :  Get current time, t

   Step 4 :  Set weighing factor W₀ and W_H such that

             Weighing factor => W₀+W_E =1, where W_E < W₀ ,if
             previous info about user is available
```

```
                  Weighing factor => W₀ =1, if previous
                  information about the user is not available

                              -(t-tO)                    -(t-tE)
Step 5 :  T (U)  =  W₀*T₀(U)*e           + W *T (U)*e
         H                                 E  E

Step 6 :  Return T (U)
                  H

Step 7 :  End
```

Once the trust value is computed it would be checked with the threshold value, which could be specified by the environment. If the trust value is greater than the threshold value then the connection is established.

3.5 Trust Computation

Trust computation can be done as in [1]. The initial trust value calculated should be updated based on the various actions by the user. This trust update should be done at specific intervals of time.

Let us consider two devices A and B, where the trust value of B computed by A is $T_A(B)$. This value can be calculated depending upon the outcomes(degree of success) of a set of dedicated set of actions that underline the transaction. Some of the possible policies that define the actions are response time, infrastructure offered by the environment, cost etc.

Let us consider $C_A(B)$ as the adjustment factor of the trust computation. The new value of trust is computed as follows

$$T_A(B) = \begin{cases} 1 & \text{if } T'_A(B) + C_A(B) \geq 1 \\ T'_A(B) + C_A(B) & \\ -1 & \text{if } T'_A(B) + C_A(B) \leq -1 \end{cases}$$

Where T'A(B) is the old trust value.

The adjustment value is calculated based on the result of the various outcomes of the interactions between the entities. The value of CA(B) is between [-1,1]. We calculate the adjustment factor as the sum of the positive effect and the negative effect of the various actions of B towards A.

$C_A(B)$ is the summation of the policy vector μ which depends upon the entity. It is given by

$$\mu=[t1_A(B) \quad t2_A(B) \quad t3_A(B) \quad \ldots \quad tn_A(B)]$$

Each entry in the vector represents the outcome of a policy based trust calculation after an interaction. $t_A(B)$ is calculated as follows:

$$t_A(B)=P_A(B)+N_A(B)$$

where $P_A(B) \rightarrow$ Positive result of the interaction

$N_A(B) \rightarrow$ Negative result of the interaction

3.6 Updating Trust Values

The trust value computed by the user must be updated in the global and local data store. The algorithm for updating the data store is provided below:

```
INPUT:Trust value given by user about environment, T_U(E)
        Trust value of the user from the environment, T_E(U)
OUTPUT    :      NONE
ALGORITHM :
 Step 1: Get the old trust value of the environment
         T_o(E)
 Step 2 : Get the average trust value of the users of
          the environment, T_avg(U)
 Step 3 : Get number of previous interactions in the
          environment, N
 Step 4 : If T_E(U) = -1 goto step 9
 Step 5 : T_n(E)=[(N*T_o(E))+(T_U(E)*(T_E(U)+1)/T_avg(U)]/(N+1)
 Step 6 : T_newavg(U)= [T_avg(U) + (T_E(U) + 1)]/(N+1)
 Step 7 : N=N+1
 Step 8: Get current time, t
 Step 8 : Update values T_n(E),N,(env),t
 Step 9 : End
```

The larger the trust value of the computing entity and the larger trust placed upon it by the entity for which trust is calculated, the greater the influence on the global data store. An untrusted entity cannot affect the trust value of another significantly in the data store.

4 Security Issues

4.1 Malicious Nodes

Malicious nodes are the ones which spreads wrong information about an entity and ultimately affects the overall trust value of the entity. So the damage caused by the malicious nodes needs to be minimized. This is already taken care of by our formula (2) and (3).

Before two entities begin to interact both of them will give permission to the DBA to allow the entities that could modify their trust values. Without the permission of the entity the DBA will not allow any other entity to modify the trust value of that entity.

4.2 Selfish Nodes

During the calculation of a trusted path few nodes might act selfish by going to the sleep state. These nodes will affect the trusted path calculation, as we cannot be sure the path will be stable and hence the whole concept of trusted path will get affected. So to remove these nodes the trust value of these nodes needs to be changed if it acts selfish. The trust values of these nodes needs to be affected dynamically depending on the power level of the node.

Table 1. Selfish Node Rule Base. Power Level.

Trust value(TV)	LOW	MEDIUM	HIGH
TV>0	Affect slightly	Affect highly	Affect highly
TV=0	Don't affect	Affect slightly	Affect highly
TV<0	Don't affect	Don't affect	Affect highly

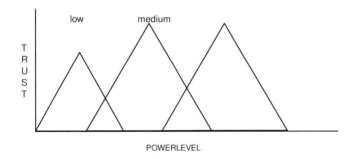

Fig. 1. Fuzzy Rule Base to determining the amount of trust to reduce based on the power level and the trust value of the node

Center of Gravity(COG) method could be used to get a crisp solution and depending on that value the DBA could decrease the trust value of the selfish node.

4.3 Group of Nodes

As seen with malicious nodes, a single node cannot affect the trust value drastically but if two or more nodes combine and work together to increase each others trust value illegally then it will result in erroneous values. So these kind of situations should be taken care of.

Table 2. Group of nodes where T_A is trustworthy. Deviation from the global trust value.

T_B	Acceptable	High	Drastic
Positive	$T_A(B)$	$T_A(B)$	$T_A(B)$
Negative	$T_A(B)$	$2*T_A(B)/3$	$T_A(B)/3$

Table 3. Group of nodes where T_A is trustworthy. Deviation from the global trust value.

T_B	Acceptable	High	Drastic
Positive	$T_A(B)$	$2*T_A(B)/3$	$T_A(B)/3$
Negative	$2*T_A(B)/3$	$T_A(B)/3$	0

To remove this security vulnerability we could enforce some constrains depending upon the trust values updated by the entities interacting and the frequency of trust update.

4.4 Hacking at the Network and the Database Layer

Hacking or interfering with the trust values at the transmitting or at the database should be dealt separately. It depends upon the security policies adopted in the network layer and in the database.

5 Performance Evaluation

A comparison between the Probabilistic Trust Model(PTM) and the proposed Global Trust Model(GTM) is done. The various metrics used are:

Number of nodes denotes the number of active nodes currently in contention in the environment such that all possible interactions take place only between a subset of these nodes.

Simulation time is a collection of different times such as the time taken to quantify trust according to the trust strategies and policies of the entities. It also includes the response times of the entities involving themselves in trust computation.

Throughput is defined as the number of packets sent successfully in unit time by an entity through to another entity via the communication medium. The trust value of an maliciousness of the entity therefore depends both on the maliciousness of the medium as well as the success rate of transmission of the network architecture.

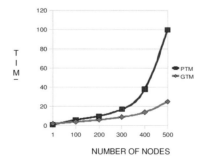

Fig. 2. Simulation time for GTM and PTM models

Number of interactions is determines by the network traffic density as well as the number of nodes in the system. The higher the number of nodes, the higher the potential number of interactions. Also, the use of recommendations may increase the number of interactions in case of higher number of nodes in PTM.

In PTM the number of transactions made to calculate the trust value depends upon the number of neighboring nodes to which the request is made. So as the number of recommendation increases to get an accurate value the network traffic also increases which results in a poor performance of the environment. In GTM the number of transactions is always a constant and is always affected by the network load.

In a PTM, we have the weighing mechanism that gives weight-age to the most recent behavior of the node. Hence, if the node is found to be malicious, then the most recent behavior outweighs the rest and communication is suspended. But the time taken to find out if the node is malicious is an overhead when a node enters the environment.

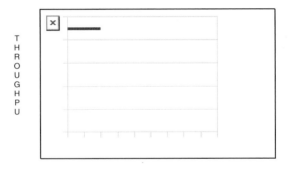

NUMBER OF INTERACTIONS

Fig. 3. Throughput of PTM versus GTM

In a GTM, this overhead is avoided because the trust value from the global data store is merged with the local data store and this value is used to decide on the threshold of trust. As a result, GTM makes a faster adjustment in cases of malicious nodes and so, there is a lower drop in the throughput- faster recovery.

6 Conclusion

In this paper, we discuss the possibility of implementing a trust management solution for a pervasive environment. In such a situation, the importance of trust as a means of security was discussed and the usage of a global and local data store was justified. We have proposed and evaluated a trust management scheme where a global data store is used along with a local data store and the combination of both the data stores in conjunction with the algorithms to compute trust. When entering a new environment where local information is not known, the weight-age is given to global data store. Also the various security issues in the GTM is also handled. This enhanced the accuracy of environment based behavior of the nodes.

References

1. Sun, T., Denko, M.K.: A Distributed Trust Management Scheme in the Pervasive Computing Environment. In: Canadian Conference on Electrical and Computer Engineering CCECE 2007, April 2007, vol. 2226, pp. 1219–1222 (2007)
2. Yuan, W., Guan, D., Lee, S., Lee, Y.: The Role of Trust in Ubiquitous Healthcare. In: 9th International Conference on eHealth Networking, Application and Services, June 2007, pp. 312–315 (2007)
3. Sun, T., Denko, M.K.: Performance Evaluation of Trust Management in Pervasive Computing. In: 22nd International Conference on Advanced Information Networking and Applications AINA 2008, March 2008, vol. 2528, pp. 386–394 (2008)
4. Wang, Y., Vassileva, J.: Bayesian NetworkBased Trust Model. In: Second International Conference on Internet Monitoring and Protection, ICIMP 2007, July 15, p. 26 (2007)
5. Black, J.P., Segmuller, W., Cohen, N., Leiba, B., Misra, A., Ebling, M.R., Stern, E.: Pervasive Computing in Health Care: Smart Spaces and Enterprise Information Systems
6. Yajun, G., Hao, C., Zhongqiang, Y., Huihui, D.: Generalized Trust Negotiation for Pervasive Computing. In: ISECS International Colloquium on Computing, Communication, Control, and Management, CCCM apos 2008, August 2008, vol. 1(34), pp. 684–687 (2008)
7. Denko, M.K., Sun, T.: Probabilistic Trust Management in Pervasive Computing. In: IEEE/IFIP International Conference on Embedded and Ubiquitous Computing, EUC apos 2008, December 2008, vol. 2(1720), pp. 610–615 (2008)
8. Xu, W., Xin, Y., Lu, G.: A Trust Framework for Pervasive Computing Environments. In: International Conference on Wireless Communications, Networking and Mobile Computing, WiCom 2007, September 2007, (2125), pp. 2222–2225 (2007)
9. Ranganathan, K.: Trustworthy Pervasive Computing: The Hard Security Problems. In: Second IEEE Annual Conference on Pervasive Computing and Communications Workshops, March 17, vol. 14
10. Ztoupis, D., Zarifis, K., Stavrakakis, I., Xenakis, C.: Towards a Security Framework for an Established Autonomous Network. In: 3rd International Symposium on Wireless Pervasive Computing, ISWPC 2008, May 2008, (79), pp. 749–754 (2008)
11. Kagal, L., Undercoffer, J., Joshi, A., Finin, T., Perich, F.: A Security Architecture Based on Trust Management for Pervasive Computing
12. Dong, C., Dulay, N.: Privacy Preserving Trust Negotiation for Pervasive Healthcare. In: Pervasive Health Conference and Workshops, November 29-December 1, p. 19 (2006)
13. Hassan, J., Sirisena, H., Landfeldt, B.: TrustBased fast Authentication for Multiowner Wireless Networks (Feburary 2008)
14. Khare, R., Rifkin, A.: Trust management on the world wide web. Computer Networks and ISDN Systems 30, 651–653 (1998)
15. Kim, T.K., Seo, H.S.: A Trust Model using Fuzzy Logic in Wireless Sensor Network
16. Wu, Z., Weaver, A.C.: Application of Fuzzy Logic in Federated Trust Management for Pervasive Computing

Reducing the Size of the Test Suite by Genetic Algorithm and Concept Analysis

S. Selvakumar[1], M.R.C. Dinesh[1], C. Dhineshkumar[1], and N. Ramaraj[2]

[1] Department of Information Technology,
Thiagarajar College of Engineering,
Madurai, India
[2] Department of Computer Science and Engineering,
G.K.M. College of Engineering,
Chennai, India
ssit@tce.edu, {dinesh.mrc,dhineshjim2006}@gmail.com,
prof.ramaraj@yahoo.co.in

Abstract. Test-suite reduction can provide us with a smaller set of test cases that preserve the original coverageoften a dramatically smaller set. One potential drawback with test suite reduction is that this might affect the quality of the test suite in terms of fault finding the problem and determine its effect when testing. Based on observations from our previous experimental studies on test suite reduction, we believe there is a need for optimized test suite with increase in fault detection. We examine the effectiveness of a test suite reduction process based on a combination of both concept analysis and Genetic algorithm. We also suggest a method for handling the tie between the groups in the lattice which will yield the cases that are most suitable for covering the requirements at that level. Our experimental study suggests that integrating concept analysis and Genetic algorithm has a positive impact on the effectiveness of the resulting test suites.

Keywords: test suite minimization, concept analysis, lattice, Genetic Algorithm, Empirical analysis.

1 Introduction

Software testing is a part of the software development lifecycle which involves detection of errors in the software. The selection of the testing objective is the initial part of the testing lifecycle [3]. Practically speaking the test quality depends upon the test suite being selected. Test suites once developed are reused and updated frequently as the software evolves. As a result, some test cases in the test suite may become redundant as the software is modified over time since the requirements covered by them are also covered by other test cases. A traditional approach to the test suite reduction consists in building a test suite of a smaller size but equivalent to the original one in terms of a selected coverage metric [2]. Test cases are selected in such a way so as to satisfy maximum testing requirements. As a result, the constructed test suite may contain of the many

N. Meghanathan et al. (Eds.): NeCoM, WiMoN, and WeST 2010, CCIS 90, pp. 153–161, 2010.

test cases that may have become redundant. The above process cannot be fully automated because the problem of determining whether a requirement is feasible is not decidable [4].

2   Problem Statement

A test suite T of test cases (t_1,t_2,t_m), a set of testing requirements (r_1,r_2,r_m) that must be satisfied for the overall coverage of the program, and subset (t_1,t_2,t_n) of T, that must be chosen to satisfy the requirements associated with the program.

2.1   Related Work

Many test suite minimization techniques involve reduction of test cases which can lead to reducing of the overall coverage of the program, thus leading to weaker fault detection. Some prior empirical studies have used the code coverage criteria for minimizing the test suites. In experiments by Wong et al., minimized test suites achieved 9 percent to 68 percent size reduction while only experiencing 0.19 percent to 6.55 percent fault detection loss. On the other hand, in the empirical study conducted by Rothermel et al., the minimized suites achieved about 80 percent suite size reduction on average while losing about 48 percent fault detection effectiveness (FDE) on average. These results are encouraging as much higher percentage suite size reduction was achieved as compared to the percentage loss in FDE of suites. There are a variety of testing criteria that have been discussed in literature, and some are finer than others. We observed that different testing criteria are useful for identifying test cases that exercise different structural and functional elements in a program, and we therefore believe the use of multiple testing criteria can be effective at identifying test cases that are likely to expose different faults in software. So the final problem evolves as to find an efficient test suite minimization technique without affecting the overall coverage and fault detection capability of the test suite which involves adding a partial amount of redundancy for extra coverage of the program.

2.2   Proposed System

The basis for forming any of the lattice structure is to first identify the concepts and subconcepts.In the approach described in this paper grouping plays a major role which is achieved through concept analysis [3]. In the test case, requirement matrix (C_1,C_2,C_3C_n) represents the objects and the requirements $(R_1R_2,R_3.R_m)$ represents the attribute set. Concept analysis is a mathematical technique for grouping objects that have common discrete attributes [17][19]. Based on the original test case requirement matrix, concept analysis derives the concepts and sub concepts[19] which are later used for forming the lattice by applying Genetic Algorithm. Concept is a tuple(O,A) where O represents the object set and A represents the attribute set. Each of these concepts have discrete values for the tuple. For eg $(((C_1,C_2,C_4),(R_1,R_4))$ to form a concept only if $((C_1,C_2,C_4)\epsilon O$, $(R_1,R_4)\epsilon$ A and (R_1,R_4) is satisfied only by $((C_1,C_2,C_4)$.Sub concepts are formed from the concepts such that CϵO , RϵA and R$\epsilon(R_1)$ ∥ RR_4. In general if (C_c,R_c) represents the concept then any of the tuple $((C_s),(R_s))$ forms the sub concept if $(R_s)\epsilon R_c$ and $(R_s)\epsilon(R_c)$. Thus the concepts and their sub concepts are formed for all the cases and requirements in the entire test case requirement matrix. These concepts and sub concepts form the basis for the conceptualGA. In our approach these concepts and sub concepts play a major role in grouping together the entire test cases that satisfy the requirements. These concepts and sub concepts together form the grouped test cases wherein for each group the set of requirements that satisfy the group are also represented for later analysis. In conceptualGA sub concepts need not be processed separately since it can be organized later while applying GA for forming the lattice structure. Thus grouped cases along with the grouped requirements are obtained through the concept analysis.

3   Genetic Algorithm

3.1   An Overview of Genetic Algorithms

Genetic algorithms are optimization algorithms based on natural genetics and selection mechanisms. GA is used to extract approximate solutions for problems through a set of operations fitness function, selection, crossover, and mutation [5][7] . Such operators are principles of evolutionary biology applied to computer science. GA search process depends on different mechanisms such as adaptive methods, stochastic search methods, and use probability for search. Using GA for solving most difficult problems that searches for accepted solution; this solution may not be the best and the optimal one for the problem. GA is useful for solving real and difficult problems, adaptive and optimization problems, and for modeling the natural system that inspired design. To apply genetic algorithms to a particular problem, it has to be decomposed into atomic units that correspond to genes[5]. Then individuals can be built with correspondence to a finite string of genes, and a set of individuals is called a population [6]. A criterion needs to be defined: a fitness function F , for every individual among a population, gives F(x), the value which is the quality of the individual regarding the problem we want to solve. Once the problem is defined in terms of genes, and fitness function is available, a genetic algorithm can be computed . As an adaptive search technique, genetic algorithms have been used to find solutions to many NP-complete problems and have been applied in many areas as well in testing.

3.2   Representation

The general representation for Genetic Algorithm is shown in the figure 1, where search space and the solution space is provided [16]. In this paper the test cases grouped through concept analysis are converted (otherwise called as encoding) into 0s and 1s as is represented in the Genotype space. Phenotype space contains

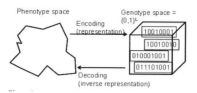

Fig. 1. Representation for Genetic Algorithm

all the grouped test cases and the set of requirements for each group. Processing is done on the encoded strings in the Genotype space by applying Genetic operators and the result is again decoded to obtain the minimized suite in the form of test cases and requirements.

3.3   Genetic Algorithms Operators

Typically, any genetic algorithm used for purpose of optimization consists of the following features: 1. Chromosome or individual representation. 2. Objective function fitness function. 3. Genetic operators (selection, crossover and mutation). Where applying GA over a population of individuals or chromosomes shows that several operators are utilized. Presenting of GA process described in this paper applies the selection operator for determining which solution candidates are allowed to participate in the next step Some of the methods for selection are: Elitism Selection, Roulette Wheel Selection, Tournament Selection, Rank Selection, and Stochastic Selection.In ConceptualGA the selection is based on Ranking. The individual containing the larger fitness value is assigned greater rank.[7]

3.4   Genetic Algorithm for Test Suite Reduction

For our problem of test-suite reduction, gene of an individual is modeled as a 0-1 string. The process involved in our approach is given below.

Choose an initial population from the previous concept analysis Evaluate Fitness value for each individual Rank the chromosomes Select the populated chromosomes in the order of their ranking Identify mutant child.

Organize them in the lattice Calculate the diversity Stopping criteria when all the test cases are being analyzed.

Here the initial population is generated from the previous step of concept analysis by prioritizing the position of test cases. If there are N cases in the initial suite then there are N number of chromosomes in the population. The number of genes present in each chromosome depends upon the number of test cases that makes sense in the context of testing. Chromosomes are represented by a string of 0s and 1s. Initial population is generated such that it contains N chromosomes. After generating initial population for each chromosome fitness value has to be evaluated. Fitness function, the source of determining the level of chromosome in the lattice is given by F(X) =X1+X2+X3.XN. The individual with the largest fitness value is the best individual [7]. The genetic algorithm uses the individuals in the current Generation to create the children that make up the next generation. Besides elite children, which correspond to the individuals in the current generation with the best fitness values, the algorithm creates Mutation children by applying random changes to a single individual in the current generation to create a child [5]. Therefore to identify the parent-children relationship, identification of mutant children is essential. Any type of mutant child present is recognized and allocated on the appropriate position in the lattice.

3.5   Genetic Algorithm for Lattice

These lattice diagrams are an important tool for researchers in lattice theory and ordered set theory and are now used to visualize data. This paper also shows a new approach how to draw a lattice diagram using genetic algorithm. A lattice is an ordered set in which every pair of elements a and b has a least upper bound, a and b, and a greatest lower bound, aand b, and so also known as Hasse diagram [5]. There are several known approaches for drawing these lattice diagrams. Let us explain our approach for drawing this in the following paragraph.

3.5.1   Create Next Generation of Solutions
The probability of being a parent depends on the fitness. There are different ways for parents to create next generation. They are by means of 1. Reproduction Use a string again unmodified. 2. Crossover Cut and paste portions of one string to another. 3. Mutation Randomly flip a bit. 4. Combination of all of the above. Of these using mutation to select the children offers a better solution for fault detection [6] and minimizes the time taken for comparison. Moreover crossover is explorative, it makes a big jump to an area somewhere in between two (parent) areas whereas Mutation is exploitative, it creates random small diversions, thereby staying near (in the area of) the parent.

3.5.2   Tie Breaking Condition
The optimized suite is obtained by considering the set of cases, which are connected by a direct edge to the bottom of the lattice. One set from each level is to be chosen. If there are more than one set from the same level connected to the bottom of the lattice then only one set among those in the same level has to be chosen which has the larger fitness value. If they have the same fitness value then any one of them can be chosen by the method as follows. In order to improve the efficiency along with obtaining the reduced suite the groups with the tie are selected. The group which has larger number of intersections with others in the same level is chosen to be the final suite to be included in the reduced suite.

4   Frame Work for Test Suite Minimization

The entire framework in the figure 2 is composed of three parts. The first part involves the use of concept analysis for deriving the concepts otherwise said to

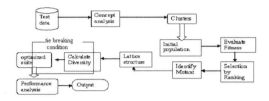

Fig. 2. Framework for Test suite minimization

be of grouped test cases. Here an iterative approach is used for effective comparison of all the available attributes in the attribute set and the test cases The Second part utilizes Genetic algorithm operators and functions with the goal of obtaining the lattice structure which is composed of initial population generated by encoding the concepts obtained by the first part, and the fitness evaluation for each of the chromosome in the generated population by the fitness function in section 4.4, then organizing the groups at each level by two methods: 1. Selecting the groups based on ranking the concepts and 2. Identifying the mutants which provides better fault detection [6] than the other genetic operators. The lattice structure is finally obtained after organizing all the grouped cases in their appropriate positions in the lattice Diversity is to be calculated for identifying the cases connected by an edge to the final requirement set at the bottom of the lattice which forms the final set to be considered for obtaining the optimized suite. After the final sets are identified Tie breaking condition is adopted to evolve the final optimized suite improving the fault detection when compared with the other existing minimization techniques [1] [3].

4.1   ConceptualGA

The conceptualGA is described where the input is the test case requirement matrix .The output for this algorithm is the minimized suite containing the reduced number of cases than the original. By using this algorithm almost half the size of the original test suite is reduced. Also in our proposed algorithm the criteria to be checked is also given as the input. The outcome to be checked is included in the requirements. So the proposed algorithm checks for both success and failure thereby improving the fault detection. Figure 3 shows the conceptualGA algorithm and is provided including all those which are essential for determining the optimized suite.

5   Performance Analysis

The conceptualGA Algorithm proposed in this paper reduces the test suite to half the percentage of what already exists and also as the test suite size increases, the size of the minimized suite still decreases to less than half of the original. Let SS be the original suite and Cl be the number of groups present. Size (SS)

```
Input:
TR : Test case requirement matrix where C={C1,C2..Cn}
R={R1,R2...Rm}
Criteria to be checked

Output:
minimized suite sel with reduced cases than original

Algorithm:
Begin
Attribute set = {R1,R2....Rm}
For each Ri where j=1,2,3 ..... m
S(i)←cluster of test cases
H(i)←cluster of requirements for corresponding test cases
All the cases with same Ri forms a cluster
If ({Cl},{Ri}) = ({Cr},Rj}) where {Cr}={Cl}
S(i)←({Cl, Cr}) H(i)←({Ri,Rj}) where {Cl=Cr} and i=j
End if
End for
For each case Cl where l=1,2 ... n-1
If {Ri} of Cl satisfies test criteria then
If {Ri} of Cl == {Rj} of Cr where r={l+1 ...n} & i=j
S(i)←({Cl,Cr}), H(i)←{Ri})
End if
End if
End for
For each i in S(i)
For j=1:n
If Cj == 'T' A(I,j)←1
Else
A(I,j)←0
End if
End for
End for
Fitness.string←A
F(x)←∑Xi where Xi∈A(I,j)
```

```
Calculate F(x) for all I in A(I)
Fitness.fit←F(x)
Label each cluster in A
Fitness.case←label
For i=1to l-1 & j=i+1 to I
if fitness(i).fit<fitness(j).fit
   swap fitness(i).fit,fitness(j).fit
   swap fitness(i).case,fitness(j).case
   swap fitness(i).string,fitness(j).string
end if
end for
[initial population is ranked and sorted based on the ranking]
plot(1)←fitness(1).label
for i=2 to size(fitness)
for each I
if fitness(i).string<fitness(i-1).string(i-1)
& fitness(i) inherits fitness(i-1).string then
plot fitness(i).string is a subplot of fitness(i-1).string
connect plot(fitness(i-1)) and plot(fitness(i)) by an edge
else
plot fitness(i).string in the same level L of fitness(i-1).string
connect fitness(i) by an edge to its parent in L-1
end if
end for
end for
for all children in each level
if fitness(children).label ≠parent
connect fitness(children).label to bottom
end if
end for
end if
replace all the 1s by appropriate test cases
ie. if A(I,j)=1
then Cj is included in the optimized suite
end if
optimized suite←all the cases in sel
End
```

Fig. 3. CGA Algorithm

$1/\propto$ Cl Let RC be the number of redundant test cases in the test suite and OS the minimized suite. As the number of redundant test cases increases the size of the minimized suite decreases since they are eliminated in the lattice structure. RC $1/\propto$size (OS) When more number of redundant test cases are included in the original suite the size of the suite increases. RC $\propto$ Size (SS) RC and SS are directly proportional to each other and hence, the number of test cases in the original suite (SS) increases and the size of the minimized suite decreases. Size(SS) $1/\propto$ size(OS) Figure 4 depicts the minimization achieved by ConceptualGA (denoted by CGA) and Harrolds approach (H). A test case in a test suite is said to be redundant if the same testing objective can still be satisfied by other test cases [2]. When there is no redundancy in the original test suite H offers lesser number of suites than CGA. But the probability is that no redundancy is present or lesser number of cases are tested is very less because whenever a software is modified and tested again there is a probability that some amount of redundancy will always be present [4]. So using CGA in these situations will offer a more or less the same percent of minimized suite as that of H. But small increase in the size of the suite is almost negligible in case of

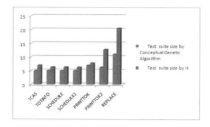

Fig. 4. Comparison of suite size reduction

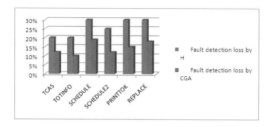

Fig. 5. Comparison of fault loss percentage

testing large number of test cases. Whenever test suite minimization is performed there is some loss in fault detection. In CGA the fault detection capacity is much greater than H. For the test case used in the experiment, Harrold approach offers a minimized suite - Case1 and Case4. When testing these cases, test is achieved only for access and one case for redir. But in order to identify the faults redir must be tested for more number of failure cases which is missing in H. CGA offers four cases to check for access as well as three cases to identify the faults to redirect. Thus in terms of fault detection, CGA performs better than H. H and CGA offers more or less the same number of minimized suites for large number of test suites. The graph for fault detection by CGA and H is shown in figure 5. The loss in fault detection in CGA is lesser than H as shown by the plotted values in figure 5.

6   Conclusion and Future Work

In this paper we proposed a new algorithm for improving the fault detection by integrating concept analysis and Genetic algorithm. We have also performed an empirical comparison of our approach to another approach for minimizing the test suite. The comparison targets two main factors of test suite reduction: Test suite minimization and fault detection. Findings of this comparison are summarized as follows. Both the approaches dramatically reduce the size of the original suite and also produce good representative sets with size of minimized suite by H slightly less than that by CGA, which doesnt affect the time or cost to a greater extent. The CGA can produce better fault detection than by H, which is very much essential for testing after software modification. Based on the above findings the framework proposed in this paper offers optimized suite and better fault detection.

Acknowledgments

We thank Dr. Gregg Rothermel, Dept. of Computer Science, University of Nebraska, for providing the Siemens suite of programs, their faulty versions and the associated test pools.

References

1. Garey, M.R., Johnson, D.S.: Computers and Intractability: A Guide to the Theory of NP-Completeness. Freeman and Company, New York (1979)
2. Korel, B., Tahat, L.H., Vaysburg, B.: Model-based regression test reduction using dependence analysis. In: Proceedings. of ICSM 2002, Montral, Canada, October 3-6 (2002)
3. Lin, J.-W., Huang, C.-Y.: Analysis of test suite reduction with enhanced tie-breaking techniques. In: Proceedings of the 31 st Internatinaol Conference on Software Engineering, vol. 51, pp. 679–690 (2009)
4. Tahat, L.H., Bader, A., Vaysburg, B., Korel, B.: Requirement- based automated black box test generation. In: Proceedings of COMPSAC 2001, Chicago,USA, October 8-12 (2001)
5. Rothermel, G., Harrold, M.: A Safe, Efficient Regression Test Selection Technique. ACM Transactions on Software Engineering and methodology 6, 173–210 (1997)
6. Jeffrey, D., Gupta, N.: Test suite reduction with selective redundancy. In: IEEE International Conference on Software Maintenance ICSM, Budapest, Hungary, pp. 549–558 (2005)
7. Hong, H.S., Cha, S.D., Lee, I., Sokolsky, O., Ural, H.: Data flow testing as model checking. In: Proceedings of ICSE 2003, Portland, USA, May 22-26 (2003)
8. Tallam, S., Gupta, N.: A Concept Analysis Inspired Greedy Algorithm for Test Suite Minimization. In: Proceedings of Workshop Program Analysis for Software Tools and Engineering (September 2005)

AODV-DS with Dominant Pruning in Mobile Ad Hoc Networks

Sonali Mote[1], Somnath Wategaonkar[2], Surekha Khot[3], and Sangita R. Wategaonkar[4]

[1] LBHSST's ICA, Mumbai-400051, India
sonalimote@gmail.com
[2] BVCOE, Navi-Mumbai-410210, India
itssomnath@rediffmail.com
[3] A.C.P.C.O.E., Navi-Mumbai-410210, India
surekhaakhot@rediffmail.com
[4] S.P.I.T., Mumbai, India
sangitarw@gmail.com

Abstract. We investigate the use of dominating-set neighbor elimination as an integral part of the distribution of route requests using the Ad hoc On-demand Distance Vector (AODV) protocol as an example of on-demand routing protocols. We use detailed simulations to show that simply applying dominant pruning (DP) to the distribution of route requests in AODV results in pruning too many route requests in the presence of mobility and cross-traffic. Accordingly, we introduce several heuristics to compensate the effects of DP and show that the resulting AODV with Dominating Set heuristics (AODV-DS) has comparable or better delivery ratio, network load, and packet latency than the conventional AODV. AODV-DS exhibits over 70% savings on RREQ traffic than conventional AODV, and in some situations, AODV-DS may have a lower control overhead using Hello packets than conventional AODV without Hellos.

Keywords: MANET, AODV, AODV-DS.

1 Introduction

Routing in an ad hoc network has several challenges not present in wire-line networks. Bandwidth and energy are limited, so one must have message efficiency. Nodes typically use a single contention-based radio channel, so in multi-hop environments – where one would need routing – all-node broadcasts are error-prone due to hidden-terminal losses. Links are ephemeral and nodes have no means to detect the creation or loss of a link except through use of the link. Mobility further complicates matters because the network topology may be in a state of constant change and a node's picture of the network graph must be continually refreshed. A number of approaches to routing in ad hoc networks have been proposed in the recent past that address the aforementioned challenges by either having all nodes act as peers (i.e., execute the same protocols and algorithms), or by defining a backbone of nodes that carry out special routing functions.

N. Meghanathan et al. (Eds.): NeCoM, WiMoN, and WeST 2010, CCIS 90, pp. 162–170, 2010.
© Springer-Verlag Berlin Heidelberg 2010

To reduce the signaling overhead on a peer-to-peer basis, on-demand routing protocols maintain routes to only those destinations for which traffic exists. A couple of examples of such protocols are DSR (Johnson & Maltz 1996) and AODV (Perkins & Royer 1999) (Perkins et al. 2002a). For the purposes of this paper, the main feature of these protocols is that a node uses a series of network-wide all-node broadcasts to disseminate its route request to discover a route to an intended destination. In most situations, the node uses an expanding-ring search to limit flooding the whole network, but this comes at additional cost to the local area of a node where the same route request is likely to be repeated several times. Hence, it would be highly desirable to limit the number of unnecessary broadcast transmissions.

Another peer-oriented approach to reducing routing overhead is exemplified by the Optimized Link State Routing (OLSR) protocol (Clausen, Jacquet, Laouiti, Minet, Muhlethaler, Qayyum & Viennot 2001), which operates by flooding link-state information and limits the overhead incurred by flooding by only having the multipoint relays (MPR) of a node forward the flooded packets. A node selects MPRs from its symmetrical one-hop neighbors. A node designates a neighbor symmetrical after verifying a bi-directional channel to that neighbor. OLSR defaults to an MPR set of all symmetric neighbors and thus floods over well-connected nodes and uses all well-connected nodes in routing computations. Each node may reduce the MPR set based on a locally tunable parameter called MPR COVERAGE, which is the minimum number of covers desired per two-hop neighbor. The algorithm suggested in (Clausen et al. 2001) uses a greedy approach to minimize the number of repeater nodes while trying to achieve the desired MPR COVERAGE.

The Topology Broadcast Reverse Path Forwarding (TBRPF) (Ogier et al. 2001) routing mechanism uses broadcasts and limits flooding through a packet cache similar to AODV. It is based on (Perkins, Beling-Royer & Das 2001a), which has the potential to limit the default blind flooding but does not have any specific mechanisms to do so. A TBRPF node may choose to not participate in routing, in which case it only receives TBRPF topology packets but does not originate any. Thus, no other node will create a route through the passive member.

There have been a few proposals for establishing a virtual backbone over which routing takes place (e.g., (Das & Bharghavan 1997, Das, Sivakumar & Bhargavan 1997)). In (Das & Bharghavan 1997) a spine is used for all communications, while in (Das et al. 1997) the backbone is used as a secondary route in case shortest-path routes fail. These approaches assume a perfectly scheduled MAC layer. Subsequent work (Wu & Li 2001) provides more advanced algorithms and more sophisticated methods to handle node movement, shutdown and power-on. (Wu & Li 2001) also suggests a way to run Dynamic Source Routing (DSR) (Johnson & Maltz 1996) over a connected dominating set of the network. The dominating set of a network is a subset of nodes such that each node is either in the dominating set, or is adjacent to a node in the dominating set. Obtaining the minimum connected dominating set of a graph is known to be NP-hard (Amis, Prakash, Vuong & Huynh 2000) (Garey & Johnson 1979) even when the complete network topology is available.

Our work is distinct from (Wu & Li 2001) and OLSR's MPR scheme in that we only use dominating sets for flooding control, not packet routing, and we construct a more robust connected dominating set through several heuristics. In particular, we address the process of distributing route requests of an on-demand routing protocol in ways that reduce the overhead incurred by the protocol without incurring a substantial negative impact on the ability of the network to deliver data packets to their destinations.

In the present work, we use Dominant Pruning (DP) (Lim & Kim 2001) as our dominating-set broadcast distribution mechanism and apply it to AODV, which we use as our example of on-demand routing protocols. Section 2 describes how DP is applied to the forwarding of route request (RREQ) packets in AODV. To facilitate DP, each node needs two-hop neighbor information. We use the neighbor-exchange protocol NXP (Mosko & Garica-Luna-Aceves 2002). Applying DP directly to AODV does not result in better performance from that obtained by the conventional AODV in many situations, due to the loss of RREQ packets. We present several heuristics to re-introduce some of redundancy. Although we have only used DP, the heuristics should apply to many dominating-set approaches. The resulting approach is called AODV-DS.

Section 3 presents the results of our simulation performance analysis between conventional AODV, AODV with DP, and AODV-DS. The results from our analysis are consistent with the findings for OLSR (Laouti, Muhlethaler, Najid & Plakoo 2002), which show that multipoint relays (MPR) significantly reduce the protocol overhead, but also results in a lower route availability and packet delivery rates, except for one topology. Our results show that AODV with DP has similar behavior: lower overhead and lower packet delivery ratio. The AODV-DS protocol using our heuristics has lower overhead and equal or higher delivery ratio.

2 Dominating Sets in AODV

This section reviews the RREQ process of AODV and the Dominant Pruning algorithm. It then describes our integration of a neighbor elimination scheme to AODV. We present several heuristics to boost the performance of dominant pruning by adding more redundancy.

In AODV, a node generates a RREQ to find a path to a specific destination, generally using an expanding ring search. The expanding ring search begins with a small TTL flood over the neighborhood of the source. If a RREQ times out, the source retransmits the RREQ with a larger TTL until it finds a route to the destination or has exceeded a threshold and terminates the search in failure. A node receiving a RREQ with positive TTL will relay the RREQ if it cannot send a Route Reply (RREP) for the desired destination. RREP packets are sent unicast. Nodes keep a packet cache of recently seen RREQ packets, and drop duplicates.

Dominant Pruning is an algorithm to achieve a minimum connected dominating set (MCDS). A connected dominating set of graph $G=(N,V)$ is a subset $S \subseteq N$ such that every node in $N-S$ has an edge to at least one node in S and that S is connected. A minimum CDS is a CDS with minimal set size. All nodes are expected to have information about the two-hop neighborhood. For a packet originated at node i, DP performs a greedy set cover (GSC) of all two-hop nodes $N2[i]$ using the one-hop node set $N1[i]$. This cover set is appended to the data packet and broadcast to the neighborhood. When a node i receives a packet from node j, i will relay the packet if it is listed in the forwarding set in the packet. When i relays the packet, it will use a last-hop specific forwarding set. i creates a last-hop effective one-and two-hop neighbor sets.

Let $N1[i,j]$ be the $N1$ set of j known at i via Hello messages. The effective one-hop set is $E1[i,j]=N1[i]\backslash N1[i,j]$. The effective two-hop set is $E2[i,j]=N2[i]\backslash N1[i,j]\backslash N1[i]$. Node i then performs a greedy set cover of $E2[i,j]$ with $E1[i,j]$ yielding the forwarding set for the relayed packet from j.

2.1 AODV-DS

It is straightforward to apply a neighbor elimination scheme to the process of flooding RREQs in an on-demand routing protocol. In the case of AODV, every node connected by the dominating set may receive the RREQ, and any node with an active route to the destination and appropriate sequence numbers may respond. Only nodes listed in the forwarder set RREQ extension may relay the RREQ. The main issues in making use of dominating sets worthwhile are how to make the dominating-set scheme more robust, and how to ensure fairness so the broadcast backbone is not unduly burdened with both broadcast and unicast traffic. Our main implementation difficulty with combining a neighbor elimination scheme with the AODV RREQ process arises from packet loss. We found that replacing the greedy set cover of DP with a *least-first* set cover (LFSC) and using hints from the AODV routing table yielded the best performance.

The AODV-DS algorithm is based on three heuristics to the DP scheme. We eliminate certain nodes from the eligible one-hop neighbors when performing the set cover of two-hop nodes, we use a LFSC rather than a GSC, and we add certain nodes to the forwarder set in addition to the LFSC results. When computing the DP cover set, we first compute the set invalid, being any broken 1-hop AODV route. We compute the DP cover set by first removing all invalid nodes from the one-hop set reported by the neighbor protocol and then compute the DP cover (which could be an empty set). We compute the cover using a LFSC, which is essentially the inverse of GSC: begin with the node whose cover size is minimal but non-zero. After we have the set cover from LFSC, we add in all nodes in the invalid set to the forwarder list. Finally, if we have any route information for the destination (either an active or broken route), we add the listed next-hop to the forwarder list.

To summarize, we construct the forwarder list on a hop-by-hop basis. We first remove from consideration any one-hop nodes listed by AODV as broken routes (but listed by the neighbor protocol as Up) and perform LFSC to get the forwarder list. We then add the excluded invalid nodes to the forwarder list. Finally, if we have any routing information for the destination from either an active route or broken route, we add the listed next-hop to the forwarder list.

3 Simulation Results

We implemented AODV draft 10 and Dominant Pruning in GloMoSim (Bajaj et al. 1999). We did not use the version of AODV distributed with GloMoSim, but rather made a new version conforming to recent AODV specification. This section first reviews our implementation of AODV, and then describes the simulation environment before finishing with the results of simulation. We used all default parameters from AODV draft 10, with the following differences. We set TTL START = 2, we use local repair, we do not use link-layer drop detection, and we do not use reboot hold.

ALLOWED HELLO LOSS only applies to conventional AODV as AODV with DP and AODV-DS use an external two-hop neighbor protocol. Following the recommendation in draft 10, we unicast RERR packets whenever there is only one destination in the precursor list.

Our version of AODV has the following implementation-specific features. If a RREQ for a destination has failed within DELETE PERIOD and a new packet arrives for that destination, it starts with a TTL of NETWORK DIAMETER. After a RREQ failure for a destination, a node will not issue another RREQ for that node for 6 seconds, and it will have a TTL of NETWORK DIAMETER. After each failure (the conventional 2 retries are allowed), queued packets are dropped. We have not investigated the Hello reduction technique that is specified in the more recent AODV specification (Perkins, Belding-Royer & Das 2002b), where only nodes participating in active routes need to issue Hello packets to maintain connectivity. All AODV control packets – broadcast and unicast – are jittered by an exponential delay with mean value of 10 milliseconds, with a minimum of 1 ms and a maximum of 100 ms.

Our simulations generally replicate (Perkins, Royer, Das & Marina 2001b) for a 50-node network. We have scenarios with 10 source nodes and 30 source nodes, transmitting 4 pack-ets/sec CBR traffic of 512 byte UDP packets. Nodes begin transmitting at 50 seconds plus an offset uniformly chosen over a 5 second period to avoid all nodes sending a packet at exactly 50s. Destination nodes are chosen uniformly from any node except the source. All simulations run for 900 seconds.

We use a random waypoint movement model with velocities between 0 and 20 m/s in a 1500m x 300m space with random initial node placement. We use six pause times of 100s, 200s, 300s, 500s, 700s, and 900s. The radio is a 2 Mbps IEEE 802.11 device with a maximum range of 280m. The radio uses an accumulated noise interference model and a two-ray path loss. We used two Hello periods of 1 second and 2 seconds. We repeated all experiments over 10 trials with different random number seeds. Each data point represents the mean over the 10 trials. We show 95% confidence intervals all graphs except some cumulative distribution plots.

Our performance metrics are similar to (Perkins et al. 2001b). We measure the delivery ratio of CBR packets received to packets transmitted, the latency of received CBR data packets, and the control overhead. The control overhead is the ratio of the total number of AODV control packets (RREQ,RREP, RERR, Hellos) to the number of data CBR packets received. In cases where we used NXP, all NXP packets are counted in the control overhead.

Table 1 presents the four performance metrics averaged over all pause times and the 95% confidence interval. Due to space, we only show graphs for the delivery ratio, RREQ load, and RREQ distribution. Any entries in a column with overlapping confidence intervals are statistically identical. AODV-DS has a statistically identical delivery ratio to AODV in all cases. AODV-DS has a significantly better delivery ratio than AODV with DP in all cases. For 10source network load, AODV-DS is statistically identical to AODV, while for 30-sources, AODVDS has about 1/3 the load of AODV. In terms of the number of RREQ packets transmitted, AODV-DS averages under 1/3 the number of AODV, but is at times an order of magnitude higher than AODV with DP. For 10-sources, AODV-DS has about double the latency of AODV, but for 10-sources, it has about 1/2 the latency of AODV.

Table 1. Performance average over all pause times

sources	nodes	hello	protocol	delivery ratio	net load	rreq load	latency (sec)
10	50	1S	AODV	0.977 ±0.009	1.943 ±0.309	558.541 ±253.097	0.029 ±0.006
10	50	1S	AODV w/ DP	0.830 ±0.032	1.648 ±0.303	34.385 ±5.257	1.281 ±0.300
10	50	1S	AODV-DS	0.981 ±0.009	1.530 ±0.316	106.130 ±46.467	0.054 ±0.012
10	50	2S	AODV	0.982 ±0.007	1.089 ±0.190	367.967 ±156.603	0.029 ±0.005
10	50	2S	AODV w/ DP	0.818 ±0.038	0.956 ±0.187	32.327 ±4.030	1.257 ±0.281
10	50	2S	AODV-DS	0.977 ±0.010	0.922 ±0.216	102.843 ±43.386	0.057 ±0.012
30	50	1S	AODV	0.790 ±0.060	3.545 ±1.373	3924.323 ±1365.625	0.687 ±0.072
30	50	1S	AODV w/ DP	0.723 ±0.026	0.822 ±0.135	150.888 ±5.169	1.595 ±0.174
30	50	1S	AODV-DS	0.833 ±0.037	1.579 ±0.460	1158.063 ±370.558	0.399 ±0.007
30	50	2S	AODV	0.793 ±0.056	3.328 ±1.270	3797.293 ±1219.152	0.739 ±0.062
30	50	2S	AODV w/ DP	0.716 ±0.025	0.512 ±0.079	141.950 ±3.698	1.661 ±0.133
30	50	2S	AODV-DS	0.851 ±0.036	1.147 ±0.353	1023.992 ±321.734	0.328 ±0.007

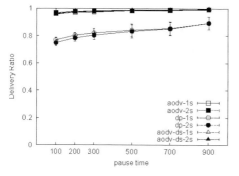

Fig. 1. Delivery ratio, 10 sources

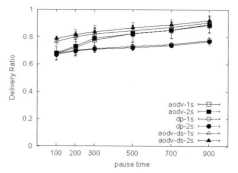

Fig. 2. Delivery ratio, 30 sources

Figures 1 and 2 shows the delivery ratio for 10 and 30 source nodes. For 10 source nodes, AODV and AODV-DS have approximately equal delivery rates. AODV with DP has a significantly lower delivery ratio, due to multiple failures of RREQs. Overall, conventional AODV averaged under 0.5 failed route requests per node (for both 1s and 2s intervals), AODVDS averaged under 1.0 failed route requests per node. AODV with DP averaged 3.3 failed route requests per node (3.29 for 1s and 3.35 for 2s hello intervals), but had the fewest number sources of transmitted RREQs. For 30 source nodes, the differences are not as pronounced as for 10 source nodes. AODV-DS has the highest delivery ratio, AODV is next, and AODV with DP has the lowest delivery ratio.

Figures 3 and 4 shows the average number of RREQ packets transmitted per node over the simulation period. For both 10 sources and 30 sources, AODV with DP transmitted significantly fewer RREQ packets than AODV or AODV-DS. On average over the ten trials, AODV with DP transmitted 34 RREQs for 1s Hellos and 32 RREQs for 2s Hello. AODV-DS transmitted between on average 104 RREQs per node, but had a very wide range between 24 and 205, depending on pause time. Conventional AODV averaged 428 RREQs per node, with a range of 109 to 965, depending on pause time. AODV-DS exhibits over a 70% savings in RREQs compared to conventional AODV and has a similar or better delivery ratio.

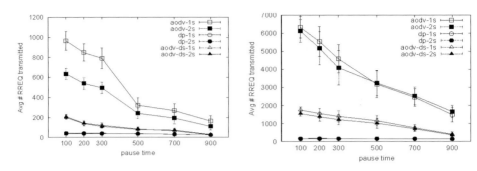

Fig. 3. Average #RREQ transmitted, 10 sources   **Fig. 4.** Average #RREQ transmitted, 30 sources

Figures 5 and 6 shows the cumulative distribution (CDF) of RREQ transmissions for a 100s and 900s pause times. The CDF measures the fraction of RREQs transmitted by nodes. These plots illustrate a sense of fairness in the routing protocol – if the CDF is linear, then all nodes bear an equal share of load. The 30-source 100-second pause time graph is closest to linear for all scenarios. The 10-source 900-second pause time graph is the least linear. Intuitively, when there are more flows and move movement, the flows spread over the graph more evenly. When there is no movement and few flows, paths become established early and do not change. In both graphs, AODV is closest to linear because it completely floods the network. AODV with DP is the furthest from linear while AODV-DS is close to AODV.

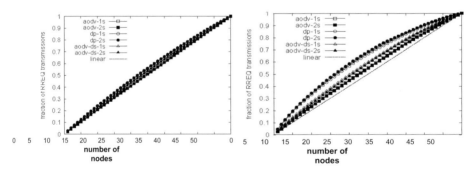

Fig. 5. RREQ distribution, 30 sources, 100s pause   **Fig. 6.** RREQ distribution, 30 sources, 900s pause

When we compare our results with those in (Perkins et al. 2001*b*), there are three significant differences between AODV in (Perkins et al. 2001*b*) and our implementation of AODV. (Perkins et al. 2001*b*) uses link-layer feedback for failed links. When the MAC layer fails an RTS/CTS/ACK handshake and has used all allowable retries, it notifies AODV that a specific packet failed. AODV immediately breaks the link. (Perkins et al. 2001*b*) does not use Hello packets, which we rely on to detect link failures and exchange two-hop data. (Perkins et al. 2001*b*) broadcasts all RERR packets while our implementation sometimes unicasts them.

In terms of delivery ratio, our simulations of AODV show similar performance to (Perkins et al. 2001*b*), which observes a 97% or higher delivery ratio for 10 source nodes and between a 76% to 85% ratio for 30 source nodes. Our results show for 10 source nodes a similar 96% or higher delivery ratio. For 30 source nodes, our work shows between 68% and 89% delivery for conventional AODV and between 75% and 92% delivery for AODV-DS.

For the control load ("routing load" in (Perkins et al. 2001*b*)), one would expect a large difference because we used Hello packets. For 10 source nodes, (Perkins et al. 2001*b*) reports a routing load of 1.0 or less, dropping towards zero as the pause time increases. For 30 source nodes, the routing load is between 1.5 and 2.4. If we look at our best results, which is for a 2s Hello interval, for 10 source nodes conventional AODV showed 0.8 to 1.5 control load and AODV-DS 0.5 to 1.3. For 30 source nodes, AODV ranged between 1.3 and 5.9 while AODV-DS ranged between 0.4 and 1.7. Interestingly, for 30 source nodes we achieved a lower control load using Hello packets and AODV-DS than (Perkins et al. 2001*b*) reported for conventional AODV without Hello packets.

4 Conclusion

We present a method to combine dominating-set broadcast distribution with the AODV RREQ process. The novelty of our contribution is in addressing the fragility of a minimum connected dominating set in the presence of mobility and cross-traffic. We develop three heuristics to fortify the dominating set process against loss by re-introducing some redundancy using a least-first set cover rather than a greedy set cover. We also use hints from the AODV routing table to compute the forwarding list. AODV-DS exhibits about a 70% savings in RREQ traffic while maintaining the same or better latency and delivery ratio for 30 source nodes in a graph of 50 nodes. AODV-DS is also about as fair as conventional AODV in distributing the RREQ burden among all nodes, except in cases of low-mobility and few source nodes. For low-mobility networks, AODV-DS is not as fair to forwarding nodes as AODV, but is better than AODV with DP.

Future work includes detailed study of over-covering two-hop neighbors for more efficient mechanisms than a LFSC. We need a more thorough understanding of the interactions between a two-hop neighbor protocol and the AODV route expiry mechanism. From the RREQ load results, it appears at times that the LFSC adds very many nodes to the cover set. Investigating how to create more tightly bound cover sets should further reduce the network load.

References

[1] Johnson, D.B., Maltz, D.A.: Dynamic source routing in ad hoc wireless networks. In: Mobile Computing, vol. 353. Kluwer Academic Publishers, Dordrecht (1996)

[2] Johnson, D.B., Maltz, D.A., Hu, Y.-C.: The dynamic source routing protocol for mobile ad hoc networks (DSR), IETF Internet draft, draft-ietf-manet-dsr-09.txt (2003)

[3] Johnson, D.B., Maltz, D.A., Hu, Y.-C., Jetcheva, J.G.: The dynamic source routing proto-col for mobile ad hoc networks (DSR), IETF Internet draft, draft-ietf-manet-dsr-07.txt (2002)

[4] Perkins, C.E., Royer, E.M.: Ad hoc on-demand distance vector routing. In: Proc. WMCSA 1999 (1999)

[5] Clausen, T., Jacquet, P.: RFC 3626: Optimized link state routing protocol OLSR (2003)

[6] Clausen, T., Jacquet, P., Laouiti, A., Minet, P., Muhlethaler, P., Qayyum, A., Viennot, L.

[7] Amis, A., Prakash, R., Vuong, T., Huynh, D.: MaxMin D-cluster formation in wireless ad hoc networks. In: IEEE INFOCOM (2000)

[8] Das, B., Bharghavan, V.: Routing in ad hoc networks using minimum connected domi-nating sets. In: Proc. ICC 1997, vol. 1 (1997)

[9] Das, B., Sivakumar, R., Bhargavan, V.: Routing in ad hoc networks using a spine. In: Proc. ICCCN (1997)

[10] Laouti, A., Muhlethaler, P., Najid, A., Plakoo, E.: Simulation results for the OLSR rout-ing protocol for wireless network, Technical Report 4414, INRIA (2002)

[11] Ogier, R.G., Templin, F.L., Bellur, B., Lewis, M.G.: Topology broadcast based on re-verse-path forwarding (TBRPF), IETF Internet draft, draft-ietf-manet-tbrpf-05.txt (2001)

[12] Bajaj, L., Takai, M., Ahuja, R., Tang, K., Bagrodia, R., Gerla, M.: GloMoSim: A scalable network simulation environment, Technical Report 990027, UCLA Computer Science Department (1999)

[13] Perkins, C.E., Belding-Royer, E.M., Das, S.: Ad hoc on demand distance vector (AODV) routing, IETF Internet draft, draft-ietf-manet-aodv-11.txt (2002b)

[14] Perkins, C.E., Royer, E.M., Das, S.R., Marina, M.K.: Performance comparison of two on-demand routing protocols for ad hoc networks. IEEE Personal Communications 8(1) (2001b)

DoS Attack Inference Using Traffic Wave Analysis

P. Jayashree, T. Aravinth, S. Ashok Kumar, and S.K.R. Manikandan

Department Of Information Technology,
Anna University Chennai, Chennai-600044
pjshree@annauniv.edu, thiyagu.ily@gmail.com,
ashok_acp@yahoo.com, skrau89@gmail.com

Abstract. DoS attacks are still remaining unsolved mystery in internet. Though various methods such as change point detection, classifier method, packet marking, use of efficient filters and gateways have been proposed to mitigate DoS attacks, all these methods lack in enough accuracy in detection and hence the false alarm. The proposed work performs network traffic monitoring by way of analyzing the generated traffic signal and determines the traffic wavelet coefficients using continuous wavelet transform and based on the wavelet coefficients and energy distribution in successive time intervals, inference of attack occurrence is confirmed. In this paper, DoS attack detection is performed using three types of wavelet functions and the efficiency of different wavelets in the attack detection is compared.

Keywords: continuous wavelet transform, denial of service, mother wavelet, wavelet analysis.

1 Introduction

DoS is a type of attack in which an attacker uses malicious code to attack a single target. This type of network anomaly occupies the resources of victim so that victim may not be allowed for further communication. DDoS attacks involve breaking into hundreds or thousands of machines all over the Internet by installing malicious software on them, allowing them to control all these machines to launch coordinated attacks on victim sites. These attacks typically exhaust bandwidth, router processing capacity, or network stack resources, breaking network connectivity to the victims.TCP SYN Flood [12], Smurf, Tear Drop, UDP Flood, ICMP Flood and peer-to-peer are common attacks reported in the present days. There are many defensive mechanisms available for DoS attack such as detection, prevention, IP spoofing, etc. Attack detection involves raising the alarm after the occurrences of attack. Prevention involves protect the network from the attack in future. IP spoofing involves the identification of the attackers involved in the attack launching.

Wavelet analysis is a mathematical technique used to represent data or functions. The wavelets used in the analysis possess some mathematical properties, and break the data down into different scales or resolutions. The wavelet transform is a powerful tool in the analysis of transient phenomena because of its ability to extract time and frequency information from the transient signal. Further choosing a mother wavelet is

N. Meghanathan et al. (Eds.): NeCoM, WiMoN, and WeST 2010, CCIS 90, pp. 171–179, 2010.

application specific. Wavelets were developed independently in the fields of mathematics, quantum physics, electrical engineering, and seismic geology. During the last ten years wavelets have been used in many applications such as image compression [15], turbulence, power analysis in transmission lines [6], [10], human vision, radar, and earthquake prediction.

2   Related Work

[7] used vector subspaces for wavelet analysis and obtain the detail signals by projection. From implementation point of view, this becomes more complex in case of continuous flooding attacks, in terms of computational cost. Here energy distribution based on wavelet analysis is used to detect DoS attacks. The use of sliding window requires more concentration, because when the size of window is small, it may lead to overlap of signals and when the size is small, the anomalies may get obsorbed and may not be revealed. While [5] eliminated the risk of using windows. CWT was used to obtain the wavelet coefficients rather than DWT, which is a major advantage. But this system modifies the amplitude and duration of the signal, due to which there are chances for many false detections and missing the duration of real attacks. The time series is constructed by considering the packet rate.

   [3] monitors only a link or node in network to detect the anomaly. This is not aptly characterize the network traffic, as the attack launching and detection can not be centralized. The authors reported that if the energy value changes and continues to remain constant then it is the result of attack. But when traffic changes from attack to normal, there will be a sharp decrement in energy value and this remains constant till next attack happens. This constant value cannot be claimed as attack. [1] uses DWT for finding wavelet coefficients. This is not as efficient as CWT because it is not assured that DWT will give wavelet coefficient for each input given. And also not all wavelets can be used in DWT. Such restrictions make DWT inefficient.

3   Need for Wavelets

It is well known from Fourier theory that a signal can be expressed as the sum of a, possibly infinite, series of sines and cosines. This sum is also referred to as a Fourier expansion. The big disadvantage of a Fourier expansion is that it has only frequency resolution and no time resolution. This means that although determining all the frequencies present in a signal is possible, the time of presence of those frequency bands is missing. To overcome this problem in the past decades several solutions have been developed which are more or less able to represent a signal in the time and frequency domain at the same time. The *wavelet transform* or *wavelet analysis* is probably the most recent solution to overcome the shortcomings of the Fourier transform. They have advantages over traditional Fourier methods in analyzing physical situations where the signal contains discontinuities and sharp spikes.

   The wavelet transform is also less computationally complex taking O(N) time as compared to $O(N \log N)$ for the fast Fourier Transform(FFT). It is also important to note that this complexity only applies when the filter size has no relation to the signal size. A wavelet without compact support such as the Shannon wavelet would require $O(N^2)$.

4 Proposed Method

The network traffic is viewed as a sequence of packets, each of which is represented using a set of 41 parameters as mentioned in KDD 1999 dataset. The times series representation of the traffic is constructed using certain significant parameters in the traffic. The parameters that are considered are protocol type, service, src bytes, count, srv count, dst_host_srv_count. The traffic signal is constructed by calculating the entropy value for the chosen parameters for each of the packets arriving at a particular time and then the average of all entropy values is plotted to obtain the time series. The time series of the traffic signal is constructed using the function as described in equation (1).

$$ f_t = \frac{1}{n}\left(-\sum_{i=1}^{n}\sum_{j=1}^{v} S_{ij} \log\left(\frac{S_{ij}}{n} \right) \right) \tag{1}$$

where the subscript i stands for a parameter out of the of n chosen parameters and the subscript j stands for the set of values existing in the traffic for the parameter i. S_{ij} is the value j of the parameter i. Then the time series is smoothened using moving average [3], with $\alpha=0.3$, in order to avoid false alarms. This smoothened time series is taken as the input for wavelet analysis. The wavelet analysis procedure involves the use of the abstract wavelet function, called mother wavelet. Here the initial analysis is performed on the mother wavelet function, while further analysis is performed with a wavelet obtained with a scaled and translated version of the same wavelet. As the original signal or function can be represented in terms of a wavelet coefficient, any further operations can be performed using wavelet coefficients itself.

Since the network traffic is continuous, it is better to choose the wavelet corresponding to continuous wavelet transform. Some of the continuous wavelets are Morlet, Gaussian, Mexican hat, etc. The energy distribution variance in traffic behaviour under DoS attack changes markedly and this change in distribution is used to detect the attacks. The energy values generated using different wavelets are compared and the properties of wavelets are anlysed to identify the most efficient one for attack detection.

4.1 Continuous Wavelet Transform

A brief description of the wavelet analysis, *continuous wavelet transform* or *CWT* is *presented.* More formally it is written as in equation (2).

$$ \gamma(s,\tau) = \int f(t)\, w^{*}_{s,\tau}(t) dt \tag{2}$$

where * denotes complex conjugation. The variables s and τ, represent scale and translation factors. It shows how a function $f(t)$ is decomposed into a set of basis functions, $w_{s,\tau}(t)$ called the wavelets. The CWT for network traffic is defined as in equation (3).

$$C(f_t) = f_t \Psi s, \tau \ (t) \ dt \qquad (3)$$

The function *f(t)* in the equation denotes the time series of network traffic f_t as said earlier. Ψ(t) is the wavelet chosen for the study, which is discussed in the following sections.

4.2 Scaling and Translation

The wavelets are generated from a single basic wavelet W(t), the so-called *mother wavelet*, by scaling and translation as shown in equation (4).

$$Ws, \tau \ (t) = (1/\sqrt{s})W((t-\tau)/s) \qquad (4)$$

The factor s-1/2 is used for for energy normalization across the different scales. The scale refers to the width of the wavelet and as the scale increases and the wavelet gets wider, it includes more of the time series, but the finer details get smeared out. So a smaller scale value of 3 is chosen for the experiment.

The translation and scaling operations applied to the mother wavelet are performed to calculate the wavelet coefficients. The wavelet coefficients are calculated for each wavelet segment. The CWT uses discretely sampled data, however the translation process is a smooth operation across the length of the sampled data, and the scaling can be defined from the minimum to a maximum chosen by the user. The effect of this translation and scaling process is to produce a time-scale representation. This process of translation and dilation of the mother wavelet is depicted in figure 1.

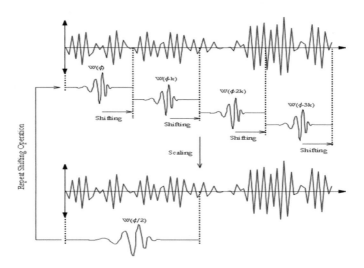

Fig. 1. Scaling and shifting of a mother wavelet

4.3 Morlet Wavelet

The wavelet basis function of Morlet [5] is given by the equation (5).

$$W = (1/(\sigma .k. \sqrt{k}))e^{-(\sigma \ t/k)^2} \ cos(2\pi ft/k) \qquad (5)$$

where $\sigma = 0.05$ is the morlet wavelet bandwidth and $f=0.9$ is the centre frequency of morlet wavelet chosen in order to satisfy the admissibility condition. The wavelet is subjected to CWT and the corresponding wavelet coefficients are obtained. Only the real part of the transform evaluation is considered.

4.4 Spline Wavelet

The B-spline wavelets satisfy all the desirable properties namely biorthogonality, compact support, smoothness, symmetry, good localization, and efficient implementation. Nowadays B-spline scaling functions find place in many applications.

B-spline wavelet is defined by the equation (6) using the three parameters of integer order parameter ($m \geq 1$), bandwidth parameter (f_b) and wavelet center frequency (f_c).

$$w(x) = \sqrt{f_b} \left(sinc(f_b x/m)\right)^x e^{2i n f_c x} \tag{6}$$

One property that is exclusively possessed by these splines is that they have the best approximation among all known wavelet families. Here the values of above said parameters are chosen as 3, 0.05 and 0.9 respectively. In order to satisfy the properties of wavelets and to have best approximation, the periodic boundary conditions are used and the length of signal must be a power of two.

4.5 Daubechies Wavelet

Daubechies D4 wavelets are commonly used as it easy to put into practice. Daubechies wavelet is widely used in solving a broad range of problems, like self-likely properties of a signal or fractal problem, signal discontinuities, etc. The wavelet scaling and translation function is given by the following set of equations (7).

$$h_0 = (1+\sqrt{3}) / (4\sqrt{2})$$
$$h_1 = (3+\sqrt{3}) / (4\sqrt{2})$$
$$h_2 = (3-\sqrt{3}) / (4\sqrt{2})$$
$$h_3 = (1-\sqrt{3}) / (4\sqrt{2})$$
$$g_0 = h_3$$
$$g_1 = -h_2$$
$$g_2 = h_1 \tag{7}$$
$$g_3 = -h_0$$
$$a_t = h_0 s_{2t} + h_1 s_{2t+1} + h_2 s_{2t+2} + h_3 s_{2t+3}$$
$$a[i] = h_0 s[2i] + h_1 s[2i+1] + h_2 s[2i+2] + h_3 s[2i+3]$$
$$c_t = g_0 s_{2t} + g_1 s_{2t+1} + g_2 s_{2t+2} + g_3 s_{2t+3}$$
$$c[i] = g_0 s[2i] + g_1 s[2i+1] + g_2 s[2i+2] + g_3 s[2i+3]$$

5 Implementation and Results

In this paper, the attack detection process is implemented on the network traffic data set provided by KDD. Morlet, Spline and Daubechies wavelets are used for the network traffic transformation and the accuracy of these wavelets in detecting the attack is compared.The continuous wavelets may be real or complex valued. For implementation purpose, only real values are considered. The selection of parameters is based on their entropy values and attack detection rate. Then the time series is constructed by taking average value of those parameters, which represent the traffic and are considered to be significant in detecting the attack.

5.1 Energy Distribution

The energy values of wavelets [7], at two different time instants t and t+ τ are given by equation (8).

$$E_i^t = (1/n_i) \sum_i |d^t (s, \tau)|^2 \ and$$
$$E_i^{t+\tau} = (1/n_i) \sum_i |d^{t+\tau}(s, \tau)|^2 \tag{8}$$

where d^t (s, τ) and $d^{t+\tau}$ (s, τ) are the wavelet coefficients obtained from CWT with a scaling factor of 3 and translation factor of 6 and n_i is the total number of samples taken in the experiment. In this paper, 5000 samples of packets from the KDD CUP 1999 data set have taken used over various runs of detection. Then the energy difference between successive wavelets are found using the equation (9).

$$\Delta E_i = log \ E_i^t - log \ E_i^{t+\tau} \tag{9}$$

The wavelet coefficients obtained using Morlet wavelet is shown in Figure 2 and the energy values obtained from above wavelet coefficients is provided in table 1.

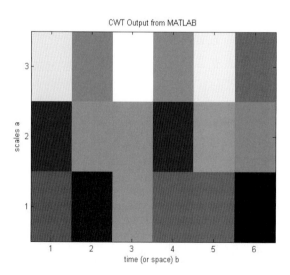

Fig. 2. CWT output for Morlet wavelet

Table 1. Energy values obtained from wavelets

Mother wavelet	Average energy value during attack $(x10^{-3})$	Average energy value during normal $(x10^{-3})$
Morlet	340.82	120.45
Daubechies	290.65	101.67
Spline	300.87	113.96

Figure 3 shows the energy values calculated using morlet wavelet over a period of 15 mins.

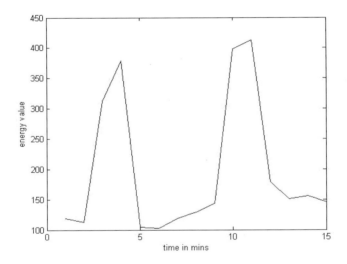

Fig. 3. Graph showing the energy values of traffic

6   Performance Comparison

With respect to wavelet properties, the analysis on the transformed traffic wave is performed. Symmetric wavelets show no preferred direction in time while asymmetric wavelets do for two different directions. A narrow wavelet functions is fast to compute but the narrowness in time implies a very large width in frequency. Conversely wavelets with large compact support are smoother, have finer frequency resolution and are usually more efficient. Regularity gives the approximate measure of the number of continuous derivative that the wavelet functions possess. The regularity therefore gives the smoothness of wavelet function with higher regularity implying a smoother wavelet. A higher vanishing moment implies that more moments will be removed from the signal.

Table 2. Performance Comparison of Wavelet properties

Property	Morlet wavelet	Daubechies D4 wavelet	Spline wavelet
Symmetry	Symmetric	Asymmetric	Symmetric
Compact support	Infinity	15	24
Vanishing moments	1	4	2
Regularity	Infinity	0.85	0.63

From tables 1 and 2, it is clear that the order of efficiency of wavelets in DoS attack detection is as follows

    i.   Morlet wavelet
    ii. Spline wavelet
    iii. Daubechies D4 wavelet.

Daubechies wavelet has a major disadvantage that although it can be used in both CWT and DWT, it is not best suited to CWT. Hence a low result is obtained. If the wavelet has highest number of vanishing moments, it may not be able to detect the attack in the traffic wave, as the attack scenario may get vanished. The traffic wave may contain some flash events and in order to avoid false detections, the wavelet should have smoother function. The table 3 gives the attack detection and false alarm raised by the proposed method, ARX model [1], FD (CUSUM) [5] and vector subspace based detection [7].

Table 3. Comparison of proposed method with existing methods.

Methodology	Attack detection (%)
Proposed method	93.27
ARX model [1]	80.34
FD (CUSUM) [5]	84.70
Vector subspace [7]	88.65

The proposed method is found to be better than the earlier ones in [1], [5], [7]. [1] used DWT for finding wavelet coefficients, but this does not give coefficients for all given inputs. This difficulty can be overcome by using CWT. [3] claimed that attack can be detected by monitoring the energy difference. But this does not detect the flooding attacks. In this paper, rather than using energy difference, the energy values are directly used to detect the attack. Hence most of the attacks can be detected. Using [5] the attack cannot be detected efficiently, because even when the packet rate is low, there is a possibility of non-flooding DoS attack. [7] used sliding windows, which needs more concentration, because when the size of window is small, it may lead to overlap of signals and when the size is large, the anomalies may get absorbed and may not be revealed.

7   Conclusion and Future Work

This paper presented the work of detecting DoS attacks by means of wavelet analysis. Further by choosing three different types of mother wavelet, analysis is done based on their properties for comparing their performance with respect to DoS attack detection. The continuous wavelet transform gives wavelet coefficients for each input value, while the discrete wavelet transform does not do so and also the number of coefficients decreases as scale increases. The multi resolution analysis of wavelets is being carried out using tree based decomposition of signal associated with selected mother wavelets.

References

[1] Lu, W., Ghorbani, A.A.: Network Anomaly Detection Based on Wavelet Analysis. EURASIP Journal on Advances in Signal Processing, Article ID 837601, 16–32 (2009)

[2] He, W., Hu, G., Yao, X., Kan, G., Xiang, H., Wang, H.: Applying Multiple Time Series Data Mining to Large-Scale Network Traffic Analysis. In: CIS 2008, pp. 394–399 (2008)

[3] Shinde, P., Guntupalli, S.: Early DoS Attack Detection using Smoothened Time-Series and Wavelet Analysis. In: Third International Symposium on Information Assurance and Security, pp. 215–220 (2007)

[4] Benetazzo, L., Narduzzi, C., Pegoraro, P.A.: Internet Traffic Measurement: A Critical Study of Wavelet Analysis. IEEE transactions on instrumentation and measurement 56(3), 800–806 (2007)

[5] Dainotti, A., Pescapé, A., Ventre, G.: Wavelet-based Detection of DoS Attacks. In: IEEE Communications Society subject matter experts for publication in the IEEE GLOBECOM, pp. 494–499 (2006)

[6] Soares, L.R., de Oliveira, H.M., Cintra, R.J.S.: Signal Analysis Using Fourier-like Wavelets

[7] Li, L., Lee, G.: DDoS attack detection and wavelets. Springer Science Telecommunication Systems 28(3, 4), 435–451 (2005)

[8] Liu, L., Li, Z., Xu, Y., Mei, C., Tan, X.: A wavelet based distributed ID model. In: Proceedings of the 2005 IEEE International Conference on Services Computing (SCC 2005), pp. 104–110 (2005)

[9] Huang, M.-C.: Wave parameters and functions in wavelet Analysis. In: Ocean Engineering, pp. 111–125. Elsevier, Amsterdam (2004)

[10] Probert, S.A., Song, Y.H.: Detection and Classification of High Frequency Transients using Wavelet Analysis. In: IEEE Power Engineering Society, pp. 801–806 (2002)

[11] Crovella, M., Kolaczyk, E.: Graph Wavelets for Spatial Traffic Analysis. In: Proceedings of ACM SIGCOMM, pp. 185–195 (2002)

[12] Cheng, C.-M., Kung, H.T., Tan, K.-S.: Use of Spectral Analysis in Defense against DoS Attacks. In: Proceedings of IEEE GLOBECOM (2002)

[13] Barford, P., Kline, J., Plonka, D., Amos, R.: A Signal Analysis of Network Traffic Anomalies. In: Proceedings of ACM IMW, pp. 71–82 (2002)

[14] Abry, P., Veitch, D.: Wavelet Analysis of Long-Range-Dependent Traffic. IEEE transactions on Information Theory 44(1), 2–15 (1998)

[15] Ramachandran, K., Vetterli, M., Herley, C.: Wavelets, subband coding, and best bases. Proceedings of IEEE 84(4), 541–560 (1996)

[16] Flandrin, P.: Wavelet analysis and synthesis of Brownian motion. IEEE transaction on Information Thoery 38(2), 910–917 (1992)

Designing 3rd Generation Long-Haul Optical Backbone Networks through a Cost-Conscious Regeneration-Aware RWA Scheme

Ariyam Das and Aveek Chakrabarti

Department of CSE, Jadavpur University, Kolkata, India
{ariyamdas,aveek.chakrabarti}@gmail.com

Abstract. In the 3rd generation long-haul optical backbone networks, an optical signal is not transmitted end-to-end solely in the optical domain due to several physical layer impairments affecting the optical fiber transmission system; intermediate 3R regeneration is essential after an optical lightpath transmits for a long distance. This study focuses on the impact of regenerators on the network design problem. We also propose a cost-conscious 3R-regeneration based Routing and Wavelength Assignment (RWA) scheme that reduces the network cost without any compromise in the network performance by allocating optimal number of regenerators in the network. The different network parameters (like blocking probability, number of regenerators, wavelengths per fiber, etc) computed on a practical subnet using this new scheme show the effectiveness of our heuristic. Our results also provide information on the system specifications required to achieve efficient network performance at an optimal cost, under different network design scenarios.

Keywords: Regenerators, Long-haul Optical Network, WDM, Wavelength Converters, Network Design.

1 Introduction

In wavelength routed networks, signal quality is subjected to a variety of impairments [1-3] which degrade the signal quality to such an extent that signal regeneration becomes inevitable. For long-haul carrier backbone networks spanning thousands of kilometers, designers overcome the adverse effect of signal impairments using per channel optoelectronic regenerators at selected network nodes. The distance upto which an optical signal can travel without any necessary regeneration even under the impact of impairments is called optical reach. With the advent of new ultra-long-haul technology in the carrier backbone networks, optical reach is extended but it is still less than usual connection requests. So, the amount of regeneration in the network is significantly reduced but not completely eliminated.

3R regeneration is most conveniently achieved using Optical-Electronic-Optical (OEO) conversion. 3R regeneration can occur in two fashions namely inline 3R regeneration, and in-node regeneration. Inline 3R regeneration is implemented when the physical distance between two end points of the optical system exceeds a maximum transmission reach (optical reach) before 3R regeneration is required. On the

N. Meghanathan et al. (Eds.): NeCoM, WiMoN, and WeST 2010, CCIS 90, pp. 180–189, 2010.

other hand, in-node regeneration occurs in an Optical Cross-Connect (OXC) node, in which some OEO transponders are deployed for the regeneration purpose. An OXC node with full OEO regeneration capability is called opaque OXC node, an OXC node with partial OEO regeneration capability is called translucent OXC node, while an OXC node without any OEO regeneration capability is called transparent OXC node. Generally, in-node 3R regeneration is more economical since OEO regenerators are shared by all the incident links to the node.

An added advantage of using regenerators in the backbone networks is that regeneration provides the opportunity of wavelength conversion [4,5]. Wavelength conversion can easily be achieved from in-node regeneration, if the OEO transponders are tuned to different wavelengths. Use of wavelength converters in WDM networks can substantially reduce the blocking ratio as discussed in [4]. So, regenerators can play an important role in the RWA problem in long-haul networks. Therefore, routing connections and assigning wavelengths to them in long-haul networks are not totally similar to that discussed in [5] for all-optical networks.

There are different approaches found in the literature on network design problem. The algorithm presented in [1] deals with impairments for metropolitan networks, covering small geographical area. The Impairment Constraint Based Routing (ICBR) discussed in [1] cannot be applied in the initial stages of the network design when the details of the fiber plant are generally not known, to obtain a good approximation. The approach proposed in [2] is for transparent optical networks. So, the techniques discussed in [1,2] are not practically useful for long-haul networks. The technique proposed in [6] uses standard offline RWA algorithms which are elaborately discussed in [5]. However, it does not fully explore the advantage of having regenerators in the network.

The rest of the article is organized as follows. In section 2 we discuss the system model. Section 3 explains the principles behind our algorithm. The proposed algorithm is discussed in section 4 with subsequent subsections. Section 5 does a time-complexity analysis of the proposed algorithm. We present simulation results for a practical subnet in Section 6. Finally, section 7 concludes the article.

2   System Model

According to Greenfield network dimensioning, the given parameters in the development of a system model for a network design problem generally include a physical network topology (lowest duct layer) and a set of traffic demands (in the client layer). The network configuration of long-haul networks that guide the development of this system model are stated below:

(a) The physical topology comprises of nodes and bi-directional links.
(b) The average nodal degree is 2 and the average link length is about 950 km.
(c) Average optical reach is between 2000 km to 4000 km.
(d) The nodes are selected as the regeneration sites.
(e) Each demand is characterized by a source-destination node pair (s,d).
(h) Given a fixed demand set, the factor regulating the network cost is the number of intermediate regenerators needed along the paths.

The assumptions related to the system model are:

(a) The fibers are single mode fibers enabling longer reach of the long-haul networks.
(b) The traffic is at the line rate (no grooming required).
(c) The distribution of traffic demands is random.
(d) The design is carried out under the 1+1 protection scheme.
(e) All the nodes in the network are either opaque OXC or transparent OXC.
(f) All the opaque OXC nodes provide full-range wavelength conversion from any
    input wavelength to any other wavelengths.

3 Proposed Approach

Routing and Wavelength Assignment are important aspects of the network design process. For each demand, if we first find a route, assign a free wavelength to it and then proceed to the next demand, we will not be able to fully utilize the advantage of using regenerators as wavelength converters in the network. Treating routing and wavelength assignment as a single problem unnecessarily adds complications. Hence, a better approach will be to treat routing and wavelength assignment as two separate problems.

Now, regenerators can be allocated in the network in two ways. In the first way, regenerators can be initially allocated in the network as wavelength converters so as to achieve maximum wavelength utilization, and then adding regenerators in all the computed routes of the network for relaying the signal according to optical reach. Alternatively, first regenerators can be allocated in all the computed paths corresponding to the given demand set for the network, according to optical reach and then using these existing regenerators as wavelength converters, wavelength assignment can be carried out. Allocating regenerators in the network as wavelength converters first makes more sense, because an efficient allocation of wavelength converters in the network can yield very high network performance as there will be maximum resource utilization. Using these existing regenerators, when other regenerators are added to the network, the total number of regenerators required will be similar to that obtained from the second method, since placing of regenerators depends on the optical reach only. So, actually the position of the regenerators will merely be shifted. Hence, the first method provides a better approach in having an optimal number of regenerators operating in the network to achieve high network performance. Based on this, our algorithm is presented in the next section.

4 Proposed Algorithm

The proposed algorithm works in three consecutive phases, namely

- Routing
- Wavelength Assignment by Optimal Allocation of Regenerators
- Final Positioning of Regenerators

4.1 Routing

For every demand in the set of connection requests, under the 1+1 protection assumption, a working path and a protection path are needed to be selected. Practical examples reveal that generally one of the first three shortest paths for a connection is the minimum regeneration path. Using k-shortest path algorithm, the first three shortest paths for a demand are identified. From them, the path giving minimum number of regenerations for the connection is selected as the working path. Next a link-disjoint minimum regeneration path is selected as the protection path. Assigning two link-disjoint paths per source-destination pair generally yields good load balancing. The step-wise algorithm for this routing phase is stated below in Algorithm 1.

Algorithm 1. Routing

Inputs: $G(V,E) \leftarrow$ connected graph; $R(s,d) \leftarrow$ Requests; ND $\leftarrow$ Number of Demands; optical_reach $\leftarrow$ average optical reach for all wavelengths.

Outputs: $P \leftarrow$ list of primary routes (working paths) corresponding to the requests in R; $S \leftarrow$ list of link-disjoint protected routes corresponding to the requests in R.

Step 1:	$i \leftarrow 1$. Initialize P and S to $\emptyset$.
Step 2:	$s \leftarrow$ source of the ith request in R.
	$d \leftarrow$ destination of the ith request in R.
	$i \leftarrow i+1$ // increment i //
	found_primary_path $\leftarrow$ false.
	Repeat step 3 to step 11 two times.
Step 3:	$k \leftarrow 1, L \leftarrow \emptyset$
	Repeat Step 4 three times.
Step 4:	$L \leftarrow L \cup \{k^{th}$ shortest path from s to d$\}$
	$k \leftarrow k+1$ // L will contain first three shortest paths between s to d //
Step 5:	Initialize variable min_Regenerations with a high value.
Step 6:	Repeat step 6 to step 9 three times
	$t \leftarrow$ obtain path from L
	$L \leftarrow L - t$
	Dist $\leftarrow 0$, Reg $\leftarrow 0$
Step 7:	Hop to adjacent node (v) of s in the route t in the direction from s towards d
	Dist $\leftarrow$ Dist + link-length between s and v
	If Dist > optical_reach then
	$\qquad$ Reg $\leftarrow$ Reg + 1
	$\qquad$ Dist $\leftarrow 0$
Step 8:	If v is not destination d, then
	$\qquad$ s $\leftarrow$ v
	$\qquad$ Repeat step 7.
Step 9:	If Reg < minRegenerations then
	$\qquad$ minRegenerations $\leftarrow$ reg
	$\qquad$ Min_Reg_Path $\leftarrow$ t
Step 10:	If found_primary_path is false then
	$\qquad$ Temp $\leftarrow$ Min_Reg_Path
	$\qquad$ P $\leftarrow$ P U Min_Reg_Path
	$\qquad$ found_primary_path $\leftarrow$ true
	$\qquad$ Delete all links from G that are in Temp
Step 11:	Else
	$\qquad$ S $\leftarrow$ S U Min_Reg_Path
	$\qquad$ Restore all links in Temp to G
Step 12:	If i$\leq$ND then
	$\qquad$ Repeat from step 2

4.2   Wavelength Assignment by Optimal Allocation of Regenerators

Regenerators are allocated in the network as full-range wavelength converters in this phase. Wavelength assignment in two successive links not sharing a regenerator (wavelength converter) must follow wavelength continuity constraint i.e. same wavelength must be assigned to both the links. However, two different wavelengths can be assigned to two successive links if they share a wavelength converter. Using the full-range wavelength conversion capability of regenerators in this phase, wavelength assignment is carried out by an optimal allocation of regenerators. This algorithm is designed to work according to the congestion in the network. It easily identifies the most congested link by calculating link load (number of times a link is being used in all the paths for routing demands) and the most congested path by calculating path load (sum of the link loads of all the links along the path). This algorithm also makes use of the First-Fit (FF) and the Least-Used (LU) wavelength assignment heuristics discussed in [5]. In this phase, first wavelength assignment is carried out subjected to wavelength continuity constraint without any wavelength conversion. Then regenerators (as wavelength converters) are allocated in the network accordingly to route the remaining demands. The algorithm for this phase is given in Algorithm 2.

Algorithm 2. Wavelength Assignment by Optimal Allocation of Regenerators

---

Inputs: $G(V,E) \leftarrow$ connected graph; $R(s,d) \leftarrow$ Requests; $P \leftarrow$ list of primary routes corresponding to the requests in R; $S \leftarrow$ list of link-disjoint protected paths corresponding to the requests in R; $W \leftarrow$ number of wavelengths per fiber with the wavelengths numbered from 1 to W.

Output: WC $\leftarrow$ set of nodes which are allocated a regenerator for full-range wavelength conversion.

Step 1:	For every unordered node pair (u,v),
	Link load of link between u and v $\leftarrow$ Number of u-v/v-u links in P
Step 2:	For every path $t \, \varepsilon \, P$, compute path load $\leftarrow \sum$ link load of all links along t
Step 3:	Initialize variable blocked to 0.
	$A \leftarrow \emptyset, L \leftarrow P$
Step 4:	$t \leftarrow$ path in L with minimum path load
	// incase of tie, any of the paths with lowest path load is chosen //
	$L \leftarrow L - t$
Step 5:	Assign wavelength to t by First-Fit.
	// first available wavelength is selected //
	$A \leftarrow A \cup t$ // Routes in A follow wavelength continuity constraint //
Step 6:	If $q_1, q_2, \ldots, q_n$ be paths in L such that for any i,
	| links in t $\cap$ links in q_i | ≥ 1, then $L \leftarrow L - q_1 \cup q_2 \cup \ldots \cup q_n$
	// L contains all link-disjoint paths to t //
Step 7:	If $L \neq \emptyset$ then
	Repeat from step 4
Step 8:	$Z \leftarrow P - A$ // Z gives set of all wavelength unassigned paths //
Step 9:	$t \leftarrow$ obtain path from Z
	$Z \leftarrow Z - t$
Step 10:	If t has a free continuous wavelength then
	$A \leftarrow A \cup t$ // assign wavelength //
Step 11:	Else if one or more links of t are out of capacity then
	blocked $\leftarrow$ blocked+1
Step 12:	Else if t has no regenerators then
	prev $\leftarrow$ least-used wavelength in the path
	Execute step 13.4
Step 13:	Else
	Break t into smaller segments starting from source to regenerator, regenerator to regenerator (if any) and regenerator to destination.
	For each segment check,
Step 13.1:	If free wavelength is available then,

Algorithm 2. (*Continued*)

	Assign wavelength
	Proceed to next segment
Step 13.2:	Else if segment is between source (s) and regenerator (d) then,
	prev ← least-used wavelength in the path
	Goto step 13.4.
Step 13.3:	Else // when segment is between two regenerators (s and d) or
	between regenerator (s) and destination (d) //
	prev←wavelength of preceeding link incident on s that is used in t
Step 13.4:	While d is not reached
	u ← node reached
	v ← next hop from u towards d
	If prev is available on current link (u-v) then
	Assign prev to current link
	Else if least-used wavelength of this segment is available on current link then
	Assign least-used wavelength
	WC ← WC U {u}
	prev ← least-used wavelength
	Else
	Assign next available wavelength
	WC ← WC U {u}
	prev ←next available wavelength
	Proceed to next link
Step 13.5:	Proceed to next segment
Step 14:	If Z ≠ Ø then
	Repeat from step 9

All the steps from step 1 have to be repeated for the protected paths in S.

4.3 Final Positioning of Regenerators

Some regenerators are already present in the network, which were added in the earlier phase. In this phase some more regenerators are allocated to the network. These regenerating nodes will be used globally over the network, as any signal transmitted over the paths routed through these regeneration sites will be regenerated, whether needed or not. Clearly, the order in which routes are chosen for regenerator site selection, affects the network design. An optimal way is to first allocate the regenerators along the working routes and then along the protected paths starting from the path with minimum hops, gradually moving towards the path with maximum hops. Some fiber types may have regions of very low dispersion leading to more nonlinear impairments, resulting in the wavelength in this region to have reduced optical reach as compared to the rest of the system spectrum. As wavelength assignment is completed in the earlier phase, we can use varying optical reach for different assigned wavelengths. However, here the algorithm is presented on the assumption that the optical reach does not vary too much for the different wavelengths and an average optical reach is used. The algorithm for this final phase is stated in Algorithm 3.

Algorithm 3. Final Positioning of Regenerators

Inputs: G(V,E) ← connected graph; R(s,d) ← Requests; P←list of primary routes corresponding to the requests in R; S←list of link-disjoint protected paths corresponding to the requests in R; A ← set of all paths which have wavelengths assigned to it; optical_reach ← average optical reach for all wavelengths; WC ← set of nodes which are allocated a regenerator for full-range wavelength conversion.

Output: Regenerators ← set of all nodes in the network which are allocated a regenerator.

Step 1:	Initialize Regenerators to Ø.
Step 2:	Regenerators ← Regenerators U WC

Algorithm 3. (*Continued*)

Step 3:	PA ← P∩A // primary routes which have wavelengths assigned //
Step 4:	Sort PA in the ascending order of the number of hops.
Step 5:	i ← 1
Step 6:	t ← obtain ith path from sorted PA
	i ← i+1 // increment i //
	s ← source of path t.
	d ← destination of path t.
	dist ← 0
	u ← s
Step 7:	Hop to adjacent node of u (v) towards d in the path t
	dist ← dist + link-length between u and v
Step 8:	If dist>optical_reach then
	Regenerators ← Regenerators U {u}
	dist ← link-length between u and v
Step 9:	If v ε Regenerators then
	dist ← 0
Step 10:	If v is not destination d then
	u ← v
	Repeat from step 7
Step 11:	If i ≤	PA	
	Repeat from step 5
	//continue till all regenerators are allocated in all the wavelength assigned primary paths //

All the steps from step 3 have to be repeated for the protected paths specified in S.

---

5   Time-Complexity Analysis

The following notations are used for time-complexity analysis of the algorithms described in the previous section.

N = number of nodes in the network
D = number of demands
H = average number of hops of all the routes for the given demand set
W = number of wavelengths per fiber
K = number of wavelength unassigned paths without any wavelength conversion
With the above notations, we compute the time complexity as follows:
$\Theta(D*H+D*N*\log N)$ = Overall time complexity for the Routing phase
$\Theta(D*H+K*H^2*W)$ = Overall time complexity for Wavelength Assignment
$\Theta(D*\log D*H)$ = Overall time complexity for final positioning of the regenerators
Overall time complexity of the algorithm = $\Theta(D*N*\log N+K*H^2*W+D*\log D*H)$
Since, D>>N>H, overall time complexity of the algorithm = $\Theta(D*N*\log N+K*H^2*W)$

6   Simulation Results

The well-known subnet (shown in Fig. 1) has been used in the simulation. It has 24 nodes and 43 duplex links. It is assumed that all the links between the nodes have same number of wavelength channels. Keeping the number of demands fixed, we have calculated the blocking ratio (number of connection requests blocked/number of demands) for different number of wavelength channels. Fig. 2 shows the number of wavelengths per fiber versus blocking ratio curve for different demand sizes. This result is particularly very important because the number of wavelengths per fiber to achieve a certain blocking probability can be determined, when the specification of the fiber is not known.

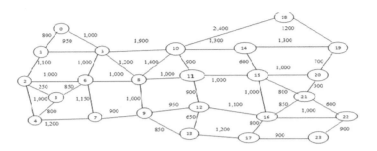

Fig. 1. Network Topology

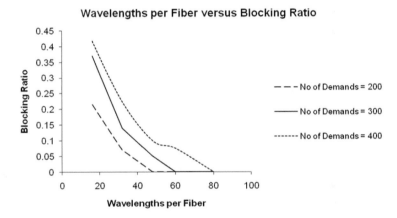

Fig. 2. Wavelengths per Fiber versus Blocking Ratio curve for different demand sizes of 200 (*dashed*), 300 (*continuous*) and 400 (*dotted*) for the network in Fig. 1

Demand size versus number of regenerators (used as wavelength converters) curve for different number of wavelengths per fiber is shown in Fig. 3. As expected, for given number of wavelength channels, wavelength converters increase with demand size. Number of wavelengths per fiber versus number of regenerators (used as wavelength converters) curve for various demand sizes is shown in Fig. 4. For fixed demand size, number of regenerators, serving as wavelength converters, decreases with increase in number of wavelength channels. The second phase of the algorithm provides the necessary specifications on how to achieve a high desirable network performance.

Demand Size vs No. of Regenerators Used as Converters

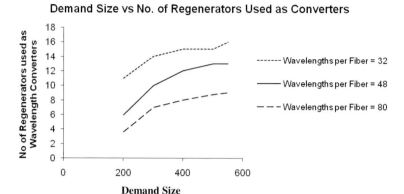

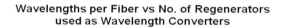

Fig. 3. Demand Size versus Number of Regenerators (used as Wavelength Convertors) curve for 32 (dott*ed*), 48 (continuous) and 80 (*dashed*) wavelengths per fiber for the network in Fig. 1

Wavelengths per Fiber vs No. of Regenerators used as Wavelength Converters

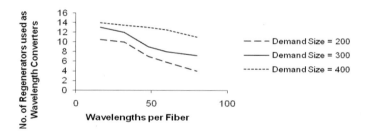

Fig. 4. Number of Wavelengths per Fiber versus Number of Regenerators (used as Wavelength Convertors) curve for different demand sizes of 200 (*dashed*), 300 (*continuous*) and 400 (*dotted*) for the network in Fig. 1

From the final phase of the algorithm, number of total regenerators required, can be known, which will provide an estimate of the cost that is required to be spent on regenerators of the network. The number of regenerators depends on the average optical reach. Demand size versus number of regenerators curve is shown in Fig. 5 for four different optical reaches. Clearly, with increase in demand size, number of regenerators increases and with increase in optical reach, number of regenerators decreases. As is evident from fig. 5, number of regenerators required for an optical reach of 4000km is only slightly less than that required for an optical reach of 2500km for the same demand size. So, at times, increasing the optical reach with expensive components such as higher power amplifier pumps, more precise lasers and filters, better forward error correcting chips, etc, might not be fruitful.

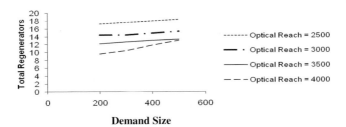

Fig. 5. Demand Size versus Total Regenerators curve for different optical reaches of 2500 km (*dotted*), 3000 km (*thickly dashed with intermediate dots*), 3500 km (*continuous*) and 4000 km (*dashed*) for the network in Fig. 1

7 Conclusions

In this article, the proposed regeneration aware Routing and Wavelength Assignment scheme has reduced the capital and operational cost of the network by reducing the number of regenerators through their optimal allocation in the network. The shortest path routing, First-Fit (FF) and Least-Used (LU) wavelength assignment heuristics have been included in this approach. The simulation over backbone network has established the feasibility and effectiveness of our proposed algorithm. The results in this article can be used to effectively design a network under different scenarios. When the fibers for the network are already specified, the results can be used to provide an estimate of the number of regenerators required in the network in future. On the other hand, when fibers are not yet bought, the simulation study presented can specify the type of fiber as well as the number of regenerators that would be required to satisfy network design goals of low network cost and better performance.

References

1. Tomkos, I., et al.: Performance Engineering of Metropolitan Area Optical Networks through Impairment Constraint Routing. IEEE Communications Magazine 42(8), 40–47 (2004)
2. Manousakis, K., Christodoulopoulos, K., Varvarigos, E.: Impairment-Aware Offline RWA for Transparent Optical Networks. In: IEEE INFOCOM 2009 (2009)
3. Ramamurthy, B., et al.: Impact of Transmission Impairments on the Teletraffic Performance of Wavelength-Routed Optical Networks. IEEE/OSA J. Lightwave Tech. 17(10), 1713–1723 (1999)
4. Strand, J., Doverspike, R., Li, G.: Importance of Wavelength Conversion in an Optical Network. Optical Networks (May/June 2001)
5. Zang, H., Jue, J., Mukherjee, B.: A Review of Routing and Wavelength Assignment Approaches for Wavelength-Routed Optical Networks. Opt. Net. Mag. 1(1), 47–60 (2000)
6. Simmons, J.M.: Network Design in Realistic "All-Optical" Backbone Networks. IEEE Communications Magazine, 88–94 (November 2006)

An Automated and Full-Proof Attendance Marking Scheme (TATTEND) Using Three Integrated Technologies

Divyans Mahansaria[1], G.S. Kartik[1], Gautam Singh[1], Himanshu Mishra[1], Kartikey Singh[1], Sandeep Sharma[2], and B. Amutha[1]

[1] Deptartment of Computer Science and Engineering,
SRM University, Kattankulathur, Chennai,
Tamil Nadu - 603 203, India
[2] Department of Electronics and Communication Engineering,
SRM University, Kattankulathur, Chennai,
Tamil Nadu - 603 203, India
divyansmahansaria@hotmail.com, kartikgs1@gmail.com,
gautamsingh2503@gmail.com, homi1388@gmail.com,
rucust@gmail.com, sandy_illuminati07@yahoo.com,
bamutha62@gmail.com

Abstract. It is an established fact that we are facing difficulties in the attendance management. Presently the attendance in most of the organizations is marked manually on paper which is an error-prone process. Specifically, in educational institutions, a significant amount of time of both students and staff is wasted while marking the attendance manually. Further, there are additional malpractices like proxy and bunking which make this system flawed. To counter these problems, we propose a system *TATTEND* which achieves full transparency and it maintains the regular and accurate updating of the attendance in the database. The three technologies have been integrated to achieve a full-proof system for effective attendance marking. The concept is innovative and a fully automated one. The three technologies include the use of RFID, IR Motion Sensor and an Electronic Deadbolt.

Keywords: TATTEND, RFID (Radio Frequency Identification), IR (Infrared) Motion Detector, Deadbolt, Attendance Marking.

1 Introduction

Radio-frequency identification (RFID) is the use of an object (typically referred to as an RFID tag) applied to or incorporated into a product, animal, or person for the purpose of identification and tracking using radio waves. Most RFID tags contain at least two parts. The first part consists of an integrated circuit for storing and processing information, modulating and demodulating a radio-frequency (RF) signal, and other specialized functions. The second part is an antenna for receiving and transmitting the signal. There are generally two types of RFID tags: Active RFID tags, which contain a battery and thus can transmit its signal autonomously, and passive RFID tags,

N. Meghanathan et al. (Eds.): NeCoM, WiMoN, and WeST 2010, CCIS 90, pp. 190–199, 2010.

which have no battery and require an external source to initiate signal transmission. These tags obtain the energy from the magnetic field of the reader. They are smaller, cheaper and can be used for long time. Passive tags when placed near the reader, detects the radio signals which is generated by the reader. After detecting the signal it transmits its data to the reader. We are going to use passive tags for our application.

A *motion detector* is a device that contains a physical mechanism or electronic sensor that quantifies motion that can be either integrated with or connected to other devices that alert the user of the presence of a moving object within the field of view. An electronic motion detector contains a motion sensor that transforms the detection of motion into an electric signal. This can be achieved by measuring optical or acoustical changes in the field of view. Motion detectors are mainly used in for security systems. For example, motion detectors are typically positioned near exterior doorways or windows of a building for monitoring the area around the building. Upon detecting motion, they generate an electrical signal that is transmitted to a preselected audible alarm or lighting device which is then activated. For our application we are going to use an Infrared motion sensor. IR motion sensors have wide usage. They are also cheap.

A *Deadbolt* or *Deadlock* is a locking mechanism which cannot be moved to the open position except by rotating the lock cylinder. It is used for security to prevent intruders or any other unauthorized person from entering into a doorway. A deadbolt lock's job is to make it simple for someone with a key to move the bolt but difficult for someone without a key to move it. Deadbolt locks provide a door with extra protection because they are stronger than regular locks. This kind of lock cannot be bumped, picked or forced open. It can go with any door. There are several different styles of bolt locks, each made for a specific function. For our application we are going to use a deadlock which will open when the connected RFID reader intercepts a valid RFID tag.

In this paper a fool-proof system TATTEND was proposed to automatically detect the presence of an individual human. This system is going to function as an autonomous attendance marking system be it for students, staffs, employee in a company etc. This system makes the task of attendance management easier while allowing recording correct attendance status and making the same data available to all concerned. This can be made feasible by synchronizing a combination of RFID and IR motion sensing technology integrated with an electronic deadbolt.

The organization of the paper is as follows. In the 1st section we presented an introduction to RFID, Motion Sensor and Deadbolt. In section 2 of the paper we present some of the related work which has already been carried out in this regard. In section 3, section 4 and section 5 we describe about our proposed system TATTEND, a flowchart depicting its operation and step by step simulation of TATTEND. Section 6 discusses the significance of using our proposed solution and section 7 discusses some of the limitations associated with it. Finally some of the application areas where this proposed system could be used before conclusion.

2 Related Works

Though there are few research proposals that have already been proposed in this area but none of them is a full proof solution which is resistant to all sorts of malpractices in the attendance management system.

Francisco Silva etal [1] proposed architecture and a prototype of a system that uses distributed RFID over Ethernet. The system architecture is shown in figure 1.

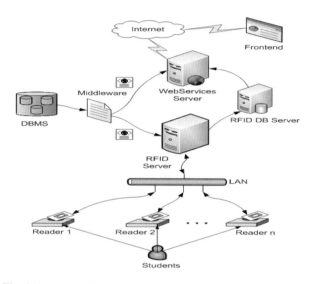

Fig. 1. System architecture as proposed by Francisco Silva et al.

In the proposed architecture one RFID reader is installed to each classroom. It is connected through LAN interface. RFID server, RFID DB Server, Frontend, Web Services Server, Middleware and DBMS which records the student attendance is present in this architecture. This system was used to mark the presence of students in an educational institution environment.

Junhuai Li etal [2] has proposed a scheme for Exercise Information System. The system architecture is shown in Fig.2.

It comprises the following layers: presentation layer, business logical layer, interface layer and data layer. The data layer acts as Database which stores information pertaining to each student and attendance data. The database interface provides access to the database while the hardware interface manages different types of hardware. The business logical layer organizes and realizes system business and the presentation layer provides user friendly interface. This system is based on RFID technology to promote students' attendance in extracurricular activities. It was used to analyze there fitness.

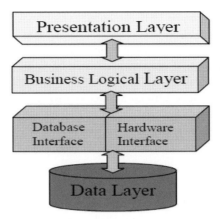

Fig. 2. System architecture as proposed by Junhuai Li et al.

Sourish Behera etal [3] proposed the use of UHF (Ultra High Frequency) tag for RFID Based Attendance Recording System. The overview of the system is shown in Fig. 3.

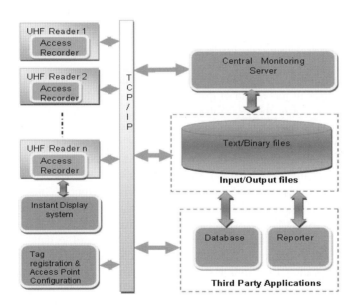

Fig. 3. Overview of the system proposed by Sourish Behera et al.

It consists of several UHF Reader situated in different areas. They are interlinked to each other and the main system over the TCP/IP network. The central monitoring server handles the actual collection of data and creation of reports. Here the novelty lies in the utilization of UHF Antennae which makes the system completely ubiquitous.

These and other proposed systems though effective in the management of attendance but suffers from certain drawbacks. A person could carry several RFID tags (including that of his colleague) with him and get the attendance marked for all the RFID tags carried by him. It is difficult to trace out whether a person is carrying more than one RFID tag. Our proposed system TATTEND counters the malpractices and is a full proof solution in the management of attendance.

3 Proposed System

In the proposed solution to the stated objective of flawless attendance marking we are going to integrate three technologies namely RFID, IR Motion Sensing and Deadbolt. Initially a Smart Card (a RFID tag which is based on low frequency radio signal) Reader is installed with specifications according to the application. There will be two Smart Card Reader installed in a doorway – one each for entering the doorway and exiting from the doorway. A user who wishes to enter or exit through the doorway has to show his Smart Card in front of the Smart Card reader. The Smart Card has been configured before use and the required data pertaining to an individual has been electronically stored in it. A Smart Card has multiple read options i.e. it can be read multiple times by the Smart Card Reader. An Infrared (IR) Motion Sensor and an Electromechanical Gateway, using off the shelf [COTS] component are the other two major components used in our system.

The IR motion detector is used to detect the motion of the individual entering the doorway. It is placed just ahead of the electromechanical doorway. When an individual enters the doorway the IR Motion Sensor records his/her presence. Therefore, even if a person is carrying more than one Smart Card still the attendance will be marked for only one individual because the Smart Card reader and IR Motion Sensor are both synchronized. Only if a motion is recorded by the IR Motion Sensor the attendance for the intercepted Smart Card will be marked. The Electromechanical doorway will open when a valid Smart Card is placed in front of Smart Card Reader. It is used for both entrance and exit for an individual. The Electromechanical doorway automatically closes after allowing passage to an individual. The individual components are synchronized using middleware and controller board. A database is set up to store the required information. The database can contain whatever information is desired. In an educational institution the details regarding student, staff such as their name, registration number etc. and other pertaining data can be stored. A user interface program is provided to manage the work of the complete system.

3.1 Flowcharts

The following Flowchart shows the steps carried out during the entrance process of TATTEND -

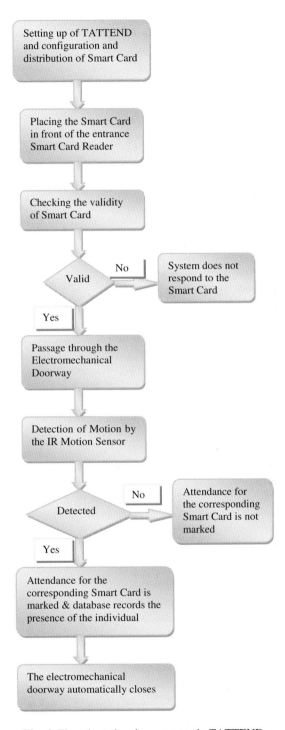

Fig. 4. Flowchart showing entrance in TATTEND

The following Flowchart shows the steps carried out during the exit process of TATTEND –

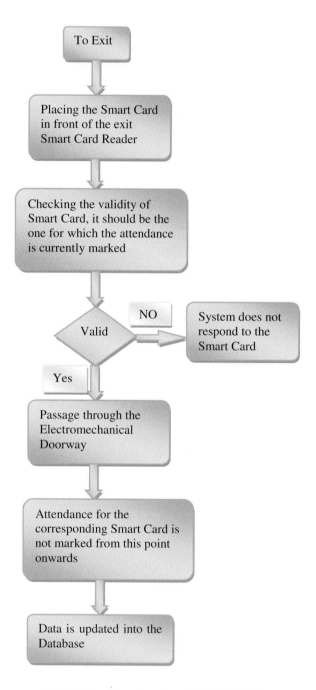

Fig. 5. Flowchart showing exit in TATTEND

4   Simulations

A step by step simulation to the preinstalled proposed system is presented here.

Step 1: A user places his Smart Card in front of the Smart Card reader in order to enter through the electromechanical doorway.

Fig. 6. A Smart Reader reading a Smart Card

Step 2: The Electromechanical doorway allows the passage to the individual on intercepting a valid Smart Card. Just ahead of the Electromechanical doorway is an IR Motion Sensor. If the individual passes through the electromechanical doorway then the IR motion sensor records motion. Only if a motion is recorded the attendance is marked for that individual. The doorway closes subsequently after allowing the passage to the individual.

Step 3: There is another Smart Card reader situated on the other side of the electromechanical doorway. When an individual wants to exit he/she again places the same Smart Card in front of the other Smart Card reader corresponding to which the electromechanical door opens. Now from that point onwards the attendance corresponding to that Smart Card is not counted. After allowing passage the electromechanical door closes again.

5   Significance

It is an established fact that we are facing difficulties in the attendance management. Presently the attendance in most of the organizations is marked manually on paper which is an error-prone process. Specifically, in educational institutions, a significant amount of time of both students and staff is wasted while marking the attendance manually. Further, there are additional malpractices like proxy and bunking which make this system flawed. To counter these problems, our proposed system achieves full transparency by maintaining the regular and accurate updating of the attendance in the database. The intrinsic process of this system is simple and reduces the workload and maximizes the accuracy. Hence, our system highlights the importance of being physically present throughout the working hours as well as providing a sophisticated yet easy to use procedure for efficient management of a large database involving a big organization.

6 Constraints

TATTEND is by far a full-proof solution and is resistant against the malpractices in the attendance marking scheme. The attendance marking scheme is fully-automated with regular update of attendance. The installation cost though initially high but requires less maintenance. The initial LAN interfacing is also cumbersome. But keeping in mind the advantages the limitations can be accepted.

7 Applications

This system has wide variety of applications. In Institutes, it could be used for marking the presence or absence of an individual in regular academic classes, in auditoriums, Hostels, Libraries etc. It could be used at several workplaces including industries as an entry and exit marking scheme, instead of gate passes. Only a Smart Card is a must at all times.

8 Conclusions and Future Work

RFID is currently being used for a wide variety of applications. What we have proposed is a novel system which integrates three technologies namely RFID, IR Motion Sensor and Deadbolt. It is by far very useful in effective attendance management. It removes the present malpractices in attendance management and is a fully automated system for attendance marking. Thus it could be deployed at several places be it in Universities, workplaces etc. The initial cost is though a bit high but operational and maintenance cost is less. We are working on the cost factor to make the system less costly.

Acknowledgements

We are grateful to Dr. D. Narayana Rao, Research Director, SRM University, India and Dr. S. V. Kashmir Raja, Dean Research, SRM University, India for helping us in our research work.

References

1. Silva, F., Filipe, V., Pereira, A.: Automatic control of students' attendance in classrooms using RFID. In: The Third International Conference on Systems and Networks Communications, pp. 384–389. IEEE Computer Society, Los Alamitos (2008)

2. Li, J., Liu, H., Zhang, J.: Design and Implementation of a RFID-based Exercise Information System. In: Second International Symposium on Intelligent Information Technology Application, pp. 216–219. IEEE Computer Society, Los Alamitos (2008)
3. Behera, S., Kushwaha, R.K.: RFID Based People Management System Using UHF Tags. In: The Proceedings of ASCNT 2009, CDAC, Noida, India, pp. 231–238 (2009)
4. Yu-Ju-Tu, S.P.: On Improving the Accuracy of RFID Tag Identification in Supply Chain Applications. In: The Proceedings of TISC 2007, Chennai, India, pp. 891–895 (2007)
5. http://www.wikipedia.com

Agent Based Adaptive Multi-constrained Multicast Routing with QoS Guarantees in MANETs

G. Santhi[1] and Alamelu Nachiappan[2]

[1] Assistant Professor, Department of IT, Pondicherry Engineering College
shanthikarthikeyan@yahoo.co.in
[2] Associate Professor, Department of EEE, Pondicherry Engineering College
nalam63@yahoo.com

Abstract. Multi-constrained Quality of Service (QoS) routing is to find a feasible path that satisfies multiple constraints simultaneously, which is a big challenge for Mobile Ad hoc Networks (MANETs) where the topology may change constantly. Most of the conventional protocols are designed to concentrate on either maximizing the throughput or decreasing the end-to-end delay. These single constrained QoS routing protocols have inherent shortcomings in real time applications where the communication requires meeting stringent requirements on delay, delay-jitter, cost and other QoS metrics. In this paper we propose an agent based Multi-Constrained QoS aware multicast routing scheme based on MAODV (MC_MAODV) which uses a set of static and mobile agent. It depicts QoS multicast model with multiple constraints which may deal with bandwidth reservation, delay constraint and packet loss to multicast session. Here the mobile agents are used to find multicast routes, create the backbone for a reliable multicasting and to adapt to dynamic topology. Multi-path strategy is introduced to reduce the time consumption of rerouting when the link fails due to node mobility. Also, the source node can utilize the best path for the data transmission to meet multiple QoS requirements. Extensive simulations have been conducted to evaluate the performance of MC_MAODV using Network Simulator (NS-2). The simulation results show that the proposed scheme performs better than traditional MAODV in terms of improving packet delivery ratio and minimizing end-to-end delay.

Keywords: MANETs, multi-constrained routing multicasting, clusters, end-to-end delay, packet loss ratio.

1 Introduction

An ad hoc mobile network is a collection of mobile nodes that are dynamically and arbitrarily located in such a manner that the interconnections between nodes are capable of changing on a continual basis [1]. In order to facilitate communication within the network, a routing protocol is used to discover routes between nodes. The primary goal of such an ad hoc network routing protocol is to provide an efficient route establishment between a pair of nodes so that messages may be delivered in a timely manner. Route construction should be done with a minimum of overhead and bandwidth

N. Meghanathan et al. (Eds.): NeCoM, WiMoN, and WeST 2010, CCIS 90, pp. 200–213, 2010.
© Springer-Verlag Berlin Heidelberg 2010

consumption. QoS is an important consideration in networking, but it is also a significant challenge [10]. QoS is more difficult to guarantee in MANETs than in other type of networks, because the wireless bandwidth is shared among adjacent nodes and the network topology changes as the nodes move. This requires extensive collaboration between the nodes, both to establish the routes and to secure the resources necessary to provide the QoS. With the extensive applications of MANETs in many domains, the appropriate QoS metrics should be used, such as bandwidth, delay, packet loss rate and cost for multicast routing. Therefore, QoS multicasting routing protocols face the challenge of delivering data to destinations through multihop routes in the presence of node movements and topology changes [13].

It is a novel way to deal with QoS routing algorithm based on mobile agent [9]. Mobile agent is a program segment which is self-controlling. They navigate from node to node not only transmitting data but also doing computation. They are an effective paradigm for distributed applications, and especially attractive in a dynamic network environment.

The mobile agents are simple packets, which move around the network and collect useful information such as node id, link latency, congestion level etc. as they visit different nodes [11]. The information carried by the mobile agents helps multicast routing protocol to find a route for a given destination, when no route exists in the multicast table to the destination. By this way, the protocol overcomes the additional delay which would have been required, in finding a new route to the destination and also reduces the control traffic generated.

The QoS multicast routing discussed in this paper is a new scheme which utilizes mobile agents for finding multiple paths and to meet the requirement of a single call under multiple QoS constraints. The rest of the paper is organized as follows. Related work is presented in the next section. In Section 3, the proposed QoS aware multicast routing is explained in detail. Section 4 presents the agent model. Some simulation results are presented in section 5. The paper concludes with section 6.

2 Related Works

Multicast routing protocols in ad hoc networks must deal with typical limitations of these networks, which include high power consumption, low bandwidth, and high error rates. These protocols may be divided into two main categories: Table and source initiated (demand-driven). Table-driven routing protocols attempt to maintain consistent, up-to-date routing information from each node to every other node in the network. It includes Destination-Sequenced Distance-Vector Routing (DSDV) [2], Cluster head Gateway Switch Routing (CGSR) [8], and the Wireless Routing Protocol (WRP) [15]. A different approach from table-driven routing is source-initiated on-demand routing. This type of routing creates routes only when desired by the source node. It includes Dynamic Source Routing (DSR) [4], Ad hoc On demand Distance Vector protocols (AODV) [3].

Multicast Ad-hoc On-demand Distance Vector (MAODV) [6] is an on-demand routing protocol that discovers the route only when a node has something to send. It is a hard state protocol, i.e., if a member node of a multicast group desires to terminate its group membership, it must request for termination. When a mobile node wants to join a multicast group or send a message but does not have a route to the group, a

Route Request (RREQ) is originated. All the nodes that are members of a multicast group together with the nodes that are not members of the group but their position are very critical for forwarding the multicast information, compose the tree structure. Every multicast group is identified by a unique address and group sequence numbers for tracing the freshness of the group situation. MAODV however is a hard state protocol and uses flooding of data packets for data discovery that affects the overall performance metrics.

On-Demand Multicast Routing Protocol (ODMRP) [7] is a mesh architecture protocol, i.e., it has multiple paths from the sender to the receivers and uses a forwarding group concept. It applies on-demand procedures to dynamically build route and maintain multicast group membership.

A Framework for QoS Multicast (FQM) to support to support QoS enabled applications is proposed. Aggregated QoS multicast (AQoSM) [5] to provide scalable and efficient QoS multicast in Diff-Serv network is also proposed. The key idea of AQoSM is to separate the concept of groups from the concept of distribution tree by mapping many groups to one distribution tree, so that multicast groups can be routed and rerouted very quickly by assigning different labels to the packets.

ABMRS [11] introduces the agent technology for multicast route discovery. This hybrid protocol works with static and mobile agents that are integrated with existing on-demand multicast routing protocols such as multicast ad hoc on-demand distance vector (MAODV) routing protocol, on-demand multicast routing protocol (ODMRP) routing protocol and others. Here, the mobile agents move around the network and collect the routing information. This routing information assists the on-demand multicast routing protocols in discovering the route. But, the system still suffers in case of random failures of links and nodes, excessive control overheads and absence of a methodology for multi-group transmissions. Also, flooding of agents in all direction, absence of cluster management provides room for enhancement of the protocol.

MOLSR (multicast optimized link state routing protocol) is one of multicast protocols using trees [19]. MOLSR builds and maintains multicast trees for any tuple (source, multicast group) in a distributed manner without any central entity and provides shortest routes from the source to the multicast group members.

The Source routing-based Multicast Protocol (SRMP) is an on-demand multicast routing protocol proposed in [20]. Route selection takes place through establishing a multicast mesh, started at the multicast receivers, for each multicast session. SRMP applies the source routing mechanism, defined by the DSR protocol in a modified manner.

It is observed from the literature that still multicast routing with QoS needs much more attention so that the routing scheme must be robust, maximize packet delivery ratio and adapt dynamically to changes un MANET topology and environment. This paper proposed a QoS aware multicast routing scheme that ensures QoS guarantees such as bandwidth reservation, delay constraint, packet loss and minimum cost to multicast sessions.

3   Proposed Work

The proposed scheme in MANETs employs a set of static and mobile agents. The scheme assumes availability of an agent platform at all the mobile nodes. However, in case of agent platform unavailability, traditional message exchange mechanisms can be used for agent communication.

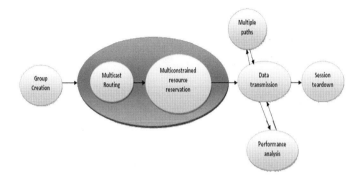

Fig. 1. Architecture of the system

This scheme operates in the following sequence. (i) Hello messages are exchanged by all the nodes in the entire network. 2) Construct a backbone for multicasting using agents. 3) Use of agent technology to find the multicast tree with multiple QoS constraints which may deal with the delay, delay-jitter, bandwidth and packet-loss metrics. 4) Agents are used to discover multiple feasible paths during route discovery and select the path with minimum cost as the primary route. 5) Due to mobility, when a link failure occurs, the agents use the alternate routes for data transmission. Cluster management and link failures are handled by agents to significantly reduce the overhead of constructing a multicast tree with multiple QoS constraints.

3.1 Network Environment

A MANET comprising of several nodes that are distributed across a given geographical area is considered. Multicast group members may be located in any part of a given geographical area. Mobile nodes may randomly move in any directions. All the nodes maintain their QoS parameters. All the reliable nodes support multicast operations whereas intermediate nodes just forward packets from one node to another.

The existing zone based clustering algorithm is used for topology construction. Cluster heads are chosen based on Reliability Factor (RF). RF is computed based on the availability of power, bandwidth, memory and mobility of a node. The reliability factor of each node is recorded and the node which has more reliability factor is selected as cluster head. The mobile agents resides at every cluster head collects information from all the other cluster heads through intermediate nodes of the multicast group if it exists. This cluster head maintains the control information between clusters and for individual nodes. The mobile agents also monitors for a change in the reliability factor to declare a new cluster head thus accounting for dynamic topological changes.

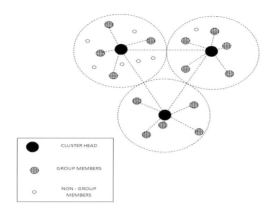

Fig. 2. Nodes organization in the cluster

3.2   QoS Aware Multi-constrained Routing Model

The multi-constrained QoS routing for a mobile ad hoc network is to find a route in the ad hoc network that satisfies all the QoS requirements such as bandwidth, delay and packet loss ratio of the incoming traffic and at the same time reduces constrained resources consumption as much as possible to provide a better throughput. The routes will be discarded even if any one of the parameter is not satisfied. So it is necessary to satisfy all the basic constraints.

As far as routing is concerned, a network is usually represented as a weighted digraph $G = (V, E)$, where V denotes the set of nodes and E denotes the set of communication links connecting the nodes. Let Φ denotes the set of multicast nodes, $\Phi \subseteq V$. $|V|$ and $|E|$ denote the number of nodes and links in the MANET, respectively. Let $s \in \Phi$ be source node of a multicast tree, and $M \subseteq \{\Phi - \{s\}\}$ be a set of end nodes of the multicast tree. Let R be the positive weight and R^+ be the nonnegative weight.

- For any Link, $e \in E$, we can define some QoS. metrics: delay function *delay (e)*: $E \rightarrow R$, packet loss ratio *plr(e)*: $E \rightarrow R$, bandwidth function *bandwidth(e)*: $E \rightarrow R$ and delay jitter function *delay jitter(e)*: $E \rightarrow R$.
- Similarly, for any node $n \in V$, one can also define some metrics: delay function *delay(n)*: $V \rightarrow R$, packet-loss function *packet-loss(n)*: $V \rightarrow R^+$, delay jitter function *delay jitter(n)*: $V \rightarrow R^+$

We also use T (s, M) to denote a multicast tree in which the following relationships hold:

$$Delay\ (p(s,t)) = \sum\nolimits_{e \in P(s,t)} delay(e) + \sum\nolimits_{e \in P(s,t)} delay(n)$$
$$Bandwidth\ (p(s,t)) = min\{bandwidth(e), e \in P(s,t)\}$$
$$Packet\text{-}loss\ (p(s,t)) = 1 - \Pi_{\in P(s,t)}\ (1\text{-}packet\text{-}loss(n))$$
$$Delay\text{-}jitter\ (p(s,t) = \sum\nolimits_{e \in P(s,t)} delay - jitter(e) + \sum\nolimits_{n \in P(s,t)} delay - jitter(e)$$

where p(s, t) denotes the path from source s to end node t of T(s,M).

Delay Constraint : delay(p(s,t))≤ Dt
Bandwidth Constraint : bandwidth(p(s, t))≥B
Packet loss Constraint : packet-loss(p(s,t)) ≤ L
Delay jitter Constraint : delay-jitter(p(s,t)) ≤ J

where, D is delay constraint, B is bandwidth constraint , L is packet loss constraint and J is the delay Jitter constraint.

3.3   Route Discovery Process

In MC-MAODV, the route discovery process is initiated whenever a source node needs to communicate with another node for which it has no routing information in its table. The source node initiates the path discovery by broadcasting a route request (RREQ) packet to its neighbors. The route request packet contains the following fields.

PACKET HEADER FORMAT OF RREQ IN MAODV
rq_src seqno
rq_ timestamp
rq_type
reserved
rq_hop_count
rq_bcast_id
rq_dst
rq_dst_seqno
rq_src

(a)

PACKET HEADER FORMAT OF RREQ IN MCMAODV
rq_src seqno
rq_ timestamp
rq_type
reserved
rq_hop_count
rq_bcast_id
rq_dst
rq_dst_seqno
rq_src
rq_bandwidth
rq_delay
rq_plr

(b)

Fig. 3. Packet header format of (a) MAODV (b) MC-MAODV

In our proposed MC-MAODV, we define three more fields in the existing MAODV packet header: total bandwidth requested (rq-bandwidth), expected end-to-end delay (rq-delay) and the (rq-plr) represents the minimum packet loss ratio. This change has been done to the packet format so as to provide the route discovery by satisfying the QoS parameters like bandwidth, packet loss ratio and end-to-end delay.

When a node receives a new RREQ, it looks in its route table for the destination. If it does not know any route, the node rebroadcasts the RREQ to its own neighbors after increasing the hop count if it satisfies all the QoS constraints. If it knows the fresh route or if the node is the destination, the node stores the information transported by the RREQ and sends the RREP(reply) back to the source.

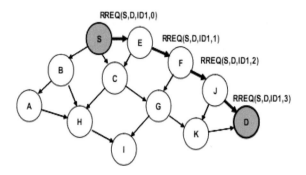

Fig. 4. Route discovery broadcast initiated by the source

When the intermediate node receives back a RREP, it updates in its table and makes the resource reservation and forward the packet to the source which begins to send data after the first received RREP. To set up a reverse path and then to be able to forward a RREP, a node records the address of the neighbor from which it received the first copy of the RREQ.

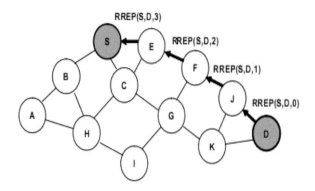

Fig. 5. Route reply unicast from the destination

3.4 Adaptive Multi Path Routing Mechanism

MANETs are typically characterized by high mobility and frequent link failures that result in low throughput and high end-to-end delay. To reduce the number of route discoveries due to such broken paths, multi path routing can be utilized so that alternate paths are available [12]. In this approach multiple paths are formed during the route discovery process. All the paths are maintained by means of periodic update packets along each path. At any point of time only the path with minimum cost is chosen for data transmission as primary path. When the primary path breaks due to node movement, one of the alternate paths can be chosen as the next primary path and data transmission can continue without initiating another route discovery [14]. Here, we use the link-disjoint approach for route discovery. In which paths are allowed to have nodes in common, but the links still must be unique. To discover link-disjoint paths, each node forwards only one route request (RREQ) towards the destination during the route discovery process. The destination node sends a route reply to each of the unique previous hops from which it received a route request.

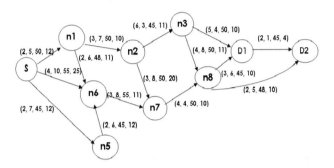

Fig. 6. Finding Link Disjoint paths

In the above Fig. 3, node 's' is the multicast source. D_1 and D_2 are the destinations. The network's edge are described by four tuples (D,J,B,C) . In this example, suppose delay constraint D=15, delay-jitter J=30, Bandwidth constraint B=45 and Cost C = 60. When D_1 is the destination, it computes the paths according to the multiple QoS constraints. The paths S→ n1→n2→n3→D1, S→n1→n2→n3→n8→→d1 and path S→n6→n7→n8→D1 does not satisfy the delay constraint. The paths s→n1→n6 →n7→n8→d1 and s→n5→n6→n7→n8→d1 satisfies the delay constraint, delay-jitter constraint, bandwidth constraint and cost constraints. Furthermore, the path s→n1→n6→n7→n8→d1 has minimum cost among these paths. Therefore the primary path should be the path s→n1→n6→n7→n8→d1. When d2 is the destination, it computes the path s→n1→n6→n7→n8→d2 which should satisfy delay, delay-jitter, bandwidth constraints and also have minimum cost.

3.5 Broken Link Maintenance

When a link failure occurs due to the node mobility, the corresponding node invalidates its routing table entry for that destination and sends and Route Error (RERR) message towards the source. Each node along the active path receives route error and invalidates its corresponding route table entry. Once the source node receives RERR, it switches its primary path to the next best alternate link-disjoint path. If no alternate path is available, at the source it initiates a route discovery.

In this example (Fig. 4)   when node 'n1' moves out of the transmission range, the path s→n5→n6→n7→n8→d1 could be used as alternate route to reach d1.

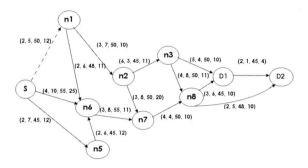

Fig. 7. Finding alternate paths due to node mobility

4 Multicast Routing Scheme Using Agents

The proposed scheme employs a set of static and mobile agents. The traditional programming paradigm uses functions, procedures, structures and objects to develop software for performing a given task. This paradigm does not support developments of flexible, intelligent and adaptable software and also does not facilitate all the requirements of Component Based Software Engineering (CBSE) [17]. Nowadays, agent technology is making its way as a new paradigm in the areas of artificial intelligence and computing which facilitates sophisticated software development with features like flexibility, scalability, adaptability and CBSE requirements [18]. Agents are the autonomous programs activated on an agent platform of a host. Agents use their own knowledgebase to achieve the specified goals without disturbing the activities of the host. The primary goal of an agent is to deliver information of one node to others in the network. Here, the agents are used to find the multicast routes and to create the backbone for reliable multicasting. An agent consists of three components. (a) agent identifier (b) agent program (c) agent knowledgebase. The knowledgebase maintains a set of network state variables such as status of the node (cluster head, source, intermediate, others) RF value, available power, bandwidth, number of movements made in recent interval, delay between adjacent nodes etc. Agents use the knowledgebase for reading and updating.

To initiate multicasting, the mobile agent which resides in the source node provides group ID and distributes multicast key to all the group members. The source node examines all the QoS metric values of next intermediate node using the knowledgebase of agents. If it satisfies all constraints data transmission takes place among all multicast members. When an intermediate node either moves out of the range or fails, the static agent resides at the node that monitored such a situation will find out the new alternate path with minimum cost between the nodes. The alternate path and its connectivity to the network are broadcast, so that the new forwarding table is generated at every node. The agents update their knowledgebase with more recent values. The agent based architectures provide flexible, adaptable and asynchronous mechanisms for distributed network management, and also facilitate software reuse and maintenance.

5   Simulation

The proposed scheme has been simulated in various network scenarios using NS-2 simulator. A discrete event simulation is done to test operation effectiveness of the scheme. In this section we describe the simulation model and the simulation procedure.

5.1   Simulation Model

A mobile ad hoc network consisting of 'n' nodes is generated by using a random placement of the nodes and allowed for the free movement within the area of 'l x b'm^2. Each node starts from a random location and moves in all directions. A maximum number of movements allowed per node every period 'per' is 'move_max'. The communication range for each node is selected as 'C_ran'. All nodes are considered to be non-malicious and are included in the clustering scheme. All nodes must support an agent server, interpreter and transport mechanism. Every node has enough memory to support the agent's knowledge database. Every mobile agent is only allowed three hops from the parent node to avoid network congestion.

Table 1. Simulation parameters

Parameters	Value
MAC Layer	IEEE 802.11
Simulation area(m)	1000*1000
Simulation Time	60 secs
Number of nodes	25
Node mobility speed	0-60m/s
Mobility pattern	Random way point
Traffic flow	CBR
Packet size	512 bytes
Transmission range	250m

5.2   Simulation Procedure

To illustrate some results of the simulation, we have taken n = 50, l = 1000 m and b = 1000 m, per = 100 s, move_max = 2, C_ran = 225 m. D=16, J=30, B=45, C=60 are given as user input for various scenarios. The proposed routing scheme is evaluated in terms of packet delivery ratio, end-to-end delay and control overhead.

- Packet delivery ratio: The ratio of the average number of data packets received by the destination node to the number of data packets transmitted by the multicast source.

- End-to-end delay: The time when a data packet is sent by the source to the time the data packet is received at the destination node.
- Control overhead: The total number of control received by the destination node.

5.3 Analysis of Results

5.3.1 Packet Loss Ratio

Fig 8.a) shows the performance of the average packet loss ratio under various mobility speeds. The packet loss ratio is increased with increasing mobility due to more link breaks. This resulted in more multicast tree partitions for MAODV and MC-MAODV. When the mobility is low, the multicast tree structure was mostly static and therefore the packet loss ratio is low. In MC-MAODV, we used the multipath scheme to avoid the reconstruction of new tree when the links broke down due to mobility. Hence the packet loss ratio of MC-MAODV is higher than that of MAODV.

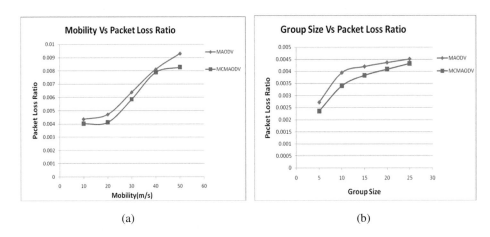

(a)   (b)

Fig. 8. (a) Packet loss ratio vs. mobility speed; (b) Packet loss ratio vs. group size

Packet loss ratio of the proposed system is less than MAODV for all group size values (Fig. 8.b). This is because of finding more reliable path and managing node breakage thereby avoiding the recomputation of route. As the group size increases packet loss ratio also increases since the entire nodes share the common wireless medium for transmission of packets.

5.3.2 End-to-End Delay

Fig.9. shows the performance of the end-to-end delay under various mobility speeds. As the mobility speed increases average end to end delay also increases. Packet delivery latency is significantly less than that for MC-MAODV compared to MAODV (Fig 6.4) even at higher node mobility for constant group size. This is due to the fact that, forwarding nodes chosen are reliable nodes and are less prone to scarcity of re-source. Also once the transmission path breaks, the intermediate node chooses another backup path immediately for transmitting the data.

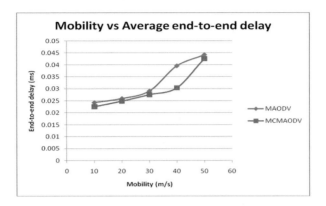

Fig. 9. End-to-end delay vs. mobility speed

5.3.3 Control Overhead
Fig.10. shows the performance of the control overhead under various mobility speeds. As was expected the control overhead increased as the number of nodes increases. The reason is that the inclusion of extra fields in RREQ packer header. Also, the number of route broadcasts increased when the group size increases.

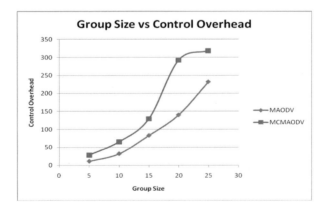

Fig. 10. Control overhead vs. Group size

6 Conclusions

This paper proposes a multi path multicast routing algorithm with multiple constraints based on mobile agents. It effectively routes data packets to group members even in case of high mobility and frequent link failures. A set of static and mobile agents are used to carry out route discovery and route maintenance process. It has higher packet delivery ratio as compared to MAODV and reduces end-to-end delay. This work can further be extended to include the mobile prediction scheme for multiple multicast trees.

References

[1] Junhai, L., Danxia, Y., et al.: A survey of multicast routing protocols for Mobile ad-hoc networks. IEEE Communication surveys & Tutorials 11(1), 78–90 (First Quarter 2009)

[2] Perkins, C.E., Bhagwat, P.: Highly dynamic Destination Sequenced Distance-Vector routing (DSDV) for mobile computers. In: Imielinski, T., Korth, H. (eds.) Proceedings of SIGCOMM 1994 Conference on Communications Architectures, Protocols and Applications, pp. 234–244. ACM, London (1994)

[3] Perkins, C.: Ad-hoc On-Demand Distance Vector (AODV) routing, RFC3561[S] (2003), http://www.ietf.org/rfc/rfc3561.txt

[4] Johnson, D.B., Maltz, D.A., et al.: The dynamic source routing protocol for mobile ad hoc networks, Internet draft, draft-ietf-manet-dsr-10.txt (2004)

[5] Cui, J.H., Lao, L., et al.: AQoSM: Scalable QoS multicast provisioning in Diff-Serv networks. Computer Networks 50, 80–105 (2005)

[6] Royer, E.M., Perkins, C.E.: Multicast operation of the ad-hoc on-demand distance vector routing protocol. In: Proc. ACM MOBICOM, August 1999, pp. 207–218 (1999)

[7] Gerla, M., Lee, S.J., et al.: On-demand multicast routing protocol (ODMRP) for ad-hoc networks, Internet draft, draft-ietf-manet-odmrp-02.txt (2000)

[8] Chiang, C.C.: Routing in clustered multi hop mobile wireless networks with fading channel. In: Chua, T.S., Pung, H.K., Kunii, T.L. (eds.) Proceedings of the IEEE Singapore International Conference on Networks, pp. 197–211. Springer, Singapore (1997)

[9] Amantilla, C., Marzo, J.L.: QoS Routing in Mobile Ad-Hoc Networks using Agent Technology. In: Proceedings of Med-Hoc-Net 2004, Bodrum, Turkey, June 2004, pp. 30–36 (2004); ISBN 975-98840-0-3

[10] Junhai, L., Liu, X., Danxia, Y.: Research on multicast routing protocols for mobile ad-hoc networks. Computer Networks 52(5), 988–997 (2008)

[11] Manvi, S.S., Kakkasageri, M.S.: Multicast routing in mobile ad hoc networks by using a multiagent system. Inf. Sci. 178(6), 1611–1628 (2008)

[12] Tarique, M., Tepe, K.E., et al.: Survey of multipath routing protocols for mobile ad hoc networks. Journal of Network and Computer Applications 32, 1125–1143 (2009)

[13] Zhu, X., Lian, J.: A QoS multicast routing protocol with mobile prediction based on MAODV in MANETs. In: International Conference on Computer Science and Software Engineering, pp. 355–357 (2008)

[14] Wu, H., Jia, X.: QoS multicast routing by using multiple paths/tress in wireless ad hoc networks. Ad Hoc Networks 5, 600–612 (2007)

[15] Shree, M., Garcia-Luna-Aceves, J.J.: An efficient routing protocol for wireless networks. ACM Mobile Networks and Applilcation Journal 1, 183–197 (1996)

[16] Saghir, M., Wan, T.C., Budiarto, R.: A new cross-layer framework for QoS multicast applications in mobile ad hoc networks. International Journal of Computer Science and Network Security 6, 142–151 (2006)

[17] Griss, M.L., Pour, G.: Development with agent components. IEEE Compuiter magazine 34, 37–43 (2001)
[18] Manvi, S.S., Venkataram, P.: Applications of agent technogy in Communications: a review. Computer Communicatuions 27, 1493–1508 (2004)
[19] Jacquet, P., Minet, P., Laouiti, A., Viennot, L., Clausen, T., Adjihh, C.: Multicast Optimized Link State Routing Protocol Extensions, Technical Report, IETF Internet Draft (March 2001)
[20] Mousatafa, H., Labiod, H., Godlewski, P.: A Reactive Random Graph (RRG) Model for Multicast Routing in MANETS. In: Proc. IEEE Globecom 2005 (November 2005)

FPGA Implementation of High Speed Pulse Shaping Filter for SDR Applications

Rajesh Mehra and Swapna Devi

Faculty Members of Electronics and Communication Engineering Department,
National Institute of Technical Teachers' Training & Research,
Sector-26, Chandigarh, India
rajeshmehra@yahoo.com

Abstract. In this paper an efficient approach is presented to design and implement a high speed RRC pulse shaping filter for digital up converter (DUC) section of Software Defined Radios (SDR). The implementation is based on efficient utilization of embedded DSP48E slices of the target device to enhance the speed of complex multipliers used in implementation of pulse shaping filters. It is an efficient method because the use of DSP48E slices not only increases the speed but also saves the general purpose resources on the target device. The root raised cosine (RRC) filter is designed and simulated in direct and transposed form with Matlab and Xilinx AccelDSP, synthesized with Xilinx Synthesis Tool (XST), and implemented on Virtex-5 based XC5VSX50T FPGA device. The proposed transposed structure can operate at an estimated frequency of 146.5 MHz as compared to 69.1 MHz in case of direct form structure by consuming almost same embedded DSP48E slices to provide cost effective solution for mobile and wireless communication systems.

Keywords: DUC, FPGA, RRC, SDR, XST.

1 Introduction

The wide diffusion of wireless terminals like cellular phones is opening new challenges in the field of mobile telecommunications. Besides, the possibility to transmit not only voice but even data between terminals and end users of many kinds has fostered the development of new technologies and new standards for cellular communications [1]. Recently, there is increasingly strong interest on implementing multi-mode terminals, which are able to process different types of signals, e.g. WCDMA, GPRS, WLAN and Bluetooth. These versatile mobile terminals favor simple receiver architectures because otherwise they'd be too costly and bulky for practical applications [2].

The answer to the diverse range of requirements is the *software defined radio*. Software defined radios (SDR) are highly configurable hardware platforms that provide the technology for realizing the rapidly expanding digital wireless communication infrastructure. Many sophisticated signal processing tasks are performed in SDR, including advanced compression algorithms, power control, channel estimation, equalization, forward error control, adaptive antennas, rake processing in a WCDMA (wideband code division multiple access) system and protocol management.

As digital technology ramps up for this century, an ever-increasing number of RF applications will involve the transmission of digital data from one point to another.

N. Meghanathan et al. (Eds.): NeCoM, WiMoN, and WeST 2010, CCIS 90, pp. 214–222, 2010.

The general scheme is to convert the data into a suitable baseband signal that is then modulated onto an RF carrier. Pulse shaping filters are used at the heart of many modern data transmission systems like mobile phones, HDTV, SDR to keep a signal in an allotted bandwidth, maximize its data transmission rate and minimize transmission errors. The ideal pulse shaping filter has two properties:

i. A high stop band attenuation to reduce the inter channel interference as much as possible.
ii. Minimized inter symbol interferences (ISI) to achieve a bit error rate as low as possible.

The RRC filters are required to avoid inter-symbol interference and constrain the amount of bandwidth required for transmission [3]. Root Raised Cosine (RRC) is a favorable filter to do pulse shaping as it transition band is shaped like a cosine curve and the response meets the Nyquist Criteria [4]. The first Nyquist criterion states that in order to achieve an ISI-free transmission, the impulse response of the shaping filter should have zero crossings at multiples of the symbol period. A time-domain sinc pulse meets these requirements since its frequency response is a brick wall but this filter is not realizable. We can however approximate it by sampling the impulse response of the ideal continuous filter. The sampling rate must be at least twice the symbol rate of the message to transmit. That is, the filter must interpolate the data by at least a factor of two and often more to simplify the analog circuitry. In its simplest system configuration, a pulse shaping interpolator at the transmitter is associated with a simple down sampler at the receiver. The FIR structure with linear phase technique is efficient as it takes advantage of symmetrical coefficients and uses half the required multiplications and additions [5].

Today's consumer electronics such as cellular phones and other multi-media and wireless devices often require digital signal processing (DSP) algorithms for several crucial operations[6]. Due to a growing demand for such complex DSP applications, high performance, low-cost Soc implementations of DSP algorithms are receiving increased attention among researchers and design engineers. There is a constant requirement for efficient use of FPGA resources [7] where occupying less hardware for a given system that can yield significant cost-related benefits On one hand, high development costs and time-to-market factors associated with ASICs can be prohibitive for certain applications while, on the other hand, programmable DSP processors can be unable to meet desired performance due to their sequential-execution architecture [8]. In this context, reconfigurable FPGAs offer a very attractive solution that balance high flexibility, time-to-market, cost and performance. Therefore, in this paper, RRC pulse shaping filter is implemented on FPGA.

2   Pulse Shaping Filters

Before delving into the details of pulse shaping, it is important to understand that pulses are sent by the transmitter and ultimately detected by the receiver in any data transmission system. At the receiver, the goal is to sample the received signal at an optimal point in the pulse interval to maximize the probability of an accurate binary decision. This implies that the fundamental shapes of the pulses be such that they do not interfere with one another at the optimal sampling point. There are two criteria that ensure non interference. Criterion one is that the pulse shape exhibits a zero crossing at the sampling point of all pulse intervals except its own. Otherwise, the residual effect of other pulses will introduce errors into the decision making process. Criterion two is that the shape of the pulses be such that the amplitude decays rapidly outside of the pulse interval.

This is important because any real system will contain timing jitter, which means that the actual sampling point of the receiver will not always be optimal for each and every pulse. So, even if the pulse shape provides a zero crossing at the optimal sampling point of other pulse intervals, timing jitter in the receiver could cause the sampling instant to move, thereby missing the zero crossing point. This, too, introduces error into the decision making process. Thus, the quicker a pulse decays outside of its pulse interval, the less likely it is to allow timing jitter to introduce errors when sampling adjacent pulses. In addition to the non interference criteria, there is the ever-present need to limit the pulse bandwidth.

The rectangular pulse, by definition, meets criterion number one because it is zero at all points outside of the present pulse interval. It clearly cannot cause interference during the sampling time of other pulses. The trouble with the rectangular pulse, however, is that it has significant energy over a fairly large bandwidth. In fact, because the spectrum of the pulse is given by the familiar sinc response, its bandwidth actually extends to infinity. The unbounded frequency response of the rectangular pulse renders it unsuitable for modern transmission systems. This is where pulse shaping filters come into play. If the rectangular pulse is not the best choice for band-limited data transmission, then what pulse shape will limit bandwidth, decay quickly, and provide zero crossings at the pulse sampling times? The raised cosine pulse is used to solve this problem in a wide variety of modern data transmission systems.

3 Raised Cosine Filter

The magnitude spectrum, $P(\omega)$, of the raised cosine pulse is given by:

$$P(\omega) = \tau$$
$$for\, 0 \le \omega \le \frac{\pi(1-\alpha)}{\tau}$$
$$P(\omega) = \frac{\tau}{2}\left[1 - \sin\left[\left[\frac{\tau}{2\alpha}\right]\left[\omega - \frac{\pi}{\tau}\right]\right]\right]$$
$$for\, \frac{\pi(1-\alpha)}{\tau} \le \omega \le \frac{\pi(1+\alpha)}{\tau} \tag{1}$$
$$P(\omega) = 0$$
$$for\, \omega \ge \frac{\pi(1+\alpha)}{\tau}$$

The inverse Fourier transform of $P(\omega)$ yields the time-domain response, $p(t)$, of the raised cosine pulse. This is also referred to as the impulse response and is given by:

$$P(t) = \frac{\left[\sin c \dfrac{t}{\tau}\right]\left[\cos \dfrac{\alpha \pi t}{\tau}\right]}{1 - \left[\dfrac{2\alpha t}{\tau}\right]} \qquad (2)$$

Unlike the rectangular pulse, the raised cosine pulse takes on the shape of a sinc pulse, as indicated by the leftmost term of $p(t)$. Unfortunately, the name "raised cosine" is misleading. It actually refers to the pulse's frequency spectrum, $P(\omega)$, not to its time domain shape, $p(t)$. The precise shape of the raised cosine spectrum is determined by the parameter, α, which lies between 0 and 1. Specifically, α governs the bandwidth occupied by the pulse and the rate at which the tails of the pulse decay. A value of $\alpha = 0$ offers the narrowest bandwidth, but the slowest rate of decay in the time domain. When $\alpha = 1$, the bandwidth is $1/\tau$, but the time domain tails decay rapidly. It is interesting to note that $\alpha = 1$ case offers a double-sided bandwidth of $2/\tau$. This exactly matches the bandwidth of the main lobe of a rectangular pulse, but with the added benefit of rapidly decaying time-domain tails. Conversely, inverse when $\alpha = 0$, the bandwidth is reduced to $1/\tau$, implying a factor-of-two increase in data rate for the same bandwidth occupied by a rectangular pulse. However, this comes at the cost of a much slower rate of decay in the tails of the pulse. Thus α parameter gives the system designer a trade-off between increased data rate and time-domain tail suppression. The latter is of prime importance for systems with relatively high timing jitter at the receiver.

4 Proposed RRC Design and Simulation

The raised-cosine filter is obtained by truncating the analytical impulse response and it is not optimal because it results in higher filter order. In this proposed work Raised cosine filter has been designed using Matlab and Xilinx AccelDSP by taking filter order 25 and roll off factor 0.5. The proposed design is an efficient realization of RRC filter by using embedded DSP48E blocks of target FPGA to perform the fast multiply-and-accumulate (MAC) operations.

4.1 Matlab Code

```
function [P,F]=aw_psd(X,NFFT,Fs)
if (min(size(X))~=1)
   disp('aw_psd only operates on row or column vectors')
   return;
end
% Convert input to column vector
X=X(:);
% Set default values if not specified
if (nargin < 3)
   Fs = 2;
end
if (nargin < 2)
   if (length(X)<256)
```

```
      NFFT = length(X);
    else
      NFFT = 2^8;
    end
  end
  RealVal = isreal(X);
  if (RealVal == 0)
    Fs=Fs*2;
  end
  % Zero pad input if needed
  if (length(X) < NFFT)
    X = [X;zeros(NFFT-length(X),1)];
  end
  % Determine available averaging
  if (length(X) > NFFT)
    AVE = floor(length(X)/NFFT);
    X = X(1:AVE*NFFT);
  %    X = [X;zeros(AVE*NFFT-length(X),1)];
  else
    AVE = 1;
  end
  X=reshape(X,NFFT,AVE);
  %Create Hanning Window
  if ~rem(NFFT,2)
    % Even length window
    m=(NFFT)/2;
    w = .5*(1 - cos(2*pi*(1:m)'/(NFFT+1)));
    w = [w; w(end:-1:1)];
  else
    % Odd length window
    m=(NFFT+1)/2;
    w = .5*(1 - cos(2*pi*(1:m)'/(NFFT+1)));
    w = [w; w(end-1:-1:1)];
  end
  hm=kron(ones(1,AVE),w);
  %Compute PSD
  P=abs(fft(X.*hm)).^2/((length(X))/2);
  P=mean(P,2)*1.332;
  if (RealVal == 1)
    P=P(1:end/2,:);
    NFFT=NFFT/2;
  end
  F=linspace(0,1-1/NFFT,NFFT)*Fs/2;
  if (nargout == 0)
    plot(F,10*log10(P),'r')
    grid on
    xlabel('Frequency')
    ylabel('Power Spectrum Magnitude (dB)')
  end
```

The first step in design flow is to develop m-code for RRC filter with required specifications using Matlab as shown in Fig.1. The floating point output has been generated from m-code file which is then verified and analyzed.

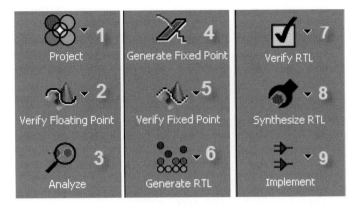

Fig. 1. Design Flow

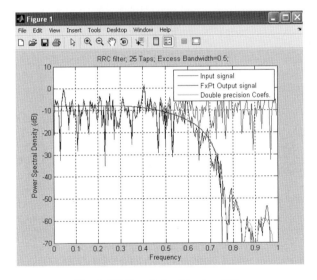

Fig. 2. RRC as Pulse Shaping Filter

Then the equivalent fixed point file is generated and verified by AccelDSP whose output has been shown in Fig.2. The red plot shows the input to the filter and blue plot is the output from RRC filter.

Then RRC filter has been scaled by a factor of 1.4172 and delayed by 4 samples to obtain the normalized error as shown in Fig.3.

The proposed RRC implementation is shown in Fig.4. In this implementation each coefficient has been processed by one multiplier in a parallel style and pipelined registers are used to enhance the speed performance of the filter.

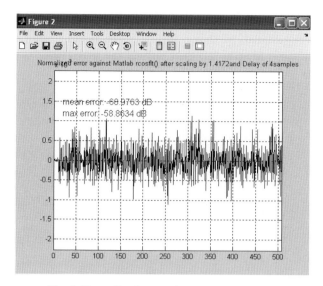

Fig. 3. Normalized error after delay and scaling

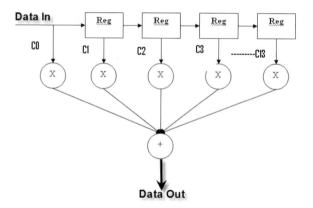

Fig. 4. Proposed RRC Filter Structure

5 Hardware Implementation Results and Discussions

To observe the speed and resource utilization, RTL is generated, verified and synthesized. The proposed RRC pulse shaping filter has been implemented on Virtex5 based XC5VSX50T target device using direct and transposed form structures. The proposed transposed design can be operated at an estimated frequency of 146.5 MHz as compared to 69.1 MHz in case of direct form design by using almost same number of embedded DSP48E slices of the target FPGA as shown in Table1 and 2. The resource utilization of both implementations is shown in Table3 and 4 respectively.

Table 1. Transposed Form Performance Evaluation

Clock Name	Requested Frequency	Estimated Frequency	Estimated Period	Max Throughput	Input Sampling
Clock	100.0 MHz	146.5 MHz	6.8250 ns	1	146.520 MSPS

Table 2. Direct Form Performance Evaluation

Clock Name	Requested Frequency	Estimated Frequency	Estimated Period	Max Throughput	Input Sampling
Clock	100.0 MHz	69.1 MHz	14.4760 ns	1	69.080 MSPS

Table 3. Transposed Form Resource Utilization

Information	Count	Percentage Use
Slice Registers added for Registered Inputs	17	
Slice Registers	689 of 32640	2%
Slice LUTs	690 of 32640	2%
Slice LUTs used as Logic	690 of 32640	2%
LUT Flip Flop pairs used	754	
LUT Flip Flop pairs with an unused Flip Flop	65 of 754	8%
LUT Flip Flop pairs with an unused LUT	64 of 754	8%
Fully used LUT-FF pairs	625 of 754	82%
Unique control sets	3	
IOs	52	
Bonded IOBs	0 of 480	0%
DSP48Es	14 of 288	4%

Table 4. Direct Form Resource Utilization

Information	Count	Percentage Use
Slice Registers added for Registered Inputs	17	
Slice Registers	450 of 32640	1%
Slice LUTs	544 of 32640	1%
Slice LUTs used as Logic	544 of 32640	1%
LUT Flip Flop pairs used	893	
LUT Flip Flop pairs with an unused Flip Flop	443 of 893	49%
LUT Flip Flop pairs with an unused LUT	349 of 893	39%
Fully used LUT-FF pairs	101 of 893	11%
Unique control sets	3	
IOs	52	
Bonded IOBs	52 of 480	10%
BUFG/BUFGCTRLs	1 of 32	3%
DSP48Es	13 of 288	4%

6 Conclusion

In this paper, an efficient method is presented to minimize the time to market factor. A pulse shaping filter for DUC section of SDR has been designed and implemented in direct and transposed form by using embedded DSP48E slices of target device. The results have shown enhanced performance in terms of speed. The proposed transposed design can be operated at an estimated frequency of 146.5 MHz as compared to 69.1 MHz in case of direct form. The proposed structure has consumed almost same embedded DSP48 slices to provide cost effective solution for mobile and wireless applications.

References

1. Wei, W., Yifang, Z., Yang, Y.: Efficient Wireless Digital Up Converters Design Using System Generator. In: IEEE 9th International Conference on Signal Processing, ICSP 2008, pp. 443–446 (2008)
2. Huang, K.B., Chew, Y.H., Chin, P.S.: A Novel DS-CDMA Rake Receiver: Architecture and Performance. In: IEEE International Conference on Communications, ICC 2004, pp. 2904–2908 (2004)
3. Macpherson, K., Stirling, I., Garcia, D., Rice, G., Stewart, R.: Arithmetic Implementation Techniques and Methodologies for 3G Uplink Reception in Xilinx FPGAs. In: IEE Conference on 3G Mobile Communication Technologies, IEE 2002, pp. 191–195 (2002)
4. Zawawi, N.M., Ain, M.F., Hassan, S.I.S., Zakariya, M.A., Hui, C.Y., Hussin, R.: mplementing WCDMA Digital Up Converter In FPGA. In: IEEE International RF and Microwave Conference, RFM 2008, pp. 91–95 (2008)
5. Chandran, J., Kaluri, R., Singh, J., Owall, V., Veljanovski, R.: Xilinx Virtex II Pro Implementation of a Reconfigurable UMTS Digital Channel Filter. In: IEEE Workshop on Electronic Design, Test and Applications, DELTA 2004, pp. 77–82 (2004)
6. Allred, D.J., Yoo, H., Krishnan, V., Huang, W., Anderson, D.: A Novel High Performance Distributed Arithmetic Adaptive Filter Implementation on an FPGA. In: Proc. IEEE Int. Conference on Acoustics, Speech, and Signal Processing ICASSP 2004, vol. 5, pp. 161–164 (2004)
7. Macpherson, K.N., Stewart, R.W.: Area efficient FIR filters for high speed FPGA Implementation. IEE Proc.-Vis. Image Signal Process 153(6), 711–720 (2006)
8. Longa, P., Miri, A.: Area-Efficient FIR Filter Design on FPGAs using Distributed Arithmetic. In: IEEE International Symposium on Signal Processing and Information Technology, pp. 248–252 (2006)
9. Mazzini, G., Setti, G., Rovatti, R.: Chip pulse shaping in asynchronous chaos-based DS-CDMA. IEEE Trans. Circuits Syst. I 54(10), 2299–2314 (2007)

Feature Selection and Classification of Intrusions Using Genetic Algorithm and Neural Networks

T. Subbulakshmi[1], A. Ramamoorthi[2], and S. Mercy Shalinie[3]

[1] Senior Grade Lecturer, Department of Computer Science and Engineering,
Thiagarajar College of Engineering, Madurai
subbulakshmitce@yahoo.com
[2] IME CSE, Department of Computer Science and Engineering,
Thiagarajar College of Engineering, Madurai,
armoorthi@gmail.com
[3] HODCSE, Department of Computer Science and Engineering,
Thiagarajar College of Engineering, Madurai
shalinie_m@yahoo.com

Abstract. Intrusion Detection Systems are one of the emerging areas of Information Security research. They can be implemented using Soft computing techniques. This paper, focuses on multi class classification process whose performance can be significantly enhanced by selecting an optimal subset of input features that is used for training in multi layer feed forward network thereby reducing the false alarm rate. A feed forward network called the back propagation network is trained to classify data as being normal or intrusive. Five training functions are used and analysis is done to decide which training function gives an optimal performance. In addition, the selection of a subset will reduce the dimensionality of the data samples and eliminate the redundancy and ambiguity introduced by some attributes. The user classifier can then operate only on the selected features to perform the learning process. Experiments are performed using kddcup99 dataset. The optimality of the obtained feature subset is then tested and a classification rate of 86% is obtained.

Keywords: Neural Networks, Intrusion Detection, Genetic Algorithm, Feature Selection.

1 Introduction

An intrusion is defined to be a violation of the security policy of the system. Intrusion detection refers to the mechanisms that are developed to detect violations of system security policy. Intrusion detection is based on the assumption that intrusive activities are noticeably different from normal system activities and thus detectable. Intrusion detection is intended to complement existing security measures and detect actions that bypass the security monitoring and control component of the system. Intrusion detection is therefore considered as a second line of defense for computer and network systems. IDS try to perform their task in real time. However, there are also IDS

N. Meghanathan et al. (Eds.): NeCoM, WiMoN, and WeST 2010, CCIS 90, pp. 223–234, 2010.
© Springer-Verlag Berlin Heidelberg 2010

that do not operate in real time because of the nature of the analysis. There are some intrusion detection systems that try to react when they detect an unauthorized action. IDS must therefore reduce the amount of data to be processed. This is very important if real-time detection is desired. Some data may not be useful to the IDS and thus can be eliminated before processing. In complex classification domains, features may contain false correlations, which hinder the process of detecting intrusions. Further, some features may be redundant since the information they add is contained in other features. Extra features can increase computation time, and can have an impact on the accuracy of the IDS. Feature selection improves classification by searching for the subset of features, which best classifies the training data.This paper focuses the use of Artificial Neural Network and Genetic Algorithm in relationship with IDS.ANN in implementing IDS' s is to include an intelligent agent in the system that is capable of disclosing the latent patterns in abnormal and normal connection audit records, and to generalize the patterns to new and slightly different connection records of the same class. Neural networks are, therefore, well suited to picking up new patterns of attacks readily, although some learning time is required. Genetic algorithms are a particular class of evolutionary algorithms also known as evolutionary computation that use techniques inspired by evolutionary biology such as inheritance, mutation, selection, and crossover also called recombination.

2   Existing Methods

In this section a brief overview of the existing methods has been presented. In the research work reported by K,M.Faraoun and A.Rabhi,. et. al [1], has explained the data dimensionality reduction based on genetic selection of feature subsets. Experiments are performed using the KDD99 dataset to classify DoS network intrusions, according to the 41 existing features. The optimality of the obtained features subset is then tested using a multi-layered neural network. Obtained results show that the proposed approach can enhance both the classification rate and the learning runtime.

In the research work reported by Chebrolu S, Abraham A,..et al[2], intrusion detection systems examination towards all data features to Detect intrusion or misuse patterns is described. The purpose of this paper is to identify important input features in building IDS that is computationally efficient and effective. This investigates the performance of two feature selection algorithms involving Bayesian networks (BN) and Classification and Regression Trees (CART) and an ensemble of BN and CART. Empirical results indicate that significant input feature selection is important to design an IDS that is lightweight, efficient and effective for real world detection systems. Hybrid architecture has been used for combining different feature selection algorithms for real world intrusion detection.

In the research work reported by Anup Goyal et al [5], a machine learning approach known as Genetic Algorithm (GA) is proposed to identify attack type of connections. The algorithm used considers different features in network connections such as type of protocol, network service on the destination and status of the connection to generate a classification rule set. GA is implemented and trained it on the KDD Cup 99 data set to generate a rule set that can be applied to the IDS to identify and classify different types of attack connections.

In the research work reported by Diaz-Gome, P. A., and D. F. Hougen et al [7],the improved offline intrusion detection system using genetic algorithm is explained. Various architectures and approaches have been proposed including: Statistical, rule-based approaches; Neural Networks; Immune Systems; Genetic Algorithms; and Genetic Programming. This study discusses a fitness function independent of variable parameters to overcome this problem. This fitness function allows the IDS to significantly reduce both its false positive and false negative rate.

In the research work reported by Li, W., et al [11],a technique of applying Genetic Algorithm to network Intrusion Detection Systems is described. A brief overview of the Intrusion Detection System, genetic algorithm, and related detection techniques is presented. Parameters and evolution process for GA are discussed in detail. This work is focused on the TCP/IP network protocols.

In this research work reported by H. Güneş Kayacık et al [12],a feature relevance analysis is made on KDD 99 dataset. Numerous researchers employed the datasets in KDD 99 intrusion detection competition to study the utilization of machine learning for intrusion detection and reported detection rates up to 91% with false positive rates less than 1%. To substantiate the performance of machine learning based detectors that are trained on KDD 99 training data, it investigates the relevance of each feature in KDD 99 intrusion detection datasets. To this end, information gain is employed to determine the most discriminating features for each class.

In this paper an IDS is built on some of the components. An ordinary expert system component has a task to monitor logs and, according to the defined policy, search the intrusions. It is a signature based IDS. Another component is a neural network that can observe the behavior of a user and send the alarm if the observed behavior is violated. This work shows how neural network can be used in combination with expert systems and improves intrusion detection qualities.

3 Dataset Description

The datasets contain a total of 24 training attack types, with an additional 14 types in the test data only. There are 41 features for a single connection record and 42nd feature specifying its characteristic namely normal or its attack type. Some of the features are duration, protocol_type, service, flag, src_bytes, dst_bytes, land, su_attempted, num_root, num_file_creations, num_shells, is_host_login, is_guest_login, count, srv_count, srv_serror_rate, rerror_rate, dst_host_serror_rate, dst_host_srv_rerror_rate.

Table 1. Darpa dataset

S.No	Attacks	Training Phase(10, 000- 4000 normal, 6000 attacks)	Testing phase(5,000 – 2000 normal, 3000 attacks)
1.	DoS	1350	350
2.	U2R	1650	650
3.	R2L	1455	455
4.	Probe	1545	545

4   System Design

In this paper, an off-line intrusion detection system is implemented using Multi Layer Feed Forward network. Different structures of the network are examined to find a minimal architecture that is reasonably capable of classification of network connection records. The use of the GA offers a practical approach to feature selection for attacks taken from the KDDcup99 dataset. The genetic search in our work is guided using the proposed fitness measure that compute the information gain of a given features subset. The result of the search is then an optimal features subset, which will be used with a multi-layer feed forward network to learn the class's discrimination. The results show that a feed forward network with two layers of hidden neurons and minimal feature subset can generate satisfactory classification results. promising results show the potential applicability of Neural Network with Genetic Algorithm for developing practical Intrusion Detection Systems.

4.1   Feature Selection Using Genetic Algorithm

The module comprises of

- Encoding of connections
- Fitness Function
- Genetic Parameters

4.1.1   Encoding of connections

Every network connection in the KDD Cup data set contains 41 features out of which, four including the label are strings, 14 fields are float type values in the range 0.00-1.00, while the remaining 23 fields are integer values. With 41 different fields having varying types of values, the hypothesis search space which is the number of possible individuals in every population becomes alarmingly large and will thus necessitate a very large population size requiring ultra-scale computing to select fit individuals. Due to this, the hypothesis space is restricted by calculating the upper and lower bounds for every field from the training set and allowed for values only within this range in the random population generated at the start of the experiment. The fields that carry string type of values were represented using positive numbers which were calculated from the summation of ASCII value of each letter of the string.

4.1.2   Fitness Function

The fitness value of a given features subset is proportional to its information gain. In the computation of the information gain for only one feature according to the classes is proposed like the following:

Let S be a set of training set samples with their corresponding labels. Suppose there are m classes and the training set contains si samples of class i and s is the total number of samples in the training set. Expected information needed to classify a sample is given by:

$$I(S_1, S_2, \ldots S_m) = \sum_{i=1}^{m} \frac{S_I}{S} \log_2 \left(\frac{S_I}{S}\right) \tag{1}$$

A feature F with values { f1, f2, ..., fv } can divide the training set into v subsets {S1, S2, ..., Sv } where Sj is the subset which has the value fj for the feature F. Furthermore let Sj contain sij samples of class i. Entropy of the feature F is:

$$E(F) = -\sum_{J=1}^{V} \frac{S_{1i} + S_{2i} + ... + S_{mi}}{S} . I(S_{1i} + S_{2i} + ... + S_{mi}) \qquad (2)$$

Information gain for F can be calculated like following :

$$Gain\ (F) = I\ (S_1, S_2, ..., S_m) - E\ (F) \qquad (3)$$

The value of the gain as shown gives information gain of a feature F with regard to all classes. To measure the gain of the feature a given class k, consider the problem as binary classification one. considering two classes: the class k and the remaining of classes will constitute one other class. So the new Expected information needed classify a given sample will be:

$$I(S_k, S_{k1}) = -\left(\frac{S_K}{S} \log_2 \frac{S_K}{S} \right) \frac{S_{K1}}{S} \log_2 \frac{S_{K1}}{S} \qquad (4)$$

Where k' denote the complemented class of the class. The entropy of a feature F according to the class k is:

$$E(F) = \sum_{J=1}^{V} S_K + S_{K1} . I(S_K + S_{K1}) \qquad (5)$$

Information gain for F can be calculated as:

$$Gain\ (F) = I\ (S_k, S_{k1}) - E(F) \qquad (6)$$

The value of the information gain is always bounded by the value of the expected information to classify a given record. It is always preferable to have a fitness function limited in the interval [0,1], this can help to stop the genetic process when the value of the best chromosome reaches the maximum possible one. For this reason, the normalized information gain measure has been introduced as the following:

$$NormGain\ (C) = \frac{Gain\ (F)}{I\ (S_1, S_2, ... S_m)} \qquad (7)$$

4.1.3 Genetic Parameters
Generation count: it is the maximum number of generations that the GA will proceed and is set to 100.

- Population size: it is the number of chromosomes created in each generation and is set to 100.
- Crossover rate: it is the probability of crossover. It is set to 0.7.
- Mutation rate: it is the probability of mutation. it is set to 0.1.
- Maximum chromosome length: it specifies the maximum number of features that must be used in each chromosome. It is set to 20.

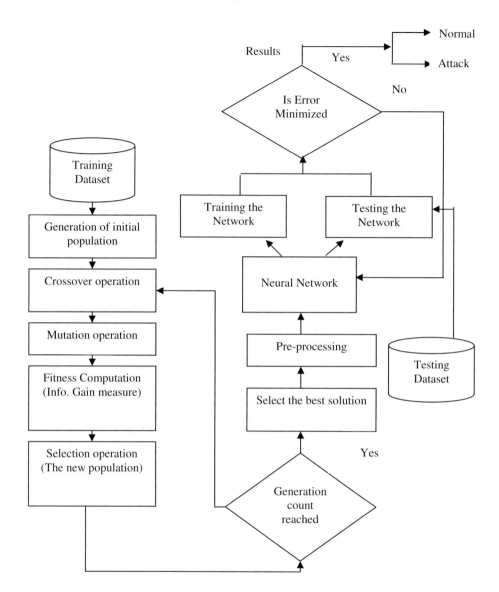

Fig. 1. Intrusion Detection System Model

4.2 Data Pre-processing

The model reads the TCP/IP dump data and sends it first to the pre-processing model, which process the raw data into a form acceptable for the Neural Network. The pre-processing module also converts 41 features into a standardized numeric representation. In matlab, the default datatype is double, so all the features are converted into double. The String datatypes like tcp,http,SF are converted using 'sum of all the ascii characters'. For example, ascii for t (116)+ascii for c(99)+ascii for p (112)=327.

4.3 Neural Network Classification

The Model comprises 3 modules namely,

1. Creation of the Network
2. Training the Network
3. Testing the Network

4.3.1 Creation of the Network

Network created is a feed forward network with 3 layers, 2 hidden layers with 73 and 15 neurons and an output layer with 5 neuron, one for normal and one for each category of attack. The activation function used is a sigmoid function namely 'transig'. The input layers contain 41 neurons corresponding to the input data. The number of neurons for each layer is got by trail and error method. The network is created using,

Net = newff ([73, 15, 5], {'tansig', 'tansig', 'tansig'}, 'traingd');

The following table describes the performance for some different combination of the neurons tried.

Table 2. Selection of Neurons in each layer

S.No	No of Neurons	Performance goal	Epochs
1.	41, 20, 10, 5	0.0259	3825
2.	41, 25, 10, 5	0.0408	6875
3.	41, 20, 15, 5	0.0501	7250
4.	41, 25, 25, 5	0.0234	8725
5.	41, 73, 17, 5	0.0001	417
6.	41, 73, 16, 5	0.0001	370
7.	41, 73, 14, 5	0.0001	282
8.	41, 73, 15, 5	0.0001	240

It is clear from this table that though a two layered network is successful in classifying the attack, the computation and classification performance is better in a three layered network. Thus it is obvious that the number of layers and the number of neurons play an important role in optimizing the performance. Thus the number of neurons is set as 73, 15 and 5.

4.3.2 Training the Network

The Network training is done with 10,000 records of KDD cup data set. Out of which nearly 4000 are normal packet, and remaining are attacks from all the four categories. The target is set in such a way that, the value for the corresponding unit alone is set to 1 and all other units are set to 0. The first output is fixed for normal, second for DOS, third for U2R, fourth for R2L and finally for probe. For example, the target for the normal packet is set to [1, 0, 0, 0, 0, 0], the target for DOS attack is set to [0, 1, 0, 0, 0, 0] and so on. We tried 9 learning algorithms as listed in table 3. and made a comparative study of these algorithms.

4.3.3 Testing the Network

For testing the network, 5000 records are used, with evenly distributed attacks and normal packet. The dataset used here is different from the records used for training. The testing is done using 'sim' command,

$$Obsveredtarget = sim(net,testinput);$$

The resulting observed target is matched with the desired output, and if match is found the packet has been correctly identified, if not falsely identified.

5 Results

5.1 Using Neural Network

The training and testing results of Neural Networks with different training functions is given in Table 3 and 4. The True Positives, True Negatives and False Alarms are shown.

Table 3. Training Phase performance using 10,000 results

S.No	TRAINING FUNCTION	NO OF EPOCHS	PERFORMANCE
1.	Traingd	6800	0.000475642
2.	Traingda	3703	0.000103014
3.	Triaingdm	5546	0.000102319
4.	Traingdx	6547	0.000101932
5.	Trainrp	42	9.95818e-005
6.	Trainscg	270	9.98748e-005
7.	Traincgf	129	9.86234e-005
8.	Traincgp	273	9.82378e-005
9.	Traincgb	512	9.83289e-005

(traingd – Steepest Descent, traingda-Steepest descent with adaptive learning rate, trainrp- Resilient back propagation, trainscg- scaled conjugate gradient algorithm, traincgf- Fletcher-Reeves Update)

Table 4. Testing Phase performance using 5,000 results

S.No	TRAINING FUNCTION	(TP)	(TN)	FA (FP+FN)	PERFORM-ANCE (%)
1.	Traingd	1871	1469	2562	57
2.	Traingda	1936	1820	2241	59
3.	Triaingdm	1948	1836	2178	58
4.	Traingdx	1643	1247	2379	53
5.	Trainrp	2511	1597	2162	76
6.	Traincgf	2758	1545	1245	84
7.	Trainscg	2823	1647	1028	86
8.	Traincgp	2340	2371	3249	84
9.	Traincgb	2438	1236	1237	82

(TP-True Positive, TN-True Negative, FA-False Alarm)

5.2   Using Genetic Algorithm with Neural Networks

The Classification results of using Genetic Algorithm are shown in Table 5. for every attack class the optimal subset of features are selected by the Genetic algorithms and the classification accuracy has been increased since the number of epochs for classification has been reduced to acceptable levels. For ip sweep attack the number of epochs has been reduced from 389 to 248 and the features required for effective classification has been reduced from 41 to 17 and the reduction in percentage of epochs for effective classification is exactly half.

Table 5. Classification Performance using different input classes

S.No	Feature	Number of epochs with reduced feature set	Number of epochs with whole feature set	No. of Reduced Features	Reduced Percentage (%)
1.	Normal	134	523	16	75
2.	Neptune	150	346	10	57
3.	Smurf	161	457	11	65
4.	Back	165	245	10	63
5.	Teardrop	155	457	14	67
6.	Pod	170	423	13	78
7.	Land	169	354	14	53
8.	Buffer_ Overflow	213	259	12	64
9.	Loadmodule	296	344	10	61
10.	perl	282	497	17	53
11.	rootkit	314	581	19	55
12.	Ftp_Write	277	467	15	69
13.	Guess_passwd	310	519	18	49
14.	imap	357	623	16	43
15.	multihop	264	487	11	46
16.	phf	340	412	15	51
17.	spy	327	623	17	57
18.	warezclient	280	512	20	63
19.	Warezmaster	247	502	16	58
20.	nmap	296	497	13	49
21.	Portsweep	331	524	14	52
22.	satan	317	575	13	65
23.	ipsweep	248	389	17	50

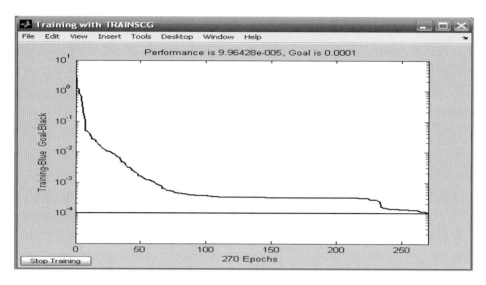

Fig. 2. Training with 'scg' function without feature selection

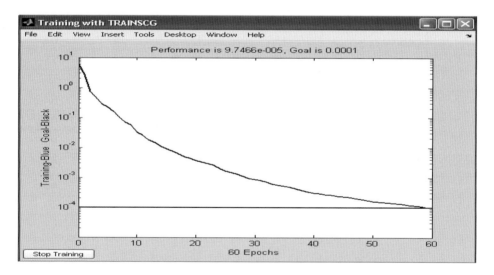

Fig. 3. Training with 'scg' function with feature selection

6 Conclusion

This paper presents the application of multi layer feed forward network for learning previously observed behaviour in order to detect future intrusions against the systems. The results show the viability of this approach for detecting intrusions. It should be mentioned that the long training time of the neural network was mostly due to the huge number of training vectors. However, when the neural network parameters were determined by training, classification of a single record was done in a negligible time. Therefore the neural network based Intrusion Detection system can operate as an online classifier for the attack types that it has been trained for. The results show that the classification is better and computationally memory efficient with a three layered feed forward network. A new approach for selecting best discriminated features subset using genetic algorithms is presented. The goal is to select the best combination that is sufficient to perform a good classification and obtain acceptable rates. This task can not be realized with any iterative or exhaustive approach, so we have use an evolutionary genetic algorithm to explore the huge space of all possible features subsets. To drive this search process correctly to the best solution, a new measure of subset quality is proposed and used as fitness function. In this paper, a feature relevance analysis is performed on KDD 99 training set, which is widely used by machine learning researchers. Feature relevance is expressed in terms of information gain, which gets higher as the feature gets more discriminative. In order to get feature relevance measure for all classes in training set, information gain is calculated on binary classification, for each feature resulting in a separate information gain per class.

References

1. Yang, J., Honavar, V.: Feature subset selection using a genetic algorithm. IEEE Intelligent Systems 13, 44–49 (1998)
2. Raymer, M.L., Punch, W.F., Goodman, E.D., Kuhn, L.A., Jain, A.K.: Dimensionality reduction using genetic algorithms. IEEE Transactions on Evolutionary Computation 4, 164–171 (2000)
3. Faraoun, K.M., Rabhi, A.: Data dimensionality reduction based on genetic selection of feature subsets (2007)
4. Chebrolu, S., Abraham, A., Thomas, J.P.: Feature Deduction and Ensemble Design of Intrusion Detection System. Computer & Security 24(4), 295–307 (2005)
5. Goyal, A., Kumar, C.: GA-NIDS: A Genetic Algorithm based Network Intrusion Detection System. Northwestern university
6. Ghosh, A., Schwartzbard: A study in using neural networks for anomaly and misuse Detection. In: 8th USENIX Security Symposium, pp. 141–151 (1999)
7. Diaz-Gome, P.A., Hougen, D.F.: Improved off-line intrusion detection using a genetic algorithm. In: Proceedings of the Seventh International Conference on Enterprise Information Systems, Miami, USA (2005)
8. Sung, A.H., Mukkamala, S.: Identifying important features for intrusion detection using support vector machines and neural networks. In: Proceedings of International Symposium on Applications and the Internet (SAINT 2003), pp. 209–17 (2003)
9. Mukkamala, S., Sung, A.H., Abraham, A.: Intrusion Detection Using an Ensemble of Intelligent Paradigms. Journal of network and computer applications 28(2), 167–182 (2005)
10. Bobor, V.: Efficient Intrusion Detection System Architecture Based on Neural Networks and Genetic Algorithms, Department of Computer and Systems Sciences, Stockholm University / Royal Institute of Technology, KTH/DSV (2006)

11. Li, W.: Using Genetic Algorithm for Network Intrusion Detection. In: Proceedings of the United States Department of Energy Cyber Security Group 2004 Training Conference, Kansas City, Kansas, USA, May 24-27 (2004)
12. Güneş Kayacık, H., Nur Zincir-Heywood, A.: Heywood, M.I.: A Feature Relevance Analysis on KDD 99 Intrusion Detection Datasets
13. Srinivas, M., Sung Andrew, H., Ajith, A.: Intrusion detection using ensemble of soft computing paradigms. In: Third international conference on Intelligent systems design and applications. Advances in soft computing, pp. 239–248. Springer, Germany (2003)

An Algorithm for Designing Controllers

Sankalp Bagaria

Centre for Development of Advanced Computing, Mumbai, India
Sankalp@cdacmumbai.in

Abstract. In control engineering, any system that takes some input signals, processes it and gives output signals, e.g. an electrical transformer, a mechanical lever, a car's hydraulic brake system, a country's economy, population of a country etc., can be treated like a black – box plant. Any given plant should be stable and also should perform well in terms of speed, accuracy and other properties. If it does not behave so, another system called controller is designed which is used in conjunction with the plant. In this paper, we propose an alternative, easy-to-use algebraic method to find the transfer function of the controller with better accuracy than graphical methods like root locus and bode plot. Our algorithm has complexity O(n^3).

Keywords: Plan; Controller; Transfer function; Design; Algorithm.

1 Introduction

A system can be electrical, mechanical, chemical, fluid, financial, biological etc. The mathematical modeling of the system, its analysis and the controller design is done using control theory in the time, complex – s or frequency domain depending on the nature of the control design problem. Control Theory is an interdisciplinary branch of engineering and mathematics. It deals with the behavior of dynamical systems. The desired output of system is called the reference. When one or more output variables of a system need to follow a certain reference over time, a controller manipulates the inputs to the system to obtain the desired effect on the output of the system.

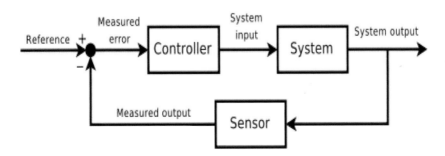

Fig. 1. A Typical Control System

N. Meghanathan et al. (Eds.): NeCoM, WiMoN, and WeST 2010, CCIS 90, pp. 235–242, 2010.

Take a fan for an example. The regulator (controller) controls the voltage sent to the motor of the fan (system). If the voltage is high, the fan has higher speed. It is an example of open – loop system. Now, take an air – conditioner. A thermometer (sensor) measures the temperature of the room and this data is used to control the time for which the cooling system is on so that the temperature desired (reference) is maintained. It is an example of on – off controller. If the difference between the reference temperature and the actual temperature is greater than zero, AC is switched on and otherwise, it is switched off.

2   Control System Design Problem

The output of the system y(t) is fed back through a sensor measurement F to the reference value r(t). The controller C then takes the error e (difference) between the reference and the output to change the inputs u to the system under control P. This is shown in the figure. This kind of controller is a closed-loop controller or feedback controller.

This is called a single-input-single-output (SISO) control system; MIMO (i.e. Multi-Input-Multi-Output) systems, with more than one input/output, are also used.

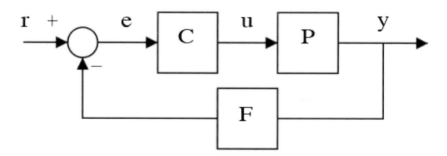

Fig. 2. Feedback Control System

If we assume the controller C, the plant P and the sensor F are linear and time-invariant (i.e.: elements of their transfer function C(s), P(s), and F(s) do not depend on time), the systems above can be analysed using Laplace transform on the variables. This gives the following relations:

$$Y(s) = P(s)U(s)$$
$$U(s) = C(s)E(s)$$
$$E(s) = R(s) - F(s)Y(s).$$

Solving for Y(s) in terms of R(s) gives:

$$Y(s) = \left(\frac{P(s)C(s)}{1 + F(s)P(s)C(s)} \right) R(s) = H(s)R(s).$$

The expression $H(s) = \dfrac{P(s)C(s)}{1 + F(s)P(s)C(s)}$ is referred to as the closed-loop transfer function of the system. The numerator is the forward (open-loop) gain from r to y, and the denominator is one plus the gain in going around the feedback loop, the so-called loop gain. If $|P(s)C(s)| \gg 1$, i.e. it has a large norm with each value of s, and if $|F(s)| \approx 1$, then Y(s) is approximately equal to R(s). This means simply setting the reference controls the output.

Most of the systems in our world, ranging from a simple lever to PID controllers in industry, can be modeled as LTIL systems. Usually such a system is expressed as a differential equation in time domain (an equation relating input and output) and is converted to an algebraic equation in s – domain using Laplace. The output is studied for knowing about system's stability, its rise time, settling time ie, how fast or slow is the response of the system to change in input. The sensitivity of the system to the disturbances and the noise is studied. If the system's response is not satisfactory, a controller is designed. Its Laplace equation is found and then used to make the system.

3 Guidelines for Designing a Stable, Useful System

Time domain specifications:

1. Peak overshoot < 10 %
2. Settling time < 5 seconds
3. Rise time a small as possible
4. Steady state error < 10 %

Frequency domain specifications:

1. Bandwidth < 10 krad/sec
2. Gain margin > 20 decibels
3. Phase margin > 45 degrees

4 Some Heuristics for Designing the Closed-Loop Transfer Function

1. For a system to be stable, all the poles of its transfer function should be in the left half of the s-plane ie, their real part should be negative.
2. Settling time is approximately 4.5 * time – constant
3. Poles nearer to the real line cause lesser overshoot but the system becomes sluggish.
4. A system should not only be absolutely stable but relatively stable too so that it is robust and should tolerate noise, disturbances and perturbations.

5 Design Problem

Let the denominator of the closed loop transfer function calculated above be ø(s). Also, let the transfer function of the plant P(s) be Np/Dp and that of the controller C(s) be Nc/Dc.

Closed - loop transfer function is then

$$\frac{\dfrac{Nc\ Np}{Dc\ Dp}}{1 + \dfrac{Nc\ Np}{Dc\ Dp}} \qquad = \qquad \frac{Nc\ Np}{NcNp + DpDc}$$

Now, we have the transfer function Np/Dp of the plant and the closed – loop transfer function. We have to find suitable Nc & Dc, such that NpNc + DpDc = ø(s).

6 Algorithm for Computing Controllers for SISO System

1. Compute the desired characteristic polynomial ø(s). Degree of ø(s) must not be less than that of Np & Dp.
2. Choose degree of Nc & Dc such that it is the difference of the degrees of ø(s) and the larger of the degrees of polynomials Np and Dp.
3. Assign arbitrary variables to the unknown coefficients of polynomials Nc & Dc.
4. Equate the coefficients of various terms of NpNc + DpDc & ø(s) and form the equations in the variables representing the coefficients of Nc, Dc.
5. Solve the equations of step 4 for the unknown coefficients of Nc, Dc. If there are too many equations, Gaussian elimination method maybe used.
6. Thus the values of the coefficients of Nc, Dc will be obtained, given the desired characteristic polynomial ø(s). If the equations could not be solved for any value of the variables, the desired characteristic polynomial will have to be changed by increasing its degree (adding a single pole or a pair of conjugate poles to closed – loop transfer function) and the steps be repeated from step 2.

Examples:

1. Np=1   Nc = a

   Dp=s-1   Dc = b

   Ø=s+10   (Pole at s = -10)

   1*a + (s-1)*b = s+10

   s:b=1

   const : -b+a=10 => a=11

   Nc = 11

   Dc

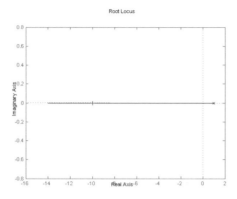

Fig. 3.

The figure 3 is the root locus of example 1. It shows how a compensator gain of 11 in a feedback system will place the pole of the overall transfer function at -10.

2. $Np = 2$ $Nc = as + b$

$Dp = s-1$ $Dc = cs + d$

$\emptyset = s2 + 2s + 1$ [Poles at s = -1, -1]

$2(as + b) + (s - 1)(cs + d) = s2 + 2s + 1$

$=> s2 : c = 1$

$\quad s1 : 2a + d - c = 2 => 2a + d = 3$

$\quad$ const: $2b - d = 1$ $=> 2b - d = 1$

Choosing d as the parameter,

$a = \dfrac{3-d}{2}$

$b = \dfrac{1+d}{2}$

$c = 1$

$d = d$

One possible choice is $(d = 2)$

$\dfrac{0.5s + 1.5}{s+1} = \dfrac{s + 3}{2(s+2)}$

The figure 4 shows root locus of the example 2. It shows how a constant gain compensator for the above example can never yield two poles in the desired transfer function of the overall system. So, we add a first – order compensator (degree of the rational function of the compensator being 1) to the system and get the root locus shown in figure 5. We then get the desired pole – zero configuration as shown in the figure.

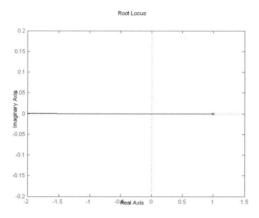

Fig. 4.

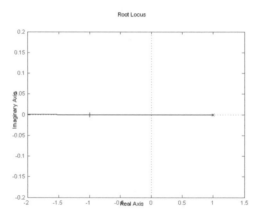

Fig. 5.

3.   Np = s+2

   Dp = s2 + s + 4

   Desired poles: -2,-3 ± 3i

   Ø = (s+2)(s2+6s+18)

     = s3 + 8s2 + 30s + 36

   (as + b)(s + 2) + (cs + d)(s2 + s + 4)

         = s3 + 8s2 + 30s + 36

   s 3 : c = 1

   s 2 : a + d + c = 8   => a + d = 7

   s1: 2a + b + 4c + d = 30   => 2a + b + d = 26

   const.: 2b + 4d = 36   => b + 2d = 18

Substituting a = 7-d and b – 18-2d into 2a + b + d = 26, we get

2(7 – d) + (18 – 2d) + d = 26

⇨   14 – 2d + 18 – 2d + d = 26

⇨   -3d = -32 + 26 = -6

⇨   d = 2.

=> a = 7 – d = 5

   b = 18 – 2d = 14

Nc = 5s+14

Dc   s+2

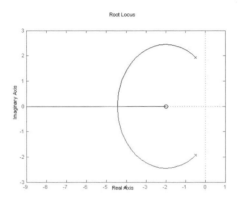

Fig. 6.

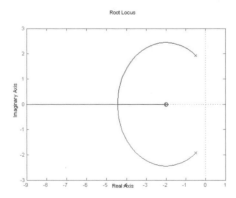

Fig. 7.

The figure 6 is the root locus of the example 3. It shows how a two – pole plant cannot give three desired poles. So, we add a first – order compensator and use our algorithm to find the coefficients of the compensator. The root locus (figure 7) is then drawn again to show how the desired pole – zero configuration is achieved. If the number of poles in the transfer function of the desired over-all system is greater than two, we can add more number of poles and zeroes in our compensator to yield the desired transfer function.

7 Conclusions

If n is the degree of the characteristic polynomial, the complexity of this algorithm is $O(n^3)$ as Gausian elimination is used to solve the equations in step 5. This control system algorithm has been verified by comparing designs with root locus drawn using MATLAB. Further restrictions on the coefficients of controller transfer function can be integrated with this procedure to get even better suited controllers. We described the procedure for signals continuous in time and used Laplace transform to convert from time – domain to complex-s domain. As can be easily seen, the method hold for systems involving discrete – time signals, which can be mapped to complex – z domain using z – transform and the controller can be designed accordingly. As further work, this method can be extended to MIMO (Multiple Input, Multiple Output) systems by converting state space design to transfer function based pole placement design and then obtaining the coefficients of the controller matrix by the above method.

References

1. Cormen, T., Leiserson, C., Rivest, R.: Introduction to Algorithms
2. Tsang, C.: Linear system theory and design
3. Dorf, R., Bishop, R.: Modern Control Systems
4. The online encyclopedia: Wikipedia

Decision Support with RFID for Health Care

Yannick Meiller[1,2], Sylvain Bureau[1,2], Wei Zhou[1,2], and Selwyn Piramuthu[2,3]

[1] Information Technologies & Modeling, ESCP Europe, Paris, France
[2] RFID European Lab, Paris, France
[3] Information Systems and Operations Management, University of Florida, USA
{yannick.meiller,sylvain.bureau,wzhou}@escpeurope.eu,
selwyn@ufl.edu

Abstract. The health care environment is rife with issues that are urgently in need of solutions that can readily be addressed using appropriate tools for decision support. Recent developments in RFID technology facilitate this process through continuous provision of instantaneous item-level information. We consider an existing decision support framework and instantiate this framework using an example from the health care domain using RFID-generated item-level information. We illustrate the process by developing a health care knowledge-based system and evaluate its performance.

Keywords: RFID, Health Care, DSS.

1 Introduction

Systems for decision support as well as automation have been used in the health care domain for several decades. However, even if the underlying work flow and processes in general may seem similar to those in other domains, the general health care environment is characterized by somewhat different perspectives due to invaluable human lives that are directly at stake. For example the health care environment typically has a higher than average safety factor, high tolerance for longer payback period on investments, and an overall conservative approach. Simultaneously, researchers and practitioners are continually searching for improvements in process efficiency while safely and uncompromisingly delivering health care services. While it is difficult to achieve dramatic improvements in efficiency in the delivery of health care processes, it is possible to provide appreciable improvements in several scenarios that when put together results in the overall improvement of the health care delivery process in terms of patient outcome, efficiency, accuracy, and cost.

RFID tags are increasingly being used in the health care environment with varying levels of success (e.g., Tu et al., 2009, Meiller et al., 2010). For example, tagging pharmaceutical items to prevent counterfeiting as well as tagging items in a hospital environment for inventory purposes have been fairly successful. However, certain RFID applications have faced resistance in a hospital setting where their electromagnetic interference could affect normal operation of medical instruments (e.g., Ashar and Ferriter, 2007; Seidmann et al., 2010; Togt et al., 2008). Nevertheless,

N. Meghanathan et al. (Eds.): NeCoM, WiMoN, and WeST 2010, CCIS 90, pp. 243–249, 2010.

in spite of some issues, there is a large potential for RFID applications in health care organizations.

We consider a scenario from the context of health care delivery in France that lends itself to improvements in efficiency and effectiveness (Meiller and Bureau, 2009). This scenario relates to the sharing of ancillaries used in prosthesis implantation and extraction among hospitals. We modify and instantiate an adaptive knowledge-based system framework to this scenario and study the dynamics. We utilize a framework (Piramuthu and Shaw, 2009) that has been successfully instantiated in disparate domains including intelligent tutoring systems, machine scheduling, automated supply chain configuration, CRM, among others.

The remainder of this paper is organized as follows: in Section 2, we provide a brief introduction to the scenario considered. In Section 3, we introduce the modified adaptive knowledge-based system framework adapted to the scenario considered. We also illustrate the instantiation of this modified framework to the health care scenario of interest. We conclude the paper with a brief discussion in Section 4.

2   The Scenario

We discuss the scenario of interest in this section. Specifically, we consider ancillaries that require tracking. The ancillaries of interest here are those that are used in the implantation and extraction of prosthesis in humans. Each of these ancillaries is designed to be used only with a specific brand, model, and type (e.g., hip, knee) of prosthesis. I.e., hip prostheses from two different brands or even models are sufficiently different that they are not interchangeable. This level of specialization has its related consequence of high unit cost and the sheer number of different ancillaries translates to reduced frequency of use for each ancillary. Given its infrequent use and the large number of available ancillaries, buying every (or, even a large number of) available ancillary is an expensive proposition both in terms of the cost of acquisition and the resources (e.g., storage, maintenance, accounting) that are necessary for their proper maintenance and use. This has led to the prostheses providers renting ancillaries to hospitals that use their corresponding prosthetic part. Renting naturally signifies the movement of these ancillaries among different hospitals throughout their lifetime.

This movement of ancillaries necessitates some means to keep track of their instantaneous location as well as history. This has to be done on each individual ancillary in the system. This scenario naturally lends itself to automation through an appropriate knowledge-based system with learning capability.

3   Adaptive Knowledge-Based System Framework

The adaptive knowledge-based framework (Piramuthu and Shaw, 2009) we consider (Figure 1) has been fairly successfully instantiated in disparate domains. We extend this existing stream by modifying and instantiating the adaptive knowledge-based learning system framework for the scenario under consideration. This adaptive framework comprises four primary components including Simulation, Learning,

Problem-Solving, and Performance-evaluation. Given that this is a knowledge-based system, the Learning component is used to generate the knowledge-base which forms the core of this system. Without appropriate and necessary knowledge, this system will not be able to perform intelligently. The Problem Solving component comprises the Knowledge-base and the Problem-solver. The knowledge-base contains learned knowledge on the domain of interest. The Problem-solver uses the knowledge-base and an instantaneous snap-shot of the environment to generate the most appropriate decision. A common characteristic of a knowledge-base in any dynamic environment is its tendency to become stale sooner or later. This can be addressed through consorted effort by the other three (i.e., Learning, Simulation, and Performance-evaluation) components.

The Performance-evaluation component constantly keeps track of the performance of the system. When it determines that the adaptive knowledge-based system is beginning to perform below par, it generates the specifications for new training examples and the Simulation component generates appropriate training examples based on these specifications. The training examples thus generated are input to the Learning component, which incrementally learns new knowledge and accordingly updates the knowledge-base.

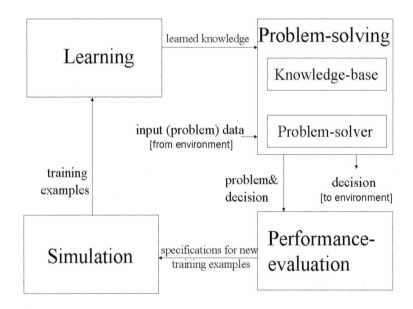

Fig. 1. Adaptive DSS framework

We modify this adaptive knowledge-based system framework for our purposes. The result of such modification to accommodate RFID-embedded systems in a health care environment is given in Figure 2. In this framework, the Learning component performs a similar function as the Learning component in the framework given in Figure 1. The Measurement and Evaluation components perform a similar function as the Performance-evaluation component in Figure 1. The knowledge base in the modified framework comprises four sub-components to accommodate the different functionalities that are required of the system including delivery routing and frequency, patterns of local demand and service provisions. The remainder of the components and sub-components in Figure 2 perform the functionalities of the Problem-solving component in Figure 1.

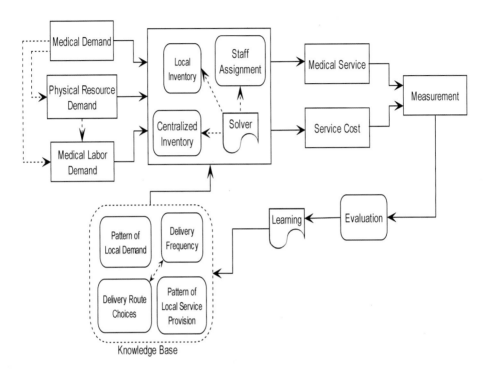

Fig. 2. RFID enabled Adaptive Learning framework for Health Care

The exogenous factors include the actual medical requirements that further become the demand on both physical and medical labor resources. With these inputs, the problem solver determines the appropriate local and centralized inventory, and effective assignment of staff in charge of inventory management. After a medical service is performed, both service quality and associated cost are determined and evaluated. Based on evaluation, associated benchmarks, and the extent of possible potential improvements, appropriate remedial measures are recommended and implemented.

3.1   Modified Adaptive Knowledge-Based Framework for Tracking Ancillaries

We model four hospitals in this scenario. All ancillaries are RFID tagged, and provide instantaneous information when needed. We consider both centralized and decentralized decision making scenarios. A schematic of the modeled scenario for the decentralized case is given in Figure 3. The scenario is operationalized as follows:

The ancillary provider has the option of either providing a centralized coordination mechanism whereby a hospital that needs an ancillary orders and receives the same from the central location. Once used, the ancillary is then returned to the central location by the hospital. The hospital pays rental fee on the ancillary to the ancillary provider for each day it has the ancillary in its possession. The other option modeled here is the decentralized case where the hospital pays the ancillary provider 100% of the daily rental charge only for the days in which it uses the ancillary. When no longer needed, the ancillary is transferred directly from this hospital to another hospital that has a need for this ancillary. The hospital in possession of the ancillary, in a sense, acts as its temporary repository when it's not in use. Moreover, the hospital pays a deeply discounted rental amount for the days it is in possession of an ancillary and the ancillary is not used. Here, each of the hospitals has its own local inventory of the ancillaries that it recently used until the next demand for this item is realized. This is beneficial for the hospital since it avoids the round-trip time (in the centralized case) and local inventory is beneficial in emergency circumstances.

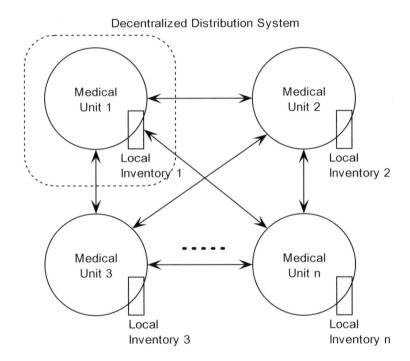

Fig. 3. Schematic of the modeled scenario for tracking ancillaries

We model these two (centralized and decentralized) cases and illustrate the proposed framework using simulation. We simulated the system for 365 days after a warm-up period of seven days, and the results are provided in Tables 1. The proposed framework was used to model both centralized and decentralized cases. To keep the model simple and yet be able to convey the gist of the scenario, we consider two identical ancillaries to be shared among four hospitals We modeled the rental cost in normalized form where all ancillaries cost the same for a day's rental (of 1 currency unit) when it is used and the rental charge is a small fraction of this amount for the days in which the ancillary is not used but is physically present at the hospital. This fraction is listed under the "Relative Cost" column in Table 1. The "Overall Cost" column lists the cumulative cost incurred by the hospital and it includes the deeply discounted rental charges for the decentralized case. The "# Items" column lists the number of ancillaries that were delivered to the requesting hospital. The "Cost/Item" column lists the unit cost of ancillaries that were delivered and used by the hospital. The "# Balked" column lists the number of hospital requests that went unfulfilled.

Table 1. Results for the centralized and decentralized scenarios

	Relative cost	Overall Cost	# items	Cost/item	# Balked
centralized	N/A	158	122	1.295	46
decentralized	0.005	165.595	154	1.075	9
decentralized	0.01	166.19	154	1.079	9
decentralized	0.02	167.38	154	1.087	9
decentralized	0.1	176.9	154	1.149	9
decentralized	0.2	188.8	154	1.226	9
decentralized	0.3	200.7	154	1.303	9

As can be seen in Table 1, the number of requests from hospitals that were not fulfilled is more in the centralized case. This is primarily due to the fact that in the centralized case, the round trip for an ancillary from a hospital to the central coordinating center and then to another hospital takes time. The other distinguishing characteristic of the decentralized case is in the cost/item, which is lower than a similar centralized case for low levels of the discounted rent value. With the parameter settings used in this study, the relative cost (i.e., discounted rental value) is about a third of the regular rental rate for the cost/item to be similar in both (centralized and decentralized) the cases. I.e., the ancillary provider can afford to charge a third of the regular rental price for days on which the ancillary is not used and still come even with cost. Note that we are ignoring the higher transportation cost in the centralized case (vs. the decentralized case for similar demand dynamics) because of the round-trips involved (vs. the one-way trip in the decentralized case). We are also ignoring inventory storage cost in the centralized case, and it is taken care of by the deeply discounted rent in the decentralized case. Including these would make the case for decentralized even stronger.

4 Discussion

We considered an existing adaptive knowledge-based decision support system framework and instantiated it to accommodate a scenario in the health care domain. Specifically, we considered the scenario where ancillaries are shared among multiple hospitals. RFID tags have begun to permeate a wide variety of application areas. Health care applications, where there is a need to accurately track and trace individual items at any point in time as situations dictate, and RFID tags are in a sense complementary to each other and can be synergistically used to improve performance. We showed that the proposed modified framework results in automating the processes involved. Moreover, we illustrated means to develop an adaptive knowledge-based system for health care applications.

References

1. Ashar, B.S., Ferriter, A.: Radiofrequency Identification Technology in Health Care: Benefits and Potential Risks. JAMA 298, 2305–2307 (2007)
2. Meiller, Y., Bureau, S.: Logistics Projects: How to Assess the Right System? The Case of RFID Solutions in Health Care. In: Proceedings of the Americas Conference on Information Systems, AMCIS (2009)
3. Meiller, Y., Bureau, S., Zhou, W., Piramuthu, S.: Simulation of a Health Care Knowledge-based System with RFID-generated Information. In: Proceedings of the Asian Simulation Technology Conference (ASTEC 2010), Shanghai (2010)
4. Park, S.C., Piramuthu, S., Shaw, M.J.: Dynamic Rule Refinement in Knoweldge-based Data Mining Systems. Decision Support Systems 31, 205–222 (2001)
5. Piramuthu, S., Shaw, M.J.: Learning-Enhanced Adaptive DSS: A Design Science Persprctive. Information Technology & Management 10(1), 41–54 (2009)
6. Seidman, S.J., Brockman, R., Lewis, B.M., Guag, J., Shein, M.J., Clement, W.J., Kippols, J., Digby, D., Barber, C., Huntwork, D.: In vitro tests reveal sample radiofrequency identification readers inducing clinically significant electromagnetic interference to implantable pacemakers and implantable cardioverter-defibrillators. HeartRhythm 7(1), 99–107 (2010)
7. Togt, R.v.d., van Lieshout, E.J., Hensbroek, R., Beinat, E., Binnekade, J.M., Bakker, P.J.: Electromagnetic Interference from Radiofrequency Identification Inducing Potentially Hazardous Incidents in Critical Care Medical Equipment. JAMA 299, 2884–2890 (2008)
8. Tu, Y.-J., Zhou, W., Piramuthu, S.: Identifying RFID-embedded Objects in Pervasive Health Care Applications. Decision Support Systems 46, 586–593 (2009)
9. Zhou, W.: RFID and Item-Level Visibility. European Journal of Operational Research 198(1), 252–258 (2009)

An Algorithm to Determine Multicast Meshes with Maximum Lifetime for Mobile Ad Hoc Networks

Natarajan Meghanathan and Srilakshmi R. Vavilala

Jackson State University
Jackson, MS 39217, USA
{nmeghanathan,srilakshmi.r.vavilala}@jsums.edu

Abstract. We propose an algorithm called *OptMeshTrans* to determine a sequence of stable meshes that connect the source nodes and receiver nodes of a multicast session in Mobile Ad hoc Networks (MANETs). *OptMeshTrans* uses the following greedy strategy: Whenever a mesh connecting a set of source nodes to a set of receiver nodes is required, we choose the mesh, called the Stable-Static-Mesh, which exists for the longest time. In this pursuit, we determine a long-living minimum edge Steiner tree connecting the source nodes to the receiver nodes and the Stable-Static-Mesh is an extension of this Steiner tree by including in the mesh, all the edges that exist between the constituent nodes of the tree. When such a Stable-Static-Mesh gets disconnected, leading to the absence of a path from any source to any receiver node, we use the above greedy principle to construct another long-living mesh. The sequence of long-living Stable-Static-Meshes determined over the duration of the multicast session time is called a Stable-Mobile-Mesh. The lifetime of the meshes determined using algorithm *OptMeshTrans* forms the benchmark for maximum mesh lifetime in multicast routing. Simulation results indicate that the lifetime of the meshes determined using the classical mesh-based On-Demand Multicast Routing Protocol (ODMRP) is significantly lower than the optimal lifetime of the stable meshes determined using *OptMeshTrans*.

Keywords: Mesh, Multicast Routing, Optimality, Stability, Simulation.

1 Introduction

A mobile ad hoc network (MANET) is an autonomous, dynamic distributed system of mobile nodes connected through wireless links. The wireless nodes have limited battery charge and operate with limited transmission range. Hence, routes in MANETs are mostly multi-hop in nature, with a node, apart from being a source or receiver, also routing packets for other nodes in the network. Multicasting has emerged as a desirable and essential technology for several distributed applications in wireless networks such as audio/ video conferencing, distance learning, collaborative and groupware applications and etc. The mobility of nodes, with the constraints of limited battery charge and bandwidth, makes multicast routing a very challenging problem in MANETs [1]. It is advantageous to use multicast rather than multiple unicast, especially in ad hoc environments, where bandwidth comes at a premium. MANET multicast routing protocols can be classified into two types based on the multicast topology [1]: *tree-based* and *mesh-based*. In tree-based protocols, there

N. Meghanathan et al. (Eds.): NeCoM, WiMoN, and WeST 2010, CCIS 90, pp. 250–259, 2010.
© Springer-Verlag Berlin Heidelberg 2010

exists only a single path between a source-receiver pair, whereas in mesh-based protocols there are multiple paths between a source-receiver pair. The presence of multiple paths adds to the robustness of the mesh-based protocols at the cost of multicast efficiency. We focus on mesh-based multicast protocols in this paper.

In this paper, we propose an algorithm called *OptMeshTrans* to determine a sequence of long-living stable multicast meshes connecting a set of source nodes to a set of receiver nodes for MANETs. The *OptMeshTrans* algorithm uses the following greedy strategy: Whenever a mesh connecting a set of source nodes to a set of receiver nodes is required, we choose the mesh, called the Stable-Static-Mesh, which exists for the longest time. In this pursuit, we determine a long-living minimum edge Steiner tree connecting the source nodes to the receiver nodes and the Stable-Static-Mesh is an extension of this Steiner tree by including in the mesh, all the edges that exist between the constituent nodes of the tree. We use the Kou et al.'s heuristic [2] (refer section 2) to approximate a multicast Steiner tree connecting the set of source nodes to the set of receiver nodes using the minimum number of links. When such a Stable-Static-Mesh gets disconnected, leading to the absence of a path from any source to any receiver node, we use the above greedy principle to construct another long-living mesh. The sequence of long-living Stable-Static-Meshes determined over the sequence of the multicast session time is called a Stable-Mobile-Mesh.

The lifetime of the stable meshes determined using algorithm *OptMeshTrans* forms the benchmark for the optimum (maximum) mesh lifetime that is obtainable in a given network. We conduct extensive simulations of algorithm *OptMeshTrans* and the classical mesh-based On-Demand Multicast Routing Protocol (ODMRP) [3] and compare their performance with respect to mesh lifetime, number of edges per mesh and the hop count per source-receiver path. ODMRP basically determines minimum hop paths between every source-receiver pair and the congregate of such minimum hop paths by including the edges that exist between the forwarding nodes of the paths forms the multicast mesh. Simulation results indicate a tradeoff between {mesh lifetime and number of edges per mesh} vs. {hop count per source-receiver path}. The meshes determined using algorithm *OptMeshTrans* have longer lifetime and relatively fewer edges, but have a larger hop count per source-receiver path compared to the meshes discovered using ODMRP.

The rest of the paper is organized as follows: Section 2 describes algorithm *OptMeshTrans* in detail, analyzes its complexity and also provides proof of correctness. Section 3 presents and analyzes the simulation performance results comparing *OptMeshTrans* with ODMRP. Section 4 concludes the paper. Throughout the paper, the terms 'link' and 'edge', 'node' and 'vertex' are used interchangeably.

2   Algorithm to Determine Stable-Mobile-Mesh

We model an ad hoc network as a unit disk graph [4] $G = (V, E)$, wherein V is the set of vertices representing the wireless nodes and E is the set of undirected edges representing the wireless links. An edge exists between two vertices if the corresponding nodes are within the transmission range of each other. Let S be the set of source nodes and R be the set of receiver nodes. The multicast group is represented as set $SR = S \cup R$, i.e., the union of the set of source nodes and receiver nodes. Algorithm *OptMeshTrans* uses the notion of a mobile graph [5] to represent the sequence of network topology changes.

A *mobile graph* [5] is defined as the sequence $G_M = G_1G_2 \ldots G_T$ of static graphs representing network topology changes over a time scale T. In the simplest case, the mobile graph $G_M = G_1G_2 \ldots G_T$ can be extended by a new instantaneous graph G_{T+1} to a longer sequence $G_M = G_1G_2 \ldots G_T G_{T+1}$, where G_{T+1} captures a link change (either a link comes up or goes down). We sample the network topology periodically for every 0.25 seconds, which could be the instants of data packet origination at the source.

We use the Kou et al's [2] well-known $O(|V||SR|^2)$ heuristic (|V| is the number of nodes in the network graph and |SR| is the size of the multicast group comprising of the source nodes and the receiver nodes) to approximate the minimum edge Steiner tree in graphs representing snapshots of the network topology. An *(S-R)-Steiner-tree* is defined as the multicast Steiner tree connecting the set of source nodes, S, to the set of receiver nodes, R. We give a brief outline of the heuristic in Figure 1.

Input: An undirected graph $G = (V, E)$
        Multicast group $SR \subseteq V$
Output: An *(S-R)-Steiner-tree* for the set SR in G

Step 1: Construct a complete undirected weighted graph $G_C = (SR, E_C)$ from G and SR where $\forall (v_i, v_j) \in E_C$, v_i and v_j are in SR, and the weight of edge (v_i, v_j) is the length of the shortest path from v_i to v_j in G.
Step 2: Find the minimum weight spanning tree T_C in G_C (If more than one minimal spanning tree exists, pick an arbitrary one).
Step 3: Construct the sub graph G_{SR} of G, by replacing each edge in T_C with the corresponding shortest path from G (If there is more than one shortest path between two given vertices, pick an arbitrary one).
Step 4: Find the minimal spanning tree T_{SR} in G_{SR} (If more than one minimal spanning tree exists, pick an arbitrary one). Note that each edge in G_{SR} has weight 1.
Step 5: Construct the *(S-R)-Steiner-tree*, from T_{SR} by deleting the edges in T_{SR}, if necessary, such that all the leaves in the *(S-R)-Steiner-tree* are members of SR.

Fig. 1. Kou et al's Heuristic [2] to find an Approx. Minimum Edge Steiner Tree

2.1   Description of Algorithm *OptMeshTrans*

We now describe the *OptMeshTrans* algorithm proposed to determine the sequence of multicast meshes connecting a set of sources (S) to a set of receivers (R), such that the meshes exist for the longest possible time and the number of mesh transitions is minimal. The pseudo code is given in Figure 2. Algorithm *OptMeshTrans* operates according to the following greedy strategy: Whenever a multicast mesh connecting all the source nodes (S) to all the receiver nodes (R) of a multicast group is required, the multicast mesh, called the Stable-Static-Mesh, represented as $(S\text{-}R)_{Stable\text{-}Static\text{-}Mesh}$, which exists for the longest time is selected.

A mobile graph $G_M = G_1G_2 \ldots G_T$ is generated by sampling the network topology at regular time intervals $t_1, t_2 \ldots t_T$. At time instant t_i, when a multicast mesh is required, a mobile sub graph $G(i, j) = G_i \cap G_{i+1} \cap \ldots \cap G_j$ is constructed such that there exists at least one mesh connecting every source $s \in S$ to every receiver $r \in R$ in $G(i, j)$ and no mesh exists in $G(i, j+1)$. A minimum edge *(S-R)-Steiner-tree* connecting every source s ($\in S$) to every receiver r ($\in R$) is constructed based on the Kou's heuristic and the Steiner tree is extended to a mesh by including all the edges (represented by the set *Additional-Edges* in the pseudo code, Figure 2) that exist between the constituent nodes of the tree in the mobile sub graph $G(i, j)$. The above procedure is repeated until time instant $j+1 \leq T$, where T is the duration of the multicast session. The Stable-Mobile-Mesh, represented as *(S-R)*$_{Stable-Mobile-Mesh}$, is a sequence of such maximum lifetime Stable-Static-Meshes and will undergo the minimum number of mesh transitions (i.e., mesh changes).

If T is the duration of the multicast session and k is the sampling rate (k samples of static graphs collected per unit time) used to form the mobile graph, the Kou et al.'s heuristic has to be run $T*k$ times, each time on a graph of $|V|$ nodes. During each such iteration, we will also have to form the set of *Additional-Edges* to extend the minimum edge Steiner tree to a multicast mesh. At the worst case, there would be $O(|V|)$ vertices in the minimum edge Steiner tree and it would take $O(|V|^2)$ time to determine whether an edge between every pair of vertices in the Steiner tree exists in the mobile sub graph for inclusion in the set of *Additional-Edges*. Hence, the run-time complexity of *OptMeshTrans* would be $O((|V||SR|^2 + |V|^2) T*k)$, where SR is the union of the set of sources and receivers of the multicast group.

Input: $G_M = G_1 G_2 ..... G_T$, Set of source nodes - S, Set of receiver nodes - R
Output: *(S-R)*$_{Stable-Mobile-Mesh}$ // Stable-Mobile-Mesh
Auxiliary Variables: i, j, *Additional-Edges*
Initialization: $i=1$; $j=1$; *(S-R)*$_{Stable-Mobile-Mesh}$ = ϕ, *Additional-Edges* = ϕ
Begin *OptMeshTrans*

1. **while** *(i<= T)* **do**
2.   Find a mobile sub graph $G(i, j) = G_i \cap G_{i+1} \cap ... \cap G_j$ such that there exists at least one *(S-R)-Steiner-tree* connecting every source $s \in S$ to every receiver $r \in R$ in $G(i, j)$ and {no such *(S-R)-Steiner-tree* exists in $G(i, j+1)$ or $j = T$}
3.   **if** $\exists$ a *(S-R)-Steiner-tree* in $G(i, j)$ **then**
4.   **for** (every vertex u and v in *(S-R)-Steiner-tree*)
5.   **if** (edge $(u, v) \in G(i, j)$ and edge $(u, v) \notin$ *(S-R)-Steiner-tree*) **then**
6.   *Additional-Edges = Additional-Edges* U $\{(u, v)\}$
7.   **end if**
8.   **end for**
9.   *(S-R)*$_{Stable-Static-Mesh}$ in $G(i, j)=\{(S-R)\text{-}Steiner\text{-}tree$ in $G(i, j)\}$ U *Additional-Edges*
10. $i = j + 1$
11.   *Additional-Edges* = ϕ
12.   **end if**
13. **end while**
14. **return** *(S-R)*$_{Stable-Mobile-Mesh}$

End *OptMeshTrans*

Fig. 2. Pseudo code for *OptMeshTrans* algorithm

2.2 Proof of Correctness of Algorithm *OptMeshTrans*

Given a mobile graph $G_M=G_1G_2.....G_T$, set of sources S and the set of receivers R, let the number of mesh transitions generated by *OptMeshTrans* in the Stable-Mobile-Mesh, $(S-R)_{Stable-Mobile-Mesh}$ be m. We use the proof by contradiction technique to prove the correctness of the *OptMeshTrans* algorithm. To show that m is optimal, we assume the contrary as the hypothesis for our proof, i.e., there exists another Stable-Mobile-Mesh $(S-R)'_{Stable-Mobile-Mesh}$ with m' number of mesh transitions, such that $m'<m$.

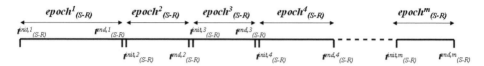

(a) Sampling Time Instants for $(S-R)_{Stable-Mobile-Mesh}$ (Algorithm *OptMeshTrans*)

(b) Sampling Time Instants for $(S-R)'_{Stable-Mobile-Mesh}$ (Hypothesis for the Proof)

Fig. 3. Sampling Time Instants to Prove the Correctness of Algorithm *OptMeshTrans*

Let $epoch^1_{(S-R)}$, $epoch^2_{(S-R)}$,......, $epoch^m_{(S-R)}$ (refer Figure 3a) and $epoch^1_{(S-R)'}$, $epoch^2_{(S-R)'}$,......, $epoch^{m'}_{(S-R)'}$ (refer Figure 3b) be the set of sampling time instants in $(S-R)_{Stable-Mobile-Mesh}$ and $(S-R)'_{Stable-Mobile-Mesh}$ respectively, wherein no mesh transitions exist. Let $t^{init,j}_{(S-R)}$, $t^{init,k}_{(S-R)}$ be the initial and $t^{end,j}_{(S-R)}$, $t^{end,k}_{(S-R)}$ be the final sampling time instants of $epoch^j_{(S-R)}$ where $1 \le j \le m$ and $epoch^k_{(S-R)'}$ where $1 \le k \le m'$ respectively. Since $(S-R)_{Stable-Mobile-Mesh}$ and $(S-R)'_{Stable-Mobile-Mesh}$ exist over the same time period T, the initial and final sampling time instants are same (i.e., $t^{init,1}_{(S-R)} = t^{init,1}_{(S-R)'}$ and $t^{end,m}_{(S-R)} = t^{end,m'}_{(S-R)'}$). As our hypothesis is that the number of transitions in $(S-R)'_{Stable-Mobile-Mesh}$ is less than that of $(S-R)_{Stable-Mobile-Mesh}$, there should exist a mesh in $(S-R)'_{Stable-Mobile-Mesh}$ that has longer lifetime than that in $(S-R)_{Stable-Mobile-Mesh}$, $m'<m \Rightarrow \exists j, k$ where $1 \le j \le m$ and $1 \le k \le m'$ such that $epoch^j_{(S-R)} \subset epoch^k_{(S-R)'}$, i.e., $t^{init,k}_{(S-R)'} < t^{init,j}_{(S-R)} < t^{end,j}_{(S-R)} < t^{end,k}_{(S-R)'}$). In other words, there should exist a $(S-R)'_{Stable-Static-Mesh}$ in $[t^{init,k}_{(S-R)'} ,..., t^{end,k}_{(S-R)'}]$. But, in *OptMeshTrans* algorithm, a transition was made at $t^{end,j}_{(S-R)}$ as the mesh that started to exist at $t^{init,j}_{(S-R)}$ does not exist beyond $t^{end,j}_{(S-R)}$. So, $t^{end,k}_{(S-R)'}$ should be less than or equal to $t^{end,j}_{(S-R)}$ and cannot be greater. There is no common $(S-R)'_{Stable-Static-Mesh}$ in $[t^{init,j}_{(S-R)'} ,..., t^{end,k}_{(S-R)}]$ and hence there is no common $(S-R)'_{Stable-Static-Mesh}$ in $[t^{init,k}_{(S-R)'} ,..., t^{end,k}_{(S-R)'}]$. Therefore, the lifetime of all the meshes in $(S-R)'_{Stable-Mobile-Mesh}$ has to be less than or equal to that of $(S-R)_{Stable-Mobile-Mesh}$ i.e., $m' \ge m$. This is in contradiction to the hypothesis. Hence, m, the number of transitions in *OptMeshTrans* algorithm is optimal (minimum) and *(S-R)*$_{Stable-Mobile-Mesh}$ is the Stable-Mobile-Mesh connecting the set of sources *S* to the set of receivers *R*.

3   Simulations

We implemented ODMRP and *OptMeshTrans* in a discrete event simulator developed by us in Java. The network dimensions are 1000m x 1000m. The transmission range of each node is 250m. We vary the density of the network by conducting simulations with 50 nodes (low density) and 100 nodes (high density). The simulation time is 1000 seconds. The IEEE 802.11 Medium Access Control (MAC) protocol [6] has been used as the link-layer protocol for ODMRP. The mobility model used is the Random Waypoint model [7], wherein the velocity of a node is uniform-randomly selected from $[0,...,v_{max}]$ every time the node incurs a direction change to travel to a randomly selected location within the network. The v_{max} values used are 5 m/s and 50 m/s, characteristic of low and high node mobility respectively. For each v_{max} value, we generated five mobility profiles of the nodes for the simulation time of 1000 seconds.

The values for the number of sources used are: 2, 4 and 8; and the values for the number of receivers used are: 3, 6 and 9. The data packet size is 512 bytes and the packet sending rate from each source to the set of receivers is 4 packets per second. For each value of the number of sources and receivers, we created one list of source nodes and five lists of receiver nodes. All the node lists are generated randomly; but, we made sure a node acts at most only as a source or a receiver; not both. Simulations for a given number of sources were run for each of these five lists using the five mobility profiles generated for each v_{max} value. Each data point obtained for ODMRP [3] and *OptMeshTrans* in the performance figures 4, 5 and 6 is the average value obtained from these 25 experiments for a given number of sources and v_{max} value.

The following performance metrics are measured for the ODMRP protocol and the *OptMeshTrans* algorithm under the different simulation conditions described above.

(i)   Lifetime per Mesh – average of the lifetimes of the sequence of multicast meshes discovered over the duration of the entire multicast session.
(ii) Edges per Mesh – time-averaged value of the number of edges per mesh connecting the set of sources to the set of receivers, for the multicast session.
(iii) Hop Count per Source-Receiver Path – time-averaged hop count of the paths from the source to each receiver, considering all the source-receiver pairs and computed over the entire multicast session.

3.1   Average Mesh Lifetime

It is imperative to form multicast meshes with larger lifetime because each time a new mesh is to be formed, a global network-wide broadcast of the control messages from each source node is initiated. The larger the value for the mesh lifetime, the lower will be the number of times such resource-consuming global broadcast of control messages will be needed in the network. The Stable-Mobile-Meshes are relatively more stable (have larger lifetime) than compared to ODMRP meshes. The meshes formed using algorithm *OptMeshTrans* have 400%-450% (on average) and 830%-1450% (at the worst case) longer lifetime than the meshes formed using ODMRP.

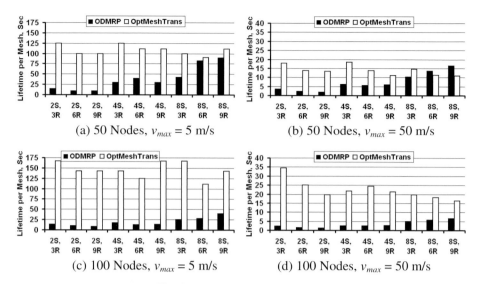

Fig. 4. Average Lifetime per Mesh

For a given node mobility and network density, the lifetime of meshes formed using ODMRP increases with increase in the number of sources. This is due to the increase in the number of edges to ensure connectivity in the mesh with increase in the number of sources. With an increased number of edges, there is an increase in the number of alternate paths between a source-receiver pair in a mesh, resulting in larger lifetime between two successive mesh transitions. The lifetime of meshes formed using *OptMeshTrans* does not relatively change much with increase in the number of sources. This is because the algorithm looks into the future topology changes and considers a mobile sub graph that consists of the minimum number of edges that will exist for a longer time as well as constitute a mesh.

For fixed node mobility and number of sources, with increase in node density, the average lifetime per mesh discovered using ODMRP decreases. This can be attributed to the decrease in the hop count per source-receiver path with increase in node density, leading to an increase in the probability of a path break in the near future. As node density increases, the Stable-Mobile-Mesh comprises of relatively better stable paths in which the physical Euclidean distance between the end nodes of the constituent links is close to only 50-60% of the transmission range of the nodes.

For fixed node density and number of sources, with increase in node mobility, the neighbors of each node move very fast, leading to a larger probability of link break in the near future. Hence, the lifetime per mesh for both ODMRP and *OptMeshTrans* would naturally be lower with increase in node mobility. For a fixed node density, mobility and number of sources, the lifetime per mesh is more likely to decrease with increase in the number of receivers as it becomes difficult to maintain the connectivity of a mesh involving more receiver nodes, but a fixed number of source nodes.

3.2 Average Number of Edges Per Mesh

The meshes formed using the *OptMeshTrans* algorithm have relatively few edges compared to those discovered using ODMRP. This is due to the decrease in the number of edges in the mobile sub graph which is an intersection of the static graphs of the network in the future. The ODMRP protocol focuses on discovering minimum hop paths between a source-receiver pair available at the current instant and the congregation of such locally optimal paths forms the mesh. There is no inclination to reduce the number of edges in the mesh when the individual paths are discovered in the case of ODMRP. On the other hand, *OptMeshTrans* looks at the future and is based on the minimum edge Steiner tree heuristic. Hence, it focuses on discovering a mesh that will exist for a longer time with a reduced number of constituent links.

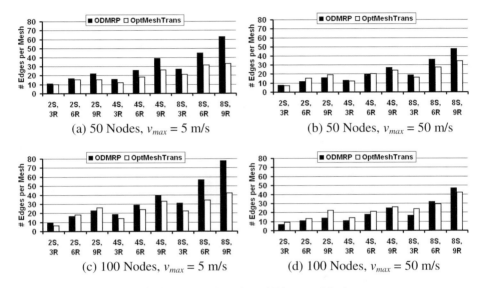

Fig. 5. Average Number of Edges per Mesh

As node mobility increases, the number of edges per mesh decreases for both ODMRP and *OptMeshTrans*. For fixed node mobility, the number of edges also increases for both of them, with increase in node density. For different node mobility and density scenarios, the number of edges per mesh increases with increase in the number of sources. We can also observe an increase in the number of edges with increase in the number of receivers with different node density and node mobility values. As the number of sources and receivers increases, the number of edges per mesh increases to maintain connectivity in the mesh. However, for all the above scenarios, the rate of increase in the number of edges per mesh discovered using the *OptMeshTrans* algorithm is lower than that observed with ODMRP. The meshes formed using algorithm *OptMeshTrans* have 13%-20% (on average) and 45%-48% (at the worst case) fewer edges than that of the meshes formed using ODMRP.

3.3 Average Hop Count Per Source-Receiver Path

The average hop count per source-receiver path is a measure of the end-to-end delay per data packet. The source-receiver paths that are part of the meshes discovered using algorithm *OptMeshTrans* have a larger hop count compared to those discovered using ODMRP. This can be attributed to the relatively fewer number of edges in the meshes discovered using algorithm *OptMeshTrans*. With fewer edges, some of the paths between a particular source node and receiver node in the mesh could be relatively longer (i.e. more hops). ODMRP looks at the current network topology and determines minimum hop paths between individual source and receiver nodes.

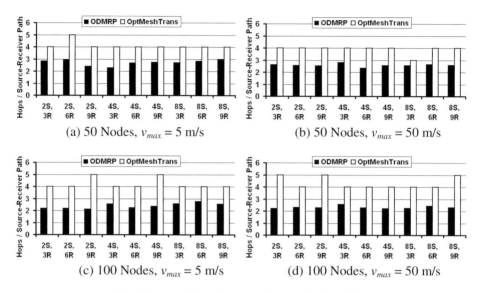

(a) 50 Nodes, v_{max} = 5 m/s   (b) 50 Nodes, v_{max} = 50 m/s

(c) 100 Nodes, v_{max} = 5 m/s   (d) 100 Nodes, v_{max} = 50 m/s

Fig. 6. Average Hop Count per Source-Receiver Path

For fixed node mobility, the average hop count per source-receiver path in the meshes discovered using ODMRP increases with increase in the number of sources and receivers, but the increase is below 25%. The average hop count per source-receiver path in meshes discovered using ODMRP decreases with increase in node density, but the decrease is below 20%. For different node mobility and node density, the average hop count per source-receiver path in the meshes discovered using *OptMeshTrans* is not affected much by the number of sources and receivers. The difference in the hop count per source-receiver path in the meshes formed using *OptMeshTrans* and those formed using ODMRP increases with increase in density.

4   Conclusions and Future Work

The high-level contribution of this paper is the development of a theoretically optimal algorithm *OptMeshTrans* that forms a sequence of stable meshes. The complexity of *OptMeshTrans* would be O(($|V||SR|^2 + |V|^2$) $T*k$), where SR is the union of the set of sources and receivers of the multicast group, T is the duration of the multicast session and k is the sampling rate, number of static graphs collected per unit time. The lifetime of the meshes determined using algorithm *OptMeshTrans* forms the benchmark for maximum possible mesh lifetime in multicast routing.

Simulation results indicate that the meshes formed using algorithm *OptMeshTrans* have significantly longer lifetime than those formed using ODMRP. Hence, there is still lot of scope to improve the stability of the meshes discovered by the multicast routing protocols. With respect to the number of edges per mesh (a measure of bandwidth efficiency and also energy-efficiency), the meshes formed using algorithm *OptMeshTrans* have fewer edges than those formed using ODMRP. However, the hop count per source-receiver path in the Stable-Mobile-Meshes is significantly larger compared to those discovered using ODMRP. This indicates the tradeoff between ODMRP and *OptMeshTrans* and our future research will be on developing a distributed version of *OptMeshTrans* that can minimize this {mesh lifetime and number of edges per mesh} vs. {hop count} tradeoff.

References

1. Murthy, C.S.R., Manoj, B.S.: Ad Hoc Wireless Networks: Architectures and Protocols. Prentice Hall, Upper Saddle River (2004)
2. Kou, L., Markowsky, G., Berman, L.: A Fast Algorithm for Steiner Trees. Acta Informatica 15, 141–145 (1981)
3. Lee, S.-J., Gerla, M., Chiang, C.-C.: On-Demand Multicast Routing Protocol. In: Wireless Communications and Networking Conference, pp. 1298–1302. IEEE, New Orleans (1999)
4. Kuhn, F., Moscibroda, T., Wattenhofer, R.: Unit Disk Graph Approximation. In: Joint Workshop on Foundations of Mobile Computing, pp. 17–23. ACM, Philadelphia (2004)
5. Farago, A., Syrotiuk, V.R.: MERIT: A Scalable Approach for Protocol Assessment. Mobile Networks and Applications 8(5), 567–577 (2003)
6. Bianchi, G.: Performance Analysis of the IEEE 802.11 Distributed Coordination Function. IEEE Journal of Selected Areas in Communication 18(3), 535–547 (2000)
7. Bettstetter, C., Hartenstein, H., Perez-Costa, X.: Stochastic Properties of the Random-Way Point Mobility Model. Wireless Networks 10(5), 555–567 (2004)

Distributed Weight Based Clustering with Efficient Channel Access to Improve Quality of Service in Mobile Ad-Hoc Networks (DWCA)

Mohd. Amjad[1] and M.N. Doja[2]

[1] Asstt. Professor, Department of Computer Engineering
[2] Professor, Department of Computer Engineering
Faculty of Engineering & Technology, Jamia Millia Islamia
New Delhi, 110025, India
amjad2k3@yahoo.com, ndoja@yahoo.com

Abstract. Mobile ad hoc network is a set of mobile nodes connecting with each other without physical infrastructure and centralized computing. Factors such as variable wireless link quality, propagation path loss, fading, multiuser interference, power expended, and topological changes, become relevant issues. Quality of Service (QoS) is a set of service requirements that needs to be met by the network while transporting a packet stream from a source to its destination. QoS support for Mobile Adhoc Networks (MANETs) is a challenging task due to the dynamic topology and limited resources. The clustering algorithm presents a logical topology to the routing algorithm, and it accepts feedback from routing algorithm in order to adjust that logical topology and make clustering decisions. In this algorithm we have introduced a new metric, next hop availability, which is a combination of two metrics. It maximizes path availability and minimizes travel time of packets and therefore offers a good balance between selection of fast paths and a better use of network resources. In the conclusion it provides simulation result of DWCA Algorithm performed on network simulator.

Keywords: Clusters, Quality of Service support, Ad hoc network.

1 Introduction

Mobile ad hoc network (MANET) is a collection of wireless hosts that communicate with each other through multi-hop wireless links. Due to the absence of fixed infrastructure, nodes must collaborate between them to accomplish some operations like routing and security. Some envisioned MANETs, such as mobile military networks or future commercial networks may be relatively large (e.g. hundreds or possibly thousands of nodes per autonomous system). A way to support the increasing number of nodes in MANET is to subdivide the whole network into groups, and then create a virtual backbone between delegate nodes in each group. In ad hoc network this operation is called clustering, giving the network a hierarchical organization.

N. Meghanathan et al. (Eds.): NeCoM, WiMoN, and WeST 2010, CCIS 90, pp. 260–269, 2010.

A cluster is a connected graph including a cluster head responsible of the management of the cluster, and (possibly) some ordinary nodes. Each node belongs to only one cluster. Some MANETs, such as mobile military networks or future commercial networks may be relatively large (e.g. hundreds or

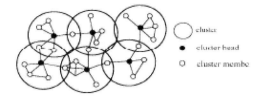

Fig. 1. Clustering in MANET

possibly thousands of nodes). A way to support the increasing number of nodes in MANET is to subdivide the whole network into groups, and then create a virtual backbone between delegate nodes in each group. In ad-hoc network this operation is called clustering, giving the network a hierarchical organization.

2   Clustering in MANETs

A way to support the increasing number of nodes in MANET is to subdivide the whole network into groups, and then create a virtual backbone between delegate nodes in each group. In ad-hoc network this operation is called clustering, giving the network a hierarchical organization. Several cluster based adaptations has been proposed for existed routing protocols and other protocol as ZRP (zone routing protocol), CBRP (cluster based protocol) have originally exploited this concept. Clustering for security can simplify the management of Certificate Authority in a Public Key Infrastructure (PKI) by affecting the full or a subset of Certificate Authority services to cluster heads, ensuring in this way the availability of the Certificate Authority. The Hierarchal organization consists of:

Cluster Head: A cluster head, as defined in the literature, serves as a local coordinator for its cluster, performing inter-cluster routing, data forwarding and so on. In our self-organized clustering scheme the cluster head only serves the purpose of providing a unique ID for the cluster, limiting the cluster boundaries.

Cluster Gateway: A cluster gateway is a non cluster-head node with inter-cluster links, so it can access neighboring clusters and forward information between clusters.

Cluster Member: A cluster member is a node that is neither a cluster head nor a cluster gateway.

Clustering has several advantages:

1) First, clustering allows the reuse of resource which can improve the system capacity, in the way that information is stored once on the cluster head.
2) Secondly, clustering may optimally manage the network topology, by dividing this task among specified nodes which can be very useful for routing since any node is identified by its identity and the identity of the cluster-head of the cluster to which it belongs, simplifying by this way the forwarding of messages.

3 Related Work

3.1 Highest-Degree Heuristic

The Highest-Degree, also known as connectivity-based clustering, in which the degree of a node is computed based on its distance from others. Each node broadcasts its id to the nodes that are within its transmission range. A node x is considered to be a neighbor of another node y if x lies within the transmission range of y. Experiments demonstrate that the system has a low rate of clusterhead change but the throughput is low under the Highest-Degree heuristic. As the number of nodes in a cluster is increased, the throughput drops and hence a gradual degradation in the system performance is observed.

3.2 Lowest-ID Heuristic

The Lowest-ID, also as known as identifier-based clustering, was originally proposed by Baker and Ephremides. This heuristic assigns a unique id to each node and chooses the node with the minimum id as a clusterhead. Thus, the ids of the neighbors of the clusterhead will be higher than that of the clusterhead. However, the clusterhead can delegate its responsibility to the next node with the minimum id in its cluster. A node is called a gateway if it lies within the transmission range of two or more clusterheads. The concept of distributed gateway (DG) is also used for inter-cluster communication only when the clusters are not overlapping. DG is a pair of nodes that lies in different clusters but they are within the transmission range of each other.

3.3 Node-Weight Heuristic

Basagni proposed two algorithms, namely distributed clustering algorithm (DCA) and distributed mobility adaptive clustering algorithm (DMAC). In this approach, each node is assigned weights (a real number > 0) based on its suitability of being a clusterhead. A node is chosen to be a clusterhead if its weight is higher than any of its neighbor's weight; otherwise, it joins a neighboring clusterhead. The smaller node id is chosen in case of a tie.

4 Limitations of Existing Algorithm

None of the above three heuristics leads to an optimal election of clusterheads since each deals with only a subset of parameters which can possibly impose constraints on the system. To be precise, the Highest-Degree heuristic states that the node with the largest number neighbors should be elected as a clusterhead. However, a clusterhead may not be able handle a large number of nodes due to resource limitations even if these nodes are its immediate neighbors and lie well within its transmission range. In other words, simply covering the area with the minimum number of clusterheads will put more burdens on the clusterheads. On the other hand, a large number of clusterheads will lead to a computationally expensive system. Although this may result in good throughput, the data packets have to go through multiple hops thus implying high latency.

Since the node ids do not change with time, those with smaller ids are more likely to become clusterheads than nodes with larger ids.Thus, certain nodes are prone to power drainage due to serving as clusterheads for longer periods of time.

5 Our Algorithm

5.1 Modifications over Existing Algorithms

The most of algorithms proposed in literature have giving solution to only some specific problems of ad hoc networks. However none of them deals with the entire characteristics of ad hoc networks (mobility, transmission range, size of the network, capabilities of the node). For example, the highest-degree, lowest-ID algorithms create one hop clusters, which are too small for large networks resulting on a big number of clusters, which complicate the virtual backbone management. They are also sensitive to small changing in the topology. The WCA and Mobility based algorithms try to include the mobility (stability) of nodes as a factor in the election procedure, in order to elect the most stable node as cluster-head. But their methods to compute stability are based on some assumptions which are not always valid in all ad hoc networks. Another method proposed in mobility based d-hop algorithm relies on the idea that nodes have equal antennas and transmit with the same power, to compute an estimate value of the distance between nodes. However this supposition is rarely guarantied because ad hoc networks are composed by heterogeneous nodes having different capabilities and antennas. Another observation is related to security features which are not included in the above algorithms. As mentioned in security problem must be taken into consideration in all schemes devoted to ad hoc networks.

5.2 The Design Approach

The main basic concepts used to derive the needed parameters are given below:

The Max Value: Represents the upper bound of the number of nodes that can simultaneously be supported by a cluster-head.

The Min Value: Represents the lower bound of the number of nodes that belong to a given cluster before proceeding to the extension or merging mechanisms.

D hops Clusters: As one hop clusters are too small for large ad hoc networks, therefore DWCA creates D hops clusters where D is defined by the underlying protocol or according to the cluster-head state (busy or not).

Identity (ID): It is a unique identifier for each node in the network to avoid any spoofing attacks or perturbation in the election procedure. We propose to use certificate as identity.

Weight: Each node is elected cluster-head according to its weight which is computed from a set of system parameters. The node having the greatest weight is elected as cluster-head.

Global Weight: using all parameters cited above every node in the network computes its global weight. Depending on this weight a given node can be elected as cluster-head or not.

We denote WT , WD , WB ,WM ,WS the partial weights and FT , FD , FB ,FM,FS are the weight factors corresponding respectively to Trust value, Degree, Battery, Max Value, and Stability. The global weight is computed as follows:

$$WG=FT \times WT + FD \times WD + FB \times WB + FM \times WM + FS \times (-WS)$$

As we can observe the value of WS is retrieved from the global weight in order to elect the node with the greatest weight, because the stable node is the node with the smallest value of WS, which keeps the equation coherent for our assumption.

5.2.1   Election Procedure

This operation is invoked whenever a neighborhood has no cluster-head, or whenever one of the cluster-heads isn't able to achieve its responsibilities. Discovery stage: The purpose of this step is to get information about the neighborhood where the election procedure is invoked. Thus nodes desiring to be clusterhead send cluster-head_ready beacons within the radius of D hops. Each node when receiving this beacon estimates a trust value and sends it back to the asking node. After a discovery period Td, nodes having initiated this operation can derive from the received responses the following information:

- *Degree*
- *Stability:*
- *Trust value*

Computing weight: After the discovery stage, each node adds to the previous parameters the state of its battery and the max value, then combines them with the corresponding weight factors and computes the global weight.

Elaboration of the virtual backbone: Whenever the previous steps are successfully achieved, each cluster head need to discover each other to elaborate a virtual backbone to ensure inter-cluster services. Thus every new elected cluster-head broadcast a discovery request over the entire network; cluster-heads receiving this request register the certificate of the new clusterhead and send him their certificate.

5.3   Description of Algorithm

- Each node declares itself a clusterhead.
- Each node broadcasts the list of nodes that it can hear, that is, the set of nodes that are within the communication range of the original node. If a node A hears from a node B with a higher number of neighbors than itself, node A sends a message to B requesting to join B's cluster. If B already has resigned as a clusterhead itself, B returns a rejection, otherwise B returns a confirmation. When A receives the confirmation, A resigns as a clusterhead.
- When the previous step is completed, the entire network is divided into a number of clusters. This process can be repeated several times, depending on what the maximum cluster diameter is considered to be in this case. Each node keeps track of the id of its clusterhead, the first step in the path to its clusterhead, the distance to the clusterhead, the time the node has been a member of its current cluster, as well as the number of nodes in the cluster. A clusterhead also keeps track of the time each node in its cluster has been a member of that cluster.

- It is possible for a cluster to grow too large. Consider a situation when a cluster is just below the maximum allowed size, and several nodes join simultaneously.
- A node can leave a cluster, either because the situation described above, or because it is moving away from the cluster. Even if it loses contact with the node that is the first step to the clusterhead, it might still be able to connect to another node in the cluster. However, if the node is more than d-hops away from the clusterhead, it must leave that cluster. When a node leaves a cluster, it tries to find another cluster to connect to. That cluster must be smaller than the maximum allowed size, and the node cannot be more than d hops away from the clusterhead. If several such clusters are found, the node joins the largest one. If no such cluster is found, the node forms a cluster with itself as clusterhead and only member.

5.3.1 Cluster Initialization
The Init procedure is executed by each node in a no determinist status. A node with this status is a node which isn't attached yet to any cluster, this may be caused by a link failure, a roaming, or whenever a node coming for the first time to the network.

5.3.2 Cluster Division
A node can't serve for ever as CH (Cluster Head), because it has limited resources (battery, memory, etc). So, whenever it becomes busy (can't support the increasing number of nodes), the CH launches a cluster division procedure to divide the cluster into two small clusters with reasonable number of nodes. Therefore the CH broadcasts, Cluster_Division request to its CMs (Cluster Merge). Whenever this request is received, each CM computes its weight and sends it back to the CH. Then the CH chooses as a new CH the farthest node with the maximum weight and sends him a grant response. Then the new CH begins sending beacons and creates its own cluster.

5.3.3 Cluster Size Reduction
This operation is executed after the division of the cluster and aims to reduce the cluster radius from D to D-1, which means that beacons don't reach the boundaries of the cluster, resulting on the roaming of boundaries nodes to other clusters including new cluster creation.

5.3.4 Cluster Merging
In the algorithms taken from the literature, no lower bound is defined to limit the minimum number of nodes in a cluster, resulting on some clusters with two or one nodes which is not suitable. Therefore, in our algorithm we propose to merge such clusters immediately with the nearest cluster if it exists by executing the merging procedure. First, the CH begins to listen if there are any neighboring CHs; if this is the case it broadcast a merging request. Then it wait until receiving all confirmation from its CMs or the expiration of the delay TM to choose the nearest cluster and roams to that cluster.

6   Implementation and Performance Evaluation

The DWCA implemented algorithm is using GloMoSim (Global Mobile Information System Simulator), is a scalable network simulation environment for mobile ad-hoc networks, developed at UCLA Parallel Computing laboratory. And PARSEC (PARallel Simulation Environment for Complex systems) is a C-based discrete-event simulation language. GloMoSim has the capabilities to simulate thousands of mobile nodes without disregarding the details in the lower layer protocols. GloMoSim simulation library is built using the PARSEC simulation environment. With GloMoSim we are building a scalable simulation environment for wireless network systems. It is being designed using the parallel discrete-event simulation capability provided by Parsec discrete event simulation engine.

6.1   Transmitting a Hello Packet to the Nodes

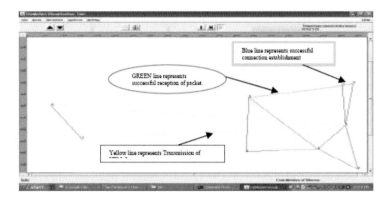

Fig. 2. Tx Packet to a node

Table. 1. Simulation Parameter

Network Size	300 X 300 m
Mobility of Nodes	20,40 and 50 Nodes
Range of each Node	625 m
Mobility Model	Random
Minimum Node Speed	5-20 m/sec
Pause Time	0,4,8 and 16sec
Data Rate	One Message per minute
Time	500 seconds

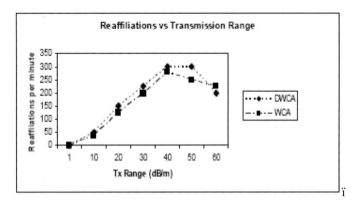

Fig. 3. Reaffiliations Vs Tx Range

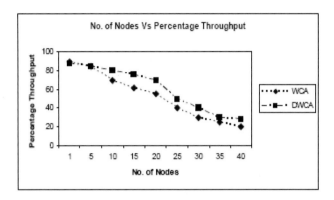

Fig. 4. Node Vs Throughput

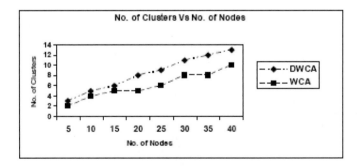

Fig. 5. Clusters Vs Nodes

7 Conclusion

We have presented a distributed algorithm, DWCA for the efficient partitioning of the nodes of an ad hoc wireless network into clusters with a clusterhead and some ordinary nodes. This is a practically important task, especially for all those network algorithms/applications that assume a mobility- adaptive hierarchical organization of the network. A new weightbased criterion is introduced for the cluster formation that allows the choice of the clusterheads based on node mobility, battery power, degree, cumulative link strength and data rate that were not available in previous clustering algorithms. It is seen that a tradeoff between network stability and effective clusterhead selection process is to be made. WCA compromises on the latter by not always selecting the best nodes as clusterheads, whereas our algorithm, DWCA improves upon the clustering process and the network organization in terms of well spread out clusters while sacrificing a bit of network stability. It also combines easiness of implementation with full adaptation to the mobility of the nodes, even during clustering set up.

References

1. Ganesan, D., Govindan, R., Shenker, S., Estrin, D.: Highly-resilient, Energy-efficient multipath Routing in Wireless Sensor Networks. Mobile Computing and Communications Review 4(5) (October 2008)
2. Mhatre, V., Rosenberg, C., Koffman, D., Mazumdar, R., Shroff, N.: A minimum cost heterogeneous sensor network with a lifetime constraint. IEEE Transactions on Mobile Computing (TMC) 4(1), 4–15 (2005)
3. Arboleda, L.M., Nasser, N.: Comparison of Clustering Algorithms and Protocols for Wireless Sensor Networks. In: Canadian Conference on Electrical and Computer Engineering (CCECE 2006), Ottawa, May 2006, pp. 256–261 (2006)
4. Akkaya, K., Younis, M.: A Survey on Routing Protocols for Wireless Sensor Networks. Elsevier Ad Hoc Network Journal 3(3), 325–349 (2005)
5. Luo, J., Hubaux, J.-P.: Joint Mobility and Routing for Lifetime Elongation in Wireless Sensor Networks. In: 24th Annual Joint Conference of the IEEE Computer and Communications Societies, INFOCOM 2005, Miami, March 2005, pp. 1735–1746 (2005)
6. Barbeau, M., Kranakis, E., Krizanc, D., Morin, P.: Improving Distance Based Geographic Location Techniques in Sensor Networks. In: 3rd International Conference on ADHOC Networks and Wireless, Vancouver, British Columbia (July 2004)
7. Muruganathan, S.D., Ma, D.C.F., Bhasin, R.I., Fapojuwo, A.O.: A Centralized Energy-Efficient Routing Protocol for Wireless Sensor Networks. IEEE Communications Magazine 43, 8–13 (2005)
8. Dasgupta, K., Kalpakis, K., Namjoshi, P.: An Efficient Clustering-Based Heuristic for Data Gathering and Aggregation in Sensor Networks. IEEE Wireless Communications and Networking 3, 1948–1953 (2003)
9. Bandyopadhyay, S., Coyle, E.: An Energy-Efficient Hierarchical Clustering Algorithm for Wireless Sensor Networks. In: Proceedings of IEEE INFOCOM (April 2003)
10. Michiardi, P., Molva, R.: Core: A Collaborative Reputation mechanism to enforce node cooperation in Mobile Ad Hoc Networks. In: Communications and Multimedia Security Conference (2002)

11. Younis, O., Fahmy, S.: Distributed Clustering in Ad-hoc Sensor Networks: A Hybrid, Energy-Efficient Approach. In: Proceedings of IEEE INFOCOM, vol. 1, pp. 629–640 (March 2004)

12. Mhatre, V., Rosenberg, C.: Design guidelines for wireless sensor networks: communication, clustering and aggregation. Ad Hoc Networks 2(1), 45–63 (2004)

13. Akkaya, K., Younis, M.: A survey on routing protocols for wireless sensor networks. Ad Hoc Networks 3(3), 325–349 (2005)

14. Choi, W., Shah, P., Das, S.K.: A framework for energy-saving data gathering using two-phase clustering in wireless sensor networks. In: Proceedings of International Conference on Mobile and Ubiquitous Systems, August 2004, pp. 203–212 (2004)

15. Liu, J.S., Lin, C.H.: Energy-efficiency clustering protocol in wireless sensor networks. Ad Hoc Networks 3(3), 371–388 (2005)

16. Lin, C.R., Gerla, M.: Adaptive clustering for mobile wireless networks. IEEE Journal on Selected Areas in Communications 15(7), 1265–1275 (1997)

17. He, T., et al.: SPEED: a stateless protocol for real-time communication in sensor networks. In: Proceedings of International Conference on Distributed Computing Systems, Providence, RI (May 2003)

18. Estrin, D., Culler, D., Pister, K., Sukhatme, G.: Connecting the physical world with pervasive networks. IEEE Pervasive Computing, 59–69 (January- March 2002)

19. Akyildiz, I.F., Su, W., Sankarasubramaniam, Y., Cayirci, E.: Wireless sensor networks: A survey. Computer Networks 38(4), 393–422 (2002)

20. Vyas, N., Mahgoub, I.: Location and Mobility Pattern Based Routing Algorithm for Mobile Ad Hoc Wireless Networks. In: International Symposium on Performance Evaluation of Computer and Telecommunication Systems, Montreal, Canada (July 2003)

21. Barbeau, M., Kranakis, E., Krizanc, D., Morin, P.: Improving Distance Based Geographic Location Techniques in Sensor Networks. In: 3rd International Conference on ADHOC Networks and Wireless, Vancouver, British Columbia (July 2004)

22. Kadri, B., M'hamed, A., Feham, M.: Secured Clustering Algorithm for Mobile Ad Hoc Networks. IJCSNS International Journal of Computer Science and Network Security 7(3) (March 2007)

WACA: A New Weighted Adaptive Clustering Algorithm for MANET

Ira Nath[1], Rituparna Chaki[2], and Nabendu Chaki[3]

[1] West Bengal University of Technology, West Bengal, India
ira.nath@gmail.com
[2] Department of Computer Sc. & Engineering, West Bengal University of Technology, India
rchaki@ieee.org
[3] Department of Computer Science & Engineering, University of Calcutta, India
nabendu@ieee.org

Abstract. This paper aims towards a critical retrospection of some of the most bugging limitations of cluster formation and cluster head selection. Based on this, a new Weighted Adaptive Clustering Algorithm (WACA) has been proposed. The proposed methodology is aimed at reducing the transmission overhead, total required time and increasing the stability of the formed cluster. WACA can dynamically adapt itself to the frequently changing topology of ad-hoc network.

Keywords: Cluster, topology, adhoc network, cluster head.

1 Introduction

Mobile Ad hoc Network (MANET) can be typically described as a group of mobile nodes connected by wireless links. *MANET plays a critical role* in places where a wired (central) backbone is neither available nor economical to build, such as law enforcement operations, battle field communications, and disaster recovery situations, and so on. Such situations demand a network where all the nodes including the base stations are potentially mobile. Many Mobile AD-HOC routing protocols started with a simple concept. Then, essential features like route maintenance or packet salvation for staying ahead in the competition among protocols are added. Mobile ad hoc Network (MANET) consists of a number of wireless hosts that communicate with each other through multi-hop wireless links. In MANET, the flat routing schemes do not scale well in terms of performance. With an increase in the size of the networks, its performance rapidly decreases. Another disadvantage of flat routing scheme is that the routing tables and topology information in the mobile stations also get tremendously large. It may result in low bandwidth utilization in large networks with high load and longer source routes. To solve this problem some kind of organization is required in large MANET. This is possible by grouping a number of nodes into easily manageable set known as cluster [5, 6]. Certain nodes, known as cluster heads, would be responsible for the formation of clusters and maintenance of the topology of the networks. Clustering algorithms in MANETS should be able to maintain its cluster structure as stable as possible while the topology changes [1]. Naturally, there are many ways in which a

N. Meghanathan et al. (Eds.): NeCoM, WiMoN, and WeST 2010, CCIS 90, pp. 270–283, 2010.

network can be partitioned into clusters and cluster head chosen. This is reflected in the large number of clustering protocols, developed by the MANET. In this paper, we compare four clustering algorithms. The compared algorithms are Lowest-ID [9], [10], Highest-Connectivity [11], [12], Weighted clustering Algorithm (WCA) [8] and Enhanced Weighted Clustering Algorithm (EWCA).

A comparative study of the above mentioned clustering algorithms lead to the observation that the performance of Enhanced Weighted clustering algorithm (EWCA) is the best. However, EWCA does not consider neighbor cluster heads for cluster head election procedure. Thus the stability of the created cluster is a confusing issue considering the mobility factor. For this reason, EWCA cannot be applied for an isolated node who wants to join as a cluster member of an existing cluster or declare itself as a cluster head separately. However, the performance of Enhanced Weighted clustering algorithm (EWCA) can be improved by considering some more parameters. In order to eliminate the above-mentioned major drawbacks, we propose a new cluster formation algorithm named Weighted Adaptive Clustering Algorithm (WACA).

The paper is organized as follows. A brief review on some of the well-referred clustering algorithms is presented in Section 2. The description of the proposed WACA clustering algorithm is in Section 3. We have partially simulated our method and some of the results of our experiments are in section 4. The paper ends with concluding remarks in section 5.

2   Related Works

In this section, we present a brief description of four of the clustering algorithms that are often referred before comparing their performances.

2.1   Lowest-ID Algorithm

The Lowest-ID algorithm [9], [10], is also known as identifier based clustering. In this algorithm, each node is assigned a distinct ID. Then each node periodically broadcasts the list of nodes that it can hear. A node becomes a cluster head (CH) if it only hears nodes with ID higher than itself. The lowest- ID node that a node hears is its cluster head, unless it gives up its role as a cluster head. A node is called gateway if it can hear two or more cluster heads [13]. Otherwise this node is an ordinary node.

Figure 1 shows an example with seven nodes. Nodes 1 and 4 are respective cluster heads and node 7 is the gateway node. This Lowest- ID algorithm has some drawbacks. It is totally based on the ID of nodes. In a MANET all the nodes are mobile. So, a node being more mobile but having Lowest ID should not be made the cluster head. A cluster head has to perform additional tasks for the other nodes in the cluster. Thus certain nodes in the Lowest-ID heuristic are prone to power drainage due to serving as cluster heads for longer periods of time. Further, the lower-ID heuristic does not attempt to balance the load uniformly across all the nodes. The node ids are randomly assigned numbers and the qualifications of a node or its topological position are not considered for a cluster head election procedure. In Lowest-ID when a non-cluster head node moves into another cluster, none of both cluster heads will change. Only cluster members are changed. A cluster head change

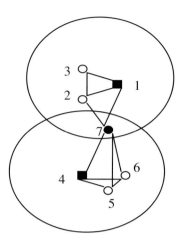

Fig. 1. Cluster Formation by Lowest ID

occurs only if two cluster heads come into one cluster leading to a situation where someone has to give up its cluster head position according to lowest-ID or one of the nodes moves out of range of all cluster heads.

2.2 Highest-Connectivity Clustering Algorithm

The Highest-connectivity cluster algorithm is also known as Highest-Degree algorithm [11], [12]. A node that has not yet elected its cluster head is called an "uncovered" node. Otherwise a node with an assigned cluster-head is termed as a "covered" node. Each node in the cluster formation procedure broadcasts the list of nodes that it can hear. If a node is the most highly connected node of all its "uncovered" neighbor nodes, it is elected as a cluster head. Figure 2 shows again an example, where nodes 1 and 4 are cluster heads; any of the two nodes, 3 and 2 may be the gateway node. All the other nodes are cluster members.

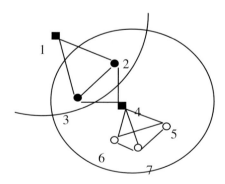

Fig. 2. Highest Connectivity Cluster Formation

This Highest-Connectivity cluster algorithm has some drawbacks. In general, the clustering algorithm must be performed as early as possible, so that each cluster head can take and maintain control of its members efficiently. However, in a highly mobile environment, nodes keep on forming newer links and dropping the existing ones. Thus the current cluster-head may fail to be re-elected as a cluster head. One may have to constantly look for re-electing the cluster heads. Thus the cluster formation procedure lacks in stability comparing methods like the Lowest-ID algorithm. Further, a cluster head may not be able to handle a large number of nodes due to resource limitations even if these nodes are its immediate neighbors and lie well within its transmission range.

2.3 Weighted Clustering Algorithm (WCA)

To decide a node as a cluster head, WCA clustering algorithm [8] considers Node's degree, Transmission power, Mobility, and Battery power. In WCA clustering algorithm, the cluster head election procedure is not periodic and is invoked as rarely as possible. Each cluster head can ideally support only δ (a pre-defined threshold) nodes. In this cluster formation procedure, less power is needed for a node to communicate with other nodes if they are close to each other. It is desirable to elect a cluster head that does not move quickly to avoid frequent cluster head changes. A cluster head is able to communicate better with its neighbor having closer distances from it with the transmission range. Considering these features, combined weight for each node is calculated. The node with the smallest weight is then chosen as the cluster head.

2.4 Enhanced Weighted Clustering Algorithm (EWCA)

Enhanced Weighted clustering algorithm [14] elects cluster heads based on the degree-difference, the sum of the distances, the mobility, and the battery power.

EWCA finds out the ideal neighbors (δ) of each node in its transmission range. Ideal neighbors of a node are the nodes that reside within the transmission range of that node and are on a single-hop distance from it.

EWCA calculates the combined weight W_m for each node m, as:

$W_m = w_1 \Delta m + w_2 \overline{D}_m + w_3 \overline{V}_m + w_4 P_m$, where, w_1, w_2, w_3 and w_4 are the weighing factors for the corresponding system parameters.

For each node m, Δm (Degree- difference) is defined as

$\Delta m = |N - \delta|$ for every node m, where,

δ = The total number of ideal neighbors of node m.

N = Degree (Number of neighbors) of node m = $\Sigma\{dist(m_i, m_j) < t_{x\ range}\}$ for $m_j \in M$, $m_j \neq m_i$

EWCA finds the sum of the distances, D_m, for every node and its neighbors as

D_m = Sum of distances

$= \Sigma\sqrt{(X_{mi} - X_{mj})^2 - (Y_{mi} - Y_{mj})^2}$ for $(m_i, m_j \in M)$ and

Average relative distances $\overline{D}_m = D_m/N$

Then EWCA finds the running average of the speed, Vm, for every node until the current time T to calculate mobility, as

Running average relative speed

$$\overline{V}_{m_i, m_j, t} = 1/N \sum_{i=1}^{N} |V(m_i, m_j, t)|$$

Running relative speed with its neighbor nodes = $V(m_i, m_j, t) = v(m_i, t) - v(m_j, t)$

Running average of the speed $v_m = 1/T [\sqrt{(X_t - X_{t-1})^2 + (Y_t - Y_{t-1})^2}]$

where, T = the time for node m motion from the coordinates of (X_{t-1}, Y_{t-1}) to (X_t, Y_t) at time (t-1) and t   respectively.

The cumulative time, P_m, during which a node m acts as a cluster head is obtained. The node with the smallest Wm is then chosen as a cluster head. This means that the neighboring nodes of the selected cluster head are no longer allowed to participate in the election procedure. The above procedure would be repeated for the remaining nodes that have not been selected neither as a cluster head nor assigned to a cluster.

The sum of the weighing factors equals to 1 where each weighing factor is determined based upon the application requirements.

EWCA Clustering Algorithm manages motion of each node hierarchically and forms the forwarding groups based on cluster heads. All the neighbors of the chosen cluster head are no longer allowed to participate in the election procedure. EWCA better fits to manage the large scale and multi-environment wireless networks.

The main drawback of EWCA Clustering Algorithm is as the number of cluster members in a formed cluster increases, and then computation overhead also (i.e. transmission rate decreases) increases. EWCA has no proper method to solve this problem.

Table 1. Performance Comparison between Clustering Algorithms

Algorithm	Topology-driven	Energy-efficient	Mobility	Stability	Message Complexity
Lowest-ID	Not considered	Poor – the cluster head may run out of power	Permits mobility of nodes and cluster head	Relatively stable	Uses broadcasting
Highest-Degree	Considers degree of a node as the deciding parameter	The instability leads to overall drainage of power	Not good for highly mobile environment	Not stable	Uses broadcasting
WCA	Takes into account the topology of the network to select a cluster head	Energy-efficient	Low mobility of cluster head	Relatively stable	Exchanges messages only with nodes at close proximity
EWCA	Aimed for large-scale multi-environment wireless networks	Not meant to be energy efficient – draws a lot of power for larger clusters	Mobility is higher than WCA.	Lacks in stability	Exchanges messages only with nodes at close proximity

3 Weighted Adaptive Clustering Algorithm (WACA)

EWCA algorithm does not consider neighbor cluster heads for cluster head election procedure. A new node has no knowledge about the weight of its neighbor nodes and EWCA does not provide this knowledge to a new entrant. Thus, the EWCA cannot tally the weight of the newly entered node with other existing neighbor cluster heads. So, this newly entered node neither can join as a cluster member of an existing cluster head nor declare itself as a cluster head. As a result, the stability of the created cluster using EWCA is rather restricted.

We address this issue in the proposed Weighted Adaptive Clustering Algorithms (WACA).

3.1 Assumptions

- Two cluster heads are not allowed to be one-hop neighbors of each other.
- Gateway nodes connect two overlapping clusters.
- All the ordinary nodes are one-hop from their cluster heads.
- Each node that requests for an entry permit must keep track of the respective weights broadcasted by the neighbor nodes.

3.2 Data Dictionary

A	A node in the cluster formation procedure.
W_A	Combined weight of each node A.
PC_{WT}	Minimum weight among all W_A.
PC	Possible Clusterhead.
X [ ]	Neighbor cluster heads in the transmission range of PC.
CHMsg	Cluster head selection message.
Weight []	Weights of all neighbor cluster heads in the transmission range of PC.
th1	Threshold value 1 (associated with weights of newly selected cluster head).
th2	Threshold value 2 (associated with weights of newly selected cluster head and existing neighbor cluster heads in the transmission range of PC).
n	Total number of existing cluster heads in the whole network.
C	The total number of existing cluster heads in the whole network whose weights are greater than a specified value.
B	Any neighbor node in the transmission range of node A.

3.3 Weight Function Calculation for the Proposed Algorithm

The WACA considers various important parameters for cluster formation procedure. These parameters are degree-difference, average relative distances, mobility, battery power, transmission rate and transmission power.

When cluster formation is to be performed by WACA, the nodes can change their position randomly (moves away from each other) due to mobility. The communication among them may become difficult when they place themselves outside the transmission range (t_x) of the node from which data has to be transferred. For this reason, transmission power of each node is required for weight calculation.

Mobility produces the randomly changed position of each node. But the rates of data transfer capability (t_r) are not same for all the nodes in a cluster formation procedure. It shows the amount of data can be delivered in a certain period of time by a node to all the other nodes in its transmission range.

These two parameters have been considered for overall improvement in performance.

Using the following formula we calculate the combined weight W_m for each node m, where

$$W_m = \frac{(w_1*\Delta m + w_2*\bar{D}_m + w_3*\bar{V}_m + w_4*P_m)}{(w_5*t_r + w_6*t_x)} \tag{1}$$

where, w_1, w_2, w_3, w_4, w_5 and w_6 are the weighing factors for the corresponding system parameters.

The values of w_1, w_2, w_3, w_4, w_5 and w_6 are assigned arbitrarily such that the sums of all the weighing factors are 1, $(w_1 + w_2 + w_3 + w_4 + w_5 + w_6 = 1)$.

In our implementation, the weights w_1, w_2, w_3, w_4, w_5 and w_6 are initialized as follows: $w_1=0.1$, $w_2=0.2$, $w_3=0.5$, $w_4=0.1$, $w_5=0.05$ and $w_6=0.05$.

Data transfer rate $(t_r) = (C1*60)/T1$ packets/min where,

T1 = Packet transfer duration in second.
C1 = Number of packets transferred in T1 seconds.

For each node, the range of transmission is $t_x \propto (T_2 - T_1)/2$. At time T_1 the HELLO message is at co-ordinate (X_{T1}, Y_{T1}) and after $(T_2 - T_1)/2$ time the message reached the co-ordinate $(X_{((T_2-T_1)/2)} - Y_{((T_2-T_1)/2)})$.

Thus, the transmission range is

$(t_x) = \sqrt{((X_{((T_2-T_1)/2)} - X_{T_1})^2 - (Y_{((T_2-T_1)/2)} - Y_{T_2})^2)}$

T: Specified period of time such that,
$T \geq \{Max ((T_2 - T_1)$ for all N nodes $)\}$

Each node that wishes to join a cluster must keep information about weights of its neighbor cluster heads. To maximize the resource utilization, we can choose to have the minimum number of cluster heads to cover the whole geographical area over which the nodes are distributed. The whole area can be split up into zones. The size of each zone can be determined by the transmission range of the nodes, selected as cluster heads.

3.4   The Logic Behind

Initially, each node A in the cluster formation procedure broadcasts HELLO message along with its node ID (assigned) and status bit 00 periodically. Then weight of each entered node is calculated by equation number (1). Each node of the cluster formation procedure broadcasts its own calculated combined weight within its transmission range. The minimum among all the calculated weights is selected. The ID of that particular node with minimum weight is selected as Possible Cluster Head PC and then its status bit changes into 01. The PC finds out all the Neighbor Cluster Heads in the transmission range. PC broadcasts the CHMsg within its transmission range. PC collects weights of all the neighbors cluster heads. That is, it collects those nodes with status 11 (status bit of cluster heads is 11) within its transmission range.

If the weight of the possible cluster head PC is less than all the calculated weights of the neighbor cluster heads within its transmission range then PC is elected finally as cluster head and its status becomes 11. Otherwise PC joins as an ordinary node of the neighbor cluster head X whose calculated weight is lowest among all neighbor cluster heads in the transmission range of PC. Then the status of that newly joined cluster member becomes 10. So, the status bit of newly entered nodes, Possible Cluster Heads, Cluster Heads and Cluster members are 00, 01, 11 and 10 respectively.

In order to find out the total number of existing cluster heads (that is to count the total numbers of node-ids with status 11) in the whole network we take a threshold value th1.

Lemma 1. The total number of cluster heads in the whole network, when the weight of the newly selected cluster head is less than or equal to the threshold value (th1), is one.

Proof. If the weight of a newly selected cluster-head (A) is less than a very small threshold value th1 (say), then all the neighbor cluster-heads are included in the cluster of A. All the neighbor cluster members remain under the sub-cluster heads.

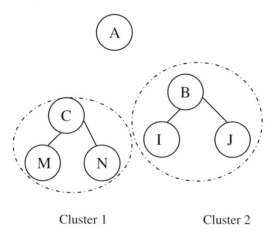

Cluster 1   Cluster 2

Fig. 3. A is the newly selected cluster head. Cluster 1 headed by node C and Cluster 2 headed by node 2.

For example, suppose th1==4 and PC$_{WT}$ <=4. Then all-existing neighbor cluster heads (B and C) join as the cluster members of recent Cluster Head (whose weight is PC$_{WT}$). Then total number of Cluster Head in the whole network becomes 1.

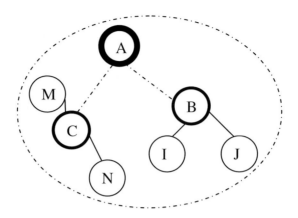

Fig. 4. Multi-level Hierarchical clustering (1)

Lemma 2. If th1< value of PC$_{WT}$ < th2, then the total number of cluster heads in the whole network would be ((n+1)-c), where c is the number of cluster heads in the whole network whose weights are greater than th2. n is the total number of existing cluster heads in the whole network.

Proof. This is due to the fact that the cluster heads with weight greater than th2 (the allowed high limit), they shall join as sub-clusters of the new cluster-head A. As for example, suppose th2==15, so 4< PC$_{WT}$ <=15.

Then the neighbor cluster heads whose weights are greater than 15 (let total number of c=3) join as the cluster members of the recent selected new Cluster Head (whose weight is PC$_{WT}$). Then the total numbers of Cluster head in the whole network are ((n+1)-c) or ((10+1)-3) or 8, where, n = is the total number of existing neighbor cluster heads=10 (suppose).

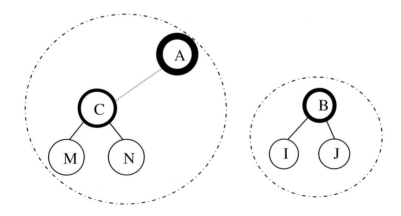

Fig. 5. Multi-level Hierarchical clustering (2)

Lemma 3. If PC_{WT}>th2 then the total number of existing cluster heads in the whole network would be (n+1), i.e., the total number of existing cluster heads would be increased by 1.

Proof. If the PC sends CHMsg and PC does not belong to the neighbor Cluster X then it joins in the formed cluster X as the ordinary node (one of the cluster members). If any of the associated nodes fails to return back any ACK message (i.e. acknowledgment) after receiving the HELLO message from its neighbor within a specified period of time, then two mobile nodes are considered disconnected. Cluster (X) represents a formed cluster headed by node X. The link between node A and node B (where B is any neighbor of A) is removed. If a cluster member is able to hear HELLO messages from another node of another cluster, it assumes the role of a gateway; otherwise it declares itself to be an ordinary node.

Let, the total numbers of entered nodes in the cluster formation procedure are k. Then, we repeat the above-mentioned entire procedure for k times.

After the cluster formation, if there is no link between any ordinary node and the selected cluster head in the formed cluster then restart the whole procedure once again and select the next smallest weighted node as possible cluster head (i.e. PC) and continue the next whole process.

Algorithm WACA
```
Begin
For each node (A)
If (Broadcast (HELLO) ==true)
{
For each node (A)
    WA = CalNodeweight (A)
    Broadcast (WA)
       End For
  PCWT =min (WA)
  PC=PossibleClusterHead=return(address (PCWT))
  X= NeighborClusterHead (PC)
  For each clusterhead X
    Broadcast (CHMsg, PC)
    If (PCWT <Weight (X))
    {
    Clusterhead=PC
                If (PCWT <=th1)
           NoOfClusterhead=1
       End if
     If (th1<PCWT<=th2)
           NoOfClusterhead = (n+1)-c
         End if
      If (PCWT >th2)
           NoOfClusterhead = (n+1)
         End if
  }
```

```
              Else
      {
      If (CHMsg (PC) = = true)
       If PC ∧ cluster (X)
             Cluster (X). Add (PC)
       End if
                 End if
      }
       End if
         End For
  Else
  {
        If (HELLO (A) ==true&& ACK (B) ==false)
        Remove (A, B)
        End if
        }
       }
  End if
  End For
  End
```

4   Simulation Experiment and Results

We conducted simulation experiments to evaluate the performance of the proposed algorithm and compare these finding against two existing algorithms Lowest-ID and the Weighted Clustering Algorithm (WCA) .We assumed a variety of systems running with 20, 30, 40, 50 and 60 nodes to simulate ad hoc networks with varying levels of node density. Two nodes are said to have a wireless link between them if they are within transmission range of each other. The performance was simulated with the transmission range of the nodes set to 50, 100, 150, 200 and 250 length units. The entire simulation was conducted in a 600×600 unit region. The nodes were then allowed to move at random in any direction at a speed of not greater than ½ the transmission range of a node per second. T he simulation for 2000 seconds, and the network was sampled every 2 seconds. Some of the more noteworthy simulation statistics measured was: Average number of Clusters with changing transmission range and Number of Cluster heads with increasing number of nodes. In each of the graph below, one of the parameters (e.g., the number of nodes in the network space or the transmission range) was varied for the Lowest-ID, WCA and WACA algorithms while the other parameters were kept constant.

Figure 6 shows the variation in the number of clusters with respect to the transmission range. Here, we observe that the number of clusters decrease with the increase in the transmission range of each node. The possible reason for this kind of behavior is that a cluster head with a large transmission range will cover a larger area. However, as the transmission radius increases even further, the rate of reduction in the number of clusters decreases due to the increase in overlap between adjacent clusters, and these results in an increase in the number of nodes belonging to multiple clusters.

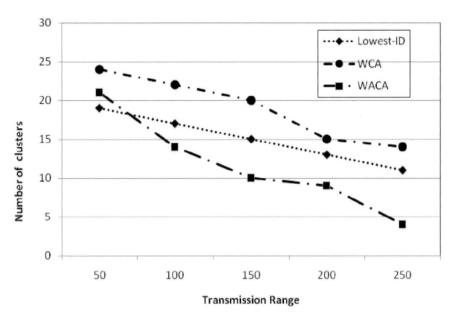

Fig. 6. Number of Clusters vs. Transmission Range

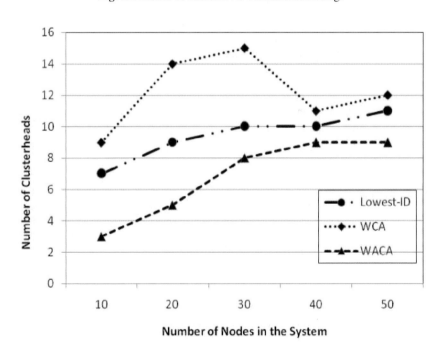

Fig. 7. No. of Cluster heads vs. No. of Nodes

It can be seen from the graph that WACA is much better (as it forms multilevel hierarchical clusters) than the other two algorithms. WCA gives the worst performance.

Figure 7 shows the number of clusters formed for the three clustering algorithms as a function of number of nodes. It can be seen from the graph that the algorithm WACA performs very well. For larger number of nodes the WCA algorithm is found to perform better than the Lowest-ID algorithm, but not better than WACA.

4.1 Performance Analysis

WCA vs. WACA
Stability
In WCA, the weights of the neighbor cluster heads are not considered in cluster formation procedure. This is one of the main drawbacks of WCA. So a newly entered node cannot tally its calculated combined weight with the weights of the already existing neighbor cluster heads. For this reason the stability of the created cluster using WCA is a confusing issue for mobility purpose.

But in the proposed algorithm WACA the neighbor cluster heads come into field of cluster head chosen. So, the stability of the formed cluster has increased here.

Multi-level hierarchical clusters
Using WCA algorithm it is not possible to create multi-level hierarchical clusters. But in contrary to WCA, WACA creates multi-level hierarchical clusters.

Lowest-ID vs. WACA
In Lowest-ID algorithm, each node is assigned a distinct ID. To find out the cluster head, the combined weight is not considered here. So, transmission range, transmission rate, mobility, battery power and degree of each node are not considered here. As a result, these basic factors of each node that has direct relation with the new cluster head creation or re-election of a node as a cluster head are totally hampered. That is, this algorithm starts its work with an arbitrary assignment operation by the user who wants to create clusters. This algorithm is totally user dependent. On the other hand, qualifications of each node in the cluster formation procedure are not considered here.

WACA considers qualifications (transmission range, transmission rate, mobility, battery power and degree) of each node separately for calculation of combined weight of each node. No arbitrary assignment operation to each node is occurred in my proposed algorithm. So, this algorithm is totally user independent.

5 Conclusion

This paper proposes a new Weight Based Adaptive Clustering Algorithm aimed at reducing the transmission overhead, total required time and increasing the stability of the formed cluster by EWCA. We conducted simulation experiments to measure the performance of my clustering algorithm and demonstrate that it performs significantly better. Results have shown that the average number of cluster heads can be decreased using WACA. WACA can create multi-level hierarchical clusters. Additionally, the WACA algorithm works on local information only and supports well-formed multi-hop clusters, realized by introducing cluster sub-heads.

References

[1] Lin, C.R., Gerla, M.: Adaptive clustering for mobile wireless Networks. IEEE Journal on Selected Areas in Communications 15(7), 1265–1275 (1997)

[2] McDonald, A.B., Znati, T.F.: A mobility-based framework for Adaptive clustering in wireless ad hoc networks. IEEE Journal on Selected Areas in Communications 17(8), 1466–1486 (1999)

[3] Perkins, C.E. (ed.): Ad Hoc Networking. Addison-Wesley, Reading (2001)

[4] Basagni, S.: Distributed clustering for ad hoc networks. In: Proceedings of International Symposium on Parallel Architectures, Algorithms and Networks, June 1999, pp. 310–315 (1999)

[5] Lin, C.-H.R., Gerla, M.: A distributed control scheme in multi-hop Packet radio networks for voice/data traffic support. In: Proceedings of IEEE GLOBECOM, pp. 1238–1242 (1995)

[6] Lin, C.-H.R., Gerla, M.: A distributed architecture for multimedia in dynamic wireless networks. In: Proceedings of IEEE GLOBECOM, pp. 1468–1472 (1995)

[7] Basagni, S.: Distributed and mobility-adaptive clustering for multimedia Support in multi-hop wireless networks. In: Proceedings of Vehicular Technology Conference, VTC, vol. 2, pp. 889–893 (Fall 1999)

[8] Chatterjee, M., Das, S., Turgut, D.: WCA: A Weighted Clustering Algorithm for Mobile Ad-hoc Networks. Journal of Cluster Computing Special Issue on Mobile Ad Hoc Networks 5(2), 193–204 (2002)

[9] Baker, D., Ephremides, A.: The architectural organization of a Mobile radio network via a distributed algorithm. IEEE Transactions on Communications COM-29 (11), 1694–1701 (1981)

[10] Baker, D., Ephremides, A.: A distributed algorithm for organizing Mobile radio telecommunication networks. In: Proceedings of the 2nd International Conference on Distributed Computer Systems, pp. 476–483 (April 1981)

[11] McDonald, A., Znati, T.: A mobility-based framework for adaptive Clustering in wireless ad hoc networks. IEEE Journal on Selected Areasin Communications (JSAC) 17(8), 1466–1487 (1999)

[12] Gerla, M., Tsai, J.: Multicluster, mobile, multimedia radio network. ACM Wireless Networks (WINET) 1(3), 255–265 (1995)

[13] Bölöni, L., Turgut, D.: YAES - A Modular Simulator for Mobile Networks. In: Proceedings of the 8th ACM/IEEE International Symposium on Modeling, Analysis and Simulation of Wireless and Mobile Systems (MSWiM), October 2005, pp. 169–173 (2005)

[14] Sun, X.-M., Liu, W.-J., Zhang, Z.-Q., Zhao, Y.: Cluster-based On Demand Multicast Routing Protocol

A Topology and Context Aware Query Distribution System in Middleware for Wireless Sensor Networks

Dhrubajyoti Saha[1] and Dibyendu Mallik[2]

[1] Software Engineer at IBM ISL
dhrubajyotisaha2008@gmail.com
[2] MTech student of CSE at IIT Kharagpur
dmallik@cse.iitkgp.ernet.in

Abstract. The continuous miniaturization of hardware components has contributed greatly to developement of wireless sensor nodes, that have greater computing capabilities. One major drawback of these sensor nodes, however, is that they have to operate in diverse environments without adequate maintenance in terms of power recharging. Thus reducing the amount of computation, and data transmission in such cases is of paramount importance. In this paper, we look at an approach in which a publish/subscribe based middleware arcitecture can be made both context and topography aware. We aim at decomposing complex queries, coming from the subscribers, and distributing the subqueries depending on the topography of the network. We also implement a feedback mechanism, which fine tunes this redistribution, at runtime. The redistribution is context aware (ie, dependant on the collected data and the computational power of the individual sensors), and is aimed at allowing the individual nodes to share greater computaional responsibilities. The ultimate aim is to minimize the computaion and data transmission load on each individual node.

1 Introduction

A communication network is composed of nodes, each of which have certain computing power, and can transmit and receive messages over communication links wireless or cabled [12]. The advancements, in the field of microelectronics, have led to the development of miniaturized sensing devices (nodes). A network formed with these nodes as the central component for aggregation of data, and then transmitting them via wireless media is known as Wireless Sensor Networks.

The sensor nodes have to operate without significant maintenance for long periods of time (e.g. Environment monitoring application). According to [10], WSN nodes must operate unattended, which means that middleware for WSN has to provide new levels of support for automatic configuration and error handling. The midleware can thus play a vital role in making network systems self sufficient in monitoring, and redistributing tasks within itself to achieve a better and cheaper mean of communication and data aggregation.

N. Meghanathan et al. (Eds.): NeCoM, WiMoN, and WeST 2010, CCIS 90, pp. 284–295, 2010.
© Springer-Verlag Berlin Heidelberg 2010

A middleware is a layer of software abstraction, that is placed between the operating system and the application programs, hiding the underlying system complexities and providing an interface to the clients. In recent years, middleware for WSN s have adopted the data centric model of communication, giving high emphasis on the publish/subscribe message passing model (e.g. The Mires Architecture[14]).

Retrieving queries, from network can also be done more effectively, if the query is split and redistributed, over the individual network components. The COUGAR project has contributed substantially in this respect [7]. However, matching the processing power of the individual nodes to the complexities of the generated subqueries, introduces some comstraints on the redistribution of queries. We, in this paper have introduced a topography aware middleware that will transmit queries based upon it's knowledge of the network topology. Since a full knowledge of the topography is an additional overhead, we make a tradeoff, and take decisions based on partial topographical knowledge.

However, since this method is not an optimum one, also have a feedback mechanism, through which a capable node can request more complex queries from the query dispatcher.

2   Basic Concepts

2.1   The Publish/Subscribe Paradigm

The Publish Subscribe model of Middleware architecture aims at minimizing the amount of data being transmitted by the nodes, and thus prolonging the lifetime of the system.

The model works in the following manner. The nodes advertise their topics (detectable parameters) to the server. The server informs the remote client/user of the available topics. When the user selects (subscribes to) a topic, this information is broadcast to all the nodes via the server. When an event occurs, which has been subscribed to, the nodes transfer the relevant data to the server, via the sink node. The server is then responsible for sending the data to the remote user. The nodes are the Publishers, since they publish the data on demand. The remote application is the Subscriber since it subscribes to the topic of its interest.

Another perspective from which a WSN can be looked at is the *database approach*, which approaches each sensor nodes as a potential storage space for data. from the sensors.

2.2   Distributed Query Processing in WSN

The foremost work in this regard has been done by the COUGAR project[4]. The basic concept is to distribute query elements to various nodes. In distributed database systems, a query is subdivided in to several smaller queries. The fitness of these generated subqueries can be determined by several factors. In traditional relational database management systems, determine the best possible query plan by evaluation two key factors: the time required for figuring out the query plan, and the time required to implement it. Whatever, the approach, a query has to be decentralized (based upon the parallelism constraints) and then computed. This leads to lessening of redundancy of data collection, as well as easing the load on a particular resource (ie, the sensor node).

There are several methods by which optimization of queries and generation of a query plan can be handled. Several of these are described in[11].

In WSNs the distribution of queries, should take into account not only the computing power of the nodes, but also the network topography and the event generation rates. The capability of considering such statistics is termed context awareness, in distributed systems.

2.3   Context Awareness

Context aware systems are those systems that can alter their behavior with respect to certain key elements in their environments such as location, neighbourhood, resources available. Context awareness is a key feature in mobile communication as well as multimedia based systems [5][6]. This feature is gaining importance in the field of Wireless Sensor Networks as well. Several strategies have been deviced and exploited. The major ones are cited in [9].

3   The Proposed Architecture

This section describes in detail, the proposed architecture.

Fig. 1 gives a broad overview of the system architecture. The middleware application interacts with the application programs via messages. These messages when coming from the application to the middleware, is in the form of queries. On the

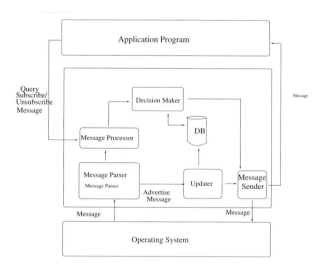

Fig. 1. The Proposed Middleware Architecture

other hand, when the data is being sent back to the application program, it is in the form of a notification message, containing the result of a query, and an indication of the subject of the query (which acts as a reference for the generated message).

The query which is received by the middleware can be of the three types:

1. A Subscribe/Unsubscribe Message
2. An Advertise Message
3. A Notify Message

Each of these messages, has to be handled differently. That is why, the message received is first sent to the message parser module, which determines the type of the message. Then depending on the type of the message, it is sent to the Message Processor, or the Updater Modules.

The Message Processor Module, handles the messages which are of type 1 or 2. The Message Processor is a module whose functionality depends on several factors, such as the computational power of the individual node and the amount of data storage available. Evidently, the strongest Message Processor module is available to the server itself. All others, implement a lightweight version, with limited capabilities.

3.1 Message Processor

The basic functionality of this module is the recognizing the capability of the individual computing power and thereafter, choosing a task for self and distributing the rest.

Server Message Processor. The server side Processor has to play the vital role in recognizing potential for parallelism in the input query. Depending upon it's nature, the input query, may be broken into several smaller queries, which can execute in parallel. Here we introduce a concept called the "query ranking", whereby, each generated subquery can be ranked according to the system requirements for it to be executed. The Message Processor, thus creates these queries based upon the ranking scheme, and hands it over to a decision making module. This module determines, which of the queries are to be transmitted based upon it's knowledge of the topography of the network.

General Message Processor. The generalized message processor, has a few simple functionalities. It's method of operation is as follows. First, check the rank of the query that is received. Choose from the queries, the one that requires a rank that is closest ($\leq$) to it's own. Then register the query in it's own internal database. Else, send the message to the decision making module, which will determine, whether, a neighboring node has similar rank. If no such nodes exist, the query is dropped altogether. Otherwise the query is broadcast.

The dependence upon the topography reduces the number of messages that will be sent from a particular node. This however, also creates a problem. If a node (of rank x say) is surrounded by nodes of rank $< x$, then all queries intended for nodes having rank $> x$ will be discarded at the previous node. To overcome this problem whenever a data which satisfies a certain query is generated, the generating node checks to see if the function associated with that particular query is equal to it's own rank. If this is not the case (which means that the query is of lesser rank), then the node sends out a message requesting a higher ranked query.

When this query is propagated forward, any node which has the required query, sends out the same. In this way, an adaptive mechanism is followed, by which queries are distributed to the regions of the network, where data is being generated in greater concentration.

4   A Simple Example

In this section we consider a simple example to look into the working of our proposed architecture.

4.1   Building the Topography Database

At the onset, let us consider that we have the WSN system and the nodes in place. Firstly, all nodes transmit messages which state their capabilities in terms of hardware, memory, sensing capabilities. These messages can be intercepted by the middleware, to create a local database of the neighboring nodes. Henceforth, we shall call this list as the "Topography List".

Current MAC layer protocols, require a partial or full view of the topography of the network. Moreover, publish/subscribe mechanism, requires the individual nodes to advertise their sensing capabilities. That is why, these messages sent at the onset will provide no extra overhead.

There are several ways by which neighboring nodes may be detected. For an example, the sender field can be verified and the most common nodes may be assumed to be neighboring ones.

There are certain tradeoffs involved, with keeping the partial information about the topography. Any node (in this architectural scheme) has no data concerning the capabilities of nodes that lie beyond it's immediate neighbors.For data aggregation purposes, certain nodes might thus be overlooked, because the server acts as the chief dispatcher of the queries. Thus only the nodes, which are near (in the neighborhood) the server or are connected by powerful nodes, will participate in data aggregation.

However, due to the memory and processing power constraints, we have aimed at minimizing the amount of stored data, and the amount of message transmission. We also have a mechanism, which we will explain later on, by which other nodes (located away from the server), can also participate in the aggregation process.

4.2   Query Splitting

When a query is submitted to the server, it is first parsed, and then the scope for parallelism is determined. For example, consider the query:

if (AVERAGE(TEMPERATURE) $\geq$ 90)
SUBSCRIBE QUERY { SELECT HUMIDITY
WHEN TEMPERATURE $\geq$ 100 }

This queries can be parsed to form the parse tree. If these queries can be processed by different nodes, a certain amount of cost efficiency in transmission can be saved. For example, if the result of a "if condition " is known beforehand, then the following statement (subscribe query) can be executed directly, thus saving computation time. Moreover, it is better to send a boolean value (true or false), which is the result of the "if condition" over the network, rather than sending individual temperature values, or even the average value of the temperature.

However each of the subqueries thus created will have system requirements of it's own. Since a WSN is composed of heterogeneous nodes, all nodes might not be able to process the entire query. For the specific example, it is not feasible to send the details of a cumbersome "subscribe query" operation over the network, unless it is certain, that, by doing so, some future transmission/computation can be saved. Hence, the scope of parallelism has to be explored, taking into consideration the cost of each function.

Each in-built function that the SQL like database (provided by the middleware) acknowledges, should thus have a unique rank. This rank should reflect the memory and computational requirement of the function. Similarly each node should have a ranking scheme, reflecting it's own memory/processing capabilities. As already stated, each node is aware of it's own system specifications, and thus it's own rank. The ranking system must be rigid,because the ranking of the database functions are static. For the sake of simplicity, let us consider that the memory and power of the nodes are not decreasing considerably in short span of time.

Backward Compatibility Issues. It is to be observed that the subqueries produced by splitting, cannot be disjoint. This is because of the uncertainty in the nature of the messages received by any node. For example, let us consider that a subquery of rank "x" is registered with a node. The node in question should also have the resources to calculate all subqueries of rank less than "x". This is because, data might be coming to the particular node, from other nodes, which have queries of rank less than "x-1". The Sever side processor will thus create several queries out of the submitted query. In this case the following are the subqueries that will be created.

- Rank <SOME HIGH VALUE>
  full query
- Rank <SOME INTERMEDIATE VALUE>
  subquery1 { select 1 when AVG(TEMPERATURE) $\geq$ 90 }
- Rank 0
  select TEMPERATURE

Note that the query we have selected in this example does not face the backward compatibility issue described in the previous section.

4.3   Query Distribution

The server needs to maintain a table of sub queries corresponding to each query. The server and all nodes also need to identify the main query as well as all the related subqueries. A tuple data (<query−id>,<subquery-id>) , should be associated with each subquery. Each server needs to maintain this data in a table like structure. Let us call this structure "SubQuery Map". Another list having all the subqueries also needs to be maintained. Let us call this the "SubQuery List". Every time a subquery is generated.

After the subqueries are generated, the server, checks it's Topography Table to determine which queries to broadcast. The matching algorithm is simple.

For each subquery s

Add(<query-is>, <subquery-id>) to SubQueryMap.

1. For each entry n in it's Topography Table
   if rank(n) = rank (s)
   broadcast (s)
2. Add s to "SuBQuery List"

The server also needs to maintain a subquery specific view of the entire query. This is required to reduce computation, when subqueries are being computed in a distributed fashion.

Receiver Nodes. The receiver nodes, need to maintain an account of the queries that it is currently handling. A small data structure is also maintained to assist the decision making in case a message is received. The structure that needs to be maintained is (<query-id>,<subquery-id>,<subquery-rank>). The receiver nodes, on receiving a subscribe message, does the following: For a message containing (<newquery-id>,<newsubquery>,<newsubquery-id>,<newsubquery-rank>), the algorithm is explained in algorithm 1.

Algorithm 1. The Subscription Algorithm

1: $i \leftarrow 0$
2: **if** $i > node\ list\ length$ **then**
3:     *Send out Message*
4: **else**
5:     **if** $rank(msg) > rank(node[i])$ **then**
6:         $i \leftarrow i + 1$
7:         **go to step 2.**
8:     **else**
9:         *Send out Message*
10:    **end if**
11: **end if**
12: **if** $rank(msg) < own\ rank$ **then**
13:     **if** $rank(msg) > rank(existing\ msg)$ **then**
14:         update query DB
15:     **end if**
16: **end if**

4.4   Adaptive Query Propagation

When data is gathered by a sensor node, it is reported via the operating system to the overlying middleware. The middleware, conducts a series of logical operations on these data, and then makes a decision to send it or not. The raw data collected by the sensor, is processed serially for each query that is registered into the middleware of the sensor.

In our proposed architecture, a case might arise when a node has a subquery such that, $subquery - id < rank$. In such cases, the resources of the nodes remain unutilized. This problem becomes quite acute, when a series of data are generated, all of which satisfy the condition for notification (broadcast of data).

A node having a rank > 0, may actually using subquery meant for a node ranked 0. In our example, then it will be sending all TEMPERATURE data as and when generated to the sink. This is highly unreasonable, because subquery1, which is of a higher rank, would have substantially decreased it's transmission. In other cases, where transmission may not be appreciably reduced (non decision making functions), the computational capabilities of a greater portion of a network may be utilized.

Algorithm 2. The Notification Algorithm

```
 1: i ← 0
 2: while i < number of queries do
 3:     Perform query[i]
 4:     if satisfied(query[i]) = true then
 5:         if rank(query[i]) < own rank then
 6:             Generate msg(data + request)
 7:         else
 8:             Generate msg(data)
 9:         end if
10:         Send out message
11:     end if
12:     i ← i + 1
13: end while
```

Algorithm 3. Aggregation Algorithm

```
 1: if isRegisteredQuery(query) = true then
 2:     if rank(own subquery) > rank(message subquery) then
 3:         Process Message
 4:         return
 5:     end if
 6: end if
 7: Forward Message
 8: if a higher query is there then
 9:     Send out Request
10: end if
```

A node, in such a situation, thus broadcasts a request, seeking a higher ranked subquery (for the same query). The message contains the following information (<query-id>,<node-rank>). If any node is using has such the appropriate subquery, it transmits the subquery to the requesting node.

Algorithm 2 explains how a data collected at a particular node is processed. Algorithm 3 explains how data received from other nodes will be processed. The above scheme ensures that queries are propagated and forwarded to only those nodes where appropriate data collection is occurring.

5   Evaluation

In this section, evaluate our middleware framework. We compare it to a middleware framework in which topology oriented message passing is not implemented. In other words, data packets are forwarded regardless of the neighboring nodes' ranks. Let us call the later framework the "Normal" framework.

5.1   Evaluation Setup

To evaluate our middleware architecture, we have simulated a WSN using Java. The simulator generates a random topology, given the number of nodes and the highest possible node rank. It then transmits data according to the "Normal" framework, and our framework respectively. For the simulation, we executed runs with 10, 20 and so on number of nodes. The maximum rank of the nodes were kept at 2 (ie, ranging was 0, 1, 2). We created the following query and sent it out into the network. We followed the query in the example showed in section 4.2. The evaluation was done using Java 1.5. The evaluation was run on a dual core Intel system running at 2.2 GHz.

5.2   Results

Fig. 2 shows the comparison between our model and the "Normal" model. The total data transmission rate for the Normal model has been normalized. We can

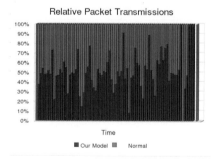

Fig. 2. Comparisons (10 random nodes)

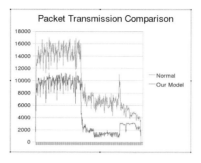

Fig. 3. Comparisons (20 random nodes)

find that there is a significant saving of nearly 30% considering the amount of data transmissions.

We have also simulated the same on a larger scale.

Fig. 3 shows the difference in the data transmissions when the number of nodes are 20. We find that the savings in the amount of data transmission is again close to 30 %.

Thus it can be inferred, though not conclusively, that the model that we propose can reduce the amount of data transmission between the nodes. Thus we have achieved power efficiency by using topology oriented message passing.

6   Related Work

The database approach towards sensor networks have been highlighted by COUGAR [1], SINA [2] and tinyDB [13]. COUGAR and tinyDB have focussed on treating each sensor node as a storage space of a relational database table, thus middleware funtionality is limited to extracting queries from a distributed data storage environment. To reduce data transmission, COUGAR project had introduced "in network query processing"[8] as early as 2002. Future works have focussed on creating and executing a more sophisticated query plan for queries.

SINA, on the other hand,introduces a scripting interface, by which small pieces of scripts can be transferred between nodes,thus increasing the diversity of the applications that can be developed over it.

MiLAN [16], is a middleware architecture which discovers services on the network as and when required. The application can communicate it's requirements to the middleware. MiLAN then finds out the appropriate node (or set of nodes) which are available to suit the requirement.

Taherkordi et al. [15] describes a context aware middleware framework. Taherkordi et al, borrows heavily from a framework called the COSMOS [3]. The COSMOS architecture is concerned with gathering context data from the environment and then adapting to these changes. Every node might not be capable of adaptation. These nodes communicate the data to respective higher level nodes, which in turn induce a context adaptation.

7   Conclusions and Future Work

We, in this paper have proposed a novel context aware query distribution scheme using node rankings. We have also proposed a topography aware query distribution scheme. We have implemented the proposed middleware architecture, and shown it to perform significantly better than a middleware which is not topology aware.

Such a middleware would be of great advantage in an environments where queries are injected with lesser frequency, and longetivity of the network is important. Certain kinds of queries(e.g. queries containing decision making problems) are also favourable for the proposed architecture.

There are certain drawbacks to the architecture as well. The architecture will perform better if either the high ranking nodes are nearer to the server, or are placed at distances of regular intercals from the server. If neither condition is satisfied, then the higher ranked queries will not be propagated initially. Moreover, when nodes ask for higher ranked queries, it is more likely that the request will be propagated as far back as the server.

There are certain aspects of this architecture which would need furthar investigation and research. Firstly it is thus important to have a dynamic rank allocation strategy, since the rank is dependant on the power and memory that a node holds. Moreover, an event which has just occured, may not occur again in the near future, and as such requesting a query, just because the current query conditionwas satisfied, may not be efficient. It might be better to have a threshold value for the number of events, after which a node will request a higher ranked query.

These aspects would provide the basis for future improvements in the proposed architecture.

References

1. Bonnet, P., Gehrke, J., Seshadri, P.: Towards sensor database systems. In: Tan, K.-L., Franklin, M.J., Lui, J.C.-S. (eds.) MDM 2001. LNCS, vol. 1987, pp. 3–14. Springer, Heidelberg (2000)
2. Srisathapornphat, C., Shen, C.-C., Jaikaeo, C.: Sensor information networking architecture and applications. IEEE Personal Communications 8(4), 52–59 (2001)
3. Rouvoy, R., Conan, D., Seinturier., L.: Scalable processing of context information with cosmos. In: Indulska, J., Raymond, K. (eds.) DAIS 2007. LNCS, vol. 4531, pp. 210–224. Springer, Heidelberg (2007)
4. COUGAR, http://www.cs.cornell.edu/bigreddata/cougar/index.php
5. Davidyuk, O., Riekki, J., Rautio, V.-M., Sun, J.: Context-aware middleware for mobile multimedia applications. In: MUM 2004: Proceedings of the 3rd international conference on Mobile and ubiquitous multimedia, pp. 213–220. ACM, New York (2004)
6. Dietze, S., Domingue, J.B.: Towards context-aware multimedia processing through semantic web services. In: EuroITV 2009: Proceedings of the seventh european conference on European interactive television conference, pp. 129–132. ACM, New York (2009)

7. Fung, W.F., Sun, D., Gehrke, J.: Cougar: the network is the database. In: SIG-MOD 2002: Proceedings of the 2002 ACM SIGMOD international conference on Management of data, p. 621. ACM, New York (2002)
8. Fung, W.F., Sun, D., Gehrke, J.: Cougar: the network is the database. In: SIG-MOD 2002: Proceedings of the 2002 ACM SIGMOD international conference on Management of data, p. 621. ACM, New York (2002)
9. Henricksen, K., Robinson, R.: A survey of middleware for sensor networks: state-of-the-art and future directions. In: MidSens 2006: Proceedings of the international workshop on Middleware for sensor networks, pp. 60–65. ACM, New York (2006)
10. Mattern, F., Romer, K., Kasten, O.: Middleware challenges for wireless sensor networks. Mobile Computing and Communications Review 6(2)
11. Kossmann, D.: The state of the art in distributed query processing. ACM Comput. Surv. 32(4), 422–469 (2000)
12. Lewis, F.L.: To appear in Smart Environments: Technologies, Protocols, and Applications. John Wiley, New York (2004)
13. Madden, S.R., Franklin, M.J., Hellerstein, J.M., Hong, W.: Tinydb: an acquisitional query processing system for sensor networks. ACM Trans. Database Syst. 30(1), 122–173 (2005)
14. Souto, E., Guimares, G., Vasconcelos, G., Vieira, M., Rosa, N., Ferraz, C., Kelner, J.: Mires: a publish/subscribe middleware for sensor networks. Personal Ubiquitous Comput. 10(1), 37–44 (2005)
15. Taherkordi, A., Rouvoy, R., Le-Trung, Q., Eliassen, F.: A self-adaptive context processing framework for wireless sensor networks. In: MidSens 2008: Proceedings of the 3rd international workshop on Middleware for sensor networks, pp. 7–12. ACM, New York (2008)
16. Carvalho, H.S., Heinzelman, W.B., Murphy, A.L., Perillo, M.A.: Middleware to support sensor network applications. IEEE Network 18(1), 6–14 (2004)

On-Demand Table-Driven Topo-Aware Routing Protocol for Wireless Mesh Networks

Ramesh Babu Battula[1], Srikanth Vemuru[1], Rajasekhara rao Kurra[1],
Pavan Kumar Tummal[1], and Jatindra Kumar Deka[2]

[1] K L University, School of Computing,
Vijayawada, Andhra Pradesh, India
[2] Indian Institute of Technology,
Guwahati, India
battula@alumni.iitg.ernet.in,
{srikanth_ist,rajasekhar.kurra,pavankumar_ist}@klce.ac.in,
jatin@iitg.ernet.in
http://www.kluniversity.in, http://www.iitg.ac.in

Abstract. Wireless Mesh Networks(WMNs) are emerging and low-cost next generation wireless networks. WMNs are able to provide communication for all types of networks with its backbone composed of low mobile or stationary Mesh Routers(MR). In WMNs, most of the traffic is generated by either Mobile Clients(MC) or Mesh Points(MP). MRs and MCs are two different mobile nodes in WMNs with different resources. Due to low mobility at MR level, proactive scenario performs well and proactive approach effectively utilizes the resources. The main constraint is at mobile client side, which have less resources and high mobility. So at this level reactive scenario performs well and it helps to utilize less resources in a good way.

In On-demand Table-driven approach, based on the topology proactive or reactive routing is used. At backbone level, the topology information is collected and maintained in the form of routing tables. At MC level, one-hop neighbors information is collected. Rouitng is mainly between the gateways(MP) and MCs, MPs use table-driven approach to communicate MCs and MCs use on-demand approach to communicate with MPs or MCs. MRs are intermediate routers, topology information are collected and provide instant route to either MPs or MCs. On-demand Table-driven approach reduces end to end delay,routing overhead and packet loss ratio.

Keywords: On-demand, Table-driven, Virtual Cluster, AODV and OFLSR.

1 Introduction

Wireless Mesh Networks(WMN) are next generation wireless networks with their promising and low-cost technology. It provides high-speed Internet access for future broadband applications. WMNs are flexible, mobile, reliable and scalable wireless networks. WMNs reduce the initial investment and deployment time

N. Meghanathan et al. (Eds.): NeCoM, WiMoN, and WeST 2010, CCIS 90, pp. 296–305, 2010.

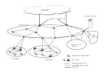

Fig. 1. Hybrid Wireless Mesh Networks

compared to traditional broadband Internet access technologies [1]. In WMNs 802.11 based multi-hop communication is used for delivering fast services to end-users, WMNs are not used for any fixed Access point networks like Wireless Local Area Networks(WLAN). WMNs are extremely reliable with its mesh connection. If any node fails or drop of packet in the network occurs, it uses another route as activce route.

Wireless mesh networks (WMN) is an emerging technology. Existing definitions are simply based on Mobile Ad hoc Networks (MANETs), which are variants of WLAN. WMNs are considered as special MANETS [3,5]. Wireless Mesh Networks(WMNs) are self-organized, self-configured, ease and can rapidity change with the network deployment [2,4,5]. Wireless Mesh Network consists of three types of nodes. **Mesh Points(MP), Mesh Routers(MR)**, and **Mesh Clients(MC)**.

In wireless networks routing protocols are broadly categorized into proactive, reactive, and hybrid. These protocols are either distance-based or link state-based. Proactive routing protocols are "table-driven", where it maintains every nodes information. So every node maintains one or more tables based on the protocol and timely broadcasts the table information to its neighbors and exchange the tables, in which control overheads play key a role and it degrades protocol performance. Reactive routing protocols are "source routing protocols", it reduces the control overheads, and it performs well in highly mobile networks [6,7,8,9].

2   Cluster Formation

2.1   Cluster Formation at Mesh Router Level

2.2   Cluster Formation at MC Level

In client level, cluster formation is mainly based on its connectivity with MR, MR has radio transmission, MCs within that range and one-hop neighbors can directly communicate with the MR and at same time all MC also maintains two-hop neighbors communication list in its route cache. The list is based on its ETT value. MC level clusters heads are MRs. In the same fashion, any dynamic changes in the cluster is identified and updated in the MC route caches and MR routing tables. ETT routing metric provide traffic load information in the cluster. Load on MR is controlled to know the traffic load in the cluster, when the load is high and cluster does some changes. Periodically sending hello message clearly defines the cluster size and its topology changes in the network.

Algorithm for Backbone level
Step 1 A node send hello massage to its one hop neighbors, hello message contain hop Count Field it increases at every node.
Step 2 if ((hop count = = k) or (hop count! =k and Link (i, j) = = NULL) Then assign weights from k-hop to source node in increasing order (1 to k); Calculate Link Weight factor (ETT = ETX × ($\frac{S}{B}$)) at each link; (ETT = Expected transmission time, ETX = Expected transmission count; t = $\frac{S}{B}$=Avg. Time for single packet delivered, S = Packet size and B = Bandwidth). Go to step 4.
Step 3 else increment hop count and direct to next link; go to Step 2.
Step 4 Calculate all nodes Sum = $\sum_{\forall(links)}(\sum_{i=1,j=i+1}^{i=k-1,j=k} ETT_{i,j} \times W_i)$;(k is maximum hop cout, i and j are link interfaces,W is weight).
Step 5 If x and y Mesh Routers are least SUM routers, these two elect as a cluster sub-head1 and Sub-head2. Least sum Mesh Router elect as Gateway and second least MR elect as cluster head. More then two are same Sum nodes, and then select highest weight nodes.

Algorithm for Client Mesh Level
Step 1 First MR generate hello message to communicate with its one-hop neighbors
Step 2 if it is mesh client and one-hop neighbor of MR then it find its k-hop neighbors,generate Hello message and send to client mesh.
Step 3 while it is k-hop or no link to forward the hello message.calculate SUM so go to Step 6
Step 4 else increment hop count and direct to next link;
Step 5 at acknowledgement passing time, calculate ETT value and assign weights to its hop with Increasing order 1 to k. (here k=2).
Step 5 Calculate SUM at all nodes in the cluster SUM = $\sum_{i=1,j=i+1}^{i=k-1,j=k} ETT_{i,j} \times W_i$; (k is maximum hop cout, i and j are link interfaces,W is weight).
Step 6 MR one-hop neighbors (Mesh clients) collect the information about all links and store its in route cache.we use this algorithm when any new one-hop router within the MR radio range. otherwise every node in the cluster use hello messages and update k-hop neighbors list, Path information and its ETT value.
Step 7 Once MC set its route cache, send information to be cluster head that is MR.Hello Messages generate at regular intervals, at this time we update any information.route cache details propagate upto k-hop nodes. if any changes in its one-hop neigbors, MR also update route cache.

2.3 Performance Metrics for Routing Protocols

Performance metrics calculations can be classified as follows, *Passive monitoring*: traffic coming in and out of bandwidth estimation done. *Piggyback Probing*: Measurements done by include probing information into regular traffic. It is commonly used for measure delay. *Active probing*: Special packets generated to measure properties of a link. Some performance metrics are Packet Loss Ratio [11,12], Hop Count [11], Blocking [11] and etc.

2.4 ETX (Expected Transmission Count)

Expected Transmission Count is defined as the number of required successfully delivered packets over a wireless link [14]. ETX measures the expected transmissions and retransmissions needed to successfully deliver a packet from sender to receiver. The ETX of a link is the predicted number over a link; the ETX of a route is the sum of the ETX for each link over the route. The derivation of ETX starts by measuring the underlying packet loss probability in both the forward and reverse directions denoted by d_f and d_r. Let p denote the probability that the packet transmission from node x to y in a link is not successful.

$$p = 1 - (1 - p_f) \times (1 - p_r) \tag{1}$$

Also, assume the probability that the packet will be successful received by node y after k attempts denoted by s (k). Then, s(k) = $p^k \times$(1 - p). Finally, ETX is acquired mathematically using series theory:

$$ETX = \sum k \times s(k) = \frac{1}{(1-p)} \qquad k = 1 \ \ to \ \ \infty \tag{2}$$

When ETX is measured in a link of a real network,

$$ETX = \frac{1}{(d_f \times d_r)} \tag{3}$$

d_f and d_r mean the probability of the successful packet delivery in the forward or reverse direction.

2.5 ETT (Expected Transmission Time)

The Expected Transmission Time metric (ETT) has the goal to incorporate throughput into its calculation. Let S be the size of the probing packet and B be the measured bandwidth of a link, then the ETT of this link is defined as follows.

$$ETT = ETX \times \frac{S}{B} \tag{4}$$

Similar to ETX, the expected transmission time of a path is computed as the sum of the links ETT along the path.

Where β is a tunable parameter less than 1 and X represents the number of times channel j is used along path p.

3   Proposed Rouitng Protocol

The proposed routing protocol uses Neighbor discovery, Route discovery, and Route maintenance processes.

- **Neighbor discovery process**: Is used to discover neighbors and to update the routing table using hello messages and topology control messages.
- **Route discovery process**: Is used to find the destination by on-demand table driven manner.
- **Route maintenance process**: Any failure/repair/loss in the network will be handled by this process.

3.1   Neighbor Discovery

This mechanism is responsible for establishing and maintaining neighbors relationship among the nodes in the entire network. Neighbor nodes can communicate with each other by simply transmitting special packets (Hello and Topology control messages), broadcast through Multi Point Relay (MPR) nodes (Topology control messages) over the medium. In this, HELLO packets are periodically broadcasted and nodes within the transmission range of the sending node will hear these special packets and record them as neighbors. Each node associates an ACTIVETIME value in the node's route cache or routing table for each neighbor. When it does not hear a HELLO packet from a particular neighbor within the ACTIVETIME period, it will remove that neighbor from the neighbor list and it will maintain in precursor table for a short-period of time. Suppose if it hears HELLO packet, it will be updated, otherwise it removes the routing entry information from the routing table. ACTIVETIME values are reset when a HELLO message is heard. HELLO Packets also contain the list of routers whose HELLO Packets have been seen recently. Nodes can use this information to find the links. In this proposed protocol hello message processing is shown in the figure - 2. In our proposed routing protocol, Topology control messages are used to collect the topology information at backbone level. Topology control messages at SCOPE level is used to collect topology information in the network to describe hop distance. Time interval is different for each and every SCOPE level. Topology control message processing shown in figure 3.

Fig. 2. Hello Message Processing

Fig. 3. Topology Control message Processing

In this, Topology control message uses scope level information with a field in packet format. Scope level contains three types which are shown in figure 3. In topology packet format, if scope level field contains 1, it collects the two hop away topology information, if it is 2, it collects three-hop away nodes information and if it is 3, it collects four-hop away information. Scope levels uses different time interval sets to reduce the number of control messages in the network. Multi Point Relay (MPR) concept similar to OSLR is used to send messages. In routing table, it calculates ETT values which is used as a metric and sums all ETT values when the acknowledgement passes to source. Topology control messages uses differnt times and diffrent ETT values to find cluster head to form a virtual cluster.

3.2 Route Discovery

In Route Discovery mechanism, Route Request(RREQ) message is used to discover and set a path to the destination. A node broadcasts RREQ when it needs a route to destination, which is not available in the routing table, This happens when destination is unknown, or if a valid route is expired. If Route reply(RREP) is not received within the time period, it rebroadcasts the RREQ message. If any intermediate or destination node receives the route request message, it processes as shown in the figure-4.

Whenever a node has to send data, it checks whether it has a route to destination; if not it starts the route discovery phase. The route discovery mechanism has three phases: route request, route formation, and route reply. In route request, RREQ generates either Mesh Point(MP)or Mesh Client(MC).

Fig. 4. Route Request Message Processing at Destination/Intermidiate

Table 1. Route Discovery Process

Step 1	recevRREQ destinationID
Step 2	Check for Destination NodeID is same for Current NodeID
Step 3	if Destination ID and CurrentNodeID Same then
Step 4	Check for U bit in RREQ (U = 1 bit one Means Unknown Sequence Number)
Step 5	if U bit is 1 then
Step 6	Generate RREP with Destination Sequence Number
Step 7	Forward RREP to source node
Step 8	Else Forward RREP to Source NodeID
Step 9	Else LookUp for Destination ID in Routing Table
Step 10	if Routing Entry for DestinationID in Routing Table
Step 11	Check for U bit in RREQ
Step 12	if U bit is 1 then
Step 13	Generate RREP with Destination Sequence Number
Step 14	Forward RREP to source node
Step 15	Else Forward RREP to Source NodeID
Step 16	Else Check for NodePt is less then 250
Step 17	(we use in our simulation Mesh Router Radio range is 250m)
Step 18	if NodePt is less then 250
Step 19	Broadcast RREQ to it's one-hop Neighbors
Step 20	one-hop neighbors receive RREQ it will start from STEP 1
Step 21	Else Forward RREQ to it's Four-hop Neighbors in Routing Table
Step 22	Four-hop neighbors receive RREQ it will start from STEP 1

After a route to the destination is found, the whole route from source to destination is formed by the intermediate/destination nodes. This phase is called the route formation phase. When a route is formed, a route reply with the entire route information is sent to the source node, which is the last phase of route discovery. If the receiving node exists in the same region or ad hoc component as the sending node, only reactive routing is used. The RREP discovers the possible routes and data is send through the discovered routes. If the receiving node and the sending nodes are not in a same region or ad hoc component then route discovery is done by using both reactive and proactive routing protocols. The route request phase is uses on-demand table driven technique and process the route request and route replay messages in the network, so the receiving node MR using table-driven and on-demand procedures are used. In this proposed routing protocol, any intermediate/destination node receives the RREQ message.

3.3   Routing Maintenance

Route maintenance is invoked when a link has broken or when the intermediate node detects when the next hop in the route is unreachable. Intermediate router sends route error packet back to sender, after receiving route error it may use different routes or may perform route discovery.

The knowledge of network topology of a region can be used to provide better route maintenance. In Router infrastructure, the feature of the above protocol is incorporated in the router with multiple paths, a multiple path routing will provide reliability, load balancing, and better route maintenance with little delay and less control traffic. Once link failure happens, the node will become forging node. When it want to connect back it has to join as the neighbor. In our routing maintenance scheme, node failure or link failure will detect neighbor nodes and inform to its neighbors. Suppose it is in a ACTIVE path it uses another path from that node and informs to the source node. Route maintenance is easy because of mesh connectivity between the nodes.

4 Simulation and Results

4.1 Simulation Environment

Simulation environment is explained in table 2. In this simulation, compare the results of proposed protocol with AODV and DSDV routing protocols.

Table 2. Simulation parameters

1	Examined Protocols	AODV,DSDV and HWMP
2	Simulation time	200sec
3	Simulation Area	620×620,860×860, etc
4	Propagation Model	Two-ray ground Reflection
5	Mobility Model	Random Way Point
6	Mobility for Mesh clients	0,5,10,15,20,25 and 30 m/s
7	Transmission range	MR - 250m and MC - 40m
8	Packet Type and Size	CBR - 512 bytes and TCP - 552 Bytes
9	Packet Rate	32
10	Number of Radios	Single radio for MR and MC

In this simulation, examined already existing protocols in Mobile ad-hoc networks (MANET), AODV and DSDV these two protocols are leading protocols in the wireless networks. Proposed protocol compare its performance efficiency with AODV and DSDV.

4.2 Simulation Results

- *Routing Overhead*: The total number of sent or forwarded control packets that are usefull to route the data packets. Ratio of total sent and forwarded control packets to total sent and forward data packets is called routing overhead of a protocol.
- *End-to-End Delay* : It is defined as the averaged time needed for a data packet to be delivered from source to destination.
- *Packet Loss Ratio*: The number of packets that were lost due to unavailable or incorrect routes, MAC layer collisions or through the situation of interface queues.

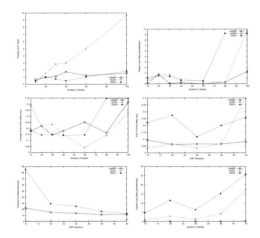

Performance parameters are compared with the number of nodes. Simulation results are proved that the packet loss ratio, routing overhead and end-to-end delay of On-Demand Table-Driven Topo-Aware Routing Protocol is better when compared with traditional routing protocols in wireless mesh networks.

5   Conclusion

The proposed routing protocol collects topology information at mesh router level using hello messages and topology messages. Topology message will be used up to four hops away from the source to construct a virtual cluster. Cluster maintenance and cluster overhead is reduced using topology messages. These control messages uses MPR concept in the network to reduce the number of control messages. Proactive concept is used to collect the topology information and reactive concept is used to route the packets. Proactive scenario improves the end-to-end delay and provides efficient routing in the network. Reactive scenario improves packet delivery ratio and reduces packet loss ratio in the network.

References

1. Jun, J., Sichitiu, M.L.: MRP: Wireless Mesh Networks Routing Protocol, 3rd edn.
2. Akyildiz, I.F., Wang, X., Wang, W.: Wireless Mesh Networks: a survey. Elsevier, Amsterdam (2004)
3. Akyildiz, I.F., Wang, X.: A Survey on Wireless Mesh Networks. IEEE Radio Communication, 523–530 (2005)
4. Nandiraju, N., Nandiraju, D., Santhanam, L., He, B., Wang, J., Agrawal, D.P.: Wireless Mesh Networks: Current Challenges and Future Directions of Web-in-the-Sky. IEEE Wireless Communications, 1536–1284 (2007)
5. Zemmermann, A., Gijnes, M., Wenig, M., Meis, U., Titzerfeld, J.: How to study wireless mesh networks: a testbed approach. In: 21st International conference on advanced networking and applications, AINA2007 (2007)

6. Akyildiz, I.F. (Georgia Institute of Technology) Wang, X., Kiyon: A Survey on Wireless Mesh Networks (2005)
7. Nandaraju, N., Nandaraju, D., Santhanam, L., He, B., Wang, J., Agrawal, D.P.: Wireless Mesh Networks: Current Challenges and Future Directions of Web-in-the-sky. University of Cincinnati, USA (2006)
8. Akyildiz, I.F., Wang, X., Wang, W.: Wireless mesh netwoks: a survey (2004)
9. Pirzada, A.A., Portmann, M.: High performance AODV routing protocol for Hybrid wireless mesh networks (2007)
10. Chen, J., Lee, Y.-Z., Maniezzo, D., Gerla, M.: Performance comparison of AODV and OFLSR. Wireless Mesh Networks (2007)
11. Rainner, SimonJhonson: 96 and Andres and Mario. A survey on routing metrics (2006)
12. Zakrzewska, A., Koszalka, L., Poszalka-Koszalka, I.: Performance study of routing protocols. In: IEEE 19th international conference on system engineering (2008)
13. Waharte, S., Ishibashi, B., Boutaba, R., Meddour, D.: A Performance Study of Wireless Mesh Networks Routing Metrics. IEEE Wireless Communications (2008)
14. De Couto, D., Aguayo, D., Bicket, J., Morries, R.: A high throughput path metric for multi-hop wireless routing. In: Mobicom 2003, ACM, New York (2003)
15. Information Sciences Institute, NS-2 Network Simulator, Software Package (2003), http://www.isi.edu/nsnam/ns/
16. Chen, J., Lee, Y.-Z., Maniezzo, D., Gerla, M.: Performance comparison of AODV and OFLSR in wireless mesh networks. In: IEEE Conference (2006)
17. Johnson, D.B., Maltz, D.A.: Dynamic Source Routing Protocol for Wireless Networks. In: Imielinski, Korth (eds.) Mobile Computing. Kluwer Academics Publisers, Dordrecht (1996)
18. Das, S.R., Perkins, C.E., Royer, E.M.: Performance Comparison of Two On-Deamnd Routing Protcols. In: Proceedings of the IEEE conference on computer communications, INFOCOM (March 2000)

An Efficient Quality of Service Scheduling Strategy for IEEE 802.16 Broadband Wireless Access Systems

Prasun Chowdhury[1] and Iti Saha Misra[2]

Electronics and Telecommunication Engineering
Jadavpur University, Kolkata, India
prasun.jucal@gmail.com, itisahamisra@yahoo.co.in

Abstract. In this paper, an efficient QoS scheduling strategy is proposed for IEEE 802.16 BWA systems that satisfies both throughput and delay guarantee to the applications such as video and audio streaming, online gaming, video conferencing, Voice over IP (VoIP), File Transfer Protocol (FTP) and Web Browsing. The proposed QoS scheduling strategy is compared with an existing QoS scheduling scheme proposed in literature in recent past. Simulation results show that the proposed scheduling architecture can provide a tight QoS guarantee for all types of traffic as defined in the standard hence maintain fairness and helps to eliminate starvation of lower priority class services.

Keywords: IEEE 802.16; MAC; QoS; Packet Scheduling.

1 Introduction

WiMAX (Worldwide Interoperability for Microwave Access), is a technology aimed at providing last-mile wireless broadband access at a cheaper cost. The "last mile" is the final leg of delivering connectivity from the service provider to the customer [1]. This leg is typically seen as an expensive undertaking because of the considerable costs of wires and cables. The core of WiMAX technology is specified by the IEEE 802.16 standard that provides specifications for the Medium Access Control (MAC) and Physical (PHY) layers. The term WiMAX was created by the WiMAX forum that promotes conformance and interoperability of the standard.

In WiMAX network such as, traffic from the Base Station (BS) to the Subscriber Stations (SSs) is classified as downlink traffic while that from the SSs to the BS is classified as uplink traffic. A scheduling algorithm implemented at the BS has to deal with both uplink and downlink traffic. In some cases, separate scheduling algorithms are implemented for the uplink and downlink traffic. Typically, a Call Admission Control (CAC) procedure is also implemented at the BS that ensures the load supplied by the SSs can be handled by the network [1-5]. A CAC algorithm will admit a SS into the network if it can ensure that the minimum Quality of Service (QoS) requirements of the SS can be satisfied and the QoS of existing SSs will not deteriorate. The performance of the scheduling algorithm for the uplink traffic strongly depends on the CAC algorithm.

N. Meghanathan et al. (Eds.): NeCoM, WiMoN, and WeST 2010, CCIS 90, pp. 306–315, 2010.

Packet scheduling [5-14] is the process of resolving contention for shared resources in a network. The process involves allocating bandwidth among the users and determining their transmission order. Scheduling algorithms for a particular network need to be selected based on the type of users in the network and their QoS requirements. QoS requirements vary depending on the type of application/user. For real-time applications such as video conferencing, voice chat and audio/video streaming, delay and delay jitter are the most important QoS requirements. Delay jitter is the inter-packet arrival time at the receiver and is required to be reasonably stable by the real-time applications. On the other hand, for non-real time applications such as file transfer (FTP), throughput is the most important QoS requirement. Some applications, such as web-browsing and email do not have any QoS requirements. In a network, different types of applications, with diverse QoS requirements, can co-exist. A scheduling algorithm's task in a multi-class network is to categorize the users into one of the pre-defined classes. Each user is assigned a priority, taking into account its QoS requirements. Subsequently, bandwidth is allocated according to the priority of the users as well as ensuring that fairness between the users is maintained.

Packet scheduling algorithms are implemented at both the BS and SSs. A scheduling algorithm at the SS is required to distribute the bandwidth allocation from the BS among its connections. A scheduling algorithm at the SS is not needed if the BS grants bandwidth to each connection of the SS separately i.e. the Grant per Connection (GPC) procedure is followed. If the Grant per Subscriber Station (GPSS) procedure is followed, the scheduling algorithm at the SS needs to decide on the allocation of bandwidth among its connections. The scheduling algorithm implemented at the SS can be different than that at the BS [8].

The focus of our work is on scheduling algorithms for the uplink traffic in WiMAX i.e. traffic from the SSs to the BS. A scheduling algorithm for the uplink traffic is faced with challenges not faced by an algorithm for the downlink traffic. An uplink scheduling algorithm does not have all the information about the SSs such as the queue size. An uplink algorithm at the BS has to coordinate its decision with all the SSs where as a downlink algorithm is only concerned in communicating the decision locally to the BS.

K. Wongthavarawat et al. propose a hybrid scheduling algorithm in [1] that combines Earliest Deadline First (EDF), Weighted Fair queuing (WFQ) and First in First out (FIFO) scheduling algorithms. The overall allocation of bandwidth is done in a strict priority manner i.e. all the higher priority SSs are allocated bandwidth until they do not have any packets to send. The EDF scheduling algorithm is used for SSs of the rtPS class, WFQ is used for SSs of the Non-Real Time Polling Service (nrtPS) class and FIFO for SSs of the Best Effort (BE) class. Besides the scheduling algorithm, an admission control procedure and a traffic policing mechanism are also proposed. All these components together constitute the proposed QoS architecture. A drawback of this algorithm is that lower priority SSs will essentially starve in the presence of a large number of higher priority SSs due to the strict priority overall bandwidth allocation.

J. Lin et al. [8] propose architecture called Multi-class Uplink Fair Scheduling Structure (MUFSS) to satisfy throughput and delay requirements of the multi-class traffic in WiMAX. The proposed scheduling discipline at the BS is Modified Weighted Round Robin (MWRR), although details of the modifications to the

Weighted Round Robin (WRR) discipline are not provided by the authors. The model is based on Grant per Subscriber Station (GPSS) bandwidth grant mode and thus schedulers are implemented at the SSs to distribute the bandwidth granted among their connections. At the SS, Modified WFQ (MWFQ) is used for Unsolicited Grant Service (UGS) and Real-Time Polling Service (rtPS) connections, MWRR is used for nrtPS connections and FIFO is used for BE connections.

K. Vinay *et al.* [9] propose a hybrid scheme that uses EDF for SSs of the rtPS class and WFQ for SSs of the nrtPS and BE classes. This algorithm differs from the one in [1] in a couple of ways. First, the WFQ algorithm is used for SSs of both nrtPS and BE classes. Secondly, the overall bandwidth allocation is not done in a strict priority manner. Although the details of overall bandwidth allocation are not specified, it is briefly mentioned that the bandwidth is allocated among the classes in a fair manner. Since SSs of the BE class do not have any QoS requirements, using a computationally complex algorithm such as WFQ for them is not needed. Here Author made the comparative study of the scheduling algorithms implemented in GPSS and GPC and found that GPSS gives better end-to-end delay.

M.Settembre *et al.* [10] propose a hybrid scheduling algorithm that uses WRR and Round Robin (RR) algorithms with a strict priority mechanism for overall bandwidth allocation. In the initial portion of the algorithm, bandwidth is allocated on a strict priority basis to SSs of the rtPS and nrtPS classes only. After that the WRR algorithm is used to allocate bandwidth among SSs of rtPS and nrtPS classes until they are satisfied. If any bandwidth remains, it is distributed among the SSs of the BE class using the RR algorithm. This algorithm will starve lower priority SSs in the presence of a large number of higher priority SSs. The algorithm can also result in low fairness among SSs as it selects SSs with the most robust burst profiles first.

J. SUN *et al.* [11] proposed that the scheduler inside the BS may have only limited or even outdated information about the current state of each uplink connection due to the large Round Trip Delay (RTD) and possible collision occurred in the uplink channel transmission. So there is a need of an additional scheduler in each SS to reassign the received transmission opportunities among different connections. Since the uplink traffic is generated at SS, the distributed scheduler is able to arrange the transmission based on the up-to-date information and then provide QoS guarantee for its connections. But here the proposed algorithm is suffered by a problem called as *starvation of lower priority class services*.

In the proposed method the uplink traffic is scheduled based on current queue information at SS similarly in the way proposed in [11]. But a different hybrid algorithm has been implemented at the SS scheduler which helps to eliminate the starvation of lower priority class services. In the proposed method the BS scheduler can guarantee the minimum bandwidth for each service flow and ensure fairness and QoS in distributing excess bandwidth among all connections. At the same time, the scheduler in SS can provide differentiated and flexible QoS support for all of the four scheduling service types. In this paper EDF algorithm is applied for rtPS class of services and Deficit Fair Priority Queue (DFPQ) algorithm found in literature [12],[13] is applied for nrtPS and BE class of services. It can both reduce the delay of real-time applications and guarantee the throughput of non-real-time applications such as nrtPS and BE.

The rest of the paper is organized as follows; The QoS related features of IEEE 802.16 standard are discussed in section 2. Then the proposed scheduling algorithms are introduced in section 3. Section 4 provides simulation model and results analysis. Finally, this paper is ended up with the conclusions drawn in section 5.

2   QoS Features of IEEE 802.16

The first version, known as 802.16, was completed in October 2001. It specified a Single Carrier (SC) air interface for fixed point-to-multipoint (PMP) BWA systems operating between 10-66 GHz. The second amendment, 802.16a, was published in January 2003. It extends the physical environment towards lower frequency bands below 11 GHz. The next approved version is 802.16d, which is published in June 2004 and also known as FIXED WiMAX (802.16-2004). It incorporates all the previous versions to provide fixed BWA. In 2005, IEEE is undertaking the standardization of 802.16e, which is expected to support full mobility up to 70-80m/s [6]. Four service types are defined in IEEE 802.16d-2004 (Fixed) standard, which includes UGS (Unsolicited Grant Service), rtPS (Real-time Polling Service), nrtPS (Non Real-time Polling Service), and BE (Best Effort). The UGS is designed to support real-time service flow that generates fixed-size data periodically, such as T1/E1, VoIP without silence suppression [1], [6]. The rtPS is designed to support real-time service flow that generates variable size data, such as video streaming services while the nrtPS deals with FTP in similar manner. The BE perform tasks related to e-mail and web browsing. The guaranteed delay aspect is also taken care in video streaming and VoIP.

Since IEEE 802.16 MAC protocol is connection oriented, the application first establishes the connection with the BS as well as the associated service flow (UGS, rtPS, nrtPS or BE). BS will assign the connection with a unique connection ID (CID) [1], [6]. All packets from the application layer in the SS are classified by the connection classifier based on CID and are forwarded to the appropriate queue. So the scheduler inside the BS has outdated information about the current state of each uplink connection due to the large Round Trip Delay (RTD) and possible collision occurred in the uplink channel transmission [14].

3   Proposed Scheduling Algorithm

In the proposed method, the uplink bandwidth allocation at BS is done based on the per connection requests from SSs. Because a SS may have multiple connections at the same time, the bandwidth request messages should report the bandwidth requirement of each connection in SS. After that the allocated bandwidth per connection is pooled together and granted to each SS. Then SS re-distribute the received transmission opportunities among its connections according to their QoS requirement. Therefore an additional scheduler is needed in each SS to reassign the received transmission opportunities among different connections. Since the uplink traffic is generated at SS, the distributed scheduler is able to arrange the transmission based on the up-to-date information and then provide tight QoS guarantee for its connections.

Since the BS scheduler has limited information on the traffic generated at SS, the computing of bandwidth allocation should just consider the bandwidth request and reservation for each connection.

Let $BWMIN_i$ denote the minimum reserved bandwidth for connection i, and $BWREQ_i$ represent the bandwidth currently demanded by the connection i. Since the connection will never get more resources than it has requested, the bandwidth actually allocated during this phase is

$$BWALLOCATE_i = \min \{BWMIN_i, BWREQ_i\} \tag{1}$$

For rtPS and nrtPS, $BWMIN_i$ is specified by the QoS parameter termed Minimum Reserved Traffic Rate. Clearly, to guarantee the contracted bandwidth, the sum of minimum reserved bandwidth for all the connections should not exceed the available bandwidth B. After each connection gets its guaranteed bandwidth, if there is still excess uplink bandwidth remained, BS scheduler should distribute the residual bandwidth in proportion to the pre-assigned connection weight. The algorithm in this phase can be described as:

```
BWREMAIN = B - ∑ BWALLOCATE_i;
              i
While BWREMAIN > 0
{
      If (BWALLOCATE_i < BWREQ_i)
      {
                                    n
            BWADD_i = BWREMAIN*W_i / ∑W_k;
                                   k=1
            BWALLOCATE_i = BWALLOCATE_i + BWADD_i;
            BWREMAIN = BWREMAIN - BWADD_i;
      }
}
```

Where BWREMAIN is the remaining bandwidth, $BWADD_i$ is the amount of excess bandwidth allocated to connection queue i and W_i is the weight of connection queue i. Now the allocated bandwidth per connection is pooled together and granted to each SS.

SS scheduler will select the packet to be transmitted from the highest priority queue. The priority of the queue is maintained in the following way UGS > rtPS > nrtPS > BE.

- Scheduling algorithm for UGS queues
UGS generate fixed size data packets on a periodic basis. This service has a critical delay and delay jitter requirement. So SS scheduler will firstly guarantee the bandwidth for UGS queues.

- Scheduling algorithm for rtPS queues
For rtPS service, Each packet entering the rtPS queues should be marked with a delivery deadline equal to t + tolerated delay, where t is the arrival time and tolerated delay is

the Maximum Latency for such a service flow. The packet with smaller deadline will be transmitted earlier. This greatly reduces the end-to-end delay of rtPS service.

- Scheduling algorithm for nrtPS and BE queues
For nrtPS and BE services Deficit Fair Priority Queue (DFPQ) algorithm found in literature [12], [13] is employed. DFPQ is almost similar to Deficit Round Robin (DRR) algorithm. This algorithm has been applied because of the following reasons.

1. The algorithm is mostly suited for datagram networks where packet sizes vary.
2. Since this algorithm requires accurate knowledge of packet size, it is suitable for the uplink traffic at SS scheduler.
3. The algorithm is flexible enough as it allows provision of quanta of different sizes depending   on the QoS requirements of the SSs. With this algorithm employed, SS scheduler can guarantee the minimum bandwidth for every non real time services such as nrtPS and BE connection and hence maintain an acceptable throughput. *Thereby eliminate starvation of lower priority service classes.*

In each service round, the nrtPS queue will be served first until its assigned bandwidth is deficit. If the assigned bandwidth is deficit for the nrtPS queue, the BE service flow queue will have chance to be served. Similar to [12], in DFPQ algorithm, a Quantum Q is assigned to each queue i. The quantum of a queue i $(Q[i])$ represent the maximum number of bits that can be serviced in the first round. The scheduler visits each nonempty queue and determines the number of bandwidth requests in this queue. If there are more packets in the queue i after servicing $Q[i]$ bits, the remaining amount of bits is stored in a queue state variable called *Deficit Counter (DC[i])* and the scheduler moves on to serve the next non-empty queue. In subsequent rounds, the amount of bandwidth usable by this flow is the sum of $DC[i]$ in the previous round added to $Q[i]$. The $Q[i]$ is the Maximum Sustained traffic rate (rmax) of a certain service flow. In case *rmax* = 0 (BE service flow), *rmin* is used instead. As a result of using the quantum variable, connections with larger quantum are serviced more.

DFPQ algorithm is shown below. Here *Ltotal* is defined to be the remaining total capacity of the frame after servicing UGS and rtPS queues and *La* to be its remaining capacity. p(i,k) denotes k[th] packet of ith connection, i belongs to nrtPS and BE connections. The algorithm can be described as follows,

Each service queue i of nrtPs and BE is initialized with

```
La = Ltotal;
DC[i] = Q[i];

While La > 0
{
        While DC[i]>0 and p (i, k) is available
        {
            DC[i] = DC[i] - p(i,k);
            La =La - p(i,k);
```

```
            k++;
        }
        DC[i] = DC[i] + Q[i];
        i = (i % n) + 1;
    }
Go to UGS scheduling for next frame
```

4   Simulation Model and Result Analysis

To evaluate the effectiveness and efficiency of the proposed scheduler, the IEEE 802.16 MAC layer protocol is analyzed using MATLAB. A number of simulations are conducted in this section. At first, the simulation environment and parameters are described. And then the simulation results will be presented for discussion.

4.1   Simulation Environment and Parameters

As mentioned before, basically PMP MAC operation is focused in this article. A TDD-OFDM system is used in our simulation with the MAC layer configuration parameters as shown in table 1 and the network is configured as consists of one BS and multiple SSs as shown in fig 1.

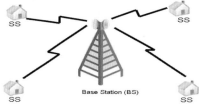

Fig. 1. Proposed model architecture

Table 1. MAC layer configuration parameters

Bandwidth	4.3MHz
Frame duration	10 ms
Duplex	TDD
Delay	20ms

4.2   Simulation Result and Discussions

The simulated 802.16 network consists of one BS and four SSs with different traffic patterns. The first SS is configured with all types of traffic flows nominated as UGS-_1, rtPS_1, nrtPS_1 and BE_1, the second SS has UGS_2, rtPS_2, nrtPS_2 and BE_2, the third SS has UGS_3, rtPS_3, nrtPS_3 and BE_3, the fourth SS runs UGS_4, rtPS_4, nrtPS_4 and BE_4. Two scenarios - with and without SS scheduler are simulated to study the effect of SS scheduler.

Our proposed method is compared with the proposed method in [11]. Here, "without SS scheduler" and "BS-(service class)" means that BS scheduler will designate bandwidth to individual connection. On the other hand, "with ss-scheduler1" and "SS1-(service class)" means that SS scheduler will designate bandwidth to individual connection in our proposed method. Again "with ss-scheduler2" and "SS2-(service class)" means that SS scheduler will designate bandwidth to individual connection

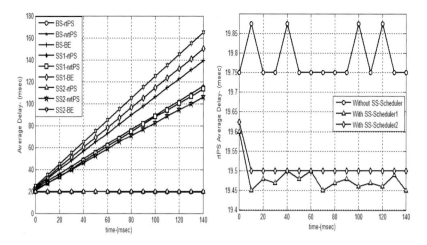

Fig. 2. Service delay comparison   **Fig. 3.** Service delay comparison of rtPS

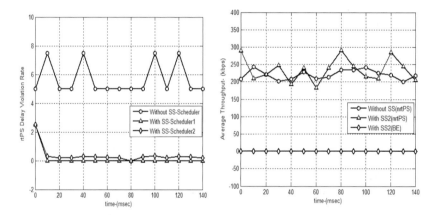

Fig. 4. % of packet drop comparison   **Fig. 5.** Throughput comparison proposed in [11]

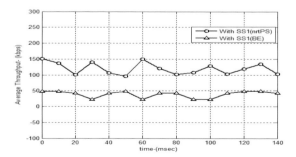

Fig. 6. Throughput comparison in our proposed strategy

proposed in [11]. Here service class refers to UGS, rtPS, nrtPS and BE. As UGS generate fixed size data packets on a periodic basis so delay is negligible and throughput is constant and hence it is not shown in our simulation result. Fig. 2 displays the end-to-end delay of different services with and without SS scheduler. The curves show that after SS scheduling, low priority service suffered longer delay. From rtPS, nrtPS to BE, the end-to-end delay increased with the service priority decreased. The fundamental requirement of QoS scheduling for IEEE 802.16 systems is achieved.

To further demonstrate this benefit, we simulated the rtPS performance under the same number of background SS in Fig. 3. From fig.4 we can see that the SS scheduler can effectively reduce the QoS violation rate of rtPS service flow. Here, the QoS violation rate is defined as the amount of packets whose delay is larger than the Maximum Latency to the total amount of packets that have been received from network interface.

By introducing DFPQ algorithm for nrtPS and BE services on priority order, SS scheduler can guarantee the throughput of nrtPS service as well as BE service. Though BE services do not require any QoS but in our proposed algorithm fairness is maintained for all type of service classes. But this fairness is not maintained in [11] where we got throughput of BE service is zero shown in fig.5. But our simulation result shows that SS scheduler guarantees the throughput of nrtPS service as well as BE service shown in Fig.6 where throughput of BE service is greater than zero throughout simulation time, hence maintain fairness of all the services and eliminate the problem of starvation of lower priority class services.

5   Conclusion

We proposed an efficient packet scheduling scheme for IEEE 802.16 WiMAX to satisfy both delay and throughput guarantees for the admitted connections. An architecture model was developed to demonstrate the performance of the proposed scheme. The simulation results show that the proposed scheme is the best choice for QoS scheduling in WiMAX in terms of delay and throughput of all connections of the system compared to schemes proposed in [11]. Simulation results prove that the BS scheduler can guarantee the minimum bandwidth for each service flow and ensure fairness and QoS in distributing excess bandwidth among all connections. At the same time, the scheduler in SS can provide differentiated and flexible QoS support for all of the four scheduling service types. It can both reduce the delay of real-time applications and guarantee the throughput of non-real-time applications. Thereby eliminate starvation problem of lower priority class services.   Therefore, the proposed QoS scheduling architecture can provide good optimized QoS guarantees for all types of traffic classes as defined in the scheduler standard.

Acknowledgement. The authors deeply acknowledge the support from DST, Govt. of India for this work in the form of FIST 2007 Project on "Broadband Wireless Communications" in the Department of ETCE, Jadavpur University.

References

1. Wongthavarawat, K., Ganz, A.: Packet scheduling for QoS support in IEEE 802.16 broadband wireless access systems. International Journal of Communication Systems 16(1), 81–96 (2003)
2. Wang, H., Li, W., Agrawal, D.P.: Dynamic admission control and QoS for IEEE 802.16 Wireless MAN. In: Proc. of Wireless Telecommunications Symposium (WTS 2005), April 6-7, pp. 60–66 (2005)
3. Niyato, D., Hossain, E.: Connection Admission Control Algorithms for OFDM Wireless Networks. In: Proc. of IEEE Globecom, pp. 2455–2459 (2005)
4. Suresh, K., Misra, I.S., Saha (Roy), K.: Bandwidth and Delay Guaranteed Call Admission Control Scheme for QOS Provisioning in IEEE 802.16e Mobile WiMAX. In: Proceedings of IEEE GLOBECOM (December 2008)
5. Jiang, C.-H., Tsai, T.-C.: CAC and Packet Scheduling Using Token bucket for IEEE 802.16 Networks. In: 3rd IEEE, Consumer Communications and Networking Conf., CCNC 2006, January 8-10, vol. 1, pp. 183–187 (2006)
6. Andrews, J.G., Ghosh, A., Muhamed, R.: Fundamentals of WiMAX-Understanding Broadband Wireless Networking. Pearson Education, London (March 2007)
7. Chowdhury, P., Misra, I.S.: A Comparative Study of Different Packet Scheduling Algorithms with Varied Network Service Load in IEEE 802.16 Broadband Wireless Access Systems. In: IEEE Proc. Int. Conf. Advanced Computing & Communications, Bangalore (December 2009)
8. Lin, J., Sirisena, H.: Quality of Service Scheduling in IEEE 802.16 Broadband Wireless Networks. In: Proceedings of First International Conference on Industrial and Information Systems, August 2006, pp. 396–401 (2006)
9. Vinay, K., Sreenivasulu, N., Jayaram, D., Das, D.: Performance evaluation of end-to-end delay by hybrid scheduling algorithm for QoS in IEEE 802.16 network. In: Proceedings of International Conference on Wireless and Optical Communication Networks, 5p. (April 2006)
10. Settembre, M., Puleri, M., Garritano, S., Testa, P., Albanese, R., Mancini, M., Lo Curto, V.: Performance analysis of an efficient packet-based IEEE 802.16 MAC supporting adaptive modulation and coding. In: Proceedings of International Symposium on Computer Networks, pp. 11–16 (June 2006)
11. Sun, J., Yao, Y., Zhu, H.: Quality of Service Scheduling For 802.16 Broadband Wireless Access System. In: Advanced system technology telecom lab, China, Beijing, IEEE, Los Alamitos (2006)
12. Shreedhar, M., Varghese, G.: Efficient Fair Queuing using Deficit Round Robin. IEEE/ACM Transactions on Networking 1(3), 375–385 (1996)
13. Safa, H., Artail, H., Karam, M., Soudah, R., Khyat, S.: New Scheduling Architecture for IEEE 802.16 Wireless Metropoliton Area Network, American university of Beirut, Lebanon. IEEE, Los Alamitos (2007)
14. Chu, C., Wang, D., Mei, S.: A QoS architecture for the MAC protocol of IEEE 802.16 BWA system. IEEE Communications, 435–439 (July 2002)

Comparison of VoIP Performance over WiMAX, WLAN and WiMAX-WLAN Integrated Network Using OPNET

Anindita Kundu[1], Suman Bhunia[1], Iti Saha Misra[2], and Salil K. Sanyal[2]

[1] School of Mobile Computing and Communication, Jadavpur University,
Kolkata, India
kundu.anindita@gmail.com, sumanbhunia@gmail.com
[2] Electronics and Telecommunication Engineering, Jadavpur University,
Kolkata, India
iti@etce.jdvu.ac.in, s_sanyal@ieee.org

Abstract. Voice over IP is expected to be in practice in the next generation communication networks. The target of this paper is to analyse its performance in the next generation networks. Among the most competing networks like WiMAX, Wifi, etc., WiMAX having higher bandwidth accommodates more users but with degraded performance. Hence, an integrated network using Wi-MAX backbone and WLAN hotspots has been developed and VoIP has been setup using SIP. Since, OPNET 14.5.A provides a real life simulation environment, it is chosen as the simulation tool. Quality of the service is critically analysed with parameters like jitter, MOS and delay for various voice codecs. Finally, it is concluded that the WiMAX-WLAN integrated network provides improved and optimal performance over WLAN and WiMAX network with respect to network capacity and quality of service.

Keywords: WiMAX, WLAN, Integrated network, backbone, hotspot, VoIP, Codecs, OPNET.

1 Introduction

Wireless networking has become an essential part in the modern telecommunication system. The demand of high speed data transfer with quality has led to the evolution of technologies like WiMAX and WLAN and is still increasing. Hence, new ways to enhance quality and speed of connectivity are being searched for.

WLANs [1] are mostly designed for private wired LANs and have been enormously successful for data traffic but voice traffic differs fundamentally from data traffic in its sensitivity to delay and loss [2]. Voice over WLAN is popular, but maintaining the speech quality is still one of many technical challenges of the VoIP system. VoIP is spreading rapidly and there is need to support multiple concurrent VoIP communications but WLAN support handful number of users [3] [4].

The IEEE 802.11 MAC specifies two different mechanisms, namely the contention-based Distributed Coordination Function (DCF) [1] and the polling-based Point Coordination Function (PCF) [1]. The DCF uses a carrier sense multiple access with collision avoidance (CSMA/CA) scheme for medium access and the optional

N. Meghanathan et al. (Eds.): NeCoM, WiMoN, and WeST 2010, CCIS 90, pp. 316–325, 2010.
© Springer-Verlag Berlin Heidelberg 2010

four way handshaking request-to-send/clear-to-send [1] mechanism (RTS/CTS). Incapability of providing differentiation and prioritization based upon traffic type results in providing satisfactory performance for best-effort traffic only, but inferior support for QoS requirements posed by real time traffic. These requirements make the DCF scheme a less feasible option to support QoS for VoIP traffic. The PCF mode enables the polled stations to transmit data without contending for the channel. Studies on VoIP over WLAN in PCF mode [5] shows that the polling overhead is high with increased number of stations in a basic service set (BSS). This results in excessive delay and poor performance of VoIP under heavy load conditions. Thus, both DCF and PCF have limited support for real-time applications. Supporting VoIP over WLAN using DCF mode poses significant challenges, because the performance characteristics of their physical and MAC layers are much worse than their wired counterparts and hence considered in our system.

WiMAX (Worldwide Interoperability for Microwave Access) [6][16] on the other hand is designed to deliver a metro area broadband wireless access (BWA) service. So, while wireless LAN supports transmission range of up to few hundred meters, WiMAX system ranges up to 30 miles [6]. Unlike a typical IEEE 802.11 WLAN with 11Mbps bandwidth which supports very limited VoIP connections [4], an IEEE 802.16 WiMAX with 70Mbps bandwidth [7] can support huge number of users. These motivations led to study and comparison of the VoIP quality of service in IEEE 802.11b WLAN and IEEE 802.16 WiMAX network.

IEEE 802.16 support 5 types of service classes, namely UGS (Unsolicited Grant Service), rtPS (real time Polling Service), nrtPS (non-real time Polling Service), BE (Best Effort Service), ertPS (extended rtPS service) [8]. UGS supports fixed-size data packets at a constant bit rate (CBR). It supports real time applications like VoIP or streaming applications but wastes bandwidth during the off periods. rtPS supports variable bit rate(VBR) real-time service such as VoIP. Delay-tolerant data streams such as an FTP is designed to be supported by the nrtPS. This requires variable-size data grants at a minimum guaranteed rate. The nrtPS is similar to the rtPS but allows contention based polling. Data streams, such as Web browsing, that do not require a minimum service-level guarantee is supported by BE service. BE connections are never polled but receive resources through contention. ertPS was introduced to support VBR real-time services such as VoIP and video streaming. It has an advantage over UGS and rtPS for VoIP applications as it carries lower overhead than UGS and rtPS [9] and hence is modeled in the system.

Since, WiMAX is expected to create the opportunity to successfully penetrate the commercial barrier by providing higher bandwidth, establishing wireless commons becomes an important factor. Also, bandwidth crunch and network integration are some of the major technical and social challenges regarding the future of the community-based Wi-Fi networks [10]. According to [10], the foundation of the WiMAX PTP commons is the process of hot-spot interconnection and integration. Instead of global Internet connectivity, many current applications and businesses are expected to be better utilized by using the localized Wi-Fi constellation.

With a step towards the next generation, it is expected that an integrated network as shown in Figure 1, comprising of both the WiMAX and WLAN network and using mobile nodes with dual stack is expected to provide a better performance than a similar WiMAX or WLAN network.

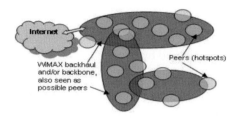

Fig. 1. Wi-Fi integration using WiMAX [10]

VoIP has been widely accepted for its cost effectiveness and easy implementation. A VoIP system consists of three indispensable components, namely 1) codec, 2) packetizer, and 3) playout buffer. Analog voice signals are compressed, and encoded into digital voice streams by the codecs. The output digital voice streams are then packed into constant-bit-rate (CBR) voice packets by the packetizer. A two way conversation is very sensitive to packet delay jitter but can tolerate certain degree of packet loss. Hence a playout buffer is used at the receiver end to smooth the speech by removing the delay jitter.

Quality of noise sensitive VoIP is usually measured in terms of jitter, MOS and packet end-to-end delay. Perceived voice with zero jitter, high MOS and low packet end-to-end delay is considered to be the best. With the two competing wireless networks namely WLAN and WiMAX, this paper analyses the perceived voice quality as measured using OPNET simulation environment.

2 Voice over IP

Voice is analog and is converted to digital format before transmitting over Internet. This process is called encoding and the converse is called decoding and both are performed by voice codecs [11]. With bandwidth utilization becoming a huge concern, voice compression techniques are used [11] to reduce bandwidth consumption. Voice compression by a codec adds an additional overhead of algorithmic delay. Thus, a codec is expected to provide good voice quality even after compression, with minimum delay.

Table 1 shows the bandwidth requirements of some common codecs. G.711 is the international standard for encoding telephone audio. It has a fixed bit rate of 64kbps. G.723 and G.729 are low bit rate codecs at the expense of high codec complexity. G.723 is one of the most efficient codecs with the highest compression ratio and is used in video conferencing applications. G.729 is an industry standard with high bandwidth utilization for toll-quality voice calls [12]. G.726 uses ADPCM speech codec standard, and transmits at rates of 16, 24, 32, and 40 kbps. G.728 officially codes speech at 16 Kbit/s using low-delay code excited linear prediction [13]. For example, during a call using G711 as codec, the amount of data transfer for both uplink and downlink will be 87.2 x 2 = 174.4Kbps = 0.1703 Mbps = 10.21 MB per minute. So, G 711 uses 10.21 Mb/min per VoIP call where as G 729 uses 0.5MB/min per voice call in the same way.

Table 1. Bandwidth Requirement of Some Common Codecs [11][14]

Codecs	Algorithm	Bandwidth (Kbps)	Ethernet Bandwidth Usage (Kbps)
G 711	PCM(Pulse Code Modulation)	64	87.2
G 729	CS-ACELP (Conjugate Structure Algebraic-Code Excited Linear Prediction)	8	31.2
G 723.1	Multi Rate Coder	6.3	21.9
G 723.1	Multi Rate Coder	5.3	20.8
G 726	ADPCM(Adaptive Differential Pulse Code Modulation)	32	55.2
G 726	ADPCM(Adaptive Differential Pulse Code Modulation)	24	47.2
G 728	LD-CELP (Low-Delay Code Excited Linear Prediction)	16	31.5

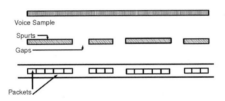

Fig. 2. Packet Creation based on voice activity

Moreover, recently voice codecs are developed to detect talk-spurt [15] and silence lengths [15] within a conversation. Silence in a communication period leads to packetization of the background noise and sending it over the network. This causes bandwidth wastage. Usually, during a conversation we talk 35% of the time and remain quiet rest of the time [15]. With silence suppression during the silence period, the codec does not send data as shown in figure 2. This decreases channel utilisation and thereby saves bandwidth.

Voice communication is noise sensitive. Noise causes the signal to reach the destination with a lead or lag in the time period. This deviation is called jitter. Lead causes negative jitter and lag causes positive jitter and both degrade the voice quality. The time taken by voice to be transmitted from the mouth of the sender to the ear of the receiver is called packet end-to-end delay. The packet end-to-end delay should be very less for voice communication. Perceived voice quality is typically estimated by the subjective mean opinion score (MOS), an arithmetic average of opinion score. MOS of a particular codec is the average mark given by a panel of auditors listening to several recorded samples. It ranges from 1(unacceptable) to 5 (excellent). It depends on delay and packet dropped by the network. The E-model, an analytical model defined in ITU-T recommendation, provides a framework for an objective on-line quality estimation based on network performance measurements like delay and loss and application level factors like low bit rate codecs. The result of the E-model is the calculation of the R-factor (best case 100 worst case 0) [5].

$$R = R_0 - I_s - I_d - I_e + A. \tag{1}$$

Where R_0 groups the effects of noise, I_s includes the effects of the other impairments related to the quantisation of the voice signal, I_d represents the impairment caused due to delay, I_e covers the impairments caused by the low bit rate codecs and packet losses. The advantage factor A compensates for the above impairments under various user conditions. A is 10 for mobile telephony but 0 for VoIP [5]. R_0 is considered to be 94.77 and I_s is considered to be 1.43 in OPNET 14.5.A. The relation between MOS and R-factor:

$$MOS = 1 + 0.035R + 7.10-6R(R - 60)(100 - R) \tag{2}$$

The purpose of this modeling is to compare the performance parameters for the voice codecs considering both with and without silence suppression in WiMAX 802.16d, WLAN 802.11b and their integrated network and thereby show that the integration provides optimal network capacity and quality of service.

3 Simulation Environment

Figure 3 show WiMAX network setup. The Wireless Deployment Wizard of OPNET is used to deploy a 7 celled WiMAX network, with multiple subscriber stations.

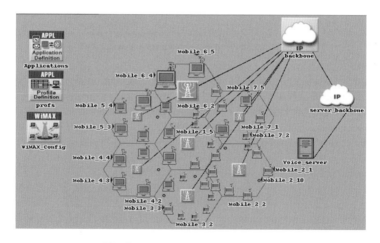

Fig. 3. Network Model for WiMAX

The base stations are connected to the voice server configured as the SIP server via an IP backbone and a server backbone. These nodes represent the service provider company network. The Base Station and subscriber station parameters are as shown in Table 2. The number of subscribers in cell 2 and cell 3 are 10 and VoIP calls are configured between them in mesh.

Table 2. WiMAX and WLAN Network Parameters

WiMAX Parameters	Values	WLAN Parameters	Values
WiMAX Service Class	ertPS	Physical Characteristics	Direct Sequence (DSSS)
BS Transmission Power	10W	Data Rate	11Mbps
SS Transmission Power	0.5W	Transmission Power	0.005 W
PHY profile	WirelessOFDMA 20MHz	Buffer Size	2048000 bits

Similar to the WiMAX network, a WLAN 802.11b network is also deployed by the Wireless Deployment Wizard of OPNET where a 7 celled WLAN network with multiple subscriber stations. Unlike the WiMAX network, the WLAN network has access points (APs) in place of the base stations and the mobile nodes of WiMAX are replaced by mobile nodes of WLAN. The APs are also connected to the core network. The APs are connected to the voice server configured as the SIP server via an IP backbone and a server backbone. These nodes represent the service provider company network. Similar to the WiMAX network, the VoIP calls are setup between the subscribers of cell 2 and cell 3 in mesh. The parameters of the access points and the subscriber stations are as shown in Table 2.

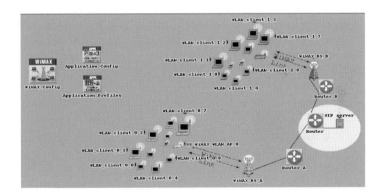

Fig. 4. Network Model for WiMAX-WLAN Integrated Network

Like figure 1, a WLAN integrated network using WiMAX is developed as shown in figure 4. Two WiMAX Base Stations are connected to each other and a SIP server via routers. A special type of node called SS_WiMAX_WLAN_AP having dual stack of both WiMAX and WLAN as shown in figure 5, is configured as the subscriber station of WiMAX network and Access Point for the WLAN network. This node is a bridge between the WLAN subscriber stations and the WiMAX base station. There are 10 WLAN subscriber stations under each SS_WiMAX_WLAN_AP. VoIP calls are setup between 10 users of two such SS_WiMAX_WLAN_AP. The parameters of the WiMAX Base Station and the WLAN subscriber stations are same as that shown in Table 2.

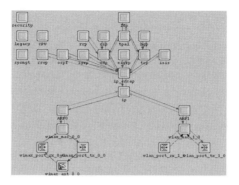

Fig. 5. Protocol Stack of SS_WiMAX_WLAN_AP

4 Simulation Results and Discussion

The variation of jitter with variation of the voice codecs with and without silence suppression is shown in Fig 6a and 6b. From 6a, we see that the average voice jitter is almost 0 for WiMAX implying very good quality of voice while WLAN has a positive jitter varying from about 0.0007 to 0.001 seconds. The integrated network shows jitter variation from about 0.0004 to 0.0006 seconds. For G 723.1, the average jitter is almost 0 irrespective of the network indicating a very good performance. This is because the bit rate of G 723.1 is 6.3 or 5.3 Kbps which results in generation of small packets. But modem and fax signals cannot be carried by G 723.1 [15]. It can be used only for narrow band communications.

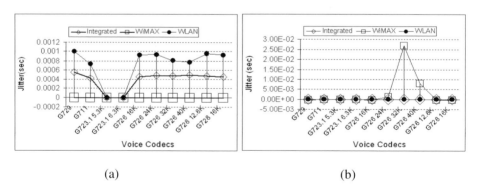

(a)   (b)

Fig. 6. Average jitter, (a) Without silence suppression (b) With silence suppression

With silence suppression, as shown in Fig 6b, the result is different. Like G711, G 726 has its roots in the PSTN network. It is primarily used for international trunks to save bandwidth. Unlike G711, G 726 uses 32Kbps to provide nearly the same quality of voice [17] because 32 Kbps is the de facto standard. As shown in Figure 6b, the average voice jitter is almost 0 for all codecs in both WLAN and WLAN-WiMAX integrated network where as the WiMAX network shows a slight deviation for the voice codec G 726. The deviation is highest for G 726 with 32kbps and is about

0.03sec. Though G 726 supports data rate of 16 , 24, and 40Kbps also, the 24 and 16 Kbps channels are used for voice in Digital Circuit Multiplication Equipment (DCME) and the 40 Kbps is for data modem signals (especially modems doing 4800 Kbps or higher) in DCME. But G 726 with 32 Kbps follows the de facto standard and the jitter is within the consideration limit.

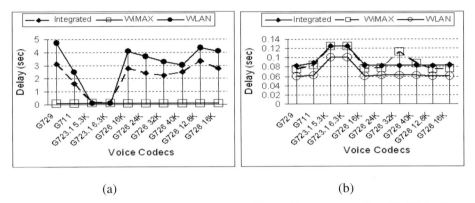

(a)   (b)

Fig. 7. Average Packet End-to-end Delay (a) Without silence suppression (b) With silence suppression

As shown in Figure 7a, the packet end-to-end delay for voice without silence suppression is less than 0.5 seconds for WiMAX where as for WLAN high bit rate codecs it is very high. This is because the silence periods is also packetised and send thereby creating huge bandwidth requirement and congestion in the WLAN network. Integration results in increased capacity. Hence, the integrated network shows delay less than the WLAN network as increased capacity results in less congestion.

Figure 7b shows, the packet end-to-end delay with silence suppression for WiMAX is more than WLAN and the integrated network has the same almost as that of WiMAX network. This is because with silence suppression, the number of packets to be send decreases thereby releasing the congestion in the WLAN network and also the distance to be traversed by the packet for WiMAX is much higher than the distance to be covered by the packet in case of WLAN and even for the integrated network the distance traversed by the packet is almost is as huge as that of WiMAX. For WLAN the packet end-to-end delay is about 0.06 seconds except for G 723.1 for which it is about 0.1 seconds where as for WiMAX and WLAN-WiMAX integrated network, the delay varies from 0.08 seconds for G 729 and G 711 to 0.13 seconds for G 723.1.

Figure 8a shows the variation of MOS for all networks with variation of the voice codecs without silence suppression. As mentioned before, MOS depends on the packet end-to-end delay and packets dropped. As the figure shows, MOS value obtained for WiMAX is above 3, for WLAN is almost 1 and for the integrated network is about 1.5 except for G 723.1 for which it is about 2.5. This is because G 723.1 being a low bit rate codec creates numerous packets which results in increased delay due to packet reassembly. Hence, low MOS in case of WiMAX. On the other hand it has low bandwidth requirement and hence less packets are dropped for this codec in WLAN network. Hence higher MOS compared to the other codecs.

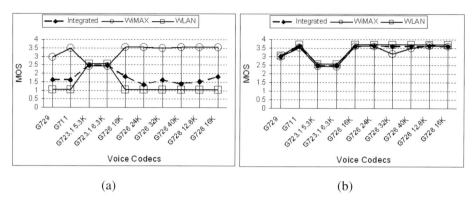

Fig. 8. Average voice MOS (a) Without silence suppression (b) With silence suppression

The result with silence suppression is totally different and is shown in Fig 8b. As shown in figure, WLAN perform better among the three networks with a MOS value of above 3.5 except for G711 for which it is about 3 and for G 723.1 for which it is about 2.5. This is because with the silence suppression the number of packets in the network decreases thereby releasing the congestion in the WLAN network. This decreases the amount of packet dropped considerably and thereby increases the MOS value. The codec G 723.1 is a low bit rate codec having bit rate of 5.3 kbps and 6.3kbps and the packet end-to-end delay is larger for G 723.1 in comparison to the other codecs. Hence the MOS decreases.

5   Conclusion

In this paper extensive simulation based performance analysis for VoIP application is done over a WiMAX based BWA network, a WLAN (IEEE 802.11b), and also on a WLAN-WiMAX integrated network. For this we have used OPNET 14.5.A simulation platform. Multiple competing traffic sources using SIP signalling over the networks are generated and the trace of traffic and measurements for different performance parameters discussed in this paper are obtained.

Close observation of the results reveal that WiMAX network performs better on the basis of jitter, MOS and packet end-to-end delay than conventional WLAN 802.11b in case of voice applications when no silence suppression is considered, i.e. with no bar on the bandwidth usage, but when more users are to be accommodated, bandwidth becomes a constraint and hence silence suppression has to be used. With silence suppression, WLAN provides a better voice quality than WiMAX. Though, the WiMAX network provides high capacity, degradation of the voice quality is observed i.e. reflected from the MOS value. WLAN on the other hand has less capacity but provides a better voice quality. Hence, the integrated deployment of WiMAX and WLAN is expected to be competent enough to provide optimal voice quality with optimal network capacity.

Acknowledgment. The authors deeply acknowledge the support from DST, Govt. of India for this work in the form of FIST 2007 Project on "Broadband Wireless Communications" in the Department of ETCE, Jadavpur University.

References

1. Crow, B.P., Widjaja, I., Kim, J.G.: IEEE 802.11 Wireless Local Area Networks. IEEE Communications (1997)
2. Malone, D., Clifford, P., Leith, D.J.: On Buffer Sizing for Voice in 802.11 WLANs. IEEE Communications Letters (2007)
3. http://voip.biz-news.com/news/tags/en_US/VoIP
4. Smart Mobile^{TM}: Next-Generation Wlan Architecture For High Performance Networks, A Trapeze Networks White Paper (November 2006)
5. Chen, D.Y., Garg, S., Kappes, M., Trivedi, K.S.: Supporting VBR VoIP traffic with IEEE 802.11 WLAN in PCF mode. In: Proceedings of OPNETWork 2002, Washington D.C. (August 2002)
6. Retnasothie, F.E., Ozdemir, M.K., Y' Cek, T., Celebi, H., Zhang, J., Muththaiah, R.: Wireless IPTV over WiMAX: Challenges and Applications. In: IEEE WAMICON (2006)
7. Cai, L.X., Shen, X. (S)., Mark, J.W., Cai, L., Xiao, Y.: Voice Capacity Analysis of WLAN With Unbalanced Traffic. IEEE Transations on Vehicular Technologies 55(3) (May 2006)
8. Nagarajan, N., Rajeev, Kaarthick, B.: Performnance analysis of Video Conferencing and Multimedia application Services over WiMAX. In: IEEE International Advance Computing Conference (IACC 2009), Patiala, India, March 6-7 (2009)
9. Chu, G., Wang, D., Mei, S.: A QoS Architecture for the MAC protocol of IEEE 802.16 BWA System. In: IEEE 2002 ICC, Circuits and Systems, July 2002, vol. 1, pp. 435–439 (2002)
10. Angelov, B., Rao, B.: The Progression of WiMAX Toward a Peer-to- Peer Paradigm Shift. Annual Review of Communications 59 (2007)
11. http://whirlpool.net.au/wiki/?tag=VoIP_Codecs
12. http://en.wikipedia.org/wiki/G.726
13. Trad, A., Munir, F., Afifi, H.: Capacity Evaluation of VoIP in IEEE 802.11e WLAN Environment. In: IEEE CCNC 2006 Proceedings (2006)
14. http://wiki.snom.com/Bandwidth_requirements_and_QoS
15. Hersent, O., Petit, J., Gurle, D.: IP Telephony- Deploying Voice-Over-IP Protocols. John Wiley & Sons, Ltd., Chichester (2005)
16. Ghosh, A., Wolter, D.R., Andrews, J.G., Chen, R.: Broadband Wireless Access with WiMax/802.16: Current Performance Benchmarks and Future Potential. IEEE Communications Magazine (February 2005)
17. http://www.voip-info.org/wiki/view/ITU+G.726S

A Generalized Trust Framework for Mobile Ad Hoc Networks

Revathi Venkataraman[1], M. Pushpalatha[1], and T. Rama Rao[2]

[1] Assistant Professor, Computer Science & Engg
[2] Professor, Telecomunication Engg
revathi@ktr.srmuniv.ac.in, ramarao@ieee.org

Abstract. Mobile ad hoc networks (MANET) are formed when two or more nodes come within the communication range of each other. Since the wireless range is very short, all the nodes in the network have to extend their complete co-operation for efficient functioning of the network. This paper proposes a generalized trust framework for any ad hoc routing protocol to curb selfish and malicious nodes in a MANET. The trust relationships existing between the nodes determine the routing path to be taken for data transfer. The trust framework is combined with any MANET routing algorithm. The performance analysis of this framework is currently done with two reactive protocols. Jointly, they form a trusted network to curb various attacks originating in the ad hoc network. This type of a trusted framework established in a MANET, would be most suited for tactical environments.

1 Introduction

Security is one of the major issues to be considered in the deployment of MANETs in a tactical network environment. Since, today's world is moving toward Network-Centric Warfront [1], the requirements and functionalities of ad hoc networks are much more than their wired counterparts. MANETs should provide all services like routing, data forwarding, resource availability which are typically offered by infrastructure-based networks, in a most secure environment. In addition, the participating entries in the network should be capable to self-organizing among themselves in a dynamically changing topology with limited resources. The absence of centralized infrastructure or server component in mobile ad hoc networks poses the greatest security challenge [2]. Since no monitoring or detection software can be deployed for the network, the mobile devices which form the network have to take care of routing, security and all other server functionalities. Hence, all mobile devices are expected to extend their co-operation in exchanging routing information, forwarding of data packets etc. It is easily possible that after the deployment of these mobile devices, some of the nodes may be implanted by enemies in a tactical environment [1]. These nodes may behave maliciously, disrupting the networking services. Therefore, it is very essential to safeguard the ad hoc networks which are deployed in a tactical environment. Effective solutions to these security issues need to be proposed for widespread deployment of mobile ad hoc networks.

N. Meghanathan et al. (Eds.): NeCoM, WiMoN, and WeST 2010, CCIS 90, pp. 326–335, 2010.

The wireless links are more susceptible to various types of attacks like passive eavesdropping, active modification of messages, disruption of service, replay attacks and impersonation attacks [2]. The compromised nodes makes use of the unreliable links and dynamic topology of ad hoc networks and introduce inconsistencies in the routing table information exchange. It is very difficult to detect these nodes because there is no central server component wherein key management and monitoring software can be installed. Hence, detection of attacks and countermeasures to be taken in the midst of these attacks will be very complex. Establishment of trust relationship between the nodes will lead to the detection of these attacks and isolation of compromised nodes [2].

To curb selfish behavior of nodes in mobile ad hoc networks, three broad strategies are identified: reputation-based methods, credit-based methods and game theory solutions [3]. In reputation-based schemes, the neighboring nodes are observed and their behavior is quantified and used for routing and packet forwarding. In credit-based techniques, the co-operating nodes are benefited from their benevolent behavior. In game-theory based approaches, the entire forwarding process is modeled as a game and individual participants are expected to find an optimal strategy.

This paper is an initiative towards providing a security solution which spans the entire protocol stack of a MANET. The attacks under consideration for this paper are black holes, grey holes and flooding attacks. A comprehensive trust framework is suggested which will improve the efficiency of the network even in the presence of these attacks. The rest of the paper is organized as follows. Section 2 describes the related works and literature review done on security issues in mobile ad hoc networks, as well as various trust establishment schemes. Few works on flooding attacks prevention and wormhole detection strategies are also analyzed. Section 3 briefs about the proposed strategies to prevent the abovementioned subset of attacks. A Trust architecture to be incorporated in each mobile node is discussed. Section 4 describes about the performance analysis of the proposed methods. Section 5 mentions about further enhancements to be made to the trust model.

2   Related Works

The lack of trusted environment in an ad hoc network results in many security lapses. This is considered as one of the major concerns in the large scale deployment of ad hoc networks [4]. Trust establishment algorithms [5, 6, 7] have been developed which addresses few of the security attacks possible in an ad hoc network. The participating nodes should know in advance regarding the type of security attack in the network and run the corresponding algorithm to detect the misbehaving nodes in the network. Most of the techniques are suited to prevent or detect a specific type of attack. These schemes do not provide any comprehensive framework for securing the ad hoc network resources.

The Dynamic Source Routing(DSR) protocol for dependable routing as presented in [8] has the possibility of flooding and sinkhole attacks in the network. Again, this scheme is suited for DSR and it has to be customized for other proactive and reactive protocols. An improvised protocol version is presented in [9] for DSR and Ad hoc On-demand Distance Vector (AODV). Some of the cryptographic protocol schemes [10, 11, 12] presented have the overheads associated with the secure routing at all times. Also, distribution of certificates and key management is again an issue in mobile ad hoc networks. The presence of a server or a central monitoring component is inevitable in these schemes. Computational overheads involved in executing a cryptographic algorithm are considerable. The battery power and computational overheads assume great importance in a resource constraint MANET environment. These schemes will be impractical for deployment of wireless ad hoc networks in real world.

Resisting flooding attacks in ad hoc networks as in [13, 14] describes two flooding attacks: Route Request (RREQ) and Data flooding attack. In RREQ flooding attack the attacker selects many IP addresses which are not in the network or select random IP addresses depending on knowledge about scope of the IP address in the network. A single threshold is set up for all the neighbor nodes. The given solution is neighbor suppression. In Data flooding attack the attack node first sets up the path to all the nodes and send useless packets. The given solution is that the data packets are identified in application layer and later path cutoff is initiated. . Similar solutions are proposed in [15] where a rate-limitation component is added in each node. This component monitors the threshold limit of request packets sent by the neighboring nodes and accordingly, drops the packets if the limit is exceeded. Flooding by data packets is not addressed.

The work presented in [16, 17, 18] provides a generalized trust metric scheme to be used for neighbor evaluation. The direct trust refers to the trust computed for all the nodes which are adjacent to the evaluating node. Recommendation trust is an indirect trust given by a node i, about node j to a node k. Two schemes are presented: distance semiring, which aggregates the trust from one node to another along a particular path; path semiring, which aggregates the trust from one node to another along different (parallel) paths. Even though these schemes are useful in collecting a global trust value for a particular node in the network, the overheads associated with these techniques needs to be analyzed. And the practical limitations of computing a trust value for a node, taking the feedback of every other node in the network needs to be studied in an ad hoc environment where all the information are localized.

Hence, our proposed system considers only the direct trust values based on the experience of the node with its neighbors. The trust concept was introduced in DSR protocol and its performance analyzed in [19]. Furthermore, a proposal for flooding attack prevention using the trust scheme is made in [20]. Initially, at the time of initiation of an ad hoc network all the nodes will be strangers with unknown trust values. Later, the observations and behaviors of the neighboring nodes are recorded and an analyzed and the neighboring nodes are categorized.

3   Proposed Model

The trust establishment algorithms will run below any MANET routing algorithm. Fig.1 shows the security issues in a wireless protocol stack. Every participating node in an ad hoc network will be fortified with the trust architecture as shown in Fig.2. The trust relationships between individual nodes in an ad hoc network may belong to any type as shown in Table 1.

Table 1. Trust Relationships existing between ad hoc nodes

Relationship: Node i→ Node j	Trust significance
Stranger	The neighbor node is not evaluated. Default value
Acquaintance	Neighbor node is evaluated for relatively short duration. Upgraded from stranger status.
Friend	Neighbor node is one among the trusted nodes in the network. The relationship is evaluated over a period of time. Upgraded from acquaintance.
Malicious	Blacklisted neighbor nodes. These nodes are evaluated to over a short duration and their co-operation is not satisfactory. Degraded from stranger.

At the time of initiation of the ad hoc network, all the nodes will be strangers to each other. At that time, no routing packets exchange or data transfer would have taken place. Hence, the nodes in the network would not have had a chance to evaluate their neighbors. Once, the first request for data transfer comes in a participating node, it initiates the ROUTE DISCOVERY process by broadcasting the RREQ message. The trust estimator in the node will be in promiscuous mode overhearing the transmission of the neighboring nodes. The counter which records the RREQ message broadcast will be incremented or decremented based on the behavior of the neighboring node. Similarly, black hole attacks of the neighboring nodes can be detected. Table 2 lists the metrics for estimating the trust relationship of a neighboring node.

The overall trust relationship with a neighboring node is computed by performing the aggregation of individual metrics. The Ordered Weighted Averaging(OWA) operator is used for aggregation of individual constraints.

Table 2. Trust metrics defined in an individual node

Trust Metrics
Number of RREQ packets successfully forwarded
Number of DATA packets successfully forwarded
Number of instances with matched message digest values in packet transmission
Number of RREQs received from the neighboring node
Number of DATA packets received from the neighboring node
Time taken to respond to a RREQ message

$$OWA(T_1, T_2 ..... T_n) = \sum_{j=1}^{n} w_j T_{\sigma(j)} \tag{1}$$

Where $T1, T2 ..... Tn$ are individual trust metrics, wj are positive weights associated with each trust metric and $\sigma(j)$ is the permutation ordering of the metric. $Wj > 0$ and $\sum_{j=1}^{n} w_j = 1$. The purpose of assigning weighted trust metric is to give different weights to different trust metric. The aggregated trust value is normalized within limits (0 to 1). The normalized trust value from Eqn 2 will determine whether the neighboring node is a friend, acquaintance, stranger or malicious as shown in Table 3.

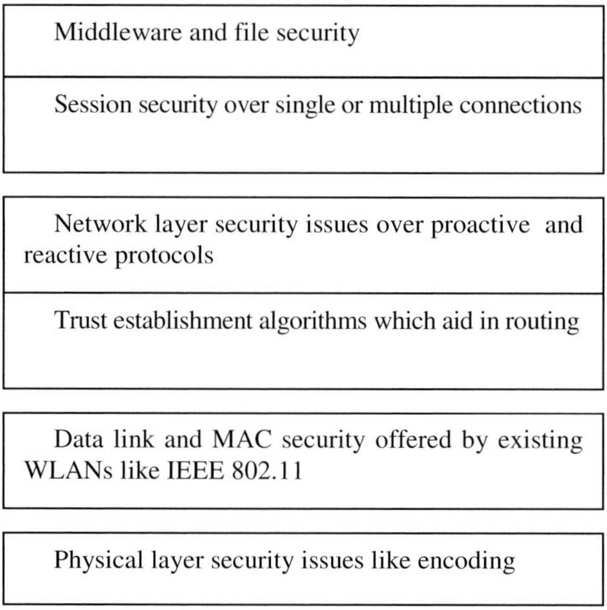

| Middleware and file security |
| Session security over single or multiple connections |

| Network layer security issues over proactive and reactive protocols |
| Trust establishment algorithms which aid in routing |

| Data link and MAC security offered by existing WLANs like IEEE 802.11 |

| Physical layer security issues like encoding |

Fig. 1. Security Issues in a wireless ad hoc protocol stack

$$\text{Normalized trust } T = \frac{(A_c - A_{min})(L_{max} - L_{min})}{A_{max} - A_{min}} + L_{min} \tag{2}$$

Where A_c - current aggregated trust

A_{min} - minimum possible aggregated trust

L_{max} - 1

L_{min} - -1

A_{max} - maximum possible aggregated trust

These computed trust values are stored along with routing information in the route cache table. These observations are used in choosing the right path for data transmission. After discovering the routes and updating the information in the route cache, the data transfer will be initiated. Before transmission of data packets, a message digest is computed for the packet and sent to the neighboring node. The current node will switch to promiscuous mode and listen to the packet transmission of the neighboring node. It will recompute the message digest of the packet transmitted from neighboring node. If the values match, no content modification of the packet is done by the neighboring node. Accordingly, another counter keeps track of this behavior of the node and records it.

Some of the neighboring nodes may act malicious by frequently involving ROUTE DISCOVERY process. These nodes may use the stale route table information and initiate the route discovery process for destination nodes which never exist in the network. They may involve in RREQ Flooding attacks. Hence, all the neighboring nodes which receive the RREQ will remain in the active mode participating in the route discovery process. This scenario will exhaust the network resources; drain the battery power, thereby reducing the battery life of the ad hoc devices. To curtail flooding attacks, the proposed trust model in the ad hoc node, monitors this activity. Any node can accept only a certain number of RREQs from its neighboring node. If it exceeds the RREQ threshold limit set for its trust relationship, which it maintains with the current node, further RREQs will be destroyed. A similar setup is used for DATA Flooding attacks by the malicious nodes. A neighboring malicious node may be cooperative in route discovery process. Once the data transfer begins, it may start sending junk packets for transmission. Even though, the content of the packet can not be viewed at the network layer, depending on the volume of data transfer, restrictions can be applied over the incoming traffic from neighboring node. To prevent DATA Flooding, incoming packets for data transfer can be accepted from a neighboring node till a certain threshold is reached. Since the packet arrival from a neighboring node is assumed to follow a randomized Poisson distribution, any deviation from the distribution pattern indicates malicious intention of the neighboring node and their behavior is recorded. The cumulative probability Pn of getting n junk packets from a neighboring node is expressed using Poisson distribution in Eqn 3.

$$P_n = \sum_{k=0,n} e^{-\lambda} \lambda^n / k! \qquad (3)$$

where k is the number of times incoming packets were processed from the neighboring node at a constant rate λ.

Table 3. Trust threshold limits

Relationship with neighboring node	Trust Threshold (normalized)
Friend	> 0.75
Acquaintance	>0.3 and < 0.75
Stranger	<0.3 and positive
Malicious	-1

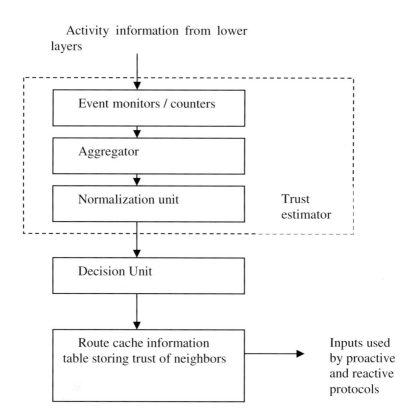

Fig. 2. Trust Architecture in an individual node

4   Simulations and Performance Analysis

4.1   Test 1: Few Black Holes as Neighbors over DSR Protocol

In a standard MANET running DSR protocol, compromised nodes are introduced into the network. These intermediate malicious nodes involve in active attack by receiving the data packets, not meant for them and simply not forwarding them. Simulations are carried out in OPNET Modeler in a 500 X 500 Sq.m area and the mobility model chosen is Random Waypoint. There are 25 nodes moving about with a speed of 20m/s and the transmitted power of these nodes is 1 mW. Fig.3 compares the throughput of standard DSR and modified DSR by varying the number of malicious nodes in the network. The modified DSR copes up well in an environment where the number of malicious nodes in the network is less than six out of twenty five. The performance of the trusted network is analyzed with six different scenarios as shown in Fig.4. In all the scenarios except scenario 5, the percentage of malicious nodes in the network is 40%. Scenario 1 represents a network by decreasing the node density in an area. Scenario 2 is with increasing node mobility speed. Scenario 3 is with slight increase in transmitted power of the participating nodes. Scenario 4 represents a

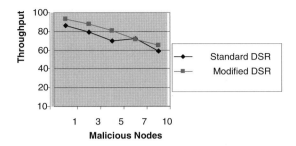

Fig. 3. Comparison of Throughput by varying malicious nodes in scenario 25 nodes, 20m/s, 20 connections

network with increased number of nodes. In scenario 5, number of malicious nodes is decreased to 5%. Scenario 6 represents an extreme case with many failed connections. In all these environments, the trusted network over DSR protocol offers increased throughput compared to standard DSR. The neighboring nodes behaving as black holes are detected and an alternate path is found to destination over the trusted nodes.

4.2 Flooding Attacks over AODV

Simulations are carried out over a mobile ad hoc network running AODV protocol. The simulation parameters are same as Test1. In default scenario, four nodes are made malicious by making them to transmit RREQ packets frequently with different identifiers which are meant for various destinations not existing in the network. Fig.5 shows the delay of packet transfer in seconds for the entire network. In modified AODV, all the nodes in the network run the trust establishment algorithm and evaluate their neighbors. Based on their observations, they accept RREQ packets from their neighbors depending on their respective thresholds. If their neighbors exceed their limit, their RREQ packets are dropped. The reduction in delay of packet transfer is accounted for by the involvement of the nodes in data transfer rather than participating in the RREQ flooding traffic caused by malicious nodes. From Fig.4, we can conclude that the superfluous routing packets sent by malicious nodes are immediately destroyed by its neighboring node.

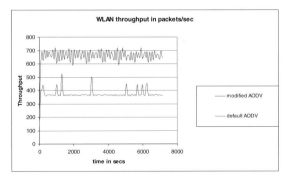

Fig. 4. Routing traffic received from a malicious node in packets/sec

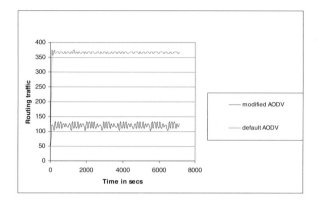

Fig. 5. WLAN throughput in packets/sec

Fig. 5 shows the increase in the WLAN throughput using the modified AODV. Thus, adding a trust establishment framework in every mobile node in an ad hoc network, curtails flooding attacks and improves the performance of the WLAN networks.

5   Conclusion

Wireless ad hoc networks are more prone to security attacks because of the vulnerable environment, frequently changing topologies and absence of centralized infrastructure. Since security is one of the major issues to be considered in the large scale deployment of mobile ad hoc networks, our work is an initiative towards the development of a foolproof trust model which can detect and isolate a wide set of security attacks possible in an ad hoc environment.

A generalized trust framework is formulated and every node in the network will incorporate the trust architecture. The neighbor behavior and relevant events are observed and given as input to the routing algorithms. These trust information help in choosing the best path for data transfer in an ad hoc communication. In addition, the nodes protect themselves from their malicious neighbors by retaining their resources like power and computation time. Our trust model currently detects *black holes*, *grey holes* and *flooding attacks* in the neighborhood. The efficiency of this model is tested over DSR and AODV protocols.

Acknowledgements. We sincerely thank our colleague Mr.K.Senthil Kumar, Assistant Professor, Dept of CSE, SRM University for his valuable suggestions in the preparation of this paper.

References

[1] Burbank, J.L., Chimento, P.F., Haberman, B.K., Kasch, W.T.: Key Challenges of Military Tactical Networking and the Elusive Promise of MANET Technology. IEEE Communications Magazine 44(11), 39–45 (2006)

[2] Buttyán, L., Hubaux, J.-P.: Security and Co-operation in wireless networks. Cambridge University Press, Cambridge (February 2007)

[3] Yoo, Y., Agrawal, D.P.: Why Does It Pay To Be Selfish In A Manet? IEEE Wireless Communications (December 2006)

[4] Conti, M., Giordano, S.: Multihop Ad Hoc Networking: The Reality. IEEE Communications Magazine 45(4), 88–95 (2007)

[5] Li, J., Kato, J.: Future Trust Management Framework for Mobile Ad hoc Networks. IEEE Communications Magazine (April 2008)

[6] Sun, Y., Han, Z., Liu, K.J.R.: Defense of trust management vulnerabilities in distributed networks. IEEE Communications Magazine (February 2008)

[7] Sun, Y., Yu, W., Han, Z., Liu, K.J.R.: Information Theoretic Framework of Trust Modeling and Evaluation for ad hoc networks. IEEE JSAC 24(2) (February 2006)

[8] Pirzada, A.A., Datta, A., McDonald, C.: Incorporating Trust and Reputation in the DSR protocol for Dependable Routing. Computer Communications, Special issue on Internet Communications Security 29, 2806–2821 (2006)

[9] Pirzada, A.A., Datta, A., McDonald, C.: Performance Comparison of Trust-based reactive routing protocols. IEEE Transactions on Mobile Computing 5(6) (June 2006)

[10] Papadimitratos, P., Haas, Z.J.: Secure Data Communication in Mobile Ad hoc Networks. IEEE JSAC 24(2) (February 2006)

[11] Papadimitratos, P., Haas, Z.J., Samar, P.: The Secure Routing Protocol (SRP) for Ad Hoc Networks, IETF Internet Draft (March 2004), http://www.potaroo.net/ietf/idref/draft-papadimitratos-secure-routing-protocol

[12] Zhou, L., Haas, Z.J.: Securing Ad hoc Networks. IEEE Networks 13(6), 24–30 (1999)

[13] Yi, P., Dai, Z., Zhong, Y., Zhang, S.: Resisting Flooding Attacks in Ad Hoc Networks. In: International Conference on Information Technology, Coding and Computing, ITCC 2005, April 2005, vol. 2, pp. 657–662 (2005)

[14] Ping, Y., Yafei, H., Yiping, B., Shiyong, Z., Zhoulin, D.: Flooding Attacks and defence in Ad hoc networks. Journal of Systems Engineering and Electronics 17(2), 410–416 (2006)

[15] Balakrishnan, V., Varadharajan, V., Tapakula, U., Gaup Moe, M.E.: Mitigating Flooding attacks in Mobile Ad hoc Networks Supporting Anonymous Communications. In: Proceedings of the 2nd International Conference on Wireless and Ultra Wideband Communications, Auswireless, p. 29 (2007)

[16] Theodorakopoulos, G., Baras, J.S.: On trust models and trust evaluation metrics for ad hoc networks. IEEE Journal on Selected Areas in Communications 24(2), 318–328 (2006)

[17] Theodorakopoulos, G., Baras, J.S.: A Testbed for Comparing Trust Computation Algorithms. In: Proceedings of the 25th Army Science Conference, Orlando, FL, November 27-30 (2006)

[18] Theodorakopoulos, G., Baras, J.S.: Trust evaluation in ad-hoc networks. In: WiSe 2004: Proceedings of the 3rd ACM workshop on Wireless security, PA, pp. 1–10 (2004)

[19] Venkataraman, R., Pushpalatha, M.: Security in Ad Hoc Networks: An extension of dynamic Source Routing in Mobile Ad Hoc Networks. In: Proceedings of the 10th IEEE International Conference on Communication Systems (2006)

[20] Venkataraman, R., Pushpalatha, M., Khemka, R., Rao, T.R.: Prevention of Flooding attacks in Mobile Ad hoc Networks. In: ICAC3 2009: Proceedings of the International Conference on Advances in Computing, Communication and Control, January 2009, pp. 525–529 (2009) ISBN:978-1-60558-351-8

Adaptive Routing Techniques in Disruption Tolerant Networks

Mohammad Arif[1] and Abu Daud[2]

[1] Department of CSE, GSMVNIET, Palwal, Haryana, India
arif_mohd2k@yahoo.com
[2] Department of CSE, AFSET, Faridabad, Haryana, India
abu.daud@gmail.com

Abstract. It is very tough to use today's Internet efficiently on poles, disasters or in the environments which are characterized by very long delay paths and frequent network partitions. DTN is a new area of research to improve network communication when connectivity is periodic, intermittent, and/or prone to disruptions. Delay Tolerant Networks (DTNs) is used to interconnect devices in regions in which an end-to-end connection may never be present. It is based on store and forward principle as to make communication possible, intermediate nodes stores the data and forward it as the opportunity arises. In a DTN, however, an end-to-end path may be unavailable at all times, routing is performed to achieve eventual delivery by employing long-term storage at the intermediate nodes. This paper surveys the area of routing in delay tolerant networks and presents a system for classifying the proposed routing strategies.

Keywords: Routing, Delay Tolerant Network, Ad-hoc Networks, Intermittent Connectivity, Routing Protocols, Wireless Communication.

1 Introduction

The traditional Mobile Ad-hoc Network (MANET) routing protocols establishes end-to-end paths between communicating nodes and thus support end-to-end semantics of existing transports and applications. In contrast, DTN-based communication schemes imply asynchronous communication (and thus often require new applications) but achieve better reachability, particularly in sparsely populated environments. [7]

Delay tolerant network can be said as a type of network of regional networks. It is an overlay on top the regional network including Internet. DTN is used between and within regional networks. DTN accommodates the mobility and limited power of evolving wireless communication devices. Delay Tolerant Networks (DTNs) is a class of useful but challenging networks. DTN have many challenges. First is to cope up large transmission delays. These delays may result either from physical link properties or extended periods of network partitioning. A second one is efficient routing in the presence of frequent disconnection, pre-scheduled or opportunistic link availability. In some cases, an end-to-end path may not even exist at any single point in time. A third challenge is that high link-error rates make end-to-end reliability difficult. Finally,

N. Meghanathan et al. (Eds.): NeCoM, WiMoN, and WeST 2010, CCIS 90, pp. 336–348, 2010.

heterogeneous underlying network technologies (including non-IP-based internetworks) with very different communication characteristics may need to be embraced [3].

The rest of the paper is organized as follows: Section 2 presents the description of Delay Tolerant Network and its evolution. Section 3 explains routing process, routing issues and some routing algorithms. Section 4 presents various routing strategies and explains the overall categorization of routing approaches in broad way and Section 5 summarizes the matter.

2   DTN Architecture

The present Internet service model as explained in [14] provides end-to-end communication using a concatenation of potentially dissimilar link-layer technologies. In IP protocol, the mapping into network-specific link-layer data frames at each router supports interoperability using the packet-switching model. A number of key assumptions are also made regarding the overall performance characteristics: an end-to-end path exists between source and its peer(s), the maximum round-trip time between any node pairs in the network is not excessive, and the end-to-end packet drop probability is low. Unfortunately, classes of *challenged networks*, which may violate one or more of the assumptions, are becoming important and may not be well served by the current end-to-end TCP/IP model. Examples include:

- **Terrestrial Mobile Networks:** These networks are unexpectedly partitioned due to node mobility or changes in signal strength, while others may be partitioned in a periodic, predictable manner.
- **Exotic Media Networks:** These include near-earth satellite communications, very long distance radio or optical links, audio links in air or water, and some free-space optical communications.
- **Military Ad-Hoc Networks:** These systems operate in the environments where mobility, environmental factors, or intentional jamming may be cause for disconnection. In addition, data traffic on these networks may have to compete for bandwidth with other services at higher priority.
- **Sensor/Actuator Networks:** These networks are characterized by extremely limited end-node power, memory, and CPU capability. Communication within these networks is often *scheduled* to conserve power, and sets of nodes are frequently named (or addressed) only in aggregate. [14]

The Delay Tolerant Networking (DTN) architecture mentioned in [16] wants to address the communication needs of these challenged environments. This proposes a message based store-and-forward overlay network that uses a set of convergence layers to adapt to a wide variety of underlying transports.

3   Routing in a Delay Tolerant Network

3.1   Example: Connecting a Remote Village

In this example the scenario of communications to remote and rural areas is shown. A digital courier service provides disconnected Internet access to schools in remote villages of a country [14]. In this example, a courier on a motorbike, equipped with a USB storage device, travels from a village school to a large city which has permanent Internet connectivity. It takes a few hours for the courier to travel from the village to the city. Thus, we consider a simple scenario, based on this real-world example, which motivates the DTN routing problem. Figure 1 shows a village served by a digital courier, a wired dialup Internet connection, and a store-and-forward LEO satellite. These satellites have low bandwidth (around 10 Kbps) and are visible for 4-5 short periods of time ("passes") per day (lasting around 10 minutes per pass, depending on the orbit inclination and location on Earth).

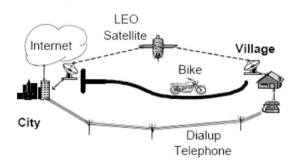

Fig. 1. Scenario illustrating a variety of connectivity options between a remote village and a city. Even in this simple scenario, many route choices are possible.

Depending on the type of connection used, buffering constraints should also be considered. The digital courier service represents a high-bandwidth, high-latency contact, the dialup represents a low-bandwidth, low-latency contact, and the LEO satellite represents a moderate-bandwidth, moderate-latency contact. The problem is to select which contacts should carry messages. Selection of route depend on a variety of factors including source and destination, message size, time of request, available contacts, traffic in the system, or other factors (e.g. cost, delay, etc.).

3.2   DTN Routing Issues

This section explains a number of important issues in any routing algorithm including the routing objective, the amount of knowledge about the network required by the scheme, when routes are computed, the use of multiple paths, and the use of source routing. Here we focus on these issues in the context of the DTN routing problem.

3.2.1   Routing Objective
There are various routing objectives, among them are: to select a shortest path, to maximize the probability of message delivery and to minimize the delay of a message (the time between when it is injected and when it is completely received). Minimizing delay lowers the time messages spend in the network, reducing contention for resources (in a qualitative sense). Therefore, lowering delay indirectly improves the probability of message delivery. [12]

3.2.2 Proactive Routing vs. Reactive Routing

In *proactive routing*, routes are computed automatically and independently of traffic arrivals. Most Internet standard routing protocols and some ad-hoc protocols such as DSDV (Destination Sequenced Distance Vector) and OLSR (Optimized Link-State Routing) are examples of this style [13]. Despite the drawback that they fail to provide paths to nodes which are not currently reachable, proactive network-layer routing protocols may provide useful input to DTN routing algorithm by providing the set of currently-reachable nodes from which DTN routing may select preferred next hops.

In *reactive routing*, routes are discovered on-demand when traffic must be delivered to an unknown destination. Ad-hoc routing protocols such as AODV (Ad-hoc On-demand Distance Vector) and DSR (Dynamic Source Routing) are examples of this style [13]. In these systems, a route discovery protocol is employed to determine routes to destinations on-demand, incurring additional delay. These protocols work best when communication patterns are relatively sparse. They fail in the sense that they fail to return a successful route.

3.2.3 Source Routing vs Per-hop Routing

In *source routing* the source node is responsible for determining the complete path of a message and encoding in some way in the message. The route is therefore determined once and does not change as the message traverses the network. In *per-hop routing* at each hop along its forwarding path the next-hop of a message is determined. Per-hop routing allows a message to utilize local information about available contacts and queues at each hop, which is typically unavailable at the source. Thus, per-hop routing may lead to better performance.

3.2.4 Message Splitting

The splitting of a message is done in such a way that different parts (fragments) are routed along different paths. This technique may reduce the delay or improve load balancing among multiple links. It can be used in DTNs because messages can be arbitrarily large and may not fit in a single contact. However, splitting complicates routing because, in addition to determining the sizes of the fragments, we also have to determine corresponding paths for the fragments.

3.3 Knowledge

The figure shows that more knowledge is required to attain better performance.

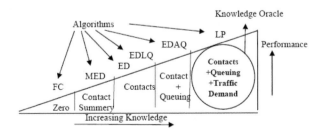

Fig. 2. Conceptual performance vs knowledge trade-off

In Figure 2, the x-axis depicts the amount of knowledge (increasing in the positive direction). The y-axis depicts the expected performance that can be achieved using a certain amount of knowledge. Labels on top show algorithms developed in this paper using the corresponding oracles.

3.3.1   Routing with Zero Knowledge

a) First Contact (FC)
Knowledge Oracles: None
An edge is chosen randomly among all the current contacts and the message is forwarded along it. If all edges are currently unavailable, the message waits for an edge to become available and is assigned to the first available contact. FC poorly performs because the chosen next-hop is random and forwarding along the selected edge may not make any progress toward the destination. A message may also oscillate forever among a set of nodes or be delivered to a dead end. FC requires only local knowledge about the network and is easy to implement. [12]

3.3.2   Routing with Partial Knowledge

a) Minimum Expected Delay (MED)
Knowledge Oracles: Contacts Summary
As the route of a message is independent of time so a proactive routing approach can be used. MED uses the same path for all messages with the same source-destination pair. No mechanism is employed to route around congestion or avoid message drops if storage space is unavailable. The key property of MED is that it minimizes the average waiting time.

b) Earliest Delivery (ED)
Knowledge Oracles: Contacts
Paths are computed by the Dijkstra's shortest path algorithm, so loop free. The route is determined once at the source making, ED a form of source routing. Paths are computed without considering the availability of storage (buffers) at intermediate nodes on the path and this may lead to drops when buffers overflow. ED is efficient if the nodes on the selected path have no queued messages or if buffers are large. Paths computed by ED do not take into account queuing delays. However, if many other messages are ahead in the queue, the contact may finish before the message is sent.

c) Earliest Delivery with Local Queuing (EDLQ)
Knowledge Oracles: Contacts
In EDLQ, we recomputed the route at every hop (per-hop routing), unlike ED. The EDLQ may lead to loop formation and the messages may oscillate forever which can be avoided by performing a re-computation of fixed routes (e.g. calculated using ED) when a loop is detected. Like ED, messages might get dropped because of buffer overrun.

d) Earliest Delivery with All Queues (EDAQ)
Knowledge Oracles: Contacts, Queuing
EDAQ uses the queuing oracle to determine the instantaneous queue sizes across the entire topology at any point in time. After computing the best route for a message,

edge capacity must be reserved for the message over all edges along its path. Such reservations ensure that messages will have been moved in sufficient time to avoid missing scheduled contacts. A bandwidth reservation is a challenge for a DTN, where communication with some nodes may be significantly delayed. For systems where centralization is practical bandwidth allocation would be greatly simplified. In EDAQ an optimal route is determined for a new message given existing reservations for the previous messages. EDAQ is also unaware to available buffer capacity. Comparison is mentioned in Table 1. [12]

Table 1. Overview of different routing algorithms. All Dijkstra-based, incorporate a cost functions sensitive to edge propagation and transmission delays. Costs are ascertained by consulting the respective oracles. [12]

Abbr.	Name	Description	Oracle Used
FC	First Contact	Use any available contact	None
MED	Minimum Expected Delay	Dijkastra with time invariant edge costs based on waiting time	Contacts Summery
ED	Earliest Delay	Modified Dijkastra with time varying cost function based on waiting time	Contacts
EDLQ	Earliest Delay with Local Queue	ED with cost function incorporating local queuing	Contacts
EDAQ	Earliest Delay with all Queue	ED with cost function incorporating queuing information at all nodes & using reservation	Contacts & Queuing

4   Routing Strategies for DTN

4.1   Unicast Routing in DTN

As DTN can be represented as a directed multi-graph, thus there may exist multiple edges between two nodes. As in [12] each edge represents a connection between nodes having two arguments i.e. time-varying capacity and propagation delay. The capacity of an edge is zero when the corresponding connection is unavailable. A *contact* is defined as an opportunity to send data between nodes, i.e., an edge and the time interval during which the edge capacity is positive.

4.2   Anycast Routing in DTN

In Anycast a node is allowed to send a message to at least one, and preferably only one, of the members in a group. DTN Anycast means that a node wants to send a message to any one of a destination group and intermediate nodes help to deliver the message when no direct path exists between the sender node and any node of the destination group. DTN anycast can be used in a disaster rescue field, in which people may want to find a doctor or a fireman without knowing their IDs or accurate locations. In DTN anycast, the destination can be any one of a group of nodes. The path to a group member and the destination can change dynamically according to mobile device movement situation during routing.

4.3   Delay-Tolerant Broadcasting

It is also called BBR (Broadcast Based Routing).In this method the data is forwarded in the form of chunks through mobility of wireless nodes. It is a receiver-driven system. It has a public broadcast channels, which is used for both transmission and reception. This system is useful where the population of users is dense. In broadcasting each channel provides a particular type of content. Contents originated from the mobile nodes could be broadcast without any infrastructure. The data chunks can be delivered in or out of order, with or without assured completeness. There are many applications for which order and completeness are not necessary such as the distribution of a mixture or music, news, traffic and weather information [4].

4.4   Multicasting Routing in DTN

As DTN has a unique characteristic of frequent partitioning, multicasting is a considerably different problem in DTNs. DTN applications often requires different network support communication. In a disaster recovery scene, it is essential to distribute information about victims and risks among rescue workers. In a battlefield, soldiers need to inform each other about their surrounding situation. Although unicast can be used by sending a separate unicast packet to each user of the group. This approach suffers from poor performance. The efficient multicast services are needed as available bandwidth and storage are generally limited.

There may be no end-to-end path between nodes in DTNs. Thus multicast routing in DTNs needs to operate in the presence of network partitions. As proposed in [11], data transfer in DTNs is in application data units called *messages* (or bundles). This is different from the use of flows in traditional multicasting. Information about nodes joining or leaving a group may be available only after significant. As DTN can have large transfer delays group membership may change during a message transfer. So it is necessary to make a distinction between *group members* which may change with time as endpoints join and leave the group and the *intended receivers* which are fixed based on group membership.

4.5   Multicast Routing Algorithms

4.5.1   STBR
In Static Tree Based Routing (STBR), a shortest path tree in the DTN graph is constructed from the source to the intended receivers at message generation time. As a node enters or leaves the group, nodes update the shortest path tree. Messages are then forwarded along the tree. In STBR, the route is static. Thus if a message does not get a contact with a node, it waits for the next opportunity to connect to this node, which may increases the delay. The use of static routes does not allow nodes to use local information to forward messages along better paths. [11]

4.5.2   DTBR
This is a Dynamic Tree-Based Routing (DTBR) designed for DTNs. In DTBR, the receiver list will be assigned to the downstream nodes by upstream node. The bundles

will be forwarded to only those receivers which are mentioned in the list, even if a new path is discovered for another receiver. In Figure 3(a), suppose link 1-2 is not available when the multicast bundle reaches node 1. Then, node 1 will use node 3 as intermediate node to deliver to nodes 5 and 6 and store a copy of the bundle so that node 1 can send to node 2 when the link 1-2 becomes available again since this is the only route to reach node 4. DTBR assumes that each node has complete knowledge or the summary of the link states in the network. [11]

4.5.3 OS-multicast

The On-demand Situation-aware multicast (OS-multicast) approach is a dynamic tree-based method that integrates DTN multicasting with the situation discovery mechanism provided by the underlying network layer. For each bundle a unique tree is constructed and this tree is adjusted according to the current network conditions. Upon receiving a bundle, the node will dynamically update the tree based on its current knowledge of the network conditions. Thus any newly discovered path can be quickly utilized. For example, in Figure 3(b), the link between 2-5 is broken but when the bundle reaches node 3, it will send a copy to both nodes 5 and 6. The drawback of the OS-multicast approach is that a receiver may receive many copies of the same bundle. [17]

4.5.4 CAMR

It is also a multicast routing scheme based on node-density. The authors of [2] showed that CAMR scheme achieve better message delivery ratio, with higher transmission efficiency and similar delay performance especially when the nodes are very sparsely connected or the network scenarios where an instantaneous end-to-end path between a source and destination may not exist because of opportunistic links. It is a node-density based adaptive multicast routing scheme for DTNs that is based on five components: (a) Local Node Density Estimation, (b) 2-Hop Neighbor Contact Probability Estimate, (c) Route Discovery, (d) Route Repair, and (e) Data Delivery.

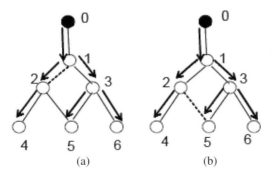

(a)   (b)

Fig. 3. Multicast approaches in DTN (a) DTBR, (b) OS multicast: when link 2→5 is unavailable and link 3→5 becomes available, node 3 will take advantage of the current available link immediately.

Table 2. Comparison between some multicast techniques

	Delivery Ratio	Average Delay	Data Efficiency
CAMR	90.5%	21 seconds	0.32
DTBR	74.0%	0.2 seconds	0.42
OS-multicast	48.9%	20 seconds	0.08
u-multicast	42.0%	0.1 seconds	0.46

4.6 Mobility Pattern Based Routing Scheme

This is designed on the basis of mobility patterns for routing in a delay tolerant network (DTN). As DTN architecture defines scheduled, opportunistic, and predicted types of contacts. Scheduled contacts exist between a base station on earth and a low earth orbiting relay satellite. Opportunistic contacts exist between two entities at the same place that was neither scheduled nor predicted. In predicted contacts predictions of their existence can be made. They are also not scheduled.

The mobility pattern based routing schemes are compared against the following:

- **Epidemic:** As described by [6] each time two nodes meet, they exchange their bundles. It provides the optimum path and thus the minimum delay. In general, there is high buffer occupancy and high bandwidth utilization.
- **Opportunistic:** In this method it involves only one transmission per bundle. A node has to wait to meet the destination in order to transfer its bundle.
- **Random:** When the bundle's destination in not there and the node are at a location, the node transfers the bundle to a randomly chosen neighbor. Bundles will jump to other nodes without any preference ordering. This makes extraordinarily high average route lengths.

The author of [5] tested two variants of the mobility pattern based routing scheme. In the first, it is assumed that a node that is sending a bundle has full knowledge of the destination's mobility pattern, and that it addresses the bundle accordingly. In the second, it is assumed that nodes communicate only the major components of their mobility patterns. By this, the amount of traffic exchanged between nodes is reduced.

4.7 Mobility Profile Based Routing

In this method we assume that a user regularly visits a small set of socially significant and geographically distant places called "hubs". By using the knowledge of the users' sociological hub based orbital mobility profiles, throughput of routing protocols can be increased and overhead can be decrease. The main contribution of the author is a routing protocol called *SOLAR-HUB* that takes advantage of user mobility profiles to perform "hub-level" routing. In SOLAR-HUB, when the sender, or an intermediate user carrying the message, moves into the hub(s) where the receiver can retrieve the message, a message from a sender will be routed to one or more hubs visited by the receiver called destination hub(s). Such a hub-level routing differs from any contact-probability based routing in several aspects. First, the contact probability of two users based on all users' hub-visit probabilities can be computed but not vice versa (since most users' contact information is location independent). Secondly, we can generalize the concept of hub-based routing such that a user may deliver a message to another by giving the message to a destination hub(s) even when the contact probability of the two users may be zero, which is possible when the two are never in the same hub at the same time and there are no other intermediate users in the system. [8]

4.8 Redundancy-Based Routing

In DTN the exact contact information between any two nodes is usually unknown in advance. So there is a class of routing in DTN that uses redundancy to reduce the delay and increase the delivery rate. One simple redundancy-based scheme is flooding-based routing which can cause too much overhead for the network and overflow the buffer of the nodes. To control the overhead of flooding-based routing schemes, the authors of [9] propose to dispatch a certain number of identical message copies to a fixed number of relay nodes, instead of every node in the network. When a message is generated by a source node, a "quota" is attached to that message, which represents how many identical copies of the message can be inserted in the network. When a node forwards a copy to another node, the remaining quota of the message is distributed between the two copies on the two different nodes. The node will not forward the message to somebody else if the carried message does not have enough quota.

The author proposed a model using continuous time Markov chain with absorbing state to study the performance. The non-absorbing states of the Markov chain are the number of relays carrying copies of the same message. When the message is successfully delivered to its destination node, the chain enters its absorbing state.

4.9 Spray and Wait Scheme

Spray and Wait is highly scalable having good performance under a large range of scenarios, unlike other schemes. It is simple to implement and optimize in order to achieve given performance goals in practice.

Definition: *Spray and Wait routing consists of the following two phases:*

- Spray phase*: for every message originating at a source node, L message copies are initially forwarded by the source and possibly other nodes receiving a copy to L distinct "relays".*
- Wait phase*: if the destination is not found in the spraying phase, each of the L nodes carrying a message copy performs direct transmission i.e. will forward the message only to its destination.* [10]

In Spray and Wait the total number of copies and transmissions per message are bound, without compromising performance. Under low load, Spray and Wait results in much fewer transmissions and smaller delays than flooding-based schemes. In case of high load, it gives better delays and fewer transmissions than flooding-based schemes. It exhibits good and predictable performance for a large range of network sizes, node densities and connectivity levels. As the size of the network and the number of nodes increase, the number of transmissions *per node* decreases in order to achieve the same performance. When enough copies have been spread to guarantee that at least one of them will find the destination, it stops and lets each node carrying a copy perform direct transmission. Its performance is better with respect to both number of transmissions and delay than all other practical single and multi-copy schemes, in most scenarios considered. [10]

4.10   Inter-domain Routing Schemes

There are two methods for interdomain routing for delay tolerant networks. [15]

4.10.1   GBIR

Gateway-Based Inter-domain Routing (GBIR) has following three components.

a) Leader Selection and Transfer
The node will be selected as the leader which sends the claim first and which are one hop away from the center of the subnetwork. If more than one leader succeeds almost the same time, the one closest to the subnetwork center will be selected. When a leader moves out of the one hop area from the center, it checks all its neighbors and chooses the one which is closest to the subnet center to take over its leadership.

b) Gateway registration, deregistration and transfer
A node sends a gateway registration message to the leader of its own subnet when it hears messages from other groups. Since the leader is always within the one-hop area from the subnet center, geographical routing will be used to forward registration message. Thus the gateway can register successfully with its leader without knowing the identity of its current leader. The registration message contains gateway location information. If a registered gateway does not hear from other groups, it sends a de-registration message to its leader. If a gateway node is away from the overlapping area, it finds a neighboring subnet, currently in the overlapping area to take over.

c) Data Delivery
Node requires gateway information to send data to another group. The leader does not provide the exact location of the gateway that is why upon receiving the response from the leader it uses the multihop routing to send the data to the gateway.

4.10.2   FBIR

Assumptions for Ferry-Based Inter-domain Routing (FBIR) are that each group has one ferry which sends inter-group messages and that each group member knows the identifier of its own group's ferry. A ferry can be either local to its own group or roaming i.e. visiting other groups. When a ferry crosses the area of its own group, it broadcasts a service announcement message periodically to discover nodes from other groups. Ferry periodically checks its buffered packets to see that are there *some packets queued for more than w seconds* or the *buffer capacity exceeds 99%*. If any of the above conditions occurs, the ferry will start moving towards the destination group of the oldest message among those queued messages. If buffer exceeds then the ferry will visit the destination group which has maximum number of queued messages. As ferry knows the approximate location of the destination group, it issues hello messages periodically to look for nodes from the destination group and transfers the message when node is discovered. The ferry will move to other groups only if there are messages destined to other groups the buffer otherwise, the ferry stays in its own group. [15]

5 Conclusion

In this paper, we have surveyed many existing algorithms for evaluating DTN routing algorithms. While discussing abut DTN routing it is necessary to pay attention on various tasks like selection of paths, transmission schedules, estimated delivery performance, and management of buffers. The problem of frequent disconnection in devices which may be mobile is more important. In many such cases, communication opportunities may be predictable. The algorithms mentioned in this paper focus on these situations. This survey suggests that in situations where resources are limited smarter algorithms will be beneficial. Our survey and classification also enabled us to make the following observations.

First, hybrid techniques that are based on both knowledge of the topology and replication will give high delivery ratio with low resource consumption. But determining the correct balance between consumption of resources and redundancy of replication is a challenge. Second, epidemic routing will be useful in the cases where message are small.

References

[1] Gong, Y., Xiong, Y., Zhang, Q., Zhang, Z., Wang, W., Xu, Z.: Anycast Routing in Delay Tolerant Networks. In: IEEE GLOBECOM 2006 proceedings (2006)

[2] Yang, P., Chuah, M.C.: Context-Aware Multicast Routing Scheme for Disruption Tolerant Networks. In: Proceeding of PE-WASUN 2006, Torremolinos, Malaga, Spain, October 6 (2006)

[3] Brunner, M., Eggert, L., Fall, K., Ott, J., Wolf, L.: Seminar on Disruption Tolerant Networking. ACM SIGCOMM Computer Communication Review 35(2) (July 2005)

[4] Karlsson, G., Lenders, V., May, M.: Delay-Tolerant Broadcasting. In: The proceedings of SIGCOMM 2006 Workshops, Pisa, Italy, September 11-15 (2006)

[5] Leguay, J., Friedman, T., Conan, V.: DTN Routing in a Mobility Pattern Space. In: The proceedings of SIGCOMM 2005 Workshops, Philadelphia, PA, USA, August 22–26 (2005)

[6] Vahdat, A., Becker, D.: Epidemic routing for partially connected ad hoc networks. Technical Report CS-200006, Duke University (April 2000)

[7] Ott, J., Kutscher, D., Dwertmann, C.: Integrating DTN and MANET Routing. In: The proceedings of SIGCOMM 2006 Workshops, Pisa, Italy, September 11-15 (2006)

[8] Ghosh, J., Ngo, H.Q., Qiao, C.: Mobility Profile based Routing Within Intermittently Connected Mobile Ad hoc Networks (ICMAN). In: The proceedings of IWCMC 2006, Vancouver, British Columbia, Canada, July 3-6 (2006)

[9] Liao, Y., Tan, K., Zhang, Z., Gao, L.: Modeling Redundancy-based Routing in Delay Tolerant Networks. In: The proceedings of IEEE 2007, pp. 212–216 (2007)

[10] Spyropoulos, T., Psounis, K., Raghavendra, C.: Spray and wait: an efficient routing scheme for intermittently connected mobile networks. In: WDTN 2005: SIGCOMM 2005 DTN workshop, pp. 252–259 (2005)

[11] Zhao, W., Ammar, M., Zegura, E.: Multicasting in Delay Tolerant Networks: Semantic Models and Routing Algorithms. In: The proceedings of SIGCOMM 2005 Workshops, Philadelphia, PA, USA, August 22–26 (2005)

[12] Jain, S., Fall, K., Patra, R.: Routing in a Delay Tolerant Network. In: The proceedings of SIGCOMM 2004, Portland, Oregon, USA, August 30–September 3 (2004)

[13] Broch, J., Maltz, D.A., Johnson, D.B., Hu, Y.C., Jetcheva, J.: A Performance Comparison of Multi-Hop Wireless Ad Hoc Network Routing Protocols. In: ACM Mobicom (August 1998)

[14] Fall, K.: A Delay-Tolerant Network Architecture for Challenged Internets. In: The proceedings of SIGCOMM 2003, Karlsruhe, Germany, August 25-29 (2003)

[15] Yang, P., Chuah, M.: Performance Comparison of Two Interdomain Routing Schemes for Disruption Tolerant Networks

[16] Warthman, F.: Delay Tolerant Networks – A Tutorial. DTN Research Group Internet Draft, Vreson No. 1.1 (March 2003), http://www.dtnrg.org

[17] Ye, Q., Cheng, L., Chuah, M., Davison, B.D.: On-Demand Situation Aware Multicasting in DTNs. In: Proceedings of IEEE VTC, Spring (2006)

Adaptive Valid Period Based Concurrency Control without Locking in Mobile Environments

Mohammed Khaja Nizamuddin* and Syed Abdul Sattar

[1] Associate Professor, DCET, Hyderabad, India
mknizams@yahoo.com
[2] Professor, Royal Institute of Technology and Science, Chevella, India
syedabdulsattar1965@gmail.com

Abstract. In a mobile computing environment, clients can access data irrespective of their physical location. Data is shared among multiple clients and can be updated by each client independently. This leads to inconsistency of the data. Due to limitations of mobile computing environment traditional techniques cannot be used. Several concurrency control techniques are proposed in literature to prevent data inconsistency. In this paper we first analyze the existing scheme of concurrency control without locking and justify its Performance limitations. A new scheme is proposed which adaptively set the validity period of the cached data items based on the number of data items required and current load of the database server. Experimental results show performance benefits and increase in commit rate of the transactions *abstract* environment.

Keywords: Absolute Validity Interval, Valid Period, semaphore, data count, Mobile Host, Fixed Host.

1 Introduction

Concurrency control is one of the essential characteristics of transaction management to ensure consistency of database. In mobile computing environment, data management becomes a challenging issue due its limitations i.e. variable bandwidth, frequent disconnections, limited resources on mobile host etc [6]. Several valuable techniques are proposed in literature to provide concurrency control in mobile environments, however most of them are based on locking, time stamp and optimistic concurrency control.

In reference [9], a new concurrency control technique is proposed without using locks. In this scheme Absolute validity interval (AVI) value is used to achieve concurrency control [3]. This scheme has a problem of predicting new AVI value of the data item based on the update history. In this paper we justify that predicting new AVI value based on history may result in abortion of the next transaction. Several performance limitations of the scheme is also mentioned. In

---

* Corresponding author. Research scholar, Rayalaseema University, Kurnool, India.

N. Meghanathan et al. (Eds.): NeCoM, WiMoN, and WeST 2010, CCIS 90, pp. 349–358, 2010.

this paper we also proposed a scheme for achieving concurrency control in mobile environments by eliminating limitations of the existing scheme and increasing commit rate of the transactions.

The rest of the paper is organized as follows. Section 2 reviews existing concurrency control schemes. Section 3 describes mobile database environment. In Section 4 we discuss performance limitations of the existing lockless scheme. Section 5 explores proposed concurrency control scheme. Section 6 specifies performance metrics. Section 7 concludes the paper.

2   Related Work

In mobile database environment any mobile client can access data item irrespective of its physical location. Providing consistency of the data items is a challenging issue in case of concurrent access. Various valuable attempts are made in providing solutions for data management in mobile environments.

The conventional two phase locking protocol is not suitable as it requires clients to communicate continuously with the server to obtain locks and detect the conflicts [7]. An optimistic concurrency control technique has the problem of delayed response [11]. In [12] timeout based Commit Protocol is proposed which faces the problem of the time lag between local and global commit and more rollbacks of the transactions due to starvation.In [5] the proposed Mobile 2PC protocol preserves the 2PC principle and minimizes the impact of unreliable wireless communication.

An Optimistic Concurrency Control with Dynamic Time stamp Adjustment Protocol requires client side write operations. However because of the delay in execution of a transaction, it may never be executed [2]. In [1, 4], the conventional optimistic concurrency control algorithm in enhanced with an early termination mechanism on conflicting transactions. In [8] dynamic timer management is used for achieving concurrency control. This suffers from the problem of frequent rollbacks due to regular expiry of the timer and wastage of computation. In [10] preemptive dynamic timer adjustment strategy is proposed to enhance throughput of the system. This scheme is based on assumption of execution time and not scalable.

3   Mobile Database Environment

In mobile database environment (fig.1) the network consists of Mobile Host (MH), Fixed Host (FH) and Base station. A MH is connected with Base station through wireless links. The communication of the MH with the FH is supported by Base station. The area covered by a base station is called cell. Mobile Hosts in a particular cell cannot directly communicate with each other, instead they have to communicate through the base station. Base stations are directly connected with the power terminals, hence there is no problem of power consumption at base station. FH is connected with a wired network and usually has a large

database server, which performs all operations of a DBMS. MH may have storage capabilities and DBMS modules to perform database operations. However
it has small screen size, less processing capability and variable bandwidth. Also
the communication asymmetry between MH and base station makes receiving
by the MH preferable than sending to base stations. A MH may not always be
connected with the network. It may be disconnected or in doze mode to same
battery consumption. Hence disconnections are treated as normal events and not
as failures [7]. The execution of the transactions may be completely on FH or
on MH or partially on both.

In our scheme we assume that transactions copy all data items required from
FH to local physical memory of the MH. The transactions then disconnect from
the FH to decrease network load and execute transaction locally. The updates
are recorded on the FH in Write through manner.

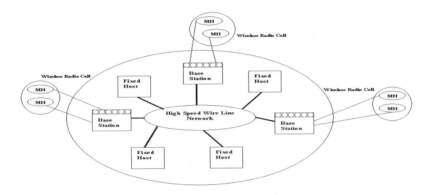

Fig. 1. Mobile Database Environment[8]

4   Performance Limitations of Existing Scheme

1. The AVI value is proposed to do cache invalidation. New value is assigned
   based on the last update period of the data item. This assumption leads
   to abortion of the next transaction if it uses this data item after slightly
   more period. This results is expiry of the data item and there may not be
   any transaction waiting for this data item. Hence predicting the new AVI
   value based on update history of the data item may lead to more number of
   transaction aborts.
2. The TLU value used by the server to save last update time of the data item
   is not required in maintaining concurrency control. This is included only to
   predict the AVI value and increasing the computation cost at the server.
3. The AVI value is set two times once at the time of copy of the data item
   from server and once at the time of update onto the server. Setting the new
   AVI at the time of update on the server is not required since there may not
   be any transactions waiting to acquire this data item. Also, at update time

the operations such as write the data value, log record entry etc. will already delay the commit of the transactions.

5   Proposed Concurrency Control Scheme

5.1   Proposed Scheme Features

1. We define a variable VALID PERIOD (VP) of a data item as time quantum in which a MH should use this value in its local execution. This value is deduced based on the remaining number of data items a transaction has to copy from the server to the local memory of the MH. Predicting the validity period of a data item based on total number of data items a transaction further requires to be copied from the server will give a reasonably close valid period for the current transaction than last update time, as time at which the data item is used in execution of the transactions varies. For example, transaction T1 on MH1 may copy data item X as its last data item from server and start local execution. If T1 has only 3 data items then X will be updated in next 4 time units. Hence new AVI value of X will be utmost 4.Next Transaction T2 on MH2 may copy X as its first data item which has a data count of 10.The X value is used in the local execution only after at least 9 time units. This will make X to expire without any reason.
2. We define a parameter DATA COUNT (DC) of a transaction as the remaining number of data items a transaction has to copy from the server to the local memory of the MH.
3. The VP value is a times enhanced based on the number of transactions currently present in the system. This parameter will adaptively set the VP value by considering the current network load on the Fixed Host. Since more number of concurrent transaction results in increased waiting time and data conflicts.
4. Read and Write operations of a transaction are clearly separated to ensure serializability.

The data stored on the fixed host has the following new format to control concurrent access.

Table 1. Data Item Format stored on Fixed Host

Data-Id	Semaphore	VP	Data

1. Data-ID denotes a unique-Id of the data item.
2. Semaphore denotes a binary variable, which has either 0 or 1 value.
3. VP denotes the Valid Period, i.e. the time period for which the data item value should be used in local execution of the MH.
4. Data denotes the current value of the data item.

5.2   Proposed Client (MH) Algorithm

1. MH Connects to the fixed host. Checks the availability of all the data items required by comparing its semaphore value to zero.
2. MH then encounters any one of the two cases.

   Case(A):If semaphore=0 is true, then MH submits data count (DC)(number of data items required) value to the FH, copies the data item format and decrements DC.

   Case(B): If semaphore=0 is false, then wait in the queue till the data item is available.
3. Repeat step (2) for all data items until DC=0.
4. Start execution of the transaction locally on the MH.

   Case(A): for read operation of the data item directly execute step (5).

   Case(B): for write operation of the data item check the following equation
   $Current access time \geq timestamp + valid period$ ————————————————-(1)
   (Timestamp is the time at which the data item is read by the mobile host)

   i) if equation (1) if true, it means that the period for which the data item is given for update is exceeded. Hence the current value of the data item may be invalid. Increment DC and execute from step (1).
   ii) if equation (1) is false, it means that the data item is still valid. Execute step (6).

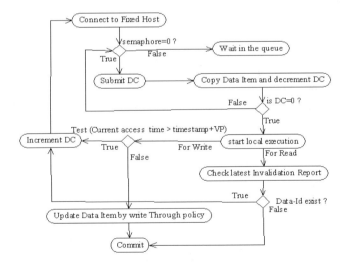

Fig. 2. Activity Diagram of MH

5. Search the Data-Id of the data item in the latest invalidation report.
   Case(A): If Data-Id exist, it means that the value of the data item is updated on the server and the current value is invalid. Increment DC and execute from step (1).

Case(B): If Data-Id does not exist, it means that the value of the data item is still valid.

6. Write data item locally and to maintain consistency, update the value of the data item on the server by write through policy. Write through policy is, whenever the data item is updated in the local memory at the same time it should also be updated on the server by changing the semaphore value to zero (=0).

7. If all data items are updated on the Fixed Host then transaction on Mobile Host commits.

5.3   Proposed Server (FH) Algorithm

1. Create the data item format for each data item by initializing semaphore, Data-Id and Data value. Set valid period zero (VP=0).
2. Start timer.
3. Wait for data item request from MH.
4. If request arrives check semaphore value of the data item.

   Case(A): If Semaphore=1, add this transaction in waiting queue.

   Case (B): If Semaphore=0, allow the MH to read the data item. If the MH wants to perform a write operation then set the semaphore value to '1' and assign new valid period ($VP = \alpha * DC$).
5. Wait for data item update or expiry of valid period.
6. Case(A): If valid period expired before update, then set the semaphore value and valid period of the data item to zero. Invoke the next transaction waiting in the queue. Execute from step (4)

   Case(B): If update request of a data item comes, then generate invalidation report by including Data-Id of the data item updated and send only to those

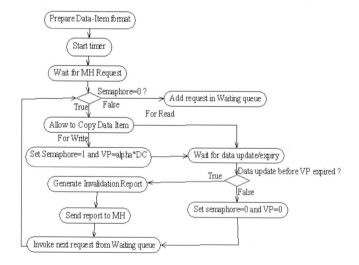

Fig. 3. Activity Diagram of FH Server

MH which has a copy of this data item. Set the semaphore value and valid period of the data item to zero. Invoke the next transaction waiting in the queue. Execute from step (4).

6   Performance Metrics

Same concurrent execution scenario of the transactions as presented in [9] is taken to show performance enhancement. The table. 2 depicts execution steps of the transactions. X,Y,Z are the data items. Each Mobile Host (MH) requires two data items. Copy denotes the operation of copying the data item from Fixed Host (FH) to MH. Read, Write, commit are the operations of normal transaction execution.

Table 3. represents the above Mobile Host transactions execution schedule by the existing scheme [9].The Current Access Time depicts the time of the each logical operation of transaction execution. RW (A) represents copying the data item into the private memory and performing the write operation on A. R (A) represents copying the data item into the private memory for performing read

Table 2. Execution Steps of transactions

MH1	MH2	MH3
Copy(X)	Copy(Y)	Copy(Z)
Copy(Y)	Copy(Z)	Copy(X)
Write(X)	Read(Y)	Write(Z)
Write(Y)	Write(Z)	Write(X)
Commit	Commit	Commit

MH=Mobile Host

Table 3. Transaction Execution on MH [9]

CT	MH1	MH2	MH3	AVI			Timestamp		
				X	Y	Z	MH1	MH2	MH3
11	RW(X)	R(Y)	RW(Z)	5	6	4	X(11)	Y(11)	Z(11)
12	RW(Y)	WAIT(Z)	WAIT(X)	5	6	4	Y(12)	–	–
13	WRITE(X)	—	—	3	6	4	–	–	–
14	WRITE(Y)	Inv.Report	RW(X)	3	5	4	–	–	X(14)
15	COMMIT	RW(Z)	ABORT	2	5	7	–	Z(15)	–
16	—	R(Y)	—	-	5	7	–	Y(16)	–
17	—	WRITE(Z)	—	-	-	5	–	–	–
18	—	COMMIT	—	-	-	-	–	–	–

CT=Current Access Time , AVI=Absolute Validity Interval

only operation. WAIT (A) specifies that the mobile host is waiting to acquire the data item A. WRITE (A) denotes write through policy for updating the data item A. A (T) denotes the time T at which the data item A is copied by the Mobile Host.

In the above schedule MH3 aborts due to wrong prediction of AVI of data item Z, Since by the time it acquires Z after waiting for it, transaction MH2 acquires it violating Serializability. Hence MH3 aborts execution.

Table 4. represents Mobile Host transactions execution schedule with the proposed scheme. For the present scenario $\alpha = 3$.MH3 now commits due to appropriate assignment of the VP (valid period) value of the data item Z. With a cost of 1 time unit the system is able to give full commit rate, though some waiting time of the transaction may increase. The results of the scheme over increased number of transactions given more commit rate. The number of parameters required to update by the server is also minimized. The server updates the values of the data item format only when some transaction uses it.

Table 4. Transaction Execution on MH in proposed scheme

CT	MH1	MH2	MH3	VP			DC			Timestamp		
				X	Y	Z	MH1	MH2	MH3	MH1	MH2	MH3
10	–	–	–	0	0	0	2	2	2	0	0	0
11	RW(X)	R(Y)	RW(Z)	6	0	6	1	1	1	X(11)	Y(11)	Z(11)
12	RW(Y)	WAIT(Z)	WAIT(X)	6	3	6	0	1	1	Y(12)	–	–
13	WRITE(X)	–	–	0	3	6	0	1	1	–	–	–
14	WRITE(Y)	Inv.Report	RW(X)	3	0	6	0	1	0	–	–	X(14)
15	COMMIT	–	WRITE(Z)	3	0	0	0	1	0	–	–	–
16	–	RW(Z)	WRITE(X)	0	0	3	0	0	0	–	Z(16)	–
17	–	R(Y)	COMMIT	0	0	3	0	0	0	–	Y(17)	–
18	–	WRITE(Z)	–	0	0	0	0	0	0	–	–	–
19	–	COMMIT	–	0	0	0	0	0	0	–	–	–

DC=DATA COUNT   VP=VALID PERIOD $VP = (\alpha * DC)$ $\alpha = 3$

Table 5. represents data item format values stored on the server while concurrent execution of the transactions.

6.1   Advantages of Proposed Scheme

1. Valid Period (VP) value of a data item is decided based on remaining number of data items a transaction has to copy from Fixed Host. This ensures sufficient time Period in which a transaction use this data item and successfully complete its execution. Hence commit rate of the system increases.
2. Parameter 'α' enhances the VP of a data item based on number of transactions active in the system. Considering current work load of the Fixed Host while assigning new VP of a data item appropriates data sharing period of the concurrent transactions.

Table 5. FH data item status while execution

CT	VP			Semaphore		
	X	Y	Z	X	Y	Z
10	0	0	0	0	0	0
11	6	0	6	1	0	1
12	6	3	6	1	1	1
13	0	3	6	0	1	1
14	3	0	3	1	0	1
15	3	0	0	1	0	0
16	0	0	3	0	0	1
17	0	0	3	0	0	1
18	0	0	0	0	0	0

3. The Value of VP a data item is set to zero after update, since when no transaction requests for that data item, the value will not be invalid without update. It is set only when a transaction request the data item for Write.

7   Conclusion

In this paper we have shown the limitations of the existing concurrency control scheme. We also justified that predicting the AVI value based on update history is not desirable. The proposed concurrency control scheme improves the drawbacks of the existing scheme by adaptively selecting validity period of the data items based on required number of data items and current load of Fixed Host server. It also increases the overall commit rate of the system.

References

1. Anand, Y., Wen, C.H., Chih, F.W.: Improving Concurrency Control in Mobile Databases. In: Lee, Y., Li, J., Whang, K.-Y., Lee, D. (eds.) DASFAA 2004. LNCS, vol. 2973, pp. 642–655. Springer, Heidelberg (2004)
2. Ho, J.C., Byeong, S.J.: A Timestamp- Based Optimistic Concurrency Control for Handling Mobile Transactions. In: Gavrilova, M.L., Gervasi, O., Kumar, V., Tan, C.J.K., Taniar, D., Laganá, A., Mun, Y., Choo, H. (eds.) ICCSA 2006. LNCS, vol. 3981, pp. 796–805. Springer, Heidelberg (2006)
3. Joe, C.H.Y., Chan, E., Lam, K.Y., Leung, H.W.: An Adaptive AVI-based Cache Invalidation Scheme for Mobile Computing Systems. In: 11th International Workshop on Database and Expert Systems Applications (DEXA 2000), p. 155. IEEE computer society, USA (2000)
4. Minsoo, L., Sumi, H.: HiCoMo:High Commit Mobile Transactions. In: Distributed and Parallel Databases, vol. 11, pp. 73–92. Kluwer Academic Publishers, Dordrecht (2002)

5. Nadia, N., Anne, D., Habiba, D.: A Two-Phase Commit Protocol for Mobile Wireless Environment. In: 16th Australasian Database Conference, Australia, pp. 135–143 (2005)
6. Patricia, S.A., Claudia, R., Michel, A.: A Survey of Mobile Transactions. In: Distributed and Parallel databases, vol. 16, pp. 193–230. Kluwer Academic Publishers, Dordrecht (2004)
7. Salman, A.M., Lakshmi, R.: An Algorithmic approach for achieving Concurrency in Mobile Environment. In: INDIACom, India, pp. 209–211 (2007)
8. Salman, A.M., Lakshmi, R.: Single Lock Manager Approach for Achieving Concurrency in Mobile Environments. In: Aluru, S., Parashar, M., Badrinath, R., Prasanna, V.K. (eds.) HiPC 2007. LNCS, vol. 4873, pp. 650–660. Springer, Heidelberg (2007)
9. Salman, A.M., Nizamuddin, M.K.: Concurrency Control Without Locking in Mobile Environments. In: 1st International Conference on Emerging Trends in Engineering and Technology, pp. 1336–1339. IEEE Computer society, USA (2008)
10. Salman, A.M., Lakshmi, R.: Concurrency Control Strategy to Reduce Frequent Rollbacks in Mobile Environments. In: International Conference on Computational Science and Engineering, pp. 709–714. IEEE Computer society, USA (2009)
11. Victor, C.S., Kwok, W.L., Son, S.H.: Concurrency Control Using Timestamp Ordering in Broadcast Environments. The Computer Journal 45(4), 410–422 (2002)
12. Kumar, V., Prabhu, N., Dunham, M.H., Seydim, A.Y.: TCOT- A Timeout based Mobile Transaction Commitment Protocol. IEEE Transactions on Computers 51(10), 1212–1218 (2002)

An Associativity Based Energy Aware Clustering Technique for Mobile Ad Hoc Networks

Tahrima Rahman and A.M.A. Elman Bashar

Department of Computer Science & Engineering
Eastern University, Bangladesh
{tahrima,elman}@easternuni.edu.bd

Abstract. Node clustering is a widely used approach to address the scalability issue of large-scale mobile ad hoc networks(MANETs). It eases the implementation of routing and resource management by constructing an abstract hierarchy of the flat network architecture of MANETs. Its effectiveness however depends largely on the clusters stability which is measured by the lifetime of the clusters. The aim of this paper is to propose a fully distributed clustering algorithm that addresses the stability of mobile nodes in terms of neighborhood associativity and remaining energy. The algorithm maximizes the cluster lifetime by choosing those nodes as clusterheads which have the highest neighborhood associativity and remaining energy. It also tries to minimize the number of clusters in the network by giving priority to higher degree nodes. Simulation results show that the algorithm identifies clusters that are stable with respect to cluster lifetime and the frequency of reaffiliations of mobile nodes.

Keywords: Mobile Ad Hoc Networks, Clustering Algorithm, Associativity.

1 Introduction

Mobile ad hoc networks are autonomous systems of mobile hosts that communicate by multi-hop wireless links without any fixed infrastructure or predetermined connectivity. There are no specialized routers for path discovery and packet routing in such networks. Instead intermediate nodes between a source and destination act as routers by relaying packets between them. These intermediate nodes are mobile in a MANET. Mobility of such nodes cause link failures which in turn cause established routing paths between the source and destination to break. Once an established path is broken a new path has to be discovered. Path discovery algorithms incur extra overhead in the network. This problem becomes acute as mobility increases in the network. For this reason, it is always desirable to select a path that is more stable over time. One solution to this problem is to partition the network into group of clusters[1]. By keeping nodes with a stable neighborhood in the same cluster, the topology within a cluster becomes less dynamic. This minimizes link breakage and packet loss. The number

N. Meghanathan et al. (Eds.): NeCoM, WiMoN, and WeST 2010, CCIS 90, pp. 359–368, 2010.

of nodes in a cluster is smaller than the number of nodes in the entire network. Thus each node needs to store only a partial information of the entire network topology. This reduces the number of entries in the routing table and the exchange of routing information between nodes. Thus clustering helps to mitigate topology information and improves network scalability.

Under a cluster structure, mobile nodes may be assigned different roles, such as clusterheads, cluster gateways or cluster members. A clusterhead is elected to serve as a local coordinator for its cluster performing intra-cluster transmission arrangement, data forwarding, and so on. A node that has a packet to send to another node can obtain routing information from its clusterhead. A cluster gateway is a non-clusterhead node with inter-cluster links, so it can access neighboring clusters and forward packets between them. A cluster member is usually called an ordinary node, which is a non-clusterhead node without any inter-cluster links[3].

Since the purposes of forming clusters are to stabilize the end-to-end communication paths and to improve the network scalability, the cluster stability must be considered, which is defined to be the lifetime of the clusters[6]. Unstable clusters could jeopardize both objectives. Many existing clustering algorithms do not consider the cluster stability as the design goal and, therefore, experience frequent cluster changes. This paper proposes a new clustering algorithm. The basis of the algorithm is a scheme that predicts the stability of each mobile host based on the associativity with its neighborhood and its remaining energy. The concept of associativity (relative stability of nodes) is used to get long-lived routes[7]. On the other hand high remaining energy of a node indicates that the node is stable in the energy sense. Choosing associativity and remaining energy in the selection of clusterheads increases the temporal stability of the clusters. In addition to these parameters, node's degree is also taken into consideration. Nodes with degrees greater than a predetermined value are given priority in the clusterhead election process to reduce the number of clusters throughout the network.

The rest of the paper is organized as follows. In Section 2, we summarize related work with a particular focus on a recent algorithm named Distributed Score Based Clustering Algorithm(DSBCA)[2]. In Section 3, we propose the new clustering algorithm. Simulation results are presented in Section 4 while conclusions are drawn in Section 5.

2   Related Work

Many clustering techniques have been proposed over the past years to manage MANETs effectively. Each technique has its own strengths and weaknesses. Some of the well-known algorithms are the Lowest-ID[4] and the Highest-Degree[5] Algorithms, the Weighted Clustering Algorithm(WCA)[10] and the Distributed Weighted Clustering Algorithm(DWCA)[13]. The Lowest-ID algorithm chooses the node with the minimum identifier in the neighborhood as the clusterhead. Since node ID does not change over time, lower ID nodes are prone to power drainage due to serving as clusterheads for longer periods of time resulting in shorter system life time. In the Highest-Degree algorithm the node with the highest degree in the neighborhood is elected as the clusterhead. It performs much worse than the Lowest-ID algorithm in terms of stability of clusters. The WCA algorithm combines system parameters such as degree, transmission power, mobility and battery power with certain weighing factors to calculate the weight of a node. The node with the smallest weight in its neighborhood is chosen as the clusterhead. The overhead induced by WCA is very high.

The DSBCA[2] is a more recent algorithm based on the idea of WCA. The algorithm considers the Battery Remaining, Number of Neighbors, Number of Members, and Stability in order to calculate a node's score with a linear function. After each node calculates its score independently, the neighbors of the node are notified about it. Each node selects one of its neighbors with the highest score to be its clusterhead. The algorithm was compared with WCA and DWCA in terms of number of clusters, number of re-affiliations and the lifespan of nodes in the system. Although simulation results showed that DSBCA achieved better performance than WCA and DWCA it has some inherent deficiencies. The following subsections describe the identified deficiencies of DSBCA.

2.1 Neighboring Time as the Metric of Node Stability

DSBCA defines the stability of a node to be the total time in which the neighbors of a specific node have spent their time beside the node. It is calculated as follows-

$$S_{(DSBCA)} = \sum_{i=1}^{n}(T_{RL} - T_{RF}) \tag{1}$$

Where n is the number of node's neighbor, T_{RL} is the time of the last packet reception from a neighbor and T_{RF} is the time of the first packet reception from the same neighbor. A higher stability simply means that the neighbors of a certain node has spent a longer time in its transmission range. But it can also be seen that a node with many new neighbors (high degree) might have the same stability value as a node with very few old neighbors. This is because the calculation of S takes into account the neighboring time of both stable and unstable neighbors of a node. Thus it becomes a poor representation of stability of a node in some situations.

2.2 Adjacent Cluster Heads

Two clusterheads might be in direct communication with each other in DSBCA. This is because in DSBCA, instead of clusterheads announcing their leadership, nodes send membership messages to their elected clusterheads. As a result clusterheads might become adjacent nodes. This will create inter-cluster interference, which is not desirable.

2.3 Problem with Weight Based Clustering Technique

In DSBCA two neighboring nodes may have the same weight. But it does not mention how to break such tie. As a result a node might elect more than one clusterhead. This increases the number of clusters in the network.

The proposed algorithm in this paper tries to eliminate the above drawbacks of DSBCA. Unlike DSBCA's general concept of weight, our algorithm takes the actual values of the system parameters such as stability, remaining energy and degree into account and quantitatively measures each node's suitability to become a clusterhead.

3   Associativity Based Energy Aware Clustering Algorithm

In this section we formally describe our new clustering algorithm, named Associativity Based Energy Aware Clustering Algorithm. The algorithm works in a distributed manner. As mentioned in the previous section it takes three attribute values of a node-stability, remaining energy and degree. The nodes in the network exchange these attribute values with their neighbors by means of periodic advertisements. Every node makes its own decision to become a clusterhead after having collected the attribute values from each of its neighbors and comparing them against it's own. The following subsections give a detailed description of how these three attribute values are measured.

3.1   Stability

In our algorithm the stability of mobile nodes is defined in terms of their neighborhood associativity. In the networking context, associativity means periods of spatial, temporal, connection and signal stability[7]. The associativity between nodes is measured in associativity ticks that are calculated from broadcasted packets. All nodes in the network periodically send out Advertisement packets to signify their existence. A node counts the number of Advertisement packets received from a neighbor by a counter variable called Associativity Tick(AT). Whenever it receives an Advertisement packet from the neighboring node, it increments the AT value corresponding to that neighbor. On the other hand, if it does not receive any Advertisement packets within a timeout period, it decrements the neighbor's corresponding AT value. When a neighbor's AT value reaches a desired threshold S_{th}, it is marked as *stable*.

As an example, assume there are two mobile nodes A and B each having a transmission and reception range of 10m in diameter[8]. Initially they are not in radio connectivity with each other but each sends an Advertisement packet every two seconds. If B is migrating at 1m/s speed and it starts to enter A's radio range and move through it, then both A and B record at most 5 Advertisements each. Hence this is the associativity threshold. If only 5 or less Advertisements are recorded, then one can assume that the other mobile host is migrating past it, and this situation is viewed as ***associatively unstable***. Otherwise, if the mobile host is moving but is constantly within the radio coverage of its neighbor, then more than 5 Advertisements will be recorded and hence the node will be noted as ***associatively stable***.

The associativity measure of a node is used as the primary basis for electing clusterheads in the proposed algorithm. It will serve as an indication of a node's stability. The associativity of any node 'x' in the network is defined to be the sum of associativity ticks of its *stable neighbors* only whose $AT \geq S_{th}$. Neighbors whose AT values are below the threshold S_{th} are not considered. Thus the sum of associativity ticks of a node 'x' is defined as

$$\sum AT(x) = \sum_{v=1}^{S(x)} AT(v) \tag{2}$$

Where $S(x) = \{v \subset N(x) \mid AT(v) \geq S_{th}\}$, where $N(x)$ is the neighborhood of x. A node that has the highest $\sum AT$ among its neighbors signifies its highest stability and hence the highest priority in becoming the clusterhead. By selecting nodes with high associativity values, a cluster is expected to be long-lived.

3.2   Remaining Energy

The remaining energy of a node plays a subsidiary role in determining its stability. A node with greater remaining energy than its neighbors can serve for a longer period of time and hence can be considered to have greater stability in the energy sense. NS-2's[9]simple energy model is used to calculate the remaining energy of a node. This model states that, every time a packet is received(transmitted), the total energy is decreased by the value:

$$DecEnergy = P_{rcv}(P_{tx}) \text{ x rcvTime(txTime)}$$

Where $P_{rcv}(P_{tx})$ is the power consumed during receiving(transmitting) a packet and rcvTime(txTime) is the time to receive(transmit) the packet. The remaining energy of a node will be

$$Remaining \ Energy = Energy - DecEnergy$$

3.3   Degree

Degree of a node is defined to be the existing neighbors of the node that are within its transmission range. If two nodes have the same associativity and energy levels but varying degrees then the node with the higher degree is chosen to be the clusterhead. Higher degree nodes are preferred to reduce the number of clusters throughout the network.

Two nodes may have the same values in all three attributes. In such an unlikely case, the node with the lowest identifier is used to break the tie.

3.4   Algorithm Description

The proposed clustering algorithm executes in three different phases. They are

1. Neighborhood Discovery by Advertisement of Attributes
2. Clusterhead election
3. Cluster Formation and Finalization of Roles

The following subsections present these three phases in detail.

3.4.1 Neighborhood Discovery by Advertisement of Attributes

Every node periodically broadcasts Advertisement packets to its neighborhood. A node includes its up-to-date stability value ($\sum$AT), its remaining energy (E) and its degree (D) in the Advertisements. Every node maintains a neighborhood table to keep a record of the received Advertisements. For each neighbor, the table keeps the neighbor ID, its AT, its $\sum$AT, its D, its E, and the time of receiving the latest Advertisement from it. When an Advertisement is received, the corresponding entry in the table is updated and its AT value is incremented by 1. If a node does not receive an Advertisement from an existing neighbor within a time out period, it decrements the AT value of that neighbor. When the AT of a neighbor becomes zero, its entry is deleted from the neighborhood table.

3.4.2 Clusterhead Election

Initially, all the nodes in the network are free or in the UNDECIDED state. The nodes use their neighborhood tables to determine their respective roles. It takes at most three steps to select a clusterhead from a neighborhood table. These step are described below. It is important to note that all the operations of clusterhead election take into account only the stable neighbors of a node(those whose AT$\geq$S$_{th}$)

Step 1: A node first sorts its neighborhood table from the highest $\sum$AT to the lowest $\sum$AT, including itself. Since cluster stability is the main concern, a node will select the neighbors having the highest $\sum$ATs.

Step 2: The list of nodes from Step 1 is next sorted from the highest energy (E) to the lowest energy (E). Nodes having the highest energy (E) are selected for the next step.

Step 3: The node with the highest degree from step 2 becomes the clusterhead. In case of a tie, the node with the lowest ID becomes the clusterhead.

If a node selects itself as the clusterhead, it switches to the HEAD state and broadcasts a ClusterHead Beacon message; otherwise it remains in the UNDECIDED (free) state.

As an example, consider the neighborhood table of an arbitrary node n (Tab. 1) which is about to select its clusterhead. The associativity threshold (S_{th}) of the network is set to 6. The node has three neighbors 1,8 and 19, all of which are stable. It calculates its own $\sum$AT as follows,

$$\sum AT(n) = AT(1) + AT(8) + AT(19) = 6 + 6 + 6 = 18$$

Table 1. Neighborhood Table of Node n

ID	AT	$\sum$AT	D	E	Last time heard from this node
1	6	6	1	90.0	T_1
19	6	18	3	95.75	T_{19}
8	6	18	3	100.0	T_8

Step 1: The node first sorts the records in its Neighborhood table by $\sum$AT, including itself. The result of the sorting is shown in Tab. 2

Table 2. Neighborhood Table of Node n (sorted by $\sum$AT)

ID	AT	$\sum$AT	D	E	Last time heard from this node
19	6	18	3	95.75	T_{19}
8	6	18	3	100.0	T_8
n	–	18	3	100.0	–
1	6	6	1	90.0	T_1

Step 2: Since all three records have the same $\sum$AT, they are next sorted by the field E(remaining energy). Nodes n and 8 have the same highest remaining energy. So selection will continue to step 3 which is based on node degree.

Step 3: Both nodes n and 8 have the same degree. So to break the tie, the lowest ID node will be selected to be the clusterhead.

During the clusterhead selection phase, no new nodes are allowed to join the cluster, even if they reach the required stability level. In that case the node is not marked as stable. This is to help the selection mechanism to be simple and fast.

3.4.3   Cluster Formation and Finalization of Roles

A node that wins the election, switches to the HEAD state and broadcasts a Clusterhead Beacon (CHB) packet to notify its leadership. A node in UNDE-CIDED state receiving a CHB packet from a neighboring clusterhead will become the member of the corresponding cluster. It will switch from the UNDECIDED state to the MEMBER state and send a Member Beacon (MB) message to the respective head. A node receiving multiple CHB packets from different neighboring heads will assume the role of a gateway and switch to the GATEWAY state. A clusterhead receiving a CHB packet will simply discard it. A cluster member(gateway) maintains a **Clusterhead Table** which keeps the ID(s) of its head(s). Likewise, a head node maintains a **Member Table** containing the IDs of all its members and gateways. Re-clustering only takes place when a head node loses contact with all its members or when a member(gateway) node loses contact with its head(s).

4   Simulation

To simulate the new clustering algorithm and compare its performance against DSBCA, Network Simulator version 2.31[9] was used. The simulations were carried out on an 800m X 800m area with N nodes as in DSBCA. The value of N was varied between 10 and 60. Radio range for each node was set to 250 meters. The nodes in the simulations moved according to the random way point

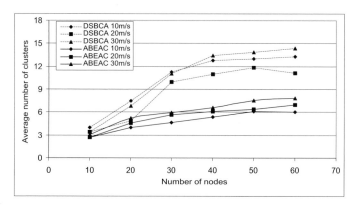

Fig. 1. Comparison of average number of clusters for varying speed and node density

model[11]. The nodes moved randomly in all directions with maximum speed of 10m/s, 20m/s,30m/s. AODV [12] was used as the underlying routing protocol.

4.1   Performance Metrics

Three metrics were chosen to compare the performance of our clustering algorithm with DSBCA: (i)the average number of clusters, (ii)the average number of reaffiliations and (iii)the average lifetime of clusters. Our algorithm showed better performance than DSBCA on all three metrics.

4.1.1   Average Number of Clusters

Figure 1 shows the comparison of the average number of clusters formed in DSBCA and our algorithm. It can be seen that the average number of clusters increase with node mobility in both algorithms. This is because as the mobility of nodes increase, their stability decreases. As a result more clusters are formed. But the important thing to note is that our algorithm forms less clusters in comparison to DSBCA regardless of this node speed, which is desirable.

4.1.2   Average Number of Reaffiliations

Figure 2 depicts the comparison of the average number of reaffiliations in the proposed algorithm with DSBCA for different speed values. According to the result, our algorithm gives less reaffiliations than DSBCA. If a node detaches itself from its current clusterhead and attaches to another clusterhead, then the involved clusterheads update their member list instead of invoking the election algorithm. Re-clustering takes place only when a head loses contact with all its members or when a member(gateway) loses contact with its head(s). A non-clusterhead never challenges the status of an existing clusterhead. Thus the clusterheads change as infrequently as possible resulting in longer duration of stability of the topology.

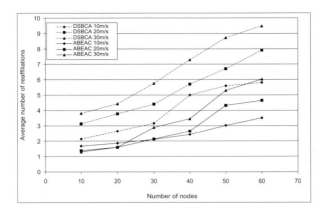

Fig. 2. Comparison of average number of re-affiliations for varying speed and node density

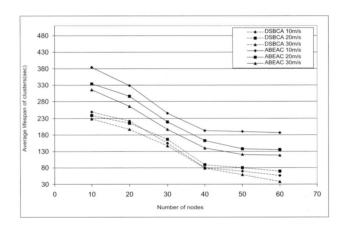

Fig. 3. Comparison of average lifespan of clusters for varying speed and node density

4.1.3   Average Lifespan of Clusters

Figure 3 shows a comparison of the average lifespan of clusters in DSBCA and our algorithm. As the mobility and node density increases, nodes consume more battery power[2]. Consequently the minimum lifespan of nodes decreases in both algorithms. The proposed algorithm provides longer lifespan of clusters. Since the stability of clusters in the proposed algorithm is high and the re-clustering frequency is less, nodes send and receive comparatively less messages than DS-BCA. This leads to longer battery lifetime and thus longer lifespan of clusters.

5   Conclusion

In this paper we have proposed a new clustering algorithm and proved by simulations that our algorithm achieved its functional goals. The algorithm showed better performance in terms of smaller number of clusters, a longer lifespan of clusters and much less reaffiliations which is an indication of cluster stability. It is believed that the proposed clustering algorithm will be suited best for small to medium sized networks. In future, an associativity based hierarchical routing protocol can be implementing on top of this clustering technique. The routing protocol's main objective would obviously be to find stable enough links between the source and the destination.

References

1. Lin, C.R., Gerla, M.: Adaptive clustering for mobile wireless networks. IEEE J. on Selected Areas in Communications 15(7), 1265–1275 (1997)
2. Adabi, S., Jabbehdari, S., Rezaee, A., Adabi, S.: A Novel Distributed Clustering Algorithm for Mobile Ad Hoc Networks. J. Computer Science 4, 161–166 (2008)
3. Yu, J.Y., Chong, P.H.J.: A survey of clustering schemes for mobile ad hoc networks. IEEE Communications Surveys and Tutorials 7, 32–48 (2005)
4. Gerla, M., Tzu-Chieh Tsai, J.: Multicluster, mobile, multimedia radio network. Wireless networks 1(3), 255–265 (1995)
5. Parekh, A.K.: Selecting routers in ad-hoc wireless networks. In: Proceedings SBT/IEEE Intl. Telecommunications Symposium, pp. 420–424 (1994)
6. Wu, Y., Wang, W.: MEACA: Mobility and Energy Aware Clustering Algorithm for Constructing Stable MANETs. In: Military Communications Conference, MILCOM 2006, pp. 1–7 (2006)
7. Toh, C.-K.: Associativity-Based Routing For Ad-Hoc Mobile Networks. Kluwer Wireless Personal Communications 4(2), 103–139 (1997)
8. Tenhunen, J., Typpo, V., Jurvansuu, M.: Stability-based multi-hop clustering protocol. In: 16th Annual IEEE International Symposium on Personal Indoor and Mobile Radio Communications, PIMRC 2005 (2005)
9. McCanne, S., Floyd, S.: NS network simulator (1995)
10. Chatterjee, M., Das, S.K., Turgut, D.: WCA: A weighted clustering algorithm for mobile ad hoc networks. Cluster Computing 5(2), 193–204 (2002)
11. Johnson, D.B.: Routing in Ad Hoc Networks of Mobile Hosts. In: Workshop on Mobile Computing and Applications (1997)
12. Perkins, C.E., Royer, E.M.: Ad-Hoc on-Demand Distance Vector Routing. In: Proc. of IEEE WMCSA 1999, New Orleans, LA (February 1999)
13. Choi, W., Woo, M.: A Distributed Weighted Clustering Algorithm for Mobile Ad-hoc Networks. In: AICT/ICIW (2006)

Frequency Domain Equalisation for OFDMA System in Multipath Fading Channels

R.J. Susan[1] and Sakuntala S. Pillai[2]

[1] Department of Electronics and Communication,
College of Engineering,
Thiruvananthapuram - 695016, Kerala, India
[2] Department of Electronics and Communication,
Mar Baselios College of Engineering and Technology,
Thiruvananthapuram - 695015, Kerala, India

Abstract. High speed wireless data transmission requires systems to operate with high spectral efficiency in wideband channels The physical layer should facilitate multiuser/multirate transmissions to support a number of users and applications with diverse needs. Orthogonal Frequency Division Multiple Access (OFDMA) is a multiple access technique that can accommodate many users with widely varying applications, data rates and Quality of Service requirements with increased spectral efficiency. OFDMA is attractive due to the fact that it exploits the computational efficiency associated with frequency domain equalization (FDE). This paper presents analysis of transmission of multiple data rates by using Orthogonal Variable Spreading Factor (OVSF) codes in an OFDMA system with frequency domain equalization. The performance of the system is analyzed using bit error rate (BER), for Vehicular A and Pedestrian B channel models.

Keywords: OFDMA, Frequency domain equalization, Multiple data rate.

1 Introduction

OFDMA is an attractive choice to meet requirements for high data rates, with correspondingly large transmission bandwidths, and flexible spectrum allocation [1]. Higher capacity can be achieved by simultaneously allocating the available bandwidth to multiple users. One possible technique offering high spectrum efficiency is the multicarrier modulation technique, Orthogonal Frequency Division Multiplexing (OFDM). This paper examines the application of Minimum Mean Square Error (MMSE) frequency domain equalization to OFDMA system in Multipath fading channels. OVSF codes are used to achieve multiple data rate.

Multiple access strategies attempt to provide orthogonal i.e., non-interfering communication channels for each active link. Frequency division multiple access (FDMA) can be readily implemented in OFDM system by assigning to different users their own sets of subcarriers. Simplest of allocation scheme is static allocation of subcarriers to each user. There could also be uneven allocations, with high data rate users

N. Meghanathan et al. (Eds.): NeCoM, WiMoN, and WeST 2010, CCIS 90, pp. 369–377, 2010.

being allocated more subcarriers than low rate users. Different bandwidths are realized by varying the number of subcarriers used for transmission, while the subcarrier spacing remains unchanged.

Frequency domain equalization has been used for reducing interference due to frequency selective fading. MMSE criterion aims at reducing mean square error between transmitted symbol and received symbol. The equalization coefficients based on MMSE criterion is applied independently per carrier.

Transmission at different rates as per the requirement of each user can be achieved by combining different messages with different spreading factors, while maintaining orthogonality between them [1]. In digital communication systems, variable length Walsh codes are also called OVSF codes. A range for code-length can be chosen, depending on the maximum and minimum bit rates to be supported. In this system multiple rate transmission for different users is realized using OVSF code which gives variable spreading factor, without using uneven allocation of subcarriers to achieve multiple bit rates.

2   OFDMA System

In cellular mobile communication systems, the increasing number of users, demand for high and different user data rates and multipath fading channels, cause degradation in performance of the system. Multiple access schemes are used to allow many users to share a finite amount of spectrum. For high quality communication this must be done without severe degradation in performance of the system.

OFDMA is a superior access technology for broadband wireless data network compared to traditional access technologies. OFDM divides total bandwidth into spectrally overlapping, narrowband subchannels. In OFDMA system subcarriers are allocated using assignment map defined by subcarrier allocation scheme, before modulation [2]. Data of kth user can be received by knowledge of subcarrier mapping. Subcarrier allocation can be static or dynamic depending on current traffic, channel and user data rate. In OFDMA, base station allocates to each user a fraction of subcarriers, preferably in a range where they have channel with good quality transmission.

OFDM achieves orthogonal frequency multiplexing using Inverse Discrete Fourier Transform (IDFT) implemented using Inverse Fast Fourier Transform (IFFT). The subcarriers assigned have overlapping sidelobes but signal waveforms are designed to be orthogonal. OFDM symbol duration should be smaller than coherence time of the channel and subcarrier spacing should be smaller than coherence bandwidth of the channel. OFDM system help to convert a frequency selective channel to multiple flat fading subchannels, resulting in the use of simple equalization at the receivers.

OFDMA is more sensitive to frequency offset and phase noise as compared to other techniques. Frequency synchronization is critical to reduce intercarrier interference. The problem is even more significant at high mobile speed due to Doppler effect. One of the major drawbacks of multicarrier transmission is the high peak-to-average power ratio (PAPR) of the transmit signal.

3   System Model

In this communication system, data bits of users are transmitted with different data rates over the multipath fading channel. The block diagrams (Figures 1 and 2) show the transmitter and receiver models.

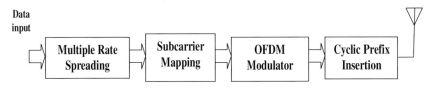

Fig. 1. Block diagram of transmitter

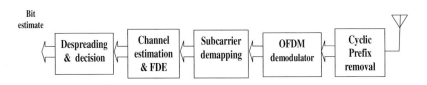

Fig. 2. Block diagram of receiver

Users are assigned spreading codes with different spreading factor depending on the bit rate. Corresponding code sequences are used at receiver to get bit estimates. Spread data after subcarrier mapping is given to OFDM modulator as blocks of length N symbols each. After taking IFFT at the transmitter a cyclic prefix (CP) of length M greater than channel impulse response (CIR) length L is added to the beginning of each OFDM symbol to avoid intersymbol interference.

The channel is modeled as discrete time multipath slow fading channel with Rayleigh distribution. Block type pilot based channel estimation is performed by inserting pilots to all subcarriers of OFDM symbols. At the receiver after IFFT, MMSE frequency domain equalization is used to recover the transmitted signal. This is followed by despreading and detection.

3.1   Multiple Rate Spreading

OVSF code sequence can be used to assign various spreading factors to active users, according to users requirement on bit rate without losing the orthogonality among code sequence. OVSF codes support simultaneous multiple data rate transmission by using variable spreading factor (SF) while keeping the transmission bit rate same for all carriers. For realization, codes with maximum spreading factor are allotted to low rate users. For a user with double the bit rate, codes with spreading factor half the maximum value is chosen for spreading of data symbols [2]. Higher data rates require shorter length Walsh codes than lower data rate (R_b, figure 3). This operation requires short and long Walsh codes to be orthogonal (1), which is achieved using OVSF codes [3].

$$\int_{-\infty}^{\infty} c_k(t) c_l^*(t)\, dt = 0 \tag{1}$$

Orthogonal Walsh Hadamard codes are simple to generate recursively by using Hadamard matrix generation. The maximum number of available orthogonal spreading codes determines maximum number of users. The generated code (Fig. 3) of same layer constitutes a set of Walsh codes and they are orthogonal. Any two codes of different layers are also orthogonal except for the case that one of the two codes is a mother code of the other. When a user is assigned a code, another low rate user should not be assigned any of the two codes into which it branches [4][5], to ensure that orthogonality condition is satisfied.

For spreading factor m assigned to a user, the spread data signal of the user can be written as in (2):

$$d_k(t) = \sum_i b_k(i) c_k(t - imT_c) \tag{2}$$

where $b_k(i)$ and $c_k(t)$ represents i^{th} data symbol and the spreading waveform of kth user, T_c the chip duration.

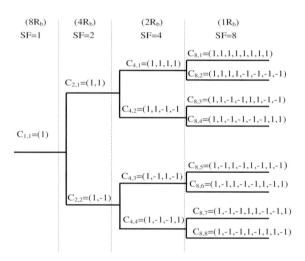

Fig. 3. Code tree for generation of OVSF code

3.2 Transmitted Signal

Data set X(k), k = 0,….,N-1 denote information bearing symbols of a block to be transmitted on N subcarriers, X(k) is the data symbol to be transmitted on the kth subcarrier. OFDM modulation is achieved by taking IFFT of the data block (3).

$$x(n) = IDFT(X(k)) = \frac{1}{\sqrt{N}} \sum_{k=0}^{N-1} X(k) e^{\frac{j2\pi kn}{N}} \qquad 0 \leq n \leq N-1 \qquad (3)$$

To avoid intersymbol interference (ISI) a cyclic prefix (CP) of length M greater than channel impulse response (CIR) length L is added to the beginning of each OFDM signal block [6](4).

$$\begin{aligned} s(k) &= x(k+N) & -M \leq k < 0 \\ &= x(k) & 0 \leq k \leq N-1 \end{aligned} \qquad (4)$$

The N subcarriers are chosen to be orthogonal, subcarrier frequency $f_k = k \, \Delta f$, where Δf is taken as $(1/NT)$ and T is the original symbol period.

3.3 Multipath Channel Model

In mobile radio channels, the Rayleigh distribution is commonly used to describe the statistical time varying nature of the received envelope of a fading signal. Local propagation effects may differ at different positions. This is modeled as a case in which transmitted signal reaches a stationary receiver via multiple paths. The channel is modeled as AWGN and slow fading channel with Rayleigh distribution, with the assumption that direct wave is obstructed and the receiver receives only the reflected waves.

Discrete time multipath channel response vector is described by L tap complex random vector $\mathbf{h}$ represented as $\mathbf{h} = [h(0) \; h(1) \; \dots \; \dots \; h(L-1)]^T$, where h[i]'s represents independent zero mean complex Gaussian random variables. Due to insertion of CP at the transmitter and removal of CP at the receiver, the dispersive channel is represented as NxN circulant matrix $\tilde{\mathbf{H}}$ with $\left[\tilde{\mathbf{H}}\right]_{i,j} = h((i-j) \bmod N)$. When channel is time invariant within the block, $\tilde{\mathbf{H}}$ becomes a cyclic matrix.

3.4 Received Signal

At the receiver N dimensional signal vector after removal of cyclic prefix is given by (5) where $\mathbf{n}$ represents zero mean additive white Gaussian noise.

$$\mathbf{y} = \tilde{\mathbf{H}} \, \mathbf{x} + \mathbf{n} \qquad (5)$$

Transforming to frequency domain as given in (6), using DFT matrix $\mathbf{F}$ gives

$$\mathbf{Fy} = \mathbf{F\tilde{H}x} + \mathbf{Fn} = \mathbf{F\tilde{H}F^H Fx} + \mathbf{Fn} \qquad (6)$$

where $\mathbf{F^H F} = \mathbf{I}_N$ as $\mathbf{F}$ is a unitary matrix.
$(.)^H$ denotes Hermitian transpose operation.

Thus $\tilde{\mathbf{H}}$ can be diagonalised by $\mathbf{F}$ as $\mathbf{F\tilde{H}F^H} = \mathbf{H}$ where $\mathbf{H}$ represents the channel frequency response matrix defined as $\mathbf{H} = diag(H(0), \dots \dots H(N-1))$, equation (7).

$$H(k) = \sum_{n=0}^{L-1} h(n)e^{-j\frac{2\pi k n}{L}} \qquad 0 \le k \le N-1 \tag{7}$$

The kth subcarrier output is given by equation (8)

$$Y(k) = H(k)\,X(k) + W(k) \qquad 0 \le k \le N-1 \tag{8}$$

Y[k], X[k] and W[k] represents received signal, transmitted signal and noise represented in frequency domain. As taking IFFT at the transmitter and FFT at the receiver diagonalises the circulant matrix $\tilde{\mathbf{H}}$, we obtain ISI free model of OFDM symbol [7]. Received signal of kth subcarrier equals transmitted one scaled by channel frequency response at frequency k. MMSE frequency domain equalization can be performed independently for each frequency. It is assumed that guard interval is longer than maximum channel delay and synchronization is perfect.

3.5 Channel Estimation and Equalisation

A dynamic estimation of the channel is required as radio channel is frequency selective and time varying. When the channel can be estimated and this estimate sent back to the transmitter, the transmission scheme can be adapted relative to the channel characteristics. The intersymbol interference due to multipath fading can span up to 100 or more data symbols when the data rates are of the order of tens of megabibits per second. In such cases the conventional RAKE receiver seems to be ineffective and the complexity of time domain equalization methods become exhorbitant. In such cases the FDE proves to be a computationally simpler and effective solution. Block type pilot channel estimation, has been developed under the assumption of slow fading channel.

A block type channel estimation has been used, in which the pilot tones are inserted into all of the subcarriers of OFDM symbols and channel estimation is based on these known pilot symbols [8]. In block-type pilot-based channels, the estimators are usually calculated once per block and are used until the next pilot symbol arrives.

The estimates of channel frequency response of the subchannels is obtained as in (9).

$$\hat{H}(k) = \frac{Y(k)}{X(k)}$$

$$= H(k) + \frac{W(k)}{X(k)} \qquad 0 \le k \le N-1 \tag{9}$$

MMSE equalization minimizes the mean square value of error between transmitted signal and the estimated output for each subcarrier [9]. MMSE equalization weights E(k) for subcarrier k is given by equation (10)

$$E(k) = \frac{H^*(k)}{|H(k)|^2 + (SNR)^{-1}} \qquad\qquad 0 \le k \le N-1 \qquad (10)$$

where SNR is the signal to noise ratio. By applying MMSE FDE the estimate of transmitted signal X(k) is obtained as in (11).

$$\hat{X}(k) = E(k)Y(k) \qquad\qquad 0 \le k \le N-1 \qquad (11)$$

This is followed by despreading and detection to get the bit estimates.

4 Simulation

In this work the performance of multiple rate transmission for OFDMA system using MMSE FDE is analyzed. Simulation was done for 16 users, simultaneously transmitting data with different bit rates, each user is assigned a Walsh code with different spreading factors, namely, 16, 8 and 4 to achieve transmission rates of 1, 2 and 4, respectively. Perfect subcarrier synchronization with no frequency offset is assumed for simulation. Performance of the system was analyzed using bit error rate by varying signal to noise ratio (SNR) in dB. The channel estimated at the beginning of the block is used for all the following symbols of the block.

Channel models used for simulation are Vehicular A and Pedestrian B models. Figure 4 shows performance with and without equalization for Vehicular A and Pedestrian B channel models respectively. Figure 5 gives performance comparison of equalization for different number of subcarriers 16, 64 and 256 for the two models. Figure 6 gives the mean square error (MSE) for the two channels for different Doppler shifts in comparison to AWGN channel.

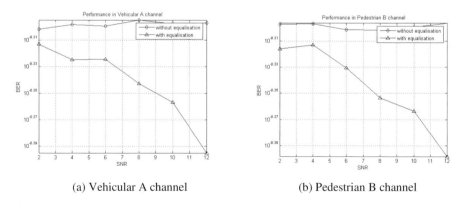

(a) Vehicular A channel   (b) Pedestrian B channel

Fig. 4. Performance with and without equalization

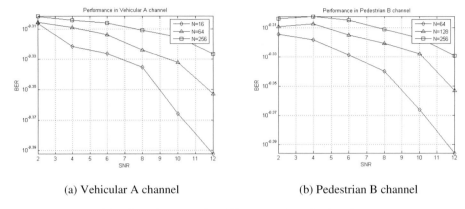

(a) Vehicular A channel   (b) Pedestrian B channel

Fig. 5. Performance for different number of subcarriers

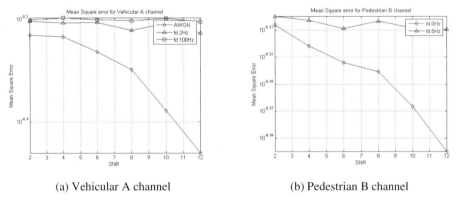

(a) Vehicular A channel   (b) Pedestrian B channel

Fig. 6. Mean Square error in comparison with AWGN channel

5   Conclusion

In this paper performance of multiple data rate OFDMA system using frequency domain equalization is presented. Simulations are done for Vehicular A channel and Pedestrian B channel models. The BER for multipath transmission will depend on the number of paths, attenuation and delay for each path. It was found that system performance improves with frequency domain equalization. BER increases with increase in Doppler shift. Increase in error was also observed with increase in number of subcarriers. Mean square error is lesser for AWGN channel as compared to other channel models.

References

1. Husain, I., Husain, S., Khokhar, I., Iqbal, R.: OFDMA as a technology for the next generation mobile and the Internet. In: Proc. of the third international conference on Wireless and mobile communication, p. 14 (2007)

2. Ha, J.B., Park, J.: A code grouping interference cancellation receiver in OVSF DS CDMA downlink, pp. 694–797. ICCS (2002)
3. Maeda, N., Kishiyama, Y., Atarashi, H., Sawahashi, M.: Variable spreading factor OFCDM with two dimensional spreading that prioritizes time domain spreading for forward link broadband wireless access, pp. 127–132. IEEE, Los Alamitos (2003)
4. Adrian, C., de Leon, G.D., Garcia, J.s., Bean, M.C., Alberto, L.: MC CDMA/VSF for the downlink physical layer in next generation wireless local area networks, pp. 221–226. IEEE, Los Alamitos (2006)
5. Takyu, O., Ohtsuki, T., Nakagawa, M.: Orthogonal Variable Spreading Factor Code Selection for Peak Power Reduction in Multi Rate OFCDM Systems, pp. 117–121. IEEE, Los Alamitos (2003)
6. Wang, Z., Giannakis, G.B.: Wireless Multicarrier Communication. IEEE Signal Processing Magazine 17(3), 29–48 (2000)
7. Louveaux, J., Vadendorpe, L., Sartenaer, T.: Cyclic Prefixed Single and Multicarrier Transmission : Bit Rate Comparison. IEEE Communications Letters 7(4), 180–182 (2003)
8. Takeda, K., Adachi, F.: Pilot Assisted Channel Estimation based on MMSE Criterion for DS CDMA with Frequency Domain Equalisation. VTC 1, 447–451 (2005)
9. Falconer, D.: Frequency Domain Equalisation for Single Carrier Broadband Wireless Systems. IEEE Communications Magazine, 58–66 (2002)

Energy Aware Data Sharing in Mobile Ad Hoc Networks

M. Pushpalatha[1], Revathi Venkataraman[1], and T. Ramarao[2]

[1] Department of Computer Science and Engineering, S.R.M University, Chennai, India
[2] Department of Telecommunication and Engineering, S.R.M University, Chennai, India
lathamarudappa@yahoo.co.in, revathivenkat@yahoo.com
ramarao@ieee.org

Abstract. In mobile ad hoc networks (MANET) ,computation devices are battery powered. Limited energy in battery constrains the computation and communication of each device. Hence services like sharing a data or information among users becomes a challenging issue in critical environments like military applications, rescue operations etc. To overcome this, we have proposed a replication model which replicates shared data in suitable nodes. It addresses how data sharing can be done effectively by periodically checking the remaining energy of each node that holds the replica. If the remaining energy falls below a threshold level, replica can be relocated to appropriate nodes that has the maximum energy. Therefore our proposal ensures file availability, improves the network life time, decreases query response time, increases energy utilization, decreases number of packet drops due to battery depletion of a node.

Keywords: Mobile Ad hoc networks, Pro_active Replication, Re_active Replication, Lifetime, Residual Energy, Access Frequency.

1 Introduction

Mobile Ad hoc Networks allow any where , any time network connectivity with complete lack of control , ownership and regulatory influence. The limited energy capacity of the mobile devices made power awareness as an important factor in sharing a data and in designing a energy aware routing protocols[1][2]. In order to maximize the life time of a mobile node, it is important to reduce the energy consumption of a node in ad hoc networks[3]. The mobile nodes that are located at the centre of the network may act as a router or a shared data holder for other nodes. Since these nodes need to transmit a data or forward the messages many times, they consume more power than the other host as shown in Fig. 1. Hence frequently accessed mobile host exhaust their batteries and leave the network, and thus, data accessibility becomes lower.

To facilitate data sharing, the feasible solution is to replicate data in several nodes. Thus we have proposed a replication allocation algorithm which periodically checks the energy consumption of a node that holds the replica, calculates the lifetime of a node. If the lifetime of a particular node goes below a threshold then `replicas in that node are redistributed to appropriate nodes that has more energy. Many issues related to data replication in MANET makes replication process very complex. These issues are addressed in next subdivision. As a initial step, we have addressed the power consumption and response time as the major issues in our replication model.

N. Meghanathan et al. (Eds.): NeCoM, WiMoN, and WeST 2010, CCIS 90, pp. 378–387, 2010.

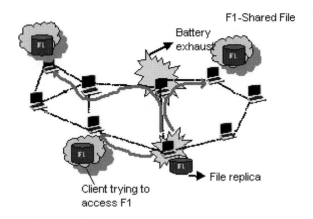

Fig. 1. Decrease of remaining amount of battery by frequent file or data access

1.1 Issues Related to Data Replication in MANET

The following are the issues related to file replication in MANET [9]:

Power Consumption
All mobile devices in the MANET are battery powered. If a node with less power is replicated with many frequently accessed data items, it soon gets drained and it cannot provide services any more. Thus replication algorithm should replicate data in the nodes that has sufficient power by periodically checking the remaining power of each node.

Node Mobility
Nodes in the MANET are mobile which leads to dynamic topology. The replication algorithm has to support mobility prediction such that if a node is likely to move away from the network, its replicas will be replaced in some other nodes which is expected to remain in the network for a particular period of time.

Resource Availability
Since nodes that participates in MANET are portable devices, memory capacity is limited. Before sending a replica to the node, the algorithm has to check whether a node has sufficient memory capacity to hold the replica.

Network Partition
If a node is in one partition it cannot provide services to other nodes in different partition. Therefore shared data will be replicated in all the partitions of the network.

Replica Relocation
This topic addresses issues related to when, where, who and how replicas are allocated. Due to dynamic topology, static allocation of replicas is not possible. Thus replicas will be relocated dynamically to improve data availability [5].

Consistency Management

If the data shared is read only , performance can be improved by fully replicating the data in all the nodes. But if a replica is frequently updated, other replicas becomes invalid. Hence a mechanism is required to manage the consistency of data in the network.

The paper presented here is organized as follows, Section 2 briefs about the related work done on energy aware replication in MANET. Section 3 gives a detail description of our proposed model. Section 4 depicts our simulation results and analyzes the performance issues in our model. Section 5 concludes our work by pointing to future work.

2 Related Work

Considerable amount of work has been done related to data replication by considering various issues related to replication. In paper[4], the authors have proposed a replica allocation scheme based on the locality of data and it is adjusted regularly in order to reduce the power consumption of a node and thus extending the survival time of the network. Replica allocation method proposed in [5] balances power consumption among the mobile hosts and improves the data availability. Data replication technique proposed in [6] improves the data accessibility by considering the limitation in energy. It replicates only the hot data items(items that are accessed frequently) at the servers that have maximum energy. In Paper[7], a method is identified for data replication which composes of two main phases. The first phase aims at creating replicas from new data in the network and second phase deals with redistribution of replicas in order to overcome the impact of dynamic changes of the topology. The algorithm discussed in paper [8] determines when and where to place the replica in order to meet the availability goals. The model proposed in it is effective in predicting the number of replicas required. The issues of data replication is discussed in[9] and an attempt is made to classify the existing data replication techniques in MANET. A new metric called Lifetime of a node is addressed in[10][11] which serves as a best routing metric to transmit packets from source to destination. This parameter is integrated in our method to replicate data.

3 Proposed Model

Assumptions made in our proposed model are the link between the nodes are bidirectional, data shared are read only, nodes in the network always remain connected even in the failure of few nodes i.e no partition occurs. It basically consists of three kinds of nodes which are as follows:

Primary Servers(P)

They are the original owners of the data or a file. They decides when and where to create replica and how many number of replicas are to be created. These servers can be the secondary servers for other data and also act as a client to access other files.

Secondary Servers(S)
They are the nodes that contain replicas and thus maintaining data availability. They may act as a client if they request for a shared data from other nodes. They can also act as a primary servers, if primary server gets disconnected from the network.

Client (C)
Nodes that request data or access data are clients. They may act as a forwarder or router when one node communicaates with another node.

Each node is represented by a unique identifier denoted as N_i and can be designated as P_j or S_j based on shared data O_j where P and S are primary servers and secondary servers whereas i and j are the identifier of the node and the data object. Initially each node has full battery capacity. Our proposed model is classified into two schemes as **Pro_Active replication algorithm** and **Re_Active replication algorithm.** The former algorithm is executed for initial distribution of the replicas when network is initialized. The later is executed to redistribute the replicas based on the energy consumption of primary servers and secondary servers.

3.1 Pro_Active Replication Algorithm

This is the initial replica distribution algorithm which is initiated by the primary servers and followed by the secondary servers when they decide to replicate the data. This algorithm distributes and replicate the data in uniform fashion by evaluating the distance between the replicas by counting the number of hops say "K". The value of K is decided based on the size of the network N and care should be taken such that no two immediate neighbors hold the replica of same data.

The messages used by servers and other nodes participating in pro_active replication are as follows:

Get_nd_nl (Node$_{id}$, Designation , HopCount=n) – This message is used to get the node degree and neighbor list of a node when its hopcount reaches K. Node$_{id}$ is the identifier of node sending this message. Designation can be P or S..HopCount determines the number of hops which takes the values 0 to K.

Put_nd_nl (S$_{id}$ Nd, Nl, D$_{id}$) – This mesaage is a reply send by the node that reaches hopcount equals to K. It sends its own id as S$_{id}$,its node degree and its neighbor list and D$_{id}$ is the address of the node which initiates **Get_nd_nl().**

Distibute replica(S$_{id}$, Designation, O$_j$, D$_{id}$, Data) – This message replicates data in the node which has reached the hop count = K. Here the designation is the sender's designation which can be the primary server(P) or secondary server(S). O$_j$ is the identifier of data where j=1to n. Data is the object to be replicated.

Createreplica(S$_{id}$,D$_{id}$,O$_j$): This message is send from one server(Por S) to another server to replicate data object in other nodes that has satisfied the condition hopcount=K.

3.1.1 Pro_Active Replication Algorithm

Step 1: Initialize the size of the network N, and Hop Count =0;

Step 2: Determine K.

Step 3: If a node N_i is a server it decides to replicate its O_j by sending **Get_nd_nl (Node$_{id}$, Designation , hopcount=0)** to neighbors.

Step 4: If Neighbors are not available then Go to Step7;
   Else On reception of this message, neighbors do the following :
      If <hopcount<>k)then
         set hopcount= hopcount + 1;
         Forward **Get_nd_nl (Node$_{id}$, Designation , hopcount=n)** to its neighbors;
      Else if (hopcount==K) then send
         Put_nd_nl(S_{id} Nd, Nl, D$_{id}$) to the server;

Step 5: On receiving **Put_nd_nl(S_{id} Nd, Nl, D$_{id}$)** the server waits until all the nodes with hopcount =K puts their information in the information table of the server. Then the server checks whether the nodes in the table are adjacent to each other in the network.
   If (true)
   Find Max(N1(d),N2(d)....Nj(d) /*Find the node with maximum degree to ensure more coverage*/
   return D_{id}= N_j then send
   Distibute replica(S_{id}, Designation, O_j, D$_{id}$, Data)to N_j and to rest of the nodes that are not adjacent;
   Else
   Distibute replica(S_{id}, Designation, O_j, D$_{id}$, Data) to all nodes in the information table;

Step 6: Server after distributing the replicas it sends a **Createreplica(S_{id},D$_{id}$,O$_j$) message to** all the servers , it has just created. On reception ,the server continue from Step 3 until no neighbors are found./* To balance the load in the network*/

Step 7: Finally, the primary server keep record of all its secondary server in a Replica Keeper Table.

3.2 Re_active Replication Algorithm

This algorithm is invoked periodically to cope up with the changes in the topology i.e is the node failure due to energy depletion. Objective of the algorithm is to redistribute the replica to appropriate nodes if the life time of one of the servers becomes low. The main parameters used in this algorithm are L(i) ,$E_r(t)$, $E_c(t)$ and AF where L(i) is called as lifetime of a node N_i , $E_r(t)$ is the residue energy of a node at time t, $E_c(t)$ is the energy consumption of a node N_i at time t and AF is the access frequency of a data object O_j at node N_i. Access frequency is defined as how many times the particular data object O_j is accessed in node N_i. Each node has to compute its lifetime in every T seconds. The procedure for life time computation is as follows:

3.2.1 Lifetime Computation

For every T seconds, nodes predict its own lifetime. Each node monitors its energy consumption and estimates its lifetime based on current interval t and past interval t-1. It calculates how much average energy is consumed by node N_i per t seconds during the interval. This value represents how long the remaining energy can keep up the connections with these conditions. The formula [10][11]to calculate node N_i its life time is given in (Eq.1).

$$L(i) = C * (E_r(t) / E_c(t)) + (1-C) *(E_r(t-1) / E_c(t-1)) \qquad (1)$$

Where:

L (i): Lifetime of node N_i.

$E_r(t)$: Residual energy of node N_i at time t

$E_c(t)$: Energy Consumption of node N_i at time t

$E_r(t-1)$: Residual energy of node N_i at time t-1

$E_c(t-1)$: Energy Consumption of node N_i at time t-1

C: It is a contant which takes the value 0.7 to give more weight for current time interval.

The total amount of energy, $E_c(t$ consumed at a node N_i is determined as:

$$E_c(t) = E_{tx}(Ni) + E_{rx}(N_i) + (N-1)* E_o(N_i) \qquad (2)$$

where $E_{tx}(Ni)$, $E_{rx}(N_i)$, and E_o denote the amount of energy expenditure by transmission, reception, and overhearing of a packet, respectively. N represents the average number of neighboring nodes affected by a transmission from node N_i.

The energy consumed for transmitting a packet is measured in Joules and it is given as :

$$E_{tx}(N_i) = P_t * T \qquad (3)$$

Where

$$T= Data\ size\ /\ Data\ rate \qquad (4)$$

$$P_t = TX\_I * V \qquad (5)$$

Here TX_I is the transmit current and V is the voltage.

The energy consumed for receiving a packet measured in Joules is given as:

$$E_{rx}(N_i) = P_r * T \qquad (6)$$

Where

$$P_r = RX\_I * V \qquad (7)$$

Where RX_I is the receive current and V is the voltage. $E_o(N_i)$ remains the same as $E_{rx}(N_i)$.

The lifetime threshold ∂ determines whether a node is alive or not. It is set to 30% of the intial energy level. When a node is likely to fail in the network ,its life time reaches ∂. Using this prediction ,the node itself invokes Re_active Replication algorithm if it is a secondary server and also checks the Access Frequency(AF) of the data object O_j it holds. If the access frequency is zero, no replication take place. Otherwise it sends a message to its neighbors to calculate their life time. Collect the lifetime of all the neighbors and choose the neighbor which has the maximum life time as a replica holder. In addition before computing the life time , every server checks the AF of every data object O_j. If the AF has reached the threshold α say 20, the server finds which node has frequently accessed this object by maintaining a counter. It then distributes the replica of O_j to the corresponding node. Hence the two parameters Access Frequency (AF) and Lifetime L_i increases the network life time and improves data availability.

3.2.2 Re_active Replication Algorithm

Step 1: For every T seconds each node in the network checks it AF of every data object O_j.

> If $(AF == \alpha)$ then find the node id which has frequently accessed
> send **Distibute replica(S_{id}, Designation, O_j, D_{id} , Data)**;

Step 2: Each node in the network calculates its life time by using the above mentioned formulas(3.3.1).

Step 3: If node Ni lifetime equals to ∂ then
> If Ni is a secondary server of data object O_i checks its AF
> If $(AF==0)$ quit(); /* No replication take place*/
> Else
> Collect the lifetime Li of all the Neighbors by sending getLi(Sid,Did);
> Find the Max(L1, L2... Li) of the neighbors and select the node with maximum lifetime;
> Set that node as a secondary server for object O_j.

Step 4: If Ni is a primary server repeat the step 2 and Step 3 and set the selected node as a primary server for object O_j.

4 Simulation Set Up and Results

We simulated our proposal using Opnet 15.0 [13]. In our experiments 25 nodes are arranged in a rectangular area of 1500m X 300m. Each node uses IEEE 802.11 standard MAC layer. The radio range is of 250m. Each packet (data) size is 512 bytes and data rate is 11 Mbps. Initial energy of a battery of each node is 2000 Joules which is mapped to 100%. The power consumed for transmission of each packet is 280 mA and reception of each packet is 180 mA. Power supply V is of 5 volts Simulation had run for 3700 seconds.

The results shown in Fig. 2 and Fig. 3 implies that the query response time is minimum if file replication technique is implemented in MANET i.e when client send their query to access the data object, the servers that are in their proximity respond immediately by sending the data object. To implement replication, many messages flows across the network which may lead to communication overhead and may decreases the performance of the network. But the result shown in Fig. 4 implies that the throughput is not degraded much and therefore the performance of the network is not affected.

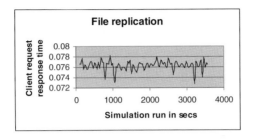

Fig. 2. Response time with file replication

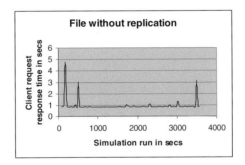

Fig. 3. Response time without file replication

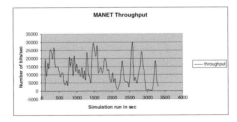

Fig. 4. MANET Throughput with replication technique

5   Conclusion and Future Work

Our proposed work deals with how data availability or accessibility can be increased by replicating the shared data using energy aware replication scheme. This scheme is well suitable for environments like military applications and rescue operations where sharing information is very important and battery is a critical resource. The algorithm we have proposed ensures data availability even if the owner of the data get disconnected from the network, decreases query response time, increases network life time, conserves the energy utilization of the nodes in the network. As a future work, our proposal will be extended to mobility aware, security aware and partition aware replication in MANET.

Acknowledgement

The authors wish to acknowledge the support of the SRM University, Chennai, India to carryout this research work.

References

1. Sivaram Murthy, C., Manoj, B.S.: Ad Hoc Wireless Networks, 2nd edn. Pearson Education, India (2001)
2. Safwat, A., Mouftah, H.: Energy aware routing in MANET. In: International Workshop on Modeling Analysis and Simulation of Wireless and Mobile Systems, Proceedings of the 5th ACM international workshop on Modeling analysis and simulation of wireless and mobile systems, pp. 46–53 (2002)
3. Tamilarasi, M., Palani Velu, T.G.: Integrated Energy-Aware Mechanism for MANETs using On-demand Routing. International Journal of Computer, Information, and Systems Science, and Engineering 2;3 © (Summer 2008), http://www.waset.org
4. Wang, Y., Yang, K.: Research of power aware dynamic adaptive replica algorithm in mobile ad hoc networks. In: Pan, Y., Chen, D.-x., Guo, M., Cao, J., Dongarra, J. (eds.) ISPA 2005. LNCS, vol. 3758, pp. 933–944. Springer, Heidelberg (2005)
5. Shinohara, M., Hara, T., Nisheo, S.: Data replication considering power consumption in Ad hoc networks. In: International Conference on mobile data management, IEEE Explore, May 2007, vol. 1, pp. 118–125 (2007)
6. Padmanabhan, Prassana: Managing data replication in MANET. In: International Conference on Collaboarative Computing, Networks, Applications and Work Sharing, ACM proceedings, vol. 17, pp. 1–10 (2006)
7. Moussvi, S., Badache, N.: Data Replication in Mobile ad hoc networks. In: Cao, J., Stojmenovic, I., Jia, X., Das, S.K. (eds.) MSN 2006. LNCS, vol. 4325, pp. 685–697. Springer, Heidelberg (2006)
8. Ranganathan, K., Iamnitchi, A., Foster, I.: Improving data availability through dymanic model driven replication in peer to peer communities. In: Proceedings of IEEE/ACM International symposium on cluster computing and the grid (2002)
9. Vallur: A survey of data replication technique for mobile ad hoc networks. International journal of very large databases, ACM digital library 17, 1143–1164 (2008)
10. Garcia, D.K., Cano: Power aware routing based on the energy drain rate for Mobile ad hoc Networks. In: IEEE Proceedings/International conference on Communication and Netwoks (2002)

11. Faezeh, C., Akbari, Majid, S.: Equalization of Energy Consumption in ad hoc Networks Using learning automata. International Journal of Computer Science and Network security 9(12) (2009)
12. Prasanna, A., Greenwald: Managing data replication in mobile ad hoc networks database. In: International Conference on Collaborative Computing, pp. 1–10 (2006) (1-4244-0429-0)
13. Laura: Energy Consumption Model for performance analysis of routing protocols in MANET. Journal of mobile networks and application (2000)
14. OPNET Technologies, http://www.opnet.com

Security Enhancement in WEP Mobility

S.M.K.M. Abbas Ahmad[1], E.G. Rajan[2], A. Govardhan[3], and Juluru Peraiah[4]

[1] Associate Professor, Dept. of E.C.E., Hi-Tech College of Engg & Tech, Hyderabad, India
Tel.: +919440434385
smkmabbas@rediffmail.com
[2] Managing Director, Pentagram Research Foundation, Hyderabad, India
Tel.: +91849164747
rajaneg@yahoo.co.in
[3] Principal, JNTUH Engineering College, Karimnagar, India
Tel.: +919440887733
govardhan_cse@yahoo.co.in
[4] Lecturer, Dept. of Natural & Computational Science, Debre Markos University, Ethiopia,
mail2juluru@rediffmail.com

Abstract. The Wired Equivalent Privacy (WEP) protocol protection technique suggested for ad hoc network falls short of the objective of data privacy, data integrity and authentication. Various security standards such as IEEE 802.11i, WAP, IEEE 802.1X were suggested to address the security issues in 802.11. Despite their efficiency, these standards do not provide any security approach for monitoring the authentication in a distributed architecture. In this paper we present a self monitored security approach for self-monitoring of key authentication for security protocol in ad hoc networks for the efficient monitoring of the authentication issue in ad hoc network. The processing overhead for the suggested approach is evaluated for a threshold based cryptographic approach.

Keywords: self monitoring, ad hoc network, WEP protocol, authentication, key certificate.

1 Introduction

Wireless technology has advanced tremendously over the past decade, introducing a wide range of devices with networking abilities. Wireless connectivity is certainly available for many devices, but it is limited to few hotspots, and requires subscription to specific services. Furthermore, the quality of connection is rarely adequate for any high-bandwidth applications, which are expected to drive the market for these devices. These are formed by a group of wireless enabled devices that connect together and form a network, without the assistance of a pre-existing infrastructure, like a base station [1]. The commonly used 802.11b MAC protocol includes support for an ad-hoc mode of operation. Such networks are often used in cases of rapid deployment, in places lacking adequate infrastructure, or to facilitate direct communication between nodes when the base station becomes the bottleneck. Ad hoc networking is an attractive concept and has various possibilities for different kinds of applications. In some

N. Meghanathan et al. (Eds.): NeCoM, WiMoN, and WeST 2010, CCIS 90, pp. 388–399, 2010.
© Springer-Verlag Berlin Heidelberg 2010

application environments, such as battlefield communications, disaster recovery etc., the wired network is not available and multi-hop wireless networks provide the only feasible means for communication and information access. This kind of network is called Mobile Ad hoc network (MANET). It is also expected to play an important role in civilian forums such as campus recreation, conferences and electronic classrooms etc. A MANET can be seen as an autonomous system or a multi-hop wireless extension to the Internet. As an autonomous system, it has its own routing protocols and network management mechanisms. As a multi-hop wireless extension, it should provide a flexible and seamless access to the Internet. Recently, because of the rising popularity of multimedia applications and potential commercial usage of MANETs, QoS support in MANETs has become an unavoidable task. By definition, a mobile ad hoc network does not rely on any fixed infrastructure; instead, all networking functions (e.g. routing, mobility management, etc) are performed by the nodes themselves in a self-organizing manner[4]. For this reason, securing mobile ad hoc networks is challenging and in some applications this requires modifications with respect to the traditional security solutions for wire line networks. Mobile ad hoc networks do not provide any online access to communicating nodes. As they exhibit frequent partitioning due to link and node failures and due to node mobility maintenance of a centralized security system is not possible. Hence traditional security solutions that require centralized authorities are not well suited for securing ad hoc networks. There are two extreme ways to introduce security in mobile ad hoc networks: 1) through a single authority domain, where certificates and/or keys are issued by a single authority, typically in the system setup phase or 2) through full self-organization, where security does not rely on any trusted authority or fixed server, not even in the system initialization phase[7]. In contrast with conventional networks, mobile ad hoc networks usually do not provide on-line access to trusted authorities or to centralize servers and they exhibit frequent partitioning due to link and node failures and to node mobility. For these reasons, traditional security solutions that require on-line trusted authorities or certificate repositories are not well suited for securing ad hoc networks. For the authentication of adhoc network.

In this paper, we propose a fully self-monitored key management system that allows users to generate their key pairs, to issue certificates and to perform authentication regardless of the network partitions and without any centralized services. A self organizing key management system that allows users to create, store, distribute and revoke their keys without the help of any trusted authority or fixed server[11].

2 Security in Ad Hoc Network

Security is a fundamental issue that needs resolution before ad hoc networks will experience large-scale deployment. Vehicular ad hoc networking is a good example of a MANET application with some serious security implications. Failure of the security mechanisms may result in the loss of human life. The characteristics of mobile ad hoc networks, pose numerous challenges in achieving conventional security goals. Since the nodes are responsible for basic network functions, like packet forwarding and routing, network operations can be easily jeopardize if countermeasures are not integrated into these network functions at the early stages of design. For example, some existing routing protocols for mobile ad hoc networks may be able to manage the dynamic network topology of mobile ad hoc networks, but none of these protocols incorporate mechanisms to prevent, tolerate or defend against attacks from malicious adversaries. Due to the close relationship between security and the characteristics of ad hoc networks these protocols will have to be fundamentally altered or re-designed to effectively incorporate security mechanisms. Researchers in the ad hoc network security field initially focused on secure routing protocols. The focus of these protocols are:

1. To provide a robust routing mechanism against the dynamic topology of MANETs.
2. To provide a robust routing mechanism against malicious nodes.

Routing protocols use various security mechanisms to ensure robustness of the routing scheme. Some of these mechanisms are listed below:

1. Redundancy exploitation.
2. Diversity coding.
3. Authenticated route discovery and network nodes.
4. Guaranteed route discovery.
5. Route maintenance techniques.
6. Fault or intrusion tolerant mechanisms.
7. Cryptographic techniques, procedures, schemes, tools or mechanism.

It is widely acknowledged that cryptographic techniques can provide some of the strongest mechanisms to ensure the authenticity, integrity and confidentiality of routing information. Secure key management with a high availability feature is at the center of providing network security. However, all routing schemes neglect the crucial task of secure key management and assume pre-existence and pre-sharing of secret key pairs. This leaves key management considerations as an open research area in the ad hoc network security field [7].

3   Wired Equivalent Privacy Protocol

The WEP was designed by a group of IEEE volunteer members, aiming at giving some layer of security to wireless networks. This layer offers the following services:

1. Data Privacy: it is the basic service offered by the WEP. Transiting data can be read only by authenticated communicating members;
2. Data Integrity: WEP offers a guarantee to the receiver that data was not altered;
3. Access Control: depends strongly on data integrity; a corrupted message is considered as non authenticated and is automatically rejected.

A. WEP's Security Mechanisms
In this section, we will describe WEP functioning process, which includes mechanisms used to implement security services.

   Initially, both of the communication entities share a secret key k. k will be used further to encrypt transmitted data. Let S be a source which sends a message M to a receiver R. S begins by calculating a checksum using the CRC (Cyclic Redundancy Check) algorithm widely used in network protocols. Let us note T=(M,CRC) the message produced by a simple concatenation of M and its CRC.

Then, S encrypts T using the RC4 algorithm [2]. RC4 is a stream cipher [3]: It generates a keystream KS using two inputs:

- The key k shared between S and R, which is 40 bits length;
- An Initialization Vector iv, used principally to minimize probability of feeding RC4 with the same entries (which leads to the same keystream in output). KS is XORed with T to produce the cipher text C. To decrypt C, R needs to reconstruct the same keystream KS and XOR it with C, indeed: However, to reproduce KS, R needs to know iv. In WEP, iv is concatenated to the cipher text C before sending it. Figure 1 illustrates this encryption process. Note that iv is sent as clear text, without any kind of encryption. This process ensures:
- Data Privacy: all transmitted data is encrypted and only communication entities can decrypt it;
- Data Integrity and Authentication: the checksum is verified upon receiving the message. Thus, all modifications of the message during its transmission will be detected.

All WEP weaknesses come from four main conception flaws:

i)   The initialization vector is transmitted as clear text. Beside the fact that this weakens the power of encrypting, attackers are in a position to detect every iv reuse.

ii) The key is rarely renewed.

Key (k) updating techniques are completely leaved as implementation details. Thus, manufacturers are free to use the techniques that they find suitable. The worst, an implementation that doesn't plan key renewing is within the norm.

iii) Data Source Authentication.

The WEP has not planed a mechanism to ensure data source authentication. As mentioned above, using CRCs   allows attackers to forge their own messages and send them as coming from a known entity (this hole is called impersonation). Using Message Authentication Code (MAC) would be an efficient solution to this problem. MACs are usually used to guarantee data source authentication.

Another solution is to secure enough the privacy mechanism, so that nobody will be able to access the CRC. This is what WEP intended to do but failed to achieve.

iv) Security services are all implemented using only one mechanism. All the security scheme is based upon the strength of the mechanism of data privacy service. Thus, once the privacy of data is broken, all other services - data integrity and access control- are directly broken.

4   Security Approach

In a security concept, typically striving for goals like authenticity, integrity, confidentiality, non-repudiation and availability, authentication of communicating entities is of particular importance as it forms the basis for achieving the other security goals: e.g., encryption is worthless if the communication partners have not verified their identities before. Various methods were suggested before to provide these security approaches.

i)   Threshold cryptography: Several methods of authentication have been proposed for ad hoc networks. The threshold cryptographic method is found to be the most commonly used current method. In threshold based cryptographic method, authentication and communication including data transfer is based on centralized node concept.

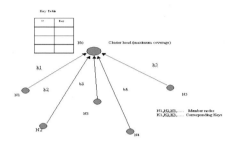

Fig. 1. Threshold cryptographic method

For the above illustrated network considered, node with id N0 is chosen as the centralized server node or the cluster head. All the other nodes N1 to N5 send their corresponding keys (K1 to K5) to the centralized node i.e.N0. Node N0 forms the repository table.

If any node needs to send a message or communicate with any other node in the network, the network performs route establishment. All the possible routes from source node to destination node are found out. This is carried out using a routing protocol Dynamic Source Routing (DSR) that gives all the possible routes that go from source node to destination node.

Table 1. Repository table at node N0

ID	KEY
N1	K1
N2	K2
N3	K3
N4	K4
N5	K5

Threshold based cryptography method is based on the centralized node for monitoring the keys .The key distribution and Authentication is completely relied on centralized node. Any failure in key generation may result in wrong authentication. All nodes depend on the centralized node for authentication.

5   Self Monitoring Approach

The main problem of any key based security system is to make each user's key available to others in such a way that its authenticity is verifiable. In mobile ad hoc networks, this problem becomes even more difficult to solve because of the absence of centralized services and possible network partitions. More precisely, two users willing to authenticate each other are likely to have access only to a subset of nodes of the network (possibly those in their geographic neighborhood). The best-known approach to the key management problem is based on key certificates [10]. A key certificate is a data structure in which a key is bound to an identity (and possibly to some other attributes) by the digital signature of the issuer of the certificate. In this system, the users themselves create users' keys. For simplicity, it is assumed that each honest user owns a single mobile node. Hence, same identifier is used for the user and her node (i.e., both user u and her node will be denoted by u). Unlike in the previous method, where certificates are mainly stored in centralized certificate repositories, certificates in our system are stored and distributed by the nodes in a fully self-monitored manner. Each certificate is issued with a limited validity period and therefore contains its issuing and expiration times. Before a certificate expires, its issuer issues an updated version of the same certificate, which contains an extended expiration time. Each node periodically issues certificate updates, as long as its owner considers that the user-key bindings contained in these certificates are correct.

The self-organizing concept includes two stages

1) Key Distribution /Initialization
2) Authentication

In an ad hoc network, in order for the nodes to communicate, it is essential that each node have the information about the rest of the nodes in the network. In particular, the keys of the nodes that are in its communication range are the most important parameter.

In self-organization method, key distribution is the first phase [11]. It is the initial phase for an ad hoc network to perform any task within the network.

Initialization Phase: The initial phase of the system is executed in three steps: each node creates a key pair; each node creates a self-certificate, issues certificates to other nodes and constructs an non updated certificate repository; nodes exchange certificates; and create updated certificate repositories. Each of these steps is illustrated in Figure.

Step-1: Creation of Key Pairs: Users locally create their own private key and corresponding key.

Step-2: Key distribution: Communication range of each user depends on the power level of each user. Depending up on the communication range of the nodes, they find out their nearest neighbors or the nodes that can be reached in one-hop. Once the nodes generate their keys, key distribution takes place. During broadcast period, each user broadcasts its key to all its nearest neighbors or one-hop neighbors. This is a synchronous process i.e. every node does this simultaneously. Now all the users in the network are aware of the keys of their neighbors.
Distribution of keys to neighbors

Step-3: issuing of Key Certificates/Certificate exchange

Every node receives a set of keys from all its neighbors. A node up on receiving a key from a particular neighbor, issues a certificate comprising the sending node id, key along with its own key. This indicates that the node believes in the sender's identity.

That is each node acknowledge back to the sender node with the certificate for the received node key. All the nodes in the network do this simultaneously.

Issuing of key certificates
Certificate issued is of the following form. It consists of ids and keys of the two nodes involved in exchange of certificates.

5.1 Authentication

Each node collects the certificates from all its one-hop neighbors. The Exchanged certificates are saved in the form of a repository table at each node. Consider node n issued a certificate to node m. The certificate includes node m's id and key Pm along with node n's id and key Pn. The exchanged certificate gives the authentication of the key received (Pm) by presenting the key of node-m which it received, with it' s own key (Pn). The authentication of the key is done by the node m by checking the second field of the certificate i.e. it's own key(Pm)as received by node-n. That means that node m believes that node n has its valid key and communication can be carried out. The certificate exchange process has a low communication cost since certificate exchanges are only performed locally in a one-hop fashion.

Every node will store the repository table in its memory. The form of the non-updated repository table is given in the figure below:

The following figure shows the formation of repository tables by the nodes in the network.

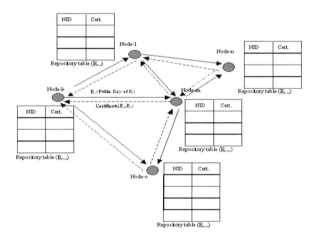

Fig. 2. Formation of repository tables

5.2 Construction of Updated Certificate Repositories

Every network has a work cycle period during which network operations are carried out. This work cycle is known as a beacon period. This beacon period includes the time taken for initialization of the network as well as communication. Initialization phase is nothing but the time taken by the nodes to know about all the other nodes in the network. This period is called the broadcast period or setup period.

Since the mobile ad hoc networks are open, any number of the existing nodes may leave the network or new nodes may join the network. The nodes or the users may keep on changing their location even. So the network is dynamic in nature. The changes that may occur to the network during any beacon period are not taken in to consideration till the completion of beacon period. That is these changes do not effect the communication that is being carried out. Once the beacon period is completed, what ever the repository table each node has is taken as a back up. Then each and every node again tries to find out their neighbors. These neighbors may be same as those, which the node encountered, in the previous beacon period or the node may encounter some new nodes The process of broadcasting the keys and certificate exchange again begins. When a node starts receiving the new certificates, it checks whether its back up repository table contains the similar certificate or not. If it already has similar certificate in its back up non-updated repository table, the newly received certificate is ignored. Like this every new certificate is verified. Scenario when one new node is added to the network after a beacon period is shown in the following figure.

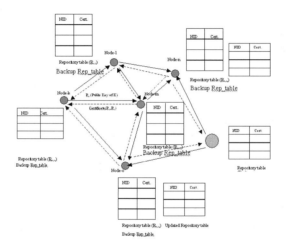

Fig. 3. Certificate exchange with newly added node

Finally certificates are saved in the new repository table are the certificates given by the nodes that entered the network lately. Users can revoke any issued certificate to other users in the instance of distrust in the key binding. Similarly users can also revoke their own certificate if they believe that their private key has been compromised. This new repository table is known as the updated repository table. Clearly the size of the updated repository table becomes less as time goes on. In the similar way, further communication will be carried out. After more and more beacon periods, the trustiness among the nodes increases. The proposed self-monitored key management system is completely independent in operation. Does not rely on any centralized node for key. The method performs certificate exchange so the authentication is most secure without involving any third party or central server. The approaches described were compared using various analysis factors. 1) Propagation delay, 2) Average packet delivery,3) Repository updation factor as shown.

6 Simulation Results

The proposed self-monitored key management scheme is implemented on an ad hoc network. The network is created with randomly distributed nodes. Network is considered with the following properties:

No of nodes (n): 20
Network area: 200 x 200
Band width: Random
Routing Algorithm: DSR
Optimizing algorithm: SWP
Network distribution: random
Neighbor Discovery: Range factor
Communication: non-interfering
Head discovery: coverage

Several ad hoc networks are tested for various cases of network load. Even variable number of nodes is taken into account. Performance of both threshold based cryptography and self monitored approach are tested. The three analysis factors mentioned in the previous section are evaluated in both the cases.

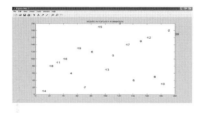

Fig. 4. Simulated network with the stated specifications

Case 1: With No Add-on nodes, Source node:18, Destination node:12, Route taken for communication from source to destination: 18 → 4→ 6 → 17→ 12

(a)   (b)

Fig. 5. (a) Average Packet Delivery & (b) Propagation delay plot

Case 2: Source node:14, Destination node:20, With No Add-on nodes, Route taken for communication from source to destination: 14 → 4 → 6 → 3 → 9 → 20

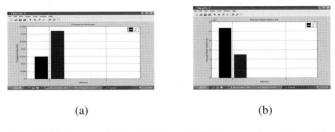

(a) (b)

Fig. 6. (a) Average Packet Delivery & (b) Propagation delay plot

Case 3: Source node:14, Destination node: 20, Generated load: four bytes, With no add on nodes, Route taken for communication from source to destination: 14 → 4 → 6 → 3 → 9 → 20

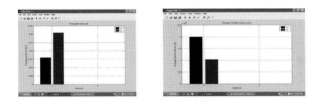

Fig. 7. Average Packet Delivery plot

Case 4: Source node: 14, Destination node: 20,Generated load: four bytes, With 2 add on nodes, Route taken for communication from source to destination: 14 → 4 → 6 → 3 → 9 → 20

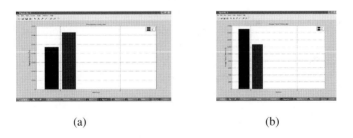

(a) (b)

Fig. 8. a) Average Packet Delivery & (b) Propagation delay plot

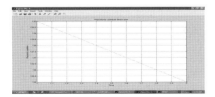

Fig. 9. Repository Updation plot

Case 5: Source node: 14, Destination node: 20, Generated load: four bytes, With 2 add on nodes and 1 remove node Route taken for communication from source to destination: 14 → 4 → 6 → 3 → 9 → 20

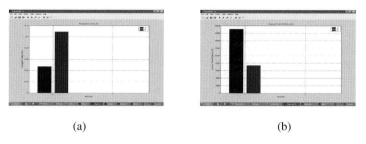

(a)   (b)

Fig. 10. (a) Average Packet Delivery & (b) Propagation delay plot

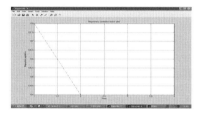

Fig. 11. Repository Updation plot

7   Conclusion

In this work, the problem of key management in mobile ad hoc networks is addressed. A fully self-monitored key management system for mobile ad hoc networks is developed and it is observed that two users in a mobile ad hoc network can perform key authentication based only on their local information, even if security is performed in a self-monitored way, it is shown that with a simple local repository construction algorithm and a small communication overhead, the system achieves high performance on a wide range of certificate graphs; it is also shown that nodes can have mobility to facilitate authentication and to detect inconsistent and false certificates. An important feature of this scheme is that key authentication is still possible even when the network is partitioned and nodes can communicate with only a subset of other nodes. In this method the involvement of all the nodes are required only when their key pairs are created and for issuing and revoking certificates; all other operations including certificate exchange and construction of certificate repositories are self monitored.

References

1. Pfitzmann, A., Pfitzmann, B., Schunter, M., Waidner, M.: Trusting Mobile User Devices and Security Modules. In: IEEE, Information infrastructure for virtual environment (1997)
2. Zhou, L., Haas, Z.J.: Securing Ad Hoc Networks. IEEE network (November/December 1999)

3. Papadimitratos, P., Haas, Z.J.: Secure Routing for Mobile Ad hoc Networks. In: SCS Communication Networks and Distributed Systems Modeling and Simulation Conference (CNDS 2002), San Antonio, TX, January 27-31 (2002)
4. Asokan, N., Ginzboorg, P., Seng, C.Y.: Key Agreement in Ad-hoc Networks. (Presentation)
5. Johnson, D.B.: Routing in Ad Hoc Networks of Mobile Hosts, Computer Science Department, Carnegie Mellon University, Pittsburgh. IEEE, Los Alamitos (1995)
6. Sayın, E., Levi, A.: Open Trust Scheme for Ad Hoc Networks (2006)
7. Roberts, N.C., Bradley, R.T.: Research Methodology for New Public Management. In: The International Public Management Network workshop, Siena, Italy, July 28-30 (1999)
8. Yi, S., Naldurg, P., Kravets, R.: A Security-Aware Routing Protocol for Wireless Ad Hoc Networks, University of Illinois, Urbana-Champaign, Urbana, IL 61801
9. Vanhala, A.: Security in Ad-hoc Networks. Research seminar on Security in Distributed Systems, University of Helsinki
10. Stajano, F., Anderson, R.: The Resurrecting Duckling:Security Issues for Ad-hoc Wireless Networks. In: Malcolm, J.A., Christianson, B., Crispo, B., Roe, M. (eds.) Security Protocols 1999. LNCS, vol. 1796, p. 215. Springer, Heidelberg (2000)
11. BlaZevit, L., Buttyan, L., Tapkun, S., Giordano, S., Hubaux, J.-P., Le Boudec, J.-Y.: Self-Organization in Mobile Ad Hoc Networks: The Approach of Terminodes. IEEE communication Magazine (June 2001)
12. Buttyan, L., Hubaux, J.-P.: Stimulating Cooperation in Self-Organizing Mobile Ad Hoc Networks., Laboratory for Computer Communications and Applications Swiss Federal Institute of Technology EPFL-IC-LCA, CH-1015 Lausanne, Switzerland, March 19. ACM/Kluwer Mobile Networks and Applications, MONET (2002)

TCP – AP and LRED over Single and Multiple TCP Flows in Multihop Wireless Channel

G. Sankara Malliga[1] and Dharmishtan K. Varughese[2]

[1] Research Scholar, Anna University, Coimbatore, Tamilnadu, India
[2] Professor/ECE, Karpagam College of Engineering, Coimbatore

Abstract. The Transmission Control Protocol (TCP) was designed to provide reliable end-to-end delivery of data over unreliable networks. In practice, most TCP deployments have been carefully designed in the context of wired networks. Ignoring the properties of wireless Ad-hoc Networks can lead to TCP implementations with poor performance. In a wireless network, however packet losses occur more often due to unreliable wireless links than due to congestion. When using TCP over wireless links, each packet loss on the wireless link results in congestion control measures being invoked at the source. This causes severe performance degradation. If there is any packet loss in wireless networks, then the reason for that has to be found out and then only congestion control mechanism has to be applied. This work shows the performance of TCP with Adaptive Pacing (TCP-AP) and Link Random Early Discard (LRED) as queuing model over Single and Multiple TCP flows in multihop transmission when the source and destination nodes are in mobile nature. The adaptive pacing technique seeks to improve spatial reuse. The LRED technique seeks to react earlier to link overload. This paper consists of simulated environment results under three different network scenarios. Simulations are done with the use of NS2.

Keywords: Wireless Networks, TCP, Congestion Control, Adaptive Pacing, Link Random Early Discard.

1 Introduction

Wireless networks are becoming very popular and are being installed almost everywhere. Reliable transport protocols such as TCP are tuned to perform well in traditional networks where packet losses occur mostly because of congestion. [1] However, networks with wireless and other lossy links also suffer from significant losses due to bit errors and handoffs. TCP responds to all losses by invoking congestion control and avoidance algorithms, resulting in degraded end-to-end performance in wireless and lossy systems [2]. As a result, many modifications and new solutions have been proposed to improve TCP's performance, such as forward error correction schemes, retransmissions at the link layer, split connections like MTCP(Mobile TCP), Explicit Loss Notification, link layer TCP Aware like Snoop, Performance Enhancing Proxies, Indirect TCP (I-TCP), MAITE(Mobility Awareness Incorporated as TCP Enhancement), etc. Available performance evaluations of TCP over wireless networks are usually incomplete, meaning that the most important TCP versions and the most

N. Meghanathan et al. (Eds.): NeCoM, WiMoN, and WeST 2010, CCIS 90, pp. 400–410, 2010.

important solutions are not studied and compared all together [1]. Therefore, we still donot have a good idea about what is the best combination.

TCP is an adaptive transport protocol that controls its offered load (through adjusting its window size) according to the available network bandwidth. It additively increases its congestion window in the absence of congestion and throttles down its window when a sign of congestion is detected. In the wired Internet, congestion is identified by packet loss, which results from buffer overflow events at the bottleneck router [9].

Over the past few years, the problem of congestion control has received wide spread attention, both in the Internet context as well as in an ad-hoc network context. Most of this research has focused on modeling, analysis, algorithm development of end-to-end control schemes (such as TCP), and adaptation of such schemes to ad-hoc networks. Given routing path and bandwidth constraints, algorithms have been developed which converge and have a stable operation. Unfortunately, when packets are lost in networks for reasons other than congestion, these measures result in an unnecessary reduction in end-to-end throughput and hence, suboptimal performance. Communication over wireless links is often characterized by sporadic high bit-error rates, and intermittent connectivity due to handoffs. TCP performance in such networks suffers from significant throughput degradation and very high interactive delays [3].

Recently, several schemes have been proposed to alleviate the effects of non-congestion-related losses on TCP performance over networks that have wireless or similar high loss links [2], [3], [5]. These schemes choose from a variety of mechanisms, such as local retransmissions, split-TCP connections, and forward error correction, to improve end-to-end throughput. However, it is unclear to what extent each of the mechanisms contributes to the improvement in performance.

In TCP, reliability is achieved by retransmitting lost packets. Thus, each TCP sender maintains a running average of the estimated round trip delay and the average deviation derived from it. Packets will be retransmitted if the sender receives no acknowledgment (ACK) within a certain timeout interval (e.g., the sum of smoothed round trip delay and four times the average deviation) or receives duplicate acknowledgments. Due to the inherent reliability of wired networks, there is an implicit assumption made by TCP that any packet loss is due to congestion[3]. To reduce congestion, TCP invokes its congestion control mechanisms whenever any packet loss is detected. Consider the problem of congestion control over wireless multihop networks. Nodes in such networks are radio equipped, and communicate by broadcasting over wireless links. Communication paths between nodes which are not in radio range of each other are established by intermediate nodes acting as relays to forward data toward the destination. The diverse applications of such networks range from community based roof-top networks to large-scale adhoc networks.

2   TCP'S Challenges in AD-HOC Networks

The performance of TCP degrades in Ad-hoc networks. This is because TCP has to face new challenges due to several reasons specific to these networks: lossy channels, hidden and exposed stations, path asymmetry, network partitions, route failures, and power constraints [4]. Some of them are discussed here.

2.1 Channel Errors

In wireless channels, relatively high bit error rate because of multipath fading and shadowing may corrupt packets in transmission, leading to the losses of TCP data segments or ACKs. If it cannot receive the ACK within the retransmission timeout, the TCP sender immediately reduces its congestion window to one segment, exponentially backs off its Retransmission Time-Out (RTO) and retransmits the lost packets. Intermittent channel errors may thus cause the congestion window size at the sender to remain small, thereby resulting in low TCP throughput.

2.2 Mobility

Cellular networks are characterized by handoffs due to user mobility. Normally, handoffs may cause temporary disconnections, resulting in packet losses and delay. TCP will suffer a lot if it treats such losses as congestion and invokes unnecessary congestion control mechanisms. Similar problems may occur in wireless LAN, as mobile users will also encounter communication interruptions if they move to the edge of the transmission range of the access point.

2.3 Asymmetry

In wireless networks, the wireless link between a base station and a mobile terminal in nature is asymmetric. Compared with the base station, the mobile terminal has limited power, processing capability, and buffer space. Another asymmetry stems from the vastly different characteristics of wired links and wireless links.

2.4 Lossy Channels

The main causes of errors in wireless channel are the following: Signal attenuation: This is due to a decrease in the intensity of the electromagnetic energy at the receiver (e.g. due to long distance), which leads to low signal-to-noise ratio (SNR). Doppler shift: This is due to the relative velocities of the transmitter and the receiver.

Multipath fading: Electromagnetic waves reflecting off objects or diffracting around objects can result in the signal traveling over multiple paths from the transmitter to the receiver.

In order to increase the success of transmissions, link layer protocols implement the following techniques: Automatic Repeat reQuest (ARQ), or Forward Error Correction (FEC), or both. For example, IEEE 802.11 implements ARQ, so when a transmitter detects an error, it will retransmit the frame, error detection is timer based. Bluetooth implements both ARQ and FEC on some synchronous and asynchronous connections. Note that packets transmitted over a fading channel may cause routing protocol to incorrectly conclude that there is a new one hop neighbor. This one-hop neighbor could provide a shorter route to even more distant nodes. Unfortunately, this new shorter route is usually unreliable. 4.5. Hidden and Exposed stations In Ad-hoc networks, stations may rely on physical carrier sensing mechanism to determine idle channel, such as in the IEEE 802.11 DCF function. This sensing mechanism does not solve completely the hidden station and the exposed station problems. Before explaining these problems, we need to clarify the "transmission range" term. The transmission range is the range, with respect to the transmitting station, within which a transmitted packet can be successfully received.

2.5 Routing Failures

In wired networks route failures occur very rarely. The main cause of route failures is node mobility. Another factor that can lead to route failures is the link failures due to the contention on the wireless channel, which is the main cause of TCP performance degradation. If TCP sender's does not have indications on the route re-establishment event, the throughput and session delay will degrade because of the large idle time. Also, if the new route established is longer or shorter, in term of hops, than the old route TCP will face a brutal fluctuation in Round Trip Time (RTT).

3 Problems and Related Studies

Fu et al. [9] pointed out the hidden terminal problem in wireless multihop networks and experimentally showed that for a chain topology the optimal windows size for which TCP achieves best throughput, is roughly given by 1/4 of the hop count of the path. Furthermore, they proposed two enhancements on the link layer: adaptive pacing to distribute traffic on the link layer among intermediate nodes in a more balanced way and link layer RED to throttle TCP senders when incipient congestion is detected. Using simulation, they showed that depending on the scenario, these link layer enhancements improve TCP goodput by 5% to 30% due to better spatial reuse. Xu et al. [16] proposed the neighborhood RED (NRED) scheme on routing layer to throttle TCP senders when incipient congestion is detected, by purposely dropping TCP packets on intermediate nodes. Nodes forming a neighborhood manage a virtual distributed queue in order to coordinate the packet drops of individual nodes. Using simulation, the authors showed that NRED could substantially improve fairness in multihop wireless networks.

Sundaresam et al. [17] and Chen et al. [18] introduced two new special-purpose transport protocols for multihop wireless networks. Both protocols employ pure rate-based transmission of packets, where the transmission rate is determined using feedback from intermediate nodes along the path. In [17], the authors propose to dynamically adjust the transmission rate according to the maximum packet queuing delay on intermediate nodes along the network path. Chen et al. [18] also proposed an explicit ratebased flow control scheme for multihop wireless network. Using cross-layer information from both the MAC and the routing layer, the sending rate of a flow is conveyed from intermediate nodes along the path in special control headers attached to each data packet.

In contrast to [5], [17], TCP-AP retains the end-to-end semantics of TCP without relying on any cross-layer information from intermediate nodes along the path. As a consequence, TCPAP can be incrementally deployed, since TCP-AP is not only TCP-friendly, but also TCP compatible. Altman and Jiménez [19] proposed a dynamic scheme for delaying ACKs in order to improve TCP throughput in multihop wireless networks. Using simulation, they showed that for an n hop chain, delaying ACKs yields around 50% more throughput for TCP NewReno.

Several authors introduced TCP enhancements for coping with mobility in ad hoc wireless networks over IEEE 802.11. Yu [20] proposed two cross-layer communication mechanisms that further improve TCP performance in case of packet losses due to mobility.

4 Improving TCP Performance

This section describes two techniques to improve TCP performance over multihop wireless networks[4]. The link RED(Random Early Discard) technique seeks to react earlier to link overload. The adaptive pacing technique seeks to improve spatial reuse. The combination of these two techniques is able to improve TCP throughput by as much as 30%.

4.1 Distributed Link RED (LRED)

Our Link RED (LRED) algorithm is based on the observation that TCP can potentially benefit from the built-in dropping mechanism of the 802.11 MAC. The main idea is to further tune up wireless link's drop probability, based on the perceived link drops. While the wired RED provides a linearly increasing drop curve as the queue exceeds a minimum value min_th, LRED does so as the link drop probability exceeds a minimum threshold.

Algorithm 1. L-RED: LinkLayerSend(Packet p)

Require: avg_retry is the average MAC retries for each packet

1: **if** $avg\_retry < min\_th$ **then**
2:     $mark\_prob \leftarrow 0$
3:     $pacing \leftarrow ON$
4: **else**
5:     $mark\_prob = min\{\frac{avg\_retry - min\_th}{max\_th - min\_th}, max\_P\}$
6:     set $pacing$ OFF
7: **end if**
8: mark p with $mark\_prob$
9: MacLayerSend(p, $pacing$)
10: $retry$ = GetMacRetries()
11: $avg\_retry = \frac{7}{8}avg\_retry + \frac{1}{8}retry$

In LRED, the link layer maintains the average number of the retries for recent packet transmissions. The head-of-line packet is dropped/marked from the buffer with a probability based on this average number. At each node, if the average number of retries is small, say less than min th, which means that the node is rarely hidden, packets in the buffer are not dropped/marked. When it gets larger, the dropping/marking probability is computed, and the minimum value of the computed drop probability and a maximum bound max P is used. A feature of this algorithm is that it can integrate with ECN enabled TCP flows. Instead of blindly dropping packets, we can simply mark them at the link layer, and thus allow ECN enhanced TCP flows to adapt their offered load without losing any packets. TCP performance is further improved, by paying the moderate cost of a slightly more complex link-layer design.

To summarize, LRED is a simple mechanism that, by monitoring a single parameter –the average number of retries in the packet transmissions at the link-layer, accomplishes three goals: a) It helps to improve TCP throughput, b) It provides TCP an early sign of network overload, and c) It helps to improve interflow fairness.

4.2 Adaptive Pacing

Our second technique seeks to take an adaptive pacing approach at the link-layer. The goal is to improve spatial channel reuse, by distributing traffic among intermediate nodes in a more balanced way, while enhancing the coordination of forwarding nodes along the data path. This design works in concert with the 802.11 MAC.

In the current 802.11 protocol, a node is constrained from contending for the channel by a random backoff period, plus a single packet transmission time that is announced by its immediate downstream node. However, the exposed receiver problem [6] persists due to lack of coordination between nodes that are two hops away from each other. Adaptive pacing solves this problem, without requiring nontrivial modifications to the 802.11, or a second wireless channel [8]. The basic idea is to let a node further back-off an additional packet transmission time when necessary, in addition to its current deferral period (i.e. the random backoff, plus one packet transmission time). This extra backoff interval helps in reducing contention drops caused by exposed receivers, and extends the range of the link-layer coordination from one hop to two hops, along the packet forwarding path.

Algorithm 2. Adaptive Pacing

Require: $extra\_Backoff = 0$

1: **if** received ACK **then**
2:      $random\_Backoff \leftarrow ran\_backoff(cong\_win)$ {DATA transmission succeeded. Setup the backoff timer}
3:      **if** $pacing$ is ON **then**
4:          $extra\_Backoff = TX\_Time(DATA) + overhead$
5:      **end if**
6:      $backoff \leftarrow random\_Backoff + extra\_Backoff$
7:      start $backoff\_timer$
8: **end if**

The algorithm works together with LRED as follows: Adaptive pacing is enabled by LRED. When a node finds its average number of retries to be less than min th, it calculates its backoff time as usual. When the average number of retries goes beyond min th, adaptive pacing is enabled and the backoff period is increased by an interval equal to the transmission time of the previous data packet. This way, a better coordination among nodes is achieved under different network load.

5   Simulation Model and Results

Here ns-2 network simulator with the CMU extensions for IEEE 802.11 wireless LAN is used. Here, the two network scenario are considered. In one scenario, that consists of 3 nodes and in another scenario, the second one that consists of 10 nodes and the third one that consists of 30 nodes. The routing protocol chosen for analysis is AODV. The analysis done in four cases such as: (i) Simple TCP NewReno with queuing DropTail (ii) TCP-AP with queuing DropTail (iii) TCP NewReno with queuing LRED (iv) TCP-AP and queuing LRED.

5.1   Simulation Scenario I

This scenario runs a single TCP connection having a 2-nodes network over an area of a size of 500m and 400m. The initial locations of nodes 0 and 1 are (5,2) and (390,385). At time 10 sec, node 0 starts moving towards (20,18) at a speed of 1m/sec. At time 50 sec, node 1 starts moving towards (25,20) at a speed of 15m/sec. The network chosen for analysis is shown in Fig. (1). The simulation lasts at 150 sec.

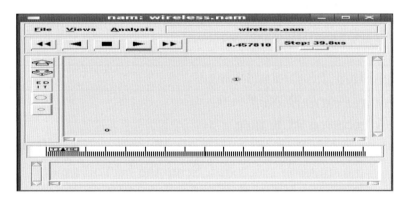

Fig. 1. Simulation Scenario 1 at Simulation Time nearly 10 sec

5.2   Simulation Scenario II

This scenario also runs a single TCP connection between two mobile nodes over an area of 500m by 500m. The initial conditions of nodes 0 and 1 are (50,90) and (450,410) respectively. All other eight nodes are at (250,250). At time 0.1 sec, node 0 moves to (420,100) and node 1 moves to (10,460) with a speed of 5m/s and also all other eight nodes are moving that will be shown in Fig. (2). Once again at time 100s, node 0 moves towards (2,450) with speed 25 m/s and node 1 moves to (490,40) with 15 m/s speed.

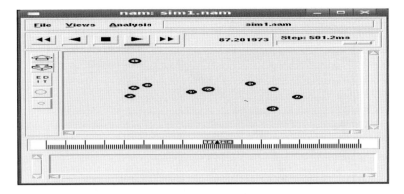

Fig. 2. Simulation Scenario 2 at Simulation Time nearly 87sec

5.3   Simulation Scenario III

This scenario consists of 30 nodes moving around the workspace area of 750m x 750m. The nodes are having random motion. The simulation time taken is 500 seconds. Multiple TCP connections and a single TCP connection are provided. That is analyzed. Nodes 8 and 15, 0 and 1, 5 and 12 are initially having single hop and then having multiple hops. The network chosen for analysis is shown in Fig. (3).

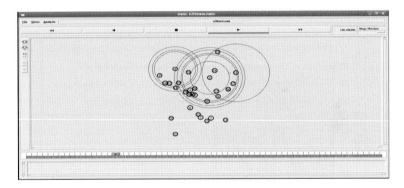

Fig. 3. Simulation Scenario 3 at Simulation Time nearly 127 sec

5.4   Analysis of Simulation Results

For the Network Scenario 1, at the beginning, the nodes are too far away and a connection cannot be set. The first TCP signaling packet is transmitted at time about 40 sec. After 150 sec also node 1 had moved and far away so that transmission can not take place. At the time during 40 sec to 150 sec, node 0 and 1 are able to initiate TCP connection between node 0 and node 1. During that time only performance is good and window size increases and reaches maximum. All other time the window size will be nearly one. This is due to the mobility nature of the node. The AODV routing protocol is creating an alternative route for transmission. The window evolution for the above mentioned cases is given in Fig. (4).

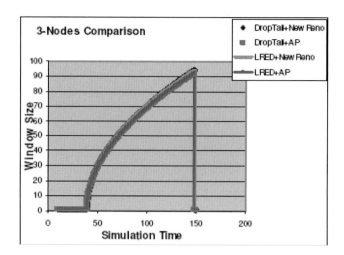

Fig. 4. Window Size for TCP with AP and LRED for Network Scenario 1

For the Network Scenario 2, during the time 10sec to 75sec, their will be multiple hop between the nodes 0 and 1. So that LRED gives maximum window size during that time. During 80 sec to 120sec, nodes 0 and 1 are closer together, so that window size will be decreased than the previous situation. The window evolution for the above mentioned cases is given in Fig. (5).

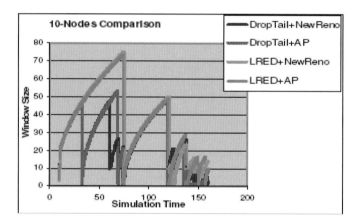

Fig. 5. Window Size for TCP with AP and LRED forNetwork Scenario 2

For the Network Scenario 3, at the beginning, the nodes are placed in random position and then moving with different speeds to different position. When multiple TCP connections are provided, window size is low only. When single TCP connection is provided, according to the number of hops between the source and destination, the performance is varied. Whenever multiple hops are provided, the window size is increased. Between 250s and 325s, nodes 0 and 1 are having multiple nodes in between them. Like that nodes 5 and 12 are having multiple hops during the time 130s to 470s.

And also nodes 8 and 15 are having multiple hops during 140s to 345s. So that in those cases, the window size in increasing up to the maximum of 100. The window evolution for the above mentioned cases is given in Fig. (6).

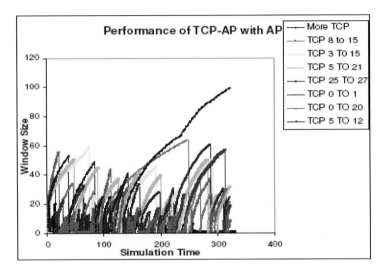

Fig. 6. Window Size for TCP with AP and LRED for Network Scenario 3

6 Conclusion

TCP is a natural choice for reliable data delivery in these scenarios. This work systematically studies the impact of node mobility on TCP performance in wireless networks. Here when the destination node moved due to mobility, that impacts the performance of TCP. To gain more insight, proposed the two link layer techniques, LRED and Adaptive Pacing, which improve the window size of TCP flows by much better. In this work, only the window size is taken as the parameter for analysis. In future, Throughput, queuing delay and packet loss have to be considered. The performance of TCP-AP and LRED are better when the source and destination nodes are having multiple hops. Whereas when the nodes are close enough, the performance will be low compared to the previous case. TCP-AP and LRED are the techniques for solving Hidden and Exposed terminals in wireless networks. In addition to that channel errors and Energy Bandwidth tradeoff of the nodes have to be considered that is going to be implemented in Enhanced LRED.

References

1. Vangala, S., Labrador, M.A.: Performance of TCP over Wireless Networks with the Snoop Protocol. In: 27th Annual IEEE Conference, pp. 600–601 (2002)
2. Balakrishnan, H., Padmanabhan, V.N., Seshan, S., Katz1, R.H.: A Comparison of Mechanisms for Improving TCP Performance over Wireless Links. ACM SIGCOMM Computer Communication Review, 256–269 (1996)

3. Caceres, R., Iftode, L.: Improving the Performance of Reliable Transport Protocols in Mobile Computing Environments. IEEE Journal on Selected Areas in Communications, 850–857 (1995)
4. Chen, X., Zhai, H., Wang, J., Fang, Y.: A Survey on Improving TCP Performance over Wireless Networks. ACM Computing Surveys (CSUR) archive, 357–374 (September 2002)
5. Yavatkar, R., Bhagwat, N.: Improving End-to-End Performance of TCP over Mobile Internetworks. Mobile Computing Systems and Applications, 146–152 (1994)
6. Bharghavan, V.: Performance Analysis of a Medium Access Protocol for Wireless Packet Networks. Wireless Networks, 519–529 (September 2004)
7. Khayat, I.E., Geurts, P., Leduc, G.: Improving TCP in wireless networks with an adaptive machine-learnt classifier of packet loss causes. In: Proceedings of the International Conference on Networking, pp. 549–560 (2005)
8. Gerla, M., Bagrodia, R., Zhang, L., Tang, K., Wang, L.: TCP over Wireless Multihop Protocols: Simulation and Experiments. Proceedings of IEEE, 1089–1094 (1999)
9. Fu, Z., Zerfos, P., Luo, H., Lu, S., Zhang, L., Gerla, M.: The Impact of Multihop Wireless Channel on TCP Throughput and Loss. In: IEEE INFOCOM 2003, pp. 1744–1753 (2003)
10. Ali, I., Gupta, R., Bansal, S., Misra, A., Razdan, A., Shorey, R.: Energy Efficiency and Throughput for TCP Traffic in Multi-Hop Wireless Networks. In: IEEE INFOCOM 2002, pp. 210–219 (2002)
11. Chen, X., Zhai, H., Wang, J., Fang, Y.: TCP performance over mobile ad-hoc networks. In: Proceedings of the 10th annual international conference on Mobile computing and networking, pp. 231–244 (2004)
12. Vicente, E., Mujica, V., Dorgham Sisalem, R., Zeletin, P., Wolisz, A.: TCP-Friendly Congestion Control over Wireless Networks (2004)
13. Gerla, M., Tang, K., Bagrodia, R.: TCP Performance in Wireless Multihop Networks. In: Proceedings of IEEE WMCSA 1999 (1999)
14. Yawen, S.B.D.: Enhancing Congestion Control for Wireless Links. In: ACM SIGCOMM (2003)
15. DeSimone, A., Chuah, M.C., Yue, O.C.: Throughput Performance of Transport-Layer Protocols over Wireless LANs. In: Proc. Globecom 1993, pp. 542–549 (1993)
16. Xu, K., Gerla, M., Qi, L., Shu, Y.: Enhancing TCP Fairness in Ad Hoc Wireless Networks using Neighborhood RED. In: Proc. ACM MOBICOM 2003 (2003)
17. Sundaresan, K., Anantharaman, V., Hsieh, H.-Y., Sivakumar, R.: ATP: A Reliable Transport Protocol for Ad Hoc Networks. In: Proc. ACM MobiHoc, Annapolis (2003)
18. Chen, K., Nahrstedt, K., Vaidya, N.: The Utility of Explicit Rate-Based Flow Control in Mobile Ad Hoc Networks. In: Proc. IEEE Wireless Communications and Networking Conference, WCNC 2004 (2004)
19. Altman, E., Jimenez, T.: Novel Delayed ACK Techniques for Improving TCP Performance in Multihop Wireless Networks. In: Conti, M., Giordano, S., Gregori, E., Olariu, S. (eds.) PWC 2003. LNCS, vol. 2775, pp. 237–250. Springer, Heidelberg (2003)
20. Yu, X.: Improving TCP Performance over Mobile Ad Hoc Networks by Exploiting Cross-Layer Information Awareness. In: Proc. ACM MOBICOM (2004)

A Secure Prioritized Trust Based Multi-path Routing Protocol for Ad Hoc Networks

Poonam, K. Garg, and M. Misra

Dept. of Electronics & Computer Engineering
IIT Roorkee, Roorkee, India
{pgeradec,kgargfec,manojfec}@iitr.ernet.in

Abstract. Security in infrastructure-less networks like MANETs (Mobile Ad Hoc Networks) has proven to be a challenging task. Multipath routing protocols were initially proposed in order to design robust and secure networks. These protocols improve network performance in terms of delay, throughput, reliability and life time. It is hard to find a single protocol that can improve all these performance parameters. In this paper we propose a secure prioritized trust based multi path routing protocol. It ensures reliable communication with low overhead and minimum delay. This is realized by discovering and selecting reliable path based on the trust information. We take the advantage of multiple paths to increase reliability and robustness of data through context aware routing. Results show the effectiveness of our protocol.

Keywords: Trust, misbehaving node, Multipath routing.

1 Introduction

A mobile ad-hoc network (MANET) is a collection of wireless mobile nodes organized to create a temporary connection between them. Neither pre-defined network infrastructure nor centralized network administration exists to assist in the communication in MANETs. Each node act both as hosts and routers, and thus cooperatively provide multi-hop strategy to communicate with other nodes outside their transmission range.

The premise of node cooperation induces various challenging security issues. One of the main issues in the process of routing of messages in the aforementioned class of networks is that the cooperation of nodes cannot be assumed in general. It can be beneficial for nodes to misbehave during the process of routing/forwarding, e.g. to save resources such as energy. A common attack is to drop messages of other nodes.

Such node misbehavior results in a severe state for the critical applications, i.e. disaster and emergency surveillance. The presence of misbehaving nodes degrades the performance of network, as the packet drop by misbehaving nodes result in resending of the packet which outcome in large end-to-end delay. As we know bandwidth is also limited in an ad hoc network, routing along a single path may not provide enough bandwidth for a connection which also results in further increase in end to end delay.

In this paper, we propose an end-to-end method aimed at providing prioritized service, safeguarding data transmission from the above node misbehavior. In our method

N. Meghanathan et al. (Eds.): NeCoM, WiMoN, and WeST 2010, CCIS 90, pp. 411–420, 2010.

we have discovered multiple secure path based on the trust information and the data is delivered on these path based on its priority and its requirements. In our method the source node distributes the load in such a manner that the delay per packet or average end to end delay is lower. Reliability of data transfer is also increased without duplicating it, by selecting the trustworthy path excluding misbehaving nodes.

The rest of this paper is organized as follows. In Section II the related work is given, followed by a detailed description of our solution in Section III. In Section IV we evaluate the efficiency of our method through exhaustive simulation. An analysis of the proposed method is also presented. Finally, the last section concludes the paper.

2 Related Work

Much research work has been done to make the route discovered by Dynamic Source Routing (DSR) secure.

The Watchdog and Pathrater mechanism [8] has been specifically designed to optimize the forwarding mechanism in the (DSR) protocol [6]. The Watchdog is responsible for detecting selfish nodes that do not forward packets. The Pathrater assigns different ratings to the nodes, based upon the feedback that it receives from the Watchdog. These ratings are then used to select routes consisting of nodes with the highest forwarding rate.

A Trust based routing is proposed by Pirzada [10] in which the trust agent derives trust levels from events that are directly experienced by a node. A Reputation agent shares trust information about nodes with other nodes in the network. A Combiner computes the final trust in a node based upon the information it receives from the Trust and Reputation agents. The trust value is propagated by piggybacking the direct trust value of the nodes along with RREQ packets [11]. Each forwarding node selects the next hop in the path having the highest direct trust value.

Wang et al. [14] have also proposed a Routing Algorithm based on Trust. They have assumed that the trust values of all nodes are stored at each node in advance. Trust for the route is calculated at the source node based on the weight and trust values are assigned to the nodes involved in the path at the source node. The protocol uses the path with the largest trust value of route and least packet delay, unlike the standard DSR protocol that only uses minimum hop count.

CONFIDANT (Cooperation Of Nodes, Fairness In Dynamic Ad hoc NeTworks) [3] adds a trust manager and a reputation system to the Watchdog and Pathrater scheme. The trust manager evaluates the events reported by the Watchdog (monitor in this case) and issues alarms to warn other nodes regarding malicious nodes. To verify the source of alarms, a mechanism similar to Pretty Good Privacy [4] is employed. The reputation system maintains a black-list of nodes at each node and shares them with nodes in the friends-list. It implements a punishment based scheme, by not forwarding packets of nodes whose trust level drops below a certain threshold.

In the TDSR [14] model, trust among nodes is calculated as a combination of direct trust and indirect trust. The direct trust score is modified when misbehavior has occurred by a number of times exceeding a threshold. The indirect trust score is modified when a node receives a message reported by neighbor nodes. If the trust score of a node in the table has deteriorated so much as to fall out of a tolerable range. Such nodes are added to the blacklist. In the route Discovery phase, node A does not sends a RREQ packet to node B if node B exists in its blacklist.

A Trust based multi path DSR protocol is proposed by Poonam et al. [12] in which uses multi-path forwarding approach. In this approach each node forwards the RREQ if it is received from different path. Through this method detect and avoid misbehaving nodes which were previously included due to vulnerability in DSR route discovery. In their protocol each node broadcast the packet embedding trust information about the node from which the packet is receive. At the source node a secure and efficient route to the destination is calculated as weighted average of the number of nodes in the route and their trust values.

In summary, we conclude that all these trust based protocol treat all the packets in same manner, regardless of disparate contributions of packets to the application. Each packet has a different requirements based on the application for example lesser end to end delay or require desired reliability. Multipath routing protocol is able to provide the desired reliability but they provide it by sending the packet through multiple paths therefore mounting network load. Our protocol is distant from all these multipath protocols as the main goal of them is reliability but our aim is to provide information-aware routing.

3 Secure Prioritized Trust Based Multipath Routing

Aiming at providing differentiated service in the ad hoc network, information-aware classification of packets is employed. We assume that the source node is able to categorize the packet it generates based on its importance. Content-awareness can be achieved in the framework described in [1]. A priority field is assigned to the each packet at the source node to classify the packets. The priority of packet is assigned based on its importance. High priority packets are send through most trustworthy and shorter paths which ensures the secure delivery of the packet resulting in higher throughput and lower end to end delay.

In this paper, we assume that the priority level goes down from 1 to M, where M is the maximum integer value of the priority level. Packets of the highest priority are forwarded on the optimal path among the m-paths to the destination.

In our method we discover multiple paths between two source and destination. In the route discovery phase the trust information is embedded in the RREQ and RREP packets. This is essential for an ad hoc network to be able to tolerate attack-induced path failures and provide robust packet delivery [15].

3.1 Multiple Path Initialization

To discover multiple paths from a source to a destination, we have modified the basic route discovery mechanisms of DSR protocol to discover multiple node-disjoint and trust-worthy paths. We avoid any RREP from the intermediate nodes. Each intermediate node forward the RREQ if it is received from a different node and it itself is included in the source route of the packet to avoid route loop. In our method, intermediate nodes do not reply from cache, only the source nodes maintain route information to destinations. Therefore memory is saved due to evasion of route cache at interme-diate nodes, but packet header size increases due to trust information embedded in it.

The assumption of our protocol is that each node creates a trust table and maintains the trust value for its immediate neighbors. The trust value is assigned in the range from 0 to 1. A node having trust value >= 0.5, is considered as well behaved node otherwise as a malicious node. The trust value of a node is computed and updated by trust agents that reside on network nodes [7].

To decrease the routing overhead and increase the network performance all the one hop neighbors of destination unicast the RREQ packet. In DSR there is no procedure to know the one hop neighbors of destination as no next hop table is maintained. Therefore to address the above problem we maintain neighbor table as shown in table 1 at every node in MANETs. This table is used to maintain all the one hop neighbors of the intended destination. It has two fields which are destination Id in which we store the destination Id to whom the RREQ packet is designated and the other field is one hop neighbor which store the hop neighbor of the specified destination. This table is created when a new RREQ packet is received at each intermediate node.

Table 1. Neighbor table

Destination ID	One hop neighbors
30	29
30	21

Route Discovery at source node. The source node initiates a route discovery process by broadcasting a RREQ packet. The RREQ packet header is modified by adding a *p_trust* field. *p_trust* denotes the trust value of the path up to that node and is initial-ized as 0 at source node.

$$RREQ: \{IPd, IPs, Seq\ num\} \| p\_trust \tag{1}$$

After broadcasting the RREQ packet, the source node sets a timer whose time period T is equal to the 1-way propagation delay and is calculated using formula given below:

$$T = 2*TR/S + C \tag{2}$$

Where TR is maximum transmission range, S is Speed of the wireless signal, C is constant value, TR/2*S as used in our simulation. The value of timer indicates the time needed to receive a RREP packet from one hop neighbors. If the packet arrives before the timer expires, it is accepted if path length is equal to 1 else it is rejected and the neighbor table is also updated.

RREQ processing at intermediate nodes. An intermediate node is not allowed to reply from its route cache. In our method, an intermediate node forwards the RREQ packet if it received from a different node and itself is node included in the source route of RREQ to avoid route loop. Each RREQ packet is modified to include the trust value of the node from which the packet is received. For example, if there are two nodes A and B in the network, when B broadcasts a RREQ packet and node A receives it, it updates the *p_trust* field as:

$$p\_trust = p\_trust + T_{AB} \tag{3}$$

where T_{AB} is the trust value that is assigned by node A to B and signifies how much node A trusts B. An intermediate node delays the forwarding of RREQ by a time equal to the 1-way propagation delay after receiving the RREQ packet. If the intermediate node overhears a RREP packet with hop count equal to 1 before the timer expires, it and node that forwarded the RREQ packet are both one hop neighbors of destination. So the neighbor table is updated.

RREP at Destination node. The RREP packet header is modified such that it contains two fields p_trust and n_trust in addition to other fields. The updated RREP is:

$$RREP : \{IPs, IPd, Seq num\} \| p\_trust \| n\_trust \tag{4}$$

where *p_trust* is assigned from the RREQ packet received at the destination and *n_trust* is initialized to 0. It has the same significance as *p_trust* in the RREQ packet and denotes the trust value of the path up to that node from the destination.

RREP processing at intermediate nodes. When an intermediate node receives a RREP, it checks if it is the intended next recipient. If yes, it modifies *n_trust* in the same manner as *p_trust*. For example, when node X receives RREP from node Y, it updates *n_trust* as:

$$n\_trust = n\_trust + T_{XY} \tag{5}$$

The intermediate node forwards the RREP along the route in the source route of RREP. If an intermediate node overhears a RREP and it is not the intended next recipient, then it adds the first node in source route of RREP to its neighbor table. The first node in source route is the one hop neighbor of destination.

Path Selection. After the initiation of route discovery process, there arise other issues, like how to select a suitable path or a set of paths from all the discovered paths and what node should make this selection namely, the source or the destination. In our method that path is selected which induces minimum delay in the network and it does not include any misbehaving nodes. The selection process is carried at both source and destination.

Path selection at destination node: The destination node RREP for the first received RREQ satisfying equation 6. Thus the selected the path has minimum delay and having average node trust value as 0.5. So, this is fastest replied trust-worthy path also called as primary path. Afterwards, destination node sends the RREP for RREQ which are node disjoint from the primary path.

$$p\_trust / n_i >= 0.5 \tag{6}$$

where n_i is the number of nodes in i_{th} path.

Path selection at source node: When the selected RREP packet reaches the source node, the secure paths are selected. It calculates *path_trust* which is the trust value associated with the path. The *path trust* is weighted average of based on the trust values *p_trust* and *n_trust* received in the RREP packet and the number of nodes in the path as shown in equation 6, 7. The path selected is the one which has the maximum path trust.

Trust value of i_{th} path:

$$path\_trust_i = ((p\_trust + n\_trust)/2) * w_i \qquad (7)$$

$$\text{where, } w_i = 1/n_i / \sum_{i=1}^{n} 1/n_i \qquad (8)$$

$$\text{and, } path\_trust_{s-d} = \max(path\_trust_i) \qquad (9)$$

n_i is the number of nodes in i_{th} path. n is the total number of paths from s to d. w_i is the weight assigned to the i_{th} path. *path_trust$_i$* is the trust value of the i_{th} path. *path_trust$_{s-d}$* is the trust value of the path selected as the most trust-worthy path. The source node computes the *path_trust* of each of RREP received it select the path which are node disjoint and having *path_trust* greater than threshold. Through exhaustive simulation we have set threshold as 0.6.

Here we refer to the "optimal" path in sense of the path with the highest *path_trust*. The main aim of our method is enhance the secure and reliable delivery of the packet with minimized end-to-end delay. A route priority table is maintained at the source node which stores priority, next hop, *path_trust* of the packet. The path discovered are assigned priority based on the *path_trust* or we can say that:

$$Priority \; \alpha \; path\_trust \qquad (10)$$

Higher the *path_trust* value of the RREP packet higher the priority of the route. Next hop is the IP address of the first node in the source route of RREP.

3.2 Priority Level Slicing Model

At the end of the route establishment stage, every source node connects to the destination through M routes. If we deal with the whole M sets of routes concurrently, it would be very sophisticated and bewildering. So we use "priority level slicing" to gain a plain view of the connectivity graph. In "priority level slicing", the entire route graph is sliced into M layers corresponding to M priority levels. In the ith layer, only routes with i priority level are present. Fig. 1 shows the layering of a topology with two priority-level routes.

In this way, we separate M level routes into different layers and handle each layer separately. Every layer has a much simpler topology than the original one. Combining all those M layers, we get the original connectivity of the whole network. As the path discovered are node disjoint so the topology change in one layer is isolated with other layer.

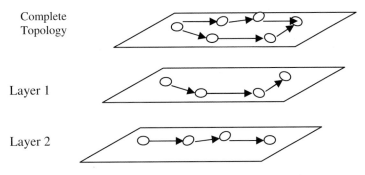

Fig. 1. Priority level slicing model

Fig. 1 shows the sliced layers of the complete network topology along with corresponding priority wise node disjoint routes extracted in each layer. Consequently, slicing facilitates the maintenance of the intricate topology due to the large amount of paths. The ad hoc network is modeled as a directed graph G = (V,E), where V is the set of vertices (nodes) and E is the set of all edges (links). Let E_p be the set of paths with priority p. The path at every layer is a directed-out tree, which is rooted at the source node to destination.

3.3 Route Utilization

Our method is designed to meet the requirements of differentiated packets. After the discovery of prioritized routes, they are used to serve this purpose. In an intuitive manner routing is performed by routing the packets at each layer according to their priorities. Upon receiving a packet the source node assign the packet priority p, based on its requirement. Afterward the route is selected from the priority routing table and the packet is routed on it. This simple method can achieve good performance under uniform traffic pattern, because no layer would experience starvation.

3.4 Route Maintenance

If a node X realizes that an established link with a neighboring node Y is broken, then it sends a Route ERRor (RERR) packet in the upstream direction of the route. The RERR contains the route to the source, and the immediate upstream and downstream nodes of the broken link. Upon receiving this RERR packet, the source removes every entry in its route table that uses the broken link (regardless of the destination). Route rediscovery is delayed as the active session is delayed if there exist at least a valid route. When the source is informed of a route disconnection, it uses the next priority route valid route to deliver data packets.

4 Performance Evaluation

In this section we discuss the performance of the proposed method based on simulation using some metrics defined here.

4.1 Simulation

We have used the QUALNET network simulator (version 4.5) developed by Scalable Network Technologies Inc. [13] to evaluate the effectiveness of the proposed method. Different scenarios are defined in a 400 * 400 m square area with 30 nodes. The source and destination nodes are randomly selected. A traffic generator was developed to simulate constant bit rate (CBR) sources. In each scenario, each node moves in a random direction using the random waypoint model [2] with a speed randomly chosen within the range of 0–20 m/s. The transmission range of each node is 100 m. We randomly choose 10 flows with the packet generation rate of 1Packet/S. The generated packet randomly chooses priority from 1 to 3. We assume that there are 0-40% malicious nodes in the network. To evaluate the performance of the proposed scheme, we use the following metrics:

- *End to End delay*: It is defined as the time taken to find the best path from source to destination, in the presence of malicious nodes.
- *Throughput*: It is the ratio of the number of data packets received by the destination node to the number of packets sent by the source node.

4.2 Results

In this section we show the results for the proposed method and compare these with those obtained from standard DSR protocol, by varying the number of malicious nodes in the network.

Throughput is defined as the number of received packets of a particular priority satisfying the specified delay requirement to the total number of packets of that priority generated by source node. Since DSR does not perform different routing for prioritized packets, its throughput is almost the same. We have shown the throughput of one of the three priorities for DSR.

When the network is free from malicious nodes the throughput of PTMDSR of packets with priority 1 is superior to DSR, but packets with lower priorities have lower throughput than DSR. Throughput for DSR steeply degrades with the increase in number of misbehaving nodes in the network as shown in Figure 4. Throughput of PTMDSR also decreases with the increase of malicious nodes but it is very less compared to DSR. PTMDSR makes effective use of its inherent multipath feature and selects the trustworthy path excluding misbehaving nodes; hence it is able to forward a large number of all its packets of different priority with minimal loss as seen in fig. 4. The packets of priority 1 are delivered through the optimal path. It leads to maximum throughput as 98% when the system is free from misbehaving nodes. The throughput of PTMDSR also degrades with the increase of misbehaving nodes in the network. But the degradation is very less compared to DSR.

For PTMDSR, packets with priority 1 have the lowest E2E delay, followed by priority 2, with priority 3 the highest. As the priority 1 packet is forwarded through the most trustworthy path so does not suffer from packet drop attack. The delay reaches its peak when 40% of the nodes in the network turn to misbehaving as shown in figure 5. However, as the trusted protocols endeavor to find the most trusted paths in the network, the selected paths may sometimes deviate considerably from the optimal

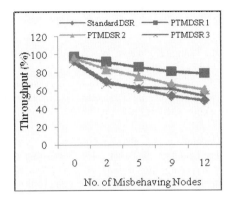

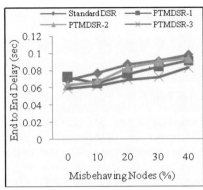

Fig. 2. Throughput   **Fig. 3.** End to End Delay

paths. This increases the length of the paths, thereby increasing the latency of the network. But the *end to end delay* of the network is lower for the multipath protocols compared to DSR, where routing decisions are only made once.

PTMDSR has the lowest end to end delay as in fig. 3 because it uses multi path simultaneously and if one of route is disconnected the data is transmitted to next available route. Hence no route acquisition latency is required. As number of misbehaving nodes increases in the network it simultaneously increases the rate of route recovery due to the attack launched by misbehaving nodes. So, end to end delay in DSR increases significantly with respect to increase in misbehaving nodes in the network. This route recovery is delayed in PTMDSR as path discovered are trust-worthy. In PTMDSR, all the paths are node disjoint so the impact of misbehavior or link failure is limited only to specified path. Due to data transmission through all the trustworthy paths, it results in less data buffering which ultimately decrease in the end to end delay.

5 Conclusion

In this paper we present a novel method which meets the challenges of differentiated routing in MANETs. It provides differentiated service to meet the demand of various applications and services. Our proposed method is able to discover a path free from misbehaving nodes which increases the network performance in data delivery and other phases. When RERR message is generated due to link breakage or due to malicious exploit done by misbehaving node, a next trust worthy route is selected from the route priority table. The route discovered are node disjoint, this lead to an advantage, as the impact of a misbehaving node is limited only to the path which includes it. The route discovery is delayed till there is a trustworthy path in route cache of source node. We have utilized multiple paths between the source and destination to satisfy the delay and reliable delivery requirements of different traffic types.

Simulation results obtained from PTMDSR are compared against the results obtained using traditional algorithm DSR. Our protocol is able to provide high throughput and lesser delay to highest priority packets in the presence of misbehaving nodes. When 40% of the nodes in the network turn to be misbehaving then also 80% of the highest priority packets are delivered.

References

1. Blake, S., Black, D., Carlson, M., Davies, E., Wang, Z., Weiss, W.: An Architecture for differentiated services. Internet draft IETF RFC 2475 (1998)
2. Broch, J., Maltz, D.A., Johnson, D.B., Hu, Y.C., Jetcheva, J.G.: A performance comparison of multihop wireless ad hoc network routing protocols. In: Proceeding of International Conference Mobile Computing and Networking (MobiCom), pp. 85–97. ACM Press, New York (1998)
3. Buchegger, S., Boudec, J.: Performance Analysis of the CONFIDANT Protocol: Cooperation of Nodes—Fairness In Distributed Ad hoc NeTworks. In: Proceeding ACM Workshop Mobile Ad Hoc Networking and Computing, Switzerland, pp. 226–236 (2006)
4. Garfinkel, S.: PGP: Pretty Good Privacy. O'Reilly and Associates, Sebastopol (1995)
5. IEEE Computer Society LAN MAN Standards Committee, Wireless LAN Medium Access Protocol (MAC) and Physical Layer (PHY) Specification, IEEE Std. 802.11-1997. The Institute of Electrical and Electronics Engineers, New York, NY (1997)
6. Johnson, D.B., Maltz, D.A., Hu, Y.C., Jetcheva, J.G.: The dynamic source routing protocol for mobile ad hoc networks (DSR). Internet draft IETF RFC 3561 (2003), http://www.ietf.org/rfc/rfc3561.txt
7. Marti, S., Giuli, T.J., Lai, K., Baker, M.: Mitigating routing misbehavior in mobile ad hoc networks. In: Proceeding of Sixth Annual International Conference Mobile Computing and Networking (MobiCom), pp. 255–265. ACM Press, New York (2000)
8. Pirzada, A.A., Datta, A., McDonald, C.: Propagating trust in ad-hoc networks for reliable routing. In: Proceeding of IEEE International Workshop Wireless Ad Hoc Networks, Finland, pp. 58–62 (2004)
9. Pirzada, A.A., Datta, A., McDonald, C.: Trust-based routing for ad-hoc wireless networks. In: Proceeding of IEEE International Conference Networks, Singapore, pp. 326–330 (2004)
10. Poonam, Garg, K., Misra, M.: Trust based multi path DSR protocol. In: Proceedings of Fifth International Conference on Availability, Reliability and Security, Poland (February 2010)
11. QUALNET simulator, http://www.scalable-networks.com
12. Yong, C., Chuanhe, H., Wenming, S.: Trusted Dynamic Source Routing Protocol. In: IEEE International Conference on Wireless Communications, Networking and Mobile Computing, Athens, Greece, pp. 1632–1636 (2007)
13. Zhou, L., Haas, Z.J.: Securing ad hoc networks. IEEE Network Magazine 13(6), 1–12 (1999)

Reducing Handoff Latency in IEEE 802.11b with the Help of Neighbor Graph Using Carrier to Interference Ratio

Debabrata Sarddar[1], Joydeep Banerjee[1], Souvik Kumar Saha[1], Utpal Biswas[2], and M.K. Naskar[1]

[1] Dept. of Electronics and Telecommunication Engg., Jadavpur University, Kolkata – 700032
`dsarddar@rediffmail.com, jogs.1989@rediff.com,`
`souviksaha@ymail.com, mrinalnaskar@yahoo.co.in`
[2] Dept. of Computer Science and Engg, University of Kalyani, Nadia, West Bengal, Pin –741235
`utpal01in@yahoo.com`

Abstract. IEEE 802.11 wireless networks have gained ever greater popularity nowadays. Handoff is a critical issue in IEEE 802.11 based wireless networks and latency in the handoff process is a major concern.

In this paper, we propose to reduce handoff latency for IEEE 802.11 wireless networks with Neighbor Graphs (NG) pre-scanning mechanisms. IEEE 802.11 uses 11 channels of which the channels 1, 6 and 11 do not mutually overlap. So these channels are expected to have a lower carrier-to-interference ratio (CI) compared to the other channels present under the same base station, which increases the channel's availability during handoff. Based on the NG pre-scanning mechanism, when handoff criterions have been met, we design an algorithm to first scan the channels 1, 6 and 11, if present under the next Access Point (AP), to reduce the scanning delay. We also introduce pre-authentication mechanism, which will effectively reduce the message processing delay.

Keywords: Handoff, Neighbor Graph, Selective channel scanning mechanism, Carrier-to-Interference (CI) Ratio.

1 Introduction

IEEE 802.11b based wireless and mobile networks [1], also called Wi-Fi commercially, are experiencing a very fast growth upsurge and are being widely deployed for providing variety of services as it is cheap, and allows anytime, anywhere access to network data. However they suffer from limited coverage range of AP, resulting in frequent handoffs, even in moderate mobility scenarios. Handoff, an inherent problem with wireless networks, particularly real time applications, has not been well addressed in IEEE 802.11, which takes a hard handoff approach [2]. Here a mobile host (MH) has to break its connection with its old access point (AP) before connecting to a new AP, resulting in prolonged handoff latency called link switching delay. Now-a-days, soft handoff procedure is in use. Here a mobile node is connected to its old AP

N. Meghanathan et al. (Eds.): NeCoM, WiMoN, and WeST 2010, CCIS 90, pp. 421–430, 2010.

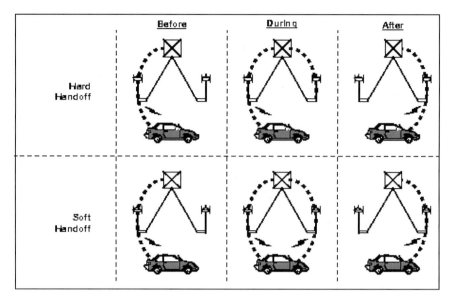

Fig. 1. Diagram showing mechanism of hard and soft handoff

till it makes connection with the new AP. This effectively reduces the packet losses incurred by hard handoff. A schematic diagram showing hard and soft hand off is given in Fig1 taken from [3].

With the advent of real time applications, the latency and packet loss caused by mobility became an important issue in Mobile Networks. The most relevant topic of discussion is to reduce the IEEE 802.11 link-layer handoff latency. IEEE 802.11 MAC specification [4] defines two operation modes: *ad hoc* and *infrastructure mode*. In the ad hoc mode, two or more stations (STAs) recognize each other through beacons and hence establish a peer-to-peer relationship. In infrastructure mode, an AP provides network connectivity to its associated STAs to form a Basic Service Set (BSS). Multiple APs form an Extended Service Set (ESS) that constructs the same wireless networks.

IEEE 802.11 standards for wireless LAN function on physical and lap layers; as IEEE 802.11b standard is compatible with the 802.11g standard; we focus on the former, since the proposed architecture also holds for 802.11g with slight changes. 802.11b uses 11 of 14 possible channels distributed over the range from 2.402GHz to

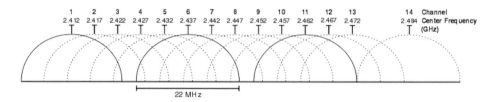

Fig. 2. The channel distribution diagram for IEEE 802.11 standards

2.483 GHz (as in Fig 2) with each channel being 22 MHz wide. Of these channels 1, 6 and 11 do not overlap.

We now describe the handoff procedure with its various phases.

1.1 Handover Process

The complete handoff procedure can be divided into 3 distinct logical parts: scanning, authentication and re-association. In the first phase, an STA scans for AP's by either sending Probe Request messages or by listening for beacon message. After scanning all channels, an AP is selected using the Received Signal Strength Indication (RSSI) and CI ratio, and the selected AP exchanges IEEE 802.11 authentication messages with the STA. Finally, if the AP authenticates the STA, the STA sends Re-association Request message to the new AP.

1.2 Scanning

Scanning can be divided into *active* and *passive* scans. During an active scan, the STA broadcasts a probe request packet asking all APs in those specific channels to impart their existence and capability with a probe response package. In a passive scan, the STA listen passively for the beacons bearing all necessary informations like beacon interval, capability information, supported rate etc. about an AP. The active scans introduce two parameters:

'*Min Channel Time*' represents the arrival time of the first probe response. So a client must listen for this period of time to decide whether there are any APs on this channel. It is recommended to be set as 3-7 ms.

'*Max Channel Time*' is the estimated time to collect all probe responses. It is supposed to be of the magnitude of tens of milliseconds. For all practical implementation, the maximum channel time is set to 30 ms [5].

1.3 Authentication

Authentication is necessary prior to association. Authentication must either immediately proceed to association or must immediately follow a channel scan cycle. In pre-authentication schemes, the MN authenticates with the new AP immediately after the scan cycle finishes. Exchanging null authentication frames takes about 1-2 ms.

1.4 Re-association

Re-association is a process for transferring associations from one AP to another. Once the STA has been authenticated with the new AP, re-association can be started. Previous works has shown re-association delay to be around 1-2 ms.

The overall delay is the summation of scanning delay, authentication delay, and re-association delay. According to [5], 90% of handoff delay comes from scanning delay. The range of scanning delay is given by "$N \times T_{min} \leq T_{scan} \leq N \times T_{max}$", where N is the total number of channels according to the spectrum released by a country, T_{min} is Min Channel Time, T_{scan} is the total measured scanning delay, and T_{max} is Max Channel Time. Here we focus on reducing the scanning delay.

The total handoff process is shown is Fig 3.

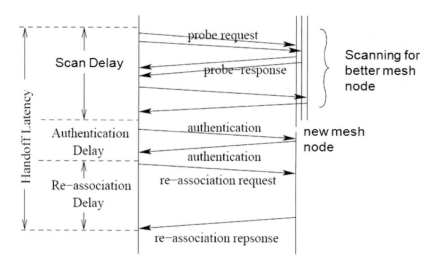

Fig. 3. The total handoff process in brief

We divide our paper into the following sections: Section-2 discusses the related works in this field; the proposed method is explained in Section-3. Section-4 discusses our simulations and experimental results, followed by conclusions and future works, and finally the references.

2 Related Works

Most of the related works focus on reducing this delay in the scan phase, as delay in the potential phase is hardware dependent and in the authentication phase is negligible in an open wireless environment. The process of AP scan and reconnection is intolerably slow, of the order of 200-300 ms or even longer, of which 80-90% delay is attributed to *probe delay* [4]. In real scenario, it is seen that maximum handoff latency for Voice over IP (VoIP) applications is 50 ms [5]. To reduce handoff latency in wireless LAN using IAPP [7], an algorithm on context transfer mechanism using 'Neighbor Graph' (NG) [4] was suggested in [7]. However, IAPP was only reactive in nature and creates an additional delay in a handoff. One approach on Physical layer (PHY) is the method using two trans-receivers, where a wireless mobile node (MN) has two Wireless Network Interface Cards (WNICs) [4], one for keeping connection to current AP and the other for scanning channels to search for alternate APs [8].

In this paper, we propose a selective scanning mechanism using NG to solve the problem of handoff latency. CI ratio forms an essential part in channel selection process during handoff, though traffic plays a more dominant role. IEEE 802.11b uses 11 channels out of 14 possible channels, of which only channels 1,6,11 do not mutually overlap. So these channels will have a very low interference with other frequency. It may have a noticeable interference only if the same channel is used by any other APs within its frequency re-use range. Thus it is quite evident that these channels will have a high probability of having a greater CI ratio as compared to the other channels within the same AP. So based on this fact, when the MN responds to handoff, according to the pre-scanning mechanism of NG, it first looks for the potential AP and then first scans the channels 1, 6 and 11, if present. If this fails, it will start scanning the other channels. In addition, we propose to reduce the authentication delay by pre-authentication method, where the authentication process is performed during the scan phase.

3   Proposed Method

The maximum range up to which the signal can be transmitted is determined by the height of the antenna and the power of the signal is inversely proportional to the square of the distance from the AP. But due to fading, the signal strength is never equally spread in all direction even for an omni-directional antenna. There are mainly two types of fading responsible for the uneven distribution of the signal strength from the AP. They are namely *fast fading* (fading due to scattering of the signal by object near transmitter) and *slow fading* (fading due to long term spatial and temporal variations). Ideally without fading, the cell's coverage area would be circular, but due to fading it becomes an undefined contour. Signal strength contours for two APs operating in ideal condition without fading is given in Fig 4 (a) and operating in real condition with fading is given in Fig 4 (b) both of which are taken from [3] . Here we define the coverage area of each AP to be concentrated within a hexagon of certain edge length, which is the best approximation so far considering uneven distribution of signal.

The same frequency band or channel used in a cell can be reused by another cell as long as the cells are far apart and the signal strength does not interfere with each other (this mechanism is shown in Fig 5 where the three yellow marked cells can use the same frequency channel to avoid frequency interference). Thus frequency channels are allocated in such a way that the interference due to any two neighboring APs, i.e., the co-channel interference is minimum. But within a cell, the channels used may be mutually overlapped and this may lead to interference within the same AP. We cannot reduce both the types of interference simultaneously. But for optimizing it to a minimum value, the channel allocation protocol is designed in such a way so that at least one of channels 1, 6 and 11 are made available to each AP. This is due to the fact that the channels 1, 6 and 11 are mutually non-overlapping. Due to increasing traffic, the need of greater frequency range is realized. Hence, by implementing the above procedure, we can thus use a maximum number of channels in one AP with at least one channel having minimum interference even in regions where signal strength is very low, thereby increasing the net *signal to noise ratio* (SNR).

Now handoff is primarily dependent upon signal strength received and the CI ratio. The term CI ratio is the ratio between the frequency band allocated to the MN and the interference associated with this frequency band. Thus as per our theory, channels 1, 6 and 11 are expected to have a greater CI ratio than the others. So, during handoff, if we scan channels 1, 6 and 11, if present, first, then there will be a greater probability that the call is transferred to any of these channels of the next AP. So based on CI ratio, it is seen that scanning non over-lapping channels is better for reducing the latency due to scanning delay.

Second generation wireless systems and most of the research works follow Frequency Division Multiple Access (FDMA) or Time Division Multiple Access (TDMA) for multiple access of a single channel frequency band. In TDMA, one channel is used by several users, with AP assigning time slots for different users, and each user is served in a round-robin method. In FDMA, the allocated frequency band for one channel is subdivided into many sub-bands and each sub-band is allocated by the AP to each user. Thus, in FDMA, it may be seen that a particular sub-band is allocated to a user which falls between the interference zones of channels within the same AP. Thus, protocols using FDMA techniques have a certain probability that during handoff, even when the channel is free, the user is allocated such a sub-band within the above mentioned region. Thus, it will encounter a very low CI ratio and the MN ceases to operate on that channel and scans for the next channel. During scanning of the non over-lapping channels, this problem will not be faced. So our method works even better in cases where FDMA is used for multiple access of a single channel.

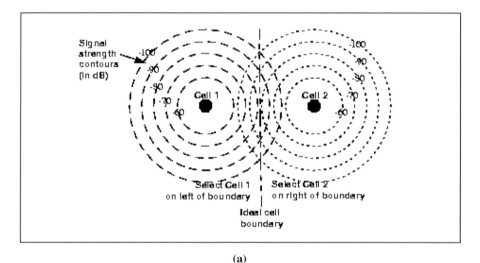

(a)

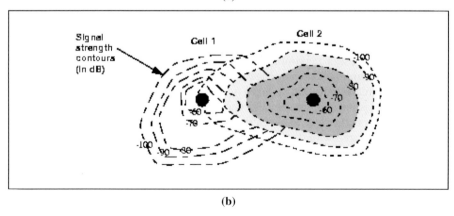

(b)

Fig. 4. (a) It shows the distribution of signal strength of APs in ideal condition ; (b) It shows the distribution of signal strength of APs in real condition

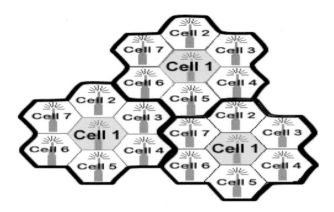

Fig. 5. Diagram representing cells that can use the same frequency channels

With these assumptions, we propose (i) a selective channel scan, as in [4], and (ii) pre-authentication scheme with the help of neighbor graph for reducing the total handoff delay.

3.1 Selective Channel Scanning

As in [3], the MN downloads from the server the data which not only contains the neighbor of the AP on which it is presently operating, but also the channels used by the neighboring APs. However the MN must wait for min channel time or max channel time as the MN does not know how many APs would respond to the probe request. So here we use unicast instead of broadcast which selects the potential APs to which the call may be handed off and scans only the channels associated with those APs. Selective channel probing with the help of unicast instead of broadcast brilliantly reduces the handoff delay by a massive percentage when compared with selective scanning or basic active scanning. Moreover, it was also stated that the MN has to wait for only the *'round trip time'* (rtt) for scanning each channel instead of the min channel time or the max channel time. We know that IEEE uses 11 out of the 14 possible channels, out of which 1, 6 and 11 are mutually non-overlapping. When the MN responds to handoff, according to the pre-scanning mechanism of NG, it first looks for the potential AP and then first scans the channels 1, 6 and 11 if present. If this fails, it will start scanning the other channels. As proposed in [4], the expected scanning delay using selective scanning is $t = N' \times \tau + \alpha$, where 't' is the scanning delay, N' is the number of channels scanned, 'τ' is the round trip time and α is the message processing time. 'τ' is the summation of the time taken for the Probe Request to be sent to the selected AP's and for the Probe Response to be received, which, in our case, is nothing but the Min Channel Time, which has been estimated to be around 3-7 ms.

3.2 Pre Authentication

To reduce the message processing delay, authentication is done during scanning phase. By this method, the authentication delay vanishes and the message processing delay, α, is composed only of the re-association time. Thus the parameter 'α' is reduced by at least half of its initial value and hence the net time delay, t, as proposed in [3], is greatly reduced. This can be implemented as proposed in [9] and [10].

Thus, the authentication time, which was very minute in proportion as compared to scanning phase delay of previous methods, would now command a greater percent of time delay, because, in our case, the scanning phase delay has been much reduced. However, by the process of pre-authentication, even this delay is nullified. So our method reduces the net handoff latency by a great extent as compared to the previous proposed methods. The experimental results are given in the forthcoming section. It gives a brief overview of the simulation process and the results obtained conform to our theory.

4 Experimental Results

For the simulation part, we used a 2D-plane with APs on centre of hexagons packed together. The heights of each antenna were considered to be the same and the topology distribution was also considered to be similar. We used hexagons for specifying the range of the APs as hexagons can fit side by side like honey combs and is mainly used by all research workers for this category of simulations. The frequency was allocated as per the protocols that are generally followed in frequency allocation in IEEE 802.11 standards. Calls originate on a memory less basis, that is, they follow Poisson distribution function and use the channel within the AP on whose range the call is created. The channel allocated to it is determined by the AP. The channel allocation is considered to be static and FDMA was used for multiple accesses. The CI ratio was calculated for each channel within each AP which is an important parameter for our method. Moreover, separate CI ratios were calculated for all the sub bands when a single channel was used by multiple users. The sub bands' CI ratio takes into account the CI ratio of the channel on which the multiple access is carried on. Now, we considered various instances of time where there is a case where a randomly generated MN has a need for handoff. The different parameters, like the number of existing MNs in the two APs, the CI ratios etc. at that instance of time were taken into consideration. Then we applied our method, i.e, the MN first looks for the potential AP and then first scans the channels 1, 6 and 11 if present. If this fails, it will start scanning the other channels. We also neglect the authentication delay as pre-authentication was done during the scan phase. We considered the round trip time to be 3 ms and the message processing time which comprises of only the re-association time was neglected to carry out our calculations.

We made a sample run of our simulation and calculated the time required for handoff at regular intervals of time. We calculated 100 such instances and calculated the total time required for the handoff to take place. From a particular sample run we got the average time delay for all 100 instances as 6.1129 ms. The graph of this simulation is plotted in Fig 6, which shows the various handoff delay times in the 'Y' axis in milliseconds, for each instance, which is shown in the 'X' axis. The variation of results obtained from other simulation was negligible. So we can consider that our method reduces the net handoff delay to a minimum of around 6 ms in the best case which is much lower than the previous results.

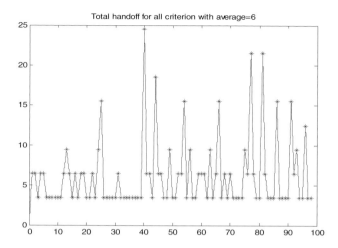

Fig. 6. Graph showing the handoff delays at various instances

5 Conclusion and Future Work

In this paper, we claim our contributions as discussed. Firstly, we have discussed a pre-scanning procedure using channels 1, 6 and 11, which greatly reduces the scanning time. Here, we have set a best scenario time of about 6 ms, which is an improvement on the best scenario time of 18 ms previously set [9]. Secondly, we have used pre-authentication in which the STA authenticates the new AP just after the scanning phase, thus minimizing the message processing delay.

Our discussion is based on IEEE 802.11b standard, even though the proposed set-up is also valid for IEEE 802.11g with minor adjustments.

As is evident, the discovery phase is still the most time consuming phase of the handoff process. Future simulations may be done using different topologies with modifications regarding selective scanning and pre-authentication using IAPP.

Moreover, our method works best in networks where FDMA is used for multiple accesses. Though networks using TDMA has also reduced handoff latency by this method, but still in the best case scenario, the net time delay is a bit more than that of networks using FDMA. So, further research work can be done in this field.

We have considered link layer handoff delay only. For intra-system handoff, a bit more time will be required due to increase in message processing delay. Though we have nullified the authentication delay, yet the re-association delay cannot be neglected while doing the simulations. But for this case, as the re-association delay is very small as compared to the handoff delay, so we can neglect it for our experimental results.

References

1. Wireless LAN Medium Access Control (MAC) and Physical Layer (PHY) Specifications. IEEE Standards (1999)
2. Puangkor, W., Pongpaibool, P.: A Survey of Techniques for Reducing Handover Latency and Packet Loss in Mobile IPv6

3. Taylor, M.S., Waung, W., Banan, M.: Internetwork Mobility The CDPD Approach. Pearson Education, Inc., London
4. Kim, H.-S., Park, S.H., Park, C.-S., Kim, J.W., Ko, S.-J.: Selective Channel Scanning for Fast Handoff in Wireless LAN using Neighbor Graph (July 2004)
5. Teng, J., Xu, C., Jia, W., Xuan, D.: D-scan: Enabling Fast and Smooth Handoffs in AP-dense 802.11 Wireless Networks
6. Zhai, H., Chen, X., Fang, Y.: How well can the IEEE 802.11 wireless lan support quality of service? IEEE Transactions on Wireless Communications 4(6), 3084–3094 (2005)
7. Huang, P.-J., Tseng, Y.-C.: A Fast Handoff Mechanism for IEEE 802.11 and IAPP Networks
8. Ohta, M.: Smooth Handover over IEEE 802.11 Wireless LAN, Internet Draft: draft-ohta-smooth-handover-wlan-00.txt (June 2002)
9. Powar, Y.A., Apte, V.: Improving the IEEE 802.11 MAC Layer Handoff Latency to Support Multimedia Traffic
10. Kim, E.-D., Ahn, D.-K., Kim, S.-Y., Cho, S.-J.: Improvement of Pre-authentication with Neighbor Graph for Fast Handoff in WLANs
11. Mishra, A., Shin, M., Arbaugh, W.: An Empirical Analysis of the IEEE 802.11 Mac Layer Handoff Process. In: ACM SIGCOM 2003 (April 2003)
12. IEEE, part 11: Wireless LAN Medium Access Control (MAC) and Physical Layer (PHY) Specification. IEEE Standard 802.11 (1999)

To Alleviate Congestion Using Hybrid Sink for Delay Sensitive Applications in Wireless Sensor Networks

Thanigaivelu K. and Murugan K.

Ramanujan Computing Centre, Anna University Chennai, Tamil Nadu, India
thanigaivelukotiswaran@gmail.com, murugan@annauniv.edu

Abstract. The Congestion in Wireless Sensor Networks is significantly higher and thus severely affects the network performance leading to increased data loss and end to end delay. In a normal scenario a static sink collects data from the entire network but this approach results in high traffic load in the sink's vicinity. To alleviate this problem a mobile sink is introduced in addition to already existing static sink for data collection from the network. Since the mobile sink travels through the network area, the sensor nodes deliver the data whenever the mobile sink comes near its vicinity. By this hybrid sink approach method along with efficient data collection algorithm not only reduces bottleneck around the static sink but also decreases end to end delay. This hybrid sink approach where a combination of a static sink and a mobile sink could be useful in delay sensitive applications. Analysis and simulation results show that Hybrid sink approach along with efficient data collection algorithm performs significantly better than a static sink.

Keywords: Congestion, Wireless sensor networks, Hybrid sink.

1 Introduction

Wireless sensor network (WSN) is one of the emerging fields that provide a wide variety of applications such as disaster prevention, environment monitoring, medical monitoring, habitat monitoring, military surveillance, inventory tracking, intelligent logistics, and health monitoring [1]. Sensor networks can be seen as a large collection of small wireless devices that can organize themselves in an ad hoc manner capable of sensing environmental conditions within their range and have constrained energy, processing and communication resources. Normally a sensor node periodically collects data from its target area and route data towards a sink. Since, a wireless sensor network lacks infrastructure the sensor nodes must organize themselves in order to create routes that lead to a sink. Therefore, several nodes are used in order to deliver a single packet to a remote sink. Each sensor node is equipped with a limited amount of storage, so if at any given routing node the data collection rate dominates the data forwarding rate congestion starts to build up at this node. Such type of congestion and data loss normally occurs at the nodes located in the vicinity of a static sink. Sensor nodes closer to the sink will drain their energy and use more resources than other nodes in the network, simply because they are in the path of many routes to the sink. As a result, the

N. Meghanathan et al. (Eds.): NeCoM, WiMoN, and WeST 2010, CCIS 90, pp. 431–438, 2010.

static sink's neighboring nodes will suffer from high congestion and packet losses. A mobile sink approach will not only remove the burden of the nodes closer to a sink, but it will provide a mechanism to reach and collect data from network areas that are disconnected as well as reducing the congestion near the sink. With the advances of wireless networks and the widespread use of thin mobile handhelds such as cellular phones and personal digital assistants (PDAs), a feasible strategy is employed where handhelds devices could be used as sensor data collectors (mobile sinks). The mobile sink is able to collect data from the proximity nodes at very low cost, usually involving one-hop communications. But the disadvantage using a mobile sink is there is latency or delay involved to collect data. This is because a single mobile sink does take more time to travel through the network to collect data. Hence this approach will not be suitable for applications which are delay sensitive. Hybrid sink approach is proposed wherein a combination of static sink and mobile sink is employed. This approach decreases congestion, traffic load and collisions near the static sink since the number of hops traversed by a packet in order to reach the sink is decreased significantly. Performance metrics like end to end delay, throughput and packet drop are evaluated using static sink and compared with hybrid sink. The rest of the paper is organized as follows: Related Work is discussed in section 2, proposed work is discussed in Section 3, Simulation scenario and metrics in Section 4, Simulation result and analysis in section 5 and finally, conclusions and future work are in Section 6.

2   Related Work

The problem of relieving or preventing congestion near the sink in a WSN has recently received increased attention. In this section, related work is reviewed on mobile sinks for data collection in Wireless Sensor Networks. Mobility in sensor networks has been introduced in a number of new applications as in [2] to increase the network lifetime. Different techniques have been proposed such as a using mobile sink to pick up traffic from near by sensors as it moves (also termed data mules) [3, 2]. In [4], the authors aim at assessing how local parameters such as the number of sources, the buffer size and the retransmission timeout, can be varied to globally decrease network congestion. A similar approach to congestion control is Event-to-Sink Reliable Transport (ESRT) [5]. If a node's queue level exceeds a certain value, the node notifies the sink, which in turn asks all sources to decrease their sending rate. Multi hop or multipath routing techniques utilize the dense deployment of the sensor nodes to remove congestion from WSNs. These techniques enable the routing nodes to find alternate routing paths to reach the desired destination in case of congestion at a routing link. The idea is that when a routing node senses increased data traffic and packets start to drop, it requests the neighboring nodes to become part of the routing scheme, thus creating a multi path routing topology to share the data traffic and eliminate congestion from the network [6]. Chen et al. [7] presented a congestion avoidance scheme that is based on the idea that at any given point of time client nodes have complete information about the buffer status of their parent node. Therefore, in case of congestion the client node either reduces the data that it is forwarding to the parent node or switches to some other parent node. In [8] the authors uses Beacon Based Data Collection (BBDC) algorithm for data collection using mobile sink to reduce energy dissipation and increase throughput. In [9] congestion is handled by rerouting packets to avoid hotspots while packet dropping is implemented otherwise. Majid I. Khan [10] addresses these problems by introducing a mobile sink based routing scheme for congestion avoidance and energy efficient routing in wireless sensor networks. The proposed scheme utilizes the sink mobility and an in-network storage model that is used to set up mini-sinks along the mobility trajectory of the sink. Kyriakos Karenos [11] study the problem of congestion avoidance in the context of sensor networks with a mobile sink. [12] Proposes a solution to the problem of deploying mobile data collectors in order to alleviate the high traffic load and resulting bottleneck in a sink's vicinity caused by static sink approaches.

3 Proposed Work

In a typical WSN scenario, all the data are routed back to the only static sink. Therefore, those nodes near the sink have to forward all the data from farther nodes and thus carry a heavier traffic load. This approach results in high traffic load in the sink's vicinity as the packets are forwarded to the sink. As all network traffic converges to this point, congestion builds up. To alleviate this problem Hybrid sink along with efficient data collection algorithm is employed, thereby reducing the congestion at the nodes closer to the static sink. A more detailed explanation is given in subsequent sections.

3.1 Wireless Sensor Network Model

To deliver a single message, the resources of many sensor nodes are used and a lot of energy is spent. A novel approach is catching momentum because of important applications that of having a mobile sink move inside the network area and collect the data with low energy cost. An efficient, scalable and robust data collection in wireless sensor networks is proposed in this model. A Network scenario of deploying N wireless sensor nodes is considered in a region of square region A. The sensor nodes are randomly scattered across the region A. Two approaches are considered here. One is using static sink alone and another one using both static and mobile sink. In the first approach a single static sink S alone is responsible for collecting data from all sensor nodes and it acts as a gateway for the sensor network. In the second approach mobile sink is employed along with static sink. It is assumed that the mobile sink is not energy and resource constrained. A sensor node communicates with its one-hop neighbors using its wireless radio resources. Each node is assumed to have transmission range R. Data propagation takes place in a multi-hop process. A efficient data collection scheme is proposed for hybrid sink which is explained in next section.

3.2 Algorithm for Data Collection

A mobile sink moving at a velocity v, and capable of communicating with wireless sensor nodes is introduced into the monitored area A. As the mobile sink moves around the network area it starts sending a beacon signal that carries the sink ID and a hop field h that indicates the hop level. Initially the sink starts broadcasting with initial hop count h = 1 and time to live TTL= t. Each sensor node have a table that carries its own hop level hs which indicate the number of hops a node is away from a static sink as well as next hop address in order to reach static sink. After receiving initial hop count value, the sensor node compares the field h and its own hop level h_s in order to decide whether to forward the message or simply to drop the packet. If h < h_s, the node will broadcast to its one hop neighbors after incrementing hop count by one and decrementing TTL by one. Those sensor nodes which received this message increments hop level h = h + 1 and broadcast this beacon message. Before broadcasting it updates the destination address field to reach the sink with its destination address along with sink ID. Once TTL reaches value 0, then nodes stops broadcasting. In case h > h_s, the node just drops the packet. At the end of this process, it looks like a small cluster tree with roots at the mobile sink. TTL ensures that beacon message is not propagated endlessly in the network. Each node has enough routing information to relay data packets to a sink. In other words, each node has a routing table entry that specifies the destination, i.e., neighbor's address, of the data packets in order to reach the sink specified by the field sink ID. The intermediate nodes will forward the message until it reaches the mobile sink. Since the mobile sink travels through the network, the sensor nodes deliver the data whenever the mobile sink comes near its vicinity. But since the mobile sink takes more time to reach the same point again, then the sensor node would have to wait that much amount of time to forward the packet. Hence in delay sensitive applications where it becomes very essential to send data immediately and the mobile sink is not in its vicinity, then sensor node makes a decision to deliver the data to the static sink. In this data collection scheme, the sensor node chooses the sink which require minimum number of hops thereby reducing the end to end delay.

3.3 Moving Scheme

In this work, performance metrics like delivery delay, packet drop and throughput are evaluated under Random Waypoint mobility pattern [13] where the mobile sink can move randomly towards all directions at varying speeds. S_{random} is defined as a function that implements random walk in this Network scenario. At each invocation S_{random} selects a random uniform angle in $[-\pi, +\pi]$ radians. This angle defines the deviation from the mobile sink's current direction. The speed of the movement is constant and predefined. The new position is determined by S_{random} which selects a uniform random distance d $\in$ (0, d $_{max}$) which is the distance to travel along the newly defined direction. This model includes pause times between changes in destination and speed. A mobile sink begins by staying in one location for a certain period of time (i.e., a pause time). Once this time expires, the mobile sink chooses a random destination in the simulation area and a speed that is uniformly distributed. The node then travels toward the newly chosen destination at the selected speed. Upon arrival, it pauses for a specified time period before starting the process again. Periodically a beacon message is transmitted from the sink. Each sensor node that receives a beacon attempts to acquire the medium and transmit the cached data to the sink. Transmitted data is then removed from a sensor node cache to free the memory for storing incoming sensed data. In this scenario, it is assumed that the sink and sensor nodes know their own geographic locations, by either GPS services or self-configuring localization techniques. Sensor nodes can obtain the location information of their one-hop neighbors by broadcasting notification messages. Sensor nodes receive the position notification from the sink. All sensor nodes that are away from the sink would report their data to the sink by multi-hop manner.

4   Simulation Scenario and Metrics

In order to evaluate and validate the performance of the proposed work, simulation was carried out using NS-2[14]. Sensor nodes are scattered across an area of 200×200m. All nodes have radio transmission range of 25m. The number of data source nodes is set to 50, and they are chosen randomly from the sensor field. Each source node generates 2 packets per second during the entire simulation. Simulation parameters are shown in Table 1. The performance was evaluated from different aspects, but always focusing on end to end delay, throughput and packet drop. The metrics used were:

- Average End-to-End delay: The end-to-end packet   delivery delay measured in seconds from the source node to the sink.
- Throughput: the ratio of the number of messages generated by sensor nodes to packets received by sink
- Packet drop: Number of packets received by the sink to the number of packets sent by source node

Table 1. Simulation Parameters

PARAMETER	VALUE
Number of nodes	Variable
Simulation Area	200x200
Wireless radio range	25m
Source node data rate	2pkts/sec
No of static sink	1
No of Mobile sink (hybrid)	1
Mobile sink velocity	5m/s
Packet size	512Bytes
Tx power dissipation	0.0148W
Rx power dissipation	0.0125W

5   Simulation Result and Analysis

The experimental results show that the Hybrid sink approach performs better than static sink for all the performance metrics including throughput, end-to-end delay and packet drop of a node. It is seen in general from Fig. 1, 2 and 3 that both in hybrid and static sink approach as the number of sensor nodes increases, the percentage throughput decreases, End to End delay increases and packet drop increases. The reason could be attributed to the fact that as number of sensor nodes increases more

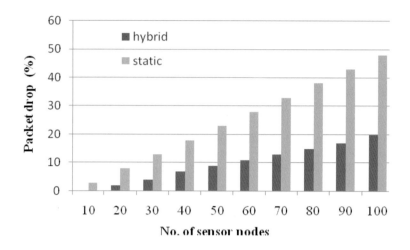

Fig. 1. Impact of Hybrid and Static sink on Packet drop

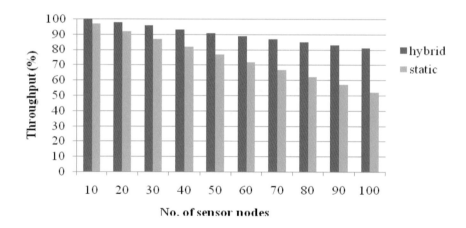

Fig. 2. Impact of Hybrid and Mobile sink on Throughput

number of packets is generated in the network. Figure 1 shows the percentage of packet dropped with respect to varying number of nodes ranging from 10 to 100. The percentage packet drop is less in case of Hybrid approach than that of Static sink approach because the traffic load is shared due to the addition of Mobile sink. Also, the number of hops required to reach the sink is reduced with introduction of the Mobile sink. The Fig 2 shows the percentage of throughput with respect to varying number of nodes. Hybrid sink approach performs better than static mainly because it reduces the number of hops traversed by data packets. This implies less traffic and, consequently, it reduces congestion near the sink as the nodes have the option of either sending data either to static or mobile sink. In Fig 3, End to end delay with respect to varying number of nodes, it is seen that end-to-end delay using hybrid sink is almost 50% lesser than single static approach. Again the reason could be that mobile sink takes the burden off from the static sink. End to end delay is further reduced using efficient data collection scheme because of the following reasons. One is the formation of cluster tree around the mobile sink which facilitates more nodes to send data to mobile sink in less time. Also the Network region covered to collect data by mobile sink is more and nodes choose the sink with fewer hops. After analyzing these results it is seen that hybrid sink approach with efficient data collection scheme performs better than that of static sink for various performance metrics and subsequently reduces congestion at the nodes in the vicinity of the sink.

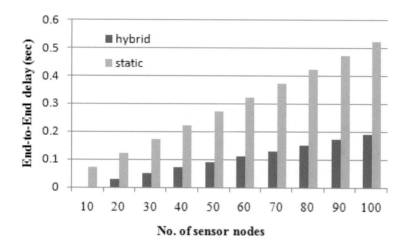

Fig. 3. Impact of Hybrid and static sink on End to End Delay

6 Conclusions and Future Work

In a typical WSN scenario, all the data are routed back to a static sink. Nodes near the sink have to forward all the data from nodes that are away from the sink and thus carry a heavier traffic load. Hybrid sink approach performs better than that of Static sink approach because the traffic load is shared due to the addition of Mobile sink. Also for delay sensitive applications where it becomes very essential to send data immediately but the mobile sink is not in its vicinity, then sensor node makes a decision to deliver the data to the static sink. This way the end to end delay is reduced. Analysis and simulation results show that using hybrid sink along with efficient data collection scheme significantly performs better than static sink for all metrics evaluated. It is further planned to study the impact of path length of mobile sink for data collection with respect to network area and for different node distributions in the network.

References

1. Akyildiz, Su, W., Sankarasubramaniam, Y., Cayirci, E.: Wireless sensor networks: a survey. Journal of Computer Networks 38, 393–422 (2002)
2. Shah, R., Roy, S., Jain, S., Brunette: Data mules: Modeling a three-tier architecture for sparse sensor networks. In: Proc. of IEEE SNPA, Seattle, WA, pp. 215–233 (2003)

3. Kansal, A., Somasundara, A.A., Jea, D.D., Srivastava, M.B., Estrin, D.: Intelligent fluid infrastructure for embedded networks. In: Proc. of 2nd Int'l. conference on Mobile systems, applications, and services, Boston, MA, pp. 111–124 (2004)

4. Vuran, M., Gungor, V., Akan, Ö.B.: On the interdependence of congestion and contention in wireless sensor networks. In: Proc. of ACM SenMetrics, San Diego, CA, July 2005, pp. 136–147 (2005)

5. Akan, O.B., Akyildiz, I.F.: Event–to–sink reliable transport in wireless sensor networks. IEEE/ACM Trans. Networking 13, 1003–1016 (2005)

6. Cerpa, A., Estrin, D.: ASCENT: Adaptive Self-Configuring Sensor Networks Topologies. The IEEE Transactions on Mobile Computing, Special Issue on Mission-Oriented Sensor Networks 3(3), 272–285 (2004)

7. Chen, S., Yang, N.: Congestion avoidance based on lightweight buffer management in sensor networks. IEEE Transactions on Parallel and Distributed Systems 17(9), 934–946 (2006)

8. Thanigaivelu, K., Murugan, K.: Reduced energy dissipation using Beacon Based Data Collection algorithm for mobile sink in Wireless Sensor networks. In: Proc of First International conference on Advanced computing (ICAC 2009), pp. 112–115 (2009)

9. Wang, C., Sohraby, K., Li, B.: Sentcp: A hop-by-hop congestion control protocol for wireless sensor networks. In: IEEE INFOCOM 2005 (Poster), Miami, FL, pp. 107–114 (2005)

10. Khan, M.I., Gansterer, W.N., Haring, G.: Congestion Avoidance and Energy Efficient Routing Protocol for Wireless Sensor Networks with a Mobile Sink. Journal of Networks 2(6), 42–49 (2007)

11. Karenos, K., Kalogeraki, V.: Facilitating Congestion Avoidance in Sensor Networks with a Mobile Sink. In: Proc 28th IEEE International Real-Time Systems Symposium (RTSS 2007), pp. 321–332 (2007)

12. Pazzi, R.W.N., Boukerche, A.: Mobile data collector strategy for delay-sensitive applications over wireless sensor networks. Journal of Computer Communications 31, 1028–1039 (2008)

13. Camp, T., Boleng, J., Davies, V.: A Survey of Mobility Models or Ad Hoc Network Research. Wireless Communication & Mobile Computing (WCMC): Special issue on Mobile Ad Hoc Networking: Research, Trends and Applications 2(5), 483–502 (2002)

14. NS-2 – The Network Simulator version 2.30, http://www.isi.edu/nsnam/ns/

Comparison of Cooperative Caching Strategies in Mobile Ad-Hoc Network (MANET)

G. Radhamani and S. Umamaheswari

School of Information Technology and Science,
Dr. G.R. Damodaran College of Science, Coimbatore, India
{radhamanig,akalyauma}@hotmail.com

Abstract. A mobile ad-hoc network (MANET) is a self-configuring network of mobile nodes. MANETs are hindred by intermittent network connections, restricted power supplies, and limited computing resources. These restrictions raise several new challenges for data access applications with the respect to data availability and access efficiency. Data caching addresses these challenges in MANETs to improve the efficiency of information access. *Cooperative caching* improves system performance because it allows sharing and coordination of cached data among multiple mobile users in the network. This paper aims to classify and compare existing cooperative caching strategies for MANETs based on their performance metrics such as query latency and cache hit ratio.

Keywords: Ad hoc networks, cooperative caching, cache replacement.

1 Introduction

A *mobile ad-hoc network* (MANET) is a self-configuring network of mobile nodes. All the nodes are routers connected via wireless links. The routers are free to move and organize themselves arbitrarily, thus, the network topology may change rapidly and unpredictably. Such a network may operate in a standalone manner, or may be connected to the larger Internet or may be used as a hybrid wireless network.

MANETs has drawn much attention in recent years due to the flexible networking solution it provides. In such networks, mobile nodes, typically battery-powered, communicate with each other through wireless medium and multi-hop routes. However, data access applications in MANETs have to face lower data availability and higher access cost caused by the special features of MANETs: wireless medium, multi-hop routing, dynamic topologies, and resource constraints.

In MANETs accessing services and data over the network can be very slow and hence, caching frequently accessed data is an effective technique for improving performance. If caching data on one device is used by itself, this mechanism does not provide a consistent framework for allowing all other devices in the network to benefit from this data. Therefore, devising an effective caching strategy for the whole MANET is of special importance since it allows for improving the performance of the network as a whole.

N. Meghanathan et al. (Eds.): NeCoM, WiMoN, and WeST 2010, CCIS 90, pp. 439–446, 2010.
© Springer-Verlag Berlin Heidelberg 2010

Caching: Caching is to copy a portion of the data from the data provider to a smaller and faster storage device (cache) interposed between the data consumer and the data provider, so that future data accesses can be resolved from the cache with less cost.

Significance of Caching: With caching, the data access delay is reduced since data access requests can be served from the local cache, thereby obviating the need for data transmission over the scarce wireless links. However, caching techniques used in one-hop mobile environment may not be applicable to multi-hop ad hoc environment since the data or request may need to go through multiple hops. Variable data size, frequent data updates, limited client resources, insufficient wireless bandwidth and clients' mobility make cache management a challenging task in mobile ad hoc networks.

Cooperative Caching: As mobile nodes in ad hoc networks may have similar tasks and share common interest, cooperative caching, which allows the sharing and coordination of cached data among multiple nodes, can be used to reduce the bandwidth and power consumption. Cooperative caching techniques have been widely studied in Wired Networks whereas little has been done to apply this technique to ad hoc networks. Due to mobility and resource constraints, techniques designed for wired networks may not be applicable to ad hoc networks. For example, most research on cooperative caching in the Web environment assumes a fixed topology, but this may not be the case in ad hoc networks due to mobility. Since the cost of the wireless link is different from the wired link, the decision regarding where to cache the data and how to get the cached data may be different. By cooperatively caching frequently accessed information, mobile devices do not always have to send requests to the data source.

2 Cooperative Caching Strategies

Cache Data

In *CacheData* [3], intermediate nodes cache the data to serve future requests instead of fetching data from the data center. The router node caches the data instead of the path when it finds that the data is frequently accessed. In this scheme, the router node caches can increase the overhead.

Cache Path

In a mobile network, the node caching the data might move or it might replace the cached data because of cache size limitations. Consequently, the node modifying the route should reroute the request to the original data source after discovering that the node moved or replaced the data. Thus, the cached path might be unreliable, and using it. To deal with this issue, a node caches the data path only when the caching node is very close. The closeness can be defined as a function of the node's distance to the data source, its distance to the caching node, route stability, and the data update rate. Intuitively, if the network is relatively stable, the data update rate is low, and its distance to the caching node is much shorter than its distance to the data source, the routing node should cache the data path.

In *CachePath* [3], mobile nodes cache the data path and use it to redirect future requests to the nearby node which has the data instead of the faraway data center. A node need not record the path information of all passing data. Rather, it only records the data path when it's closer to the caching node than the data source.

Hybrid Cache

CachePath performs better in some situations such as small cache size or low data update rate while CacheData performs better in other situations. *HybridCache* scheme [3] takes advantage of CacheData and CachePath while avoiding their weaknesses. Specifically, when a node forwards a data item, it caches the data or path based on some criteria. These criteria include the data item size, the TTL time, and the number of hops.

COOP

A Cooperative Caching service for MANETs *(COOP)* has been suggested in [7]. This scheme sits on the middleware level, acts as a proxy for user's applications, and uses underlying network stack to communicate with COOP instances running on other nodes. A running COOP instance receives data requests from user's applications, and resolves the requests using the cache resolution scheme. The cache management scheme decides what data to place/purge in the local cache of a mobile device. It discriminates primary data (non-duplicated copy) and secondary data (duplicated copy) with primary data at a higher caching priority, so that cooperated caches can store more distinctive data items to improve the overall performance.

Cache resolution: Cache resolution addresses how to resolve a data request with minimal cost of time, energy, and bandwidth. COOP's cache resolution is a cocktail scheme, which consists of three basic schemes. The first one is "Adaptive Flooding", which calculates proper flooding range based on the cost to fetch the requested data. Limited flooding is used for cache resolution, not only because it has potential to discover the closest cache around the requester, but also because flooding can serve as an announcement in the neighborhood and effectively segments the whole network into clusters, within which they can share and collaborate managing cached contents. The second scheme is "Profile-based Resolution", which maintains a historical profile of previously received data requests, and determines a closer data source for user's requests based on the profile. If a data request cannot get resolved using those two schemes, the data request is forwarded to the original data source, and the third scheme, "Roadside Resolution", is used to resolve the data request along the forwarding path.

Cache management: COOP cache management studies how to decide which data item to keep in a node's local cache. The goal is to increase cache hit ratio, which largely depends on the capacity of the cache. To maximize the capacity of cooperative caches, COOP tries to reduce duplicated caching within short-distance neighborhood, such that the cache space can be used to accommodate more distinct data items. We categorize cached data copies based on whether they are already available in the neighborhood or not. A data copy is primary if it is not available within the neighborhood. Otherwise, the data copy is secondary. The range of neighborhood is provided as a customizable option. The reason of discriminating primary and secondary data is that cache miss cost is proportional to the travel distance of a data request, and primary data usually incur higher cache miss cost than secondary data. The inter-category and intra-category rules are used to decide caching priorities of primary and second data.

Cluster Cooperative Caching

The *Cluster Cooperative (CC) Caching* [4] is to reduce the cache discovery overhead and provide better cooperative caching performance. CC partitions the whole MANET into equal size clusters based on the geographical network proximity. To enhance the system performance, within a cluster, individual caches interact with each other such that combined result is a larger cumulative cache. In each cluster, CC dynamically chooses a "super" node as cache state node (CSN), to maintain the cluster cache state (CCS) information of different nodes within its cluster domain. The CCS for a client is the list of cached items along with their time-to-live (TTL) field.

The design principle of CC is that, for a mobile client, all other mobile clients within its cluster domain form a cooperative cache system for the client since local caches of the clients virtually form a cumulative cache. In CC, when a client suffers from a cache miss (called local cache miss), the client will look up the required data item from the cluster members by sending a request to the CSN. Only when the client cannot find the data item in the cluster members' caches (called cluster cache miss), it will request the item from the client that lies on the routing path towards server. If a cluster along the path to the server has the requested data (called remote cache hit), then it can serve the request without forwarding it further towards the server. Otherwise, the request will be satisfied by the server.

Group Caching

Due to the movement of Mobile Hosts (MHs), MANETs may be partitioned into many independent networks. Hence, the requester can not retrieve the desired data from the remote server (data source) in another network. The entire data accessibility will be reduced. Also, the caching node may be disconnected from the network for saving power. Thus, the cached data in an MH may not be retrieved by other MHs and then usefulness of the cache is reduced. The MHs also decide the caching policy according to the caching status of other MHs.

GroupCaching (GC) [6] maintains localized caching status of 1-hop neighbors for performing the tasks of data discovery, caching placement, and caching replacement when a data request is received in a mobile host (MH). Each MH and its 1-hop neighbors form a group by using the "Hello" message mechanism. In order to utilize the cache space of each MH in a group, the MHs periodically send their caching status in a group. Thus, when caching placement and replacement need to be performed, the MH selects the appropriate group member to execute the caching task in the group. In this scheme, the MHs know the caching status of their neighbors and the redundancy of cached data objects can be reduced because the MHs can check the caching status of other group members for deciding the placement and replacement. Because more cache space can be utilized, each MH can store more different data objects in a group and then increases the data accessibility.

Each MH and its one-hop neighbors form a group. A one-hop neighbor can be covered in the area of transmission range from an MH. Each MH has a group member ID.

The group member ID may be the IP address or unique host ID. In order to maintain the connectivity of a group, we employ the mechanism of "Hello" messages. "Hello" messages are sent locally in each MH. These messages are sent periodically as a "Keep-Alive-Signal". In this way, each MH knows who its one-hop neighbors are. The k-hop neighbor information is obtained by piggybacking the (k–1)-hop neighbor information in "Hello" messages. However, the biggest concern is the energy consumption in MHs and constrain of wireless bandwidth. Therefore, in this GC scheme, each MH only maintains one-hop neighbors in a group. Each MH sends their caching status to its group members.

Zone Cooperative Caching

Zone Cooperative (*ZC*) scheme has been suggested in [5] for caching that exploits data utility value for cache replacement. The goal of ZC is to reduce the caching overhead and provide optimal replacement policy. The design principle of the ZC caching is that it is advantageous for a client to share cached data with its neighbors lying in the zone (i.e., mobile clients that are accessible in one hop). Mobile clients belonging to the neighborhood (zone) of a given client form a cooperative cache system for this client since the cost for communication with them is low both in terms of energy consumption and message exchanges.

In ZC caching, each mobile client has a cache to store the frequently accessed data items. The cache at a client is a nonvolatile memory such as hard disk. The data items in the cache satisfy not only the client's own requests but also the data requests passing through it from other clients. For a data miss in the local cache, the client first searches the data item in its zone before forwarding the request to the next client that lies on a path towards server. A *Least Utility Value LUV*) based replacement policy has been used to improve the efficiency of ZC caching.

COACS

A *Cooperative and Adaptive Caching System for MANETs (COACS)* is a distributed caching scheme that relies on the indexing of cached queries to make the task of locating the desired database data more efficient and reliable [1]. Nodes can take on one of two possible roles: Caching Nodes (CN) and Query Directory (QD). A QD's task is to cache queries submitted by the requesting mobile nodes, while the CN's task is to cache data items (responses to queries). When a node requests data that is not cached in the system (a miss), the database is accessed to retrieve this information. Upon receiving the response, the node that requested the data will act as a CN by caching this data. The nearest QD to the CN will cache the query and make an entry in its hash table to link the query to its response.

QDs act as distributed indexes for previously requested and cached data by storing queries along with the addresses of the CNs containing the corresponding data. The node that is requesting the data is referred as the RN, which could be any node, including a CN or a QD. The QD nodes make up the core of the caching system. To cope with the limited resources of mobile devices and to decrease the response time of the system, several QDs are used to form a distributed indexing system. If one QD receives a request that it has not indexed, the request is passed on to another QD. The desired number of QDs is a function of the various system parameters.

3 Comparison of Cooperative Caching Strategies

Cache Hit Ratio, Average Query Delay and Mean Query Generate Time are some of the performance metrics used to evaluate the performance of the data access.

Cache Hit Ratio: The percentage of accesses that result in cache hits is known as the hit rate or hit ratio of the cache.

Average Query Delay: The time interval between the time of generating a query in the requester and the time of receiving requested data object from the data source.

Table 1 provides a comparison of Cooperative Caching Strategies for data retrieval in MANETs. The HybridCache and GroupCaching deal with Cache Consistency. In order to have efficient information retrieval architecture, it is better to incorporate strong consistency in the caching schemes.

Table 1. Comparison of various Cooperative Caching Strategies

Cooperative Caching Strategy	Performance Metrics	Cache Management
Cache Data, Cache Path, Hybrid Cache	Reduces the query delay and the message complexity.	Cache Replacement and Cache Consistency
COOP	Improves data request success ratio and average response delay.	Cache Admission Control and Cache Discovery
CC Caching	Reduces the message overheads and enhances the data accessibility.	Cache Discovery, Cache Admission Control and Cache Discovery
Group Caching	Increases the hit ratio and reduces the access latency	Cache Discovery, Cache Placement, Cache replacement, Cache consistency
ZC Caching	Improves cache hit ratio and average query latency	Cache Discovery, Cache Admission Control, Cache Replacement
COACS	Improves cache hit ratio and reduces access latency	Cache Discovery

Table 2 shows the Cache hit ratio of the various Cooperative caching strategies with the Cache Size 1000 KB. Cache hit ratio is not evaluated in COOP and CC caching.

Table 2. Cache hit ratio (for 1000 KB Cache Size)

Cache Data	0.7
Cache Path	0.7
Hybrid Cache	0.8
Group Caching	11%
ZC Caching	0.8
COACS	0.7

Table 3 and Table 4 show the Average Query Delay of the various cooperative caching strategies.

Table 3. Average Query Delay (in Sec) (for 1000 KB Cache Size)

Cache Data	0.13
Cache Path	0.18
Hybrid Cache	0.11
Group Caching	34
ZC Caching	0.14
COACS	0.7
CC Caching	0.11

Table 4. Average Query Delay (in Sec) (for 100 Node Density)

Cache Path	0.7
Hybrid Cache	0.8
COOP	0.3

The Average Query Delay is evaluated in COOP with effect on the density of the nodes. For the network with 100 nodes density the delay was 0.3 sec where as it is 0.7 and 0.8 in CachePath and HybridCache respectively.

Table 5 shows the Mean Query Generate time of the caching strategies.

Table 5. Mean Query Generate Time

Hybrid Cache	100 Sec/0.06 Sec Average Delay
CC Caching	100 Sec/0.1 Sec Average Delay

4   Conclusion

Data caching is an essential concept which has to be concentrated in MANETs for improving the efficiency of data retrieval. There were many strategies suggested by various authors by concentrating various performance metrics such as hit ratio, access latency, average query latency etc.

Cache consistency is vital in every information retrieval scenario. The Hybrid-Cache and GroupCaching deal with the cache consistency whereas all the other strategies are used for managing the cache with cache placement and replacement. The cache consistency can be incorporated in these caching strategies.

The authors are working on the design and development of an effective caching strategy by incorporating cache consistency for improving the data accessibility in MANET.

References

1. Artail, H., Safa, H., Mershad, K., Abou-Atme, Z., Sulieman, N.: COACS: A Cooperative and Adaptive Caching System for MANETs. IEEE Transactions on Mobile Computing 7(8) (August 2008a)
2. Yin, L., Cao, G.: Supporting Cooperative Caching in Ad Hoc Networks. In: 2004 IEEE Infocomm (2004)
3. Yin, L., Cao, G.: Supporting Cooperative Caching in Ad Hoc Networks. IEEE Transactions on Mobile Computing (2006)
4. Chand, N., Joshi, R.C., Misra, M.: An Efficient Caching Strategy in Mobile Ad Hoc Networks Based on Clusters. IEEE, Los Alamitos (2006)
5. Chand, N., Joshi, R.C., Misra, M.: Cooperative Caching in Mobile Ad Hoc Networks Based on Data Utility. International Journal of Mobile Information Systems 3(1), 19–37 (2007)
6. Ting, Y.-W., Chang, Y.-K.: A Novel Cooperative Caching Scheme for Wireless Ad Hoc Networks: GroupCaching. In: International Conference on Networking, Architecture, and Storage (NAS 2007). IEEE, Los Alamitos (2007)
7. Du, Y., Gupta, S.K.S.: COOP – A cooperative caching service in MANETs. In: International Conference on Autonomic and Autonomous Systems and International Conference on Networking and Services (ICAS/ICNS 2005). IEEE, Los Alamitos (2005)

Framework for Probabilistic Routing in Dense MANETs

Sharmila Sankar and V. Sankaranarayanan

B.S. Abdur Rahman University, Chennai, India
{sharmilasankar,sankarammu}@yahoo.com

Abstract. On-demand ad hoc routing protocols broadcast control packets to establish route to destination nodes. In ad hoc networks that are formed by many mobile nodes, they generate a high number of broadcast packets, thereby causing contention, packet collision and battery power wastage in the mobile nodes. We propose an efficient route establishment method to decrease the transmission of control packets by using a neighborhood vector and controlled flooding technique. The goals are to: i) discover the shortest path with minimal control overhead, and ii) minimize the total resources consumed in message delivery. Through simulation, we demonstrate that our proposed method is especially efficient in dense ad hoc networks. In our proposed method, the number of control packets is decreased without lowering the success ratio of path discoveries according to the number of adjacent nodes. Furthermore, our proposed method adapts to the normal network conditions. The simulation results show [Section 3.4] that the proposal technique save up to 70% of control packets when the network is denser.

Keywords: Dense Networks, Neighborhood Vector, Saved Rebroadcast, Reachability parameter, Path Discovery, AODV, PRP.

1 Introduction

With the advent of wireless Bluetooth technology such as Wi-Fi, Bluetooth and RFID, a number of devices can be connected to each other to exchange information. These are not only stationary devices, but can also be mounted on mobile entities such as motor vehicles, thereby establishing networks and making advanced telematics a reality. Connectionless packet delivery may be an ideal match for these networks in terms of ubiquity and mobility, but packets must be routed in a network that dynamically changes its form without the presence of servers. These distributed and self-organized networks can be viewed as mobile ad hoc networks and various types of routing protocols have been designed and analyzed to support them [1].

Routing protocols for ad hoc networks can be classified into two categories: i) Table-driven: and ii) Source initiated on-demand. Table-driven protocols attempt to maintain consistent, up-to-date routing information among all nodes in the network. Table-driven algorithm requires periodic route update messages to propagate throughout the network. This can cause substantial overhead (due to the "route information" traffic) affecting bandwidth utilization, throughput as well as power usage. The advantage is that routes to any destination are always available (if within the network) without

N. Meghanathan et al. (Eds.): NeCoM, WiMoN, and WeST 2010, CCIS 90, pp. 447–456, 2010.

the overhead of a route discovery. In contrast, in On-demand routing, the entire network is flooded with RREQ packets during the route discovery phase, which leads to network congestion. Thus there is tradeoff between maintaining the paths and discovering the path to the destination.

The above mentioned protocols assume the size of the network to be several dozen mobile nodes where as the number may actually exceed one hundred, such as when many cars in a metropolitan area using wireless device or when many people gather and communicate in a small place. For this reason, performance in a highly populated (Dense) ad hoc network requires further study. The challenging issue in dense mobile ad hoc networks is the efficient way of finding a path to the destination node without congesting the network.

We propose some improvements to the flooding protocols that aim to efficiently broadcast given information in the ad hoc networks. These improvements are based on probabilistic approach and decrease the number of control packets generated [Section 3.4]. This new routing scheme establishes the connection between the two mobile hosts on demand, using the precomputed neighborhood vector. On contrast to the table-driven protocols, the proposed routing scheme uses a vector of neighbors, which drastically reduces the memory required to hold the topological information by a mobile node. When node moves to a new geographical position, they exchange HELLO messages. The path between the hosts is established on demand with controlled flooding of RREQ, which reduces the probability of the network being congested with control packets. Our proposed method attempts to combine the best of proactive and reactive protocols. The simulation results show [Section 3.4] that the proposed technique save up to 70% of control packets when the network is denser.

2   MANET Routing Protocols

In the path discovery mechanism of an on-demand routing protocol, the source node starts broadcasting the control packets and these packets gets flooded in the network. In a dense network every node will rebroadcast (except for the destination) the control packet thus causing congestion and battery power drainage. There are many approaches for an efficient path discovery. The Destination Sequenced Distance-Vector (DSDV) Routing algorithm [2] is based on the idea of the classical Bellman-Ford routing algorithm with certain improvements. Every mobile station maintains a routing table that lists all available destinations, the number of hops to reach the destination and the sequence number assigned by the destination node. The sequence number is used to distinguish stale routes from new ones and thus avoid the formation of loops. The station periodically transmits their routing tables to their immediate neighbors. A station also transmits its routing table if a significant change has occurred in its table from the last update sent. So, the update is both time-driven and event-driven. In a dense network scenario, the use of DSDV creates problems like contention and congestion of network. The tables will be of very large size, which demand more memory.

In Cluster head Gateway Switch Routing (CGSR) some nodes are elected as cluster leaders and to serve their cluster whenever a packet is destined to one among the cluster [3][6]. The cluster leaders reduce the number of control packets in the network. This will however result in draining of battery power of the cluster heads.

Ad hoc On-demand Distance Vector Routing [4] (AODV) is an improvement on the DSDV algorithm. AODV minimizes the number of broadcasts by creating routes on demand as opposed to DSDV that maintains the list of all the routes. To find a path to the destination, the source broadcasts a route request packet. The neighbors in turn broadcast the packet to their neighbors till it reaches an intermediate node that has the recent information about the destination or till it reaches the destination. A node discards a route request packet that it has already received. The entire network is thus flooded with the route request packet, which involves most of the nodes to take part in path finding.

Broadcast (diffusion of a message from a source node to all nodes in the network) is a common operation in ad hoc networks, and it is used by several routing protocols. Flooding (also called blind broadcast) is the simplest broadcast protocol: each node rebroadcasts the message and discards the duplicates. AODV, SLS, GSR, DSR and HSLS [5][7]use flooding with various improvements ("usually by changing the TTL value of the broadcast packet to limit propagation in the network). The flooding approach is reliable but has a high overhead for the routing protocol (in terms of number of packets and MAC layer access) and the number of collisions dramatically increases in the case of dense networks. The problem called *broadcast storm* due to blind broadcast, has been addressed by several papers.

It is very clear from the above discussions that there is always a tradeoff between the latency involved in path finding and bandwidth usage. We propose a hybrid routing scheme which tries to reduce the flooding of request packet (efficient usage of limited bandwidth) and reduce the size of the table maintained by a mobile host.

3 Proposed Routing Scheme

3.1 Neighborhood Vector Construction

Every node sends a HELLO message when it is up in the network to every other single hop neighbor. This enables the receiving node to populate its neighborhood vector. The neighbor nodes in turn respond with the HELLO message to enable the newcomer to populate its neighborhood vector. The neighborhood vector is thus constructed with local broadcast of HELLO messages between set of mobile nodes.

Unlike the periodic update in existing protocols, local broadcast of HELLO message is triggered when a node changes its position due to mobility and hence the neighborhood vector is updated. When a node observes mobility it broadcasts HELLO message to its single hop neighbors and constructs a new neighborhood vector. The node that moved to a new geographical position will initiate the process of constructing the new neighborhood vector. The flow diagram in Fig.1 explains the above discussed method of construction of neighborhood vector.

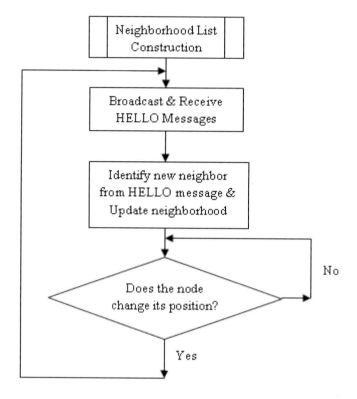

Fig. 1. Neighborhood Vector Construction

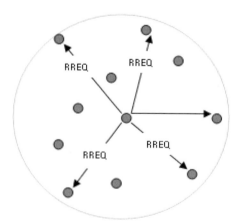

Fig. 2. Controlled RREQ broadcast in Route Discovery

3.2 Route Discovery

When a node wants to communicate with another node in the network a unique communication path is established between the sender and the receiver nodes. The source scans the neighborhood vector for the destination. If the destination node is identified to be the single hop neighbor of the source, the source node do not broadcast the RREQ packets, instead proceeds with the data transmission to the intended destination node. The transmission of the data will be uninterrupted until there is no change in the geographical positions of the source and the destination nodes.

The neighbors in the neighborhood vector are stored in the increasing order of their distances. The source node generates a RREQ packet and forwards it to n/k neighbors (where n is the total number of neighbors and K^1 – *Reachability Parameter* – a random number between 3 and 9) from the neighborhood vector, targeting the farthest nodes from the source node [9] as shown in Fig. 2. The intended neighbors check their neighborhood vectors and locate the destination else the same procedure is repeated till the destination is located. The following algorithm explains the method of finding path from the source to the destination mobile host.

```
Protocol PathDiscovery()
{ while(1)
   { for each chosen neighbor
      { if destination is in the neighborhood vector
         { unicast RREQ to the neighbor;
           exit();
         }
         Choose n/k farthest neighbors from nbr vector:
         Block the other neighbors from rebroadcasting;
         If (n/k) <= then choose the reachability factor as
         2 and unblock the neighbors to rebroadcast
      }
      PathDiscovery()
   }
}
```

3.3 Simulation Setup

We carry out the simulation in the customized event driven simulator, OMNet++ [8], which is an object modular network test-bed in C++. The mobility scenarios are obtained through mobility framework which is a part of OMNet++ distribution. The scenario generator produces the different mobility patterns such as Random Walk, Random Direction, Random Waypoint entity mobility models. The mobility model chosen for our simulation was Random Walk. The proposed method was

---

[1] K divides number of neighbors of a node to choose the candidate for rebroadcasting RREQ. If K is very less, many of the neighbors are chosen and only very few are blocked from rebroadcasting. If K is very large many neighbors are blocked and only few neighbors rebroadcast.

implemented with various densities like 50, 75, 100 and 125 nodes in an area of 350m X 350m. We compare the number of RREQ rebroadcasts in AODV routing protocol with the proposed Probabilistic Routing Protocol (PRP). The MAC layer protocol IEEE 802.11 is used in simulation with the data rate 11 Mbps. The data traffic source is set to be a Constant Bit Rate (CBR) source. The network contains one source and one destination initially, and multiple source and destination in a different scenario. Size of the message packet is set as 512 bytes. The Table 1 provides all the simulator parameter values. The performance parameters under consideration are *Path Optimality* and *Control Overheads*.

Table 1. Simulation Setup Parameter

Map Size	350m * 350m
Channel Bandwidth	11 Mbps
Channel Delay	10μsec
Simulation Time	900s
Number of Hosts	50,75,100,125
Packet Rate	3 packets/sec
Burst Length	64packets
Message Packet Size	512bytes

3.4 Results and Analysis

The simulation studies that were carried out are aimed at evaluating and comparing the performance acheived by Probabilistic Routing method and by the other routing protocol under analysis (AODV), during the Route Discovery process. The evalution comprises two metrics: Control Overhead and Path Optimality. From the simulation results we compare the number of route request rebroadcast saved with that of AODV with various network densities.

Saved Rebroadcast (SRB) is the percentage of rebroadcast saved during the path discovery from source to destination compared to AODV. SRB = (r-t)/r where r is the number of hosts receiving the broadcast message, and t is the number of hosts that actually transmitted the message. Fig.3 represents the performance of Probabilistic Routing method discussed in Section 3.4. Here the parameter K is a constant and the size of the network is varied between 50 ans 125. If the reachability parameter is chosen to be 1 then the protocol behaves as that of AODV. In AODV the number of rebroadcast saved is only 10 to 15% with single source-destination pair. The parameter K used is very useful for partial broadcast. It diffuses the information to a part of the nodes independent of the density.

A good reachability gives a worse SRB as with the case of AODV. But it can be noticed from the Fig.3 that a better SRB can be acheived with a random reachability parameter. If K is very less, many of the neighbors are chosen and only very few nodes are blocked from rebroadcasting. Therefore when the value in K is 2, for the

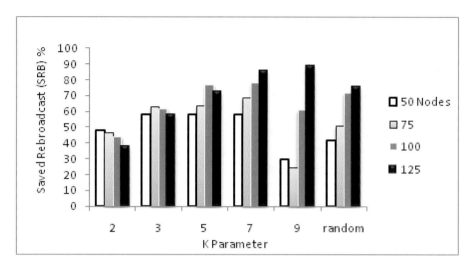

Fig. 3. Probabilistic Flooding: Parameter K vs Saved Rebroadcast

various densities, the SRB is only 40 to 45%. If the value in K is very large, only very few of the neighbors are chosen for rebroadcastingand all other neighbors of the node are blocked. In that case, there is a chance that the destination may be a neighbor to the blocked node. It may happen that, particular detination in this case may not be reached. Therefrore the K parameter should neither be too small nor be too large. It is seen from Fig.3 for K = 9, for the network densities 50 ans 75, the SRB are very less as for the densities of 100 and 125 the SRB is good. Hence it is better to have a random value in K. The last set of bars show the SRB for random value in K. From the graph (Fig. 3) we can easily realize that our protocol drastically cut down a large amount of controll overhead. Smaller control traffic translates to lower power consumption, less congestion, smaller delays, reduced memory and processing requirements and faster access to the communication channel.

The second metric is the Path Optimality. Apart from reducing the number of control packets, the path established between the source and the destination is also shortest in terms of number of hops as that of AODV. Each result in Fig.4 is the average of 50 source-destination pairs on top of 3 different network topologies for a given network density. For a smaller network size of 30, with a reachability parameter K = 2, average number of optimal paths acheived is very closer to AODV protocol which is arrived at by flooding through all nodes. It is clear form graph (Fig.4) that for a larger networks the smaller value of reachability parameter does not affect the optimal path much. Very large reachability parameter affects the path optimality. Larger the K values higher the numbers of neighbors blocked. Therefore even though there is a shortest route to the destination from the source, the packets take a longer (round about) path th the destination.

In AOVD, upon receiving the RREQ, each intermediate node checks whether it has an existing entry for the destination. If it has, a route reply (RREP) packet is generated and unicasted back to the source along the reverse path and thus the number of RREQ rebroadcasts are saved. But in the worst case, if none of the node have path

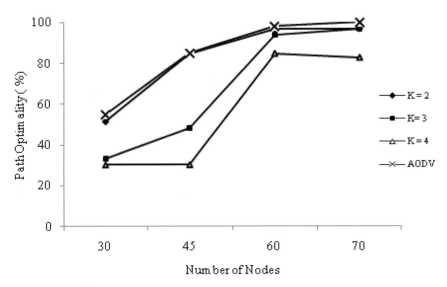

Fig. 4. Reachability for various Node Densities vs Shortest Paths

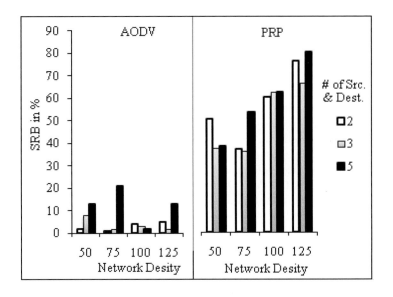

Fig. 5. Network Density vs Saved Rebroadcast forMultiple Sources and Destinations

to the destination, the RREQ packets are rebroadcasted till it reaches the destination. Broadcast Storm is caused when more number of nodes tries to establish communication path in Dense MANETs. This leads to network congestion and hence there is consistent delay in finding route in AODV.

Fig. 5 shows the variation of SRB in AODV and PRP in worst case with simultaneous paths among different sources and destinations. The scenario is based on the density of the network of size 50, 75, 100, 125 nodes. The number of active source and destinations are set as 2, 3 and 5. In PRP when the density increases the percentage of SRB also increases. On an average the 70% of rebroadcast is saved in PRP. This infers that the network is less congested even in case of many source-destination pairs trying to find routes.

SRB depends on the following factors: the topology of the network, node density and also the position of the source and destination nodes in the network. When there are 50 nodes and only two pairs of source and destinations are trying to establish path between them, ther number of RREQs generated is very less and so the links are less congested. The intermediate nodes in the path are also unique. Nodes are not overloaded with more than two paths through it to avoid congestion during data transmission. The number of RREQs generated also depends on the topology of the network. It is evident from Fig.5 that PRP saves more number of rebroadcasts as the density of the network increases and thus do not congest the network with RREQ packets even if multiple source and destination tries to discover path between them and reduce the latency involved in path discovery.

4 Conclusions

In this paper, we have proposed a new routing algorithm for mobile ad hoc networks, with a reduced overhead in case of dense networks. It is particularly efficient in case of high density and moderate mobility of nodes. Our experiments have demonstrated, through analysis and simulations, a significant reduction in the number of rebroadcast messages. Futhermore, because the nodes that rebroadcast the message are very close to the border of the radio area, the probability of acheiving the optimal path is increased. One disadvantage of this approach is that it does not guarantee a full coverage of the nodes. When the nodes are in the extreme ends and in different clusters the reachability may not be acheived. Further work in this direction is being carried out.

References

1. Royer, E.M., Toh, C.-K.: A Review of current Routing Protocols for Ad Hoc Mobile Wireless Networks. IEEE Personal Communications 6(2), 46–55 (1999)
2. Perkins, C.E., Bhagwat, P.: Highly Dynamic Destination-Sequenced Distance-Vector Routing (DSDV) for Mobile Computers. Comp. Comm. Rev, 234–244 (October 1994)
3. Chiang, C.C.: Routing in Clustered Multihop, Mobile Wireless Networks with Fading Channel. In: Proc. IEEE SICON 1997, pp. 197–211 (1977)
4. Perkins, C.E., Royer, E.M., Das, S.R.: Ad Hoc On-Demand Distance Vector Routing. IETF Draft, 33 pages
5. Johnson, D.B., Maltz, D.A.: Dynamic Source Routing in Ad Hoc Networks. In: Imielinski, T., Korth, H. (eds.) Mobile Computing, pp. 152–181. Kluwer, Dordrecht (1996)

6. Joa-Hg, M., Lu, I.T.: A Peer-to-Peer Zone-based two-level link state routing for Mobile Ad Hoc Networks. IEEE Journal on Selected Areas in Communication, Special Issue on Ad Hoc Networks, 1415–1425 (1999)
7. Johnson, D.B., Maltz, D.A.: Dynamic Source Routing in Ad Hoc Networks. IETF Draft, 49 pages
8. OmNet++ Simulator, http://www.omnetpp.org
9. Cartingny, J., Simplot, D.: Border Node Retransmission Based Protocols in Ad Hoc Networks. In: Proceedings of the 36th Annual Hawaii International Conference in System Sciences

Lightweight Management Framework (LMF) for a Heterogeneous Wireless Network for Landslide Detection

Sangeeth Kumar and Maneesha Vinodini Ramesh

Amrita Center for Wireless Networks and Applications,
AMRITA Vishwa Vidyapeetham (Amrita University),
Clappana. P. O, Kollam, Kerala - 690525, India
{sangeethk,maneesha}@am.amrita.edu

Abstract. Wireless Sensor Networks (WSN) are networks of low cost nodes with minimal power consumption, processing capabilities and maintenance, that can be used for wide area environmental monitoring. This paper discusses the main innovations, challenges, solutions and deployment experiences in designing a Lightweight Management Framework (LMF) for a real-time, 24/7 operational, heterogeneous network. The network must reliably deliver data continuously from a set of deep earth probe sensors in a remote hilly rainforest area to a data management, analysis, and visualization center at the University campus hundreds of miles away. This framework provides the ability to incorporate different heterogeneous networks such as 802.15.4, 802.11b/g, VSAT, GPRS, GSM, Internet and also proprietary wireless sensor network and hardware architectures. It also handles various network failures, data corruption, packet loss, and congestion problems. The data is analyzed to determine the factor of safety of the landslide prone area using landslide simulation software, stream data in real-time to the internet, and give automatic warnings. The architecture has been implemented in a real-time wireless sensor network deployed in the Western Ghats of Kerala, India to detect landslides. The architecture is operational in the deployment site since February 2008 and was used to issue landslide warnings during the July 2009 monsoon.

1 Introduction

Landslides are one of the catastrophic natural disasters that cause the deaths of hundreds of people annually. Continuous monitoring and real-time warning will reduce the casualties that will be caused due to this disaster. In this regard, we have deployed India's first Wireless Sensor Network (WSN) for landslide detection [1] in a landslide prone area of the mountainous Western Ghat region

---

[1] This work has been partially funded by the WINSOC project, a Specific Targeted Research Project (Contact Number 003914) co-funded by the INFSO DG of the European Commission within the RTD activities of the Thematic Priority Information Society Technologies and also by Wireless Sensor Network for Real-time Landslide Monitoring project funded by Department of Information Technology (DIT), India.

N. Meghanathan et al. (Eds.): NeCoM, WiMoN, and WeST 2010, CCIS 90, pp. 457–471, 2010.

of India. This seven acre deployment site is located just outside the town of Munnar, in the Idukki District of the southern State of Kerala, India.

Twenty wireless sensor nodes are connected to over 50 geophysical sensors measuring pore water pressure, soil moisture, rainfall, soil movement, and soil vibrations. The sensors are connected to the wireless sensor nodes. Since the sensors are deployed in hazardous areas, such as landslides, each individual sensor reading is important and could be of critical value. This mandates that the sensor data must be sent to the analysis center with very little loss and in a timely manner. The data from this wide area has to be transmitted to our university, for sophisticated data analysis and storage, which is almost three hundred kilometers away. This is achieved using a heterogeneous wireless network consisting of IEEE 802.15.4, Wi-Fi, Satellite, and GSM/GPRS, along with wired communication networks for emergency redundancy.

The establishment of this heterogeneous wireless network has brought in some complexities such as the interoperability between the networks, traffic management, the need for low overhead and low power consumption, reliability of transmission irrespective of individual network failures, the need of the user to connect to any device in the network for maintenance, and the ability to remotely monitor and control the sensors independently of the service platform. This necessitates the need for a virtual platform between the client and the sensors.

The Lightweight Management Framework (LMF) created in this work is a service oriented middleware architecture for the remote management of widespread WSN deployments using heterogeneous wireless networks. It operates in a location transparent manner and handles different rates of packet loss, data corruption, congestion and network failure during the streaming of sensor data, send alerts on analyzing the sensor data, configures the sensor nodes, and facilitates different debugging levels to troubleshoot the network.

This system has been operational for over two years, collecting continuous data. A landslide warning was issued during the monsoon in July 2009, using data monitored remotely in real-time over the internet.

Section II describes the related work. Section III elaborate the service architecture. Section IV describes the LMF components. Section V details the services from data management center. Section VI details the deployment and experimentation. Section VIII describes the conclusion.

2 Related Work

Significant research work has been conducted in the field of middleware for WSN. Yu et. al. gives an overview of design and requirements for building a WSN architecture [1]. This paper discuss the importance of light weight management architecture, layered system structure, and the distribution of a management architecture. The DSN described in Dyerl et. al. uses a middleware abstraction based architecture [2]. According the reference [2], middleware abstraction provides an easy user interface, but it needs a back bone or another hybrid network to connect to the network. The work by Ruiz et. al. provides a good explanation of the theoretical need of the wireless sensor network middleware [5]. They developed a management architecture called MANNA, with major focus on the system architecture than the network part. Aberer at. al. details the development of Global Sensor Network (GSN) middleware to provide good infrastructure for implementing a service architecture [3]. GSN uses XML to specify deployment descriptors. Currently the GSN is being used by the researchers in field deployments. Wagenknechtl et. al. describes the development of a middleware architecture called MARWIS [6]. It basically could be used only for a single type of network and it uses Agile [13] principles for full life cycle implementation of the service oriented architecture. This motivates that the service oriented technologies should combine with the real time monitoring service. The remote water monitoring application described in Dinh et. al. [10] uses a wireless sensor network. However, this system does not have a stable TCP. Therefore, the network may lose data. The volcano monitoring application described in Welsh et. al. [11], the habitat monitoring scenario described in Mainwaring [12], the soil moisture sensor network described in Oliver et. al. [13], and the environmental monitoring application using WSN described in Kranz et. al. in [14] are a few of the applications of WSN in environmental monitoring. These studies validate that LMF's can be used in these areas to stream data and control the sensors remotely.

In our real-time field deployment for landslide monitoring ([15], and [16]), we developed a robust LMF architecture framework which provides the ability to incorporate different heterogeneous networks such as 802.15.4, 802.11b/g, VSAT, GPRS, GSM, and internet as well as proprietary wireless sensor network and hardware architectures.

3   Service Architecture for Landslide Monitoring

Real-time, continuous landslide monitoring and detection using wireless sensor network requires distributed communication between the wireless sensor nodes, seamless connectivity, and data transmission with minimum delay. The wireless sensor network uses a two-layer topology for data collection from the geophysical sensors deployed at the field, as described in [15]. The data received at the gateway of the wireless sensor network has to be transmitted to our University for intensive data analysis, landslide modelling, and for alert dissemination. This is achieved through the heterogeneous wireless network architecture detailed in the reference [15]. This network is integrated with a novel lightweight management framework (LMF), a service oriented middleware architectures for the remote management of wide spread heterogeneous wireless sensor network deployments in location transparent manner using different wireless networks.

The distributed environment of the LMF is obtained through a service oriented architecture. A service oriented architecture is chosen for the LMF for a variety of reasons; 1) due to the distributed communication between the sensor nodes in the form of services, 2) it lets the heterogeneous sensor nodes expose services in an implementation independent way, 3) it is a loosely coupled system that helps in composition and reuse, 4) it allows incrementally building the system without major changes to the existing system, and 5) it communicates using well defined service interfaces.

The service oriented architecture divides the system into the application architecture, service architecture and component architecture. The application architecture focuses mainly on client interfaces for the end user, such as web pages, survey systems, and user interfaces for accessing the lower level wireless sensor node services. The service architecture provides the virtual platform for invoking the service requested by the end user in the lower level wireless sensor nodes. The component architecture focuses mainly on the hardware abstraction layer of the lower level wireless sensor nodes.

Three types of configurations are possible in the network:

- Node Level Configuration: The user has access to the node level and can log into the cluster member(CM). The user has to specify his credentials before logging in to the CM. The CM authenticates the user after verifying the user's privileges with the policy manager. The node then lists the services running in the node for the user configuration. The communication between the host and node occurs using 802.15.4 or a proprietary standard. This type of configuration is used mainly on the field for debugging the network algorithms and the sensor data in the node.
- Cluster Level Configuration: The user has cluster level access and can log into the different services in the gateway . After supplying his credentials, the user can configure the services in the gateway through the service wrappers. These services can also communicate with the cluster heads and cluster members. Since the CM's are WPAN devices they only send the id and status of the services to the gateway. The Gateway then polls its service repositories, using the service and SOURCE_ID, to get the service information for the end user. The communication between the Gateway and the host happens using the WiFi network or the Wired Ethernet connection. This provides single point of control to connect to all the nodes in the field without physically going to each node.
- Global Configuration: The user has global access of all the clusters, i.e. the entire field deployment. The user can globally log into any cluster and change the properties of a sensor or network without having knowledge of the underlying network. The user uses a VSAT or a GPRS connection for such type of configurations.

The component architecture consists of the implementation dependent modules. These modules are hardware and sensor specific and may vary between the cluster members. The component architecture is connected to the various services through abstracted management entities.

4   Lightweight Management Framework (LMF)

The LMF is a service oriented middleware architecture for the remote management of wide spread and heterogeneous wireless sensor network deployments in a location transparent manner. Various combinations of wireless networks such as 802.15.4, Wi-Fi, VSAT, GPRS, GSM can be used for connectivity. The LMF handles packet losses, data corruption, congestion and network failure during sensor data streaming, sends alerts on analyzing the sensor data, configures the sensor nodes and facilitates different debugging levels to troubleshoot the network.

4.1   Cluster Member

The sensors are connected to the cluster members in the network. The hardware of the cluster member consists of an Atmel 128L processor and the CC2420 or CC1000 transceiver. The cluster members are divided into various components, services and the management functions. In the landslide scenario, the Sensor Driver Manager (SDM) provides both analog and digital drivers. These include analog drivers such as Analog to Digital Converters (ADC), relays and digital drivers such as I2C, SPI and event detection circuits. The ADC provides 16 bit resolution for all the 8 sensors connected to it by the sensor driver manager. The digital drivers are used to connect to any digital sensors, such as the rain gauge. The I2C bus can be used by the cluster member to access the digital data.

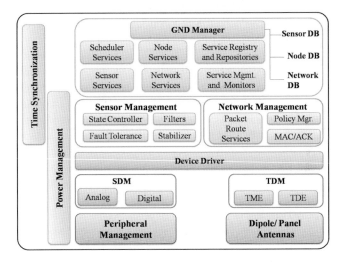

Fig. 1. Services in Cluster Member

The transceiver driver manager handles the transceiver management and the functional entities. It provides the interface that abstracts the CC2420 and the CC1000 transceiver chip sets. The Transceiver Manager Entity (TME) manages functionalities such as transmit power, which channel to use, start/stop radio transceiver, etc.

The Transceiver Data Entity (TDE) handles the data communication part of the transceiver. It transmits the data to the microcontroller along with the link quality.

Management Functions. The management functions act as an interface between the services in the cluster member and its components. Sensor management is used to handle the sensors and their generated data. The sensor state controller is used to transition the sensors between the sleep state, monitoring state, settling state and sampling state. In the sleep state the sensor are powered off. In the settling state, the sensor is given power and waits a specified time for the sensor transients to settle. Once the settling state is completed, the sensor will monitor the physical state. Finally the sensor is sampled in the sampling state, after which it again goes back to the sleep state. This process is repeated under the control of the sensor management function. The fault tolerance in the sensor management function monitors the sensor values and if any jitter or spikes occur during the sampling, it rechecks the configuration and reschedules the state transition of the sensor for repeated sampling. The filters and the stabilizer can be customized using the Node Level or Cluster Level configuration.

The network management function handles three types of packets:

- Service packets Service packets are used by 1) the sensor services which update the sensor management functions, 2) network services which update the path route service for changing the route table, and 3) node services which change the sampling time, among others. The scheduler services are used to manage all the schedulers running, preventing any race conditions between the shared resources in the node.
- Data packets The data packets are used only to send the sensor data. These packets can be of fixed size or variable size. Once the sensor values are sampled they are transferred to the path route services which decide the path to route the data based on the acknowledgement packets received.
- Data Acknowledgement (ACK) Packets Acknowledgements for the data packets received at the destination are sent. These packets are populated with time synchronization information used to synchronize the clocks in the nodes and the signal strength and link quality of the last packet received from the other node. This helps the nodes to be aware of their links before the link drops. This primarily happens because of vegetation or obstacles, causing a reduction in the link quality.
- Service Acknowledgement (SACK) Packets The Service Acknowledgement Packets are used to acknowledge service packets received. The data will be routed either to the host or to the cluster head based on the SOURCE_ID. It also sends the results of the invocation of the request. Since the packets are small it sends only the 'success' or 'failure' of the request.

Since the field deployment consists of different terrain slopes, different types of antennas with different gains are used to provide high-quality links. Panel antennas are used in the cluster members that have direct Line-of-sight with the network gateway and Omni directional antennas are used in various other locations in which broad transmission/reception are beneficial.

4.2   Cluster Heads

The cluster heads are used to disseminate and aggregate the information from the cluster members. The cluster members communicate with the gateway through the cluster heads. Among other functions, the cluster heads synchronize the clocks of the cluster members using a flooding time synchronization protocol. The cluster head will use the same services detailed in the cluster member, except the sensor driver manager (SDM).

4.3   Sensor Network Gateways (SNG)

The SNG connects the cluster heads to the Data Management Center (DMC). The cluster heads are low power devices with limited functionality that are dependent on the SNG for communication with the external world. The SNG's are battery powered devices that also must perform their work in a power efficient way. The job of the SNG is to manage the Cluster Member (CM) communication, peer-to-peer SNG Communication, and the DMC server communication.

SNG Low Overhead Design. On analyzing the above requirements, the software services and hardware components of the SNG are divided into the two loosely coupled components: the Cluster Manager and the Mesh Manager.

The Cluster Manager handles all the functionalities between the cluster members. The Mesh Manager handles all the functions and services between the SNG's and the DMC. This causes the Cluster Manager to act as the gateway to the cluster network. These two components share a persistent communication channel and all data in this channel is monitored and logged. Since the two components are totally independent of each other, if any drop happens in the network the gateway switches to the data logger mode. Once the network comes back to normal condition, it works in the network mode once again. This helps to keep the data safe in rough weather conditions where the network is very unstable. In addition, load or congestion in the SNG due to either the sensor data network or the external network will not affect the other. Both have independent monitors for resource allocation and management.

Cluster Manager. The cluster manager handles communication between the Gateways. The cluster member fetches the sensor values and hand them to the network services in the node. The end user at the DMC then receives this sensor information from the sensor service agent and does not need to be aware of the underlying transmission.

This happens because the cluster manager receives this packet, converts in into the byte stream, and inserts it into the circular queue. The scheduler checks for the availability of the Sensor Data Packet Service (SDP) and triggers the event if the channel to the SDP is free. Once the SDP service has authenticated the packet it then logs the event. The data's local sampling time is converted into global UTC time and the packet is tagged with its Metadata before placing it in the queue in the cache. The cache manager adjusts the queue size dynamically in response to the congestion and bandwidth controller. The Queue scheduler

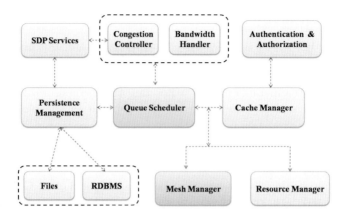

Fig. 2. Components of Cluster Manager

provides a variable buffer for the inflow and also outflow of packets using the congestion controller, which helps for different packet rates. Specifically, for sensors such as the geophone, accelerometer, etc the sampling rate will be relatively high and whenever such types of data are received, the queue scheduler automatically allocates memory for the incoming data. The cache manager also periodically checks for unused memory and reclaims it into the disk pool. The sensor data are then finally transferred to the persistence management store which saves the data in an Embedded DB or in Flat files.

Mesh Manager. The Mesh manager is responsible for connecting the clusters to the wide area network of VSAT, GPRS and Broadband. This self contained module's purpose is to reliably transfer data between the gateways and the DMC. At a low level, it uses UDP to transfer data to a particular destination. In case of packet loss in emergency conditions, the lost packets are sent via TCP. TCP is less frequently used because it has poor performance in high latency networks. The four services - Real Time Data (RTD) services, Burst Data Services (BDE), Real Time Network Configurator (RNC) services and the Acknowledgement Handler Routine (AHR) services are used for communication in the different networks. The RTD service is used for real time data, BDE is used to handle packet losses/corruptions and network failures, RNC is used to handle the configuration of cluster members from the DMC, and AHR is used to control the flow of data in the network. The data is sent in frames with varying frame slots and varying transmission frequency. Control frames are sent at the end of each frame and the destination host sends back the acknowledgment of the successful reception of the frames specified in the control frames. The AHR services are used to handle the control frames (CTRL_FRM), positive Acknowledgement frames (ACK), and Negative Acknowledge frames (NACK). The congestion and bandwidth controllers monitor the current connected network for latencies, packet losses, etc. It uses this input to generate the frequency of control frames and number of frame slots.

Sometimes the network may be terminated for longer durations. During these times a significant amount of data will be stored in the gateway, waiting for the network to reconnect. Once the network is reconnected, the current data and the cached data is sent through concurrent sockets, aiding data analysis during disaster times. The BDE service uses TCP service to transmit the lost data to the DMC. Since TCP service is a poor performance in high latency networks, the TCP Buffer and the socket time out are altered dynamically during transmission to suit different networks.

The Fig 3 shows the subset of the data model diagram of the Mesh Manager. The transport handler controls the data flow through the RTD and BDE services. Each packet is sent as an Active Message (AM) in the frames with defined slots. The Transport Handler sends this AM_GRP to the RTD which responds through res_flag whether the ACK or NACK is received. If NACK is received then the Transport handler sends the NACK Frame and the AM_grp to the BDE service which tries to send it in the TCP connection. The TCP monitors in the BDE helps to observe the TCP connection and change the buffer and TCP ACK parameters during runtime. If the TCP connection is also disconnected the BDE reconnects to the network until the data is transferred safely.

RNC services are used to communicate with the cluster node from the DMC. The RNC carries the service information through a wrapper from the DMC to the gateway. It extracts the information from the webpage or GUI in the DMC and locks the sensor id for a particular period of time before invoking the gateway service. Once the service is invoked in the gateway, it checks the user credentials and the availability of service, logs the event, and thereby invokes the corresponding service in the cluster member.

Communication between the cluster members occurs using the 802.15.4 standard or standard protocols. Communication between the Gateways uses the

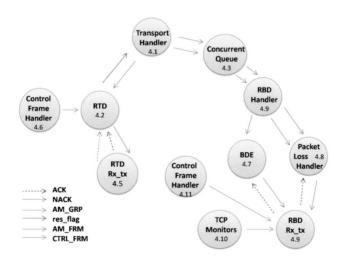

Fig. 3. Data Flow in Mesh Manger

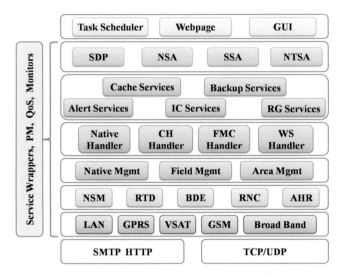

Fig. 4. Heterogeneous Network Service Stack

802.11 networks. These different Gateways are connected to the analysis center using the VSAT, GSM/GPRS, and Broadband connections.

4.4   Data Management Center (DMC)

The Data Management Center is the data center for all of the deployed cluster networks. Through the DMC, the LMF allows the user to list the services in any cluster member belonging to any cluster and to start/stop the node service.

As seen in the Fig 4, the DMC has a layered stack of services that respond to the events in the sensor networks. The references of currently running services are in the service registry. Each service has start, initialization, and stop events, which are used for initialization. The services are connected to each other using concurrent asynchronous queues.

The Layer 1 services provide interfaces for the Task Scheduler, Webpage and the GUI, which connects end users to the LMF.

The Layer 2 Sensor Data Processing (SDP) service is used to process the sensor values from the cluster members into physical units. This service extracts the sensor value, checks for CRC and passes the result to the Backup Services. The Network Service Agent (NTSA) is used to communicate with the Network Services in the cluster member. It is this service that changes the routing table entries. The Sensor Service Agent (SSA) is used for communication with Sensor Services in the Cluster Member. The Node Service Agent (NSA) is used to communicate with the node services in the cluster member for changing the sampling rate etc.

Layer 3 services, such as the Information Content (IC) service, are used to extract the byte stream and time stamp translation of the data packet from the sensors. The Cache services are used to communicate with the cache managers in the Cluster and the Mesh Manager in each gateway. The backup services are used to communicate with the Embedded Database in the gateway and also serve to archive the sensor data arriving at the DMC. The Alert Services are used to send alert messages through the Layer 4 services when it finds unusual data or that a network termination was detected. The Rain Gauge Services are used to communicate with the rain gauge sensors installed in the field.

The layer 4 services have a native handler for management of Local devices and networks. The CH Handler manages the gateway (SNG) connected to the network. The Field Management Center (FMC) is used to control the VSAT stations in the field. The Weather Station (WS) Handler is used to handle the Weather stations installed in the field.

The Layer 5 service, Field Management, is used to manage a field deployment which is connected to the overall system through a WiFi network. The Area Management service is used to manage multiple satellite connected deployments. The Native Management manages the local connections in the DMC, such as the http and smtp protocols.

The Layer 6 Service, Notification and Storage Management (NSM), is used for sending emails and database backup. The RTD, BDE, RNC and AHR communicate peer-to-peer with the same services in the gateways.

The Layer 7 Services are different type of modules that serve as the backbone for using the network protocols. For example, the VSAT satellite network uses the VSAT station to communicate with the Sensor Network Gateways (SNG), Broadband network and the GPRS connection. It uses the public IP address to connect to gateway.

Layer 8 uses low level protocols such as TCP, UDP, HTTP and SMTP. The SMTP protocol is used by the Alert services (Layer 3) to alert the user by mail if any of the gateways, hubs, or switches fail. This alert service is also used for monitoring the sensor data. If any of the sensor data exceeds a threshold then the user will notified.

5   Deployment and Validation

In the existing deployment, cluster members are comprised of Crossbow MicaZ motes using Crossbow MDA320 data acquisition boards to connect the sensors to the node. The MicaZ motes use a 802.15.4 complaint radio and an Atmel 128L Microcontroller. TinyOS is used as the WSN operating system to implement the services and the messaging formats. Different services communicate with each other using well defined interfaces in TinyOS. Each of the cluster members are connected to a cluster head, which is also a MicaZ more. Proprietary WSN nodes using ARM7TDMI processors and CC1000 chips for transmission were at times used along with the Zigbee Nodes.

In the below section we will discuss the various experiences that we faced when deploying such a system.

Table 1. Sink Node Congestion

Packets/Second	Loss (%)
30	5
40	8
50	15
60	19

5.1   Sink Node Congestion

The cluster manager in the Gateway has congestion issues when used without a
cache manager. If it received less than 20 packets per second, with a packet size
of 60 bytes, then there were no congestion issues. However, if the rate of data
transmission is increased to more than 20 packets per second then congestion
occurs. Table 1 shows the congestion as the rate of transmission is increased.

The cache manager and the queue scheduler prevent the above mentioned
packet losses by monitoring and allocating asynchronously more memory to the
sensor data. After implementing the queue scheduler, the node was tested for
18 hours while receiving packets of 51 bytes each. A total 60,000 packets were
received with 0% packet loss.

5.2   Interference

Since our current deployment of the gateway uses both the 802.15.4 standard
(2.4 GHz) and a WiFi 802.11g network, it was likely that interference would
happen due to sharing the same base frequency. During our pilot deployment,
one of the cluster members was transmitting 5 packets with a size of 51 bytes
each every 20 seconds and used different channels than the Wi-Fi channel. The
results were recorded and are shown in Table 2.

Table 2. Wi-Fi and Zigbee Interference

Time	Packet Loss (%)
1st Minute	0
2nd Minute	0
3rd Minute	0
1 Hour	10
2 Hour	15

Even if the Wi-Fi and motes are operating on different channels, many Zigbee
packets are lost due to the high power of the WiFi antenna which is located in
close proximity to the gateway antenna (WSN sink node antenna) in the field.

After replacing the whip antenna in the mote with externally mounted 2dbi
dipole antennas, for the same rate of reception, there was significantly less packet

losses. The results are given below. Due to these results, most of our sensor nodes are deployed with 2 dbi, 8dbi and 12dbi externally mounted antennas.

5.3   Packet Loss in VSAT

The packet loss in the VSAT network during data transmission was analyzed as well. It was observed that the connection was stable but there were losses of packets. The Iperf tool was used to analyze the packets sent and the packets lost. The test was conducted by running the Iperf in one end and trying to connect to the other system through the satellite. There were 5 hosts in the Satellite Hub routing the information between the sender and receiver. The delay and average RTT and the loss of packets are mentioned in Table 3.

Table 3. VSAT Packet Loss

Time Period	Total Packets	Lost Packets	Loss (%)
4 Hours	14400	234	1.6
8 Hours	28800	775	2.6
12 Hours	43200	1300	3.0

In the deployment field, all sensor nodes are powered by the solar panel and has the sensors buried underneath the soil. These wireless node (MicaZ) is kept inside one of the boxes and has the sensors are connected to the node. The 12dbi external antennas are connected to the node for communication with other nodes in the network. The data are real-time streamed to the webpage www.winsoc.org.

5.4   Validation

A landslide warning was issued in July 2009, after viewing the real-time data and its pattern through our real streaming software currently incorporated to www.winsoc.org website. Figure 5 shows the real-time streaming data from the website, for a period of July 18th, 2009 to July 20th, 2009. During this period, high rain fall was experienced at our deployment site and multiple landslides occurred all over the state of Kerala, India. In the deployment region, during the torrential rainfall, our wireless sensor network system detected certain signals that indicate vulnerability of this region to possible landslides. The real-time data analysis showed that the vunerable locations had a saturated moisture content, high rate of change in pore pressure values, and soil movements. These changes were experienced in each of the geophysical sensors deployed at the crown, middle, and the toe region. This motivated us to issue a landslide warning and the local government took the required actions.

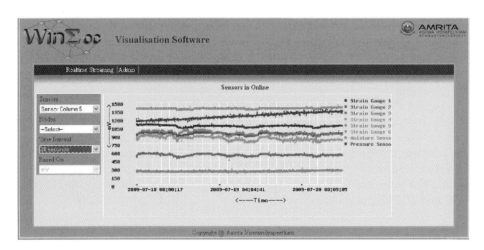

Fig. 5. Snapshot from the real streaming software, for a period of 18 July 2009 (00: 00:17) to 20 July 2009 (08:09:05) for location 5, the middle position of the hill

6 Conclusion

This research work has contributed to the development of India's first wireless sensor network for real-time landslide detection system; deployed at one of the landslide prone areas in Munnar, Southern India. The system consists of 50 geological sensors, 20 wireless sensor nodes, and heterogeneous wireless networks such as a wireless sensor network, a Wi-Fi network, a satellite network, a GPRS network, and the Internet. This work describes an innovative framework that provides the ability to incorporate different heterogeneous networks such as 802.15.4, 802.11b/g, VSAT, GPRS, GSM, Internet and also proprietary wireless sensor network and hardware architectures. This paper reveals the main innovations, challenges, solutions and deployment experiences in designing a Lightweight Management Framework (LMF). The LMF is implemented and validated in the real-time wireless sensor network deployed in the Western Ghats of Kerala, India to detect landslides. LMF showed its ability to adapt itself to handle packet losses, data corruption, congestion and network failure during sensor data streaming through heterogeneous wireless networks, in extreme environmental conditions. This frame work has send alerts on network failures, and on probable landslides. The current network is operational for the last two years and was used to issue landslide warnings during the July 2009 monsoon.

Acknowledgements. The authors would like to express gratitude for the immense amount of motivation and research solutions provided by Sri. Mata Amritanandamayi Devi, The Chancellor, Amrita University. The authors would also like to acknowledge Dr. Venkat Rangan, Mr. Jayaraj Poroor, Mr. Joshua D. Freeman, Mr. Abishek T.K, Ms. Erica (Thapasya) S. Fernandes for their valuable contribution to this work.

References

1. Yu, M., Mokhtar, H., Merabti, M.: A survey of Network Management Architecture in Wireless Sensor Network. In: Proc. of the Sixth Annual Post Graduate Symposium on The Convergence of Telecommunications Netowrking and Broadcasting (June 2006)
2. Dyer, M., Beutel, J., Kalt, T., Oehen, P., Thiele, L., Martin, K., Blum, P.: Deployment Support for Wireless Sensor Networks. In: Proceedings of KuVS Fachgesprch Sensornetzwerke, ETH Zurich (2005)
3. Aberer, K., Hauswirth, M., Salehi, A.: The Global Sensor Networks middleware for efficient and flexible deployment and interconnection of sensor networks. In: Proceedings of the 1st ACM International Workshop on Wireless Sensor Networks and Applications, LSIR-2006-001
4. Khedo, K.K., Subramanian, R.K.: A Service-Oriented Component-Based Middleware Architecture for Wireless Sensor Networks. IJCSNS International Journal of Computer Science and Network Security 9(3), 126–137 (2009)
5. Ruiz, L.B., Nogueira, J.M.S., Loureiro, A.A.F.: MANNA:A management architecture for wireless sensor networks. IEEE Communications Magazine 41(2), 116–125 (2003)
6. Wagenknech, G., Anwander, M., Braun, T., Staub, T., Matheka, J., Simon, M.: MARWIS: A Management Architecture for Heterogeneous Wireless Sensor Networks. Wireless Internet Communications, 177–188 (2008)
7. Klues, K., Hackmann, G., Chipara, O., Lu, C.: A component based architecture for Power Efficient Media Access Control in Wireless Sensor Networks. In: ACM Conference on Embedded Networked Sensor Systems (SenSys 2007) (November 2007)
8. TinyDB, http://telegraph.cs.berkeley.edu/tinydb/
9. Oscilloscope, http://www.tinyos.net/tinyos-.x/doc/tutorial/lesson6.html
10. Le Dinh, T., Hu, W., Sikka, P., corke, P., Overs, L., Brosnan, S.: Design and Deployment of a Remote Robust Sensor Network. In: IEEE Confenrence on Local Computer Networks (2007)
11. Welsh, M., Werner-Allen, G., Lorincz, K., Marcillo, O., Johnson, J., Ruiz, M., Less, J.: Sensor networks for high-resolution monitoring of volcanic activity. In: ACM Symposium on Operating Systems Principles (2005)
12. Mainwaring, A., Culler, D., Polastre, J., Szewczyk, R., Anderson, J.: Wireless sensor networks for habitat monitoring. In: ACM international workshop on Wireless Sensor Networks and Applications (2002)
13. Oliver, R.C., Smettem, K., Kranz, M., Mayer, K.: A reactive soil moisture sensor network: Design and field evalution. International Journal of Distributed Sensor Networks 1, 142–162 (2005)
14. Oliver, R.C., Smettem, K., Kranz, M., Mayer, K.: Field testing a WSN for reactive environmental monitoring. In: International Conference on Intelligent sensors, Sensor Networks and Information Processing ISSNIP (2004)
15. Ramesh, M.V.: Real-time Wireless Sensor Network for Landslide Detection. In: Proceedings of the Third International Conference on Sensor Technologies and Applications, SENSORCOMM 2009, IEEE Digital Library (2009)
16. Ramesh, M.V., Kumar, S., Rangan, P.V.: Wireless Sensor Network for Landslide Detection. In: The Proceedings of the 2009 International Conference on Wireless Networks (ICWN 2009), pp. 89–95 (2009)

Dasarathy Model Based Fusion Framework for Fire Detection Application in WSN

P.T.V. Bhuvaneswari, V. Vaidehi, and M. Karthik

Madras Institute of Technology, Anna University,
Chennai, India
ptvbmit@annauniv.edu, vaidehi@annauniv.edu,
karthikcall@gmail.com

Abstract. The accuracy of event detection is a key ingredient in wireless sensor network. It can be achieved with multi-sensor information fusion. In this paper, a fusion framework for Fire detection application using Dasarathy model is proposed .The proposed framework performs fusion with sensed data using two algorithms namely Dempster-Shafer and Fuzzy logic. The final decision about the detection of fire is decided in the sink. Further, a imprecision compensator module is also designed to minimize the imprecision present in the sensed data which results in enhancement of accuracy in fire detection. Performance of the proposed fusion framework is simulated and analyzed in MATLAB in terms of accuracy.

Keywords: Information fusion, Dasarathy model, Imprecision compensator, Dempster Shafer, Fuzzy logic.

1 Introduction

Information fusion refers to combining of data from various sources to arrive at a final decision about the occurrence of event in wireless sensor network (WSN). It is necessary because data which are sent without any redundancy tend to suffer from data loss, which in turn reduces the accuracy [4], [14]. So multiple copies of a single data or multiple sources for a single event can alleviate the problem of data loss [1], [2]. However multiple transmission of same event results in data duplication. This in turn increases the power consumption [3] in the node that leads to degradation in node's lifetime. To overcome the above mentioned problem, information fusion technique is found more suitable.

In this paper, a fusion framework based on Dasarathy model [2] is proposed for fire detection [15] application. Two fusion algorithms namely Dempster Shafer [6],[7],[10],[11] and Fuzzy [5],[8],[12],[13] are implemented in the proposed model whose performances are evaluated in terms of accuracy.

The remaining paper is organized as follows. Section 2 presents the proposed fusion framework. The simulation results are explained in section 3. Section 4 concludes the paper.

N. Meghanathan et al. (Eds.): NeCoM, WiMoN, and WeST 2010, CCIS 90, pp. 472–480, 2010.
© Springer-Verlag Berlin Heidelberg 2010

2 Proposed Fusion Framework

The proposed framework comprises of four modules namely sensing module, pre-fusion module, fusion module and post-fusion module as shown in Figure 1.

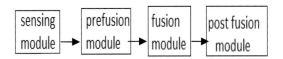

Fig. 1. Modules involved in fusion

2.1 Sensing Module

The sensing module consists of two sensors namely Temperature sensor and smoke detector that can detect the occurrence of fire. The sensed data is transmitted to pre-fusion module.

2.2 Prefusion Module

The imprecision present in the sensed data received from the sensing module are reduced in the pre-fusion module by means of sampler and imprecision compensator (IC).

The sensed data are continuously sampled over a period of observation. The sampled data output $s(j)$ can be given by

$$s_i(j) = x_i(t_{ob} * j / N) \tag{1}$$

where i = 1, 2, ... m sensors
        j = 1, 2,...., N sampling instants
        x = Continuous sensor output.

The imprecision compensator consists of three units namely reference pdf generator, mapper and level adjuster. The reference pdf generator constructs the reference pdf from the sensor characteristics namely rise time of the sensor, period of observation and decay time.

As the sampled output contains imprecision due to noise, it is mapped to the reference pdf as shown in Figure 2. The deviation that results due to imprecision is compensated by level adjuster.

Consider $\epsilon_0 = T_{room}/T_{ref}$ and q = 1 − ϵ_0. Let ϵ denote precision and t_0 denote time taken to reach ϵ = 1, then

$$\varepsilon(t) = \begin{cases} q[\dfrac{1}{q} - \exp(-\dfrac{t}{t_0})] & 0 < t < t_0 \\ 1 & t_0 < t < t_1 \\ \exp(-\dfrac{t}{kt_1}) & t_1 < t < t_{ob} \end{cases} \tag{2}$$

Where k = decay constant.

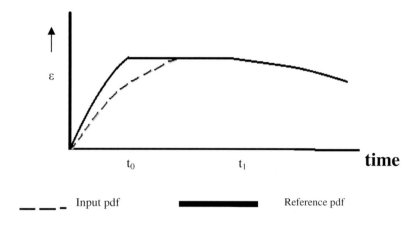

Fig. 2. Mapping of input pdf with Reference

Let

$$q' = (1 - \frac{T_{room}}{T_{max}}) \tag{3}$$

Then

$$\in'(t) = \begin{cases} q'[\frac{1}{q'} - \exp(-\frac{t}{t_0'})] & 0 < t < t_0' \\ 1 & t_0' < t < t_1' \\ \exp(-\frac{t}{kt_1'}) & t_1' < t < t_{ob} \end{cases} \tag{4}$$

Since $\in_0' = \dfrac{T_{max}}{T_{room}}$ and $p = \dfrac{T_{max}}{T_{ref}}$

It can be said that

$$\frac{\in_0'}{\in_0} = (\frac{t_0}{t_0'})^p \tag{5}$$

$$\in_0' t_0'^p = \in_0 t_0^p$$

(The above equation is linearly approximated (i.e.) p=1). t_0' is evaluated from the above equation and the number of sample instants(< rise time) that require imprecision compensation is estimated. The equation is

$$\in' = \frac{t}{t_0'} + \in_0' \tag{6}$$

So finally the difference of $\in(t)$ and $\in'(t)$ at the sampling instants is the compensation offered at time instants ($t_2, t_3, t_4 \ldots$)

Level Adjuster module just boosts up or boost down the values using the new precision values obtained from PDF.

The level adjuster module performs the following operation

$$a(n) = \frac{s_i(n)}{\in'_i(n)}$$

(7)

2.3 Fusion Module

Fusion module implements the fusion algorithms – Dempster Shafer and Fuzzy.

2.3.1 Dempster Shafer
Dempster Shafer algorithm includes 2 stages:

Category 1: Temporal fusion
Category 2: Sensor level fusion

In temporal fusion the process of data combining is repeated for prescribed number of instants, while in sensor level fusion, the fusion takes place among multiple sensors and final decision about the occurrence of fire is determined. Each sensor node maintains a frame of discernment which contains 3 possible states namely Low risk region, Medium risk region and High risk region with initial equal probabilities of 1/3. All the states have same initial probabilities. Now when each input arrives, region of interest is identified and these probabilities are modified accordingly. Then frame of discernment for successive time instant are obtained and multiplied with frame of discernment of previous time instant. From the multiplied result, the range of interest is chosen and conflict region of interest is identified. There are certain gray areas whose region is identified based on the maximum probabilities of participating frame elements.

This process is repeated for successive time instants and fused output is obtained. The same process is repeated for all sensors to complete the sensor level fusion.

From the frame of discernment the basic probability assignment (bpa) is obtained. Let $m_1(Y)$ and $m_2(Z)$ are bpa's representing temperature and smoke sensor respectively, then the rule of combination can be formulated as given below that determines the occurrence of fire.

$$m_{12}(X) = \frac{\sum_{Y \cap Z = X} m_1(Y) m_2(Z)}{1 - k}$$

(8)

Where X is the output mass function and k is probability of conflict given by

$$k = \sum_{Y \cap Z = \phi} m_1(Y) m_2(Z)$$

(9)

2.3.2 Fuzzy Logic
Fuzzification converts the sensed temperature and smoke detector data into linguistic values by computing the membership function using trapezoidal method as shown in Figure 3.

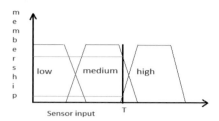

Fig. 3. Fuzzification

$$F(T)=\{F_1(T),F_2(T),F_3(T)\} \tag{10}$$

T - sensor data (temperature)
$F_1(T)$-membership of T in the fuzzy term 'low'
$F_2(T)$-membership of T in the fuzzy term 'high'.
F(T)-Linguistic or Fuzzy variable corresponding to the crisp data T.
Applying the following Fuzzy rules output fuzzy variable is obtained .

$$x \text{ AND } y = \text{Min}\{x,y\} \tag{11}$$

$$x \text{ OR } y = \text{Max}\{x,y\} \tag{12}$$

$$\text{NOT } x = 1\text{-}x \tag{13}$$

Where x,y – fuzzy terms
Fuzzy Associate Mapping (FAM) is used to map fuzzy rules in a matrix format as shown in Table1.

Table 1. FAM Table

S1/S2	LOW	MEDIUM	HIGH
LOW	VERY LOW	LOW	MEDIUM
MEDIUM	LOW	MEDIUM	HIGH
HIGH	MEDIUM	HIGH	VERY HIGH

For making the final decision about the occurence of fire, the final output fuzzy variable is converted into a crisp value by centre of gravity rule as illustrated in Figure 4.

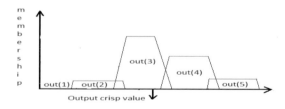

Fig. 4. Defuzzification using centre of gravity rule

In centre of gravity method the output fuzzy sets are weighted based on the output fuzzy values and the centre of gravity of the fuzzy variable is found.

$$out = \frac{out(1)out_1(c) + out(2)out_2(c) + .. + out(n)out_n(c)}{out_1(c) + out_2(c) + .. + out_n(c)} \qquad (14)$$

Where $out_n(c)$ is the Centre of gravity of nth set.
Out(n) is the value of the fuzzy term n in output fuzzy variable.
Out is the output crisp variable.

2.4 Post Fusion Module

Post fusion module evaluates performance of proposed framework in terms of accuracy. To analyze the accuracy of the developed framework, a Gaussian noise model is simulated and added to the input. The inputs without noise and with noise are both fed to the framework and their outputs are compared to evaluate the accuracy of the framework. Before passing on to stages of accuracy evaluation, formation of Probability Mass Function (PMF) for each node is performed.

The range of sensor value is scaled down to range of $0 - 10$ and then the region splitting is done as shown in Table 2.

Table 2. Sensor scale

Range	Region
0-4	Low risk
3-7	Medium risk
8-10	High Risk

These regions are demarcated with 4 pivot points. These are placed in 2 groups of 2 each

$$g_1 = \{p_1, p_2\}, g_2 = \{p_1, p_2\} \qquad (15)$$

Here g_1 denotes the region between low risk and medium risk and g_2 denotes the region between medium and high risk. p_1 and p_2 are pivot elements. Once they are obtained, the following rules are followed.

Rule 1: If p_i and p_j lies in same region, successor value is 1.
Rule 2: If p_i lies in unique region and p_j lies in overlapping region then success value is ½.
Rule 3: If p_i and p_j lies in overlapping region then successor value is ½.
Rule 4: If p_i and p_j lies in unique but conflicting region of interest then successor's value is 0. Once these values are known, the success value for each sample instants (for both cases) is evaluated and summed up. The rate of success value to no. of sampling instants gives accuracy (for both cases) The same procedure is repeated for two broader cases

Case 1: input passes on to imprecision compensator.
Case 2: input is not passed through imprecision compensator

Let **a'** be the level adjusted input with noise and '**a**' be the level adjusted input without noise. A threshold for the noise level can be given as

$$threshold = \sqrt{(E \ |(a - a')^2 |)} = \sigma_{snrt} \qquad (16)$$

$\sigma_{snrt.}$ = Tolerable standard deviation for suitable signal to noise ratio

Accuracy = success/total instants

The developed fusion framework based on Dasarathy model is illustrated in Figure 5.

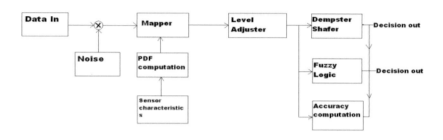

Fig. 5. Fusion Framework based on Dasarathy model

Table 3. Scenario Table

Scenario	SNR	Accuracy of Dempster Shafer		Accuracy of Fuzzy Logic	
		With Out IC	With IC	With Out IC	With IC
1	45	0.833	1	0.66	1
2	30	0.66	1	0.5	0.66
3	20	0.5	0.833	0.33	0.66
4	10	0.5	0.833	0.33	0.66
5	5	0.333	0.833	0.166	0.5
6	2	0.333	0.66	0.166	0.5
7	1	0.333	0.66	0.166	0.33
8	0.1	0.333	0.5	0.166	0.33

3   Simulation Results

The performance of two fusion algorithms in terms of accuracy with and without imprecision compensator is simulated and analysed in MATLAB R2008a as shown in Figure 6 and Figure 7.

Figure 6 represent the significance of Level Shifter(IC) that improves the accuracy of the Dempster Shafer algorithm. From the simulation result it is found that the accuracy of Dempster Shafer on an average has improved to 42.25%.

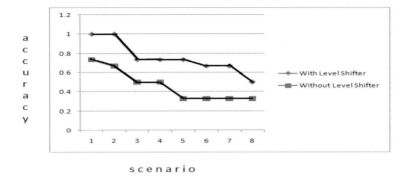

Fig. 6. Accuracy evaluation of Dempster Shafer

Figure 7 represents the accuracy analysis of fuzzy logic for different scenarios and results show that the accuracy of Fuzzy logic on an average has improved to 32.5%.

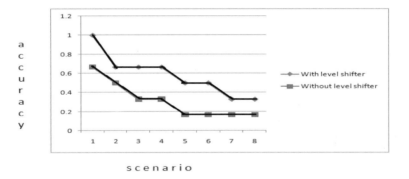

Fig. 7. Accuracy evaluation of fuzzy logic

4   Conclusion

In this paper a fusion framework based on Dasarathy model has been developed for fire detection application using Dempster Shafer and Fuzzy algorithms. Further, a Imprecision Compensator module is also designed to compensate the imprecision present in the sensed data which results in significant improvement in the accuracy of fusion. The developed framework has been simulated in MATLAB R2008a and ana-lysed for accuracy.

Acknowledgement

The authors of the paper acknowledge TATA Consultancy Services (TCS), Bangalore for funding the project titled "Power optimization in WSN".

References

1. Bors, A.G., Pitas, I., Chatziz, V.: Multimodal Decision Level Fusion for Person Authentication. IEEE transaction on Systems, Man and Cybernetics 29(6), 674 (1999)
2. Loureiro, A.A.F., Nakamura, E.F.: Information Fusion in Wireless Sensor Networks. In: Proceedings of Sigmod Conference, June 2008, p. 1365. ACM, New York (2008)
3. Jagyasi, B.G., Dey, B.K., Merchants, S.N., Desai, U.B.: An MMSE based weighted aggregation scheme for event detection using WSN. In: 14th European Signal Processing Conference, EUSIPCO 2006, September 2006, p. 332 (2006)
4. Han, B., Luo, Q., Zhao, X.: Survey on Robot Multisensory Information Fusion Technology. In: Proceedings of conference on Intelligent control and Automation, China, June 2008, p. 5019 (2008)
5. Ruzzo, F., Ramponi, G.: Fuzzy methods for Multisensory Data Fusion. IEEE transaction on Instrumentation and Measurement 43(2), 288 (1994)
6. Karray, F., Zhu, H., Basir, O.: Connectionist – Based Dempster Shafer Evidential Reasoning for Data Fusion. In: Proceedings of IEEE 13th International conference on Wireless Communication and Networking, August 2001, p. 1513 (2001)
7. Wang, G., Yuan, Z.: Sensor Deployment Strategy for Collaborative Target Detection with Guaranteed Accuracy. In: Proceedings of IEEE 4th International conference on Mobile Ad-hoc and Sensor Networks, Chicago, November 2001, p. 68 (2001)
8. Marinov, M., Dontscheva, M., Dimirtor, S., Djamiykov, T.: An Adaptive approach for linearization of temperature sensor characteristics. In: Proceedings of IEEE 27th International Spring seminar on Electronics Technology, Singapore, December 2008, p. 417 (2008)
9. Karl, H., Lobbers, M., Nieberg, T.: A Data Aggregation Framework for Wireless Sensor Network. In: PRORISC workshop on Circuits, Vancouver, November 2003, p. 256 (2003)
10. Wo, H., Yang, J., Siegel, M., Stiefelhagan, R.: Sensor Fusion using Dempster Shafer theory. In: International conference on Instrumentation and Measurement Technology, USA, May 2002, p. 193 (2002)
11. Bloch, I., Vidal-Madjar, D., Le Hegarat-Mascle, S.: Application of Dempster Shafer Evidence Theory to unsupervised classification in multisource remote sensing. IEEE transaction on Geoscience and Remote Sensing 35(4), 1018 (1997)
12. Mi, J.-S., Wo, W.-Z., Yecleung: On Generalized Fuzzy Beliefs Functions in Infinite spaces. IEEE Transactions on fuzzy systems 17(2), 123 (2009)
13. Chanussot, J., Benediktsson, J.A., Fauvel, M.: Decision Fusion for the Classification of Urban Remote Sensing Images. IEEE Transaction on Geosciences and Remote Sensing 44(4), 2828 (2008)
14. Khan, S., Alam, Z.: On the issues of linearizing a sensor characteristics over a wider response range. In: IEEE International Conference on Computer and Communication Engineering, April 2008, p. 72 (2008)
15. Lim, Y.-s., Lee, Y.-w.: A Fire detection and Rescue Support Framework with Wireless Sensor Networks. In: International Conference on Convergence IT, November 2008, p. 135 (2008)

Localization Based on Signal Strength Using Kalman Approach

P.T.V. Bhuvaneswari, V. Vaidehi, and M. AgnesSaranya

Madras Institute of Technology, Anna University,
Chennai, India
ptvbmit@annauniv.edu, vaidehi@annauniv.edu,
saran_1131@yahoo.co.in

Abstract. This paper proposes a distributed localization algorithm based on Received Signal Strength (RSS) that consists of two phases, distance estimation phase and coordinate estimation phase. In distance estimation phase the distance of the unknown node is computed based on the RSS measurements using log normal shadowing path loss model and ITU indoor attenuation model. The distance error is minimized by one-dimensional Kalman filter and the number of iterations of the filter is limited using Cramer Rao Bound value. In the second phase, the coordinates of the unknown node is estimated by lateration technique whose accuracy is improved by min-max algorithm. The RSS value is experimentally obtained in real-time indoor environment using zigbee series 1 RF module. The proposed algorithm is simulated and analyzed in MATLAB version 7. From the simulation results it is found that the proposed localization algorithm performs more efficient in terms of computational cost and accuracy.

Keywords: Received signal strength, log normal shadowing model, ITU model, one-dimension Kalman estimator, Cramer Rao bound, min-max algorithm.

1 Introduction

Localization in Wireless Sensor Networks (WSN) makes the sensed data more meaningful. It also supports in designing network layer services, such as topology control, routing, and clustering.

Using nodes equipped with GPS (Global Positioning System) receiver is costly and not energy efficient [4], [5], [8]. Hence there is a need for an efficient distributed localization algorithm to determine node's positions using distance measurements between neighboring nodes which requires two types of nodes namely, the beacon node and the unknown node. The beacon node is a node that is aware of its location while unknown node is the one whose locations is to be determined.

The distance measurement between the beacon nodes and unknown nodes can be done by three techniques [4]. In this paper, an efficient distributed localization

N. Meghanathan et al. (Eds.): NeCoM, WiMoN, and WeST 2010, CCIS 90, pp. 481–489, 2010.

algorithm based on Received Signal Strength (RSS) measurement is developed which provides an accurate and cost-effective solution.

The rest of the paper is organized as follows. Section 2 presents the proposed localization algorithm with relevant mathematical formulations. Section 3 presents the simulation results and performance analysis of the proposed algorithm. Finally, section 4 concludes the paper with future work.

2   Proposed Localization Algorithm

Consider a sensor network comprising of S_n nodes located at the coordinate $(x_i, y_i), i=1,2,...,n$, where n represents the total number of nodes in the network. Assume that there are S_k anchor nodes whose positions are known (e.g. obtained via GPS or some other "absolute" reference) and that the remaining $S_u = S_n - S_k$ nodes are located at unknown positions. Without loss of generality, assume that position of nodes $S_{k+1},..., S_n$ are unknown, whereas the locations of the nodes $S_1, S_2,..., S_k$ are known. Let θ_1, θ_2 be the coordinates of the nodes whose positions are known and unknown respectively.

$$\theta_1 = \{(x_k , y_k)\}, k = S_1, S_2,...., S_k$$
$$\theta_2 = \{(x_u , y_u)\}, u = S_{k+1}, S_{k+2},...., S_n \tag{1}$$

The proposed localization algorithm estimates the coordinates θ_2 from the given anchor node coordinates θ_1, and many pair-wise range measurement $\{\gamma_{ku}(t)\}$ taken over time t=1,2...,N where N represents number of samples. The proposed localization algorithm is shown in Figure 1.

2.1   Distance Estimation Phase

In this phase, the distance between the anchor and unknown node is estimated by one-dimension Kalman filter estimator. Initially the RSS values of anchor node's signal are measured with respect to unknown node in an indoor environment using Zigbee series 1 RF module [3]. As the medium is prone to errors due multi-path propagation, more samples are taken at different time instances for different scenario in five channels namely B, C, D, E and F. The procedure is repeated for different distances. Next by Statistical modeling the quality of channel is evaluated [1]. The channel that results with low standard deviation compared to other channels is selected as the best channel.

The distance of the unknown node with respect to anchor node is computed from the ensemble mean RSS value of the best channel. As the considered indoor environment consist of path loss and attenuation elements, two models namely path loss log normal shadowing and ITU indoor attenuation models are used in distance calculation.

2.1.1   Log Normal Shadowing Path Loss Model
The path loss between node k and node u is random and distributed log normally which can be modeled as [8], [10].

$$PL(d_{ku}')[dB] = PL(d_{ref}) + 10n_p \log(d_{ku}'/d_{ref}) + X_\sigma \tag{2}$$

where $PL(d_{ref})$ is the ensemble path loss at a short reference distance d_{ref} and X_σ is the zero mean Gaussian random variable with standard deviation σ and n_p is path-loss exponent which typically lies between 2 and 4.

The ensemble mean received power is the difference of the transmitted power and the path loss component at the specific distance d_{ku}' which is modeled as,

$$P_r(d_{ku}')[dBm] = P_t(dBm) - PL(d_{ku}')[dB] \tag{3}$$

Substituting eqn (2) in (3),

$$P_r(d_{ku}')[dBm] = P_t(dBm) - PL(d_{ref}) - 10n_p \log(d_{ku}'/d_{ref}) - X_\sigma \tag{4}$$

Where $P_r(d_{ku}')$ is the average RSS value in dBm or received power and $P_t(dBm)$ is the power transmitted.

$$PL(d_{ref}) = -10 \log(G_t G_r \lambda^2 / (4\pi^2)d_{ref}^2) \tag{5}$$

where G_t, G_r = Gain of the transmitter and receiver antennas respectively

λ = wavelength of the signal by c /f

c = Velocity of light in m/s

f =frequency of the signal in Hz.

The distance d_{ku}' computed from log-normal shadowing model can be expressed as

$$d_{ku}' = d_{ref}(10^{[(P_t(dBm)-PL(d_{ref})-X_\sigma-P_r(d_{ku}')[dBm])/(10n_p)]}) \tag{6}$$

2.1.2 ITU Indoor Attenuation Model
The ITU indoor attenuation model [11] is formally expressed as

$$PL(d_{ref})[dB] = 20 \log f + L \log d_{ref} + P_f(f_{rku}) - 28 \tag{7}$$

where   L = distance power loss coefficient
  f_{rku}= Number of floors between the node k and node u
  $P_f(f_{rku})$ = floor loss penetration factor.

Then the distance d_{ku}'' computed from ITU indoor attenuation model is obtained by substituting eqn. (7) in eqn. (6)

$$d_{ku}'' = d_{ref}(10^{[(P_t(dBm)-20\log f - L\log d_{ref} - P_f(f_{rku})+28-X_\sigma-P_r(d_{ku}')[dBm])/(10n_p)]}) \tag{8}$$

Then the distance error which is the difference between the actual distance and the calculated distance is computed which is minimized by one-dimensional Kalman filter estimator [9]. The one-dimensional Kalman estimator is modeled as average filter that combines, the distance values calculated by model 1 and 2. The standard deviations obtained from both the models are σ_1 and σ_2 which are expressed below:

$$\sigma_1 = (((d_{ku}' - m)^2 + (d_{ku} - m)^2)/(n_d - 1))^{1/2} \tag{9}$$

where $m = (d_{ku}' + d_{ku})/2$

n_d = number of samples

$$\sigma_2 = (((d_{ku}'' - m_1)^2 + (d_{ku} - m_1)^2)/(n_d - 1))^{1/2} \tag{10}$$

where $m_1 = (d_{ku}'' + d_{ku})/2$

The estimated distance $\hat{d}_{ku}$ is the average of d_{ku}' and d_{ku}'' [9] is given below,

$$\hat{d}_{ku} = d_{ku}' + K(d_{ku}'' - d_{ku}') \tag{11}$$

where $K = \dfrac{\sigma_1^2}{(\sigma_1^2 + \sigma_2^2)}$ is defined as the Kalman gain.

The accuracy of the estimator $\hat{d}_{ku}$ is then determined based on Cramer Rao Bound (CRB) value [3] which is given below,

$$\text{CRB} = \frac{\sigma^2}{n_d} \tag{12}$$

where $\sigma = (\sigma_1 + \sigma_2)/2$.

The iterations of the estimator is repeated till following condition is satisfied,

$$cov(\hat{d}_{ku}) \geq \text{CRB} \tag{13}$$

The value obtained in each iteration of the proposed algorithm is given in Table 3.

2.2   Co-ordinate Estimation Phase

Using multi-lateration model, the 2-D coordinates of the unknown node is obtained from the following expression

$$\begin{bmatrix} x_u \\ y_u \end{bmatrix} = 2 \begin{pmatrix} y_n - y_{n-1} & \cdots & y_1 - y_n \\ \vdots & \ddots & \vdots \\ x_{n-1} - x_n & \cdots & x_n - x_1 \end{pmatrix} \begin{bmatrix} (r_1^2 - r_n^2) & - & (x^2 - x_n^2) & - & (y^2 - y_n^2) \\ \vdots & & \cdots & & \cdots \\ (r_{n-1}^2 - r_n^2) & - & (x_{n-1}^2 - x_n^2) & - & (y_{n-1}^2 - y_n^2) \end{bmatrix} \tag{14}$$

where $(x_i, y_i), i=1,2,\ldots,n$, is the coordinates of the known nodes and $r_i, i=1,2,\ldots,n$ is the distance between the node i and node u.

The imperfection in the intersection of circles of trilateration are solved by min-max bounding box concept [6], in which the radio range circles are modeled as squares called Positioning Cells (PC). The set of PCs used in coordinate estimation are denoted as PCS. Then the Final Bounding Box (FBB) containing the unknown node is found by the intersection of PCs in one PCS which is given by

$$FBB = \bigcap PC_n \tag{15}$$

Where $PC_n \in PCS$.

3   Simulation Results

The experimentation is done in real-time indoor environment using zigbee series 1 RF module and the associated X-CTU software of MAXSTREAM. 20 samples of RSS values are measured at 20 different time instances for a specific distance. The experiment is repeated for five different channels (B, C, D, E and F) with five different frequencies. Figure 2 illustrate the relationship between distance and RSS measurement for channels B. It is seen that the RSS of the unknown node decreases as distance between the anchor node and unknown node increases. Similar relationship can also be obtained for the remaining channels.

Figure 3 shows the statistical modeling of channel B. Similar analysis performed for the other channels are shown in Table 1. It is found that the channel E is selected as the best channel for distance 2,4,10 and channel D for 6, 8 as they possesses low standard deviation.

The distance of the unknown node is calculated by both two models are shown in Figure 4. The distance error is computed for both the models.

Figure 5 shows distance estimation with and with out one-dimensional Kalman filter. Table 2 presents the results of Kalman estimated distance and the associated error percentage. It is seen that the error is drastically reduced by Kalman estimator. Table 4 shows the results obtained with and without min-max bounding box algorithm. It is found that accuracy is improved through min-max bounding box algorithm.

The computational complexity of the proposed algorithm is estimated as given in Table 5. So, the total computation is (9A+2D)+(2A+5D)I. The division operations involved in equation 6, 8 and 11 can be converted into multiplications by performing the division once and saving the quotient in temporary memory location to reduce the computational complexity. As division takes more time than addition and multiplication, computation of the proposed algorithm will be O((2A+I(5D)) where I is the number of iteration which is limited by the CRB value.

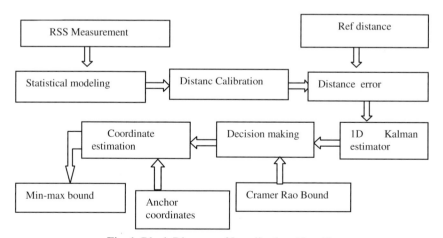

Fig. 1. Block Diagram of Localization Algorithm

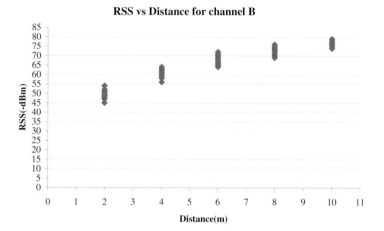

Fig. 2. RSS vs Distance in Channel B

Table 1. Standard deviation values of RSS measurements

Dist (m)	B (2.404-2.406) GHZ	C (2.409-2.411) GHz	D (2.414-2.416) GHz	E (2.419-2.421) GHz	F (2.424-2.426) GHz
2	2.39	2.13	2.62	0.92	1.69
4	1.87	1.65	1.53	1.23	1.38
6	2.13	1.67	1.26	1.37	2.05
8	1.98	1.29	1.04	1.31	1.92
10	1.11	1.44	0.96	0.61	1.18

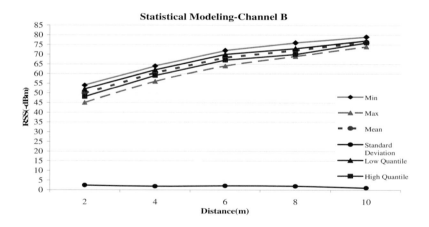

Fig. 3. Statistical modeling of Channel B

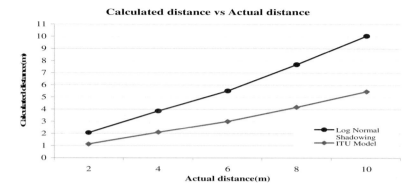

Fig. 4. Calculated distance vs Actual distance

Table 2. One-dimension Kalman Estimator

Act dist. (m)	Err (without KF)	% of error with-out KF	Err (With KF)	% of error with KF	% of imp. Acc.
2	0.4705	23.5	0.0502	2.51	89
4	1.0213	25.53	0.1524	3.81	85
6	1.7437	29.06	0.5529	9.21	68
8	2.0737	25.92	0.3507	4.38	83
10	2.2848	22.85	0.0298	0.29	98

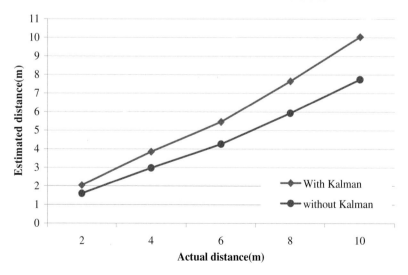

Fig. 5. Comparison of distance estimation

Table 3. Iteration algorithm of Kalman Filter

Act. dist. (m)	CRB Bound	Iteration 1		Iteration 2		Finaldist (m)
		Est. dis(m)	Var (m)	Est. dis(m)	Var (m)	
2	0.0553	2.0603	0.0603	2.0502	0.0502	2.0502
4	0.2607	3.8476	0.1524	-	-	3.8476
6	0.7601	5.4471	0.5529	-		5.4471
					-	
8	1.0751	7.6493	0.3507	-		7.6493
					-	
10	1.3050	10.029	0.0298	-	-	10.029

Table 4. Estimation of Coordinates of the unknown node

Anchor coordinates (x,y)		Distance between anchor node and unknown node(m)	Coordinates of the unknown node (x_u,y_u) without min-max algorithm	Coordinates of the unknown node(x_u,y_u) with min-max algorithm
A1	(2,1)	2.0502		
			(2.9,1.3)	(3.3,1.6)
A2	(5,4)	3.8476		
A3	(8,2)	5.4471		

Table 5. Computational Complexity

Equ. No.	Operations		
	Divisions	Additions	Loop
6	1	3	---
8	1	6	---
11	5	2	I*

I* -Index value of Iterations

4 Conclusion

In this paper, a novel cost-effective accurate distributed localization algorithm is proposed. It uses path loss and attenuation models to compute the distance of the nodes accurately. The error is minimized with one-dimensional Kalman estimator. Further the one-dimensional Kalman is not computationally heavy. The proposed algorithm can be periodically updated to address the topological changes occuring in the network due to mobility of the nodes or failure of the nodes.

Acknowledgement

The first three authors acknowledge Tata Consultancy Services for funding this Project.

References

1. Awad, A., Frunzke, T., Dressler, F.: Adaptive distance estimation and localization in WSN using RSSI measures. In: Proceedings of 10th EUROMICRO Conference on Digital System Design - Architectures, Methods and Tools, pp. 471–478 (2007)
2. Srinivasan, A., Wu, J.: A survey of secure localization in wireless sensor networks. In: Encyclopedia of Wireless and Mobile Communications, Florida Atlantic University (2008)
3. Larsson, E.G.: Cramer-Rao bound analysis of distributed positioning in sensor networks. IEEE Signal Processing Letters 11(3), 334–337 (2007)
4. Karl, H., Willig, A.: Protocols and Architectures for Wireless Sensor Networks. Wiley Publications, Chichester (2006)
5. Bachrach, J., Taylor, C.: Localization in sensor networks. In: Handbook of sensor networks: algorithms and architectures, ch. 9, 1st edn., vol. 1. Wiley Publications, Chichester (2005)
6. Yedavalli, K., Krishnamachari, B., Venkatraman, L.: Fast/Fair Mobile Localization in Infrastructure Wireless Sensor Networks. Mobile Computing and Communications Review 11(1), 29–40 (2007)
7. Patwari, N., Hero, A.O.: Demonstrating Distributed Signal Strength Location Estimation. In: SenSys 2006, pp. 353–354 (2006)
8. Sahoo, P.K., Hwang, I.-S., Lin, S.-Y.: A Distributed Localization Scheme for Wireless Sensor Networks. In: International Conference on Mobile Technology, Applications and Systems, vol. 6(7), Article No. 77, pp. 1031–1050 (2008)
9. Rojas, R.: The Kalman Filter, Technical report, Freie University of Berlin (2003)
10. Rappaport, T.S.: Wireless Communications-Principles and Practice, 2nd edn. Prentice-Hall of India Publications, India
11. ITU Model for Indoor Attenuation, http://www.wikipedia.com

Reliable Data Replication Middleware for Next Generation Web Services

G.M. Siddesh[1] and K.G. Srinivasa[2]

[1] Lecturer, Dept. of Information Science and Engineering, MSRIT, Bangalore
and
Research Scholar JNTU, Hyderbad
[2] Data Mining Lab, M S Ramaiah Institute of Technology, Bangalore
{siddeshgm,srinivasa.kg}@gmail.com

Abstract. The Web Services are interdependent among themselves in distributed environment. Offering such interdependency is a challenging task due to geographical distance of nodes in an distributed environment which results in high data accessing delay. This paper contributes an Publish/Subscribe Replication Middleware for distributed web services. This technique achieves replication of data dynamically upon the incoming transaction request from the client. This middleware framework offers: Replication services to achieve interdependency, Heterogeneity and security issues among web services. This method achieves interdependency by improving the data accessing delay and avoids reading of stale replicas. When compared to the systems with out replication/using any traditional techniques to achieve interdependency the proposed model is proved efficient through the implementation.

Keywords: Web Services, Replication, Middleware, Publish/Subscribe.

1 Introduction

An distributed system consists of large number of computers and communication links, must always function even in spite of some failures. This fault tolerance need to be achieved transparently in distributed environment.Interdependent systems in distributed environment would need to be highly available. This high availability and failure transparency is achieved through replication. Database replication addresses the problem of scalability, reliability and improves database service to web applications. Web services are autonomous software systems identified by *Uniform Resource Identifiers (*URIs) which can be advertised, located, and accessed through messages encoded according to Extensible Mark up Language (XML) based standards and transmitted using Internet protocols. Web services are the fundamental building blocks for constructing distributed systems on the Internet [1].Web services is the one true path for bringing electronic data interchange, transaction systems and business to business services in to the 21st century [2].

Simple Object Access Protocol (SOAP) is a communication protocol for inter-application communication, which achieves heterogeneity in an distributed computing

N. Meghanathan et al. (Eds.): NeCoM, WiMoN, and WeST 2010, CCIS 90, pp. 490–499, 2010.

environment. It is language-independent by using XML Schema to express message formats and invocation interfaces [3].SOAP is widely viewed as the backbone to a new generation of cross-platform, cross language distributed computing applications [4]. Effective data management in today's competitive enterprise environment is an important issue. Replication is one such widely accepted phenomenon in distributed environment, where data is stored at more than one site to achieve performance, reliability and fault tolerance [5].

There are four kinds of replication techniques [6]: active replication, semi-active (leader-follower) replication, passive replication and coordinator-cohort replication. In active replication primary server processes the client invocation and replies the client immediately. Semi-active replication is similar to active replication, where all replicas receive a request; however, one replica (the leader) plays a special role. Whenever the leader makes a nondeterministic decision, it notifies the other replicas (its followers) of its choice. The followers are then forced to take the same decision. In passive replication primary server processes the client's requests and propagates updates to other backup replica servers. Coordinator-cohort replication is another hybrid replication technique which is the combination of semi active and passive replication styles. Our approach is based on hybrid replication strategy.

A middleware is a software layer present on every node of a distributed system that uses operating system functions to provide a homogeneous high-level interface to applications for many aspects of a distributed computing environment, such as communication, naming, concurrency, synchronisation, replication, persistency, and access control [7]. Middleware is defined as a layer of software above the operating system but below application program that provides a common programming abstraction across a distributed system [8]. Replication middleware is an software layer which sits on every node of an distributed system, which achieves replication of data dynamically upon the incoming transaction request from the client.

The Publish/Subscribe model is an asynchronous, many-to-many communication model for distributed systems. It is an approach to deliver data to a large number of clients depending on their interests [9]. Publish/Subscribe communication model is an scalable approach, here information producers and consumers do not need to know about each other and a single producer may cause information to be delivered to multiple consumers [7]. This paper presents a middleware that transparently supports reliability among web services built on Publish/subscribe replication, with message filtering, publication, subscription and subscription management.

2 Related Works

There are several middleware solutions related to replication for web services in distributed world: AXIS2-based Replication Middleware for Web Services [10] proposes an active replication strategy for replication in Web Services. Primary-backup replication of Web Services is offered by Fault Tolerant SOAP middleware [11]. Lamehamedi et al. [12] proposes a method for dynamically creating replicas based on cost estimation model. Another economy-based approach for file replication proposed by Bell et al. [13] dynamically creates and delete replica of files. ADAPT [14] is a J2EE replication framework integrated into JBOSS application server which allows plug in of replication protocols. Replication for Web Hosting Systems [15] proposes a system that hosts the documents of a website and manages replication automatically.

Ranganathan et al. [16] proposes various dynamic replication strategies based on temporal and geographical locality and assumes that data access are read only so that consistency issues do not arise. Jordi Bataller, Hendrik Decker, L uis Irun and Francesc Munoz [17] proposes the architecture of the middleware package DIRECS (DIstributed REplication for Collaborative Systems). It supports the consistency of replicated data and thereby increases responsiveness, availability and failure resilience of collaborative systems. To support large numbers of users who continuously change their data and processing needs, Houda Lamehamedi, Zujun Shentu and Boleslaw Szymanski [18] has introduced scalable replica distribution topologies that adapt replica placement to meet these needs. They have designed dynamic memory middleware and replication algorithm.

Migol [19] is a Grid middleware, which addresses the fault tolerance of Grid applications and services. Migol's Replication Service uses a token-based algorithm and certificate-based security to provide secure group communication.WS-Replication [20] supports the active replication of Web services in a wide area network. The framework consists of a replication component, which implements the replication state machine on the respective node, and a multicast component, which is responsible for group communication. Globus Toolkit [21] provide base services for managing replicas: The Globus Replica Location Service (RLS) provides a simple information service, which maintains information about physical locations of file copies (replicas) using a unique logical filename. RLS instances can be hierarchically aggregated: Local Replica Catalogs (LRCs) store replica information for a local site, while Replica Location Indices (RLIs) consolidate data of a set of LRCs.

3   Proposed System

In recent years it has been shown that Replication is the major technique to achieve interdependency among distributed web services. A challenge is to keep copies consistent despite updates. We use a middleware approach which provides subject based Replication services to achieve interdependency, Heterogeneity using Simple Object Access Protocol (SOAP) based message exchange among web services, it also incorporates security issues like authentication and confidentiality.

As shown in Fig 1 Node 1, Node 2 …. Node N, are distributed and connected. Data stored in Node 1 is stored in Node 2 and is replicated at all other Nodes. Our model replicates data transparently among different nodes in distributed environment. All requests/updates are forwarded to replication service, which will multicasts all requests/updates to subscribers using an multicasting module. All subscribed nodes receive same request/update of the client and hence everyone maintains same state.

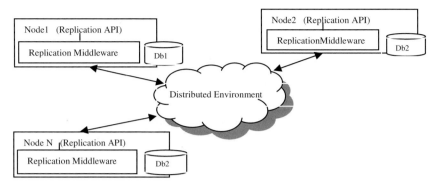

Fig. 1. Architecture of data replication in distributed Environment

As shown in Fig 2, the proposed Middleware framework consists of Interceptor module, pub/sub-rep module, multicast module, security module. To achieve fault tolerance, middleware framework and its components will be residing on each node in the distributed environment.

Execution of the proposed work consists of the following steps:

Step1: Client sends its request/update to the primary
       backup replication server.
Step2: When the transaction begins primary intercepts
       incoming SOAP messages
Step3: After client is authenticated, based on the
       subject of the request/update they are published
       in the topic.
Step4: Client request/update is multicasted through the
       SOAP communication protocol to the subscribed
       backup replication servers.
Step5: Upon reception of the replicas, backup servers
       intercept the SOAP messages and processes the
       request/update of the client.
Step6: Replies are sent to the primary from the backup
       replication servers.
Step7: Upon receiving replies from all the subscribed
       backup servers.
Step8: Primary is confirmed that all its subscribed
       backup replication servers received the copy of
       request/update of the client.
Step9: Primary replies back to the client.

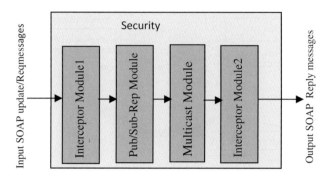

Fig. 2. Proposed middleware Frame work

3.1 Interceptor Module

Each node in the distributed environment processes the SOAP messages according to the formal set of conventions defined by SOAP. Every node is responsible for enforcing the rules that govern the exchange of SOAP messages and accesses the services provided through SOAP bindings. Interceptor Module1 accepts incoming SOAP based messages, messages are read from SOAP for invocation of requested services locally.Interceptor Module2 outgoing messages are encapsulated in to SOAP envelope, since SOAP is our communication protocol-- to achieve heterogeneity-- among web services in distributed environment to among web services.

Since SOAP messages are half duplex transmissions from a SOAP sender to a SOAP receiver, it is binded with HTTP to implement request/response model. Binding SOAP to HTTP provides the advantage of being able to use the heterogeneity and decentralized flexibility of SOAP with the rich features of HTTP. SOAP follows the HTTP request/response message model by providing a SOAP request message in a HTTP request and SOAP response message in a HTTP response.

3.2 Publish/Subscribe-Replication Module

This model is designed using Java Messaging Service (JMS) API of J2EE platform. Web components can send or asynchronously receive a JMS message. As shown in Fig 3, Clients updates/requests are published in the *topic* present in the primary backup server. Then primary backup server invokes muticast module to multicast the update/request replicas to its entire subscriber backup servers group, subscription can be done dynamically by any backup server with primary backup server, subscription is based on subject based subscription strategy. We have created *durable subscriptions*, this can receive messages even when the subscribers are not active. After intercepting incoming SOAP messages in the previous module, this module publishes the request/updates in topic of the primary, based on the subject of the request/update message of client. Subscribers status is maintained in this module. Then this module invokes multicasting module to achieve group communications.

With the reception of update/request replicas by the subscribers, corresponding services are invoked and are updated. Reply is sent to the primary backup server, after receiving replies from its subscribers primary backup server realizes that all its backup servers are updated now primary server invokes the updates/requests and is updated. Finally primary backup server replies the client back. SOAP acts as communication protocol for exchange of replicas among Primary backup server and subscriber backup servers, so that heterogeneity can be achieved among web services. SOAP Message Exchange Patterns (MEPs) have been defined to define type of interaction -- request/response interaction. However Interceptor module helps in intercepting SOAP messages. Our middleware is an primary backup replication with synchronous update propagation which performs replication on both service level & at data level.

3.3 Multicast Module

Multicast Module maintains a group membership service and group communication service which refers to the log of subscribers in the groups corresponding to their subject of subscription for replicas, since our middleware is designed on subject based subscription strategy. Multicast component provides group communication based on SOAP. SOAP group communication support has been integrated into an existing group communication stack.Having inputs from Pub/Sub-Rep module published replicas are multicasted to specific subscriber group on subject basis. Since subscription can be done dynamically by any backup server, group membership service should manage membership changes in dynamically.

In distributed environment circumstance, a group member often joins/leaves the group dynamically. When a user joins the group, the group should change the group log. Also when a user leaves a group, the original log should become invalid and the remaining member should have a new group log. So scheme should support the dynamic circumstance.

Multicast module also guarantees reliable multicast service by providing retransmission policies. This module collects responses form all the subscribers and informs pub-sub rep module, so that it should be confirmed that every one is updated with the recent request/update message of the client. After confirmation pub-sub rep module should reply back to client.

3.4 Security Module

Security Module provides authentication and confidentiality services to the middle ware frame work. Our SOAP extensibility model considers security issues during communication using SOAP protocol. To fulfill the secure group communication, each module is aware of the overall security context provided. Administrator can set policies, so that publishing and subscription of data in topic is done by privileged users. Authentication is achieved before client publishes updates/requests in primary backup server, client is authenticated at Interceptor stage itself. Confidentiality is achieved using public key cryptographic technique. Security provided here is beyond the scope of transport-level security.

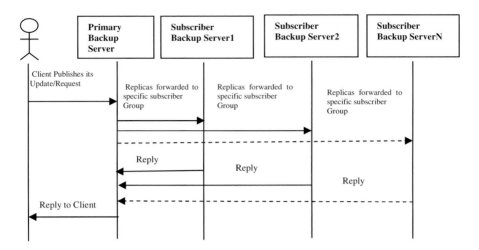

Fig. 3. UML diagram of Publish/Subscribe Replication framework

4   Performance Analysis

Performance of our Publish/Subscribe Replication Middleware is evaluated on an employee record web service. Employee record web service maintains records of employees of an organization. In this web service administrator can update the employee records. Performance of our middleware framework is measured by replicating data at 10 nodes -- 1 primary backup server, 9 subscriber backup servers. The configuration of all 10 nodes is: Intel dual core processors, 2GB RAM, Windows Vista with Service pack2.JDK is used on all nodes, we have measured performance in an Local Area Network which is having 100 Mbps capacity. Fig 4 shows the response times for update transactions to 06 different sites. It can be observed from Fig 4 that Response time is directly proportional to number of nodes (Backup servers).This technique of replication middleware is incorporated without changing the underlying database systems. Extensive experimental evaluations show a major improvement in system scalability. Employing this middleware technique improves the performance of a replicated database systems.Fig 4 depicts that as the data size increases client response time will be decreased. Fig 5 shows throughput of the number of replicas handled per second, there is an negligible overhead.Major parameter values of our experiment are show in the Table 1. Our experiment is on 10 node distributed network, network delay is based on each packet end to end transmission delay. As the data size increases, packet count will also be increased which affects in the increase of operation time, transaction period and replication overhead of the middleware. Time required to run our replication algorithm depends on replication creation time, transaction duration and operation time of request/update of the client.

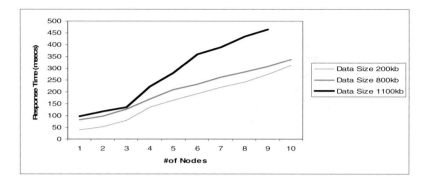

Fig. 4. Client Response time for bulk operations

Even though we need to pay a little bit for the Client response time we are completely avoiding reading of stale values at the backup servers while primary is still processing recent update/request of the client and interdependency among web services in distributed environment is achieved efficiently.

Table 1. Major parameter values of Publish/Subscribe Replication Middleware

Parameter	Value
# of Node	10
Data Size	Constant for an transaction usually ranges between 1-1024 bits among transactions.
Network Delay	2-4 ms
Transaction Duration	20 sec
Operation Time	2-6 ms
Time for replica Creation	2-3sec

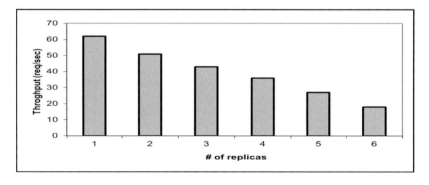

Fig. 5. Throughput based on number of replicas

5 Conclusions

In this paper we have presented an Publish/Subscribe Replication Middleware for distributed web services, which achieves fault tolerance, consistency, flexibility and security. Database replication increases widespread solutions to scalability and high availability challenges in current information systems. The proposed model achieves replication service to achieve interdependency by improving the data accessing delay and by avoiding reading out stale replicas at backup replication server, Heterogeneity among web services using SOAP based message exchange among web services, it also incorporates security issues like authentication and confidentiality. Proposed model is efficient and reliable, when compared to other models with out replication /using any traditional techniques to achieve interdependency which was proved through the implementation.

The design and implementation issues are presented and discussed in the paper, together with the experimental testing results and the discussion on the performance of the replication middleware, we conclude that the overhead by introducing our model is negligible, while the advantage it brings in is significant.As future work we can think of optimizing the middleware framework to reduce the overhead in response time for a client request/update messages, irrespective of number of subscriber back up replication nodes.Throughput overhead is negligible as number of replicas increases, due to increase in the invocation count. Invocations like one made by the client, intercepted by the primary, multicasted , interception by the subscribed backups and replying back.

References

1. Web Services Architecture Requirements, http://www.w3.org/TR/wsa-req
2. Lea, D., Vinoski, S.: Middleware for Web Services. IEEE Internet Computing (2003)
3. SOAP, http://www.w3.org/TR/2001/WD-soap12-20010709
4. Apache Axis,
   http://www.omii.ac.uk/docs/2.3.0/reference/apache_axis
5. Data Replication Strategie In: Wide Area Distributed Systems,
   http://www.gridbus.org/papers/DataReplicationInDSChapter
6. Frolund, S., Guerraoui, R.: X-ability: A theory of replication. In: Proceedings of the 9th Annual ACM Symposium on Principles of Distributed Computing, pp. 229–237. ACM, Portland (2000)
7. Hermes, P.R.P.: A Scalable Event-Based Middleware: A dissertation submitted for the degree of Doctor of Philosophy, Queens' College, University of Cambridge (2004)
8. Bakken, D.E.: Encyclopedia of Distributed Computing. Kluwer Academic Press, Dordrecht (2003)
9. Mahmoud, Q.H.: Middleware for Communications:Message-Oriented Middleware. John wiley & Sons, Ltd., Chichester (2004)
10. Osrael, J., Weghofer, M.: AXIS2-based Replication Middleware for Web Services. In: IEEE International Conference on Web Services (2007)
11. Liang, D., Chen, Lin, F.: Fault Tolerant Web service. In: Proc.10th Asia-Pacific Software Engineering Conference, pp. 10–319. IEEE Computer Society, Los Alamitos (2003)

12. Lamehamedi, H., Shentu, Z., Deelman, E.: Simulation of Dynamic Data Replication Strategies in Data Grids. In: Proceedings of the 17th International Parallel and Distributed Processing Symposium. IEEE Computer Society, France (2003)
13. Bell, W.H., Cameron, D.G., Carvajal-Schiaffino, R., Millar, A.P., Stockinger, K., Zini, F.: Evaluation of an Economy-Based File Replication Strategy for a Data Grid. In: Proccedings of 3rd IEEE International Symposium on Cluster Computing and the Grid, Tokyo Japan (2003)
14. Babaoğlu, Ö., Maverick, V., Patarin, S., Vučković, J., Wu, H.: A framework for prototyping J2EE replication algorithms. In: Meersman, R., Tari, Z. (eds.) OTM 2004. LNCS, vol. 3291, pp. 1413–1426. Springer, Heidelberg (2004)
15. Swaminathan, Szymaniak, M., Pierre, G., Vansteen, M.: ACM Computing Surveys 36(3), 291–334 (2004)
16. Ranganathan, K., Foster, I.: Identifying dynamic Replication Strategies for a High-Performance Data Grid. In: Lee, C.A. (ed.) GRID 2001. LNCS, vol. 2242, pp. 75–86. Springer, Heidelberg (2001)
17. Bataller, J., Decker, H., Irun, L., Munoz, F.: Replication for Web-Based Collaboration. In: Proceedings of the 15th International Workshop on Database and Expert Systems Applications (2004)
18. Lamehamedi, H., Shentu, Z., Szymanski, B.: Simulation of Dynamic Data Replication Strategies in Data Grids. In: Proceedings of the International Parallel and Distributed Processing Symposium (2003)
19. Luckow, A., Schnor, B.: Migol: A Fault-Tolerant Service Framework for MPI Applications in the Grid. Future Generation Computer Systems: The International Journal of Grid Computing: Theory, Methods and Application, 142–152 (2008)
20. Salas, J., Perez-Sorrosal, F., Patino-Martinez, M., Jimenez-Peris, R.: WSReplication: A Framework for Highly Available Web Services. In: WWW 2006: Proceedings of the 15th international conference on World Wide Web, pp. 357–366. ACM Press, New York (2006)
21. Foster, I.: Globus Toolkit Version 4: Software for Service-Oriented Systems. In: Jin, H., Reed, D., Jiang, W. (eds.) NPC 2005. LNCS, vol. 3779, pp. 2–13. Springer, Heidelberg (2005)

An Algorithmic Framework for Collaborative Interest Group Construction

Akshi Kumar and Abha Jain

Dept. of Computer Engineering, Delhi Technological University, Delhi, India
akshikumar@dce.ac.in, abhajain87@yahoo.com

Abstract. As organizations, both business and research-development continue to search better ways to exploit knowledge capital accumulated on the diversified Web; it fosters the need of collaboration among people with similar interest & expertise. In this paper we focus on the problem of discovering people who have particular interests or expertise. The standard approach is to build interest group lists from explicitly registered data. However, doing so assumes one knows what lists should be built, and who ought to be included in each list. We present an alternative approach, which can support a finer grained and dynamically adaptive notion of shared interests. Our approach deduces shared interest relationships between people based on interest similarity calculated by the means of entries written on their blog. Using this approach, a user could search for people by requesting a list of people whose interests are similar to several people known to have the interest in question.

Keywords: Expert finding, Interest Similarity, Blogs, Interest Groups.

1 Introduction

Ongoing increases in wide-area network connectivity promise vastly augmented opportunities for collaboration and resource sharing. A fundamental problem that confronts users of such networks is how to discover the existence of resources of interest, such as files, retail products, network services, or people. In this paper we focus on the problem of discovering people who have particular interests or expertise. We propose an Interest Group construction algorithm based on interest similarity, which can cluster researchers with similar interests into the same group and facilitate collaborative work.

Until very recently, finding expertise required a mix of individual, social and collaborative practices, a haphazard process at best. Mostly, it involved contacting individuals one trusts and asking them for referrals, while hoping that one's judgment about those individuals is justified and that their answers are thoughtful. The traditional way of providing expert assistance relied on the building a directory through manual entry of expertise data or explicitly registered data, such as X.500 directory service standard [1] or Microsoft's SPUD [2] etc. While this approach provides good support for locating particular users (the "white pages" problem), it does not easily support finding users who have particular interests or expertise (the "yellow pages" problem).

N. Meghanathan et al. (Eds.): NeCoM, WiMoN, and WeST 2010, CCIS 90, pp. 500–508, 2010.

Moreover manual collecting method requires intensive and expensive labor, and may quickly outdate due to the continuous change in people's specific expertise and skills. Recently, more attention is paid on automated systems that enhance the visibility and traceability of experts [3] [4] [5] [6] [7] [8]. These systems aim at mitigating the above shortcomings by trying to automatically discover up-to-date expertise from implicit/secondary sources instead of relying on experts and/or other human sources. The information source for these systems includes electronic mail [9], discussion groups [6] [10], personal web pages [4] [5], Web browsing pattern [3] [8], various documents/reports related to particular users [11] [12], etc.

With the advent of Web, a new type of collaborative edifying & learning method has come into being. The traditional method to learning took the teacher as the core of the system and inevitably created many *"Forlorn & Lonely"* learners. So, it is necessary to promote the cooperative activities among the members of the teaching & research communities. To solve the problem, we need to organize individuals with the same interests into the same group, so as to help them carry out cooperative research work & learning. For the reasons above, based on the idea of interest similarity, we have put forward a constructing algorithm of Interest Group.

The demand for knowledge management, including methodologies for enhancing the intellectual faculties of an organization or a community, is increasing. An important factor in knowledge management is finding a person who has a high level of expertise in a required area. In general, an expert is someone who possesses a high level of knowledge in a particular domain. This implies that experts are reliable sources of relevant resources and information. However, the conventional way of doing this relies on connections between individuals. It goes without saying that a more systematic way is required. Recently, many people have started to write their documents in electronic forms such as word processor files, e-mail messages or blogs. For engineers and researchers, this has meant a lot of their expertise written in such documents. Therefore, analyzing these documents would make it possible to estimate their expertise.

From a humble beginning as 'What's New' pages, blogs have arisen to become arguably the most popular online personal publishing platform on the internet. Many users search and read the blog sites to get grass-roots opinions, new-product evaluations, and so on. As a consequence of this trend, there are many web services that analyze blog documents and show recent topics [13]. In this paper, we put forward an approach, which deduces shared interest relationships between researchers based on the entries written on his/her blog and discuss how to extract, build and match individual researcher's interest from their blog document entries & finally detect their level of expertise in that research area. Further we organize the researchers with the same interests into the interest groups, so as to help them carry out collaborative work.

2   Determination of the Interest Similarity Relations

The difficulty and key point of constructing an Interest Group is to determine and calculate the similarity relations. This includes two steps, one is getting the dominant indication (just the Interest Vector) from the interests' recessive indication; another is calculating the Interest Similarity.

2.1 The Interest Vector

Each researcher writes blog entries according to his or her interest. Thus, it can be supposed that terms related to the researcher's interests are present in many entries in his or her blog site. The interest vector of the researcher, Vi, is represented as a bag-of-words with frequently used words being assigned high weights. The interest vector is calculated by the equation described below:

$$V_i = (s_{i1}, s_{i2}, s_{i3}, ...) \tag{1}$$

$$s_{ik} = ef_i(w_k) \times \log\left(\frac{N_u}{uf(w_k)}\right) \tag{2}$$

where s_{ik} means the strength of interest in word w_k; $ef_i(w_k)$ means the number of entries containing w_k in researchers i's site; $uf(w_k)$ means the number of researchers who use w_k; and N_u means the number of researchers. This equation corresponds to the traditional *tf-idf* weighting approach. The entry frequency, $ef_i(w_k)$, corresponds to *tf*, and inverse user frequency, $N_u/uf(w_k)$, corresponds to *idf*. Thus, a word repeatedly used in a small number of blog sites has high weight value.

2.2 Similarity Scores between Researchers

A similarity score represents how similar the interests of a pair of researchers are. If researcher *i* and *j* have similar interests, their interest vectors should be similar. Thus, we calculate the similarity score between them, Rij, using the cosine similarity of Vi and Vj as described below.

$$R_{ij} = \frac{V_i \times V_j}{|V_i||V_j|} \tag{3}$$

All elements of Vi and Vj are positive and thus the range of Rij is 0 to 1.

3 Assessing Expertise: Why It Matters?

We seek *guidance* from people who are familiar with the choices we face, who have been helpful in the past, whose perspectives we value, or who are recognized experts. In general, an expert is someone who possesses a high level of knowledge in a particular domain. This implies that experts are reliable sources of relevant resources and information. Following expert users provides more benefits:

❖ Should know the best resources with respect to a given topic.
❖ Should be quick in discovering and identifying new resources

An open problem thus arises to how can level of expertise be assessed objectively? We propose the solution for this by calculating every researcher's level of expertise [e] (that is the number of the researchers who have high interest similarity with a specific researcher).

Suppose there are m researchers, the researcher i's level of expertise will be calculated by the following formula:

$$e_i = \frac{1}{m} \sum_{j=1}^{m} ac_{ij} \tag{4}$$

In this Formula,

$$ac_{ij} = \begin{cases} 1 & \text{if } R_{ij} \geq T_1 \\ 0 & \text{otherwise} \end{cases}$$

T₁ is a pre-determined Threshold Value

4   Algorithm for Construction of Collaborative Research Interest Group

A Collaborative Research Interest Group should be a group consists of researchers in the similar area or with related interests. So, when constructing a group, try to arrange the researchers with great interest similarity into the same group. With this theory, we put forward the steps for constructing the Interest Group. The proposed method has 4 steps. Firstly we extract the researchers' Interest Vector from their blog documents; and then, with the Interest Vectors, we calculate the Interest Similarity between two researchers. Next, we compute the Level of expertise to find the experts in area and lastly, with these data, we construct an Interest group in a certain way.

Step 1: Use formula (3) to calculate the interest similarity between two researchers.

Step 2: Calculate every researcher's level of expertise [e], i.e., the number of the researchers who have high interest similarity with a specific researcher, using (4).

Step 3: Select the researcher with the highest Level of Expertise, and take him/her as the center of the group to be constructed. Pre-determine a threshold value, T_1, those researchers whose interest similarities with the centered researcher are higher than the threshold value can access into the group.

Step 4: As for the rest of the researchers, recalculate according to the step 1 to step 3, until the researchers' highest level of expertise is less than the threshold value T_1, then, stop calculating.

Some additional points to be explained:

❖ Because the interests of researchers are distributed randomly, some groups may have many members. We are not setting any restrictions on the number count and letting a pre-determined threshold value control the number of members in the interest group.
❖ In the process of constructing interest groups, we should consider that, the interests of the members in the group are in dynamic changing. So the conditions of the group are also dynamically changing. When constructing

groups, we can save the individuals interest property value as the groups' core values. Once an researcher's interest changed, calculate his/her instant interest value's similarity with relative core value. If the similarity value is less than the pre-determined threshold value, let the researcher withdraw from the community and recalculate which communities should he/she go.

❖   When constructing communities, some researchers have many different kind of interests, there may be one researcher belongs to several communities at the same time. This means he/she can take part in the activities in several communities.

5 Case Study

To clearly illustrate the effectiveness of the proposed algorithm for Construction of Collaborative Research Interest Group, a case study is presented to describe a typical scenario, where

➤   There are 5 researchers viz. i, j, k, n & m. Therefore, $N_u = 5$
➤   There are 5 entries in each of the researcher's blog site.

The following table 1 shows the blog entries of each of the researcher i, j, k, n & m.

Table 1. Sample blog entries of 5 researchers

Researcher / Entry	i	j	k	n	m
1	$W_1, W_{16}, W_3,$ W_2, W_{17}, W_9	$W_{14}, W_8, W_6,$ W_7, W_{17}	$W_{11}, W_7, W_2,$ W_9, W_{19}	$W_{13}, W_{13},$ W_{10}, W_{14}	$W_{10}, W_{15},$ W_2
2	$W_4, W_2, W_3,$ $W_{14}, W_{11},$ W_{18}	$W_1, W_{16},$ $W_{11}, W_7,$ W_{18}, W_{17}, W_6	$W_{14}, W_{10}, W_4,$ W_9, W_{19}	$W_{11}, W_{13},$ W_6, W_5	$W_{14}, W_{16},$ W_9, W_8
3	$W_1, W_2, W_6,$ W_{13}	$W_7, W_3,$ W_{18}, W_8, W_{17}	$W_9, W_{19},$ $W_{11}, W_{10},$ W_{17}	$W_{13}, W_{14},$ W_{18}, W_{12}	$W_{15}, W_{19},$ W_1, W_{16}
4	$W_1, W_2, W_4,$ W_8, W_{15}, W_{10}	$W_6, W_6, W_7,$ W_{17}	$W_{12}, W_9,$ W_{19}, W_{16}	$W_{17}, W_{13},$ W_2	$W_{11}, W_{17},$ W_6, W_{15}
5	$W_1, W_2, W_5,$ W_3, W_{19}	$W_7, W_{18}, W_{15},$ $W_2, W_{18}, W_6,$ W_{17}, W_1	$W_{19}, W_9, W_1,$ $W_{17}, W_{10},$ W_{10}	$W_{18}, W_7,$ W_{13}, W_{13}	W_3, W_{13}

5.1 Interest Vector Calculations

We have the interest vector corresponding to each of the researcher i, j, k, n & m represented as V_i, V_j, V_k, V_n, V_m. The calculation for these vectors using equation 2 is shown below:

For Researcher i: The Interest Vector is: $V_i = (S_{i1}, S_{i2}, S_{i3}, S_{i4}, S_{i5})$ where ;

$$S_{i1} = ef(w_1) \times \log[5 / uf(w_1)]$$
$$S_{i2} = ef(w_2) \times \log[5 / uf(w_2)]$$
$$S_{i3} = ef(w_3) \times \log[5 / uf(w_3)]$$
$$S_{i4} = ef(w_4) \times \log[5 / uf(w_4)]$$
$$S_{i5} = ef(w_5) \times \log[5 / uf(w_5)]$$

Now, from table 1, we find the values for ef's and uf's for the corresponding words:

$ef(w_1)=4$; $uf(w_1)=3$ => $S_{i1} = 4 * \log(5/3) = 0.8874$

$ef(w_2)=5$; $uf(w_2)=4$ => $S_{i2} = 5 *\log(5/4) = 0.4846$

$ef(w_3)=3$; $uf(w_3)=2$ => $S_{i3} = 3*\log(5/2) = 1.1938$

$ef(w_4)=2$; $uf(w_4)=1$ => $S_{i4} = 2*\log(5/1) = 1.3979$

$ef(w_5)=1$; $uf(w_5)=1$ => $S_{i5} = 1*\log(5/1) = 0.6989$

Thus, $V_i = (0.8874, 0.4846, 1.1938, 1.3979, 0.6989)$

For Researcher j: The Interest Vector is: $V_j = (S_{j6}, S_{j7}, S_{j8}, S_{j17}, S_{j18})$ where;

$$S_{j6} = ef(w_6) \times \log[5 / uf(w_6)]$$
$$S_{j7} = ef(w_7) \times \log[5 / uf(w_7)]$$
$$S_{j8} = ef(w_8) \times \log[5 / uf(w_8)]$$
$$Sj_{17} = ef(w_{17}) \times \log[5 / uf(w_{17})]$$
$$Sj_{18} = ef(w_{18}) \times \log[5 / uf(w_{18})]$$

Now, from table 1, we find the values for ef's and uf's for the corresponding words

$ef(w_6)=4$; $uf(w_6)=3$ => $S_6 = 4*\log(5/3) = 0.8874$

$ef(w_7)=5$; $uf(w_7)=2$ => $S_7 = 5*\log(5/2) = 1.9897$

$ef(w_8)=2$; $uf(w_8)=2$ => $S_8 = 2*\log(5/2) = 0.7959$

$ef(w_{17})=5$; $uf(w_{17})=4$ => $S_{17} = 5*\log(5/4) = 0.4845$

$ef(w_{18})=3$; $uf(w_{18})=3$ => $S_{18} = 3*\log(5/3) = 0.6655$

Thus, $Vj = (0.8874, 1.9897, 0.7959, 0.4845, 0.6655)$

For Researcher k: The interest vector is: $V_k = (S_{k9}, S_{k10}, S_{k11}, S_{k12}, S_{k19})$ where;

$$S_{k9} = ef(w_9) \times \log[5 / uf(w_9)]$$
$$S_{k10} = ef(w_{10}) \times \log[5 / uf(w_{10})]$$
$$S_{k11} = ef(w_{11}) \times \log[5 / uf(w_{11})]$$
$$S_{k12} = ef(w_{12}) \times \log[5 / uf(w_{12})]$$
$$S_{k19} = ef(w_{19}) \times \log[5 / uf(w_{19})]$$

Now, from table 1, we find the values for ef's and uf's for the corresponding words

$ef(w_9) = 5$; $uf(w_9) = 2$ => $S_9 = 5*\log(5/2) = 1.9897$

$ef(w_{10}) = 3$; $uf(w_{10}) = 3$ => $S_{10} = 3*\log(5/3) = 0.6655$

$ef(w_{11}) = 2$; $uf(w_{11}) = 4$ => $S_{11} = 2*\log(5/4) = 0.1938$

$ef(w_{12}) = 1$; $uf(w_{12}) = 1$ => $S_{12} = 1*\log(5/1) = 0.6988$

$ef(w_{19}) = 5$ $uf(w_{19}) = 2$ => $S_{19} = 5*\log(5/2) = 1.9897$

Thus, $V_k = (1.9897, 0.6655, 0.1938, 0.6988, 1.9897)$

For Researcher n: The Interest Vector is: $V_n = (S_{n13}, S_{n14}, S_{n20}, S_{n21}, S_{n22})$ where;

$$S_{n13} = ef(w_{13}) \times \log[5 / uf(w_{13})]$$
$$S_{n14} = ef(w_{14}) \times \log[5 / uf(w_{14})]$$
$$S_{n20} = ef(w_{20}) \times \log[5 / uf(w_{20})]$$
$$S_{n21} = ef(w_{21}) \times \log[5 / uf(w_{21})]$$
$$S_{n22} = ef(w_{22}) \times \log[5 / uf(w_{22})]$$

Now, from table 1, we find the values for ef's and uf's for the corresponding words

$ef(w_{13}) = 5$; $uf(w_{13}) = 2$ => $S_{13} = 5*\log(5/2) = 1.9897$

$ef(w_{14}) = 2$; $uf(w_{14}) = 4$ => $S_{14} = 2*\log(5/4) = 0.1938$

$ef(w_{20}) = 4$; $uf(w_{20}) = 3$ => $S_{20} = 4*\log(5/3) = 0.8874$

$ef(w_{21}) = 3$; $uf(w_{21}) = 4$ => $S_{21} = 3*\log(5/4) = 0.2907$

$ef(w_{22}) = 4$; $uf(w_{22}) = 2$ => $S_{22} = 4*\log(5/2) = 0.8874$

Thus, $V_n = (1.9897, 0.1938, 0.8874, 0.2907, 0.8874)$

For Researcher m: The Interest Vector is: $V_m = (S_{m15}, S_{m16}, S_{m23}, S_{m24}, S_{m25})$ where;

$$S_{m13}=ef\,(w_{15}) \times \log\,[5\,/\,uf\,(w_{15})]$$
$$S_{m14}=ef\,(w_{16}) \times \log\,[5\,/\,uf\,(w_{16})]$$
$$S_{m20}=ef(w_{23}) \times \log\,[5\,/\,uf\,(w_{23})]$$
$$S_{m24}=ef(w_{24}) \times \log\,[5\,/\,uf\,(w_{24})]$$
$$S_{m25}=ef(w_{25}) \times \log\,[5\,/\,uf\,(w_{25})]$$

Now, from table 1, we find the values for ef's and uf's for the corresponding words

$ef\,(w_{15})=3$; $uf\,(w_{15})=2$ => $S_{15} = 3*\log\,(5/2) = 1.1938$

$ef\,(w_{16})=2$; $uf\,(w_{16})=3$ => $S_{16} = 2*\log\,(5/3) = 0.4436$

$ef\,(w_{23})=4$; $uf\,(w_{23})=4$ => $S_{23} = 4*\log\,(5/4) = 0.3876$

$ef\,(w_{24})=5$; $uf\,(w_{24})=4$ => $S_{24} = 5*\log\,(5/4) = 0.4845$

$ef\,(w_{25})=2$; $uf\,(w_{25})=4$ => $S_{25} = 2*\log\,(5/4) = 0.1938$

Thus, $V_m = (1.1938, 0.4436, 0.3876, 0.4845, 0.1938)$

5.2 Similarity Score Calculation

Using the formula defined in equation 3, we calculate the values of Similarity Score between each of the 2 researchers:

$R_{ij} = 0.7063$; $R_{ik} = 0.7110$; $R_{in} = 0.7502$; $R_{im} = 0.8064$; $R_{jk} = 0.6688$; $R_{jn} = 0.6132$
$R_{jm} = 0.7424$; $R_{kn} = 0.8786$; $R_{km} = 0.8140$; $R_{nm} = 0.9169$

As all the elements of both the vectors taken at a time to calculate the similarity score are positive, thus the range of similarity score is between 0 to 1.
This indicates that:

➢ The value of 1 means that the 2 researchers have exactly similar interests and;
➢ The value of 0 means that the 2 researchers do not have any similar interests at all.

Therefore, we can conclude that:

➢ The researchers n & m have almost similar interests (as $R_{nm}= 0.9169$, approx 1)
➢ The researchers k & n have similar interests to a very great extent (as $R_{kn} = 0.8786$)
➢ The researchers "k & m" and "i & m" have quite a lot similar interests (as $R_{km} = 0.8140$ and $R_{im} = 0.8064$)
➢ The researchers "j & k" and "j & n" have quite less similar interests (as $R_{jk} = 0.6688$ and $R_{jn} = 0.6132$)

6 Conclusion

This paper expounds an entirely different approach to solve the problem of discovering people who have particular interests or expertise. We have put forward a constructing algorithm of Interest Group by uncovering shared interest relationships between people, based on their blog document entries, to let them arrange into groups effectively, to let them share the resources, carry out cooperative work. The practice result proves that this algorithm has the characteristics of highly effective group arranging and is easy to be extendable.

References

1. CCITT/ISO. The Directory, Part 1: Overview of Concepts, Models and Services. CCITT/ISO, Gloucester, England, CCITT Draft Recommendation X.500/ISO DIS 9594-1 (1988)
2. Davenport, T.H., Prusak, L.: Working Knowledge: How Organizations Manage What They Know. Harvard Business School Press, Boston (1998)
3. Cohen, A.L., Maglio, P.P., Barrett, R.: The Expertise Browser: How to Leverage Distributed Organizational Knowledge. Presented at Collaborative Information Seeking at CSCW 1998, Seattle, WA (1998)
4. Kautz, H., Selman, B., Shah, M.: The Hidden Web. The AI Magazine 18(2), 27–36 (1997)
5. Kautz, H., Selman, B., Milewski, A.: Agent Amplified Communication. In: Proceedings of the Thirteenth National Conference on Artificial Intelligence (AAAI 1996), Portland, OR, pp. 3–9 (1996)
6. Krulwich, B., Burkey, C.: ContactFinder: Extracting Indications of Expertise and Answering Questions with Referrals. In: Working Notes of the 1995 Fall Symposium on Intelligent Knowledge Navigation and Retrieval, Cambridge, MA. Technical Report FS-95-03, pp. 85–91. The AAAI Press (1995)
7. Mattox, D., Maybury, M., Morey, D.: Enterprise Expert and Knowledge Discovery. In: Proceedings of the 8th International Conference on Human-Computer Interaction (HCI International 1999), Munich, Germany, pp. 303–307 (1999)
8. Pikarakis, A., et al.: MEMOIR: Software Agents for Finding Similar Users by Trails. In: Proceedings of the Third International Conference on the Practical Applications of Intelligent Agents and multi-Agent Technology (PAAM 1998), London, UK, pp. 453–466 (1998)
9. Schwartz, M.F., Wood, D.M.: Discovering Shared Interests Using Graph Analysis. Communications of the ACM 36(8), 78–89 (1993)
10. Krulwich, B., Burkey, C.: The ContactFinder Agent: Answering Bulletin Board Questions with Referrals. In: Proceedings of the 1996 National Conference on Artificial Intelligence (AAAI 1996), Portland, OR, vol. 1, pp. 10–15 (1996)
11. Steeter, L.A., Lochbaum, K.E.: An Expert/Expert Locating System based on Automatic Representation of Semantic Structure. In: Proceedings of the Fourth IEEE Conference on Artificial Intelligence Applications, pp. 345–349. Computer Society of the IEEE, San Diego (1988)
12. Steeter, L.A., Lochbaum, K.E.: Who Knows: A System Based on Automatic Representation of Semantic Structure. In: RIAO 1988, Cambridge, MA, pp. 380–388 (1988)
13. BlogPulse, http://www.blogpulse.com/

Survey on Federated Identity Management Systems

Arvind Kumar Sharma[1] and Chattar Singh Lamba[2]

Research Scholar
arvind_vyas07@yahoo.co.in
Research Guide
kunjean_lamba@yahoo.com

Abstract. Federated Identity Management is a version of Single Sign-On where each device, system, and application queries a centralized database for authentication and authorization information. Federated Identity Management systems are tasked with enabling authentication and authorization data across organizational boundaries. Federated Identity Management system, authentication data can be passed across security domains from within a company to its business partners. This can enable Single Sign-On to extend past organizational boundaries. Federated Identity Management is often abbreviated *FIM*.

Keywords: Single Sign-On (*SSO*), Authentication, Authorization, Accounting.

1 Introduction

Federated Identity Management is a version of Single Sign-On where each device, system, and application queries a centralized database for authentication and authorization information. Federated Identity Management systems are tasked with enabling authentication and authorization data across organizational boundaries. Federated Identity Management system, authentication data can be passed across security domains from within a company to its business partners. This can enable Single Sign-On to extend past organizational boundaries. Federated Identity Management is often abbreviated *FIM*.

2 Federated Identity Management Standards

The leader in developing standards for Federated Identity Management is The Liberty Alliance. The Liberty Alliance is a group of more than 150 corporations, non-profit organizations, and government entities which is tasked with developing open standards for Federated Identity Management.

3 Federated Identity Management and Web Services

Federated Identity Management and Web Services are uniquely intertwined, mutually reliant on each other, and are poised to finally solve a long-running problem in both

N. Meghanathan et al. (Eds.): NeCoM, WiMoN, and WeST 2010, CCIS 90, pp. 509–517, 2010.
© Springer-Verlag Berlin Heidelberg 2010

IT and systems security. From e-business transactions over the Internet to logins for the employee HR portal, uniform access control and robust management tools are required to securely enable connectivity for customers, partners and employees. Yet user databases and access policies are often fragmented, requiring multiple logins for users and repetitive tasks for systems administrators.

The traditional approach to solving this problem has been Single Sign ON (SSO), the centralization of access control information into one server that requires special plugins (e.g., "Web agents" for Web servers) to retrieve the information. Every application needs to be "SSO enabled" by programming to the proprietary API, different for each competing vendor. The coding task usually falls to the IT organization. Overall, this technology has not been as successful as originally hoped, with many SSO implementations either behind or experiencing scalability challenges.

Traditional SSO is impractical for extranets or Web services because partners may not agree on a single SSO vendor, and it is not possible to have a unified database. Such a database might have to include up-to-date information on both companies' employees, for example, a task hampered not just by practical but also privacy and business considerations.

Where Single Sign On (SSO) relied on establishing a central server accessed using special agent libraries that had to be integrated into applications, Federated Identity Management leverages lessons from the U.S. federal system and application integration. Local applications or organizations maintain their own repositories which respond to queries from both local and remote applications with security assertions containing user attributes and roles. When encountering external users, the local applications query other federated repositories to authenticate and authorize these non-local users.

SAML (Security Assertion Markup Language) is the dominant Web services standard for federated identity management. It defines a set of XML formats for representing identity and attribute information, as well as protocols for requests and responses for access control information. The key principle behind SAML is an assertion, a statement made by a trusted party about another. For example, a federated identity management server would produce assertions about the identity and rights of users. An individual application does not need to have direct access to the user repository or trust a user, it only needs to know and trust the assertions source. Assertions can be encoded in browser requests or included in Web services transactions, enabling logins for both person-to-machine and machine-to-machine communications. This is another first, the ability to use the same standards protocol for both back-end transactions and Web portal access control.

4   Security Requirements

Regulatory and security requirements demand not just authentication, but also the other A's of AAA – fine-grained authorization and accounting. In addition to providing a means of enabling access for partners and customers, federated identity management technologies improve security by controlling access on an operation-by-operation basis and providing a detailed audit trail. SAML assertions, for example, can include the entire evidence chain used to make the access control decision. The evidence serves as a legal record of who accessed what data at what time, why and on whose authority.

This added security and accountability is especially important for unattended machine-to-machine transactions, which increasingly means Web services. With no humans to oversee transactions or assume liability, Web services rely on federated identity management instead.

Just like Web services, SAML (and other FIM technology) is not just for securing connections to external parties. It is also useful internally, since many large companies today have many internal business units with separate access control systems. Instead of attempting to replace these systems with a central server, it is now possible to leave them in place and wrap them with SAML interfaces. While the broader task of corporate identity management still remains, a federated approach based on open Web services standards makes it cheaper and more scalable.

In conclusion, federated identity management makes possible the vision of "identity as a service," where authentication and authorization functions are Web services available to any application in the enterprise SOA. It breaks the traditional lock between WebSSO shim & server, disinter mediating many access control vendors in the process. Instead of installing agents and writing custom code, single sign-on enablement is now a matter of standards support. Federated identity management applies the concept of a federal system to the ever-present problem of access control, and by using Web services standards makes secure connectivity universal. In turn, Web services use federated identity management technology to secure business transactions. And that's how these two seemingly unrelated topics are deeply intertwined.

5 Analysis

5.1 What Is It?

A system that allows individuals to use the same user name, password or other personal identification to sign on to the networks of more than one enterprise in order to conduct transactions.

5.2 How Is It Used?

Partners in a Federated Identity Management (FIM) system depend on each other to authenticate their respective users and vouch for their access to services. That allows, for example, a sales representative to update an internal forecast by pulling information from a supplier's database, hosted on the supplier's network.

5.3 Why Is It Necessary?

So that companies can share applications without needing to adopt the same technologies for directory services, security and authentication. Within companies, directory services such as Microsoft's Active Directory or products using the Lightweight Directory Access Protocol have allowed companies to recognize their users through a single identity. But asking multiple companies to match up technologies or maintain full user accounts for their partner's employees is unwieldy. FIM allows companies to keep their own directories and securely exchange information from them.

5.4 How Does It Work?

A company must trust its partners to vouch for their users. Each participant must rely on each partner to say, in effect, "This user is OK; let them access this application." Partners also need a standard way to send that message, such as one that uses the conventions of the Security Assertion Markup Language (SAML). SAML allows instant recognition of whether the prospective user is a person or a machine, and what that person or machine can access. SAML documents can be wrapped in a Simple Object Access Protocol message for the computer-to-computer communications needed for Web services. Or they may be passed between Web servers of federated organizations that share live services.

5.5 Who Is Using It?

Early adopters include American Express, Boeing, General Motors and Nokia. Another, Proctor & Gamble, had improvised its own federated-identity system using the more generic extensible Markup Language but is now moving to adopt SAML.

5.6 What Are the Challenges?

Trusting a partner to authenticate its own users is a good thing only if that partner has solid security and user-management practices. Also, while some Web access-management products now support SAML, implementing the technology still commonly requires customization to integrate applications and develop user interfaces.

6 Single Sign-On

In a Single Sign-On system, each user has *one* username and *one* password for all of the systems, devices, and applications to which she has access.

The two methods utilized by Single Sign-On systems to do this are:

- Password synchronization - The Single Sign-On system *copies* the username and password configuration to each system
- Centralized account management - Each system is configured to query a central database for user authentication and authorization

Single Sign-On systems have the promise of saving IT organizations significant resources in terms of lost user time and reduced password resets. In addition, Single Sign-On systems can significantly increase the security of an IT environment.

Single Sign-On is often abbreviated *SSO*.

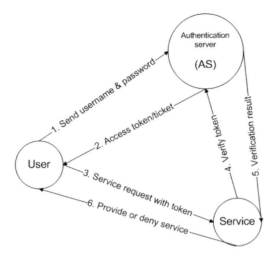

7   Authentication

Authentication is proving who you are. Authentication is the first component of the AAA (Authentication, Authorization, and Accounting) model for access control.

Authentication must precede Authorization; because you must prove *who* you are before the identity management system can determine *what* you are authorized to do.

Authentication is traditionally accomplished using passwords. More secure authentication technologies include two factor authentication and biometrics.

8   Authorization

Authorization is the second component of the AAA (Authentication, Authorization, and Accounting) model for access control.

Authorization must follow Authentication, because before the identity management system can determine *what* you are authorized to do, it must first determine *who* you are.

9   Accounting

Accounting refers to the tracking of the consumption of network resources by users. This information may be used for management, planning, billing, or other purposes. Real-time accounting refers to accounting information that is delivered concurrently with the consumption of the resources. Batch accounting refers to accounting information that is saved until it is delivered at a later time. Typical information that is gathered in accounting is the identity of the user, the nature of the service delivered, when the service began, and when it ended.

When a user connects to the network via a remote access server, VPN, firewall, router, access point, or any other RADIUS-compliant network access device, that device queries SBR to determine if the user is authorized to connect. SBR accepts or rejects the connection based on user credential information in the central security database, and authorizes the appropriate type of connection or service. When the user logs off, the network access device informs SBR, which in turn records an accounting transaction.

10 Advantages of AAA

10.1 Flexible User Authentication Methods

Works with a variety of user identity stores, helping capitalize on existing equipment and operating procedures.

10.2 Flexible User Privileges

Allows administrators to create a wide variety of user privilege profiles based on day/time access, bandwidth allocation, or access to specific segments of the WLAN. This ensures better control of user access, plus enhances enterprise user satisfaction.

10.3 Wi-Fi Visitor Access

Visitors such as customers and partners can be given secure Wi-Fi access via access points that support Virtual LANs (VLANs). Wi-Fi AAA allows administrators to create different access controls for different classes of visitors, while always protecting the enterprise.

10.4 Multi-vendor WLAN Support

Supports all major 802.1x capable WLAN access points, offering a flexible interface that allows organizations to deploy access point technology that best suits their needs.

10.5 Fast and Easy to Deploy

A Windows-based solution, Wi-Fi AAA provides quick and easy out-of-the-box deployment.

10.6 Centralized Administration Center

A browser-based interface gives network administrators the ability to manage authorization rules and access controls, plus create comprehensive usage reports.

10.7 Detailed Usage Reports

Generates accounting records that can be manipulated to create reports, including usage activity, which identifies total network usage by user name, and failed connections by time period and access point.

10.8 Scalable, Future-Proof Solution

Supports increased numbers of concurrent sessions, in increments that make good business sense, allowing enterprises to grow their system with their needs. A single server based on a basic platform can authenticate thousands of users per minute.

11 RADIUS and AAA

If the NAS receives user-connection requests, it passes them to the designated RADIUS server which authenticates the user and returns the user's configuration information to the NAS. Then, the NAS accepts or rejects the connection requests.

A full-featured RADIUS server can support a variety of mechanisms to authenticate users in addition to LDAP, including

- PAP (Password Authentication Protocol, used with PPP in which the password is sent to the client as clear text for comparison);
- CHAP (Challenge Handshake Authentication Protocol, more secure than PAP, it uses a username and password);
- the local UNIX/Linux system password database (/etc/passwd);
- other local databases.

Authentication and authorization are combined together in RADIUS. If the username is found and the password is correct, the RADIUS server returns an *Access-Accept* response including some parameters (attribute-value pairs) that grants access to the user. These parameters are configured in RADIUS and include service type, protocol type, IP address to assign the user, an access control list (ACL) or a static route to apply on the NAS, as well as other values.

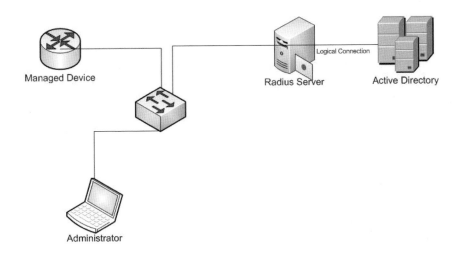

12   Lightweight Directory Access Protocol

The Lightweight Directory Access Protocol (LDAP) is an open standard that defines a method for accessing and updating information in a X.500-like directory. LDAP can be used to keep user information in a central locale to avoid having to store identical user information on each system; it can also be used to maintain and access the information in a consistent and controlled manner.

LDAP simplifies user administration tasks by managing users in a central directory. In addition to storing user information, defining users in LDAP allows for such optional features as limiting the number of logins. In this article you'll learn how a RADIUS server is configured to authenticate users against LDAP -- since the article focuses on RADIUS, I will not describe the details on the installation and configuration of an LDAP server.

13   RADIUS V/S LDAP

Most of you have already heard of RADIUS and many of you use it in your infrastructure. Have you ever wondered what's the main difference between RADIUS and user authentication databases like LDAP (and also what they have in common)? Here 're a few points:

- LDAP and RADIUS have something in common. They 're both mainly a protocol (more than a database) which uses attributes to carry information back and forth. They are clearly defined in RFC documents so you can expect products from different vendors to be able to function properly together.

- RADIUS is NOT a database. It's a protocol for asking intelligent questions to a user database. LDAP is just a database. In recent offerings it contains a bit of intelligence (like Roles, Class of Service and so on) but it still is mainly just a rather stupid database. RADIUS provide the administrator the tools to not only perform user authentication but also to authorize users based on extremely complex checks and logic. For instance you can allow access on a specific NAS only if the user belongs to a certain category, is a member of a specific group and an outside script allows access. There's no way to perform any type of such complex decisions in a user database.

- RADIUS also includes accounting. That means that you can use accounting history when making authorization decisions and get functionality like quotas (a user is only allowed 4 hours of dialup access per day regardless of how many times he connects).

- With the introduction of Extensible Authentication Protocol (EAP) you can use almost any authentication protocol known to man.

- RADIUS is extensible. You can easily extend the RADIUS schema with attributes of you choice (as long as you have a Vendor number). RADIUS servers are extensible. You can use almost any database for authentication and accounting (LDAP, SQL, password files, outside scripts). The same stands for the LDAP protocol (one of the major factors for it's popularity) and for LDAP servers although they don't get even close to the levels allowed by RADIUS servers.

References

1. Watkins, M., Wallace, K.: CCNA Security: Official Exam Certification Guide. Pearson Education, London
2. Bucker, A., Filip, W., Hinton, H., Hippenstiel, H.P., Hollin, M.: Federated Identity Management and Web Services Security With IBM Tivoli Security Solutions. IBM.Com/Redbooks
3. Windley, P.: Digital Identity. O'Reilly, Sebastopol
4. Duffy, J., Morrison, A., Wendin, C.: Information Security: A Strategic Guide for Business. PricewaterhouseCooopers LLP

Automating Reuse of Semantic Repositories in the Context of Semantic Web

Nadia Imdadi and S.A.M. Rizvi

Department of Computer Science, Jamia Millia Islamia,
New Delhi, India
nadia.imdadi@gmail.com, samsam_rizvi@yahoo.com

Abstract. In this paper a novel approach to make discovery and subsequent integration of semantic repositories, like ontologies, as seamlees and automatic as possible is presented. Reuse of semantic repositories has many advantages and it has been acknowledged time and again that it is a process which can only be partially or semi automatically be achieved. We discuss the nature of semantic repositories, the challenges and issues still to be resolved and finally the proposed framework.

Keywords: Ontology Reuse, Automatic Semantic Integration.

1 Introduction

Tim Berner Lee defined the Semantic Web as [9] "an extension of the current Web in which information is given well defined meaning, better enabling computers and people to work in cooperation. This extension is achieved by adding more dimensions in form of ontologies and rules/axioms to flat dimensional approach of the present web [1]. Since its inception several standards and languages have evolved for the creation of ontologies.

Methodologies for ontology construction is an issue that continues to be a challenge for researchers for various reasons like the dynamics of a particular domain, need of expert knowledge, costs involved. Hence the research in the field of ontology reuse methodologies has relevant significance in the context of Semantic Web.

1.1 Ontologies – Semantic Repository

Ontologies are a formal specification of a conceptualization of domains and thus can be viewed as building blocks of semantic web. They are created in knowledge representation language like the RDF/S, DAML+OIL or OWL and are expressed in logic based language to underpin specific domain knowledge. The Web Ontology Language (OWL) [11] is a family of knowledge representation languages for authoring ontologies endorsed by the World Wide Web Consortium. [15]

N. Meghanathan et al. (Eds.): NeCoM, WiMoN, and WeST 2010, CCIS 90, pp. 518–523, 2010.

1.2   Nature of Semantic Repositories

As noted earlier ontologies are represented in logic based languages and therefore inference mechanism can be applied for extraction of information from web resources on the basis of *relationships* rather than the traditional approaches of using keywords. The recall rates for any keyword based search engine may be high yet it still requires user to sift through the links which are relevant i.e. belong to the same concept or domain which the user is interested in. Ontologies provide the schema- including concept definition, axiom and rules governing a particular domain- which can be used effectively by software agents to discover knowledge about a particular resource through inference. As ontologies form the backbone of semantic web their correctness and completeness are of paramount relevance.

Thus ontology building is an important process that involves expert domain skills, and therefore is a time consuming and tedious. Over the years several semi-automated methodologies and tools have emerged [6] that have made the process of ontology building relatively easier, but most of these methods rely on syntactic and structural properties of the ontologies for their reuse during the build process.

In recent times the web has seen an increasing number of semantic web documents as can be deduced from statistics provided by Swoogle [4], also further analysis of Swoogle's database has revealed that many of these ontologies are being re-used by newer web resources, hence, the need for newer methodologies is felt so online ontologies may be reused more efficiently for ontology building.

2   Technique for Ontology Reuse

A fully automatic process is not possible for ontology creation as it requires knowledge skills in the particular domain. It is noted in literature as recent as 2009 [2], that a suitable mix of human and computing techniques will have to be applied in the process of ontology building and especially when creating ontology resources form reusing existing ones. Following four stages have been identified in the process of ontology creation by reuse.

2.1   Ontology Discovery

Several techniques have emerged for ontology discovery, details can be found in [2], some methods are semi automated, but we believe that this is one area that can be completely automated by using Swoogle search engine [10] for ontology discovery and by applying certain intelligent search strategies and word sense disambiguation techniques as discussed in the next section.

2.2   Selection of Suitable Ontologies for Reuse

This stage involves further refining of the results obtained from the ontology discovery stage and involves filtering out ontologies or repositories that may not be that relevant for the particular domain. This stage requires the need of human expert to identify most appropriate resources that may be used. So far this has been a semi automated process. Though certain aspects at this stage may be automated such as once part of ontology has been approved by the expert then the mechanism of extracting the portion may be automated. Several techniques have evolved in this area such as the traversal technique developed by F. Noy et al [5] and winnowing by H. Alani [3].

2.3 Integration of Ontologies

Till now the selection and integration stages of ontology construction by reuse have been partially automated. Details about the integration techniques and tools have been discussed by F. Noy in [6].

This stage of integration can also be fully automated by selection of appropriate mix of techniques. In particular we believe that applying word sense disambiguation may give better results as against using string and structure based similarity measures which give results based on syntactic and not semantic similarities.

2.4 Evaluation of Ontology

This is an important stage of ontology creation although not much have been reported by way of progress in this field. Hence, we conclude that ontolgy evaluation is a field that requires expert reviews. But in order to evaluate our results we will use existing online ontologies available at [7] to validate our results in terms of precision and completeness.

3 Framework for Automatic Reuse of Semantic Repositories

A basic framework for automatic semantic integration incorporating semantic repositories was proposed in [8]. We are now implementing the stages identified for ontology construction through reuse in the previous section.

3.1 Basic Framework

A modular approach to building ontology is the underlying methodology of our framework. A bottom up approach to ontology construction is employed as any domain consists of concepts, which in turn are collection of few terms, properties and relations amongst these terms. Thus based on these terms and properties an input matrix is created that is then used for concept extraction from knowledge resources which may be locally or globally imported.

The following figure shows the basic architecture of the proposed framework. Input is in form of keywords, set of concept names to query the knowledge base.

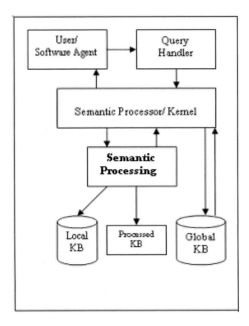

Fig. 1. Framework for automatic semantic integration of semantic repositories

3.2 Semantic Kernel

A core feature of this framework is its kernel or processor which is a first of its kind as its aim is to facilitate the make use of online semantic repositories which are scattered across the semantic web.

The functionalities of this kernel include query processing. The processor receives user inputs (term names defining a concept and properties) and prepares a input matrix to query and check with local Knowledge Base (KB) for matching resources. If the local knowledge base is able to satisfy the query the result is returned to the user if not kernel initiates a global service routine to search and retrieve relevant information from the global KB, this is where Swoogle API [10] is used.

Other role played by the processor is in the process of decision making such as when the global service routine is to be invoked and results of which have to filtered and integrated with or added to local KB.

Representation of knowledge resources in form of associated meta-data and their storage is an important aspect as local knowledge base has to be maintained for future querying, and therefore requires management by the kernel.

3.3 Implementation Overview

The Protégé-OWL[13] editor which is an extension of Protégé[12], a popular ontology building tool, that supports the Web Ontology Language (OWL), is used for implementation of this framework. The Protégé-OWL editor enables users to load and save OWL and RDF ontologies; edit and visualize classes, properties, and rules; and many other features needed in the process of ontology building. Protégé-OWL's flexible architecture makes it easy to configure and extend [13], a plugin, integrated with Swoogle web service API is being developed over the tool to retrieve online semantic repositories.

3.4   Input Processing

The input interface accepts user inputs in form of concept names and properties that describe a particular context. Each concept name is associated with a property name as it helps in determining which context the concept name is referring to eg if *book* is associated with property *publication* then it most likely means that *book* represents something that *one reads* and not related to *reserve* which may be used for referring to *ticket booking*.

This input is then processed to produce a concept name matrix where two synonyms are added, using Word Net [14], this helps in expanding the range of recall for a given set of concept names, as ontologies may use different terms to mean the same thing. Once this input matrix is ready it is executed against the local knowledge base if matches are found the result set is returned to the user else the user may invoke the global service routine to query the global knowledge base.

3.5   Global Query Processing

After analyzing the type of data structure underlying Swoogle's database [4], it is realized that Swoogle supports keyword based search on its index of ontology terms. When a keyword is searched a list of namespaces where the keyword is defined is returned.

Since multiple keyword based searches are not supported by Swoogle API, namespaces against each concept name input is retrieved and a list of those namespaces with maximum number of occurrences of a group of concept name inputs is prepared. Appropriate strategy to limit the size of resulting relevant namespace list is needed in order to keep computational time frame within acceptable limits as Swoogle indexes over 3 million semantic web documents. Presently work is on to formulate a strategy where namespaces are listed according to the coverage of most of the terms from the input matrix.

3.6   Issues and Challenges

We identify the following parameters that have to be explored for the successful implementation of the framework:

-    Defining appropriate threshold for the result set returned after initiating a global query through the global service routine.
-    Methodology for filtering irrelevant or lower significant resources.
-    Provide a service that would allow for integration, mediation and alignment of selected global repositories with the local KB.

4 Conclusions

The aim of this framework is to reuse semantic repositories present across the semantic web by automating those aspects of ontology construction which do not involve human intervention. The proposed framework will be addressing issues such as organizing and managing webKB, discovering webKB, and how knowledge is shared and exchanged amongst knowledge bases and an attempt is to arrive at a set of rules and constraints to automatically capture semantics from a variety of resources and for integration of resources based on these abstractions.

References

1. Daconta, M.C., Obrst, L.J., Smith, K.T., Fensel, D.: The Semantic Web: A Guide to the Future of XML, Web Services, and Knowledge Management. Wiley Publication, Chichester (2004)
2. Elena, S.: Reusing ontologies on the Semantic Web: A feasibility study. Data & Know. Eng., 905–925 (2009)
3. Harith, A.: Position Paper: Ontology Construction from Online Ontologies. WWW, Edinburgh, U.K (2006)
4. Lushan, H., Finin, T., Yesha, Y.: Finding Appropriate Semantic Web Ontology Terms from Words. In: Bernstein, A., Karger, D.R., Heath, T., Feigenbaum, L., Maynard, D., Motta, E., Thirunarayan, K. (eds.) ISWC 2009. LNCS, vol. 5823. Springer, Heidelberg (2009)
5. Natasha, F.N., Musen, M.A.: Specifying ontology views by traversal. In: McIlraith, S.A., Plexousakis, D., van Harmelen, F. (eds.) ISWC 2004. LNCS, vol. 3298, pp. 713–725. Springer, Heidelberg (2004)
6. Natalya, F.N.: Semantic Integration: A Survey of Ontology-Based Approaches. SIGMOD Record 33(4) (2004)
7. Protégé Ontologies,
   http://protege.stanford.edu/download/ontologies.html
8. Rizvi, S.A.M., Nadia, I.: Framework for Automatic Semantic Integration of Semantic Repositories. In: Int. Conf. on Semantic E-business and Enterprise Computing, Kerela, India (2008)
9. Tim, B.L., Hendler, J., Lassila: The Semantic Web. Scientific American 279(5) (2001)
10. Swoogle: A Semantic Web Search and Metadata Engine,
    http://ebiquity.umbc.edu/get/a/pulication/116.pdf
11. Web Ontology Language (OWL), W3C, http://www.w3.org/2004/OWL
12. What is protégé? Stanford Center for Biomedical Informatics Research,
    http://protege.stanford.edu/overview/index.html
13. What is protégé-owl? Stanford Center for Biomedical Informatics Research,
    http://protege.stanford.edu/overview/protege-owl.html
14. WordNet, http://wordnet.princeton.edu/
15. World Wide Web Consortium, http://www.w3c.org

Discovering Models from Event-Based Data Basis on a Survey of Issues and Approaches

Mohammed Shahidul Karim[1], Md. Ashiqur Rahman[1], and Abul Kalam Azad[2]

[1] Lecturer, Dept. of Computer Science & Engineering,
Southeast University, Dhaka, Bangladesh
{enggpallab,ashiq_rahman}@yahoo.com
[2] Lecturer, Dept. of Applied Physics, Electronics and
Communication Engineering, University of Dhaka, Dhaka, Bangladesh
azad@univdhaka.edu

Abstract. The constantly increasing performances of e-commerce services or telecommunication services of web services mean web model can replace more and more web applications. In design, the goal is not to just replace the solution but also to improve it by adding new functionality. To interpret the dynamic behavior of a model is crucial for being able to modify, maintain, and improve it. Model represents a complete exposition of their focus; although there may be dependencies on other aspects of the architecture: these dependencies are usually well defined. We interpret a model in two folds. Firstly, a model which is derived before implementation of a business process is defined as pre-model. Second one is post-model which is derived after implementation. Deriving Post-Model from business execution logs is one of the challenging issues in current age. In this survey, we will present different approaches of model discovery from event logs. The idea is to generalize the process discovery problem and find out research challenges.

Keywords: Process Discovery, Model Discovery, Business Process, Process Model, Event Logs.

1 Introduction

With the rampant growth of technological changes, acceptability and usability of distributed application is increasing very widely. In the distributed platform, one of the most common threads is compliance. There is different reason of being compliant. Most importantly, increasing governmental pressure of being compliant is not avoided by the business organization. For example, noncompliance of Sarbanes-Oxley act is a matter of penalty [Sox]. So information system monitoring has become a design and runtime issue for most of the distributed applications. Execution logs act as a seed for monitoring distributed applications. Correlation is one of the most important issues of grouping these logs discover patterns of running business processes in the system. Automated Business Processes are changing the way of e-business by providing

N. Meghanathan et al. (Eds.): NeCoM, WiMoN, and WeST 2010, CCIS 90, pp. 524–532, 2010.

interoperability following service-orientated architecture for creating theses applications and services. To verify compliance discovering patterns of theses running business processes are very important. Generally, automated business processes are building to deploy distributed systems. Enterprise Resource Planning (ERP), Business to Business (B2B), Workflow management Systems (WFM), Customer Relationship management (CRM) all modern information systems are maintaining event logs to maintain consistency of their system. Model Discovery aim to the automatic discovery of model. Business Processes store executing logs in log. For example, a workflow management system stores all kind transactions of the system [5]. Current trend is to support execution of such kind of workflows so that the workflow can be monitored and analyzed. Model Discovery is a way of analyzing monitoring of real-life processes. In this paper, we try to focus on the current state of the art in the area of Model Discovery. We recently have quality papers for this survey. As the problem domain is not small, it highlights on process discovery. A model is a coherent subset of architecture that typically revolves around particular aspect of the overall architecture. The techniques are based on a probabilistic analysis of the event traces. Using metrics for the number, frequency, and regularity of event occurrences, a determination is made of the likely concurrent behavior being manifested by the system. Discovering this behavior can help a workflow designer better understand and improve the work processes they are managing.

Survey Motivation: Motivation of this work is to generalize discovery problems and highlights on ongoing research in this emerging area. XML-based technology are involving in interoperability issue, whereas we are finding some concepts by which we can provide common specifications on discovery issues, obviously the specification for logging system to store the data in a meaningful way.

2   Background

In this section, we detail our view of events, concurrency, and dependencies among events that constrain concurrency. We also discuss several assumptions that underlie our work. Throughout, we use the term system to mean the whole workflow system, and the term thread to mean a sequential execution control path within the workflow, running concurrently with other threads.

Events: An event provides running time behavior of business processes that are specific, instantaneous actions. Processed models are represented in several ways. The state machines, Petri nets, procedural languages and rule based languages can be different way of representing event based process model. To store information of an action, different kinds of attributes are associated with events. As an example, time is an attribute of event. So in a different way, an event stream is the sequence of overlapping events represents the overlapping activities of a process. There are different tools that can be used for event logs.

Event Logs: Contemporary Information Systems rely on log files [5]. Event log contains the information about events referring to an activity and a process instance.

Process instance is a thing which can be customer order, job application. Event contains a list of attributes. As for example activity, case or process instance, performer or originator, timestamps are very useful to store a log event in most useful way. The idea of under given table is to provide generic view of events logs.

Directive	Description	Event	User	yyyy/mm/dd	hh:mm
	Start		pallab@seu.it	2007/04/16	11:06
task B	Processed To		pallab@seu.it	2007/04/16	11:08
task B	Expired		pallab@seu.it	2007/04/16	11:15
task B	Withdrawn		pallab@seu.it	2007/04/16	12:12
task C	Processed To		pallab@seu.it	2007/04/16	12:34
task C	Released By		pallab@seu.it	2007/04/16	12:56
task D	Processed To		pallab@seu.it	2007/04/16	13:12
task D	Released By		pallab@seu.it	2007/04/16	13:32
	Terminated			2007/04/16	13:40

Fig. 1. Event Logs

Discovery: In web service perspective, Discovery is the act of locating a machine-process able description of a Web service. It can be performed by agent or end user. Service requester needs to find services and binding information to invoke the service and use it. In systems perspective, discovery is the act of tracing event based activities of the whole system by the system itself. It can represent by a state chart diagram or inference rule or xml format that machine can understand it.

Noise in logs: The term noise is used to refer to the situation where the log is incomplete or contains errors. A similar situation occurs if a rare sequence of events takes place which is not representative for the typical flow of work (i.e., an exception). In both cases the resulting model can be incorrect (i.e., not representing the typical flow of work). Process Miner do not offer features for dealing with noise. There are mainly two types of noises in event logs [6]: incorrect conversations, and log incompleteness. In Incorrect conversations, there are many problems in event logs say for example if a message is missed it is really hard to find a complete conversation from the event logs. Partial conversation also generates incorrect conversation which is caused due to interruption of communication among different services at conversation time. Again in log incompleteness, log files are not considered as complete, because applications in execution time consider a perspective which varies on time. So, all valid conversations are not traceable from execution logs.

Correlation: Correlation is the act of grouping of events from the event logs that belong to the same conversations. As example, if L represent a log of events {e1,e2,e3,...} then each event contains a list of properties (sender, receiver, time stamp, name, header, body). So if c1{e2,e5,e7,e9}, c2{e1,e3,e4,...} represent some kind of conversation, we can represent the refined log events L{c1, c2, ...} where each c corresponds to a conversation. There are different patterns for correlation. SAP research centre have done a lot of contribution in this area. Correlation patterns can be classified in Key-based correlation, chain-based correlation, Time-based correlation, key-time based (recycling is used) correlation and chain-time based correlation.

3 Classification of Model Discovery Problem

We are considering post-model which are derived from execution log. The concept of model discovery open the way of discovering process model, protocol model, data model, behavioral model and so on. It provides the accurate view of the process model which is very important to the system analyst and to the developer whose responsibility is to maintain and work on for further development of the system. As for example, Web services provide services description and publish this description in repository to advertise the service. But this description is not enough to find the best service to fulfill customer needs. If we able to provide the customer not only the visible service description but also interaction model of different skate's holder, then the approach would be much easier for the customer for decision making. Fig. 2 provides general idea of model discovery framework.

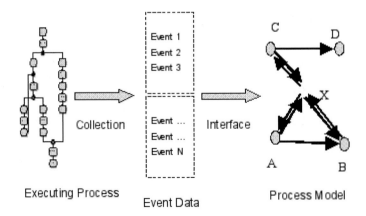

Fig. 2. Generic approach of Process Discovery

3.1 Protocol Model Discovery

Typically most of the systems need to follow for interaction. Protocols characteristic depend on the systems. For example FIPA (Federation for Intelligent Physical Agent) provides specification for interaction protocols. To communicate with agents every FIPA agents obliged to follow the specification provides by FIPA. Again if a system is complex then management of that system would be more complex and expensive. So the goal is to provide the system the functionalities to trace the events and the functionalities to discover protocol.

3.2 Data Model Discovery

Data model is description of data. It consists of rules which define logical structure of data for implementation perspective of data management system of a business organization. Desirable characteristics from data model are expressive power of data, simplicity and freedom from implementation details.

3.3 Behavioral Model Discovery

A behavioral model describes the behavior of a reactive system at some settled level of abstraction. Reactive system maintains an ongoing interaction with its environment. If a reactive system is considered as a state machine, that can change state and produce output events provided that the input events received from the environment. Like traffic control system, this must be specified and verified by terms of behavior.

4 Different Approaches for Model Discovery

Here we point out the most process-oriented systems which only store partial information about process instances, by tracing some events related to the execution of its activities.

4.1 Graph Based Process Discovery Technique

Agrawal, Gunopulus, Leymann [8] provides graphics based technique for discovering a process model. In this approach, execution logs are used for automatic discovery of a process model. The methods have been implemented and tested, using real and synthetic data. When this approach starts, use execution log files. So execution logs are traced at running time. The log file contains a list of events that records starting and finishing point of each activity also with some other attributes. The event contains a set of attributes {P,A,E,T, and O} where P is the process name, This is the name of activity, E∈{End, Start} is the type of event, T is the timestamp and O=o(A) is the output of the activity. Usually the logs are not considered as noise free. The noises inside the logs are not difficult to trace and clean. The noises occur easily due to erroneous activities. The algorithm is able to deal with noise those are anonymous traces. To correlate events, the author used some general logics which can be, for instance *If activity A is follows by activity B but A is not followed by B then B is depends on A. If*

A follows by B and B follows by A or A does not follows by B and B does not follows by A then A and B are concurrent or independent. Next for preserving consistency of the events of logs following conditions some heuristics are used. *An execution R is consistent with a process model graph G= (V,E), if the activities in R, are a subset of V' of the activities in G, and the induced sub graph G'=(V',{(u,v) € E | u, v € V'}) is connected, the 1ˢᵗ and last activities in R are process's initiating and terminating activity respectively.*

So for each dependency in the log, a path is generated in the graph. The graph represents the discovered model. The graph is acyclic. Each independent activity initiates a new dependency. For this parallelism can be occurred inside derived process. The graph is also consistent with every execution in the log. The objective of this method is to discover a graph based process model, that preserves all the dependency and also free from spurious dependencies.

4.2   Event Based Process Discovery Technique

The RNet method: The RNet method is a statistical approach based on neural network. It looks at the past behavior to specify a state. A feed forward neural network is used to predict the next state. The network use back propagation algorithm and train its layers on the basics of historical data. Once the data in the network is trained, the network is presented in the form of finite state machine. Advantage of this method is that, the method depends on the statistical data, so it has the potential, to become robust with respect to historical data. Disadvantages are that the method is very slow because of the training time. The size of the net becomes larger with the number of tokens types and arises a different kind of complexity.

The Ktail Method: Ktail is a completely algorithm based approach. The approach is followed from the work of Biermann and Feldmann [1972]. In the algorithm, grammar inference mechanism is used. The Idea of the work is that a state is defined by what future behaviours can occur from it. Thus for a given history (set of event stream), the current state is reached by the history. The ktail method is parameterized by simple threshold value, so complexity of this is controlled in a straight forward manner. The disadvantage is the uncontrolled input stream. So the approach is not effective in presence of noisy input stream.

The markov method: The approach is hybridization of algorithmic and statistical technique. Markov's method is used to find out the most probable event sequence and represent those probabilities into states transition according to the algorithm. The basic idea to use markov method is to use of probabilities for event sequences. In particular, the approach assigns the probability for event sequence. It produces probability tables considering occurrences of subsequence.

4.3   Concurrent Behavior Discovery Technique

Discovering interaction among multiple threads [2] is very useful to analysis concurrent systems and high performance computing. J.E Cook et al. provides four specific metrics that contributes as key information for the task of discovering concurrency and also provides the methodology by which these metrics are combined to discover complete models of the concurrent process. The four metrics are entropy, event type counts, periodicity and causality. Three types of correlation patterns are used for this technique which are sequential dependence (here, one event directly follows by the others), conditional Dependence (here, choice of one event from a set of events potentially followed from a given event) and concurrent dependence (based on concurrency technique). The discovering algorithm we are not discussing here as it is almost similar to sequential model discovery technique. Most workflow management systems distinguish between a buildtime component, used for the specification of workflow models, and a runtime component that is used during the invocation of workflow instances. The buildtime models are either interpreted by the runtime engine or compiled into a pseudo-code that can be executed by the runtime component. In the recent past several research projects focused on the weakening of this separation, thus enabling the modification of running process instances or the ad-hoc planning of process parts that are unknown at buildtime (cf. e. g. [8, 9]).

5   Protocol Discovery Tools

ProM Framework: The ProM framework [7] is an open-source tool specially tailored to support the development of process mining plug-ins. It is an extensible framework that supports a wide variety of process mining techniques in the form of plug-ins. This is platform independent as it is implemented in Java. Researchers and developers are open to contribute to this framework in the form of new plug-ins. This tool is currently at version 4.0 and contains a wide variety of plug-ins. Some of them go beyond process mining (like doing process verification, converting between different modeling notations etc).

DAGAMA: DAGAMA [11] is a tool which provides end to end solution from event data to a visual display of the discovered process model. It is used for the Ktail and markov process. This tool was used in an industrial process case study conducted at AT&T   Bell   Laboratories.

Business Cockpit: The project BC [10] is run by HP Labs and aims at developing a set of integrated tools that supports business and IT users in managing process execution quality. BC allows definition, monitoring and analysis of any kind of business-level metrics on top of any data source. By cleaning and aggregating process logs into a warehouse and by analyzing them with business intelligence technologies, we can extract knowledge about the circumstances in which high- or low-quality executions occurred in the past, and use this information to explain why they occurred as well as predict potential problems in running processes.

ARIS PPM: ARIS PPM [9] is a software product that leverages KPI (Key Performance Indicator) to assess real world business processes. Using actual processes, ARIS PPM generates intuitive management dashboards that display the current corporate objectives and communication relationships. An integrated early warning system (EarlyAlert) automatically monitors each step and issues an alarm in the event of deviation from planned values. ARIS PPM thus makes a key contribution to achieving sustained improvement in business processes.

6 Comparison of Different Process Mining Tools

To support the design of process model, we propose the use of process mining. Starting point for process mining is a so-called "Event-Based Data" containing information about the workflow process as it is actually being executed. In this paper, we introduce the concept of process mining and present a common format for Process Logs. Here Business Cockpit (BC) allows definition, monitoring and analysis of any kind of business-level metrics on top of any data source. ARIS PPM generates intuitive management dashboards that display the current corporate objectives and communication relationships.

Table 1. Execution of process model to follow the process Logs

Tool	Performance	Decision Point	Inspecting & cleaning log events	Analysis	Monitoring	Prediction
Business Cockpit	X	X	X	X	X	X
ProM	X	X	X	X		
ARIS PPM	X		X	X	X	

ProM is platform independent as it is implemented in Java. Researchers and developers are open to contribute to this framework in the form of new plug-ins. So if we want to measure the tools with their Event-Based Logs then the tool will match their requirement. The Logs maintain the Performance, Decision Point, analysis, Monitoring and Prediction.

7 Conclusion

The vision is to make model discovery more generalize. In this paper we try to come up with some common issues which are desirable for any kind of discovery problem. As the problem is not trivial, there are lots of factors inside, if we really want to establish our arguments of this paper. In this work, we like to highlight the most popular contributions in this area with the motivation to provide a generic platform to work with all types of model discovery problems.

While we have focused here on the use of these techniques for generating formal models, we also believe that they are useful in visualizing the data collected on a process. An engineer simply may be interested in a way to better understand the current process, as captured by the event data.

Acknowledgments. We appreciate the many helpful comments on this work provided by Rashed Mustafa and Juwel Rana. We are greatful to the J. E. Cook, David Rosenblum, Lawrence Votta, and Benjamin Zorn, as well as the reviewers of this article.

References

1. Cook, J.E., Wolf, A.L.: Discovering models of software processes from event-based data. ACM Transactions on Software Engineering and Methodology 7(3), 215–249 (1998)
2. Cook, J.E., Du, Z., Liu, C., Wolf, A.L.: Discovering models of behavior for concurrent workflows. Computers in industry 53(3), 297–319 (2004)
3. Cook, J.E., Wolf, A.L.: Software process validation: quantitatively measuring the correspondence of a process to a model. ACM Trans. Softw. Eng. Methodol. 8(2), 147–176 (1999), http://doi.acm.org/10.1145/304399.304401
4. van der Aalst, W.M.P., Reijers, H.A., Weijters, A.J.M.M., van Dongen, B.F., Alves de Medeiros, A.K., Song, M., Verbeek, H.M.W.: Business Process Mining: An Industrial Application, unpublished, Department of Technology Management, Eindhoven University of Technology, P.O. Box 513, NL-5600 MB, Eindhoven, The Netherlands, emailw.m.p.v.d.aalst@tm.tue.nl
5. Motahari Nezhad, H. R., Saint-Paul, R., Benatallah, B., Casati, F.: Protocol Discovery from Imperfect Service Execution Logs. In: Procs. of ICDE 2007, Istanbul, Turkey (April 2007)
6. Barros, A., Decker, G., Dumas, M., Weber, F.: Correlation Patterns in Service-Oriented Architectures. In: Dwyer, M.B., Lopes, A. (eds.) FASE 2007. LNCS, vol. 4422, pp. 245–259. Springer, Heidelberg (2007)
7. Agrawal, R., Gunopulos, D., Leymann, F.: Mining process models from workflow logs. In: Schek, H.-J., Saltor, F., Ramos, I., Alonso, G. (eds.) EDBT 1998. LNCS, vol. 1377, pp. 467–483. Springer, Heidelberg (1998), http://www.springerlink.com/content/0836165x01666140
8. Weske, M.: Flexible Modeling and Execution of Workflow Activities. Technical Report Angewandte Mathematik und Informatik 08/97-I, University of Muenster (1997)
9. Carlsen, S.: Conceptual Modeling and Composition of Flexible Workflow Models. PhD Thesis, Information Systems Group, Department of Computer
10. Hall, R.J., Zisman, A.: Behavioral models as service descriptions. In: Proceedings of the 2nd international Conference on Service Oriented Computing, ICSOC 2004, November 15-19, pp. 163–172. ACM Press, New York (2004), http://doi.acm.org/10.1145/1035167.1035191
11. Cook, J.E., Wolf, A.L.: Discovering models of software processes from event-based data. ACM Trans. Softw. Eng. Methodol. 7(3), 215–249 (1998), http://doi.acm.org/10.1145/287000.287001
12. Ahonen, H., Mannila, K., Nikunen, E.: Forming grammars for structured documents: An application of grammatical inference. In: Carrasco, R.C., Oncina, J. (eds.) ICGI 1994. LNCS, vol. 862, pp. 153–167. Springer, Heidelberg (1994)

Prediction of Learning Disabilities in School Age Children Using Decision Tree

M. David Julie[1] and Balakrishnan Kannan[2]

[1] MES College, Aluva, Cochin- 683 107, India
julieeldhosem@yahoo.com
[2] Cochin University of Science & Technology, Cochin - 682 022, India
Mullayilkannan@gmail.com

Abstract. The aim of this paper is to predict the Learning Disabilities (LD) of school-age children using decision tree. Decision trees are powerful and popular tool for classification and prediction in Data mining. Different rules extracted from the decision tree are used for prediction of learning disabilities. LDs affect about 10 percent of all children enrolled in schools. The problems of children with specific learning disabilities have been a cause of concern to parents and teachers for some time. This paper highlights the data mining technique – decision tree, used for classification and extraction of rules for prediction of learning disabilities. As per the formulated rules, LD in any child can be identified.

Keywords: Data Mining, Decision Tree, Divide and Conquer, Gain Ratio, Learning Disability (LD).

1   Introduction

In recent years the sizes of databases has increased rapidly. This has lead to a growing interest in the development of tools capable in the automatic extraction of knowledge from data. The term Data Mining or Knowledge Discovery in databases has been adopted for a field of research dealing with the automatic discovery of implicit information or knowledge within databases [10]. A widely accepted formal definition of data mining is given subsequently. Data mining is the non trivial extraction of implicit previously unknown and potentially useful information about data [4]. Data mining is a collection of techniques for efficient automated discovery of previously unknown, valid, novel, useful and understandable patterns in large databases. Conventionally, the information that is mined is denoted as a model of the semantic structure of the datasets. The model might be utilized for prediction and categorization of new data [1]. Diverse fields such as marketing, customer relationship management, engineering, medicine, crime analysis, expert prediction, web mining and mobile computing besides others utilize data mining [6]. A majority of areas related to medical services such as prediction of effectiveness of surgical procedures, medical tests, medication and the discovery of relationship among clinical and diagnosis data also make use of data mining methodologies [2].

Decision trees are supervised algorithms which recursively partition the data based on its attributes, until some stopping condition is reached [5]. This recursive partitioning,

N. Meghanathan et al. (Eds.): NeCoM, WiMoN, and WeST 2010, CCIS 90, pp. 533–542, 2010.
© Springer-Verlag Berlin Heidelberg 2010

gives rise to a tree-like structure. Decision trees are white boxes as the classification rules learned by them can be easily obtained by tracing the path from the root node to each leaf node in the tree. Decision trees are very efficient even with the large volumes data. This is due to the partitioning nature of the algorithm, each time working on smaller and smaller pieces of the dataset and the fact that they usually only work with simple attribute-value data which is easy to manipulate. The Decision Tree Classifier (DTC) is one of the possible approaches to multistage decision-making. The most important feature of DTCs is their capability to break down a complex decision making process into a collection of simpler decisions, thus providing a solution, which is often easier to interpret [11].

2 Learning Disability

Learning disability is a general term that describes specific kinds of learning problems. Learning disabilities are formally defined in many ways in many countries. However, they usually contain three essential elements: a discrepancy clause, an exclusion clause and an etiologic clause. The discrepancy clause states there is a significant disparity between aspects of specific functioning and general ability; the exclusion clause states the disparity is not primarily due to intellectual, physical, emotional, or environmental problems; and the etiologic clause speaks to causation involving genetic, biochemical, or neurological factors. The most frequent clause used in determining whether a child has a learning disability is the difference between areas of functioning. When a child shows a great disparity between those areas of functioning in which she or he does well and those in which considerable difficulty is experienced, this child is described as having a learning disability [7]. A learning disability can cause a child to have trouble in learning and using certain skills. The skills most often affected are: reading, writing, listening, speaking, reasoning and doing math [7]. Learning disabilities vary from child to child. One child with LD may not have the same kind of learning problems as another child with LD. There is no "cure" for learning disabilities [9]. They are life-long. However, children with LD can be high achievers and can be taught ways to get around the learning disability. With the right help, children with LD can and do learn successfully.

As many as 1 out of every 10 children, in the United States, has a learning disability. Almost 3 million children (ages 6 through 21) have some form of a learning disability and receive special education in school [2]. In fact, over half of all children who receive special education have a learning disability [3]. There is no *one sign* that shows a child has a learning disability. Experts look for a noticeable difference between how well a child does in school and how well he or she could do, given his or her intelligence or ability. There are also certain clues, most relate to elementary school tasks, because learning disabilities tend to be identified in elementary school, which may mean a child has a learning disability. A child probably won't show all of these signs, or even most of them. However, if a child shows a number of these problems, then parents and the teacher should consider the possibility that the child has a learning disability. If a child has unexpected problems in learning to read, write, listen, speak, or do math, then teachers and parents may want to investigate more. The same is true, if the child is struggling to do any one of these skills. The child may need to be evaluated to see if he or she has a learning disability.

When a LD is suspected based on parent and/or teacher observations, a formal evaluation of the child is necessary. A parent can request this evaluation, or the school might advise it. Parental consent is needed before a child can be tested [7]. Many types of assessment tests are available. Child's age and the type of problem determines the tests that child needs. Just as there are many different types of LDs, there are a variety of tests that may be done to pinpoint the problem. A complete evaluation often begins with a physical examination and testing to rule out any visual or hearing impairment [3]. Many other professionals can be involved in the testing process.

The purpose of any evaluation for LDs is to determine child's strengths and weaknesses and to understand how he or she best learns and where they have difficulty [7]. The information gained from an evaluation is crucial for finding out how the parents and the school authorities can provide the best possible learning environment for child.

3 Decision Tree

A decision is a flow chart like structure, where each internal node denotes a test on an attribute, each branch of the tree represents an outcome of the test and each leaf node holds a class label [5]. The topmost node in a tree is the root node.

Decision trees are powerful and popular tool for classification and prediction. It is a classifier in the form of a tree structure where each node is either a leaf node-indicates the value of the target attribute of examples or a decision node –specifies some test to be carried out on a single attribute-with one branch and sub tree for each possible outcome of the test[12]. Classifiers do not require any domain knowledge or parameter setting and therefore is appropriate for exploratory knowledge discovery. Decision tree can handle high dimensional data. The learning and classification step of decision tree are simple and fast.

A decision tree can be used to classify an example by starting at the root of the tree and moving through it until a leaf node, which provides the classification of the instance [11]. There are a variety of algorithms for building the decision tree that share the desirable of interpretability. In this work we are using the well known and frequently used algorithm J48 for the classification of LD.

The key requirements to do mining with decision trees are: attribute value description, predefined classes, discrete classes and sufficient data. A divide and conquer approach to the problem of learning disability from a set of independent instances leads naturally to a style of representation called a decision tree. To classify an unknown instance, it is routed down the tree according to the values of the attributes tested in successive nodes and when a leaf is reached, the instance is classified according to the class assigned to the leaf [11].

4 Classification by Decision Tree

Data mining techniques are useful for predicting and understanding the frequent signs and symptoms of behaviour of LD. There are different types of learning disabilities. If we study the signs and symptoms (attributes) of LD we can easily predict which attribute is from the data sets more related to learning disability. The first task to handle learning disability is to construct a database consisting of the signs, characteristics and level of difficulties faced by those children. Data mining can be used as a tool for analyzing complex decision tables associated with the learning disabilities. Our goal is to provide concise and accurate set of diagnostic attributes, which can be implemented in a user friendly and automated fashion. After identifying the dependencies between these diagnostic attributes, rules are generated and these rules are then be used to predict learning disability. The following checklist is used to investigate the presence of learning disability. This checklist is a series of questions that are general indicators of learning disabilities. It is not a screening activity or an assessment, but a checklist to focus our understanding of learning disability.

- has difficulty in rhyming;
- has limited interest in books and stories;
- has difficulty understanding instructions or directions;
- has trouble understanding idioms, proverbs, colloquialisms;
- has difficulty with pragmatic skills;
- has confuses similar –looking letters and numbers;
- has difficulty recognizing and remembering sight words;
- has frequently loses place while reading;
- has confuses similar looking words;
- has reverse letter order in words;

Based on the above information, a data set is generated. This set is in the form of an information system containing cases, attributes and class. A complete information system expresses all the knowledge available about objects being studied. Decision tree induction is the learning of decisions from class labeled training tuples. Given a data set $D = \{t_1, t_2, \ldots\ldots, t_n\}$ where $t_i = <t_{i1}, \ldots, t_{ih}>$. In our study, each tuple is represented by 16 attributes. The data base schema contains attributes as {DR, DS, DH, DWE, DBA, DHA, DA, ED, DM, LM, DSS, DS, DLL, DLS, STL, RG} and the class is LD. Then, Decision or Classification Tree is a tree associated with D such that each internal node is labeled with attributes DR, DSS, DH, DWE, etc. Each arc is labeled with predicate, which can be applied to the attribute at the parent node. Each leaf node is labeled with a class LD.

The basic steps in the decision tree are building the tree by using the training data sets and applying the tree to the new data sets. Decision tree induction is the process of learning about the classification using the inductive approach [5]. During this process we create a new decision tree from the training data. This decision tree can be used for making classifications. Here we are using the J48 algorithm, which is a greedy approach in which decision trees are constructed in a top-down recursive divide and conquer manner. Most algorithms for decision tree approach are following such a top down approach. It starts with a training set of tuples and their associated class labels. The training set is recursively partitioned into smaller subsets as a tree is being built. This algorithm consists of three parameters – attribute list, attribute selection method and classification. The attribute list is a list of attributes describing the tuples. Attribute selection method specifies a heuristic procedure for selecting the attribute that best discriminate the given tuples according to the class. The procedure employs an attribute selection measure such as information gain that allows a multi-way splits. Attribute selection method determines the splitting criteria. The splitting criteria tells as which attribute to test at a node by determining the best way to separate or partition the tuples into individual classes. Here we are using the data mining tool weka for attribute selection and classification. Classification is a data mining (Machine Learning) technique, used to predict group membership from data instances [9].

5 Methodology Used for Making the Decision Tree

J48 algorithm is used for classifying the Learning Disability. The procedure consists of three steps viz. (i) data partition based on cross validation test, (ii) attribute list and (iii) attribute selection method based on information gain. Cross validation approach is used for the sub sampling of datasets. In this approach, each record is used the same number of times for training and exactly once for testing. To illustrate this method, first we partition the datasets into two subsets and choose one of the subsets for training and other for testing. Then swap the roles of the subsets so that the previous training set becomes the test set and vice versa. The attribute list, attribute selection method by gain ratio and classification of our study are as given under.

5.1 Attribute List

DR : Difficulty with reading
DS : Difficulty with spelling
DH: Difficulty with Handwriting
DWE : Difficulty with written expression
DBA : Difficulty with basic arithmetic skills
DHA: Difficulty with higher arithmetic skills
DA : Difficulty with attention
ED : Easily distracted
DM : Difficulty with memory
LM : Lack of Motivation
DSS : Difficulty with study skills
DS : Does not like school
DLL : Difficulty learning a language
DLS : Difficulty learning a subject
STL : Is slow to learn
RG : Repeated a grade

5.2 Attribute Selection Method by Gain Ratio

The Information Gain Ratio for a test is defined as follows. IGR (Ex, a) = IG / IV, where IG is the Information Gain and IV is the Gain Ratio. Information gain ratio biases the decision tree against considering attributes with a large number of distinct values. So it solves the drawback of information gain. The ranked attributes based on the gain ratio is shown under.

1 DR
2 DS
6 DHA
7 DA
3 DH
14 DLS
4 DWE
5 DBA
10 LM
13DLL
16 RG
15 STL
12 DS
9 DM
8 ED
11 DSS

5.3 Classification

The correctly and incorrectly classified instances are as under.

Correctly Classified Instances   75 Nos.   75 %
Incorrectly Classified Instances   25 Nos.   25 %

The accuracy of the decision tree is given in Table 1 below. The first two columns in the table denote TP Rate (True Positive Rate) and the FP Rate (False Positive Rate). TP Rate is the ratio of low weight cases predicted correctly cases to the total of positive cases. There were 75 instances correctly predicted as low weight, and 25 instances in all that were low weight. So the TP Rate = 25/75 = 0.667. The FP Rate is then the ratio normal weight cases of incorrectly predicted as low weight cases to the total of normal weight cases, which is 0.197 in our case.

Table 1. Accuracy of Decision Tree

TP Rate	FP Rate	Precision	Recall	F-Measure	ROC Area	Class
0.667	0.197	0.684	0.667	0.675	0.767	F
0.803	0.333	0.790	0.803	0.797	0.767	T

A decision tree formed based on the methodology adopted in this paper is shown in Fig 1 below.

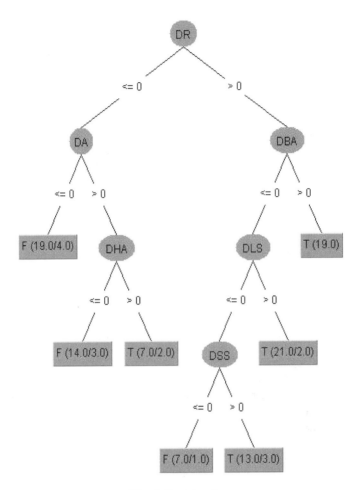

Fig. 1. Decision Tree

6   Extraction of Rules from Tree

It is easy to read a set of rules directly off a decision tree. One rule is generated for each leaf. The antecedent of the rule includes a condition for every node on the path from the root to that leaf and the consequent of the rule is the class assigned by the leaf [11]. This procedure produces rules that are unambiguous in that the order in which they are executed is irrelevant. However in general, rules that are read directly off a decision tree are far more complex than necessary and rules derived from trees are usually pruned to remove redundant tests. The rules are so popular because each rule represents an independent knowledge. New rule can added to an existing rule sets without disturbing them, whereas to add to a tree structure may require reshaping the whole tree. In this section we present a method for generating a rule set from a decision tree. In principle, every path from the root node to the leaf node of a decision tree can be expressed as a classification rule. The test conditions encountered along the path form the conjuncts of the rule antecedent, while the class label at the leaf node is assigned to the rule consequent. The extracted rules are shown below.

$$R1: (DR=N, DA=N) => (LD, N) \tag{1}$$

$$R2: (DR=N, DA=Y, DHA=Y)=>(LD,Y) \tag{2}$$

$$R3: (DR=N, DA=Y, DHA=N) => (LD, N) \tag{3}$$

$$R4: (DR=Y, DBA=N, DLS=N, DSS=N)=>(LD, N) \tag{4}$$

$$R5: (DR=Y, DBA=N, DLS=Y) => (LD, Y) \tag{5}$$

$$R6: (DR=Y, DBA=N, DLS=N, DS=Y)=>(LD,Y) \tag{6}$$

$$R7: (DR=Y, DBA=Y) => (LD, Y) \tag{7}$$

The expressiveness of a rule set is almost equivalent to that of a decision tree because a decision tree can be expressed by a set of mutually exclusive and exhaustive rules.

7 Result Analysis

The rules generated from the data sets are as shown above. If the minimum confidence threshold is, say 70%, then the above rules are output sure, the certainty of the generated rules, confidence of each rule, is calculated by considering the cases given in datasets. The accuracy obtained for the rules R1, R2, R3, R4, R5, R6 and R7 is given in Table 2 below. These rules can be used for predicting the learning disability accurately.

Table 2. Confidence of Rules

Rule	Confidence
R1	73 %
R2	72 %
R3	71 %
R4	70 %
R5	71 %
R6	73 %
R7	70 %

8 Comparison of Results

In this study, we are used the algorithm J48 for prediction of LD in children. The result obtained from this study is compared with the output, shown in Table 3 below, of a similar study conducted by using Rough Set Theory (RST) with LEM1 algorithm. From these we can see that, the rules generated based on decision tree is more powerful than those of rough set theory. From the comparison of results, we have noticed that, decision tree algorithm J48 has a number of advantages over RST with LEM1 algorithm for solving the similar nature of problems. For large data sets, there may be chances of some incomplete data or attributes. In data mining concept, it is difficult to mine rules from these incomplete data sets. In decision tree, the rules formulated will never influenced by any such incomplete datasets or attributes. Hence, LD can easily be predicted by using the method adopted by us. The other benefit of decision tree concept is that it leads to significant advantages in many areas including knowledge discovery, machine learning and expert system. Also it may act as a knowledge discovery tool in uncovering rules for the diagnosis of LD affected children. The importance of this study is that, using a decision tree we can easily predict the key attributes (signs and symptoms) of LD and can predict whether a child has LD or not.

Table 3. Confidence of Rules based on RST with LEM1 Algorithm

Rules	Confidence
R1	20 %
R2	40 %
R3	40 %
R4	20 %
R5	60 %
R6	40 %

9 Conclusion and Future Research

In this paper, we consider an approach to handle learning disability database to predict frequent signs and symptoms of the learning disability in school age children. This study mainly focuses on decision tree, because accuracy of decision-making can be improved by applying these rules. However, the study can be extended by applying clustering method also. This study has been carried out on more than 100 real data sets with most of the attributes takes binary values and more work need to be carried out on quantitative data as that is an important part of any data set. In future, more research is required to apply the same approach for large data set consisting of all relevant attributes. This study is a true comparison of the proposed approach by applying it to large datasets and analyzing the completeness and effectiveness of the generated rules.

J48 Decision Tree application on discrete data and twofold test shows that it is better than RST in terms of efficiency and complexity. J48 Decision Tree has to be applied on continuous or categorical data. Noise effects and their elimination have to be studied. The results from the experiments on these small datasets suggests that J48 Decision

Tree can serve as a model for classification as it generates simpler rules and remove irrelevant attributes at a stage prior to tree induction.

The extracted rules are very effective for the prediction. Obviously, as the school class strength is 40 or so, the manpower and time needed for the assessment of LD in children is very high. But using these rules, we can easily predict the learning disability of any child. Decision tree approach shows, its capability in discovering knowledge behind the LD identification procedure. The main contribution of this study is the selection of the best attributes that has the capability to predict LD. In best of our knowledge, none of the rules discovered in this type of study, so far, have minimum of two attributes for prediction of LD. The discovered rules also prove its potential in correct identification of children with learning disabilities.

References

1. Kothari, A., Keskar, A.: Paper on Rough Set Approach for Overall Performance Improvement of an Unsupervised ANN-Based Pattern Classifier (2009)
2. Blackwell Synergy: Learning Disabilities Research Practices, vol. 22 (2006)
3. Carol, C., Doreen, K.: Children and Young People with Specific Learning Disabilities. Guides for Special Education, vol. 9. UNESCO (1993)
4. Frawley, Piaatetsky: Shaping Knowledge Discovery in Database; an Overview. The AAAI/MIT press, Menlo Park (1996)
5. Jiawei, H., Micheline, K.: Data Mining-Concepts and Techniques, 2nd edn. Morgan Kaufmann/Elsevier Publishers (2008) ISBN : 978-1-55860-901-3
6. Chen, H., Fuller, S.S., Friedman, C., Hersh, W.: Knowledge Discovery in Data Mining and Text Mining in Medical Informatics, pp. 3–34 (2005)
7. Julie, M.D., Kannan B.: Paper on Prediction of Frequent Signs of Learning Disabilities in School Age Children using Association Rules. In: Proceedings of the International Conference on Advanced Computing, ICAC 2009, pp. 202–207. MacMillion Publishers India Ltd., NYC (2009) ISBN 10:0230-63915-1, ISBN 13:978-0230-63915-7
8. Chapple, M.: About.com Guide, http://databases.about.com/od/datamining/g/classification.htm
9. Paige, R., (Secretary): US Department of Education. In: Twenty-fourth Annual Report to Congress on the Implementation of the Individuals with disabilities Education Act-To Assure the Free Appropriate Public Education of all Children with Disabilities (2002)
10. Cunningham, S.J., Holmes, G.: Developing innovative applications in agricultural using data mining. In: The Proceedings of the Southeast Asia Regional Computer Confederation Conference (1999)
11. Pang-Ning, T., Michael, S., Vipin, K.: Introduction to Data Mining, Low Price edn. Pearson Education, Inc., London (2008) ISBN 978-81-317-1472-0
12. Witten Ian, H., Ibe, F.: Data Mining – Practical Machine Learning Tools and Techniques, 2nd edn. Morgan Kaufmann/Elsevier Publishers (2005) ISBN : 13: 978-81-312-0050-6

Co-occurrence Based Place Name Disambiguation and Its Application to Retrieval of Geological Text

N.V. Sobhana[1], Alimpan Barua[2], Monotosh Das[2], Pabitra Mitra[2], and S.K. Ghosh[1]

[1] School of Information Technology
[2] Department of Computer Science & Engineering
Indian Institute of Technology, Kharagpur 721302, West Bengal, India
{sobhanasunil,alimps,monotoshdas07}@gmail.com,
pabitra@cse.iitkgp.ernet.in, skg@iitkgp.ac.in

Abstract. This paper presents a method for resolution of ambiguity of place names and its evaluation over the Geological Corpus. We discussed the methods for generating co-occurrence models (co-occurrence matrix and co-occurrence graph) for the purpose of place name disambiguation. A graph based disambiguation algorithm is introduced to resolve the ambiguities such as synonyms and polynyms in place names. Using the neighborhoods in the co-occurrence graph, the query can be expanded with related place names after disambiguation. Experimental results on a Geological corpus (IITKGP-GEOCORP) show that query expansion with place disambiguation outperforms the baseline method.

Keywords: Co-occurrence matrix; co-occurrence graph; polynyms; synonyms.

1 Introduction

In this paper we have used co-occurrence models for the disambiguation of geological entities. Term co-occurrence model is based on the assumption that, in a sufficiently large corpus if some terms appear frequently in the same co-occurrence window, then there exists a semantic relationship between them. For higher co-occurrence frequency, semantic relations become stronger. Term co-occurrence has been used in many language processing tasks such as information retrieval, natural language processing and computational linguistics etc [1].

One of the main challenges in processing of natural language text is ambiguity. Information retrieval systems which lack of disambiguation capability often suffer in performance. The expanding of query with intended synonyms after disambiguation, can improve retrieval performance.

Geological text present a unique challenge to information retrieval and search systems because of abundance of geo-references, extent over wide spatial and temporal span. Performance of retrieval systems on geological text can be improved by place name disambiguation. This disambiguation system solves two ambiguities in place names such as synonyms (multiple place names referring to a single location) and polynyms (a single place name referring to multiple locations).

N. Meghanathan et al. (Eds.): NeCoM, WiMoN, and WeST 2010, CCIS 90, pp. 543–552, 2010.
© Springer-Verlag Berlin Heidelberg 2010

2   Related Work

Co-occurrence models have been used by Overell and Ruger for place name disambiguation. They showed that the disambiguation of polynyms and synonyms, leads to improve results in geographical information retrieval [2][3][4]. Andogah and Bouma implemented a complete place name ambiguity resolution system consisting of three components: geographical tagger, geographical scope resolver (GeoSR) and place name referent resolver (PRR) [5]. Smith and Crane implemented the toponym disambiguation system in the Perseus digital library and evaluated its performance [6]. Wacholder, Ravin, and Choi described a system that identified the occurrences of proper names in text. They analyzed the types of ambiguity (structural and semantic) that make the finding of proper names difficult in text, and described the heuristics used to disambiguate names [7]. Rauch, Bukatin, and Baker implemented a confidence-based disambiguation technique with measures of relevance to user's query [8]. Garbin and Mani implemented a corpus based method which identifies features that could help to disambiguate toponyms in news [9]. They disambiguated toponyms in a manually annotated news corpus with 78.5% accuracy.

In information retrieval often the search query is unable to express the information need of a user completely, due to its short length and inability of users to provide better terms to describe their information need [10]. The addition of related terms to a query user supplied can improve the retrieval performance. ie, query expansion assists the user in formulating better query. Number of attempts has been made to deal with the problem of selecting appropriate expansion terms. Voorhees has used Wordnet in determining expansion terms [11]. She performed experiments on TREC collection and expanded query using a combination of synonyms and hyponyms from Wordnet. The important factor that determines the effect of query expansion is the selection of appropriate expansion terms [12]. Bai, Nie and Cao used context dependent term relations for better expansion terms. They showed that Context dependent relations obtained by adding context word to the relation, performs much better than the co-occurrence relations [10]. Qiu and Frei implemented a query expansion method that expands query by adding terms that are most similar to the concept of the query, rather than selecting terms that are similar to the query terms [13]. Mandala, Tokunaga and Tanaka analyzed characteristics of different thesaurus types and propose method to combine them for query expansion. They have performed experiments on TREC collection and got better results than using single thesaurus [14].

3   Proposed System

The system builds a co-occurrence model, representing co-occurrence of place names. Disambiguator then applies the co-occurrence model to disambiguate the named entities extracted from the Geological corpus by the Named Entity Recognizer. Our disambiguation system resolves two problems such as synonyms and polynyms. The disambiguated place names are later used for query expansion.

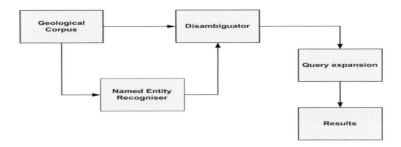

Fig. 1. The schema of the retrieval system

4 Co-occurrence Based Name Disambiguation

Term co-occurrence model captures co-occurrence information of words. Our co-occurrence based disambiguation system builds up a term co-occurrence model from geological corpus. It includes co-occurrence matrix and co-occurrence graph. The co-occurrence matrix and graph represent the places and order in which they occur. They also reveal the relationship between different places.

Each word in the co-occurrence matrix represents co-occurrence frequency of two terms. The row and column headings represent the terms of interest. The intersections of rows and columns of the matrix represent the count of the number of times a pair of places co-occur together and thus determines strength of association. The strength of the co-occurring terms comes from the number of times two terms occur together within the collection. The greater the number of times one place co-occurs with another, the stronger the association those places have. For example, India and Delhi have stronger association.

Table 1. Typical Co-occurrence matrix of Place Names

	India	Delhi	West Bengal	Maharastra	Karnataka	Tamil Nadu	Kerala
India	0	48	24	20	28	26	16
Delhi	48	0	5	3	2	2	1
West Bengal	24	5	0	3	2	2	0
Maharashtra	20	3	3	0	2	3	1
Karnataka	28	2	2	2	0	4	2
Tamil Nadu	26	2	2	3	4	0	3
Kerala	16	1	0	1	2	3	0

We define a co-occurrence graph, G (V,E) (V is the set of nodes and E is the set of edges) as a directed graph from the co-occurrence matrix. Each node p represents place names. An edge $e_{ij} \in E$ is created between two nodes p_i, p_j if they co-occur. ie an

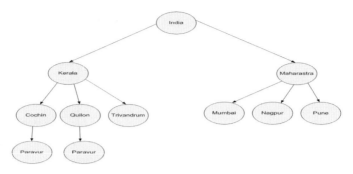

Fig. 2. Typical Co-occurrence graph

edge is formed between two nodes if place names represented by those nodes co-occur. The graph represents the direct and indirect relationship between place names.

Using Breadth First Search [16] on the co-occurrence graph we can search each node and the query can be expanded using neigbouring nodes. For example, the Maharashtra node explores as Mumbai, Bombay, Nagpur, Pune etc. Thus using the co-occurrence graph the query can be expanded using synonyms of place names.

Place name ambiguities [17][18][19] are either with synonyms (multiple place names referring to a single location) or polynyms (a single place name referring to multiple locations). The sense of a place name (i.e. meaning) is used when the place name has a number of distinct meanings.

Algorithm for handling polynyms

> Step1: Select next ambiguous polynym tp having sn senses;
> Step2: Select the context C;
> Step3: Find subhierarchies one for each sense of sn;
> Step4: Select last node in each subhierarchy of each sense; let it be node_a and node_b;
> Step5: Find co-occurrence count of node_a and node_b; let it be count_a and count_b;
> Step6: If count_a = count_b, sense cannot be disambiguated;
> Step7: If count_a < threshold value, sense related to count_a is not considered;
> Step8: if count_b < threshold value, sense related to count_b is not considered;
> Step9: if count_a ≠ count_b, select sense having higher co-occurrence count.

For example consider Paravur in Cochin and Paravur in Quilon in Kerala. From such ambiguous place names different sub hierarchies are formed in the graph. This is shown in figure II. Let the co-occurrence count of Paravur in Cochin be higher compared to the co-occurrence count of Paravur in Quilon. Then Paravur in Cochin is selected. If the co-occurrence count of Paravur in Quilon is low ie, below a threshold value, it is not considered for disambiguation.

If a place name has multiple names they are called synonyms. The sense of a place name (i.e. meaning) is used when the place name has a number of distinct meanings.

Algorithm for handling synonyms

Step 1 : select next ambiguous synonym *sm* having *sn* senses;
Step 2 : find subhierarchies one for each sense of *sn*;
Step 3 : select node in each subhierarchy of each sense; let it be *node_a* and *node_b*;
Step 4 : Find the subtree in the next level of *node_a* and *node_b*; let it be *subtree_a* and *subtree_b*;
Step 5 : if *subtree_a* = *subtree_b* and ancestor of (*node_a*) = ancestor of (*node_b*), sense related to *node_a* and sense related to *node_b* are synonyms.

For example, when Calcutta and Kolkata appear in the graph, compare the nodes in the next level of Calcutta with the nodes in the next level of Kolkata. If the number of node matches is above the threshold value then Calcutta is a synonym of Kolkata. Thus the query can be expanded with Calcutta, Kolkata etc.

5   Query Expansion Using Co-occurrence Graph

A query is expanded by adding new terms that are closely related to the original query terms. The new terms can either be statistically related to the original query words (ie, terms tend to co-occur with one another in documents) or chosen from lexical aids such as thesauri. In this work, query expansion utilizes word co-occurrence. Words co-occurring in a document or paragraph are likely to be in some sense similar or related in meaning. The advantage of co-occurrence analysis lies in the fact that information is easily generated from the documents and requires no human intervention. In this work selection of expansion terms is done by exploiting hierarchical relationships in co-occurrence graph and also by making use of synonyms. For example, Maharashtra is expanded with Mumbai, Bombay, Nagpur, Pune etc. The query expansion is described below.

5.1 Algorithm: Co-occurrence Based Query Expansion

```
Input: Fnode is the starting vertex of co-occurrence
graph. Let N be the number of vertices in  the co-
occurrence graph. Query is a pointer to a list.
Output: An array to store the order of visit of verti-
ces during traversal.
Data structure: A queue QUEUE to hold the vertices
which is initially empty. Adjacency Matrix representa-
tion of graph. Graphptr is the pointer to graph.
```

Steps

```
If   (Graphptr = NULL) then
        Print "Graph is empty"
        Exit
EndIf
Node   =   Fnode
QUEUE.INSERT_QUEUE(Node) // Enter the starting vertex
                            //into the QUEUE
While(QUEUE.STATUS() • EMPTY) do // Till the QUEUE is
                                  //not empty
        Snode = QUEUE.DELETE_QUEUE() // Delete an item
                                      //from QUEUE1
        If (SearchArray(VISIT, Snode) = FALSE) then // If
                        //Snode is not in the array
                        // VISIT
                InsertArray(VISIT, Snode ) // Store visited
                            //node Snode in VISIT
                If Snode = "query_location" // If Snode
                            //is a particular place, say
                            //West Bengal
                    For i = 1 to N do
                        Query = Query U i // Original
                            //query is expanded with
                            // children of Snode
                        Exit
                    EndFor
                else
                    For i = 1 to N do // To enter all
                            //adjacency vertices of Snode
                            //into QUEUE
                        If (Gptr[Node][i] = 1) then

                            QUEUE.INSERT_QUEUE(i)
                        EndIf
                    EndFor
                EndIf
        EndIf
    EndWhile
Return
Stop
```

This algorithm begins at the root node of co-occurrence graph, explores the neighbouring nodes and expands the query using them. For example, if *Snode* is *West Bengal*, the query is expanded with *Calcutta, Kolkata* and *Kharagpur*. It makes use of queue data structure QUEUE and adjacency matrix. VISIT stores the traversal order of visited vertices. We have used a few operations on the queue such as INSERT_QUEUE and DELETE_QUEUE.

In this work, Named Entity Recognizer recognizes geo-references i.e., place names. The machine learning technique (conditional random fields) is used to prepare baseline classifier using the annotated data and features. We have used the C++ based

OpenNLP CRF++ package for named entity recognition [21]. For evaluation of retrieval performance we have used the open source Terrier (TERabyte RetRIEveR) IR platform, (http://ir.dcs.gla.ac.uk/terrier) as implementations of the above models [22]. Many retrieval models have been used in terrier such as TF-IDF, BM25, DFR-BM25, BB2, IFB2, InexpB2, InexpC2, InL2 and PL2 [20].

Retrieval performance was evaluated using precision, recall and mean average precision. Precision is calculated as the number of correctly disambiguated synonyms and toponyms divided by the number of disambiguated synonyms and toponyms. Recall is the number of correctly disambiguated synonyms and toponyms divided by the total number of synonyms and toponyms in the collection. Mean average precision is the mean of the average precision values of a group of queries.

6 Results and Discussion

The Geological corpus (IITKGP-GEOCORP) was created out of a collection of scientific reports and articles on the geology of the Indian subcontinent. Many of these constituted reports submitted to the Earth Sciences Division of Department of Science and Technology, Government of India. The corpus consists of about 200 documents with each document about 10,000 words long, representing various aspects of geology. The lexicon consisted of several well known as well as rare geological terms. The titles of some of these documents are Coastal forms and processes of the Godavari Delta, Retreat of Himalayan Glaciers: Indicator of Climate Change, Metamorphism of the Oddanchatram Anorthosite, Tamil Nadu, South India etc. We also considered over 100 queries based on the feedback of a pool of the geological researchers. We have manually constructed a set of relevance judgments for all these documents in the corpus with help of the experts in Indian Subcontinent Geology. Some of the queries are Narmada, Gondwana, Karakonam etc.

Table 2. Precision values of various retrieval models on IITKGP-GEOCORP

N_{rt}	BM25	DFR-BM25	TF-IDF	BB2	IFB2	Inexp B2	Inexp C2	InL2	PL2
1	0.8439	0.8468	0.8811	0.7512	0.8043	0.7775	0.7751	0.8658	0.9144
10	0.8060	0.8120	0.8060	0.7794	0.8976	0.7950	0.7947	0.8236	0.9448
30	0.5992	0.6025	0.6131	0.5523	0.6229	0.5873	0.5908	0.6075	0.7708
50	0.8831	0.9043	0.9043	0.7839	0.7151	0.6954	0.6927	0.9096	0.9683
80	0.7212	0.7212	0.7212	0.7731	0.7731	0.7731	0.7212	0.7212	0.6879
100	0.7889	0.7889	0.7889	0.6227	0.8702	0.7460	0.7460	0.7889	0.7889

In Table 2 we present the precision values obtained by different models on the corpus. Gold standard was provided by human relevance judgment. The average value over hundred queries is reported. Note that both precision and recall are presented for different numbers of retrieved documents (N_{rt} = 1, 10, 30 etc). The co-occurrence based query expansion significantly improved the retrieval performance. We found that the Mean Average Precision of a system with query expansion is higher compared to a baseline system with no query expansion.

Table 3. Mean Average Precision

Retrieval models	MAP values of baseline method	MAP values of co-occurrence based query expansion
BM25	0.8610	0.9790
DFR_BM25	0.8560	0.9560
TFIDF	0.8611	0.9550
BB2	0.8456	0.9110
IFB2	0.8555	0.9520
InexpB2	0.8540	0.9440
InexpC2	0.8560	0.9460
InL2	0.8540	0.9010
PL2	0.8547	0.9560

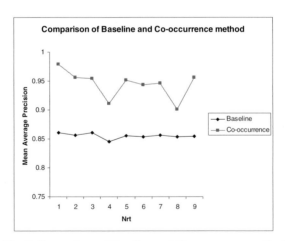

Fig. 3. Comparison of Baseline and Co-occurrence method

The Mean Average Precision (MAP) of co-occurrence based query expansion is presented in Table 3. We observed that BM25 model has a higher Mean Average Precision than other models. InL2 model has a lower Mean Average Precision than other models. Experimental results of the system with query expansion show 8.9% improvement when compared to the baseline system.

7 Conclusion

We proposed a co-occurrence graph based method of query expansion with place name disambiguation. A co-occurrence graph has been created to represent place names, relationships and resolved the problem of place name ambiguity. The results showed that co-occurrence based query expansion with resolving place name ambiguity has improved the retrieval performance. Query expansion with relevance feedback mechanisms can be explored as extension of our work.

References

1. Nan, Q.Y., Yong, Q., Di, H.: A Study on unified Term Co-occurrence Model. Information Technology Journal, 1033–1038 (2009)
2. Overell, S.E., Ruger, S.M.: Using co-occurrence models for place name disambiguation. International Journal of Geographical Information Science 22(3), 265–287 (2008)
3. Overell, S.E., Ruger, S.M.: Forostar: A system for GIR. In: Peters, C., Clough, P., Gey, F.C., Karlgren, J., Magnini, B., Oard, D.W., de Rijke, M., Stempfhuber, M. (eds.) CLEF 2006. LNCS, vol. 4730, pp. 930–937. Springer, Heidelberg (2007)
4. Overell, S.E., Ruger, S.M.: Identifying and grounding descriptions of places. In: SIGIR Workshop on Geographic Information Retrieval (2006)
5. Andogah, G., Bouma, G., Nerbonne, J., Koster, E.: Geographical Scope Resolution. In: Workshop at the 6th Conference on Language Resources and Evaluation (LREC), Paris, pp. 4–10 (2008)
6. Smith, D.A., Crane, G.: Disambiguating Geographic Names in a Historical Digital Library. In: Constantopoulos, P., Sølvberg, I.T. (eds.) ECDL 2001. LNCS, vol. 2163, pp. 127–136. Springer, Heidelberg (2001)
7. Wacholder, N., Ravin, Y., Choi, M.: Disambiguation of proper names in text. In: Proceedings of the Fifth Conference on Applied Natural Language Processing, pp. 202–208 (1997)
8. Rauch, E., Bukatin, M., Baker, K.: A confidence-based framework for disambiguating geographic terms. In: HLT-NAAL Workshop on Analysis of Geographic References (2003)
9. Garbin, E., Mani, I.: Disambiguating Toponyms in News. In: Proceedings of Human Language Technology Conference and Conference on Empirical Methods in Natural Language Processing (HLT/EMNLP), Vancouver, pp. 363–370 (2005)
10. Bai, J., Nie, J.Y., Cao, G.: Context Dependent Term Relations for Information Retrieval. In: Proceedings of the 2006 Conference on Empirical Methods in Natural Language Processing (EMNLP 2006), Sydney, pp. 551–559 (2006)
11. Voorchees, E.M.: Query Expansion using Lexical-semantic Relations. In: SIGIR 1994: Proceedings of the 17th annual international ACM SIGIR conference on Research and development in information retrieval, pp. 61–69 (1994)
12. Peat, H.J., Willett, P.: The limitations of term co-occurrence data for query expansion in document retrieval systems. JASIS 42(5), 378–383 (1991)
13. Qiu, Y., Frei, H.P.: Concept based query expansion. In: Proceedings of the 16th Annual International ACM SIGIR Conference, New York, pp. 160–169 (1993)
14. Mandala, R., Tokunaga, T., Tanaka, H.: Combining Multiple evidence from different types of thesaurus for query expansion. In: Proceedings of the 22nd annual international ACM SIGIR conference on Research and development in information retrieval, California, United States, pp. 191–197 (1999)

15. Matsuo, Y., Ishizuka, M.: Keyword extraction from a single document using word co-occurrence statistical information. International Journal on Artificial Intelligence Tools (IJAIT) 13(1), 157–169 (2004)
16. Langsam, Y., Augenstein, M.J., Tanenbaum, A.M.: Data structures using C and C++. Prentice Hall, India
17. Agirre, E., Rigau, G.: Word sense disambiguation using conceptual density. In: Proceedings of the 16th conference on computational linguistics (COLING 1996), pp. 16–22 (1996)
18. Buscaldi, D., Rosso, P.: A conceptual density-based approach for the disambiguation of toponyms. International Journal of Geographical Information Systems 22(3), 301–313 (2008)
19. Buscaldi, D., Rosso, P.: Map-based vs. Knowledge-based Toponym Disambiguation. In: Proceeding of the 2nd International Workshop on Geographic information Retrieval, GIR 2008, California, USA, pp. 19–22 (2008)
20. Manning, C.D., Raghavan, P., Schutze, H.: Introduction to Information Retrieval. Cambridge University Press, Cambridge (2008)
21. Kudo, T.: CRF++, an open source toolkit for CRF (2005), http://crfpp.sourceforge.net
22. The Terrier Information Retrieval Platform (2007), http://ir.dcs.gla.ac.uk/terrier

A Formal Method for Detecting Semantic Conflicts in Protocols between Services with Different Ontologies

Priyankar Ghosh and Pallab Dasgupta

Indian Institute of Technology Kharagpur, Kharagpur - 721302, India
priyankar.ghosh@gmail.com, pallab@cse.iitkgp.ernet.in

Abstract. The protocol between a web service and its client may lead to semantically inconsistent results if the ontologies used by the server and client are different. Given that the web is growing in a mostly un-coordinated way, it is unrealistic to expect that web services will adhere to standardized ontologies in near future. In this paper we show that if the client publishes its ontology and presents the protocol it intends to follow with a web service, then the web server can perform a semantic verification step to determine formally whether any of the possible executions of the protocol may lead to a semantic conflict arising out of the differences in their ontologies. We believe that this an approach which enables a web-server to automatically verify the semantic compatibility of a client with the service it offers before it actually allows the client to execute the protocol. We model the ontologies as graphs and present a graph based search algorithm to determine whether the protocol can possibly reach a conflict state.

1   Introduction

Ontology is regarded as a formal specification of a (possibly hierarchical) set of concepts and the relations between them. The need for developing intelligent web services that can automatically interact with other web services has been one of the primary forces behind recent research towards standardization of ontologies of specific domains of interest [1–5]. For example, if several online book stores follow the same ontology for the *book* domain, then it facilitates an intelligent web service to automatically search these book stores to find books in a particular category.

If two communicating web services use different ontologies, then they may potentially reach a state where there is a semantic conflict/mismatch arising out of the differences between their ontologies. For example, suppose the ontologies of web service A and web service B recognize the class *vehicle* and its sub-classes, namely, *car*, *truck* and *bike*. The ontology of A defines *color* as an attribute of class *vehicle*, where as the ontology of B defines *color* as an attribute of the sub-classes *car* and *bike* only. Suppose A communicates with B using the following protocol:

N. Meghanathan et al. (Eds.): NeCoM, WiMoN, and WeST 2010, CCIS 90, pp. 553–562, 2010.

Step-1. Ask B for the registration number of a vehicle, which is owned by a specific person.

Step-2. If B finds the registration number, then ask B for the color of the vehicle.

Several executions of this protocol are possible for different valuations of the data exchanged by the protocol. Semantic conflicts arising out of the differences in ontologies may occur in some of these cases, but not always. For example:

- If B does not find the registration number, then Step-2 is not executed and there is no semantic conflict.
- If B finds the registration number and the vehicle happens to be a truck, then Step-2 of the protocol will lead to a semantic conflict, since in B's ontology, the *color* attribute is not defined for trucks.
- If B finds the registration number and the vehicle happens to be a car or a bike, then Step-2 will not lead to a semantic conflict, since in B's ontology, the *color* attribute is defined for cars and bikes.

If the ontology of A and the protocol is made available to B, then B can formally verify whether any execution of the protocol may lead to a semantic conflict and warn A accordingly before the actual execution of the protocol begins. In this paper we present the formal method for performing this verification step.

There has been considerable research in recent times on matching ontologies and finding out semantic conflicts/mismatches among two ontologies [6, 7]. It is important to note that two agents can exchange information through a protocol which is mutually consistent as long as that protocol does not sensitize the parts of their ontologies in which they do not agree – a fact which is often overlooked in world politics! Therefore an approach which rules out communication between two services on the grounds that their ontologies do not match is too conservative in practice. Since the standardization of ontologies and their acceptance in industrial practice seems to be a distant possibility, we believe that the verification problem presented in this paper and its solution is very relevant at present.

The paper is organised as follows. The syntax for describing a protocol is described in Section 2. In Section 3 we present a graph based model for representing the ontologies. The proposed formal method for detecting semantic conflicts is presented in Section 4. Related works are briefly discussed in Section 5.

2   Protocol and Conflict

In this section we present a formalism similar to SQL for the specification of the protocol. It may be noted that other formalisms can also be used to specify a protocol as long as the formalism has expressive power similar to the formalism used in this paper. We present two example protocols and also describe the notion of the conflict that we have addressed in this paper.

2.1   Formal Description of the Protocol

Typically, a protocol consists of a sequence of queries and answers. The query specifies a set of variables through *"GET"* keyword and specifies a set of classes using *"from"* keyword. The valuations corresponding to the variable set are generated from those classes. Also an optional *"where"* keyword is used to specify the conditions on the variables. The answer of a query is a set of tuples, where every individual tuple is a set of valuations corresponding to the variable set specified in the query. The branching is specified using *"if-else"* statements.

2.2   Example of Protocol

Consider the protocol shown in Fig. 1. The protocol depicts a conversation between a client and a server over the publication domain. The query of the client is about the author of some specific manual. Then the client makes a query to

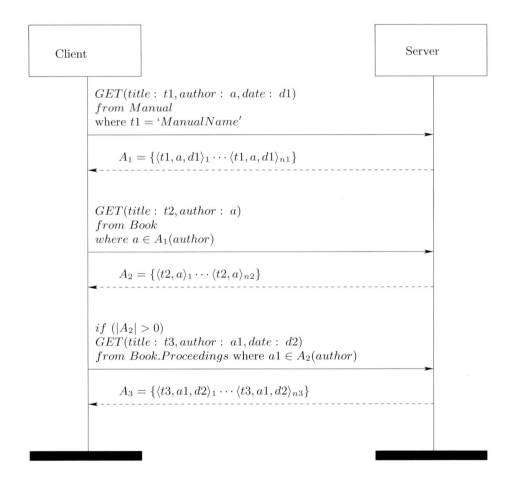

Fig. 1. Protocol on Publication Domain

retrieve the books by the authors of that manual. According to the ontology of the client, *'Proceedings'* is a subclass of *'Book'* and the client makes the next query to retrieve the proceedings by the same authors among the books. If the server does not recognize *'Proceedings'* as a sub class of *'Book'*, the query can not be answered by the server due to the mismatch in the ontologies.

In Fig. 2 we present another protocol that exchanges information about the automobile domain. The client makes a query about the brands which have sold more than a specific number of vehicles in a particular year. Then next query is made in the context of the previous query to retrive those brands which manufacture *'Red Trucks'*. According to the ontology of the client the color is a property of the vehicle class and therefore all subclasses of vehicle class will have the color attribute. However if the server recognizes *'color'* as an attribute of some of the sub-classes(suppose *'car'* and *'two-wheeler'*) instead of as an attribute of the class *'Vehicle'* itself, the query can not be answered by the server due to the mismatch in the ontology.

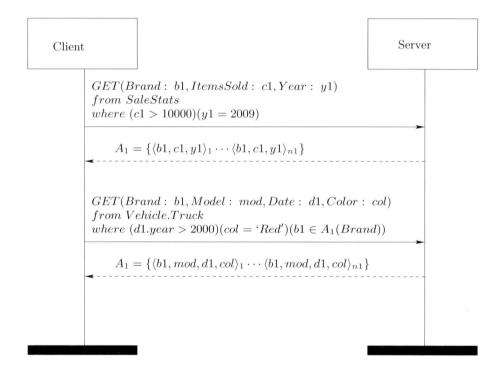

Fig. 2. Protocol on Automobile Domain

2.3   Notion of Mismatch between Two Ontologies

We focus on the following two types of mismatch between the client and server ontologies in this paper.

Specialization Mismatch(Type-1): In this type of incompatibility the client recognizes a class c_2 as the specialization of another class c_1 whereas the server recognizes c_2 as the specialization of some other class c_1'. Our first example (Fig. 1) is an instance of this type.

Attribute Assignment Mismatch(Type-2): A very common type of incompatibility arises where the client and the server both recognize classes $c_1', \ldots, c_n'$ as the specializations of another class c_1, but the client associates an attribute α with the super class c_1, whereas the server associates α with some of the sub classes $c_i', \ldots, c_j'$, $0 < i, j \leq n$. Since we view the mismatches from the query answering perspective, we use the notion of this conflict from the query perspective. If the set of variables that is used in a query q, is not available at server side, we denote that as *attribute level(Type-2)* mismatch. Our first example (Fig. 2) is an instance of this type.

3   Graph Model of Ontology

Typically the ontologies can be visualised as a combination of metadata and a set of instances. Classes, relations and datatypes form the metadata part of the ontology whereas the individuals and the valuations of the attributes are to the actual data. While describing an ontology using OWL, the class and the attributes(modeled as properties in the context of OWL) are used to represent the metadata. We use a graph based approach to model the metadata that are described as classes and attributes in OWL. While using OWL, the *properties* are used to express the attributes. Therefore we use the term property and attribute interchangeably. We define the ontology graph as follows.

Definition 1. *A **graph model** for an ontology O is $\mathcal{G} = (V, E)$ where, V is the set of vertices and E is the set of directed edges. Each node $v_i \in V$ represents a class in the OWL ontology and v_i is associated with a **property list** $\mathcal{L}(v_i)$ whose elements are the data properties of the class. There exists an edge $e_{ij} \in E$ from v_i to v_j, where $v_i, v_j \in V$, if v_j is a sub class of v_i.*

4   Overview of the Method

In this section we present the relevant formalisms and present the overall algorithm for solving the problem. The *variable set* and the *class set* specified in the query q are denoted by $S_v(q)$ and $S_c(q)$ respectively. We present a graph search based structural matching algorithm to check the semantic safety of the protocol.

Definition 2. *The specialization sequence $\sigma = \langle c_1.c_2. \cdots .c_k \rangle$ in a query q is the sequence of classes that are concatenated through the '.' operator, and for any two consecutive classes c_i and c_{i+1} in the sequence, c_i is the super class of c_{i+1}. Therefore the elements of $S_c(q)$ can be individual classes or specification sequences.*

4.1   Structural Algorithm to Check the Semantic Consistency

Algorithm 1. Check-Consistency

input : The Protocol $\mathcal{P}$ and the Server Ontology $\mathcal{O}_s$

1 $V \leftarrow \{\}$;
2 **foreach** *query q in the protocol* $\mathcal{P}$ **do**
3   **foreach** *element* τ *in* $S_c(q)$ **do**
4   **if** τ *is a specialization sequence* **then**
5              $c_1 \leftarrow$ the first concept of τ;
6              $c_t \leftarrow$ FindMatch($\mathcal{O}_s$, c_1);
7   **for** $i \leftarrow 2$ **to** $length(\tau)$ **do**
8                  $c_m \leftarrow$ the ith concept of τ;
9   **if** *any class* c_t' *equivalent to* c_m *is not found as a sub class of*
                     c_t *in* $\mathcal{O}_s$ **then** Report Mismatch at c_m;
10   **else** $c_t \leftarrow c_t'$
11   **end**
12             $V \leftarrow V \cup$ property set for c_t;
13   **else**
                /* c is an individual class   */
14             $c_1 \leftarrow \tau$;
15             $c_t \leftarrow$ FindMatch($\mathcal{O}_s$, c_1);
16             $V \leftarrow V \cup$ property set for c_t;
17   **end**
18   **end**
19   **if** $S_v(q) \subsetneq V$ **then** Report $\{S_v(q) - V\}$ as unmatched variables;
20 **end**

Function FindMatch($\mathcal{O}_s$, c_i)

1 Find the class c_t which is equivalent to c_i in $\mathcal{O}_s$;
2 **if** c_t *is not found in* $\mathcal{O}_s$ **then**
3   Report Mismatch at c_i and exit;
4 return c_i;

4.2   Working Example

We present a working example to describe how the algorithm works. Consider the protocol shown in Fig. 1. We elaborate the steps of applying Algorithm 1 with respect to the fragments of the client and server ontologies shown in Fig. 3 and Fig. 4 respectively. These fragments are taken from the benchmark provided by [8]. The benchmark has one reference ontology and four other real ontologies and the domain of these ontologies is bibliographic references. We have used the reference ontology as the server ontology and another real ontology named INRIA as the client ontology. We have used a pictorial representation which is similar to entity-relationship diagram to show the fragments of the ontologies. The classes are represented by the rounded rectangles and the ovals represent the properties of a particular class. The class hierarchy is shown using arrows,

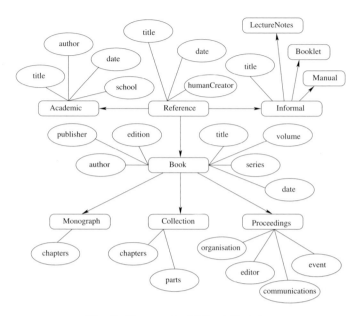

Fig. 3. Fragment of Client Ontology

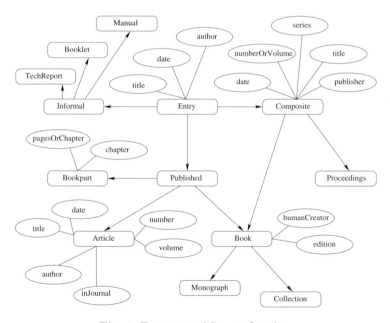

Fig. 4. Fragment of Server Ontology

that is a sub class is connected to its super class by an arrow which is directed towards the sub class. The properties that belong to a particular class are connected to the rounded rectangle corresponding to that class through a line.

Step-1: While applying Algorithm 1 to the server ontology, the individual class *'Manual'* is searched and since the search is successful, it is checked that the attributes that are associated with class *'Manual'* in the query in the protocol are actually answerable by the server and this check turns out to be successful for the ontologies that are presented here.

Step-2: The next query uses the class *'Book'*. Algorithm 1 performs the consistency checking in the way that is similar to the previous query and the check is successful.

Step-3: The third query uses a specialization sequence *'Book.Proceedings'*. Algorithm 1 searches for the *'Book'* class in the server ontology and then checks whether *'Proceedings'* is a sub class of *'Book'* in the server ontology. Algorithm 1 reports a failure since in the server ontology *'Proceedings'* is not a sub class of *'Book'*.

4.3   Proof of Correctness

Theorem 1. *[Soundness] The mismatches returned by Algorithm 1 are correct.*

Proof. Algorithm 1 reports mismatch in three cases. We observe each of the cases as follows.

Mismatch in Individual Class: If Algorithm 1 does not find a matching class c which is used in a query, a conflict is reported. Since the class is not recognized by the server, it is not possible for the server to answer the query. Therefore the outcome of the algorithm is correct.

Mismatch in Specialization Sequence: Consider a specialization sequence $\sigma = \langle c_1.c_2. \cdots .c_k \rangle$ in a query q on which Algorithm 1 returns a mismatch. We prove the correctness of the consistency checking by induction on the length k of σ.

Basis(k = 1): In this case there is only one class in the specialization sequence and this case falls under the case of mismatch in individual classes.

Inductive Step: Suppose Algorithm 1 returns the mismatch correctly for specialization sequences having length k. We prove that Algorithm 1 reports the conflicts correctly for the specialization sequences having length $k+1$. There can be two possible cases.

1. The conflict is reported for a class that appears in the ith location of the sequence, where $1 < i < k + 1$. The reported mismatch is correct according to the inductive hypothesis.
2. The conflict is reported for the $k+1^{th}$ class of the sequence. In this case there exists a matching specialization sequence at server ontology up to length k. But c_{k+1} is not a sub class of class c_k according to the server ontology. Therefore the conflict reported by Algorithm 1 is correct.

Mismatch on Variables: Suppose the set of variables that are specified by the client is V_c in a query q corresponding to the class set $S_c(q)$ and the failure is reported on some variable in V_c. Since Algorithm 1 first finds the matches corresponding to the classes in $S_c(q)$ and then checks for the answerability with respect to the variable set, in this case every class in $S_c(q)$ is matched with suitable classes in the server side. Now Algorithm 1 reports conflict if there exists any variable that is not recognized by the server as an attribute of at least one of the classes that correspond to the classes in $S_c(q)$. Therefore the reported conflict falls under the *Type-2 or attribute level* conflict category.   □

Theorem 2. *[Completeness] For any protocol $\mathcal{P}$, if there is any mismatch of type-1 or type-2, Algorithm 1 reports it.*

Proof. This proof is done by construction. For each of the type of the mismatches we show that Algorithm 1 uses a sequence of operations through which the mismatch is detected. We present the proof for each mismatch type.

Type-1 Mismatch: Consider a specialization sequence $\sigma = \langle c_1.c_2. \cdots .c_k \rangle$ which is used in query q. Algorithm 1 starts by finding the class that is equivalent to c_1 at the server side. If there is only one class in σ then Algorithm 1 reports mismatch when the corresponding class is not found in the server ontology. When the length of σ is greater than 1, Algorithm 1 continues to check whether c_i is a subclass of c_{i+1} where $1 < i < k$. A mismatch is reported by Algorithm 1 whenever c_i is a subclass of c_{i+1} for $1 < i < k$. Hence if there exists any mismatch in any specialization sequence, the algorithm reports it.

Type-2 Mismatch: Consider a query q made by the client and the set of variables is V_c in q. The set of classes is denoted by $S_c(q)$. We argue that, if there exists a *Type-2* mismatch for query q, Algorithm 1 reports it. For *Type-2* mismatches Algorithm 1 first checks the presence of the equivalent classes c_i^s in the server ontology and computes the union V_s of the attributes corresponding to every c_i^s. If there is any variable/s in V_c that are not present in V_s, a conflict is reported by Algorithm 1. Hence if there exists a *Type-2* mismatch for a query, Algorithm 1 reports it.   □

5   Related Works

Ontology plays an important role towards enhancing the integration and interoperability of the semantic web services. A significant amount of research has been done towards formalizing the notion of conflict between two ontologies. In [6], authors present a detailed classification of conflicts by distinguishing between *conceptualisation* and *explication* mismatches. In [9] authors further generalize the notion of conflicts and classify semantic mismatches into language level mismatches and ontology level mismatches. Then ontology level mismatches are further classified into conceptualization mismatch and explication mismatch. Further research in the same direction [10] adds few new types of conceptualization mismatches. Researchers in [11] present alternative types of conflicts that are primarily relevant to OWL based ontologies.

Ontology mapping primarily focuses on combining multiple heterogeneous ontologies. In [12] authors address the problem of specifying a mapping between a global and a set of local ontologies. In [13] authors discuss about establishing a mapping between local ontologies. In [14] the problem of ontology alignment and automatic merging is addressed. The problem of checking compatibility between two ontologies with respect to a protocol is new and to the best of our knowledge there is no prior work on this topic.

6   Conclusion

In this paper we addressed the problem of detecting the presence of semantic mismatch where the data exchange between two ontologies is defined in terms of a protocol. We believe that the proposed methodology will be very helpful for the integration of web services that are developed independently. Moreover the future of internet applications lie in exchanging knowledge, where semantic conflict will be a major issue.

References

1. Guo, R., Chen, D., Le, J.: Matching semantic web services across heterogeneous ontologies. In: CIT, pp. 264–268 (2005)
2. Noia, T.D., Sciascio, E.D., Donini, F.M., Mongiello, M.: Semantic matchmaking in a p-2-p electronic marketplace. In: Matsui, M., Zuccherato, R.J. (eds.) SAC 2003. LNCS, vol. 3006, pp. 582–586. Springer, Heidelberg (2004)
3. OWL Web Ontology Language, http://www.w3.org/TR/owl-ref/
4. Web Service Modeling Language, http://www.wsmo.org/wsml/
5. The Dublin Core Metadata Initiative, http://dublincore.org/
6. Visser, P.R.S., Jones, D.M., Bench-Capon, T.J.M., Shave, M.J.R.: An analysis of ontology mismatches; heterogeneity versus interoperability. In: AAAI Spring Symposium on Ontological Engineering (1997)
7. Castano, S., Ferrara, A., Montanelli, S.: Matching ontologies in open networked systems: Techniques and applications, pp. 25–63 (2006)
8. OAEI Benchmark, http://oaei.ontologymatching.org/2009/benchmarks/
9. Klein, M.: Combining and relating ontologies: an analysis of problems and solutions. In: Workshop on Ontologies and Information Sharing, IJCAI 2001, Seattle, USA (2001)
10. Qadir, M.A., Fahad, M., Noshairwan, M.W.: On conceptualization mismatches between ontologies. In: GrC, pp. 275–278 (2007)
11. Li, C., Ling, T.W.: Owl-based semantic conflicts detection and resolution for data interoperability. In: ER (Workshops), pp. 266–277 (2004)
12. Calvanese, D., Giacomo, G.D., Lenzerini, M.: A framework for ontology integration, pp. 303–316. IOS Press, Amsterdam (2001)
13. Madhavan, J., Bernstein, P.A., Domingos, P., Halevy, A.Y.: Representing and reasoning about mappings between domain models, pp. 80–86 (2002)
14. Noy, N.F., Musen, M.A.: Anchor-prompt: Using non-local context for semantic matching. In: Proceedings of the Workshop on Ontologies and Information Sharing at the International Joint Conference on Artificial Intelligence (IJCAI), pp. 63–70 (2001)

Test Suite Diminuition Using GRE Heuristic with Selective Redundancy Approach

S. Selvakumar[1], M.R.C. Dinesh[1], C. Dhineshkumar[1], and N. Ramaraj[2]

[1] Department of Information Technology,
Thiagarajar College of Engineering,
Madurai, India
[2] Department of Computer Science and Engineering,
G.K.M. College of Engineering,
Chennai, India
ssit@tce.edu, {dinesh.mrc,dhineshjim2006}@gmail.com,
prof.ramaraj@yahoo.co.in

Abstract. A testing process involves testing the given program with the designed test cases. A testing objective has to be defined before testing the program. The test cases depend upon the testing objective of the program. As new test cases are generated over time due to software modifications, test suite sizes may grow significantly. Because of time and resource constraints for testing, test suite minimization techniques are needed to remove those test cases from a suite that, due to code modifications over time have become redundant with respect to the coverage of testing requirements for which they were generated. For reducing the cost of the test execution only efficient test cases should be taken into consideration. Existing algorithms like GRE reduces the test suite by removing redundancy that may sometimes can significantly diminish the fault detection effectiveness (FDE) of suites. We present the modified GRE heuristic with selective redundancy (GSRE) for test suite reduction that attempts to use additional coverage information of test cases to selectively retain some additional test cases in the reduced suites that are partially redundant with respect to the testing criteria used for suite minimization, with the goal of improving the FDE retention of the test suites. Our experiments show that our GSRE approach can significantly improve the FDE retention of test suites without severely affecting the extent of suite size reduction.

Keywords: Software testing, testing criteria, test suite minimization, test suite reduction.

1 Introduction

Software testing is a part of the software development lifecycle which involves detection of errors in the software. The selection of the testing objective is the initial part of the testing lifecycle [3]. Practically speaking the test quality depends upon the test suite being selected. Test suites once developed are reused

N. Meghanathan et al. (Eds.): NeCoM, WiMoN, and WeST 2010, CCIS 90, pp. 563–571, 2010.

and updated frequently as the software evolves. As a result, some test cases in the test suite may become redundant as the software is modified over time since the requirements covered by them are also covered by other test cases. A traditional approach to the test suite reduction consists in building a test suite of a smaller size but equivalent to the original one in terms of a selected coverage metric [2]. Test cases are selected in such a way so as to satisfy maximum testing requirements. As a result, the constructed test suite may contain of the many test cases that may have become redundant. The above process cannot be fully automated because the problem of determining whether a requirement is feasible is not decidable [4].

2   Problem Statement

A test suite T of test cases (t_1,t_2,t_m) ,a set of testing requirements (r_1,r_2,r_m) that must be satisfied for the overall coverage of the program, and subset (t_1,t_2,t_n) of T, that must be chosen to satisfy the requirements associated with the program.

2.1   Related Work

Many test suite minimization techniques involve reduction of test cases which can lead to reducing of the overall coverage of the program, thus leading to weaker fault detection. Some prior empirical studies have used the code coverage criteria for minimizing the test suites. In experiments by Wong et al. , minimized test suites achieved 9 percent to 68 percent size reduction while only experiencing 0.19 percent to 6.55 percent fault detection loss. On the other hand, in the empirical study conducted by Rothermel et al., the minimized suites achieved about 80 percent suite size reduction on average while losing about 48 percent fault detection effectiveness (FDE) on average. These results are encouraging as much higher percentage suite size reduction was achieved as compared to the percentage loss in FDE of suites. There are a variety of testing criteria that have been discussed in literature, and some are finer than others. We observed that different testing criteria are useful for identifying test cases that exercise different structural and functional elements in a program, and we therefore believe the use of multiple testing criteria can be effective at identifying test cases that are likely to expose different faults in software. So the final problem evolves as to find an efficient test suite minimization technique without affecting the overall coverage and fault detection capability of the test suite which involves adding a partial amount of redundancy for extra coverage of the program.

2.2   Proposed System

We have proposed a new approach, GSRE heuristic for test case reduction for increasing the fault detecting effectiveness of the optimal test suite. It is based on applying multiple objectives and selective redundancy with GRE heuristic. The GSRE heuristic takes into account two or more objectives to reduce the test suite.

We focus on the minimization of the number of test cases as well as retention of partially redundant cases. A test case that may be redundant according to a particular criterion may not be redundant according to another criterion. The loss of such redundant cases can be considered as loss in fault detection where a fault detecting test case may be lost in redundancy considering only single criteria. This suggests that a combination of the testing criteria should be used for deciding the optimal representative set thus reinforcing the multi objective heuristics. The GSRE algorithm works out to reduce the test suite given a test suite T and a set of testing requirements (r_1, r_2, r_n) that must be exercised to provide the desired coverage of the program, the GSRE finds out the optimal representative set in the following manner. First the test suite is checked for 1-1 redundant cases and they are eliminated. Then the essential strategy is carried out and requirements that are satisfied by only certain test cases are selected as a part of the essential strategy. The third step involves the selective removal of test cases that have become redundant with those which have been selected. Next the greedy strategy is applied which selects the test cases which satisfies most of the unsatisfied requirements. In case of a tie, a test case can be chosen at random. Then again the selective removal of test cases that have become redundant is applied. The final set of selected cases gives the optimal representative set. The main contribution of this work is to prove that the fault detection capability of GRE algorithm can be improved by adding selective redundancy approach that allows them to clearly differentiate between fault detecting cases and fully redundant cases and at the same time allow certain amount of test case reduction.

3   Methodology and Solution

For any two sets of sets A and B, A+B denotes the set (C∪D: C∈A, D∈B). We use R and T to denote the set of all testing requirements and the test suite, respectively. In this study, we assume that both R and T are non-empty and finite. Furthermore, we assume that for every requirement r∈R, there is always a test case t in the input domain which satisfies r. Let m and n denote the cardinality of R and T, respectively. The satisfiability relation between test case t∈T and requirement rR can be represented by a binary relation S(T, R) from T to R. The satisfiability relation is defined as the set $(t, r) \in T \times R$: t satisfies r. Whenever there is no ambiguity, we use S instead of S(T,R). For any t∈T and any $T(\neq \varphi) \subset T$, we use Req(t) and Req(T) to denote the set of all requirements that are satisfied by the test case t and those test cases in T, respectively. Similarly, for any rR and any $R(\neq \varphi) \subset R$, we use Test(r) and Test(R) to denote the set of all test cases that can satisfy the requirement r and the requirements in R, respectively. A subset T_1 of the test suite T is said to be a representative set of S if $Req(T_1) = R$. The problem of test suite reduction is to find a representative set of S. A representative set T1 of S is said to be optimal if $T_1 \leq T_2$ for any representative set T_2 of S. We use REP(S) and OPT-REP(S) to denote the sets of all representative sets and optimal representative sets of S, respectively. Clearly, T is a representative set of S, and optimal representative sets of S always exist. Although optimal representative sets may not be unique, they have the same cardinality. There are two different kinds of test cases in a test suite, namely the essential test cases and the redundant test cases. A test case is said to be an essential test case of S if Req $(T/(t)) \neq$ R. Let Ess(S) denote the set of all essential test cases of S. Whenever there is no ambiguity, we use Ess instead of Ess(S).Contrary to the concept of essential test cases is the concept of redundant test cases. A test case is said to be a redundant test case of S if Req $(T/(t)) =$ R. If t is redundant, an optimal representative set of S(T/(t),R) may not be optimal with respect to S. There is a special kind of redundant test Cases known as the l-to-l redundant test cases. A test case t1ϵT is said to be redundant if there exists a test case t($\neq$ t1)ϵT such that Req(t1)ϵReq(T_{op}), where T_{op} is the test cases in the optimal set.

3.1   Greedy, Selectively Redundant and Essential Algorithm

The proposed algorithm has four main steps, they are 1-1 Redundancy: The removal of 1-1 redundant test cases. Essential: The selection of all the necessary test cases. Greedy: The selection of the test cases that satisfy maximum unsatisfied requirements. Selectively choosing from redundant test cases: Choosing a subset of redundant test cases based on additional coverage information.

3.1.1   1-1 Redundancy
The 1 -to- 1 redundancy strategy is defined as the technique of reducing the satisfiability relation S(T,R) by the removal of a l-to-l redundant test case in T. After the application of the l-to-l redundancy strategy, the original problem S(T,R) is reduced to S(T-t,R) where t is l-to-l redundant. It should be noted that l-to-l redundant test cases should be removed one at a time. Otherwise, some requirements may be left unsatisfied. For example, consider the situation that a requirement rR can only be satisfied by t_1 and t_2, and both t_1 and t_2 satisfy the same set of requirements (that is, Req(t_1)$=$ Reqt_2)). Obviously, both t_1 and t_2 are l-to-l redundant. However, we can only remove either t_1 ort_2, but not both Otherwise, r cannot be satisfied. The l-to-l redundancy strategy should be repeatedly applied until there are no l-to-l redundant test cases, because the more l-to-l redundant test cases are removed, the smaller the reduced problem.

3.1.2   Essential
In the essential step, the test cases that can only satisfy certain requirements are selected. After the application of essential strategy, the problem of D (t, r) reduces to D (t-ess, r-Req(Ess)).This can be defined as the optimal representative set after the second step of selecting essential test cases. Applying the essential strategy reduces the requirements for the next greedy strategy operation if the test case selected can satisfy extra requirements in addition to its essential requirement. So the essential strategy should be applied as soon as possible. After the selection of essential test cases the test cases left in the test suite are checked whether they have become redundant, if so they are subjected to be

```
Input
A test suite T;
Requirement coverage information for each test case in t for testing criteria C₁, C₂...,Cₖ(k>=1).
Output
RS: a reduced set of test cases from T that satisfies all testing requirements for k criteria
Algorithm reducexcitselectiverredundancy(T₁', T₂';..........Tₖ';  1≤C≥ k.  )
RS: = {}
For the primary criterion label all associated testing requirements as unmarked.
While T is not empty do

Step 1
  For all Criteria
  L'(req(t)=req(t,))
  T=T-t

Step 2
  For all requirements of primary criterion Cₚ
  Essential test case, Eₑₛₛ: =necessary test case satisfying a requirements rᵢ;
  RS: =RS U {Eₑₛₛ};
  T: =T-{Eₑₛₛ};
  Unsatisfied requirements R: =R-rᵢ;
  End for;

Step 3
  L'(requirements satisfied by the test case are already satisfied by the representative set)
  For all test cases in T;
  Redundant: =set of test cases from T that have just become redundant with the representative set;
  End for;
  T=T-{Redundant};
  Selectredundanttests (RS, Redundant, C₁...);
  End if
  End while;

Step 4
  Else
  {
  For all test cases in T
  Greedy case =test case satisfying most number of unsatisfied requirements;
  RS= RS U {Greedy case};
  T: =T-{Greedy case};
  L'(test cases become redundant with RS w.r.t. Cₚ)
  Redundant=set of test cases from T that have become redundant with RS w.r.t.Cₚ;
  T=T-{Redundant};
  Selectredundanttests (RS, Redundant, C₁...);
  End if
  End for;
```

Fig. 1. Pseudo code for our general approach to selectively redundant GSRE approach

tested through the selective redundancy function and new fault uncovering test cases are selected according to additional coverage information.

3.1.3 Greedy

A natural partner is the greedy strategy. Since the essential test cases must appear in the representative set, the greedy strategy selects all the essential test cases. Selection of the test case in this step proposes that the test case should satisfy many of the unsatisfied requirements. This can be referred to as selecting global representative through series of local optima. Clearly, the greedy heuristic G is the repeated application of the greedy strategy. After the selection of a test case according to the greedy heuristic, the other test cases in the test suite are checked if its redundant with the test case selected, if it is so, it is added to the set of redundant test cases and selectively chosen based on additional coverage

```
Input
t₁, t₂, .............tₙ :test cases in the original test suite T.
T₁ᶜ, T₂ᶜ, ............Tₙᶜ: test case sets covering each of r₁ᶜ,r₂ᶜ,.....rₙᶜ respectively for each criterion 1≤c≥k.
Output
RS: a reduced set of test cases from T that satisfies all testing requirements for k criteria.
Algorithm reducewithselectiveredundancy (T₁ᶜ, T₂ᶜ.............Tₙᶜ: 1≤ C ≥k )
Step 1
For all Criteria
If (req(t)=req(t₁))
T=T-t;
Step 2
For criterion C "unmark all tₙᶜ"
Redundant= { };
RS= { };
For each i=1.....n
If (tᵢ ε T)
RS=RS U tᵢ such that tᵢ ε R and tₙ=1;
T=T-tᵢ;
Unsatisfied Req R=R-r;
Satisfied Req=r;
Step 3
Size= T;
For j=1 to size do
If (tᵢ εT)
If (tᵢ   subset of r)
Redundant=redundant U {tᵢ}
Test = Test-tᵢ;
Selectredundanttests (RS, Redundant, C₋ᵢ);
End if
End if
End for
Step 4
Else
Merge sort (Test)
Select a test case tₓ T such that |Rₓ|=max
Test=Test-tₓ;
Unsatisfied Req R=R-r;
Satisfied req=r;
Size= T;
For j=1 to size do
If (tᵢ ε T)
If (tₙ ...subset of r)
Redundant=redundant U {tₙ};
Test = Test-tₙ;
Selectredundanttests (RS, redundant, C₋ᵢ);
End if
End if
```

Fig. 2. Algorithm for GSRE approach

```
Function Selectredundanttests(RS, Redundant, Cᵢ)

While redundant test t contributes additional Cᵢ coverage to RS do
Toadd:=the test case isn redundant contributing maximum additional coverage Cᵢ
coverage to RS;
RS: = RS U {ToAdd} ;
For each criterion label as marked the testing requirements satisfied by Toadd;
If i<k then
RedundantAgain: = the set of test cases from redundant that have just become redundant
w.r.t Cᵢ;
Redundant: =Redundant−RedundantAgain;
Selectredundanttestts(RS,redundantagain,Cᵢ₊₁);
Endif
Endwhile
```

Fig. 3. Function to Choose Selectively Redundant Test Cases

information. Let us recall that a test case t is essential if $Req(T/(t)) \neq R$. In other words, a test case r is essential if and only if there exist a requirement rR such that r can only be satisfied by r (that is, $Test(r) = (t_0)$). Hence, the worst case time complexity for identifying all essential test cases is $O(mn)$, where m And n denote the number of elements in the sets R and T, respectively. Since the time complexity of the greedy heuristic G is $O(mn*min(m, n))$, the worst case time complexity of GE is also $O(mn*min(m, n))$.

3.1.4   Selectively Choosing from Redundant Test Cases

The approach of selective redundancy is that when several test cases of the same test suite are compared on the same criterion, some test cases may exhibit redundancy while testing the same according to a different criterion may show them as not redundant i.e. like it has some extra advantages to be in consideration for the optimal set. Till the previous step of the greedy approach, some test cases can be added to the optimal representative set. This includes both the greedy cases and the essential cases. In the selective redundancy step, first the test cases that have become redundant according to the primary coverage criterion are taken and evaluated further to see if it has some additional purpose from the secondary requirements. The selective redundant test cases are added after each strategy has been carried out. An interesting property of applying the selective redundancy to this approach shows that, a test case that is selectively redundant with the primary requirements can also be essential or a much needed in the case of secondary requirements, which shows this approach can be more advantageous. This approach adds the selectively redundant cases only for a purpose and non performing test cases are not added and are not essential. Even if the essential test cases provide the full requirements to be satisfied, the secondary requirements can always be checked by the greedy strategy to add test cases that can certainly increase the fault detection capability. In this heuristic the selective redundancy is implemented after both the greedy and the essential step which implies that the greedy step can be started only after the application of selective redundancy after essential step or if there are no redundant cases after the essential step. Based on the situation of redundancy, the optimal set can be obtained after applying selective redundancy in the greedy step.

4   Performance Analysis

4.1   Representative Test Size

Fig.4 depicts the size of the representative set generated for 4 open source programs using our approach .The vertical axis denotes the representative set size. Actually our approach generated 14 precentage bigger optimal representative set when compared to the normal GRE approach. Even though the size of the set was larger, it showed a great improvement in fault detection. Most of the extra test cases generated exposed faults.

4.2   Fault Detection Capability

The following fig 5 shows the tabulation of the fault detection percentage of the algorithm. Thus we can come to the conclusion additional test cases selected exposes many faults that were previously not exposed. Experimental Results for the open source programs when the test suite was reduced by our GSRE approach showing the percentage of test case reduction and the Percentage fault Detection loss (percent fault loss).

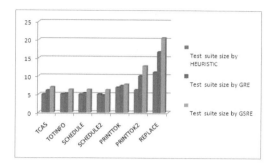

Fig. 4. Sizes of representative sets for GRE, Heuristic, and GSRE

Program	% Size Reduction	% Fault Loss
Tcas_tok	17.65	2.33
P_fac	28.43	8.92
Tot_info	32.17	12.34
sched_fac	43.22	16.78
Tot_fac	50.55	14.38
Mat_tok	52.37	4.23
Space	10.44	2.97
Select	9.66	1.63
Select_tok	22.62	0.00
Replace_tok	33.29	0.53
Sched_info	0.07	0.57
Replace_info	11.25	0.54
Info_fac	42.56	0.69
Numg_get	32.59	0.88
Num_replace	23.78	0.72

Fig. 5. Experimental Results for simulating GSRE

5   Conclusion and Future Work

In our work we discuss three strategies for test case reduction namely, the essential strategy, the greedy strategy and the selective redundancy strategy. We have the following observations, the essential strategy is to be applied first and then checked for redundancy if so, selective redundancy is applied for the test cases and then the greedy strategy is applied again with selective redundancy, the application of selective redundancy in the following approach provides more fault detection capability and a slightly bigger optimal representative set. If the application of essential strategy together with the selective redundancy is sufficient to deliver the optimal representative set, then the greedy strategy is not required. In the future, we will continue to investigate the relationship between test suite reduction and error detection by utilizing larger subject programs and by conducting further experimentation on the distribution of error revealing cases within minimized test sets. We are evaluating the use of additional mathematical programming software capable of generating alternative optimal solutions for the greedy strategy. We are also researching the effectiveness of various criteria for the GSRE test-suite reduction algorithm.

Acknowledgments

We thank Dr. Gregg Rothermel, Dept. of Computer Science, University of Nebraska, for providing the Siemens suite of programs, their faulty versions and the associated test pools.

References

1. Garey, M.R., Johnson, D.S.: Computers and Intractability: A Guide to the Theory of NP-Completeness. Freeman and Company, New York (1979)
2. Korel, B., Tahat, L.H., Vaysburg, B.: Model-based regression test reduction using dependence analysis. In: Proceedings of ICSM 2002, Montral, Canada, October 3-6 (2002)
3. Lin, J.-W., Huang, C.-Y.: Analysis of test suite reduction with enhanced tie-breaking techniques. In: Proceedings of the 31 st International Conference on Software Engineering, vol. 51, pp. 679–690 (2009)
4. Tahat, L.H., Bader, A., Vaysburg, B., Korel, B.: Requirement- based automated black box test generation. In: Proceedings. of COMPSAC 2001, Chicago, USA, October 8-12 (2001)
5. Rothermel, G., Harrold, M.: A Safe, Efficient Regression Test Selection Technique. ACM Transactions on Software Engineering and methodology 6, 173–210 (1997)
6. Jeffrey, D., Gupta, N.: Test suite reduction with selective redundancy. In: IEEE International Conference on Software Maintenance, ICSM 2005, Budapest, Hungary, pp. 549–558 (2005)
7. Hong, H.S., Cha, S.D., Lee, I., Sokolsky, O., Ural, H.: Data flow testing as model checking. In: Proceedings of ICSE 2003, Portland, USA, May 22-26 (2003)
8. Tallam, S., Gupta, N.: A Concept Analysis Inspired Greedy Algorithm for Test Suite Minimization. In: Proceedings of Workshop Program Analysis for Software Tools and Engineering (September 2005)

Mobility Monitoring by Using RSSI in Wireless Sensor Networks

Senol Zafer Erdogan

Maltepe University, Faculty of Engineering, Maltepe 34857, Istanbul, Turkey
senole@maltepe.edu.tr

Abstract. In this paper, mobility time is studied by using the changes in the received signal strenth indicator (RSSI). RSSI values are used to define mobility, non-mobility or unclear times. The experiments are conducted to investigate mobility and non-mobility times and also the poster experiment is used to determine rating ratios of posters.

1 Introduction

Wireless sensor networks are composed of small electronic devices known as sensor mote[1]. These devices are used mostly for monitoring the environmental conditions[2][3] such as temperature, humidity, light; motion detection such as monitoring animals[4], and fire detection. In recent years, wireless sensor networks have become more popular due to availability of different types of sensors and sensor applications.

Sensor motes and sensor boards are growing together with the advancements in technologic developments. Various sensor boards manufactured include sensor (CO2, NH3, NH4) boards, seismic sensor boards, acoustic sensor boards, magnetic sensor boards, barometric sensor boards. Some sensor boards include the GPS module which is used to determine the position. These developments enable many new applications.

Sensors typically operate with batteries and it is often impractical to replace these batteries. As an example, it is not practical to plug a sensor used to monitor various gas levels in a sewer system to the city power grid. Similarly, it is not possible to find an electrical outlet in a forest where sensors may be used to monitor animal movements. Accordingly, they can only be used for a limited time. As a consequence they also have limited processing resources. Several algorithms have been developed in the literature to operate these networks while taking into consideration these constraints.

Another emerging application of sensor networks is the indoor localization in which received signal strength indicator (RSSI) is used to estimate the distance, monitor mobility, and human behavior[5][6][7]. Despite the fact that RSSI values are mostly inaccurate, these problems do not yet have any other solution and the use of sensor networks is a promising approach to address the problem.

N. Meghanathan et al. (Eds.): NeCoM, WiMoN, and WeST 2010, CCIS 90, pp. 572–580, 2010.

In this study, mobility monitoring by using RSSI values are explained. The remainder of this paper is organized as follows: Section 2 gives a brief description regarding RSSI related researches in sensor networks. Section 3 provides the details of the experiment conducted for mobility monitoring in an-indoor environment. Finally, Section 4 presents the conclusions.

2   Related Work

In wireless sensor networks, several studies of sensor networks and their applications reported in the literature utilize RSSI Zhou et al[8] investigate the degree of variation in RSSI values and propose a non-circular radio irregularity model (RIM) for wireless sensor networks. Gu[9] presents a method to estimate RSSI values and use it as a Link Quality Indicator(LQI) and packet reception rate for realistic radio communication. Arias et al[10] estimate the position of all nodes using RSSI. Scott et al[11] use transmit and receive signal strengths to investigate propagation patterns. Wang et al[12] developed a method to determine a precise localization of the sensor nodes. In the study[12], RSSI is used for distance measurements between sensor nodes.

Erdogan and Hussain[13] discuss radio irregularity with respect to distance, transmission power level, directions and alignments of a sensor node from the base station. The experimental results show that proper alignment and transmission power level can reduce the energy consumption.

The variation in the received signal strength indicator values can be used to identify user mobility and environment as well. RSSI can be used for knowledge extraction.[14][5] Experiments in [5] show that the activity of a person can be determined by using the variation in RSSI values.

A sensor device can be used to detect mobility or user behavior without any wiring and provides unobtrusive monitoring at hospitals, schools, offices and homes. In doing so a person's privacy is maintained while hiding the identity.[5]

2.1   RSSI: Received Signal Strength Indicator

Received Signal Strength Indicator (RSSI) is a measurement of the power in a received signal. It is commonly known in IEEE 802.11 protocol family. RSSI parameter is used in many studies in wireless sensor networks. Some studies investigate the RSSI variation with respect to distance as well as direction and alignment from the base station.[13] shows that as the distance to the base station increases, the RSSI value decreases. Significant variation in RSSI values were observed for various distances due to alignment.[13]

In addition to distance, RSSI values can change due to mobility or physical obstruction. As a result the signal quality between two nodes is affected. Erdogan showed that a physical obstruction can result in lower RSSI value.[13]

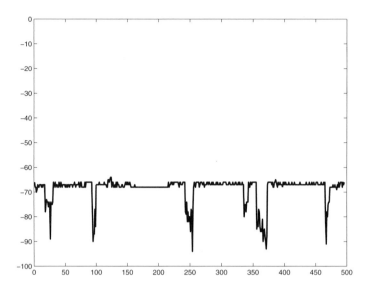

Fig. 1. The Blocking

If there is a blocking between two sensor motes, significant changes can be observed on RSSI values. If the changes are bigger than a predefined threshold, it can be said that there is a mobility or an obstruction is detected. In this paper, we conduct an experiment with two sensor motes. A person standing up between these two sensor motes blocks the motes to communicate directly with base station thereby affecting the message's RSSI value that is sent.

The RSSI values are shown in Figure 1. The x-axis specifies the time and the y-axis specifies the RSSI value obtained from the packet. There are significant changes in RSSI values at specific time intervals which means that, there is blocking at these time intervals. If these changes continue for a long time, it means that the blocking continues; On the other hand, if these changes last only a very short time, then blocking takes a short time.

3   Experimentation

We have conducted two experiments. In the first application, the entrance of a building is used for detecting the mobility. In the second application, RSSI values are used to find the most popular poster in a poster session. The details of these applications are described below:

3.1   Application 1

In this experiment,we investigated the mobility and lack of mobility times by looking at the changes of RSSI values. The entrance of a hall building of cultural organization is used. We deployed two sensor motes at the entrance of the building, left and right corners, at the main entrance door. At every half a second, one of these two motes communicate with the other. If someone goes inside, the RSSI value of the message is affected due to blocking. This way we can determine how long time there is mobility or lack of mobility in specific time intervals.

The Experiment details are as follow:

– Base station is inside the hall.
– There are 2 sensor motes besides to the door of the building enterance. The distance between motes is 4 m.
– Moteivs Tmote Sky[1] sensors are used for the base station and for 4 sensor motes.
– The time span for the experiment is 108.5 minutes.
– Every half seconds a mote communicates with the other.
– 13017 samples were collected within this period.

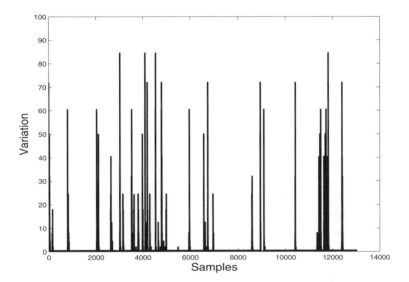

Fig. 2. The variation of RSSI changes

In Figure 2, the variations in RSSI are shown. The RSSI variation sometimes has significant changes. At these times, there is some blocking that affects the RSSI value of the message. It means that somebody goes inside or outside by passing through the door.

We analysied the data, afterwards, functions of the application are written for detecting the mobility time interval, lack of mobility time interval and unclear time intervals. We determined these values after our observations. The functions are as follows:

---

[1] http://www.moteiv.com

1. Mobility state
2. Lack of mobility state
3. Unclear state

$$
\mu_{mobility(x)} = \begin{cases} 1 & \text{-85} \geq \text{x} \\ (-83 - x)/(-83 - -85) & -85 < x < -83 \\ (x - -82)/(-80 - -82) & -82 < x < -80 \\ 0 & \text{-83} \leq \text{x} \leq \text{-82} \end{cases}
$$

$$
\mu_{nomobility(x)} = \begin{cases} 1 & \text{-83} \leq \text{x} \leq \text{-82} \\ (x - -85)/(-83 - -85) & -85 < x < -83 \\ (-80 - x)/(-80 - -82) & -82 < x < -80 \\ 0 & \text{-85} \geq \text{x} \end{cases}
$$

Table 1. Time table: It gives mobility time, lack of mobility time, unclear time and total time

States	Time(seconds)
Mobility Time	375
Non Mobility Time	5917
Unclear Time	218
Total Time	6510

In Table 1,mobility time, lack of mobility time and unclear time are shown. This experience was conducted for 6510 seconds and in this period, there is a mobility for 375 seconds and there is lack of mobility for 5917 seconds. However, there is an unclear time that can't be understood whether there is a mobility or not. This period is referred to ass unclear and unclear time and in the application it was 218 seconds in the application.

3.2   Application 2

The second experiment is conducted in a real poster session. The objective is to determine the most popular poster in a poster session. In Figure 3, there are 3 posters and 3 sensor motes under the posters. The visitors come to see the posters and they can read the posters as well. They are an obstacle between the mote and base station thereby affecting the message's RSSI value. A threshold value is used to determine whether there is a mobility or not. The changes of RSSI values illustrate that there is a blocking between the sensor mote and base station. We use this condition to determine that a person stands in front of the poster and looks it. Time period of the changes of RSSI values can give us the amount of time the visitor stands in front of the poster.

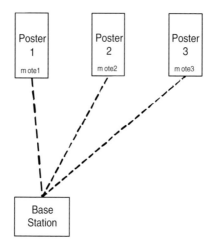

Fig. 3. Poster Placement

Experiment details are shown as below:

- Experiment is conducted in an in-door environment in a big hall.
- 3 sensor motes and 1 base station mote are used in the experiment.
- There are 3 posters in this experiment and every poster has a sensor that was deployed in front of each poster.
- Base station was placed at 6 mt. away.
- Each mote sends a message to base station in every second.
- Experiment took 500 seconds.

In Figure 4, the RSSI values are shown for each poster. Figure 4(a) shows the RSSI values of poster 1, Figure 4(b) shows the RSSI values of poster 2 and Figure 4(c) shows the RSSI values of poster 3. These three figures have some big changes at some time intervals. At these times some visitors stand in front of the posters while the sensor motes continue to send messages to the base station; However, this message's RSSI value is effected because of the blocking situation. The visitors' position makes a blocking between these two motes and the RSSI value is affected.

In Table 2, posters are shown with their rating times.After analysing the graphics, poster 1 has 63 seconds, poster 2 has 73 seconds and poster 3 has 39 seconds. So poster 2 is the most popular poster presented in this poster session.

Table 2. Popular poster time

Posters	Time(seconds)
Poster 1	63
Poster 2	73
Poster 3	39

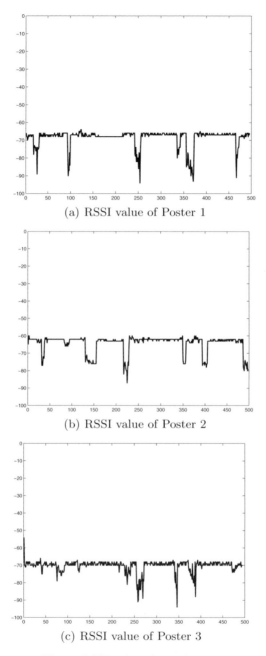

(a) RSSI value of Poster 1

(b) RSSI value of Poster 2

(c) RSSI value of Poster 3

Fig. 4. RSSI values for each poster

4 Conclusion

In this paper, we investigated the RSSI variation with respect to mobility. We conducted two different experiments to monitor mobility or lack of mobility time by looking at RSSI variation.

In the mobility monitoring application, we made some assumptions regarding the RSSI values. We decided some RSSI values for mobility situations, lack of mobility and unclear situations to guess mobility times or non-mobility times. The results of this study can be used in some places such as museums, or in any system to determine which object has a big rating ratio.

In future, we would like to increase the accuracy of our decision making process and investigate algorithms to define the number of people in front of objects using RSSI changes.

References

1. Akyildiz, I.F., Su, W., Sankarasubramaniam, Y., Cayirci, E.: A survey on wireless sensor networks. IEEE Communication Magazine (2002)
2. Werner-allen, G., Johnson, J., Ruiz, M., Lees, J., Welsh, M.: Monitoring volcanic eruptions with a wireless sensor network. In: Proceedings of the Second European Workshop on Wireless Sensor Networks (EWSN 2005) (2005)
3. Mainwaring, A., Mainwaring, A., Polastre, J., Polastre, J., Szewczyk, R., Szewczyk, R., Culler, D., Culler, D.: Wireless sensor networks for habitat monitoring, pp. 88–97 (2002)
4. Nadimi, E., Sgaard, H., Bak, T., Oudshoorn, F.: Zigbee-based wireless sensor networks for monitoring animal presence and pasture time in a strip of new grass. Computers and Electronics in Agriculture 61(2), 79–87 (2008)
5. Hussain, S., Erdogan, S., Park, J.: Monitoring user activities in smart home environments. In: Information Systems Frontiers (2008)
6. Sugano, M., Kawazoe, T., Ohta, Y., Murata, M.: Indoor Localization System using RSSI Measurement of Wireless Sensor Network based on ZigBee Standard. In: The IASTED International Conference on Wireless Sensor Networks, WSN 2006 (2006)
7. Blumenthal, J., Timmermann, D., Buschmann, C., Fischer, S., Koberstein, J., Luttenberger, N.: Minimal transmission power as distance estimation for precise localization in sensor networks. In: IWCMC 2006: Proceedings of the 2006 international conference on Wireless communications and mobile computing, pp. 1331–1336. ACM, New York (2006)
8. Zhou, G., He, T., Krishnamurthy, S., Stankovic, J.A.: Impact of radio irregularity on wireless sensor networks. In: The International Conference on Mobile Systems, Applications, and Services (MobiSys), Boston, USA (2004)
9. Gu, L., Jia, D., Vicaire, P., Yan, T., Luo, L., Tirumala, A., Cao, Q., He, T., Stankovic, J.A., Abdelzaher, T., Krogh, B.H.: Lightweight detection and classification for wireless sensor networks in realistic environments. In: The 3rd ACM Conference on Embedded Networked Sensor Systems, San Diego, USA (2005)
10. Arias, J., Zuloaga, A., Lzaro, J., Andreu, J., Astarloa, A.: Malguki: an rssi based ad hoc location algorithm. Microprocessors and Microsystems 28(8), 403–409 (2004); Resource Management in Wireless and Adhoc mobile networks

11. Scott, T., Wu, K., Hoffman, D.: Radio propagation patterns in wireless sensor networks: New experimental results. In: IEEE International Wireless Communications and Mobile Computing Conference (IWCMC 2006), Vancouver, Canada (2006)
12. Wang, X., Bischoff, O., Laur, R., Paul, S.: Localization in wireless ad-hoc sensor networks using multilateration with rssi for logistic applications. In: Proceedings of the Eurosensros XXIII conference, pp. 461–464 (2009)
13. Erdogan, S.Z., Hussain, S.: Using received signal strength variation for energy efficient data dissemination in wireless sensor networks. In: DEXA Workshops, pp. 620–624 (2007)
14. Erdogan, S.Z., Hussain, S., Park, J.H.: Intelligent monitoring using wireless sensor networks. In: Denko, M.K., Shih, C.-s., Li, K.-C., Tsao, S.-L., Zeng, Q.-A., Park, S.H., Ko, Y.-B., Hung, S.-H., Park, J.-H. (eds.) EUC-WS 2007. LNCS, vol. 4809, pp. 389–400. Springer, Heidelberg (2007)

Analyzing Web 2.0 Integration with Next Generation Networks for Services Rendering

Kamaljit I. Lakhtaria[1] and Dhinaharan Nagamalai[2]

[1] Atmiya Institute of Technology & Science, Rajkot, Gujarat, India
[2] Wireilla Net Solutions PTY LTD, Australia
kamaljit.ilakhtaria@gmail.com

Abstract. The Next Generation Networks (NGN) aims to integrate for IP-based telecom infrastructures and provide most advance & high speed emerging value added services. NGN capable to provide higher innovative services, these services will able to integrate communication and Web service into a single platform. IP Multimedia Subsystem, a NGN leading technology, enables a variety of NGN-compliant communications services to interoperate while being accessed through different kinds of access networks, preferably broadband. IMS–NGN services essential by both consumer and corporate users are by now used to access services, even communications services through the web and web-based communities and social networks, It is key for success of IMS-based services to be provided with efficient web access, so users can benefit from those new services by using web-based applications and user interfaces, not only NGN-IMS User Equipments and SIP protocol. Many Service are under planning which provided only under convergence of IMS & Web 2.0. Convergence between Web 2.0 and NGN-IMS creates and serves new invented innovative, entertainment and information appealing as well as user centric services and applications. These services merge features from WWW and Communication worlds. On the one hand, interactivity, ubiquity, social orientation, user participation and content generation, etc. are relevant characteristics coming from Web 2.0 services. Parallel IMS enables services including multimedia telephony, media sharing (video-audio), instant messaging with presence and context, online directory, etc. all of them applicable to mobile, fixed or convergent telecom networks. With this paper, this paper brings out the benefits of adopting web 2.0 technologies for telecom services. As the services are today mainly driven by the user's needs, and proposed the concept of unique customizable service interface.

Keywords: Next Generation Networks (NGN), IP Multimedia Subsystem (IMS), WWW, Web 2.0.

1 Introduction

The essential inspiration of Next Generation Networks (NGNs) [1] is to carry all types of service on a single packet-based network. This 'network convergence' allow operators to save money by having to maintain only one network platform, and to provide new services that combine different types of data. NGNs are more versatile

N. Meghanathan et al. (Eds.): NeCoM, WiMoN, and WeST 2010, CCIS 90, pp. 581–591, 2010.

than traditional networks because they do not have to be physically upgraded to support new types of service. The network simply transports data, while services are controlled by software on computers that can be located anywhere. This means that third parties can easily launch new services, not just the network operators themselves.

NGNs are based on IP, like the Internet, but they build in features that the Internet does not have, such as the ability to guarantee a certain quality of service and level of security. For example nowadays communications target to transmit a variety of of services. Those are classical telephony also the Internet traffic, data transmission, radio and television broadcasting etc. Consequently, various transmission media are used as metal and fiber cables, and microwave, millimeter wave, and optical free space communication links. Most definitions of NGN also include the principle of 'nomadicity'. This means that a user can access personal network services from different locations using a range of devices such as fixed-line phones, mobile phones and computers.

1.1 NGN-IMS Architecture

The idea of Next Generation Network (NGN) [2] is services such as voice, data and all sorts of multimedia or communication services to be transported into single infrastructure, which will be Internet Protocol (IP) based. IP Multimedia Subsystem (IMS) is one of the underlying technology components of Next Generation Network which services should be independent to any fixed or mobile networks. The IMS is introduced in order to provide converged services in IP-based network. The advent of IP Multimedia Subsystem (IMS) leads fixed and mobile communication services to convergent evolution and improves the user experience. The architecture of IMS is designed for fast deployment of services, assuring end-to-end Quality of Service and integration of different services.

Nowadays there are many services deployed over IP-based network such as instant messaging, VOIP, presence and video sharing. Service providers deploy those services in uncoordinated way. A manageable framework like IMS is required to manage those services and provide flexible integration and deployment for service providers.

With the standardization of the IMS architecture [1][2][3], the service development methods of telecom operators become more and more similar to the web development methods. Indeed, service development environment of telecom operators is based on reusability of the basic enablers (e.g. presence, messaging) which is very similar to a service oriented architecture (SOA) approach [4] that has proved its usefulness in the decade. Moreover, several operators have even opened their network through OSA/ParlayX [5] web services to facilitate the development of new telecom services. However, the promised innovative services take a long time to appear because of difficulties to manage the real time applications in the web environment. The web community has otherwise gained in experience of real time applications (e.g. googleTalk, and webMessenger) that uses web 2.0 [6] technologies such as AJAX [7][8]. Moreover, innovative applications have appeared on the public web, such a web aggregators, mashups, and social networking. These applications are characterized by the aggregation of services, sharing, participation and personalization.

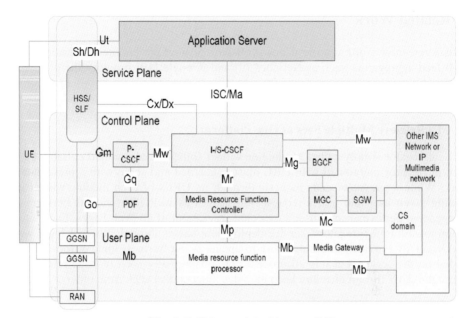

Fig. 1. IMS Layered Architecture [**]

Web aggregators (like Netvibes [9] and iGoogle [10]) are applications that give access to many web feeds (data format used to provide users with dynamic content such as news and weather) of many providers from a single web page; these feeds are displayed as independent blocs in the page (e.g. weather feeds, sport feeds, political news feeds). The goal of this paper is to show how telecom operators can benefit from web technologies to provide a unified point of access to user's services (web information and telecom services). We consider the unified interface concept as a first step toward those innovative services. Therefore, for this analysis work, research have implemented dashboard that blends both telecom real-time services and web information services on a single web page. This enables the user to access, to monitor, and to use all its preferred services simultaneously. Presented solution is implemented at the presentation layer. This is a definitely a new approach for the convergence of the telecom domain and the web domain. The real-time issues are handled using web 2.0 [6] technologies.

The rest of this paper is organized as, Section 2 Demonstrate through examples the added value of services aggregators for both the operator and the end user. While Section 3 Befits with Value Added Services with Web Aggregator implementation work discussion continues to Section 4 & 5 briefs Real-time Web aggregator implementation demonstration with their Function & Architectural descriptions. Section 6 discusses Several Implementation Issues like Security, trade-off notion of this Convergence model with respective future work path in Conclusion.

2   Related Work

Web Aggregator word simply means "collector of multiple entitites", Customizable Web feed aggregators such as Netvibes [9] and iGoogle [10] provides the user with (1) the ability to access many feeds from a single web page, (2) the ability to integrate third party feeds, and (3) personalization capabilities.

2.1   To Retrieve Multiple Fees at One Platform

Web aggregator simply called Module or widget sometime also called portal [11]. A Web aggregator mentioned with URL must concerned and serve with a presentation layer. While aggregator sends requests through its URLs of each module/widget including given user and user's request information as well. The widgets perform as independent performance of user's expected service out of all Web Pages. Each interaction regarding Aggregators' service deployment passes through business logic with AJAX. AJAX provides web framework to update as per business logic & followed by hosted on the server, but this all process not consume any need of page refreshing. Through AJAX this architecture keep modules independent each from others.

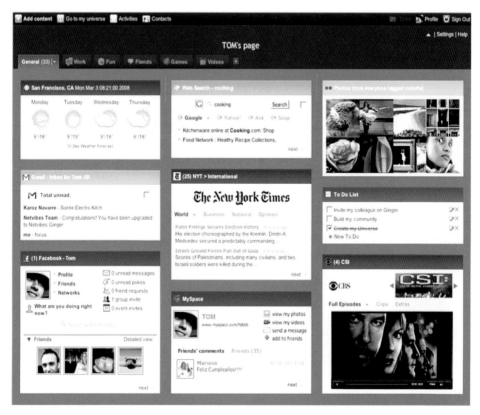

Fig. 2. Netvibes web screen shot [9] Source: www.netvibes.com

2.2   Easy Integration with Third Party Feeds and User Personalization

AJAX technologies enable aggregators to integrate modules given by different providers. Service providers as well as independent developers easily develop their own widgets. There are many ways to develop a widget. Actually, this depends on the target aggregator (whether this widget will be incorporated in iGoogle, Netvibes, or another aggregator). However, the universal widget API UWA [12] has gained a large community (Netvibes, iGoogle, Mac, Windows vista, Yahoo! Widgets, & Opera).

Moreover, W3C has initiated a standardization effort of widgets development API [13]. User able to retrieve single service from multiple time widgets there is no conflict between any Aggregator. Same way if any Aggregator service provider provides more than one fees, all fees can be presented in single web page. Web Aggregators able provide personalization; each user can personalize its aggregator by managing own modules into their Web pages. Above Figure 2 is a Netvibes [9] screenshot presented characteristics of feed aggregators.

3   Value Added Services with Web Aggregators

Web Aggregating services convergence into one web page able to provide higher benefits to user as well as service provides.

3.1   End Users Benefits

Increasing interaction between independent services: End user access their instantly. User able to retrieve more than one service. No need to navigate between services all service easily available at a single platform. User able to combine two services like select one entity from one feeds and uses that one another one as well. For example, while user uses soft phone through web feeds, any contact will retrieved as well as add to contact directory. This is main benefit that all service either provided by same provider or by different provider but once retrieved by user, then follow user's direction only. Same way using Google Map user directly fetch address and able to see location into single web platform.

Easy access to third party service providers: The user also able to retrieve services from third-party providers. Specially News Fees, Entertainment, Travel Information all managed by third party service providers only. But user easily access this all. Many developer / freelancer also provide customized Aggregators to particular services. These all services easily integrate web page.

User authentication & Personalization: User always worry for security with web Aggregators users access to their services from a single web page, the operator can perform a single authentication for all provided services. With this feature users does not requires to re-authenticate for each service. E.g. if the same operator, the user then, provides the phone service and the directory service performs a single authentication for both services. Users can personalize theirs with organizing their services into groups through tabs. They can also add, move, and delete services at the run time. All configurations (tabs configuration and modules configurations) are saved and retrieved at each disconnection and connection.

3.2 Operator Advantages

Operators able to know its users, Communication service provider as well as Entertainment and other service provides able to know gadgets used chosen by their user. With this service provide enhance and upgrade their services. Making a widget as simple as possible is the slogan of the widgets developers; indeed a widget is supposed to perform a basic function, analogous to IMS enablers [16]. Telecom operators also develop Aggregators that will enhance basic communication related services like presence and IM. Single accessing interface enables the operator to manage a single authentication for all their services. This facilitates telecom operators in the management of theirs services.

4 Contributions and Functional Description

This observation made through implementation of unified dashboard using Internet over telecom services. Presented Unified dashboard belongs to a web page that will aggregate web services as well as telecom services. Web services consist for example in web search, map, and RSS feeds. And telecom services include for instance telephony, messaging services, and videoconferencing. Users can access to their services through the dashboard, by using an Internet connection and a web browser whatever the used device like mobile phone, PDA, laptop, and desktop PC. This converged dashboard able to manage user for derive multiple services from different providers.

As per shown in Figure 3, our implemented desktop able to serve Multiple Convergence service at once. Service with short description as following:

1. Dashboard displays User's Profile, while user log-in. User able to manage his profile as well as own setting to manage Dashboard.
2. Implemented Dashboard in short performs Speed dial, where user directly select their buddy list from dashboard and make call to them, in cell phone maximum up to 9 speed dial number assigned, but with Dashboard – Buddy listing user able to add more contacts to speed dial.
3. Using API, User able to retrieve any Gadget from Web Feed Provider, mostly able to retrieve from iGoogle, Netvibes etc., in this Dashboard News Feed Tag prepared to retrieve from any News using API.
4. More Communication Service like Voice Call, Voice message also presented with this Dashboard, While User perform operation with third party Gadget/API using Feeds at that time, User Identity must provided separately to that service (e.g. in Fig. 3 Call Wave Feeds).
5. Same like Web, User able to add more Feeds for Information, Entertainment, Fun also. In this Dashboard, Picture tag is fetched using Feeds over Photo Shot Gadgets, further more user also able to connect through Video Sharing dashboard.
6. Dashboard easily integrates many different applications to a single user interface platform. Once user authentication process completes, user selected gadgets works to retrieve data into own page. For this concept the service provided with XHTML / AJAX technology.

7. Same like iGoogle, Netvibes other organization provides such service with User customization, like SkyDeck [17] and Google Voice convergence. Skydeck is online Phone, which work to provide calls, text messages, voicemails and store contacts (on Skydeck.com [17]) User can search, read, and reply to your messages (by voice or by text) from Dashboard. Google Voice is a new service that ties all your phones together with one new number that rings them all. Using Dashboard SkyDesk provide own service as well combine Google Voice too.

8. Unlike converge, Dashwire [18], an Dashboard which work to Enabling Mobile Operators, as well as Device Makers and Retailers, to quickly and cost effectively deliver a new generation of customized consumer services on open mobile phone platforms. Using this Dashboard user receive Mobile Communication as well Web-interface together.

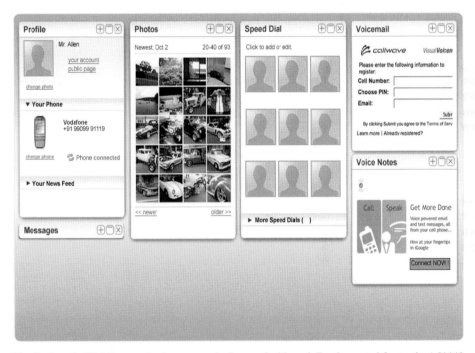

Fig. 3. Sample Web Page unite Internet and telecom dashboard (Implemented for testing) [***]

5 Architectural Descriptions

In this section we give a high-level architecture description of the proposed framework. Figure 3 displays a component overview of the framework. Components of our framework are categorized into two parts: the server side component and the client side component. Server side components of this architecture manage the persistent data such as user information with their preferences, service selection details, service configuration information and all such. For client side gadgets, all get organized and performs as per users' preference.

This architecture works in manner to perform with authentication and after verifying the web server sends all gadgets data as per user preferences. Although all information must reveals with user preference manages and components / module. More briefly each module and their abs and all such flow user settings given at the. As per discussed in section 3 users' personalization is provided with Dashboard, which tightly bound to position and each setting with only user settings. Component data received from server and presented in specified module, all modules link up with AJAX technology with that easily updates module data no need to refresh whole web page. Any voice-video-data service using NGN also provided through this modules only.

6 Implementation Issues

Our implementation of the dashboard is based on web technologies such as JavaScript, AJAX and PHP. With this dashboard we implemented a broad framework to pursue web feeds and their services aggregation. As per figure 4 the complete framework designed from End user client side to server includes service-managing tools like Billing/charging, session, user preference manager etc.

In Present architecture works from client side works in Web Browser with Java Script and AJAX, where the server side remain execute into a web server. Main issue with this Dashboard is web browser version. User works with Internet Explore and

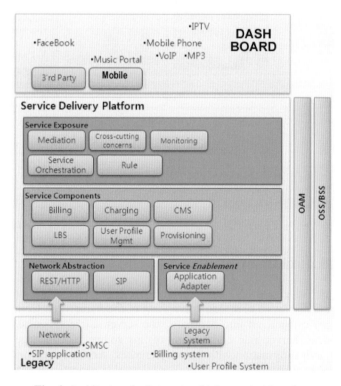

Fig. 4. Architecture for Internet and telecom dashboard

Firefox. But it is not possible all browser allows AJAX to run between multiple domains into a single web page. If browser not support instant data transfer from client to server it may cause late update of content into particular gadget.

To overcome this limit, we propose a proxy. The proxy works through same domain as the framework with the use of PHP, proxy enables and eases client side request towards server side. Some module may not able to constant render service request to server. But the proxy by pass this all requests and able to download to appropriate gadget. To this concern of security, all other AJAX security must protected outside their individual modules. This is known as module download controller component.

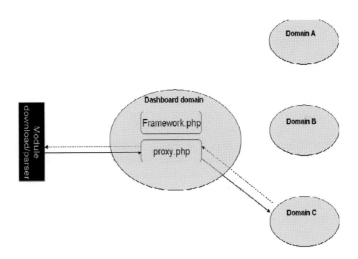

Fig. 5. Security constraint of web browsers

In this proxy, server side works with PHP. The main parts are:

1. A proxy through which gadget gets loaded all requested services.
2. A component that manages users' database.
3. A component that manages the users' preferences database.

While Module download controller receives the response in form of XHTML, the requested service through the proxy and makes the necessary modifications on the module for modules independent.

> e.g. *http://webservice.com will be transformed to*
> *http://dashboardarea/proxy.php? url=http://webservice.com*

For providing browsing into a module, this also needs to change link of and URL to AJAX requests. Such modification also avoids reloading the whole page when a user clicks on any selected module links. Moreover, the follow necessary steps also considered for manage API,

1. E.g. if the developer of the module need to handle the unclose event,
2. Use the aggregator API; Add the following statement: ON_UNLOAD = handler

7 Conclusion

Aggregating different services in a single web page is a typical web2.0 and NGN way towards access and to use telecom services. Dashboard user easily configure his own choice, data over gadgets converged into dashboard. Once service made available over dashboard then after user will no longer user particular website, definitely will derived through dashboard only. Adopting this approach, Mobile users able to access and use all his communication related services (like speed dial, calendar, visit Card) through a single web page. This is only an experimental observation but in Future work aims to implement over bulk user groups, for analyzing real time usage and Quality of Service. XHTML, XML is portable language but rather than SMIL 2.0 is also one alternate approach to consider for further implementation.

References

[1] 3GGP - IP Multimedia Subsystem (IMS); Stage 2 - 3GPP TS 23.228 V6.6.0 (2004-06)
[2] Nasser, N., Shang, M.: Policy control framework for IP Multimedia Subsystem. In: Proceedings of the 2009 conference on Information Science, Technology and Applications, pp. 53–58 (2009)
[3] Poikselka, M., Niemi, A., Khartabil, H., Mayer, G.: The IMS: IP Multimedia Concepts and Services, ISBN: 0470019069
[4] Thomas, E.: Service-Oriented Architecture: A Field Guide to Integrating XML and Web Services. Prentice Hall, Upper Saddle River (2004)
[5] Yates, M.J., Boyd, I.: The Parlay network API specification. BT Technology Journal 25(3-4), 205–211 (2007)
[6] O'Reilly, T.: What is Web 2.0. Design patterns and business models for the next generation of software. O'Reilly Media, Sebastopol (2005)
[7] Paulson, L.D.: Building Rich Web Applications with Ajax. Computer 38(10), 14–17 (2005)
[8] Zepeda, J.S., Chapa, S.V.: From Desktop Applications Towards Ajax Web Applications. In: Electrical and Electronics Engineering, September 5-7, pp. 193–196 (2007)
[9] Hoyer, V., Fischer, M.: Market Overview of Enterprise Mashup Tools. In: Bouguettaya, A., Krueger, I., Margaria, T. (eds.) ICSOC 2008. LNCS, vol. 5364, pp. 708–721. Springer, Heidelberg (2008)
[10] Casquero, O., Portillo, J., Ovelar, R., Romo, J., Benito, M.: iGoogle and gadgets as a platform for integrating institutional and external services. In: Wild, F., Kalz, M., Palmér, M. (eds.) Mash-Up Personal Learning Environments. Proc. of 1st Workshop MUPPLE 2008, Maastricht, pp. 37–41 (2008)
[11] Kaar, C.: An introduction to Widgets with particular emphasis on Mobile Widgets. Computing (October 2007)
[12] Knights, M.: WEB 2.0 MySpace, Netvibes, Wikipedia, YouTube, Goowy... the web is moving from the personal to the social. In: The process it is becoming increasingly complex, Communications Engineer -IEEE, vol. 5(1), pp. 30–35 (2007)

[13] Lee, A.: Mobile Web Widgets: Enabler of Enterprise Mobility Work. In: 2nd Workshop on Mashups, Enterprise Mashups and Lightweight Composition on the Web (MEM 2009), Spain, pp. 86–94 (2009)

[14] Knightson, K., Morita, N., Towle, T.: NGN architecture: generic principles, functional architecture, and implementation. IEEE Communications Magazine (2005)

[15] Gomez, M., de Miguel, T.P.: Advanced IMS Multipoint Conference Management Using Web Services. IEEE Communications Magazine (2007)

[16] Blum, N., Magedanz, T., Stein, H.: Service creation & delivery for SME based on SOA/IMS. In: Proceedings of the 2007 Workshop on Middleware for next-generation converged networks and applications table of contents, pp. 311–320 (2007)

[17] Banerjee, N., Dasgupta, K.: Telecom mashups: enabling web 2.0 for telecom services. In: Proceedings of the 2nd international conference on Ubiquitous information management and communication, Suwon, Korea, pp. 146–150

[18] Falchuk, B., Sinkar, K., Loeb, S., Dutta, A.: Mobile Contextual Mashup Service for IMS. In: 2nd IEEE International Conference on Internet Multimedia Services Architecture and Applications (IMSAA 2008), Bangalore (December 2008)

An Adaptive Framework for Wireless Sensor Network Application Development

Mahesh U. Patil and P. Poonguzhali

Centre for Development of Advanced Computing, Hyderabad
{maheshp,poonguzhalip}@cdac.in

Abstract. Wireless Sensor Network (WSN) is generally observed as a service layer for providing context information to Pervasive Computing applications. Acquiring this vital context information using WSN demands special skill-sets from the developer and is tightly coupled with the application requirements. The developer needs to evaluate several combination of services like routing, localization, time synchronization, security protocols to fulfill the application requirements. In this paper we justify the need and propose a system architecture of an Adaptive Framework for WSN Application (AFWA) that hosts the application workflow from development to deployment. This framework provides a flexibility for opting the required services based on the application needs and abstracts the application developer from the intricacies of WSN system components.

Keywords: WSN, Network Communication, Time Synchronization, Localization, AFWA.

1 Introduction

Wireless Sensor Networks (WSN) has been a key enabler for bridging the gap between the physical and digital world for most of the pervasive computing applications. A pervasive application requires interpreted raw physical sensed data that can be directly used in the digital workspaces. Merely, WSN systems that *sense and send* raw physical information are of less interest to the application developer. For example, receiving location information of a smart object is inadequate for a pervasive application, rather also receiving information like *what other active smart objects are in its vicinity* would support making better decisions. Also to provide this information, the WSN sub-system should be capable of relating location information from the localization service with temporal information from the time synchronization service. This location and time information from the WSN sub-system can thus avail relevant information to pervasive applications. Moreover the authenticity and confidentiality of information from the WSN workspace is of utmost important to make the right decisions. For example a malicious node providing incorrect location can potentially spread false localization information across the entire network. Such attacks thus justify the significance of security service in WSN. Another important service that

N. Meghanathan et al. (Eds.): NeCoM, WiMoN, and WeST 2010, CCIS 90, pp. 592–601, 2010.

is common across most WSN applications is Network Communication stack. Some applications, like surveillance demands event based routing while others like environmental monitoring need periodic reverse multicasting of sensed information. Thus these four services of Network Communication, Localization, Time Synchronization and Security form the basis of WSN application development. There are plethora of algorithms proposed for each of these WSN services with most of them addressing specific needs for a subset of applications [1], [2], [3], [4]. Many of these algorithms do not provide generalized Application Programming Interfaces (API) to access the services, which mandates the application developer to explore the implementation details. Thus evaluation of these services to match the application requirements expends significant development time. To fasten this development process a rapid prototyping platform is required that abstracts the application developer from the internal details of each algorithm. In this paper we propose an Adaptive Framework for WSN Application (AFWA) that would facilitate complete development to deployment workflow for WSN application developer enabling faster service evaluation iterations.

The remainder of paper is structured as follows. The second section of the paper provides a brief about existing frameworks or middleware. The third section details the overview of AFWA followed by the functional design decomposition in the fourth section. The fifth section demonstrates the feasibility of AFWA implementation. The last section of the paper presents brief concluding remarks and future work.

2 Related Work

In this section, we briefly present some of the research literature in regard to middleware frameworks for WSN applications. Most middlewares try to avoid redundancy and reimplementation of code in WSN applications.

Impala [5] is a middleware that focuses on using modular programming approach there-by enabling small updates and thus requiring low transmission energy. It aims at providing efficient updates for applications that are dynamic in nature. It addresses two major challenges of application adaptability and dynamic updates.

Mate [6] is implemented on TinyOS as a middleware solution for communication centric applications. It is ideally suited to provide a better interaction and adaptation to the dynamic changing nature of sensor networks. Mate focuses to make the network dynamic, flexible, and easily reconfigurable.

TinyCubus [7] is a flexible, adaptive cross-layer framework implemented over TinyOS and provides flexibility and adaptability. Its architecture is divided into

1. Tiny Cross-Layer Framework
2. Tiny Configuration Engine
3. Tiny Data Management Framework

Mires [8] is an publish/subscribe middleware that provides high level Application Programming Interface (API) that facilitates rapid application development. Message notification service for the subscribers and buffering are the key elements of Mires.

The other notable middlewares include TinyDB [9], Agilla [10], TinyLime [11], SINA, MiLAN [12].

This paper focusses on a framework which targets programming abstraction for WSN application development.

3 Proposed System Architecture of AFWA

AFWA consists of two software components, one that resides and executes on the motes and the other utilized on the host development platform.

It facilitates the WSN application developer to opt several services like Network Communication, Time Synchronization, Localization, and Security as shown in Fig.1. It facilitates *one time application development* and thus avoids the need of changing the WSN application code for various combination of system component by providing generalized API's to similar services. It also allows the developer to simulate and deploy the application onto the motes natively as well Over-the-Air. The framework is also designed with the flexibility to integrate customized algorithms and is being developed using defacto WSN OS called TinyOS [13], [14].

AFWA supports two user roles from the perspective of WSN Application and System developer. The major functionalities provided by AFWA to the WSN Application Developer is summarized below:

1. Facility to opt required system component for WSN Application Development
2. Facility to simulate the WSN Application
3. Facility to program the developed WSN Application Over-the-Air

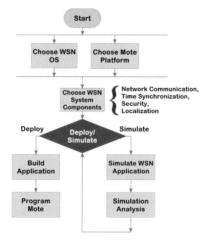

Fig. 1. Application Development Flow using AFWA

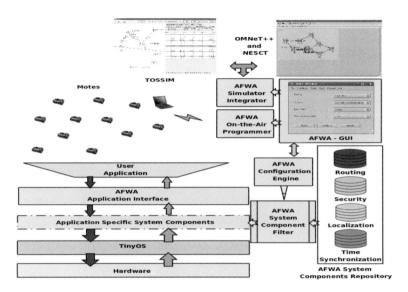

Fig. 2. AFWA System Architecture

AFWA framework from the WSN System Developers perspective facilitates easy integration of custom system components, simulators and over-the-air programming techniques.

Fig.2 represents the system architecture of AFWA. AFWA-GUI provides the graphical interface for the WSN application developer to use the facilities as mentioned in the use case. AFWA System Components Repository consists of algorithms for Network Communication, Time Synchronization, Localization and Security. Based on the user application requirement and configuration, the AFWA System Component Filter provides the interfaces for the WSN application. The AFWA Application Interface provides generic API's to similar system components which minimizes the modifications in the application code while opting different protocols. The WSN application developer can then choose to either simulate or deploy the WSN application on the motes. These functionalities are provided by the AFWA Simulator Integrator and AFWA On-the-Air Programmer respectively.

4   Functional Design Decomposition of AFWA

Fig. 3 shows the detailed functional design decomposition of AFWA. It is designed with a flexibility to support additional WSN OS and system components in future. Moreover it uses platform independent information storage using Extensible Markup Language (XML). AFWA consists of the following high-level modules:

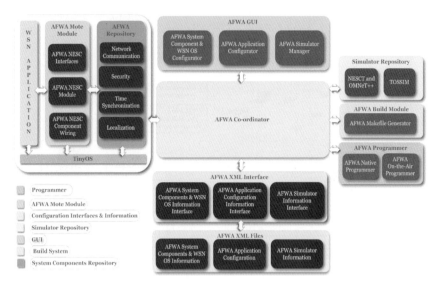

Fig. 3. AFWA Functional Decomposition

1. GUI
2. Mote Module and System Components Repository
3. XML Interfaces and Files
4. Build Module
5. Programmer

4.1 GUI

The GUI provides the graphical interface using the following sub-modules:

1. System Component Configurator
2. Application Configurator
3. Simulator Configurator
4. WSN OS Configurator
5. Programmer Configurator

The System Component Configurator allows to add, delete and edit the system component details for Network Communication, Security, Time Synchronization and Localization. It also allows adding and updating documentation related to the system components. This module would be used mostly by the WSN System Developer. The Application Configurator provides the graphical frontend for the WSN application developer to opt for WSN OS, Mote Hardware Platform, System Components, Simulator and the programming technique. The Simulator Configurator provides the graphical frontend for the WSN system developer to add and delete simulator to and from the Simulator Repository. It also manages default simulation parameters. The WSN OS Configurator provides the graphical frontend for accessing the WSN OS details and would allow integration of other

WSN OS to AFWA in future. Programmer Configurator handles the mechanism of programming the motes. It provides a graphical frontend to choose between native and Over-the-Air Programming. The frontend also allows to add new and delete existing techniques.

4.2 Mote Module and System Components Repository

Mote Module contains software that would reside on the motes. It is programmed using a specific language called nesC [15] and is also utilized for the development of TinyOS. It consists of three sub-modules as follows:

1. nesC Interfaces
2. nesC Module
3. nesC Component Wiring

The nesC Interfaces provide generic API's for different algorithms and protocols for the supported system components. These interfaces will be used by the WSN application developer for accessing the system components. All the algorithms in a system component would share the same interface. The interface would consist of commands and events that follow nesC conventions. The nesC sub-module is the bridge between the WSN application and system components. It implements the code for calling the respective commands of the system component and passing the events to the application generated from the system component. This module is provided by the WSN system developer for each of the algorithms or protocols in the system components repository. The nesC Component Wiring module provides the details about connections between the nesC Module and the system components.

4.3 XML Interfaces and Files

The XML [16] Interface module provides XML writers and parsers for different components of the AFWA tool. The following XML Interfaces are provided by this module:

1. WSN OS and Hardware Platform Information Interface
2. System Components Information Interface
3. Application Configuration Interface
4. Simulator Information Interface

The XML Files hold the information about different components of AFWA in XML format. Each component is maintained in different files as mentioned below:

1. System Components Information
2. User Application Configuration
3. Simulator Information

Sample User Application Configuration XML file

```
<AFWAWSNApp>
  <WSNOS> TinyOS-1.x </WSNOS>
  <WSNPF> MicaZ </WSNPF>
  <AFWANetComm> TinyAODV </AFWANetComm>
  <AFWASec> TinySec </AFWASec>
  <AFWASim> TOSSIM </AFWASim>
  <AFWAProgrammer> OAP </AFWAProgrammer>
</AFWAWSNApp>
```

The System Component Information holds the information about the supported system components. It also contains documentation details for each of the system component that would be useful for WSN application developer to choose the appropriate protocol. The User Application Configuration XML file as shown in the snippet above holds information about the application configuration details chosen by WSN Application developer. This information typically consists of WSN OS, Hardware Platform, opted system components, simulator and programming options. The Simulator Information holds the details about different simulators supported by AFWA. It also contains the default options for each simulator that can be used by the WSN application developer.

4.4   Build Module

The Build Module consists of the build environment for the Motes, Simulator and the Programmer. It consists of a sub-module named Makefile Generator that generates the makefile compliant with the GNU Make [17] specific to the WSN application configuration.

4.5   Programmer

Programmer facilitates programming the motes using two different mechanisms, namely:

1. Native Programmer
2. Over-the-Air Programmer

The Native Programmer would load the WSN application binary onto the mote that is connected to host development platform. The other mechanism allows the binary to be programmed Over-the-Air using one of the techniques [18].

5   Demonstrative Use of AFWA for Network Communication

To examine the feasibility of AFWA tool, we developed a test application utilizing the Network Communication service as shown in Fig. 4.

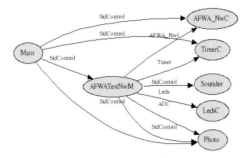

Fig. 4. AFWA System Component Independent Application

The top module of test application included components like *AFWA_NwC*, *TimerC*, *Sounder*, *LedsC* and *Photo*. The AFWA Network Communication component *AFWA_NwC* provided generic interface to call the specific API's for opted algorithm. We experimented with three routing algorithms TinyAODV, Flooding and MultiHopRouter that were available in the TinyOS repository [14]. The *AFWA_NWI* interface with common communication API's like *send* and *receive* for this service was developed. Fig. 5 shows the bubble diagram that depicts the internal connection diagram specific to each algorithm that was implemented for Network Communication. The application was then deployed and tested on the MicaZ motes.

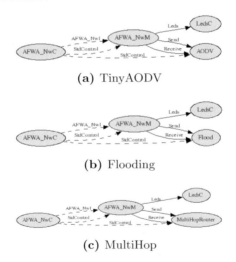

Fig. 5. Bubble diagram depicting AFWA integration with TinyAODV, Flooding and MultiHop Routing Protocols

6   Conclusions and Future Work

In this paper we proposed an Adaptive Framework for WSN Application that facilitates faster evaluation of various protocols. We provided the functional design decomposition of this framework so as to host other facilities like simulation and Over-the-Air programming that would help in the analysis and deployment of WSN application respectively. We also examined the feasibility of the framework and demonstrated a test WSN application that utilized Network Communication algorithms like TinyAODV, Flooding and MultiHopRouter.

Future work includes integration of other services like Localization, Time Synchronization, and Security with some additional Network Communication algorithms. Also integration of simulator and Over-the-Air programming techniques to the tool would be developed.

Acknowledgment. The authors acknowledge Department of Information Technology, Ministry of Communications & Information Technology, Government of India for supporting this work that is being executed by National Ubiquitous Computing Research Centre established at Centre for Development of Advanced Computing, Hyderabad.

References

1. Al-Karaki, J.N., Kamal, A.E.: Routing Techniques in Wireless Sensor Networks: A Survey. IEEE Wireless Communications 11(6), 6–28 (2004)
2. Savarese, C., Rabaey, J.M., Beutel, J.: Locationing in Distributed Ad-Hoc Wireless Sensor Networks. In: ICASSP (May 2001)
3. Sivrikaya, F., Yener, B.: Time Synchronization in Sensor Networks: A Survey. IEEE Network 18(4), 45–50
4. Walters, J.P., Liang, Z., Shi, W., Chaudhary, V.: Security in Distributed, Grid, and Pervasive Computing. In: Xiao, Y. (ed.), pp. 367–410. Auerbach Publications (April 2007)
5. Liu, T., Martonosi, M.: Impala: A Middleware System for Managing Autonomic Parallel Sensor Systems. In: Proceedings of the ninth ACM SIGPLAN symposium on Principles and practice of parallel programming, pp. 107–118 (2003)
6. Levis, P., Culler, D.E.: A Tiny Virtual Machine for Sensor Networks. In: Proceedings of the International Conference on Architectural Support for Programming Languages and Operating Systems (2002)
7. Marron, P.J., Minder, D., Lachenmann, A., Rothermel, K.: TinyCubus: An Adaptive Cross-Layer Framework for Sensor Networks. In: Information Technology 2005, pp. 87–97 (2005)
8. Souto, E., Guimar, G., Vasconcelos, G., Vieira, M., Rosa, N., Ferraz, C., Kelner, J.: Mires: A publish/subscribe middleware for sensor networks. In: Personal Ubiquitous Computing, pp. 37–44. Springer, Heidelberg
9. Madden, S.R., Franklin, M.J., Hellerstein, J.M., Hong, W.: TinyDB: an acquisitional query processing system for sensor networks. ACM Trans. Database Syst.
10. Fok, C.-L., Roman, G.-C., Lu, C.: Agilla: A mobile agent middleware for self-adaptive wireless sensor networks. ACM Trans. Auton. Adapt. Syst.
11. Curino, C., Giani, M., Giorgetta, M., Giusti, A., Murphy, A.L., Picco, G.P.: TinyLIME: Bridging Mobile and Sensor Networks through Middleware. In: Proceedings of the Third IEEE International Conference on Pervasive Computing and Communications. IEEE Computer Society, Washington

12. Hadim, S., Mohamed, N.: Middleware for Wireless Sensor Networks: A Survey. In: The First International Conference on Communication System Software and Middleware (2006)
13. Trumpler, E., Han, R.: A Systematic Framework for Evolving TinyOS. In: EmNets 2006 (May 2006)
14. TinyOS, http://www.tinyos.net
15. Gay, D., Levis, P., von Behren, R., Welsh, M., Brewer, E., Culler, D.: The nesC Language: A Holistic Approach to Networked Embedded Systems. In: Proceedings of Programming Language Design and Implementation (PLDI) (June 2003)
16. Extensible markup language (XML), http://www.w3.org/XML
17. GNU Make, http://www.gnu.org/software/make
18. Brown, S., Sreenan, C.J.: Updating Software in Wireless Sensor Networks: A Survey. University College Cork, Ireland, Technical Report no.UCC-CS-2006-13-07 (July 2006)
19. Levis, P., Madden, S., Gay, D., Polastre, J., Szewczyk, R., Woo, A., Brewer, E., Culler, D.: The emergence of networking abstractions and techniques in TinyOS. In: First Symposium on networked system design and implementation (NSDI 2004), San Francisco, California, USA, p. 1 (2004)

A Comparison of the Efficiencies of Different Wireless Sensor Network Algorithms with Respect to Time

Subrata Dutta[1], Nandini Mukherjee[2], Sarmistha Neogy[2], and Sarbani Roy[2]

[1] School of Mobile Computing and Communication, Jadavpur University
[2] Dept. Of Computer Sc. and Engg, Jadavpur University, Kolkata-700032, India
subrataduttaa@gmail.com,
{nmukherjee,sneogy,sarbani.roy}@cse.jdvu.ac.in

Abstract. In this paper we discuss different wireless routing algorithms. We compare the efficiency of those routing algorithms. The basic criterion for the comparison is to determine the time to reach a message from source to destination. In this paper we have also shown that the most efficient WSN routing algorithm may not perform best in case of every application. Different routing algorithms are suitable for different application areas. We also discuss about the limitations of WSN.

Keywords: Wireless sensor network, Flooding, Clustering, Gossiping, Directed diffusion, SPIN, Efficiency with respect to time of different wireless sensor network.

1 Introduction

A wireless sensor network (WSN) is a wireless network consisting of sensor nodes [5]. In comparison with the classical network system, there are certain differences in these networks. The main objective of a wireless sensor network is to gather some environmental data and send that data to the base station through different wireless sensor nodes. Sensor nodes can be of different types, like source node, sink node, intermediate node or base station. Source nodes collect data from the environment, sink nodes collect data from the source nodes, intermediate nodes forward data requests from a sink node to source nodes and forward data messages from source nodes to a sink node. In a homogeneous WSN, every node may act as a source node or sink node or intermediate node. Base station collects all data, which are collected by the WSN nodes. Different applications can be developed on top of Wireless Sensor Network (WSN), such as patient monitoring, disaster management, environmental monitoring etc. While developing the applications, a number of routing algorithms have been proposed by the researchers. Each individual routing algorithm has been designed with the objective of adding different capabilities to the network. Therefore these routing algorithms are used in different applications according to the specific requirements of the application. While implementing a WSN algorithm for an application, the efficiency (in respect to time) of the algorithm for transmitting data from source node to sink node must be analyzed, This paper studies some of the existing algorithms and compares their efficiencies in respect of time.

N. Meghanathan et al. (Eds.): NeCoM, WiMoN, and WeST 2010, CCIS 90, pp. 602–618, 2010.

2 Analysis of Different WSN Routing Algorithms

While analyzing the WSN algorithms, efficiency (in terms of time) to reach data from source node to sink node is considered. Let us assume that a WSN consists of N nodes and H_{opt} optimum hop counts are needed to reach a message from source node to sink node. The network topology is similar to a fully connected graph. Let us denote that number of neighbor for node number i is n_i. We also assume that if one node directly sends one message to another node, the time between sending the message and receiving is constant and that time is t. So, the time to reach a message from source node to sink node is directly proportional to the hop count between two nodes. Let the time to reach from source node to sink node is denoted by T_{wsn} and the hop count measurement from source to destination is denoted by H_{wsn}. If we ignore other constraint (Such as route congestion of any node) we can say T_{wsn} is directly proportional to the H_{wsn}.

$$T_{wsn} = H_{wsn}t \quad \text{[Since } T_T \alpha H_{opt} \text{ and } t \text{ is the time required to traverse data} \tag{1}$$
$$\text{over one hop].}$$

In case of sensor node there may not be any limitation for the size of message but the maximum packet size is constant. Suppose maximum packet size is p and total message size is m and number of packet of that message is q.

$$\text{So, } q = m/p \tag{2}$$

We also assume H_{opt} is the optimal path length from source node to destination $H_{opt} \leq (N-1)$. Now we are going to discuss the time complexities of different WSN algorithms.

2.1 Flooding

Using this algorithm in a WSN, the source node generates data and broadcasts the data to the neighboring nodes. Each neighboring node gets data and in turn broadcasts it to its neighboring nodes. Thus, a node can get the same data multiple numbers of times from different neighboring sensor nodes. Though the data message may be received through different paths, a node broadcasts a data message only once. In flooding, total number of sent and received messages required to reach a message from source to destination is high, but flooding is one of the fastest routing algorithm for dissemination of messages (assuming the topology is a connected graph). Flooding WSN routing algorithms [4] follow every possible route to reach a data message from the source to the destination. Since the optimum path is the subset of every possible path, so the data message also follows the optimum path with path length H_{opt}.

Let T_T be the total time required to reach the destination. As per (1) we can write

$$T_T = H_{opt}t \tag{3}$$

There may be two conventions for transmitting messages, each containing q packets. One convention is after getting a packet a node will broadcast the packet immediately to its neighbor nodes. We call this Flooding1. Second convention is after getting all the q packets in a message from the previous nodes, these packets will be broadcast to the neighbor nodes. We call it Flooding2.

2.1.1   Flooding1

In case of Flooding1, data message follow every possible path. The optimum path is the sub set of every possible path and thus, the data message would follow the optimum path as well. While k^{th} node receiving $(q+1)^{th}$ data packet, then $(k+1)^{th}$ node sends q^{th} packet to the next node (similar to pipeline processing) [Fig.1.].

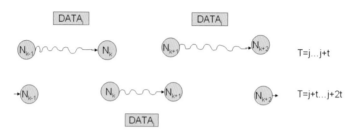

Fig. 1. Message transmission of Flooding1

A table depicting samples of data movement is given [Table1] later .The rows in the table represent the events of sent and received packets of a node sequence over a time period. S_{q^i} denotes that i^{th} packet is sent and R_{q^i} denotes that the ith packet is received. T_k and N_k are time slots and nodes that are involved.

$$T_T = ((N_N - N_1) + 2(q-1))t \tag{4}$$

$$\text{Since } \ N_N - 1 = H_{opt}$$

Table 1. Sequence table of sending and receiving message to traverse particular node sequence if message contains more than one number of packets then any node after getting packet it transmit that to the next node

	T_{j+1}	T_{j+2}	T_{j+3}	T_{j+4}	T_{j+5}	T_{j+6}	T_{j+7}	T_{j+8}	T_{j+9}	T_{j+10}	T_{j+11}
N_{i+1}	S_{q1}	R_{q2}	S_{q2}	R_{q3}	S_{q3}						
N_{i+2}	R_{q1}	S_{q1}	R_{q2}	S_{q2}	R_{q3}	S_{q3}					
N_{i+3}		R_{q1}	S_{q1}	R_{q2}	S_{q2}	R_{q3}	S_{q3}				
N_{i+4}			R_{q1}	S_{q1}	R_{q2}	S_{q2}	R_{q3}	S_{q3}			
N_{i+5}			R_{q1}	S_{q1}	R_{q2}	S_{q2}	R_{q3}	S_{q3}			
N_{i+6}				R_{q1}	S_{q1}	R_{q2}	S_{q2}	R_{q3}	S_{q3}		
N_{i+7}					R_{q1}	S_{q1}	R_{q2}	S_{q2}	R_{q3}	S_{q3}	

So, the time requirement by the algorithm for sending of q packets from source node to destination is

$$T_T = (H_{opt} + 2(q-1))t \tag{5}$$

2.1.2 Flooding2

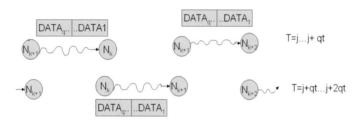

Fig. 2. Message transmission of Flooding2

In case of Flooding2, all the q packets will be received first and then they will be transmitted. Table2 depicts the scenario. The notations are similar to the previous case. Here

$$T_T = (N_N - N_1)qt \tag{6}$$

If message contains q number of packet using induction method we can write

$$T_T = H_{opt}qt \tag{7}$$

Table 2. Sequence table of sending and receiving message to traverse particular node sequence, if message contains more than one number of packets then any node gets all the packet of a particular message and then transmit to the next node.

	T_{j+1}	T_{j+2}	T_{j+3}	T_{j+4}	T_{j+5}	T_{j+6}	T_{j+7}	T_{j+8}	T_{j+9}	T_{j+10}	T_{j+11}	T_{j+12}	T_{j+13}	T_{j+14}	T_{j+15}
N_{i+1}	S_{q1}	S_{q2}	S_{q3}												
N_{i+2}	R_{q1}	R_{q2}	R_{q3}	S_{q1}	S_{q2}	S_{q3}									
N_{i+3}				R_{q1}	R_{q2}	R_{q3}	S_{q1}	S_{q2}	S_{q3}						
N_{i+4}							R_{q1}	R_{q2}	R_{q3}	S_{q1}	S_{q2}	S_{q3}			
N_{i+5}										R_{q1}	R_{q2}	R_{q3}	S_{q1}	S_{q2}	S_{q3}
N_{i+6}													R_{q1}	R_{q2}	R_{q3}

2.2 Gossiping Algorithm

However it can be shown that gossiping is an inefficient non-reliable WSN routing algorithm. Therefore we do not consider it in this paper.

2.3 Clustering Algorithm

Clustering algorithm [3,4] [Fig.4.] is a hierarchical WSN routing algorithm. A collection of some nodes is called a cluster. Every cluster has a cluster head. Simple sensor nodes collect data from the environment and then they send the data to the cluster head node associated with them. The cluster head sends the accumulated data to the next level cluster head and in this way the data reaches the base station. It is a tree like structure. Since tree is a graph without any circuit and there is one and only one path between any two nodes, the maximum hop count in a cluster is

$$H_{max} = \text{Maximum level to traverse.} \tag{8}$$

Since the route is unique, the maximum hop count is equal to the optimum hop count to reach from source to destination .It could be said that $H_{max} = H_{opt}$. Also, we can write $T_{wsn} \alpha H_{wsn}$. So, the time needed to reach data from the source to the destination is T= (Maximum level to traverse) t . [t is the time to communicate between two nodes directly, we assume t is a constant] .Let T_T is the time required to send data message from source to sink

$$T_T = H_{opt}t \tag{9}$$

There may be two conventions to transmit message, which contains q packets. One convention is after getting one packet from the previous node, the packet will be broadcast immediately to its neighbor node. We call this Clustering1. Second convention is after getting the entire q packets from the previous node, they will be broadcast to the neighbor nodes. We call it Clustering2.

2.3.1 Clustering1
If a message contains q number of packets then for every packet transmission all the above steps will be repeated q times and data message will follow optimum path. The time requirement would be same as section 2.1.1.

$$T_T = ((N_N - N_1) + 2(q-1))t \tag{10}$$

Since $N_N - 1 = H_{opt}$, the time requirement equation is

$$T_T = (H_{opt} + 2(q-1))t \tag{11}$$

2.3.2 Clustering2
In case of Clustering2 algorithm data message follow optimum path. But entire q number of packets will be received first and after that the node will transmit. If message contains q number of packets, using induction method we get the time requirement equation. The time requirement would be same as section 2.1.2.

$$T_T = H_{opt}qt \tag{12}$$

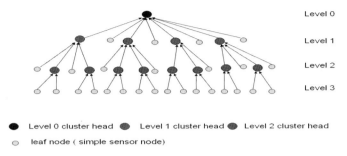

Level 0
Level 1
Level 2
Level 3

● Level 0 cluster head   ◉ Level 1 cluster head   ◉ Level 2 cluster head
○ leaf node (simple sensor node)

Fig. 3. Clustering WSN

2.4 Directed Diffusion

Directed diffusion [1] [Fig.4] is an energy efficient WSN semi mobile routing algorithm. Let us consider that at any instance of time a WSN environment consists of a source node and a sink node and $(N-2)$ multi hop nodes (assume total number of nodes to be N). At first the sink node does not have any information about source node. The sink node generates an interest message and floods that message to the network. Different intermediate nodes get that interest message from different nodes. Every intermediate node stores the information of respective previous nodes from which it gets the interest message. Thus the interest message reaches the source node through different routes. In this way we establish different route or forward gradient. The source node will wait for a finite amount of time to get interest messages from all possible paths. Now every node knows only from where it gets the interest message but not to which it sends (since it broadcast the interest message). Then the source node broadcasts an initial message to set the reverse gradient and to reinforce the best path. In the same way the source node gets the initial message (which is not data message). The sink node gets that initial message from different paths. Every message will propagate with variable hop count. By the hop count value the sink node will decide the shortest route. After that again the sink node sends (unicast sending) the request for data message along the best path. This is called the reinforcement of path. After getting the interest message second time the source node sends the data message to the sink nodes along with the best path. Let T_{F_G} is the time required to set the forward gradient. At the time of forward gradient setting we have to consider the worst case. Let worst case hop count is H_{worst} . The worst-case hop count means the maximum possible length of path from source node to destination node. The time required to traverse the H_{worst} length path is T_{worst} . Then as per (1),

$$T_{worst} \alpha H_{worst}$$

$$T_{worst} = H_{worst} t \tag{13}$$

Let best case hop count is H_{best} . The best-case hop count means the minimum possible length of path (in terms of hop count) from source node to destination node. The time required to traverse the H_{best} length path is T_{best} . Then as per (1),

$$T_{best} = H_{best}t \tag{14}$$

Let T_{worst} is the waiting time to send data message after reaching the first request from sink. If total number of nodes is equal to 2 in a WSN the maximum hop count could be 1 that means $(2-1)$. If total number of nodes is equal to 3 in a WSN the maximum hop count could be 2 that means $(3-1)$. If total number of nodes is equal to i in a WSN the maximum hop count could be $(i-1)$. If total number of node is equal to N in a WSN the maximum hop count could be $(N-1)$. There might be the path with length greater than $(N-1)$ but if the path length is greater than $(N-1)$ there must have been a loop and that path must not be considered. From the above discussion it could be said

$$T_{best} = H_{best}t \tag{15}$$

$$T_{worst} = H_{worst}t \tag{16}$$

$$H_{worst} = (N-1) \tag{17}$$

$$T_{worst\_wait} = (H_{worst} - H_{best})t \tag{18}$$

From (15) (16),(17)and (18) we get $\quad T_{worst\_wait} = (N-1-H_{best})t \tag{19}$

After reaching the first message from sink node to source node by the best possible path the sink node need to wait T_{worst_wait} time to get the request from all possible paths. But time for the gradient setting is equal to the summation of T_{worst_wait} and time to reach along the best path (T_{best}).

$$T_{F\_G} = T_{worst\_wait} + T_{best}$$
$$\text{or,} T_{F\_G} = (N-1)t \tag{20}$$

Let T_{R_G} is the time required for the reverse gradient setting. The forward and reverse gradient setting is mostly identical. In case of forward gradient setting, sink broadcasts the first interest message and source node gets that interest message from different paths. In case of reverse gradient setting source broadcasts initial message and sink gets that message from different paths. Since in both cases the approach is same, the time required for setting the reverse gradient is equal to the time required for setting forward gradient.

$$\text{Thus } T_{R\_G} = T_{F\_G}$$
$$T_{R\_G} = (N-1)t \tag{21}$$

Let T_{RI} is the time required for reinforcement of optimum path. Since H_{opt} is the hop count of optimum path.

$$T_{RI} = H_{opt}t \tag{22}$$

Let T_{DATA} is the time required to send data message from source node to the destination node. Since H is the optimum hop count

$$T_{DATA} = H_{opt}t \tag{23}$$

Let T_T be the total time needed for gradient setting and data sending. From (20), (21), (22) and (23) it could be said that

$$T_T = T_{F\_G} + T_{R\_G} + T_{RI} + T_{DATA} \tag{24}$$

$$\text{or,} \, T_T = 2(N-1)t + 2H_{opt}t \tag{25}$$

There may be two conventions for transmitting data message, which contains q packets. One convention is after getting one packet from previous node this packet will be sent immediately to the neighbor node. We call this Directed diffusion1. Second convention is after getting the entire q packets from the previous node this will be broadcast to the neighbor nodes. We call it Directed diffusion2.

2.4.1 Directed Diffusion1
In case of Directed diffusion1 after reinforcement of path data message follow the optimum path. If a message contains q number of packets then for every packet transmission all the above steps will be repeated q times and data message will follow optimum path. The time requirement would be same as section 2.1.1.

$$T_{DATA} = ((N_N - N_1) + 2(q-1))t \tag{26}$$

Since $N_N - 1 = H_{opt}$, the time requirement equation for data transmission is

$$T_{DATA} = (H_{opt} + 2(q-1))t \tag{27}$$

$$T_{DATA} = (H_{opt} + 2(q-1))t \tag{28}$$

$$T_T = T_{F\_G} + T_{R\_G} + T_{RI} + T_{DATA}$$

$$\text{or,} \, T_T = 2(N-1)t + (2H_{opt} + 2(q-1))t \tag{29}$$

2.4.2 Directed Diffusion2
In case of Directed diffusion2, after reinforcement of path data messages follow the optimum path. But entire q number of data packet will be received first and after they will be transmitted .The time requirement will be same as section 2.1.2.

$$T_{DATA} = H_{opt}qt \tag{30}$$

$$\text{Thus,}\, T_T = T_{F\_G} + T_{R\_G} + T_{RI} + T_{DATA} \tag{31}$$

$$T_T = 2(N-1)t + (q+1)H_{opt}t \tag{32}$$

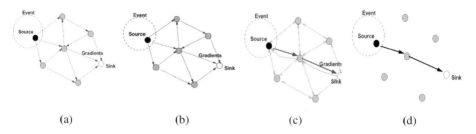

(a)   (b)   (c)   (d)

Fig. 4. [1].Directed diffusion:(a):send request or setting the forward gradient,(b): Initial gradient setting; (c): Reinforcement of optimum path; (d): Data delivery reinforced path

2.5 Sensor Protocols for Information via Negotiation (SPIN)

In case of SPIN [7] protocol, there are three kinds of messages ADV message, REQ message and DATA message. Once a sensor node senses data, it broadcasts an advertisement message (ADV message) to its neighboring nodes to inform that one data has arrived. The neighbor node sends request message (REQ message) for data to the node from which it gets ADV message. After getting the REQ message, the node sends the data message (DATA message) to its neighbor nodes individually. Again, the nodes, which get the data message from source node, broadcasts the ADV message to their neighbor nodes the above steps, are repeated. When source node generates any ADV message, the message has unique message id. Once an ADV message reaches a particular node, the node will not accept the message again from any other node. In case of SPIN WSN routing algorithm any node does not store any route information (does not maintain any routing table). To send data from one node to another node the SPIN routing algorithm takes 3 steps (ADV + REQ+DATA). So to reach DATA message from source node to destination node with distance H_{opt}, will take $3H_{opt}$ steps. Assume that T_T denotes the time required to reach data message from source to destination. From (1) we get

$$T_{wsn}\,\alpha H_{wsn}$$

$$\tag{33}$$

i.e. $T_T = 3H_{opt}t$ [t is the time required to send data from one node to another node]

If message contains q number of packet then q number packet will transmit one by one. There may be two conventions to transmit message, which contains q packet. One convention is each packet transmission will follow the full SPIN process. We could say it is the SPIN1. Second convention is after getting REQ message q massage will transmit at a stretch. We can call it SPIN2.

2.5.1 SPIN1

In case of SPIN1, data message follow every possible path and in this case each packet transmission will follow the full SPIN process. If a message contains q number of packets then for every packet transmission all the above steps (SPIN) will be repeated q times and data message will follow optimum path also. While k^{th} node receiving $(q+1)^{th}$ data packet, then $(k+1)^{th}$ node sends q^{th} packet to the next node (similar to pipeline processing) [Fig.5].

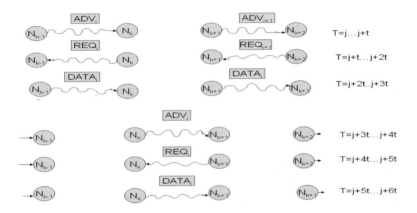

Fig. 5. Message transmission of SPIN1

A table depicting samples of data movement is given [Table3] later .The rows in the table represent the events of sent and received packets of a node sequence over a time period. S_{A_i} denotes that i^{th} ADV message is sent and R_{A_i} denotes that the ith ADV message similarly S_{R_i} and S_{D_i} denotes i^{th} REQ message and DATA message is sent .Also R_{R_i} and R_{D_i} denotes i^{th} REQ message, and DATA message is received. T_k and N_k are time slots and nodes that are involved. Table 3 depicts the scenario.

$$T_T = 3(N_N - N_1) + 6(q-1) \tag{34}$$

If message contains q number of packet using induction method we can write.

$$T_T = 3H_{opt} + 6(q-1) \tag{35}$$

Table 3. Sequence table of sending and receiving message to traverse particular node sequence in case of SPIN algorithm, if message contains more than one number of data packets then after getting one data packet it transmit that packet to the next node.

	T_{j+1}	T_{j+2}	T_{j+3}	T_{j+4}	T_{j+5}	T_{j+6}	T_{j+7}	T_{j+8}	T_{j+9}	T_{j+10}	T_{j+11}	T_{j+12}	T_{j+13}	T_{j+14}	T_{j+15}
N_{i+1}	S_{A1}	R_{R1}	S_{D1}	R_{A2}	S_{R2}	R_{D2}	S_{A2}	R_{R2}	S_{D2}						
N_{i+2}	R_{A1}	S_{R1}	R_{D1}	S_{A1}	R_{R1}	S_{D1}	R_{A2}	S_{R2}	R_{D2}	S_{A2}	R_{A2}	S_{D2}			
N_{i+3}				R_{A1}	S_{R1}	R_{D1}	S_{A1}	R_{R1}	S_{D1}	R_{A2}	S_{R2}	R_{D2}	S_{A2}	R_{R2}	S_{D2}
N_{i+4}							R_{A1}	S_{R1}	R_{D1}	S_{A1}	R_{R1}	S_{D1}	R_{A2}	S_{R2}	R_{D2}
N_{i+5}										R_{A1}	S_{R1}	R_{D1}	S_{A1}	R_{R1}	S_{D1}

2.5.2 SPIN2

In case of SPIN2, all the q packets will be received first and then they will be transmitted. Table4 depicts the scenario. The notations are similar to the previous case. Here

$$T_T = (2(N_N - N_1) + H_{opt} q)t \tag{36}$$

If message contains q number of packet using induction method we can write

$$T_T = (2H_{opt} + H_{opt} q)t \tag{37}$$

Table 4. Sequence table of sending and receiving message to traverse particular node sequence in case of SPIN algorithm, if message contains more than one number of data packets then any node gets all the packets of particular message at a stretch and then transmit to the next node

	T_{j+1}	T_{j+2}	T_{j+3}	T_{j+4}	T_{j+5}	T_{j+6}	T_{j+7}	T_{j+8}	T_{j+9}	T_{j+10}	T_{j+11}	T_{j+12}	T_{j+13}	T_{j+14}	T_{j+15}	T_{j+16}	T_{j+17}	T_{j+18}	T_{j+19}	T_{j+20}
N_{i+1}	S_A	R_R	S_{D1}	S_{D2}	S_{D3}															
N_{i+2}	R_A	S_R	R_{D1}	R_{D2}	R_{D3}	S_A	R_R	S_{D1}	S_{D2}	S_{D3}										
N_{i+3}						R_A	S_R	R_{D1}	R_{D2}	R_{D3}	S_A	R_R	S_{D1}	S_{D2}	S_{D3}					
N_{i+4}											R_A	S_R	R_{D1}	R_{D2}	R_{D3}	S_A	R_R	S_{D1}	S_{D2}	S_{D3}
N_{i+5}																R_A	S_R	R_{D1}	R_{D2}	R_{D3}

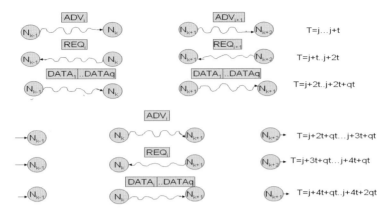

Fig. 6. Message transmission of SPIN2

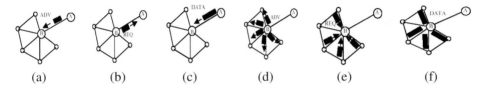

(a)   (b)   (c)   (d)   (e)   (f)

Fig.7. [7]. SPIN: (a): Broadcast ADV by node A; (b): Send REQ by node B to node A; (c): Send DATA by node A to node B; (d): Broadcast ADV message by node B; (e): Node B gets REQ message from its neighbors. (f): Node B sends DATA message to its neighbors.

Table 5. Time requirement to reaching a message contains q number of packets

WSN routing algorithms	Time
Flooding1	$T_T = (H_{opt} + 2(q-1))t$
Flooding2	$T_T = H_{opt} qt$
Clustering1	$T_T = (H_{opt} + 2(q-1))t$
Clustering 2	$T_T = H_{opt} tq$
Directed diffusion1	$T_T = 2(N-1)t + (2H_{opt} + 2(q-1))t$
Directed diffusion2	$T_T = 2(N-1)t + (q+1)H_{opt} t$
SPIN1	$T_T = 3H_{opt} + 6(q-1)$
SPIN2	$T_T = (2H_{opt} + H_{opt} q)t$

3   Results and Discussion

Fig.8. describes rate of changes in time required to reach destination with changing optimum path length keeping other parameters constant. In case of directed diffusion at the time of forward gradient setting (20) and the reverse gradient setting (21) time depends on total number of nodes. Higher number of N means the values of T_{F_G} and T_{R_G} are also high. Also $T_T = T_{F\_G} + T_{R\_G} + T_{RI} + T_{DATA}$ (from (24)) and therefore total time requirement to reach data message to the destination for directed diffusion depends on time required for gradient setting. If the gradient setting time is high then total time requirement would also be high. Thus time requirement to reach data to the destination in case of directed diffusion algorithm is higher than any other routing algorithms even when the optimum path length and single packet per message are considered. From the graph it could be said that considering the rate of change of requirement of time to reach destination the algorithms can be ordered as follows with increasing optimal hop count Clustering = Flooding < SPIN1 = SPIN2 = Directed diffusion [other parameters are const.]. Considering the total time requirement the nodes at any point is Clustering = Flooding <SPIN=SPIN2<Directed diffusion [other parameters are const.]. Fig.9. describes rate the order at of changes of time required to reach destination with changing number of packet per message keeping other parameter constant. From the graph it could be said that the change of time requirement from lower time requirement to higher time requirement with changing total number of nodes in WSN is Flooding1 = Clustering1 = SPIN1 = Directed diffusion1 < Flooding2 = SPIN2 = Clustering2 = Directed diffusion2. There are five cutting points (Flooding2 with SPIN1, Clustering2 with Directed diffusion1, Flooding2 with SPIN1, Clustering2 with SPIN1 and SPIN2 with Directed diffusion1). If we equate those equations from Table 5 we could get the theoretical values of q at those cutting points keeping other parameters constant. Let q_i, q_j , q_k , q_l, q_m are five cutting points, where q_i is the cutting point between Flooding2 graph and SPIN1 graph, q_j is the cutting point between Clustering2 and SPIN1 graph, q_k is the cutting point between Flooding2 graph and Directed diffusion1 graph, q_l is the cutting point between Clustering 2 graph and Directed diffusion1 graph, q_m is the cutting point between SPIN2 graph and Directed diffusion1 graph.

$$q_i = (3H_{opt} - 6)/(H_{opt} - 6) \tag{38}$$

$$q_j = (3H_{opt} - 6)/(H_{opt} - 6) \tag{39}$$

$$q_k = 2(N + H_{opt} - 2)/(H_{opt} - 2) \tag{40}$$

$$q_l = 2(N + H_{opt} - 2)/(H_{opt} - 2) \tag{41}$$

$$q_m = 2(N - 2)/(H_{opt} - 2) \tag{42}$$

As per our graph we can say $q_i = q_j < q_m < q_k < q_l$. From the graph we can get the order of total time requirement of any point. When message size is one [other parameters are const.] time requirement for the algorithms increases as follows: Flooding1 = Flooding2 = Clustering1 = Clustering2 < SPIN1 = SPIN2 < Directed diffusion1 = Directed diffusion2. When $1 < q < q_i, q_j$ (keeping other parameters const.). Time requirement increases as: Flooding1 = Clustering1 < Flooding2 = Clustering2 < SPIN1 < SPIN2 < Directed diffusion1 <Directed diffusion2. When $q = q_i, q_j$ (keeping other parameters const.) the order will be: Flooding1 = Clustering1 < Flooding2 = Clustering2 = SPIN1 < SPIN2 < Directed diffusion1 < Directed diffusion2. When $q_i, q_j < q < q_m$ [other parameters are const.] time will increase in the order: Flooding1 = Clustering1 <SPIN1 < Clustering2 = Flooding2 < SPIN2 < Directed diffusion1 <Directed diffusion2. When $q = q_m$ [other parameters are const.] time will increase as: Flooding1 = Clustering1 < SPIN1 < Clustering2 = Flooding < SPIN2 = Directed diffusion1 < Directed diffusion2. When $q_m < q < q_k, q_l$ [other parameters are const.] the algorithms can be ordered as: Flooding1 = Clustering1 < Flooding2 = Clustering2 < SPIN1< Directed diffusion1 < SPIN2 < Directed diffusion2. When $q = q_k, q_l$ [other parameters are const.] the time requirement will increase as Flooding1 = Clustering1 < Flooding2 = Clustering2 < SPIN1< Directed diffusion1 < SPIN2<Directed diffusion2. Total time requirement does not have much significance because if we change other parameters the order would change.

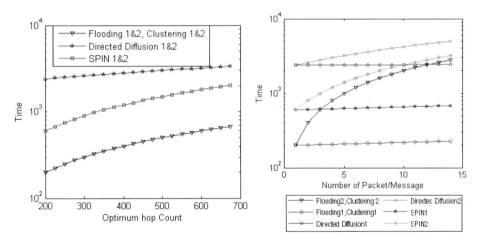

Fig. 8. Change of time requirement to reach a message from source node to destination node with changing number of optimum hop count.

Fig. 9. Changes of time to reach a message to destination with changing number of packet contains each message.

Fig.10. describes rate of changes of time required to reach destination with changing number of packets per message keeping other parameters constant. Depending upon the application, the size of message might be high due to which the total message may be needed to be segmented into many packets and sent one by one. Time required for directed diffusion depends on total number of nodes and for this reason changes in total number of nodes, time to reach destination also changes. On the contrary the time required for Flooding, Clustering or SPIN algorithms are not dependent on total number of nodes (N). So the graphs in case of Flooding, Clustering and SPIN do not exhibit any changes with respect to the horizontal axis (Number of nodes). The order of rate of changes of time requirement from lower time requirement to higher time requirement is Clustering1 =Clustering2=Flooding1=Flooding2 = SPIN1=SPIN2< Directed diffusion 1=Directed diffusion2.

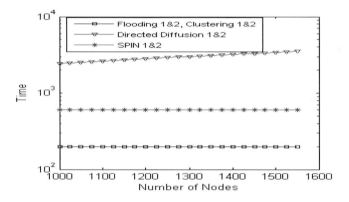

Fig. 10. Changes of time to reach a message to destination with changing number of nodes

3.1 Limitation of Mathematical Analysis

We have analyzed different WSN routing algorithms theoretically. With appropriate logic we have built up the equation for time requirement to reach a message from source node to destination node. Varying different variables we get different values for requirement of time to reach the destination. We plot that values in graph and get several graphs. Using those graphs we analyze the behavior of WSN routing algorithms. If we implement those WSN routing algorithms practically and get the real data and plot the graphs, the nature of the graphs would be slightly different. There are several reasons for the mismatch. The main reason is route collision. Messages may arrive at a particular node at the same time. Since the sensor node can read one message at a time, if more than one message come at the same time then one and only one message will be read, others will be lost. Mobility of nodes may also cause differences between analytical results and experimental results. In case of directed diffusion, after establishment of path if one node moves away, then route needs to be established again and for that effective time to reach the destination will be high. In some cases signal strength of sending message depends on distance between two sensor nodes and also time to reach a message from a node to another node directly depends on distance between two nodes. Here we assume that time to reach message from one node to the next node is constant.

4 Conclusion

In this paper we have analyzed time requirement of different WSN routing algorithms. We generate different time requirement functions to reach a message to the destination. Time requirement depends on some independent variables like optimum path length (H_{opt}), number of packets per message (q), total number of nodes in WSN (N) etc. Different routing algorithms work efficiently in different working environments. The time requirement (T_T) of SPIN and flooding algorithm is very high, but SPIN can work efficiently in the mobile environment (since SPIN does not have to store any route information). SPIN works via negotiation and for that the data security is little bit high and for that SPIN can work efficiently in the warfront. If the message size is large then the time requirement T_T is low in case of directed diffusion algorithms. The route is selected each time of message transmission and the route information is stored some finite amount of time which implies that it can work in semi dynamic environment. In case of Flooding, messages follow every possible path .As the optimum path is the sub set of every possible path, it could be said that Flooding is the most reliable and time efficient routing algorithm. The time (T_T) requirement is lowest in case of clustering algorithm. But the Clustering algorithm mostly works efficiently in the static environment where the Cluster heads are predefined. So, it could be concluded that different WSN algorithms work efficiently in different working environments. The time (T_T) requirement of a WSN routing algorithm may be high, but it could not be said that the algorithm is inefficient in a specific application area. Our analysis would help researchers to design a network for a particular algorithm.

References

[1] Intanagonwiwat, C., Govindan, R., Estrin, D., Heidemann, J., Silva, F.: Directed Diffusion for Wireless Sensor Networking. IEEE/ACM Transactions on Networking(TON) 11(1), 2–16 (2003) ISSN:1063-6692
[2] Luna-Vazquez, Israel, Supervisors: Prof. Dr. rer.nat.Roland Wismuller,Dr.-Ing. Stefan Knedlik; Master Thesis, Implementation and simulation of routing protocols for wireless sensor networks;Luna-Vazquez,Israel
[3] Wang, Y.-H., Huang, K.-F., Fu3, P.-F., Wang4, J.-X.: Mobile Sink Routing Protocol with Registering in Cluster-Based Wireless Sensor Networks. LNCS, pp. 352–362. Springer, Heidelberg, ISBN:978-3-540-69292-8
[4] Martin, G., BSc(Honours).: Software Engineering,Supervisor:Dr. Alan Tully. An Evaluation of Ad-hoc Routing Protocols for Wireless Sensor Networks
[5] Meguerdichian1, S., Koushanfar2, F., Qu, G., Potkonjak, M.: Exposure In Wireless Ad-Hoc Sensor Networks. In: International Conference on Mobile Computing and Networking Proceedings of the 7th annual international conference on Mobile computing and networking, Rome,Italy, pp. 139–150 (2001), ISBN:1-58113-422-3

[6] Bandyopadhyay, S., Coyle, E.J.: An Energy Efficient Hierarchical Clustering Algorithm for Wireless Sensor Networks. Computer Networks:The International Journal of Computer and Telecommunication Networking 44(1), 1–16 (2004), ISSN:1389-1286

[7] Kulik, J., Heinzelman, W., Balakrishnan, H.: Negotiation-based protocols for disseminating information in wireless sensor networks. In: Mobicom 1999, pp. 169–185 (2002), ISSN:1022-0038

Internal Map of the Nanostack 6LoWPAN Stack

Sergio Lembo, Jari Kuusisto, and Jukka Manner

Aalto University - School of Science and Technology
Department of Communications and Networking
P.O. Box 13000, 00076 Aalto, Finland
`firstname.lastname@tkk.fi`

Abstract. There exist several open source 6LoWPAN stacks for researchers to experiment with. However, they often lack sufficient and
in-depth description of the internal operation, which makes extending
the stacks difficult for many of us. This paper provides detailed documentation of the internal logic of an implemented and working 6LoWPAN
stack, Nanostack (v1.1). We present first the main architecture of the
stack and subsequently describe the path followed by a packet transiting
the different layers. The logic in each one of the layers is explained with
exception of the ICMP layer. Finally at the end of the paper we observe
Nanostack from user's perspective and discuss features and problems
that we noticed in the stack.

1 Introduction

Advances in micro-electro-mechanical systems (MEMS) have led to the development of wireless sensor networks (WSNs). These networks consist of individual
devices that have been interconnected wirelessly in order to perform diverse
tasks. The inter-device communication requires a suitable communication protocol that can be chosen among a diverse range of standard and non-standard
protocols. The widely adopted Internet protocol (IP) is used traditionally in
computer networks to provide a uniform and standardized way of communicating that is independent from the actual physical communication. Because IP has
many advantages (e.g. already supported standards and extensive interoperability) it is also introduced to the WSNs. 6LoWPAN defines the IP version 6 (IPv6)
networking in WSNs [1].

Currently there are few known open-source implementations of 6LoWPAN
stacks; recent surveys report four known open-source 6LoWPAN implementations [2], Nanostack [3] is one of them. Among the available open-source 6LoW-
PAN implementations, the authors selected Nanostack due to two strong facts.
Firstly, the stack operates on top of a real time kernel (FreeRTOS), making it
suitable for time critical tasks like real time control or network synchronization.
Secondly, the stack implements a mesh-under routing (in contrast of other stacks
that adopt route-over routing [2]).

Nanostack (v1.1) is an implemented and working 6LoWPAN stack distributed
under GPL license. In this paper we focus on the latest open-source Nanostack

N. Meghanathan et al. (Eds.): NeCoM, WiMoN, and WeST 2010, CCIS 90, pp. 619–633, 2010.

release, version 1.1, and hereafter refer to it simply as Nanostack. Nanostack implements most of the RFC4944 [1], namely, processing of Mesh-Header, Dispatch-Header (and its alternatives LOWPAN_HC1, LOWPAN_BC0 and IPv6), mesh-under addressing and compression of IP and UDP headers. The implementation currently does not support 6LoWPAN fragmentation and we are unable to report at what extent unicast and multicast address mapping is supported since code related to the processing of native (non-compressed) IPv6 addresses was not considered in our study. The stack was written in C language and designed to work on top of FreeRTOS kernel [4].

Despite Nanostack being an open-source stack, Nanostack authors and users never created proper documentation of the internal logic of the stack. Our main contribution in this paper is to document and analyze the internal architecture of Nanostack, followed by explanations about how it works in detail. The given details help to cope with the missing documentation and explain the internal logic at the code level. By exposing the architecture and logic of the stack, the reader can evaluate at what extent Nanostack is suitable for an intended purpose given different requirements and constraints (modularity, concurrency, real-time operation, energy consumption, memory size, etc.).

In the following sections we document the stack architecture and logic. In Section 2 we introduce the architecture of the stack. In the sections that follow (3, 4, 5, and 6) we introduce and explain the operation of each one of the layers in the stack, except the ICMP layer that is not covered in our descriptions. Finally, we present discussions and conclusions in Section 7.

2   Stack Architecture

In this section, we first introduce the main data structure used in the stack for processing packets, followed by the description of a key component in the core architecture, the "dispatcher" module. We also illustrate the overall architecture with the dispatcher module and all the layers in the stack.

2.1   Main Data Structure Used in the Stack

In the stack packets are handled by mean of instances of the data structure *buffer_t*. *buffer_t* is defined in file *buffer.h* and reproduced here in Fig. 1.

Throughout this document we denote by *b* an instance of *buffer_t*. The content of a packet is stored in the *buf* field of *buffer_t* : *b.buf*; where the notation expresses a qualified name, in this case *b* is an instance of *buffer_t* and *buf* a field belonging to *b*. (To be more precise in the actual implementation *b* is actually a pointer to an instance of *buffer_t*, and a C language notation *b−>buf* is more appropriate, although not used here to simplify the notation). Linux kernel connoisseurs can imagine *buffer_t* as a structure analogous to the socket buffer structure *sk_buff* in the Linux kernel [5][6].

Packets move through the stack by mean of instances of structure *buffer_t*. (We emphasize here that even when we say that there is a movement of packets inside the stack, Nanostack actually never moves packets but merely pointers to instances *buffer_t*). Incoming packets are directly stored in *b.buf*. Subsequent processing in the different layers of the stack parse the packet and fills accordingly the fields of *buffer_t* structure with the information extracted from the packet. Outgoing packets are constructed layer by layer; each layer adding an appropriate header in *b.buf*.

Three fields in *buffer_t* of particular importance are *b.from*, *b.to* and *b.dir*. Fields *b.from* and *b.to* indicate the previous and posterior layer that processed and will process the packet, respectively. Field *b.dir* indicates the direction of movement of the packet; the value BUFFER_UP indicates an incoming packet moving toward the Application Layer whereas the value BUFFER_DOWN indicates an outgoing packet moving toward the Network Layer.

Hereafter an instance *buffer_t*, *b*, moving in the stack can be thought as a packet under processing (parsing) when the packet is incoming or as a packet under composition when the packet is outgoing. Analogously, when talking about packets moving in the stack we always are talking of the associated instance *buffer_t*, *b*, that carries the packet in the *b.buf* field.

```
typedef struct
{
    struct socket_t *   socket;
    sockaddr_t          dst_sa;
    sockaddr_t          src_sa;
    module_id_t         from;
    module_id_t         to;
    buffer_direction_t  dir;
    uint16_t            buf_ptr;
    uint16_t            buf_end;
    uint16_t            size;
    buffer_options_t    options;
    uint8_t             buf[2];
} buffer_t;
```

Fig. 1. Main data structure used in the stack

2.2   Dispatcher of Packets and Stack Architecture

Fig. 2 shows the architecture of the stack. In the figure we observe a graphical representation of a queue labeled "Queue *events*". Queue *events* transits incoming and outgoing packets (carried in instances *buffer_t*, *b*) between different layers of the stack. The output of the queue is handled by a dedicated system task labeled *stack_main()* (file *stack.c*) that contains an endless loop checking the arrival of instances *b* from the queue (function *xQueueReceive()*). When a packet is received by *xQueueReceive()* the function *stack_buffer()* is called, passing a pointer of the *buffer_t* instance *b* as parameter. Function *stack_buffer()* behaves as a dispatcher; it contains a suitable logic that delivers the packet to the appropriate destination layer in the stack.

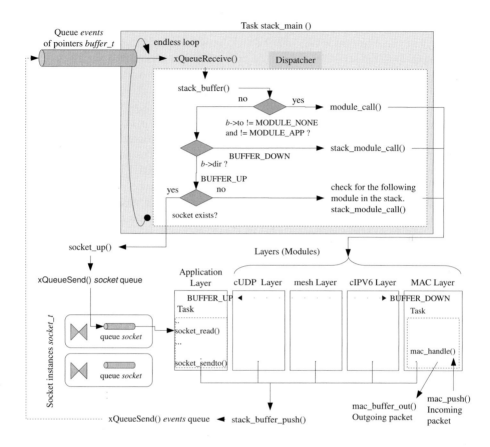

Fig. 2. Nanostack architecture

Possible destination layers are depicted below the box representing task *stack_main()*. In the figure we observe the following layers; MAC, cIPV6, mesh and cUDP. Actually the stack contains also an ICMP layer that we do not include in the current description. The details of the operation of each one of these layers are described in Sections 3, 4, 5 and 6.1. Note in the figure that the application layer is positioned outside the brace that expands under the dispatcher. The application layer is independent of the stack in the sense that it is not related to the dispatcher and instead receives/sends packets by calling socket functions.

We clarify here that the authors of the stack proposed the name cIPV6 for the layer in charge of processing the headers Mesh-Header, Dispatch-Header, and its alternatives LOWPAN_HC1, LOWPAN_BC0, IPv6, etc. (defined in [1]). And the name cUDP for the layer that processes the compressed UDP ports (HC_UDP encoding) [1]. In addition each layer is associated to a module of code that can be enabled/disabled in the stack. In this paper we assume that a module and a layer are equivalent and talk always about layers in the rest of the paper.

In the following subsections we complete the description of the stack by explaining the journey of a packet moving in the stack and introducing additional complementary details.

In the explanations below we talk about nodes. A node is defined as an entity that implements the stack and is able to transmit and receive 6LoWPAN packets.

Journey of a packet in the stack. An incoming packet enters the stack in the MAC layer through a call to *mac_push()*. In this layer a data packet is stored inside a *buffer_t* structure, in the field *b.buf*. Additional values are stored in *b* fields, for example *b.dir* = BUFFER_UP to indicate that the packet will move toward the application layer in the stack. Then the instance *b* is pushed to queue *events* by calling function *stack_buffer_push()*, which in turn calls *xQueueSend()* to input the instance into the queue (Fig. 2).

The main idea is that an instance *buffer_t b* (actually a pointer) travels among the required layers and in its journey the fields of *b* acquire the information stored in the packet by decomposing it (incoming case) or, conversely, the layers utilize the information in the fields of *b* to compose the packet (outgoing case). The movement between layers is facilitated by every time pushing the instance to queue *events*, and letting the dispatcher deliver the instance to the appropriate layer by doing a function call to a dedicated handler function in the layer and passing the instance as parameter.

After an incoming packet leaves the MAC layer and enters queue *events*, it is delivered by the dispatcher to the next layer in the BUFFER_UP direction. In the present explanation the next layer is cIPv6. Actually the layers in the stack are modular in the sense that at compilation time some layers can be added or removed from the stack. In our explanation we assume that all the layers shown in Fig. 2 are present.

Layer cIPv6 will decide (as shown in Section 4.2) the next destination layer in the stack. An incoming packet targeted for the current node will move in BUFFER_UP direction towards the application layer traveling going through the cUDP layer. Whereas a packet targeted to another node may move to the mesh layer to obtain routing information, and from there continue BUFFER_DOWN to the MAC layer for forwarding.

For outgoing packets the journey involves the displacement of *b* in the BUFFER_DOWN direction through layers cUDP, cIPV6, mesh and MAC.

In essence the processing of the packet in each layer will determine its final fate according to different situations. Subsequent sections in the paper document the different situations and decisions mandated by the logic in the stack. Of particular importance at this point is to observe the logic set in the dispatcher. The dispatcher basically selects the next layer by first checking the existence of a concrete destination in *b.to*, and if this is not present relying on the directions BUFFER_UP or BUFFER_DOWN present in the *b.dir* field (Fig. 2).

Sockets. When an incoming packet leaves the cUDP layer in the stack, it is pushed to queue *events* as usual. At this point the dispatcher recognizes that there is no concrete destination layer (*b.to* = MODULE_NONE), and that the packet is heading BUFFER_UP. At this point the dispatcher looks for an existing socket for the destination address and port number stated in the packet and if the socket exists it moves the instance b to a dedicated queue located inside the corresponding socket (queue *socket*) (Fig. 2).

Incoming packets redirected to queue *socket* are retrieved at application layer by calling *socket_read()* function.

Outgoing packets are generated at application layer by invoking function *socket_sendto()*, which will set $b.dir = $ BUFFER_DOWN in the instance b that holds the packet, and finally b is pushed to queue *events*.

Stack initialization. The stack is initialized by calling function *stack_init()*. *stack_init()* is in charge of the following:

1 Creating queue *events* by executing FreeRTOS function *xQueueCreate()*.
2 Creating a new system task *"stack_main()"* by executing FreeRTOS function *xTaskCreate()*. This task contains the endless loop shown in Fig. 2 that listens for incoming instances *buffer_t* from queue *events*.
3 Allocating memory for a defined number of instances of structure *buffer_t* (STACK_BUFFERS_MAX).
4 Initializing indexes $stack\_buffer\_rd = stack\_buffer\_wr = 0$

Allocation of pool of instances *buffer_t*. When the stack is initialized a collection (pool) of *buffer_t* instances is created. The pool of instances is arranged in a ring buffer from where the system takes and returns instances during the operation of the stack. The approach to pre-allocate memory in a pool of instances is not only to provide performance to the system. Note that this stack was designed to work in embedded microcontrollers operating with FreeRTOS. FreeRTOS is a multiplatform mini Real Time Kernel that provides memory allocation in deterministic time by means of a memory allocation API common for any platform (function *pvPortMalloc()*) [4]. In this sense the simplest RAM allocation scheme does not permit memory to be freed once it has been allocated, and hence the use of a pool of instances.

The pool of pre-allocated instances is managed by means of a ring buffer labeled *stack_buffer_pool[]*. *stack_buffer_pool[]* is indexed by two position pointers, a pointer indicating a reading position (*stack_buffer_rd*) and a pointer indicating a writing position (*stack_buffer_wr*), indicating the next available place where a *buffer_t* instance can be taken or returned respectively (Fig. 3).

The functions *stack_buffer_get()* and *stack_buffer_free()* are front end functions that will take or return a *buffer_t* instance from the pool and at the same time these functions initialize or reset the fields of the structure. Behind these functions, *stack_buffer_add()* and *stack_buffer_pull()* perform the actual load/unload of *buffer_t* pointers to/from the pool of instances *stack_buffer_pool[]* (Fig. 3).

In the stack a call to *stack_buffer_get()* is always followed by a call to *stack_buffer_free()* at some point in the life of the packet in order to recycle the finite number of instances *buffer_t*. For example, a packet is returned to the pool after transmission or after discarding it due to some exceptional condition.

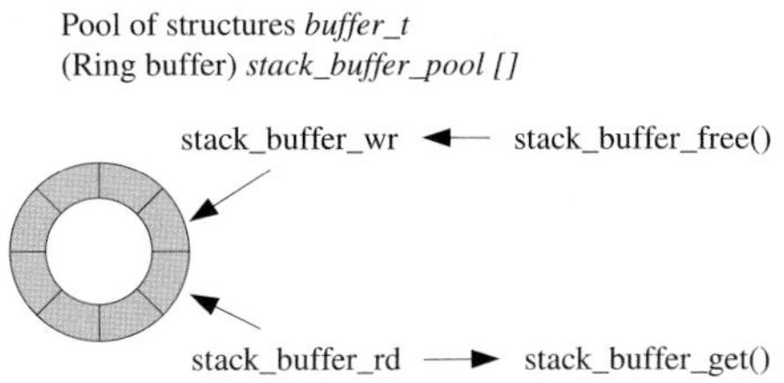

Pool of structures *buffer_t*
(Ring buffer) *stack_buffer_pool []*

stack_buffer_wr ◄——— stack_buffer_free()

stack_buffer_rd ———► stack_buffer_get()

Fig. 3. Ring buffer for *buffer_t* instances

3   MAC Layer

The processing of a packet in the MAC layer comprises the identification and incorporation of the MAC headers in the MAC sublayer part of a IEEE 802.15.4 data frame. In the following subsections we discuss the processing of a packet in the BUFFER_UP and BUFFER_DOWN direction.

3.1   Packets in BUFFER_UP Direction

A packet enters the stack by calling *mac_push()* from outside of the stack. In Nanostack 1.1 distribution for radio chip TI CC2420 *mac_push()* is called from file *rf.c* that belongs to the platform port for this radio chip.

Actually the portion of data that we call *packet* is the *MAC protocol data unit* (MPDU) (PSDU at PHY layer level) of the IEEE 802.15.4 Data Frame [7]. This portion of data is the one pointed by the *b.buf* field of the *buffer_t* instance.

Incoming packets to the stack are buffered in a ring buffer named *mac_rx[]* located in *mac_15_4.c* with prior setting of *b.dir* to BUFFER_UP value in order to let later the dispatcher move the packet in this direction.

The MAC layer has a dedicated task *mac_task()* that contains an endless loop taking care of the processing of incoming and outgoing packets. In each iteration the state of a queue used to transmit events (*mac_events* queue) is checked. When an event of type MAC_RECEIVE is received (triggered by a call to *mac_rx_push()* outside the stack), the packet buffered in the ring buffer *mac_rx[]* is retrieved by a call to *mac_rx_pull()*. Then the MAC header (IEEE 802.15.4 MPDU) is parsed by calling *mac_buffer_parse()* and the fields *b.dst_sa* and *b.src_sa*, among others, of *b* are filled with the received destination and source address. A posterior call to *mac_data_up()* (assuming that mac_mode = MAC_ADHOC) pushes the *b* instance containing the packet to queue *events* for further processing in the next layer in the stack; in this case the cIPv6 layer.

3.2   Packets in BUFFER_DOWN Direction

In this case the dispatcher makes a function call to function *mac_handle()* (the dedicated function to handle packets in this layer) and subsequently the latter calls *mac_tx_add()*. Function *mac_tx_add()* adds the instance *b* containing the packet in a ring buffer named *mac_tx[]* and triggers an event MAC_TRANSMIT. Posterior processing in the system task *mac_task()* (mentioned in the previous subsection) will process this event and retrieve the packet from the ring buffer by calling *mac_tx_pull()*. Next *mac_buffer_out()* is called and the MAC header is generated by *mac_header_generate()*. Finally the packet is output of the stack; in the case of Nanostack distribution the packet is delivered to the radio by calling *rf_write()*, function that does not belong to the stack but to the platform port for radio chip TI CC2420 in file *rf.c*.

The return status of *mac_buffer_out()* can have different states (MAC_TX_OK_ACK, MAC_TX_BUSY, etc). If an ACK is expected the packet b is kept in the system and a timer is launched. Then *mac_handle()* waits for a MAC_ACK_RX event; if an ACK never arrives the transmission is attempted up to 3 times. When an ACK is received b is returned to the pool (*stack_buffer_pool[]*).

4   cIPV6 Layer

The processing of a packet in the cIPV6 layer when it is moving in the BUFFER_UP direction comprises the identification of the 6LoWPAN headers Mesh-Header and Dispatch-Header, and the alternatives of the latter, LOW-PAN_HC1, LOWPAN_BC0 and IPv6, defined in RFC 4944 [1]. In the BUFFER_DOWN direction the processing comprises the incorporation of the 6LoWPAN LOWPAN_HC1 and LOWPAN_BC0 Dispatch-Headers.

This version of the stack (Nanostack 1.1) does not include fragmentation and it is not recognizing the Fragmentation-Header. Furthermore in our study we do not cover the processing of IPv6 and LOWPAN_BC0 headers even when these are present on the stack.

The upper part of Fig. 4 and 5 show the logic involved in cIPV6 layer. In Fig. 4 we can observe the entry point of a packet in this layer; packets are delivered by the dispatcher and can arrive either from the MAC layer (incoming packets) or from the cUDP layer (outgoing packets).

In the subsequent subsections we describe the different conditional branches that form the logic of this layer.

4.1   Exception Messages

On the top of Fig. 4 the first two conditional branches verify particular exception messages set in *b.options*. The first verification is related to an option to refresh a Time-To-Live clock counter in entries of neighbor and routing tables (described in Section 5). The second verification is related to an exception labeled *broken-link* that occurs when the stack does not receive in time an acknowledgement about the reception of a delivered packet from the destination node, or when the transmission of a packet does not succeed after exceeding a maximum number of attempts due to the unavailability of the transmitter to perform the transmission. In the *broken-link* case the MAC layer adds a flag in the packet that is identified

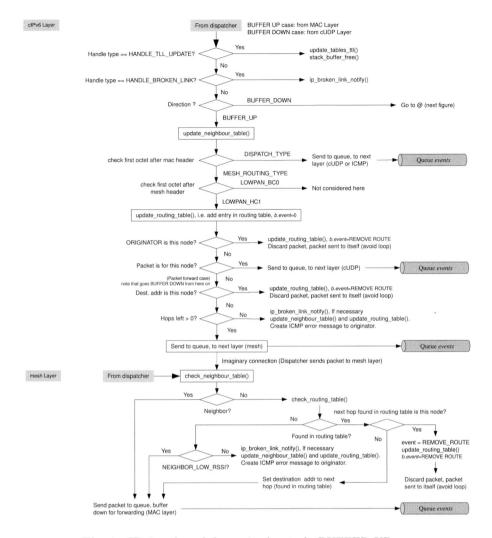

Fig. 4. cIPv6 and mesh layers in the stack: BUFFER_UP case

in this conditional branch and triggers an exception message. The exception message is delivered to the application layer for packets addressed to the current node through a dedicated queue to inform exceptions (queue *event_queue*), or otherwise delivered by means of an ICMP message to the destination address set in the packet.

Packets not involved with these conditional branches continue their journey toward the next conditional branch that verifies the direction of the packet. The logic for packets in the BUFFER_UP direction is discussed in Section 4.2 and depicted in Fig. 4. The logic for packets in the BUFFER_DOWN direction is discussed in Section 4.3 and depicted in Fig. 5.

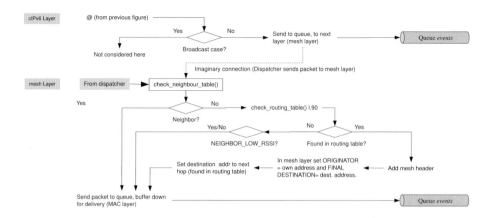

Fig. 5. cIPv6 and mesh layers in the stack: BUFFER_DOWN case

4.2 Packets in BUFFER_UP Direction

The upper part of Fig. 4 depicts the logic followed by a packet moving in the BUFFER_UP direction in this layer. The first step is to update a table called *Neighbor Table* by invoking function *update_neighbour_table()*. Studying the logic stated by the code in the stack we concluded that the criteria to define what is a neighbor and what is not is based on the principle of *"any node that can be listened is a neighbor"*. In this sense an incoming packet from other node entitles the other node to become a neighbor of the receiving node. *Neighbor Table* and a related table, *Routing Table*, are described in the next section.

The next step is to check the 6LoWPAN encapsulation header. The conditional branch checks if the header is a Dispatch-Header or Mesh-Header. When a Dispatch-Header is present, the logic verifies the existence of the type-specific header to be LOWPAN_HC1 and then pushes the packet to queue *events* for further processing in the next layers in the stack (cUDP or ICMP in this case). When a Mesh-Header is present (and assuming that routing is enabled in the stack by defining HAVE_ROUTING directive for the C preprocessor), the parsing process looks for the Dispatch-Header that follows the Mesh-Header. In the Dispatch-Header the type-specific header is checked with a conditional branch that verifies if the header is LOWPAN_HC1 or LOWPAN_BC0. The processing for the LOWPAN_BC0 case is not considered here. In the LOWPAN_HC1 case a table containing the routing of the packets, *Routing Table*, is updated by calling function *update_routing_table()*.

The next phase is to check the 6LoWPAN *originator address* (ORIGINATOR hereafter) present in the Mesh-Header and check if the ORIGINATOR is this node. If the ORIGINATOR is this node it means that the packet looped back to the original sender and therefore should be discarded. The conditional branch that follows checks if the packet is targeted for this node by comparing the *final address* present in the Mesh-Header to the own address of the node. If it is the case the packet is pushed to queue *events* for further processing in the next layer in the stack (cUDP).

A packet with a mesh *final address* other than the address of this node is a packet that reaches this node and requires forwarding. From now on the packet enters in a forwarding stage. In order to forward the packet to the proper destination its traveling direction in the stack will be now changed from BUFFER_UP to BUFFER_DOWN direction.

The first step in forwarding a packet is to check if the destination address (mesh *final address*) is the same that the own address of the node. If this is the case the packet is being sent to itself, so it is discarded. Next the number of hops left is checked. If the number of hops left is zero, a *broken-link* event is generated. Note that this *broken-link* event is a different event to the mentioned at the beginning of this section; in this case an ICMP message is delivered to the destination address set in the packet. If the number of hops is greater than zero the packet is pushed to queue *events* for further processing in the next layer in the stack, in this case the mesh layer.

As additional information we mention that at the beginning of the logic explained in this subsection, the logic checks the presence of an IPv6 header. This is not considered here and not depicted in the figure.

4.3 Packets in BUFFER_DOWN Direction

The upper part of Fig. 5 depicts the logic followed by a packet moving in the BUFFER_DOWN direction in this layer. In the figure we can observe a conditional branch that checks if the packet contains a broadcast address. The broadcast case is not considered in this document. Non-broadcast packets are pushed to the queue *events* for further processing in the next layer in the stack, in this case the mesh layer.

5 Mesh Layer

The processing of a packet in the mesh layer when it is moving in the BUFFER_UP direction comprises the execution of mesh-under routing relying on the information retrieved from the 6LoWPAN Mesh-Header in the cIPv6 layer. In the BUFFER_DOWN direction the processing comprises the incorporation of the 6LoWPAN Mesh-Header defined in RFC 4944 [1].

Routing information is stored in two main tables, *Neighbor Table* and *Routing Table*. *Neighbor Table* contains contact information related to nodes that were heard in the past, either by broadcast or unicast packets addressed to the node. *Routing Table* contains contact information for nodes that are not neighbor nodes. New entries in this table are added with callings to *update_routing_table()* setting a value $b.event$ other than REMOVE_ROUTE and ROUTE_ERR in the instance b. In the stack we identified two calls to *update_routing_table()* for adding new entries in the *Routing Table*, both mentioned in Sections 4.2 and 5.2. Here we point out that these function calls are inconsistent in the sense that the logic distributed in different points of the stack does not present a definite criterion to add initial entries in the table: The conditional statement mentioned in Section 4.2 requires the packet to have a 6LoWPAN Mesh-Header before an entry in the table can be processed, and the conditional statement mentioned in Section 5.2 requires an entry in the table before adding a 6LoWPAN Mesh-Header in the packet. Both conditions lock each other.

The lower part of Fig. 4 and 5 shows the logic involved in this layer when the packet moves in the BUFFER_UP and BUFFER_DOWN directions respectively. In the subsequent subsections we describe the different conditional branches that form the logic of this layer for the cases BUFFER_UP and BUFFER_DOWN.

5.1   Packets in BUFFER_UP Direction

The lower part of Fig. 4 depicts the logic followed by a packet moving in the BUFFER_UP direction in this layer. Actually the packet is no longer moving in the BUFFER_UP direction but hereafter in the BUFFER_DOWN direction due to the fact that the packet reaches this part in the stack from the packet forwarding case mentioned in Section 4.2. In the figure we can observe first a conditional branch that checks if the destination address of the packet to be sent matches a previously stored neighbor node (function *check_neighbour_table()*). If this is the case the packet is pushed to the queue *events* for further processing in the next layer in the stack (MAC layer). The remaining conditional branches are self explicative in the figure.

5.2   Packets in BUFFER_DOWN Direction

The lower part of Fig. 5 depicts the logic followed by a packet moving in the BUFFER_DOWN direction in this layer. In the figure we can observe first a conditional branch that checks if the destination address of the packet to be sent matches a previously stored neighbor node (function *check_neighbour_table()*). If this is the case the packet is pushed to the queue *events* for further processing in the next layer in the stack (MAC layer).

If the destination address of the packet being sent does not belong to a previously stored neighbor, the logic checks the routing table by calling *check_routing_table()*. If an entry in the *Routing Table* exists, the 6LoWPAN Mesh-Header is added to the packet with an *originator address* equal to the address of the node and a mesh *final address* equal to the intended address. The destination address in the MAC layer is set to the address found in the routing table.

If an entry in the *Routing Table* does not exist, the logic verifies whether there is a neighbor with low RSSI (Received Signal Strength Indication); state previously retrieved by *check_neighbour_table()*. Despite of the existence of a neighbor with low RSSI or not, the logic pushes the packet to the MAC layer. In other words, this means that if the node does not have the destination address registered in the neighbor or routing tables, the packet is transmitted anyway. In our opinion a more elaborated routing protocol should be developed and implemented, for example initiating a route discovery.

6   Higher Layers

In this section we describe the remaining layers that form part of the stack; cUDP layer and Application layer.

6.1   cUDP Layer

The processing of a packet in cUDP layer comprises the identification and incorporation of the 6LoWPAN header HC2, in this case for UDP HC_UDP, defined in RFC 4944.

In the BUFFER_UP direction this layer checks the HC2 encoding (HC_UDP) and extracts the port numbers. Extracted port numbers are stored in the b instance in fields $b.src\_sa.port$ and $b.dst\_sa.port$. In the BUFFER_DOWN direction this layer adds the HC_UDP header and compressed port numbers.

6.2   Application Layer

As mentioned in Section 2.2, in Fig. 2 the application layer is positioned outside the brace that expands under the dispatcher. The application layer is independent of the stack in the sense that it is not related to the dispatcher and instead receives/sends packets by calling socket functions. The application layer consists of an independent FreeRTOS task that implements the socket API to access the stack. Incoming packets are redirected to queue *socket* inside the socket structure, and are then retrieved at application layer by calling *socket_read()* function. Outgoing packets are generated at application layer by invoking function *socket_sendto()*, which sets $b.dir = $ BUFFER_DOWN in the instance b that holds the packet, and finally are pushed to queue *events* by calling *stack_buffer_push()*.

7   Discussion and Conclusions

In the previous sections we documented the architecture of the stack and each one of its layers. In this section we deviate from technical descriptions, complementing these with additional information based on the knowledge we attained using Nanostack.

In our opinion, and despite the professional design of the Nanostack, the authors of the stack failed to document their work. The source-code is limited to a brief comment per function and occasional comments in some lines of the code. A doxygen document is available but it just lists the scarce comments and data structures found in the code, not revealing the logic of the stack. On the other hand the authors provided detailed documents about how to get started with the stack at application level and in addition provided several examples ready-to-compile. Each example uses the stack with a particular application layer implementation to target a defined purpose; for example, one example retrieves sample data from an ADC connected to a sensor, other example a implements a Gateway application to relate a WSN to an IP network, etc.

In our opinion some outstanding points of this stack are: 1) The architecture offers a modularized approach. Layers can be added/removed. 2) It is suitable for researching mesh-under routing protocols, (in contrast of other stacks that adopt route-over routing [2]). 3) It is based on FreeRTOS, a well positioned real-time kernel supported by a large community of developers and in continuous evolution.

Some problems we are still facing with Nanostack are the following: 1) Despite the good architecture of the stack, some parts of the code need to be tidied up. 2) The footprint of the stack, kernel and application is just enough to fit in a node with 128 kB of flash memory. For example the footprint of the stack, kernel and a basic application to receive packets occupy around 68 kB. Expanding the functionality of the application to use an AD converter to gather data from an external sensor, report back the data, report the state of neighbor tables upon request and perform GW discovery takes around 126 kB, leaving no room for additional features.

The stack is distributed along with a platform port for the radio chip TI CC2420, programmer, tools, etc., but the required compiler is not included in the distribution. The compiler in use is a variant of SDCC with modifications to support memory banking. A notable observation is that the programming time of sensor nodes via UART takes about 4.5 minutes; not very productive for code development. Our proposed solution for this last problem is the suggestion to create a Nanostack development framework for the FreeRTOS Posix/Linux Simulator [4].

We do not have detailed knowledge of the internal characteristics of other existing open source 6LoWPAN stacks [2] to make a concise and fair comparison of advantages and disadvantages between stacks. We acknowledge that uIPv6 [8] [9] is a renowned stack; in contrast to Nanostack it is certified by the IPv6 Ready Logo Program [10] and it is maintained by a considerable number of developers and researchers. Despite these essential facts, in our selection process we favored Nanostack for several reasons. First, Nanostack supports mesh-under routing, following RFC 4944, whereas uIPv6 implements route-over routing [11]. Second, due that we needed a protocol stack based on a real time kernel (FreeRTOS), suitable for real time control processes and network synchronization [12]. And third, due that despite the complexity of the stack, the programming at application level is extremely simple, facilitated by FreeRTOS and the socket API available in the stack. We note that our selection criteria is biased by our particular needs and experiences, and acknowledge that other stacks may be more suitable under a different evaluation criteria.

As final remark we conclude that Nanostack v1.1 is a stack designed with a modular architecture that operates moving pointers to instances of data structures, and hence without misusing memory size or reducing performance. In addition the stack operates in a concurrent fashion using multiple tasks, and over a real-time kernel system. The drawbacks of the stack are the lack of documentation, the lack of code maintenance and a small community of users.

References

1. Montenegro, G., Kushalnagar, N., Hui, J., Culler, D.: Transmission of IPv6 Packets over IEEE 802.15.4 Networks. RFC 4944 (Proposed Standard) (September 2007)
2. Mazzer, Y., Tourancheau, B.: Comparisons of 6lowpan implementations on wireless sensor networks. In: Third International Conference on Sensor Technologies and Applications, SENSORCOMM 2009, 18-23 pp. 689–692 (2009)
3. NanoStack 6lowpan: Nanostack v1.1 (2008),
   http://sourceforge.net/projects/nanostack/
4. FreeRTOS: The FreeRTOS project (2009), http://www.freertos.org/
5. Rio, M.: A map of the networking code in linux kernel 2.4.20. Technical Report Data TAG-2004-1 (March 2004)
6. Wehrle, K.: The Linux networking architecture: design and implementation of network protocols in the Linux kernel. Pearson Prentice Hall, Upper Saddle River (cop. 2005)
7. IEEE Computer Society: IEEE standard 802.15.4-2006 (2006)
8. Durvy, M., Abeillé, J., Wetterwald, P., O'Flynn, C., Leverett, B., Gnoske, E., Vidales, M., Mulligan, G., Tsiftes, N., Finne, N., Dunkels, A.: Making sensor networks ipv6 ready. In: Proceedings of the Sixth ACM Conference on Networked Embedded Sensor Systems (ACM SenSys 2008), poster session, Raleigh, North Carolina, USA (November 2008)
9. Dunkels, A.: The uIP TCP/IP stack: uIP IPv6 specific features (May 2010),
   http://www.sics.se/~adam/contiki/docs-uipv6/a01110.html/
10. IPv6 Ready Logo Program (2010), http://www.ipv6ready.org/
11. Dunkels, A.: The uIP TCP/IP stack: 6LoWPAN implementation (May 2010),
    http://www.sics.se/~adam/contiki/docs-uipv6/a01109.html/
12. Mahmood, A., Jäntti, R.: Time synchronization accuracy for real-time wireless sensor networks. In: Ninth Malaysia International Conference on Communications, MICC 2009 (December 2009)

Prolonging Network Lifetime Using Ant Colony Optimization Algorithm on LEACH Protocol for Wireless Sensor Networks

Tanushree Agarwal, Dilip Kumar, and Neelam R. Prakash

Punjab Engineering College,
Chandigarh, India
tanushree26@gmail.com,
dilip.k78@gmail.com,
neelamprakash.pec.ac.in

Abstract. This paper presents a fair comparison of Low energy adaptive clustering hierarchy (LEACH) and ant colony applied on LEACH on the basis of the death of first node in the wireless sensor network (WSN) and data transfer. The simulation results show that when the ant colony algorithm is applied on the existing LEACH protocol the results show significant improvement in the network lifetime by delaying the death of first node in the WSN and thus increasing the efficiency of the system.

Keywords: Ant colony optimization, Network efficiency, Network lifetime, Sensor network.

1 Introduction

With advances in technology WSN s are becoming rapidly developing field. WSN consists of a group of sensors which are distributed spatially. They are used to monitor physical or environmental factors such as temperature, pressure or may be pollutants at times. With their growing popularity they are being used for military surveillance [3] as well. Each node is equipped with a small wireless device, a microcontroller and an energy source which can be a small battery even. The technology used may be very application specific but it shares some basic characteristics of every sensor network such as limited power supply, limited transmission range and very data centric. The aspect which needs to be rectified is its limited power supply since it is directly linked with the energy efficiency of the system, which in turn would delay the death of the first node making the system more reliable and prolonging network lifetime.

The main function of WSNs is usually for the user at the base station to collect the information of the environment that sensor nodes are monitoring.

1.1 Data Transmission

Our requirement is to transmit data between the sensor nodes and the end user. The concept of base station acts as a gateway between them. Data can be transmitted in two ways.

N. Meghanathan et al. (Eds.): NeCoM, WiMoN, and WeST 2010, CCIS 90, pp. 634–641, 2010.

1. Single hop
2. Multi hop

1. Single hop: In such kind of transmission every sensor node contacts the base station on its own i.e. there is no contact amongst the nodes which results in a chaotic situation. Consequently the chances of losing data increases as a result systems efficiency decreases as a whole. In this dense networks are a big failure. Even if sensor nodes are few in number time taken is quite large.

Fig. 1. (a) Single hop without clustering

Fig. 2. (a) Single hop with clustering

2. Multi hop:In this transmission type clustering is done. The sensor nodes forms clusters and smaller as compared to single hop. Fig. 1 depicts an application where sensors periodically transmit information to a base station [4]. It also illustrates that clustering can reduce the communication overhead for both single-hop and multi-hop networks. Periodic re-clustering can select nodes with higher residual energy to act as cluster heads.

Heinzelman [7] proposed the Low Energy Adaptive Clustering Hierarchy (LEACH) for WSNs data gathering communication. In this protocol the network is clustered, the cluster heads collects and aggregates the data from their respective clusters and sends this data to the base station. The base station has a fixed location and its distance from the nodes is much larger than the

Fig. 3. (a) Multi hop without clustering

Fig. 4. (a) Multi hop with clustering

inter-nodal distance, this means the energy requirement of the cluster head is much larger. In order that energy depletion of particular node doesnt take place random rotation of cluster head is done. LEACH [1] is an exclusive approach in terms of data gathering, clustering, and cluster head rotation since all nodes are autonomous in terms of decision making capability. No global knowledge is needed for base station location but the problem area lies in random location of cluster heads which may not ensure even clustering and another problem is that some nodes may run out of energy at a faster rate than others affecting the network lifetime and thus the efficiency of the network.

2   Proposed ACO Approach for LEACH

For simplicity and comparison the energy model for this approach is kept same as that for LEACH. Each node can communicate with all other nodes, when not in use these nodes go into idle mode or sleeping mode for energy conservation.

One thing which is common between ants and sensor nodes is the division of work amongst them according to their abilities. We can apply this to our data gathering technique [1]as well. This would save in both the parameters of time and energy. Also we can save more energy by keeping direct correspondence between the base station and the nodes. The information exchange between sensor nodes and the base station include

1. Set up information
2. In case of death of base station node, sending notification to all nodes to reconfigure the new base station.
3. Sending the TDMA schedule o sensor nodes.

Ant Colony Optimization (ACO) is a proven method of swarm intelligence. It is applicable for static and dynamic routing. In this paper we present the application of ACO algorithm on the LEACH protocol. In the ACO based approach, every ant finds a path in the network, to provide minimum cost. Ants start from a source node s and moves through neighbor repeater nodes ri and reach final destination node (sink) d. Whenever, a node transfers data to the destination which is described as a base or base station, launching of the ants is performed. After launching, the choice of the next node r is made according to a probabilistic decision rule (1):

$$P_{k(r,s)} = \frac{[\tau(r,s)^\alpha][n(r,s)]^\beta}{\Sigma_{r\epsilon R_s}[\tau(r,s)^\alpha][n(r,s)]^\beta} \quad \text{if } k\epsilon tabu^r \tag{1}$$

In ACO every arc is marked by a pheromone trail (r,s) ,this value is regularly updated in accordance with the inverse distance (d2) and n(r,s) is the heuristic related to energy, Rs is the receiver node. For node r, tabur is the list of identities of received data packages previously, and are two parameters that control the relative weight of the pheromone trail and heuristic value. Since the destination d is a stable base station, the last node of the path is the same for each ant travel.

$$n_{(r,s)} = \frac{(I - e_r)^{-1}}{\Sigma_{n\epsilon R_s}(I-e_r)^{-1}} \tag{2}$$

In (2) I is the initial energy, and er is the current energy level of receiver node r. This enables decision making according to neighbor nodes energy levels, i.e. if a node has a lower energy source then it has lower probability to be chosen. In equation (1) each receiver node decides whether to accept the upcoming packet of ant k or not, by checking its tabu list. So, the receiver node r has a choice about completing the receiving process by listening and buffering the entire packet. If the receiver node has received the packet earlier, it informs the transmitter node by issuing an ignore message, and switches itself to idle mode until a new packet arrives. After all ants have completed their tour, each ant k deposits a quantity of pheromone k (t) given in equation (3), where Jkw(t) is the length of tour wk (t) , which is done by ant k at iteration t. The amount of pheromone at each connection (l(r, s)) of the nodes is given in equation (4). In WSNs, Jkw represents the total number of nodes visited by ant k of tour w at iteration t:

$$\Delta\tau^k = \frac{1}{J_w^k(t)} \tag{3}$$

After every round, an amount of pheromone trail k (t) is added to the path visited by ant k. This amount is the same for each arc(r, s) visited on this path. This is performed by sending ant k back to its source node from the base along the same path, while it transfers an acknowledgement signal for the same data package. Increasing pheromone amounts on the paths according to lengths of tours, Jw(t), this would continuously cause an increase in the positive feedback. In order to maintain the operation, a negative feedback, the operation of pheromone evaporation after the tour is also accomplished in equation (4). A control coefficient (0,1) is used to determine the weight of evaporation for each tour.

$$\tau(r, s) = (1 - \rho)\tau(r, s) \tag{4}$$

In simulations, ACO parameters are set as =5, =0.5 and p=0.05. These parameters are experimentally found to be good.

3 Algorithm

Input: A set of N sensor nodes randomly deployed in the sensor field and a base station.

Step 1: Initialization
At first m particles are selected at random and are initialized as C1 , C2 , C3 ...Cm. Ci=node[1], node[2]node[N] where node[i]= j; meaning ith (node) member of chain has id j. The probability of becoming cluster head is initialized as p=0.05. Also the values of energy transmission and receiving are preset to a desired and feasible level. Number of iterations are bound to 5000 i.e. rmax=5000. And initially there are no cluster heads but only nodes.

Step 2: Checking if all nodes are alive Initially if all nodes are alive then all flags are cleared.

Step 3: Data transmission
Data is transmitted from nodes to their respective cluster heads and from cluster head to base station. Any node shall be declared dead if its energy level falls below or equal to zero. After each round we would have the number of alive as well as dead nodes. Now once the statistics for nodes is clear cluster head is selected. The probability of a node for becoming a cluster head is based upon its energy and this energy is compared to a preset value if the condition is satisfied then it is elected as a cluster head. And data is then transmitted from nodes to elected cluster head. These cluster heads transfer data to base station

Step 4: New loop formation
This data transmission goes on for rmax rounds and slowly all nodes die and number of alive nodes become zero. And again the loop starts.

4 Related Work

In [4] each node calculates the amount of its own energy level and then sums up the energy level of the remaining network. With the help of this comparison the node decides whether to become the cluster head or not for that round. The nodes with higher energy are more likely to become cluster heads. The drawback of this approach is that it requires extra communication of nodes with base station which in turn needs more energy.

LEACH-C (LEACH centralized)[3] also uses a centralized approach for forming clusters. The non autonomous selection of the cluster head is again the main drawback of this approach. Not only this, LEACH-C needs location information of all the nodes in the network.

P-LEACH (Partitioned LEACH) is another technique which first partitions the network into sectors and then selects the node with highest energy as the head of each sector using centralized calculations. The drawback of this approach is a considerable amount of energy is utilized for partitioning the whole network.

5   Simulation Results

The node with maximum energy and higher probability than the preset value becomes the cluster head. To evaluate the performance of our scheme, simulations were performed on 100 nodes spread over an area of 100m*100 m field. Simulations performed on MATLAB shows that our scheme out does LEACH. The base station is located at (50m, 50m) and initially every node has equal amount of energy.

Fig 5 shows that our scheme out performs leach in case of network lifetime . The 20 percent node dies in leach at 2200 while when the ant colony is applied on leach the time rises to 3300. This is almost 50 percent rise in network life time.

Fig6 depicts that since the network lifetime is prolonged in the former figure its affect can be seen on data transfer efficiency initially it is not prominent but gradually it becomes clear that as nodes start dying in the network ACO on leach proves to be a better option. Fig 6 depicts that since the network lifetime is prolonged in the former figure its affect can be seen on data transfer efficiency

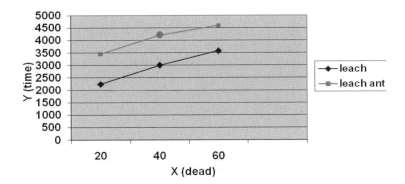

Fig. 5. Percentage of node deaths

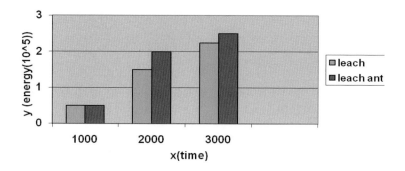

Fig. 6. Data transfer efficiency of leach and ACO on leach

initially it is not prominent but gradually it becomes clear that as nodes start dying in the network ACO on leach proves to be a better option.

6   Conclusion

The protocol studied in this paper ensures energy optimum solution and also prolonged network lifetime. It is validated by the simulations results as well. The ACO-LEACH algorithm proposed enhances the data transfer capacity too. The algorithm simplifies the work of sensor nodes and lowers the communication and computational workload.

References

1. Ding, N., Xia, P.: Data gathering communication in wireless sensor network using ant colony optimization. In: Proceedings of the 2004 IEEE conference on robotics and biometrics (2004)
2. Chakraborthy, A., Chakraborthy, K.: An energy efficient scheme for data gathering in wireless sensor networks using particle swarm optimization. Journal of applied computer science, Suceava 6(3) (2009)
3. Zhang, R., Cao, J.: A novel uneven clustering algorithm based on ant colony optimization for wireless sensor network. In: Second international conference on intelligent computation technology and automation (2009)
4. Handy, M.J., Haase, M.: Low energy adaptive clustering hierarchy with deterministic cluster head selection. In: 13th International CSI Computer Conference, CSICC 2008, Kish Island, Iran, March 9-11 (2008)
5. Seetharam, A., Acharya, A.: An energy efficient data gathering protocol for wireless sensor network. Journal of applied computer science, Suceava 1(2) (2008)
6. Acharya, A., Bhattacharya, A.: Balancing energy dissipation in data gathering wireless sensor networks using ant colony optimization. In: 10th ICDCN (2009)
7. Heinzalman, W.R.: Energy efficient communication protocol for wireless micro sensor protocol. In: Proceedings of IEEE conference Hawaai on system sciences (2000)

8. Chen, Y.: On the lifetime of wireless sensor networks. IEEE Communication letters 9(11), 976–978
9. Kumar, D., Aseri, T.C., Patel, R.B.: Energy efficient cluster head election protocol. In:International conference on advance in computing, communication and control, 75–80 (2009)
10. Kumar, D., Aseri, T.C., Patel, R.B.: Energy efficient hetrogeneous cluster head scheme for wireless sensor networks. Elsevier computer communication 32(4), 662–664 (2009)

Energy Efficient Mobile Wireless Sensor Network Routing Protocol

Getsy S. Sara, R. Kalaiarasi, S. Neelavathy Pari, and D. Sridharan

Department of Electronics & Communication Engineering, College of Engineering,
Anna University Chennai, India, 600 025
{getsysudhir,rajendranarasi}@gmail.com,
neela_pari@yahoo.com, sridhar@annauniv.edu

Abstract. Mobility in tandem with energy efficiency in wireless sensor network endows with significant challenges for routing. Sensor nodes have limited energy supply and minimizing the power consumption is crucial in Mobile Wireless Sensor Network (MWSN). This paper proposes a novel hybrid multipath energy aware routing protocol for MWSN called Energy Efficient Mobile Wireless Sensor Network Routing Protocol (E^2MWSNRP). The Energy Aware (EA) selection mechanism and the Maximal Nodal Surplus Energy estimation technique employed in this algorithm improve its energy performance. The 'readiness' concept of EA selection prolongs the network lifetime. The hybrid routing concept applied in this algorithm presents the advantages of both the reactive and proactive routing. An evaluation methodology and simulation environment to verify the operation of this algorithm is presented here. Simulation results can demonstrate that the proposed scheme can outperform the existing routing protocols in terms of energy efficiency, network lifetime and packet delivery ratio.

Keywords: Mobile Wireless Sensor network, Energy Efficiency, Surplus Energy, Network Lifetime.

1 Introduction

Mobile Wireless Sensor Network is composed of spatially distributed autonomous sensors which form the wireless ad hoc system to cooperatively monitor physical or environmental conditions, such as temperature, sound, vibration, pressure, motion or pollutants [1]. These nodes collaboratively achieve complex information gathering and dissemination. They find applications in scenarios where multiple users equipped with mobile phones move through a sensor field and interact with a WSN by querying information of interest [2] or in wildlife applications where sensors are cast in field as well as equipped on animals to be monitored [3] or in telemedicine applications where the sensors are attached to patients who move around [3] etc. MWSN are highly dynamic and the network topology may frequently change due to node mobility or link faults. Owing to these factors, various nodes will deplete their energy supplies and drop out of the network. Replacement of power resources might be impossible due to the hostile environment where they are placed. Lifetime of sensor nodes mainly depend on the energy supply. Some nodes might be very critical for forwarding the data

N. Meghanathan et al. (Eds.): NeCoM, WiMoN, and WeST 2010, CCIS 90, pp. 642–650, 2010.

packets as they alone can provide paths between certain pair of nodes and if these nodes deplete their energy and stop operating, then the whole network becomes partitioned [4]. Due to these reasons a number of researchers have focused on design of energy efficient routing protocols.

This paper is distributed as follows – Section 2 gives an idea on prior works done in this area. Section 3 gives details about Energy Efficient Mobile Wireless Sensor Network Routing Protocol (E^{2}MWSNRP). The simulation of the proposed routing protocol is given in Section 4. Finally, Section 5 summarizes this paper.

2   Related Work

Power consumption and frequent route changes are the main challenges to be endured in the design of a Mobile Wireless Sensor Network. Several researchers have focused to provide very energy efficient routing protocols for Static Sensor Network. Few of the works are oriented towards achieving energy efficiency in Mobile Wireless Sensor Network. Kisuk kweon *et al* has proposed the Grid Based Energy Efficient Routing (GBEER) [5] for communication from multiple sources to multiple mobile sinks in wireless sensor network. With the global location information a permanent grid structure is built. Data requests are routed to the source along the grid and data is sent back to the sinks. The grid quorum solution is adopted to effectively advertise and request the data for mobile sinks. The communication overhead caused by sink's mobility is limited to the grid cell. There is no additional energy consumption due to multiple events because only one grid structure is built independently of the event. Zhi-Feng Duan *et al* designed a three layer mobile node architecture [6] to organize all sensors in MWSN. Here the Shortest Path (SP) routing protocol is used to adapt sensors to update the network topology. SP provides an elegant solution to node movement in multilayer MWSN and reduces energy dissipation. In [7], Xiaoxia Huang proposed a robust cooperative routing protocol based on cross layer design with MAC layer as the anchor, operated under IEEE 802.11 MAC protocol. Robustness against path breakage is improved here thereby improving the energy efficiency of the network.

Routing protocols supporting mobility can be categorized into table driven (proactive), on demand (reactive) and hybrid protocols. The hybrid protocols incorporate the advantages of both proactive and reactive routing. The Zone Routing Protocol (ZRP) is a well known example of hybrid routing. The network is divided into different zones. Within each zone, up to date routing table is maintained by proactive component. Routes outside the zone are discovered with reactive component using route request and reply. ZRP reduces the traffic amount compared to pure proactive or reactive routing [8]. The authors in [4] have suggested Energy Efficient Ad hoc On Demand Multipath Distance Vector (E^{2}AOMDV) routing, which is an innovative multipath energy aware routing protocol for adhoc network. It includes the energy aware selection mechanism and maximal nodal surplus energy estimation in the Ad hoc On Demand Multipath Distance Vector (AOMDV) routing protocol to improve energy efficiency. The AOMDV protocol [9] applies a route update rule to establish and maintain multiple loop free routes at each node. A distributed protocol is used to find link disjoint paths. In AOMDV, different instances of RREQs are not discarded by intermediate nodes. If a new RREQ instance preserves the loop free condition and comes from a different last hop node, then a new reverse route towards the source node is logged in the intermediate node. If the intermediate node knows one or more valid forward routes to the destination, a RREP packet is produced and forwarded back to the source along the reverse path. When the destination receives more RREQ instances, in order to get multiple link disjoint routes, it replies with multiple RREP messages.

3 Energy Efficient Mobile Wireless Sensor Network Routing Protocol

It is a multipath hybrid routing protocol that can be designed mainly for highly dynamic energy deficient mobile wireless sensor network where energy dissipation reduction and reliable transmission of data is a must. Despite the real shape of the sensor field, the entire area is assumed to be circumscribed into a big square as shown in figure 1 and then divided into different square zones [10] after the sensor nodes are deployed in the field. Routing inside the zone is called IntrA Precinct Routing (IAPR). The routing done outside a zone is called IntEr Precinct Routing (IEPR).

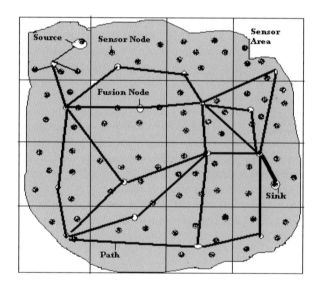

Fig. 1. Formation of precincts in MWSN

3.1 Calculation of Surplus Energy

A sensor node consumes energy when it is sensing, generating data, receiving, transmitting or in standby mode. Let e_g be the power used for sensing and generating one bit of data and e_s be the standby power of each node. The e_g and e_s value is assumed to be same for all the nodes. A node needs $E_{elec} = 50$ nJ to run the circuitry and $E_{amp} = 100$ pJ/bit/m2 for transmitting amplifier [11].

Power consumed for receiving one bit of data,

$$e_r = E_{elec} .$$ (1)

Power consumed for transmitting one bit of data to a neighboring node j [11] is given by

$$e_{ij} = E_{elec} + E_{amp} .d_{ij}^{\alpha} .$$ (2)

where

α - path loss component

d_{ij}^{α} – Euclidean distance of node i and node j respectively.

Assuming each node i has initial battery energy E_i, the uniformed mean power consumption [11] of node i is calculated as

$$w_i = [e_s + e_g . r_i + e_r. r_j + r_i. e_{ij}] .$$ (3)

where

r_i & r_j – traffic generating rate at node i and node j respectively.

Surplus energy (E_s) is calculated as

$$E_s = E_i - w_i .$$ (4)

3.2   Formation of Fusion Node

Every sensor node broadcasts its surplus energy which is considered as its budget. The virtual ID (VID) [12] is created for each sensor node as

VID = Surplus energy / Number of nodes in the precinct .   (5)

The threshold budget value is assumed to be 0.5 J. The node with the highest VID value is chosen as the fusion node. The fusion node acts as the precinct head. During communication a fusion node may exhaust its surplus energy, E_s. The surplus energy value of fusion node is always checked periodically with the threshold budget value. If E_s value is less than the threshold budget value, then the fusion node sets its VID as 0 and transfers its contents to the next fusion node. A non fusion node with the largest VID value is chosen as the next fusion node [12].

3.3   Data Announcement

When a sensor node detects an event, it becomes the source node. The source node generates the Data Announcement packet (DA packet). DA packet consists of node ID and data generation time. Many of the sensor nodes in a precinct may detect the event simultaneously and send the DA packet to the fusion node. The fusion node has to aggregate and compress these packets using data fusion algorithm [5]. Every source node sends the DA packet to the fusion node using IntrA Precinct routing.

IntrA Precinct routing. Every node in a precinct is assumed to be within the communication range of every other node in the precinct. So every sensor node can communicate with the fusion node using single hop communication. When an event is detected, the sensor node first communicates with the fusion node. The fusion node checks if the destination is within its precinct. If so, proactively the event is send to the destination

3.4   Data Forwarding

To forward the data to other precincts, the IntEr Precinct Routing is employed.

IntEr Precinct routing. It is a multipath reactive routing technique employed for communication among the fusion nodes. When a single path on demand routing protocol is used in such networks, a route rediscovery is needed in response to every route break [4]. Each route discovery is associated with high overhead and latency. This inefficiency can be avoided using multipath routing protocol. Maintaining a routing table for multipath makes the fusion node to exhaust its surplus energy faster. This can be avoided by selecting few best paths from the available multipath and routing data through them. The $E^2MWSNRP$ enables the selection of best paths from the computation of maximal nodal surplus energy [4]. The RREQ message contains the following fields:

< Source address, source precinct id, sequence no., broadcast id, hop count, destination address, maximum surplus energy>

The broadcast id is incremented whenever the source issues a new RREQ. The sequence number denotes the freshness information about a route. As the RREQ travels from a source to various destinations, it automatically sets up the reverse path from all nodes to the source. These reverse path entries are maintained for at least enough time for the RREQ to traverse the network and produce a reply to the sender. If an intermediate fusion node has a current route to the destination and if the RREQ has not been processed previously, the node then unicasts a Route Reply Packet (RREP) back to its neighbor from which it received the RREQ [13]. The RREP message contains the subsequent fields:

<Source address, destination address, destination precinct id, sequence number, hop count, readiness factor, maximum surplus energy, lifetime>.

If the readiness factor denotes 'Discard', a route error (RERR) message is propagated in the reverse path instead of RREP [4].

Four important steps are involved:

1. Energy Aware Selection Mechanism
2. Finding maximal nodal surplus energy along the best paths
3. Sorting the multipath in descending order using the nodal surplus energy
4. Forwarding the data packets through the path with maximal nodal surplus energy.

Energy aware selection mechanism. It is a mechanism to involve energetic considerations in best path selection [4]. The $E^2MWSNRP$ specification has a variable 'readiness' representing the availability of that node to act as an intermediate node. Each fusion node calculates its own energetic status and declares an appropriate readiness. The readiness selection is based on battery capacity and predicted lifetime of a node [15]. The heuristic used to associate a readiness ('Discard', 'Moderate', 'High') to a pair(battery capacity, lifetime) is shown in table 1. This mechanism permits better load balancing to be obtained.

Table 1. Energy Based Readiness Selection

Lifetime -> Battery	Short [<10ms]	Medium [10ms<lifetime<100ms]	Long [>100ms]
Low [<1J]	EA-Discard	EA-Discard	EA-Discard
High [>1J]	EA-Discard	EA-Accept moderate	EA-Accept high

It is assumed that if the surplus energy is less than 1J then it denotes low battery value. The life time of a node is calculated using drain rate value. The drain rate value (DR_i) of a node i is calculated by averaging the amount of energy consumption by that node and estimating energy dissipation per second during the given past interval. If the lifetime of a node is less than 10 seconds then it has a short lifetime and if life time is greater than 100 seconds then the node has a long life time.

Finding the Maximal Nodal Surplus Energy. When the intermediate fusion node receives a RREQ message, it checks if the sequence number specified in the RREQ message is greater than the node's sequence number. If so, it compares the surplus energy in the RREQ message and the surplus energy of the node. In case the node's surplus energy is greater than that specified in the RREQ message, the surplus energy variable in the RREQ message is updated with the nodal surplus energy. By this method it is possible to achieve the value of maximum surplus energy among all fusion nodes in the specified path. The reverse paths are set up as the RREQ travels from a source to various destinations.

Sorting Multipath and Forwarding Data Packets. The paths in the route list are sorted by the descending value of surplus energy. The path with the maximum surplus energy is chosen to forward the data packets. Once the source node receives the RREP message containing the new path with maximum surplus energy, it forwards the data packets through this path.

The structure of the routing table at each node is shown in the figure 2.The advertised hop count of a node i for a destination represent the maximum hop count of the multiple paths for destination available at i. If the maximum hop count is considered, then the advertised hop count can never change for the same sequence number. The protocol only allows accepting alternate routes with lower hop count. This invariance is necessary to guarantee loop freedom [9].

Destination
Sequence Number
Advertised-hop count
Route list { next hop1, hopcount1, readiness( ) , max-surplus energy1 } { next hop3, hopcount2, readiness( ) , max-surplus energy2 } . . { next hop n, hop count n, readiness n ( ) , max-surplus energy n}
Expiration time

Fig. 2. Structure of routing table entries at the fusion node for E^2MWSNRP

3.4   Pseudo Code to Implement IntEr Precinct Routing in E^{2}MWSNRP

```
S=0
n=i; for i=1to d
if n !=0
  Battery capacity=actual energy/initial energy;
  Lifetime=infinity;
   if (drain rate( )!=0)
     Lifetime=actual energy/ drain rate ( );
      if lifetime<10s or battery capacity<1joule then
         Readiness ( )= 'EA-Discard';
         else if 10s<lifetime<100s and  battery    capacity>1joule
      then
         Readiness ( )= 'EA-Accept Moderate';
     else if lifetime>100s or battery capacity>1joule then
     Readiness ( )= 'EA-Accept High';
     endif;
  endif;
endif;
for i=n; j=n+1;
        if readiness (i) and readiness(j)=  'EA-Accept Moderate'
     or 'EA-Accept High' then
      if (sequence number_i^d< sequence number_j^d) then
      sequence number_i^d<=sequence number_j^d;
         if (i!=d) then
         if(surplus energy_i > max-surplus energy_j^d) then
            max-surplus energy_j^d = surplus energy_i
            advertised -hopcount_i^d     = ∞;
            route-list_i^d = NULL;
            insert(j, advertised -hopcount_j^d + 1,
            max-s urplus energy_j^d) into route-list_i^d;
            else
            advertised -hopcount_i^d     = 0;
         endif;
        else  if  (sequence   number_i^d  =   sequence   number_j^d)
     and((advertised -hopcount_i^d, i) > (advertised -hopcount_j^d
     ,j)) then
      if(surplus energy_i > max-surplus energy_j^d) then
      max-surplus energy_j^d = surplus energy_i ;
         insert(j,  advertised  -hopcount_j^d  +  1,  max-surplus
      energy_j^d) into route-list_i^d;
      end if;
   endif;
endif;.
```

4   Simulation Environment and Evaluation Methodology

To implement the routing protocol, E^{2}MWSNRP the OMNET++ simulator is used
[14]. A dense sensor network of 100 nodes is being simulated in a field with 25*25
m^2 area. Each simulation last for 500 seconds. The random waypoint mobility model
with a pause time of 30 seconds is used to simulate node movement. The mobile sensor node speed is set to be between 5m/sec and 20m/sec. For radio power consumption setting, E_{elec} = 50 nJ/bit, E_{amp} = 100 pJ/bit/m2 and a path loss exponent α =2 is set
[11]. Each sensor node is assumed to have an initial energy of 5J. The transmitting

power and the receiving power of each sensor node are presumed to be 0.66W and 0.395W respectively [11]. The e_g and e_s value is taken as 50 mW and 28.36 mW respectively and the radio range of a sensor node is 250m. The data is generated at a rate of 1Kbps. The distributed coordination function (DCF) of IEEE 802.11 is used as MAC layer. Each control packet is 36 bytes long and data packet is 64 bytes long.

To evaluate the performance of E^{2}MWSNRP, three key performance metrics are assessed; total energy consumption, packet delivery fraction and network lifetime. Packet delivery fraction is defined as the ratio of data packets delivered to the destination to those generated by the source. The network lifetime is defined as the duration from the beginning of the simulation to the first time a node runs out of energy [4].

To show how EA Selection Mechanism improves the performance of a MWSN, the expiration time of connections [15] is plotted as shown in figure 3.

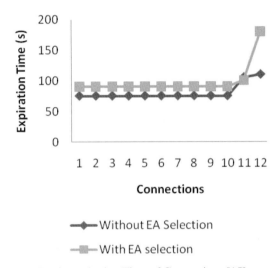

Fig. 3. Expiration Time of Connections [15]

The proposed E^{2}MWSNRP is expected to guarantee a longer network lifetime and better packet delivery ratio with less energy consumption. This is owing to the fact that this routing protocol uses hybrid routing which reduces the wastage of bandwidth and control overhead as compared to the reactive schemes [8]. It also does not stress sensor nodes with less residual energy thereby preventing the critical nodes from depleting their energy earlier and avoids route rediscovery for every route break [4]. It reduces the control traffic produced by the periodic flooding of routing information packets as seen in proactive routing [8].

5   Conclusion

This paper presents a multipath routing protocol that minimizes the energy usage for routing by mobile wireless sensor nodes. E^{2}MWSNRP is based on the AOMDV routing protocol and the Hybrid routing protocol. The key idea of this routing protocol is that it applies the hybrid routing concept. It uses the energy aware selection mechanism to choose the fusion nodes to route the data to the destination node. Distribution of energy among nodes in the sensor network is achieved by the fusion nodes and is effectual in reducing energy dissipation from global point of view. The route list consists of multipath with maximal nodal residual energy. In case of link failure and route breaks, new route discovery can be avoided. The critical nodes with less energy are not strained. All these factors of $E^2MWSNRP$ can lead to significant improvement of network lifetime and effectively reduce the energy consumption.

References

1. Wireless Sensor Network,
   http://en.wikipedia.org/wiki/Wireless_sensor_network
2. Munari, A., Schott, W., Krishnan, S.: Energy Efficient Routing in Mobile Wireless Sensor Networks using Mobility Prediction. In: 34th IEEE conference in Local Computer Networks, Zurich, Switzerland, pp. 514–521 (2009)
3. Huang, X., Zhai, H., Fang, Y.: Lightweight Robust Routing in Mobile Wireless Sensor Network. In: IEEE Military Communications Conference (MILCOM 2006), Washington DC (2006)
4. Sara, G.S., Neelavathi Pari, S., Sridharan, D.: Energy Efficient Ad hoc On Demand Multipath Distance Vector Routing Protocol. International Journal of Recent Trends in Engineering 2(3), 10–12 (2009)
5. Kweon, K., Ghim, H., Hong, J., Yoon, H.: Grid-Based Energy-Efficient Routing from Multiple Sources to Multiple Mobile Sinks in Wireless Sensor Networks. In: 4th International Conference on Wireless Pervasive Computing, Melbourne, Australia, pp. 185–189 (2009)
6. Duan, Z.-f., FanGuo, Deng, M.-x., Yu, M.: Shortest Path Routing Protocol for Multi-layer Mobile Wireless Sensor Networks. In: International Conference on Network Security, Wireless Communication and Trusted Computing, pp. 106–110 (2009)
7. Huang, X., Zhai, H., Fang, Y.: Robust Cooperative Routing Protocol in Mobile Wireless Sensor Networks. IEEE Transactions on Wireless Communication 7(12), 5278–5285 (2008)
8. Beijar, N.: Zone Routing Protocol (ZRP), Nrtworking Laboratory, Helsinki University of Technology, Finland, Nicklas, Beijar@hut.fi
9. Marina, M.K., Das, S.R.: On –demand Multipath Distance Vector Routing in Ad hoc Networks. ACM SIGMOBILE Mobile Computing and Communications Review 6(3), 92–93 (2002)
10. Liliana, M., Arboleda, C., Nasser, N.: Cluster- based Routing Protocol for Mobile Sensor Networks. In: 3rd International Conference on Quality of Service in Heterogeneous Wired/ Wireless Networks, Waterloo, Canada (2006)
11. Hua, C., Peter Yum, T.-S.: Optimal Routing and Data Aggregation for Maximizing lifetime of Wireless Sensor Networks. IEEE/ACM Transactions on Networking 16(4), 892–902 (2008)
12. Agarwal, R., Motwani, M.: Survey of Clustering Algorithm for MANET. International Journal on Computer Science and Engineering 12, 98–104 (2009)
13. Perkins, C.E., Royer, E.M.: Ad-hoc on Demand Distance Vector Routing. In: Mobile Computing Systems and Applications (WMCSA), pp. 90–100 (1999)
14. OMNET++ Simulator, http://www.omnetpp.org
15. De Rango, F., Folina, M., Marano, S.: EE-OLSR: Energy Efficient OLSR routing protocol for mobile ad- hoc network. In: IEEE- International Conference on Military Communications (MILCOM 2008), pp. 1–7 (2008)

Dynamic Service Discovery as an Optimization Problem in Wireless Sensor Networks

Kaushik Lahiri[1], Amitava Mukherjee[1], Ayon Chakraborty[2], Subhajit Mandal[2], Dipankar Patra[2], and Mrinal K. Nashkar[3]

[1] IBM India Pvt. Ltd., Kolkata-700091, India
[2] Dept. of CSE, Jadavpur University, Kolkata-700032, India
[3] Dept. of ETCE, Jadavpur University, Kolkata-700032, India
{lkaushik,amitava.mukherjee}@in.ibm.com,
{jucse.ayon,msubhajitju,deepankarbcse}@gmail.com,
mrinalnaskar@yahoo.co.in

Abstract. In a ubiquitous environment, e.g. smart home, a user is surrounded by a network of sensor nodes all around and also on his body or clothing. We modeled such a sensor network as a services network where the nodes exchange services for collaborating and smart decision taking. As the user moves around performing activities, the surrounding network also changes as wireless inter-node connections are made or broken. The challenge is to re-discover the network quickly and transparently to the user.

We used a two-step approach. First, Proximal Neighborhood Discovery identified nodes that formed the network. Second, Optimal Service Discovery determined, for each such network node, who were the best service provider nodes from the same network. We modeled this as an optimization problem and solved using a new and efficient algorithm.

We implemented the algorithm using nesC and simulated using TOSSIM interference-model. The results showed appreciable improvements over conventional approaches.

Keywords: Ubiquitous environment, sensor network, smart home, Service Discovery, nesC, TOSSIM.

1 Introduction

A Wireless Sensor Networks (WSN) consists of spatially distributed collections of small, smart and cheap, sensing and computing devices. In a traditional wireless sensor network, sensors are deployed in a specific geographical location and are required to send data to a sink. Some typical applications are habitat monitoring and military reconnaissance. Since these carry out simple tasks of remote sensing, they do not need a specific service discovery model, as routing data to the sink itself is sufficient to provide the required "service".

With the emergence of pervasive computing, users have gradually become surrounded by a variety of smart wireless computing devices. The ultimate goal is to realize a true ubiquitous computing paradigm where such devices weave themselves

N. Meghanathan et al. (Eds.): NeCoM, WiMoN, and WeST 2010, CCIS 90, pp. 651–662, 2010.

into the fabric of our everyday life by providing various different services and become invisible, as revealed by Weiser [1]. In order to realize this, we need many sensors, non-sensor smart devices and human beings moving and collaborating with each other. Together they perform multiple tasks like interfacing, querying, routing, and data acquisition.

An example is a medical application. Here, for detecting a patient's movement patterns, multiple sensors collaborate and exchange measurements perceived by light sensors and send this data to a processor sensor. This processor also receives signals from heartbeat and blood pressure monitoring devices implanted into the patient's body. It combines and digitally processes all the signals received over a period of time and sends this to the nearest available analyzer sensor. The analyzer sensor takes help from a rule server sensor to quickly find patterns in the combined data that provide vital clues to the patent's health. It then routes only the analyzed summary data to a transmitter which further compresses it and securely sends it over the internet to a medical hub. The hub takes immediate action if necessary (e.g. notifying a doctor or ambulance) or simply stores the data in the patient's medical history for future analysis and action.

In the scenario just described, some sensors and devices are worn by the patient on his or her body and others are scattered around the patient's neighborhood (e.g. in the rooms of her home). There are two implications of this – 1) the relative positional coordinates of the sensors keep changing as the patient moves. 2) The set of collaborating sensors changes, as the most convenient and nearby sensors are used for quick analysis and transmission of data.

We can look upon the sensors as each providing some services of its own (service provider) and using some services provided by others (service consumer). From the point of view of a single sensor, it operates within a service neighborhood where it has to constantly collaborate with the neighbors to send service packets (where it is the service provider) and receive service packets (where it is consumer). Because of the implications described before, the neighbors keep changing their positions and their identities also change. Whenever such changes occur, each sensor has to rediscover the set of neighbors with whom it can collaborate most effectively (considering distance and packet loss) and who can also provide the set of services it requires. These changes can happen very frequently, e.g. as the patient moves about. As a result, we need extremely efficient and dynamic service discovery protocols.

Service discovery protocols for wireless networks [8] have been a sizzling subject for researchers over the past few years. These should allow devices to automatically detect useful services offered by other devices on a network along with their service attributes which help in determining their appropriateness in a given context. It also allows devices to advertise their own capabilities to the rest of the network. A few well known service discovery protocols are SLP, Sun Micro system's Jini and Microsoft's UPnP (Universal Plug and Play). However these protocols are not suited for ubiquitous environments which are dynamic, distributed and have energy constrained sensors. For such environments, highly efficient service discovery protocols are required which can adapt to the changing network topology. Such protocols should be able to quickly discover service providers in a dynamically changing network and also, more importantly, discover those providers which can provide the required services most efficiently, which is critical in a ubiquitous environment consisting of small sensor devices.

In this paper, we present a two level hierarchical approach for efficient service discovery. First, there is Proximal Neighborhood Discovery (PND) which a prerequisite for service discovery followed by the Optimal Service Discovery (OSD). Our algorithm is a based on modern heuristic techniques like Particle Swarm Optimization [2][3] and Simulated Annealing [4]. This algorithm finds out an optimal set of service providers from a potential set of sensors identified earlier by PND. It uses optimization parameters such as the distance of the provider and whether it is able to provide the required services. The main criteria used for choosing the parameters are 1) minimizing the use of communication power (e.g. by minimizing number of packet exchanges required) and 2) maximizing the packet reception probability (e.g. by using providers which have the best communication links with the consumer). Our results show appreciable improvements over conventional approaches, not only in terms of energy efficiency, but also minimizing packet loss.

We implemented our proposed algorithm using the nesC [5] programming language running on the TinyOS [6] software platform. Simulations were conducted using the TOSSIM [7] environment. The implementation of OSD in nesC not only shows the coding feasibility of the scheme, but also verifies that it can be run on real motes like MicaZ or Mica2. An interference model provided by the TOSSIM environment to simulate the unreliable wireless links is used for studying the successful packet delivery rates which made our simulation much more realistic.

The rest of the paper is organized as follows: Sections 2 introduces the rationale behind choosing the neighborhood and Service Discovery algorithms; Sections 3 and 4 elaborate on the working of the algorithms themselves; Section 5 discusses the implementation and compares the results obtained using our algorithm and other existing algorithms. We conclude in Section 6.

2   The Rationale for Neighborhood and Service Discovery

As described in the introductory example, the network of sensors surrounding a particular sensor can change their positions quite frequently, e.g. as the patient embedded with a sensor enters or leaves a room. Whenever this happens, each sensor must quickly discover the new set of sensors surrounding it, i.e., its new neighbors. Discovering neighboring nodes (referred to as neighborhood discovery from now on) is a critical requirement for effective inter-node collaboration - inter-communication, routing and cluster formation.

Neighborhood discovery determines if direct single-hop radio communication is possible between two nodes. If the inter-node distance between the communicating nodes is greater than a certain threshold, then there is very high probability of packet loss due to larger interference and weaker signal strength. Although this situation can be partially improved by sending redundant packets or applying higher signal strength, these would drain out the resources (e.g. battery power) of the already energy-constrained sensor. Therefore it is critical to identify the right set of "neighbor" nodes (nodes with which a particular node can directly communicate by sending packets) with whom the best communication links can be established. This set of nodes can be termed as the "neighborhood" of the particular node.

Once each sensor has discovered its neighborhood, the network of sensors needs to collaborate and intercommunicate to achieve a set of objectives. When collaborating, each node acts as 1) a service provider by implementing a set of services itself and also 2) a service consumer where it depends on its neighbor nodes from whom it obtains a set of required services. In order to do this in the best possible manner, it is required that each service consumer node identifies the "optimal set of service providers" that can provide their required services. This optimal set can depend on several factors like the quality of connection with the providers, the number of bundled services that can be obtained from the same provider and the similarity of the service desired to the service provided. Considering all these factors and coming up with an optimal set of providers is the purpose of Optimal Service Discovery. Note that this optimal set should be arrived at in the fastest possible time. In fact, if there is a trade-off between the time taken for coming up with the solution and the quality of the solution itself, a higher priority should be given to a timely solution.

3   Proximal Neighborhood Discovery Algorithm

Proximal neighborhood discovery is the process by which a particular sensor discovers its neighboring nodes with which it has the best connectivity. The idea behind the discovery algorithm is simple.

Initialization: The foreign node n_0 (which enters into the network) broadcasts neighborhood request beacons periodically for $t_{MAX\_BEACONS}$ times. These beacon messages consist of the id of the transmitting node n_0. The idea behind multiple broadcasts is to account for unpredictable packet loss.

Acknowledgement: Whenever any node n_i receives a broadcast beacon from n_0, it replies back with an acknowledgement message containing its own id. Once n_0 receives back acknowledgement from n_i, it compares the received signal strength indication (RSSI) [13], S_i of the received acknowledgement message with a threshold value $S_{RSSI\_Threshold}$.

Selection: If $S_i > S_{RSSI\_Threshold}$, it selects n_i as a neighbor and adds it to the proximal neighborhood table t_{pn}. The threshold value of the signal strength is determined by factors such as the transmitting power of the node, the type of application and the physical environment in the network.

The discovery process is started immediately when the node enters a new network. Thereafter, for a particular node, inter-node communication is restricted to only those nodes that are in its proximal neighborhood table. As time passes, some nodes may leave the network or may drain out, or they might go out of range, also new nodes may join the network. Given the dynamical nature of the sensor networks and their topologies, nodes need to update themselves frequently about their neighbors by refreshing their local proximal neighborhood tables.

4 Optimal Service Provider Discovery Algorithm

As a pre-requisite for service discovery, a node first needs to know about its neighbors as described in Section 3. As a first step in service discovery, it needs to identify those neighbors that are capable for providing it with the services it needs. In a service-rich environment, more than one neighbor can provide each of the services that it needs. So the outcome of the first step can potentially be a large set of nodes. Therefore, as a second step in discovery, it needs to intelligently choose only those few service providers that are 1) necessary and sufficient for it to get all its required services and 2) able to provide the services most efficiently. Efficient service providers are chosen based on:

Distance of the provider: For service providers which are nearer, the quality of the link is also better, so there is a lesser chance of packets being lost.

The number of services provided by a single node: If the same provider can provide multiple services, then it is better, as there is a possibility for bundling of services, e.g. multiple types of information can be bundled on the same packet, thus reducing the number of packets that need to be exchanged.

"Appropriateness" of the services: Appropriateness of a service depends on how closely the consumer's requested service matches the provider's provided service. This is required as very often the services are similar but do not match exactly.

This can be looked upon as an optimization problem where, out of a set of available providers, the most efficient subset of providers must be identified.

The total set of neighbors have been already discovered (as in Section 3) and stored in the proximal neighborhood table t_{pn} as mentioned earlier. The initiator node n_0 starts by sending a service discovery beacon to each neighboring node n_i in table t_{pn}. These beacon messages consist of the id of the transmitting node n_0 and the set of services $S = \{S_{01} \ldots S_{0n}\}$ required by it. One a neighboring node gets this beacon, it checks if it can provide any of the services and replies by sending an acknowledgement message. After the initiator has waited for a sufficient period of time by which it was expecting to receive all acknowledgement messages, it prepares the Service Discovery Table.

As an input to the optimization problem, we have the Service Discovery Table, which is a relation from the set of services (S) to the set of service providers (SP). This is the set of all capable providers from which we need to identify the optimal subset of most efficient providers.

4.1 OSD Algorithm Based on Particle Swarm Optimization

Problem Formulation: If the total number of required services is n, the solution space U can be said to be a collection of "arrangements" C, each of the form $\{SP_1, SP_2, .., SP_n\}$, where SP_i denotes the service provider selected for providing the ith service in the particular arrangement. Let Q_i be the set of "all" providers capable of providing the ith service. Thus, $\bigcup_{i=1}^{n} Q_i = SP$ which is nothing but the total set of service providers and $U = \{(SP_1, SP_2, .., SP_n) \mid SP_i \in SP$ for each $i\}$. Our problem is to find the optimal arrangement C from our solution space U, i.e., the optimal way to assign service providers for each of n services that are desired by a service consumer sensor.

In order to solve this optimization problem, we start based on the idea of Particle Swarm Optimization (PSO) [2] and then apply to it the principle of Simulated Annealing (SA) [10], in order to arrive at an optimal solution in a short time. Using this idea, an arrangement C_i denotes the ith *particle* in an n-dimensional system where each dimension represents a particular service. One restriction is that the *velocity* of a particle (the number of values it can have, i.e. the number of service providers that can be assigned) along a particular dimension (service) is finite and restricted to a set of possible values, that is, the ith dimension of the particle has a domain restricted to set Q_i. We call the set Q_i the *velocity space* along a particular dimension i. If the velocity restriction is not adhered to, the arrangement would not be valid.

Formulation of the Energy Function: While formulating the energy function or cost function, we used two important thumb rules. First, the service consumer sensor should obtain as many services as it can get from a single provider, i.e., look for bundled services. This would make it possible for the single provider to combine more than one service (e.g. information on a patient) on the same packet, thereby reducing the overall number of data packets that need to be sent. Second, the service providing nodes should be as closer as possible. This is important because the signal strength between communicating nodes decreases quickly with the distance apart which means that either more energy or greater number of packets are needed to successfully send data.

Mathematically, the first goal is to minimize the 'average distance of a service' for a particular service provider node and the second goal is to minimize the sum of the service distances for all the service providers. With this goal, we formulate the energy function required for simulated annealing. For a particular arrangement C_i the energy function f(i) can be stated as,

$$\text{f(i)} = \sum_{i=1}^{\eta(sp)} d(i) / \gamma(i) \tag{1}$$

Where d(i) is the distance of the service provider with id number i, and $\gamma(i)$ is the number of services (bundled service) provided by that particular provider.

Note that a nearer service provider implies a smaller d(i) and a bundled service implies a larger $\gamma(i)$. As the ratio of d(i) and $\gamma(i)$ decreases, the arrangement C_i of service providers becomes more and more favorable. This is what we wanted to achieve in the first place. So equation (1) is a suitably formulated energy function.

As discussed before, any arrangement C_i can be looked upon as a particle in an n-dimensional space. When a particle updates its position from C_{old} to C_{new}, the energy gained is given by: $\Delta f = f(C_{new}) - f(C_{old})$. This is same as ΔE, *the energy difference* between the two states, which is an important parameter in SA.

Iterative approach to the solution based on SA: We start from an initial solution, which can be any valid arrangement and calculate its energy value. At the next step and then each subsequent step, we change the current solution to another valid solution and recalculate the energy value. We accept or reject the new solution based on a probability determined by the following *probability function* P:

$$P = 1 \qquad\qquad \text{if} \quad \Delta E \leq 0$$

$$= e^{\left(\frac{-\Delta f}{\theta}\right)} \qquad\qquad \text{if} \quad \Delta E > 0 \qquad\qquad (2)$$

Here, Θ is a variable control parameter, called the *annealing temperature*, which is initially at a high value, but gradually decreases based on a *cooling schedule*, described in section IV.

If ΔE is negative (or zero), implying lower (or same) energy value of the new solution, it is always accepted, as P=1.

If ΔE is positive and P > random (0, 1), i.e., P is greater than a random number between 0 and 1, the new solution is accepted else it is rejected.

This second decision is of utmost importance, as we accept even higher energy value solutions with a certain probability, depending on the annealing temperature Θ. This ensures that our algorithm is not stuck at a local minimal value, which implies a sub-optimal solution. We proceed in this way, iteratively towards our ultimate solution till the annealing temperature has cooled down to its desired final value.

Cooling Schedule: An important control parameter in equation (2) is Θ, called the *annealing temperature*; a parameter which is decremented, every time the system of particles approaches a better solution (or a low energy state). If Θ_i be the *initial temperature* and Θ_f be the *final temperature*, and t is the cooling time, then the designed *cooling schedule* is given by: $\Theta(t) = \Theta_f + (\Theta_i - \Theta_f)*\alpha^t$. Here α is the rate of cooling, usually $(0.7 \leq \alpha < 1.0)$ and t is the cooling time which in our case is the number of iterations.   While the SA algorithm incorporates the concept of probability through the Metropolis acceptance rule [10], it can be slow. So in our proposed algorithm, we also utilize the fast optimal search capability of PSO.

Proposed algorithm based on PSO: Input: A set of N services and the set of Service providers pertaining to each instance of a service.

Step 1: Initialization: At first, a swarm of m particles $C_1, C_2,....,C_m$ is initialized randomly:.

Here, a particle $C_i = \{SP_1^i, SP_2^i,..., SP_n^i \}$ is an arrangement of service providers where SP_k^i is the service provider which provides the kth service in the ith particle (arrangement) C_i. Here the number of services desired by the consumer is n.

The parameters Θ_i (initial temperature), Θ_f (final temperature), α (cooling rate) are initialized. A higher Θ_i gives a better result, but there is also a trade-off as this implies a larger number of iterations.

Step 2: Finding a local best solution: For each of the m particles, the next local best solution is found, at a particular temperature Θ, as described in section III. This is done by randomly selecting a member from the velocity space along a random dimension less than or equal to N. This means that any one of the N service providers is chosen randomly and replaced by another valid service provider, which also is chosen randomly. The new solution C_{new} probabilistically replaces the old solution based on the probability function described earlier in equation (2). The updated solution is referred to as C_{ilbest} or the local best.

Step 3: Updating the pbest and gbest values: For each particle, C_{ilbest} obtained in step 2 is compared to the *historically obtained best solution for that particle* C_{ipbest}. C_{ipbest} is updated by C_{ilbest} according to the following rule:

C_{ipbest} = C_{ilbest} if $f(C_{ilbest}) - f(C_{ipbest}) < 0$

= C_{ipbest} if $f(C_{ilbest}) - f(C_{ipbest}) \geq 0$

Now, comparing all the C_{ipbest} values, Cgbest (the historically obtained best solution globally across all particles) is updated by that C_{ipbest} which has the minimum energy state i.e. the minimum value of $f(C_{ipbest})$ among all particles.

Step 4: Finding new solution based on crossover: Based on the global knowledge of the swarm each particle forms a new solution from its local best (C_{ipbest}) by crossing a part of it with the global best (C_{gbest}). For example, say, C_{ipbest} = {1,5,**2,3,2**,1} and C_{gbest} = {1,3,**1,4,3**,3}. The portion {1,4,3} is randomly chosen from C_{gbest} and inserted in the same position in C_{ipbest} to obtain C_{inew}. Thus C_{inew} becomes {1,5,**1,4,3**,1}.

Note that this is slightly different from the crossover operator discussed in [11].

After the crossover, C_{ipbest} is replaced with C_{inew} if that has a lower energy state and is taken as the new individual best position. Crossover helps the particles jump out of local optimization by sharing global information about the swarm.

Step 5: Loop: The temperature $\Theta(t)$ is calculated. If either $\Theta(t)$ is less than $\Theta(f)$ or the number of iterations completed exceeds t, the algorithm comes to a halt. The best solution found is C_{gbest}. Else it goes back to step 2.

Possible extension: parameter matching and degree of association: The above algorithm can be extended to take into account the *appropriateness* of the service provider (how closely it matches the service desired by the consumer node) in cases where the types of parameters are variable. Suppose that a desired service S has parameters $\{p_1, p_2,..., p_k\}$. Also suppose that the service S is provided by Service Providers SP_1, SP_2, ..., where each of them provides the same service but with varying types of parameters. A very trivial example of varying types can be string versus integer versus floating point number. The most appropriate service provider would be the one whose parameter list matches most closely with the requested parameter list. Thus appropriateness of service provider i depends on the *degree of association* between the set $\{p_1, p_2,..., p_k\}$ and the parameter set of SP_i. Degree of association is given by:

$$D = \sum_{j=1}^{k} (p_j \Phi SP_i(p_j)) \tag{3}$$

Where, $SP_i(p_j)$ is the jth parameter in set SP_i (parameter set for the service provider providing the ith service to the service consumer) and p_j^i is the jth parameter in the parameter set for the ith service desired by the service consumer and $p_j^i \Phi SP_i(p_j)$ is the *correspondence*. The value of *correspondence* is given by:

$p_j^i \Phi SP_i(p_j) = 1$ if the type of p_j^i exactly matches the type of $SP_i(p_j)$

= 0 otherwise

The degree of association can be incorporated into the definition of distance d(i) that is used in the energy function (1). Alternatively, a strategy can be used to:

1) Produce several distinct sub-optimal particles.
2) Take the one having the maximum degree of association.

5 Simulation

Extensive simulations have been performed to judge the capability of the OSD algorithm. We have considered a sample network of 30 nodes and the existence of 10 network services. Each node provides a set of services and consumes a predefined set of services.

5.1 Implementation

We implemented the neighborhood discovery and service discovery using the nesC [5] programming language, hosted on the TinyOS [6] software platform which provides a component-based software model and an active message based communication model. The rationale behind choosing the implementation platform is to test its coding feasibility on the hardware platform (e.g., real motes like mica2, micaZ etc.) and also to utilize the interference-model provided by TOSSIM [7] to study packet-loss. NesC modules are software components that are wired together in a configuration file to form an application, much like hardware components in a schematic.

The Interference-Model: We have noticed the criticality of packet loss during transmission while simulating our scheme using the interference-model. The simulation in TOSSIM [7] considers the TOSSIM radio loss model, which is based on the empirical data (shown in Fig. 1). The loss probability captures transmitter interference using original trace that yielded the model. More detailed measurements would be required to simulate the exact transmitter characteristics; however experiments have shown the model to be very accurate.

After the nodes boot, they try to determine their neighbors. To avoid collision we have used TDMA-based approach for the nodes to transmit their neighborhood discovery messages. The implementation takes RSSI, where the signal strengths of the acknowledgement messages sent by the potential neighbors are sampled by the subject node. Our application uses a threshold value to help filter out nodes beyond a

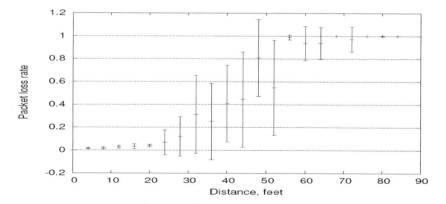

Fig. 1. TOSSIM Radio Loss Model based on empirical data

certain distance, which is directly related to the RSSI value. Results regarding relations between the RSSI values and distances have been studied in [9].

5.2 Simulation Results

The results obtained by the OSD algorithm (based on SA-PSO) were compared with results from simple PSO algorithm and a Greedy Algorithm. The PSO algorithm does not employ the notion of Simulated Annealing where as the Greedy Algorithm is more concerned only with the bundling of services from a peer.

Since all the algorithms employ an idea of random numbers the solutions produced are not at all always unique. However, the distribution of the obtained solutions varies with the algorithms. We conducted a study on this distribution, where we simulated the three algorithms for 100 times for a given network and plotted frequency of the obtained solution versus the value of energy (as in equation 1) of the obtained solution. The graph obtained is presented in figure 2.

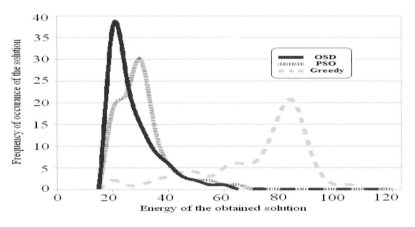

Fig. 2. Distribution of the solutions

The figure 2 shows that the graph for OSD has a greater measure of Kurtosis or *peak* than the other two. Hence the probability of the obtained optimal solution to be at a minimal energy level is greater in case of OSD, where the optimal solutions are more clustered towards the minimal energy solution. To study the merit of our approach, we performed the analysis based on the following criteria among the algorithms: a) percentage packet-loss and b) energy efficiency. The simulation was run for 50 rounds and the average number of packet losses for the three different algorithms were plotted graphically, as shown in figure 3. This simulation uses the interference-model introduced earlier. The OSD algorithm shows distinctively reliable communication compared to the others.

In case of the greedy algorithm, packet loss is the maximum as communication distance is not considered. The relatively higher packet loss in PSO shows that the application of simulated annealing technique improves the OSD algorithm. The second simulation was performed for determining the energy-awareness of the three schemes. Here, we studied the residual energy of the initiator node the number of rounds increases gradually. The energy expenditure for communication follows the first order radio model as discussed in [12]. The initiator (consumer) node is assumed to have an initial energy of 1 J. The results are shown in figure 4. The cost of communication is best in the OSD scheme. Residual energy curves show a sharper decreasing trend in the other schemes. This increases the lifetime of individual nodes resulting in increment of the network lifetime. It is clear from the above results that the OSD algorithm outperforms the other two algorithms, both in terms of higher energy conservation as well as lower packet-loss rates.

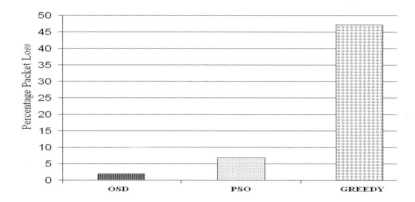

Fig. 3. Percentage packet loss for the schemes

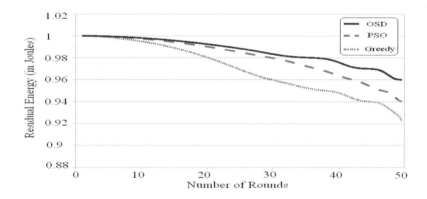

Fig. 4. Residual Mote Energy of the initiator after 30 rounds

6   Conclusion and Future Work

In this paper, we have presented a combined two-level strategy for nearest neighborhood and optimal service provider discoveries that would provide a single solution to this challenge. We described the OSD algorithm, a new optimization approach based on a combination of SA and PSO algorithms, which prevents getting stuck in local optimal solutions while at the same time quickly converges towards the final solution. We implemented this using the nesC programming language running on the TinyOS platform. We have shown that our results show appreciable improvements over two other conventional approaches. Developing applications using our approach offers two major advantages:

1. Execution time is much shorter than when using more traditional approaches.
2. The algorithm is robust, being relatively insensitive to noisy and/or missing data, as it randomly searches for the best solution over the entire solution space.

To conclude, it is our belief that optimizing the service provider selection mechanism is an important step towards minimizing energy consumption when sensor nodes collaboratively exchange services or data in a Wireless Sensor Network. For greater applicability of wireless networks in a ubiquitous environment, one should also look at the context under which different services are required and take into account the security of services being provided over an open network. Moreover, in an actual WSN, there can be intermittent total disconnection/discontinuity of services and one should take proactive steps to continue operating even under such circumstances. Our future work would endeavor to enhance our programming framework to allow these enhancements.

References

1. Weiser, M.: The Computer for the Twenty-First Century. Scientific Am. 265(3), 94–101 (1991)
2. Eberhart, R.C., Kennedy, J.: A new optimizer using particle swarm theory. In: The proceedings of the Sixth International Symposium on Micro machine and Human Science, Nagoya, Japan, pp. 39–43 (1995)
3. Shi, Y.H., Eberhart, R.C.: A modified particle swarm optimizer. In: IEEE International Conference on Evolutionary Computation, pp. 63–73 (1998)
4. Chaojun, D., Zulian, Q.: Particle Swarm Optimization Algorithm Based on the Idea of Simulated Annealing. IJCSNS International Journal of Computer Science and Network Security 6(10) (October 2006)
5. Gay, D., Levis, P., Behren, R., Welsh, M., Brewer, E., Culler, D.: The nesC language - A holistic approach to networked embedded systems. ACM SIGPLAN Notices archive 38(5) (May 2003)
6. Levis, P., et al.: TinyOS - An Operating System for Sensor Networks. In: Ambient Intelligence, Springer, Heidelberg (2005)
7. Levis, P., Lee, N., Welsh, M., Culler, D.: TOSSIM: Accurate and Scalable Simulation of Entire TinyOS
8. Lenders, V., May, M., Plattner, B.: Service discovery in mobile ad hoc networks: A field theoretic approach. In: Pervasive and Mobile Computing, Elsevier, Amsterdam (2005)
9. Lim, J.C., Wong, K.D.: Exploring Possibilities for RSSI-Adaptive Control in Mica2-based Wireless Sensor Networks. In: ICARV 2006 (2006)
10. Kirkpatrick, S., Sorkin, G.B.: Simulated Annealing. In: The Handbook of Brain and Neural Networks, The MIT Press, Cambridge (1995)
11. Hao, Z.-F., Wang, Z.-G., Huang, H.: A Particle Swarm Optimization Algorithm with Crossover Operator. In: International Conference on Machine Learning and Cybernetics 2007, August 2007, pp. 19–22 (2007)
12. Rabiner, W., Heinzelman, Chandrakasan, A., Balakrishnan, H.: Energy-Efficient Communication Protocol for Wireless Micro sensor Networks. In: The Proceedings of the 33rd Hawaii International Conference on System Sciences (2000)
13. Whitehouse, K., Karlof, C., Culler, D.: A practical evaluation of radio signal strength for ranging-based localization. SIGMOBILE Mob. Comput. Commun. Rev. 11(1), 41–52 (2007)

A New Approach for Workflow Tasks Scheduling in Distributed Heterogeneous Environment

K. Prabavathi and P. Varalakshmi

Department of Information Technology
Madras Institute of Technology, Anna University, Chromepet, Chennai-44
Tamil Nadu, India
varanip@gmail.com, kprabait@gmail.com

Abstract. Scheduling workflow tasks is a key issue in the workflow management system. Workflow Scheduling is defined as allocating suitable resources to workflow tasks in order to satisfy objective functions specified by users. This paper presents a task scheduling algorithm called LCPR algorithm for workflow tasks in heterogeneous computing environment. This algorithm focuses mainly on the tasks that are tightly coupled or that have high dependency with other tasks. This paper evaluates the algorithm with other workflow algorithms and found that LCPR gives better performance in terms of execution time and response time of the job.

Keywords: grid environment, workflow, task scheduling.

1 Introduction

Grid computing systems works in a dynamic heterogeneous environment, should support efficient execution of computational intensive and data intensive applications with different computational and data needs. Management of such environment especially in the field of resource management and scheduling of jobs gives great issue because of dynamicity and heterogeneity.

In the grid environment the jobs may be of sequential, parallel or combination of both or batch jobs or workflow jobs. [2] Presents several advantages of introducing workflow in grid like environment. Workflow is basically a flow of work between the tasks. A workflow job consists of set of tasks to execute which may be independent on each other or dependent on each other. Based on this, workflow structure or workflow pattern is broadly classified as Non- DAG and DAG respectively [3]. In grid, most of the scientific applications (large scale computation intensive and data intensive) can be modeled as complex work flows [5]. Scheduling of such complex workflow applications is a significant and essential problem in grids as it has to allocate tasks by discovering suitable resources to meet users' requirements and has to manage data transfer between selected resources. So in general, Workflow scheduling is a process that maps and manages execution of interdependent tasks on distributed resources. Due to the shared nature of these resources and the dynamic nature of the workload, different management policies and user requirements, different Qos parameters (execution time,

N. Meghanathan et al. (Eds.): NeCoM, WiMoN, and WeST 2010, CCIS 90, pp. 663–671, 2010.

cost, reliability, availability, etc.) are applied to reflect the grid tasks, and the scheduling of grid workflow applications.

In general, functions of Grid workflow management systems are characterized into build time functions and run time functions. The build-time functions are concerned with defining and modeling workflow tasks and their dependencies while the run-time functions are concerned with managing the workflow execution and interactions with grid resources for processing workflow applications [3]. This paper concentrates on the runtime functions of the workflow i.e. it focuses mainly on the improving the response time of the job submitted by the user.

The remainder of the paper is organized as follows. Section 2 describes the related work. Section 3 outlines scheduling problem and system model. The proposed LCPR workflow scheduling algorithm is described in Section 4. Implementation, experimental results and performance analysis are presented in Section 5 and 6. Finally, we conclude the paper with directions for further work in Section 7.

2   Related Work

Many algorithms and heuristics have been proposed for scheduling inter-dependent tasks in heterogeneous and homogenous environment. But still workflow scheduling faces challenges like,

- Heterogeneity of the resources makes the task performance unidentical.
- Different users compete for resources in the grid environment.
- Inter dependency between tasks makes high communication cost as data are need to be transferred between one resource to another.
- Severe dependency between tasks affects the response time and makespan of the job, this may due to the communication delay or computation delay.

Workflow scheduling algorithms are classified in to several categories [11, 12] such as group scheduling algorithms [4], list scheduling algorithms [1,14] and clustering algorithms. [4] Presents and evaluates a dynamic scheduling strategy that groups tasks based on a particular granularity size. In list scheduling algorithms the tasks are levelized and grouped for scheduling, based on some ranking factors.

The two main list scheduling heuristics proposed for workflow are Critical Path on a Processor and Heterogeneous Earliest Finish Time algorithm [1]. Both CPOP and HEFT algorithm consists of two phases, task prioritization phase and processor selection phase. HEFT algorithm selects the task with the highest upward rank at each step and the selected task is assigned to a processor that can minimize its earliest finish time where as CPOP algorithm selects the task with the highest total rank (upward rank + downward rank) at each step and schedules all critical tasks onto a host with the best performance, if a selected task is noncritical, it will be assigned to a processor which could minimize its earliest finish time, as in HEFT. LMT (Levelized Min Time) algorithm [14] groups the tasks that can be executed in parallel in a level by level fashion. It uses a greedy method that assigns each task to the "fastest" available processor with task in a lower level has higher priority than a task in a higher level. Within the same level, the task with the highest average computation cost has the highest priority. Similarly, PETS algorithm described in [7] levelizes the given workflow such that each level consists of set of independent tasks; it ranks and gives priority to the tasks at every level based on the execution and computation cost and rank of the predecessor nodes.

Clustering algorithms maps heavily communicating tasks on to an unbounded number of clusters using linear or nonlinear clustering heuristics, the selected task may not be a ready task. Then the clusters are mapped onto the set of available processors using communication sensitive or insensitive heuristics. Some examples of clustering algorithm are Clustering for Heterogeneous Processors (CHP) [10], Dominant Sequence Clustering [15].

Paper [9] says performances of the workflow scheduling are affected greatly by the rank assigned to the node, in spite of the non dedicated grid resource which also results in the performance fluctuations. So ranking the tasks is one of the important criteria to make efficient workflow task schedule. In this paper, the proposed LCPR algorithm which ranks or prioritizes tasks based on the number of sync child a task possess.

3   Scheduling System Model

Scheduling system model consists of an application, computing environment and performance criteria for scheduling. The application we are considering is workflow type of application. In the workflow, tasks that have dependencies with other tasks in are represented in the Directed Acyclic Graph G (N, E) where, N represents set of nodes and E represents the edges connecting the nodes. A typical DAG workflow is shown in figure 1. Every node in the DAG has successor and predecessor nodes except the entry node and exit node. The node is said to be entry node if it has zero predecessor nodes and non-zero number of successor nodes. Exit node is the one which has non-zero number of predecessor node and zero successor nodes. In the Figure 1, the nodes {A, B, C} are all entry nodes and nodes {L, M} are exit nodes.

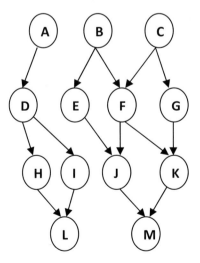

Fig. 1. A DAG Example

Any workflow job represented in DAG should maintain precedence constraint between the nodes. For a node in the DAG, the successor nodes are called parent node/task and all the predecessor nodes are called its child tasks/nodes. If a node has more than one parent tasks then the node is said to be synchronization node or simply sync node/task. In the figure 1 the nodes {F, J, K, L, M} are all synchronization nodes of the DAG.

4   LCPR Algorithm

Our proposed LCPR algorithm consists of four phases, Leveling phase, Cost assignment phase, Prioritization phase and Resource allocation phase. The first three phases talks about scheduling of tasks in the given workflow and the fourth phase handles the matching making process between task and the resources in the grid.

4.1   Leveling Phase

This phase divides the given DAG in to set of levels such that each level has set of independent tasks that can be executed in parallel. Every DAG should have single entry and single exit node. In case if no single entry or exit task available, a node with zero computation cost and zero communication cost is attached(as shown in figure 2). For the given DAG G (N, E) level l consists of set of tasks t_j and if t_k is the set of task in a level less than l then there exists atleast one edge from t_k to t_j such that t_k is in level l-1. For example in Figure 2, the entry task forms the level 0. Level 1 contains {A, B, C}, level 2 is formed by the tasks {D, E, F, G}, tasks {H, I, J, K} form level 3 and the exit tasks {L, M} forms the level 4.

4.2   Cost Assignment Phase

This phase assign cost to every node in the DAG. The assignment is based on the estimated computation cost of the node and estimated communication cost of the edge from the node. For every task T_i in the DAG (where (i=1,2…n) represents the level in which task T is present in the DAG) the average computation cost on all the available resources is calculated. The Mean Computation Cost (MCC) is calculated using equation (1),

$$MCC\ (T_i) = \Sigma\ cc\ (t_i,\ r_j)\ /\ m \tag{1}$$

Where cc $(t_i,\ r_j)$ is the computation cost of task T_i on resource r_j and m is the total number of available resources. The mean communication cost is calculated based on the available bandwidth (BW) and latency (L) and the size of the job (S_j) that the task needs to transfer to its descendant tasks which is given in equation (2)

$$C_J = (S_j\ /\ BW) + L \tag{2}$$

Where C_J is the communication cost for a job J. The cost of the node N is the sum of the value of the Mean Computation Cost and mean communication cost. The cost of the Nth node (C_N) is given by the equation (3).

$$C_N = C_J + MCC \tag{3}$$

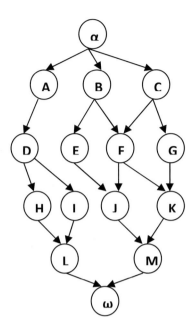

Fig. 2. Modified DAG with entry and exit task

4.3 Prioritization Phase

This phase assigns priority to all nodes in each level of the DAG. The priority is assigned at every level for the set of independent tasks. The criteria for assignment of priority are, a node must have more number of children than other nodes in the same level and/or one or more child node is a synchronization node. The higher priority is assigned to the node having high number of synchronization child nodes. In case of any tie occurs between two or more nodes, then the priority is assigned based on the cost (N_c) calculated for the node. The high cost node possesses the higher priority. Example in the figure 2, consider level 2 tasks { D, E, F, G} in that D and F has two number of children and E and G has only one child task. So the highest priority in this level goes either to D or F since both are having higher number of child tasks than others in the same level. It is noted that, out of two child tasks of F one is a sync task and D has zero sync child. So as per the criteria, higher priority is assigned for F and next higher for D. Similarly for tasks E and G, the higher priority goes to the task G than task E since task G has single sync child task unlike task E. Thus the order of priority for level 2 is (F, D, G, E). The priority table for all the tasks in the figure 2 DAG is as follows,

Table 1. Priority table

	Priority 1	Priority 2	Priority 3	Priority 4
Level 1	B	C	A	
Level 2	F	D	G	E
Level 3	J	K	I	H
Level 4	L	M		

In level 1 the task B and C has same number of child tasks and sync task. So in this case priority is assigned based on the B's and C's node cost (N_c) calculated in the previous phase. Node B's cost is found to be higher than C's, so B possess highest priority in the level 1. Similarly for the level 3 tasks, the priority is assigned based on the node cost, as all the tasks have equal number of child and sync nodes.

4.4 Resource Allocation Phase

This phase ranks the resource based on the some resource factors like CPU speed, load, memory etc. For each job the tasks are queued based on the priority at each level. The higher priority task has to be assigned to the high cost resource because the higher priority node is the one which is depend by other nodes in the DAG. A resource is said to be high cost resource if it possesses optimized measure of resource parameters like CPU speed, load, memory, hard disk etc for the grid jobs to be executed. According to our algorithm the high cost resource is the one having highest T-R (Task to Resource) value. The T-R value is calculated by considering characteristics of resource, characteristics of job and also the network parameters using equation(4),

$$TR_i = DT_i + ET_i \tag{4}$$

Where DT is the Data transfer Time of node i which is calculated based on size of the data to be transferred (d_s), available bandwidth (w_a) in the network and available latency (l_a) using the equation (5).

$$DT = (d_s/w_a) + l_a \tag{5}$$

ET(r) is the Execution Time the resource takes to execute a task. It is defined as

$$ET(r) = MCC(T_i) / (C_r + L_r + M_r) \tag{6}$$

Where C_r is the processor speed of resource r, L_r is the current load of the resource r and M_r is the memory available in the resource r. The reason for considering network parameters to calculate TR_i value is the type of job we use (workflow) depends on communication cost for successful execution. For each task TR_i value is calculated on every available resource. Let be there be n number of tasks(t) in a workflow job j and let there be m number of available resources r, then the TR_i matrix (Z) is generated as follows,

$$Z = \begin{bmatrix} (T-R)p1q1 & \cdots & (T-R)p1qm \\ \vdots & \ddots & \vdots \\ (T-R)pnq1 & \cdots & (T-R)pnqm \end{bmatrix}$$

For a task to get resource allocated, highest T-R value is chosen as the target.

5   Implementation Environment

We implemented our proposed LCPR algorithm in Centre for Advanced Computing Research and Education (CARE) laboratory, Chennai. We formed Beowulf computational cluster with several compute nodes. Our algorithm being works in meta-scheduler level, we used CARE resource broker as our meta scheduler [6]. For the network information needed to compute the communication cost, NWS (Network Weather Service) tool [17, 8] is used. Ganglia Monitoring tool [18] is used to get the available resource information in the grid environment. We used Globus Toolkit middleware [16] to communicate and access the resources in the grid.

6 Performance Analysis and Results

In this section, we present the comparative evaluation of proposed LCPR algorithm and the existing algorithm for heterogeneous system such as PETS, LMT for DAGs with various characteristics by simulation. For this purpose, we consider two sets of graphs as the workload for testing, randomly generated task graphs and the graphs that represent some of numerical real world problems such as molecular dynamic code. The metric we used to compare includes response time and execution time of the job.

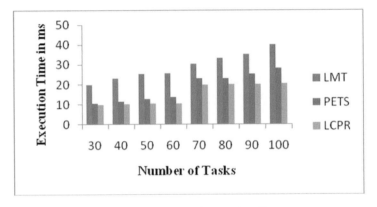

Fig. 3. Comparison of Execution Time

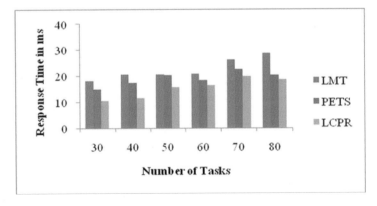

Fig. 4. Comparison of Response Time

7 Conclusion and Future Work

In this paper we propose a workflow task scheduling algorithm called LCPR algorithm which consists of four phases which describes how the workflow tasks are schedule and also chooses suitable resources to execute tasks according to resources status and the size of given job in the Grid environment. Since our algorithm gives higher priority to the synchronization tasks, the waiting time of its other dependent tasks are reduced. More over we assign tasks based on the T-R value calculated which includes parameters like job size, load and memory which is found to give good execution time for tasks. Our LCPR algorithm has been proven to be better for scheduling DAG structured applications onto heterogeneous computing system in terms of response time as simulation results confirm that LCPR algorithm is substantially better than that of the existing algorithms such as PETS, LMT.

In future, we will make efforts to study the dynamic workflow job scheduling with QoS constraints, like time and cost tradeoff and advanced resource reservation. We also intend to use our task scheduling in our real Grid platform for practical evaluations.

Acknowledgement. We would like to give thanks to all the members of CARE (Centre for Advanced Computing Research and Education) laboratory, Anna University, Madras Institute of Technology Campus, Chromepet, Chennai for their support and guidance to work in a grid environment. We would also give our hearty thanks to Department of Information Technology, MIT Anna University, Chennai for providing all the needs for our project.

References

1. Topcuoglu, H., Hariri, S., Wu, M.: Performance effective and low-complexity task scheduling for heterogeneous computing. IEEE Trans. on Parallel and Distributed Systems (2002)
2. Changsong, D., Zhoujun, H., Zhigang, H., Xi, L.: A Distributed Workflow Management System Model and its Scheduling Algorithm. In: 2008 Japan-China Joint Workshop on Frontier of Computer Science and Technology (2008)
3. Yu, J., Buyya, R.: A Taxonomy of Workflow Management Systems for Grid Computing, Grid Computing and Distributed Systems (GRIDS) Laboratory. The University of Melbourne, Australia (White Paper)
4. Muthuvelu, N., Liu, J., Soe, N.L., Venugopal, S.R., Sulistio, A., Buyya, R.: A dynamic job grouping based scheduling for deploying applications with fine-grained tasks on global grids. In: Proc. 3rd Australasian workshop on grid computing and e-research, Australia (2005)
5. Cao, H., Jin, H., Wu, X., Wu, S., Shi, X.: DAGMap: efficient and dependable scheduling of DAG workflow job in Grid
6. Somasundaram, T.S., Amarnath, B.R., Kumar, R., Balakrishnan, P., Rajendar, K., Rajiv, R., Kannan, G., Rajesh Britto, G., Mahendran, E., Madusudhanan, B.: CARE Resource Broker: A framework for scheduling and supporting virtual resource management. Future Generation Computer Systems 26, 337–347 (2010)

7. Ilavarasan, E., Thambidurai, P.: Low Complexity Performance Effective Task Scheduling Algorithm for Heterogeneous Computing Environments. Journal of Computer Sciences (2007), ISSN 1549-3636
8. Wolski, R.: Forecasting Network Performance to Support Dynamic Scheduling Using the Network Weather Service. In: Proceedings of the 6th IEEE International Symposium on High Performance Distributed Computing (1997) ISBN:0-8186-8117-9
9. Sakellariou, R., Zhao, H.: A Hybrid Heuristic for DAG Scheduling on Heterogeneous Systems. In: Proceedings of the 13th Heterogeneous Computing Workshop (2004)
10. Boeres, C., Filho, J.V., Rebello, V.E.F.: A cluster-based strategy for scheduling task on heterogeneous processors. In: Proc. 16th Symp. on Computer Architecture and High Performance Computing, SBAC-PAD (2004)
11. Dong, F., Akl, S.G.: Scheduling algorithms for grid computing: state of the art and open problems. Technical Report No. 2006-504, School of Computing, Queens University Kingston, Ontario (2006)
12. Hall, R., Rosenberg, A.L., Venkataramani, A.: A comparison of DAG-scheduling strategies for internet-based computing. In: Proc 22nd international parallel and distributed processing symposium, IPDPS (2007)
13. Mandal, A., Kennedy, K., Koelbel, C., Marin, G., Mellor-Crummey, J., Liu, B., Johnsson, L.: Scheduling strategies for mapping application workflows onto the grid. In: IEEE international symposium on high performance distributed computing, HPDC 2005 (2005)
14. Iverson, M., Ozguner, F., Follen, G.: Parallelizing existing applications in a distributed heterogeneous environment. In: Heterogeneous Computing Workshop (1995)
15. Yang, T., Gerasoulis, A.: DSC: Scheduling Parallel Tasks on an Unbounded Number of Processors. IEEE Trans. on Parallel and Distributed Systems 5(9) (September 1994)
16. http://www.globus.org/toolkit/
17. Swany, M., Wolski, R.: Representing Dynamic Performance Information in Grid Environments with the Network Weather Service. In: Proceedings of the 2nd IEEE/ACM International Symposium on Cluster Computing and the Grid, CCGRID 2002 (2002)
18. Massie, M.L., Chun, B.N., Culler, D.E.: The ganglia distributed monitoring system: design, implementation, and experience. Parallel Computing 30, 817–840 (2004)

A Range Based Localization Algorithm Using Autonomous Speed Mobile Sink (MOBISPEED) in Distributed Wireless Sensor Networks

B. Amutha[1], M. Ponnavaikko[2], and N. Karthick[3]

[1] Research Scholar, School of Computer Science and Engineering, SRM University
Tamil Nadu - 603 203, India
[2] Vice Chancellor, Bharathidasan University
[3] Department of Computer Science and Engineering, Valliammai Engineering College
bamutha62@gmail.com, ponnav@gmail.com,
b.d.best.4ever@gmail.com

Abstract. Ubiquitous computing technology is expected to become very small and reasonably cheap in the future, large amounts of electronic items can be deployed almost everywhere. Localization of sensor nodes is important in many respects in wireless sensor networks. First, it informs the remote end user of the precise location within a network where the specific "event' of interest took place. Second, in case of node failure, identification can be made for the network area within the sensor network which is affected. Similarly, the known location of sensor node helps in coming up with efficient routing paths to the sink, which is mobile, is used to track the event driven sensor nodes in the path of the event, thus conserving energy and time. In wireless sensor networks, the capabilities of individual sensor nodes are extremely limited and therefore collaboration is required with minimum energy expense.

As Information without location is meaningless in sensor networks, Localization plays an important role in coming up with an efficient inter-node collaboration. With this scheme, the ordinary sensor nodes do not need to spend energy on neighboring interaction for localization. The localization mechanism has been implemented in TOSSIM. The simulation results show that our scheme performed better than other range-based schemes.

Keywords: Mobile Sink, Location sensing, Range based location scheme, Beacon, IDSQ.

1 Introduction

Due to advances in wireless technologies, Wireless Sensor Networks can be used for many applications such as military, home, health, industries etc. Wireless Sensor Network is a dynamic network formed on-the-fly as mobile nodes move in and out of each others' transmission ranges [1]. In general, the mobile ad hoc networking model followed by wireless sensor networks make no assumption that nodes know their own locations. However, recent research shows that location-awareness can be beneficial to fundamental tasks such as routing and energy-conservation [2]-[16]. Because of the

N. Meghanathan et al. (Eds.): NeCoM, WiMoN, and WeST 2010, CCIS 90, pp. 672–681, 2010.

deployment of a large number of sensor nodes, it is often not possible to hand place these sensor nodes. On the other hand, the cost and limited energy resources associated with common low-cost nodes prohibit them from carrying relatively expensive devices such as Global Positioning System (GPS). The capabilities of individual sensor nodes are extremely limited and their collaboration is required with minimum energy expenses.

This paper proposes a mechanism that allows non-GPS equipped nodes in the network to derive their exact locations from a limited number of GPS-equipped nodes. In this method, a mobile sink is introduced, which has the prior knowledge about the sensor field. The mobile sink is used for data collection whenever any event occurs. It is used to travel in the sensor field in a randomized way with dynamic speed. During its travel, it broadcasts its location to all sensor nodes within the sensor field. A mobile sink can compute the location of sensor nodes when it selects the entry and exit point over the communication circle of the sensor node.

1.1   Related Work

Many applications need to know the physical location of objects. Several schemes have been proposed to locate the objects which are broadly classified into two categories such as range-based and range-free. Range Based Localization introduced ways to localize nodes based on range (i.e. distance or angle) information. Several mechanisms have been proposed under range based approaches [2]-[4], provide high accuracy with less than few meters in location error. But they all require more hardware on sensor nodes.

1.1.1   Using Mobile Beacons

On the other hand, Range free localization approaches expect no knowledge about communication range to be available; instead they include other metrics to calculate a node's position. Several approaches have been proposed to estimate location without distance or angle information, but they typically need a large amount of stationary reference points for achieving higher accuracy and extensive communication among neighboring sensor nodes [5]-[9].

Many schemes have been introduced, using mobile sink as a beacon node, in estimating the location of sensor nodes in a wireless sensor network. One of the scheme proposed by Sichitiu and Ramadurai, uses a single mobile beacon transmitting its current location [10].

Another Scheme proposed by Dutta and Bergbreiter, estimates the distance from a sensor node to a mobile object based on ultrasound technology [11]. Neighboring sensor nodes cooperated to evaluate the distance between them by exploiting common tangent concept. As long as the node-to-node distances are available, the position of a sensor node can be measured by range-based schemes.

Sun and Guo proposed probabilistic localization schemes with a mobile beacon [12]. The approaches use TOA technique for ranging and utilize Centroid formula with distance information to calculate a sensor node's position. The above approaches need to integrate with range information for localization. Galstyan et al. proposed a coarse-grained range-free localization algorithm to lower the uncertainty of their positions using radio connectivity constraints [13]. With each received beacon, the receiver's location is bounded in the transmission area of the sender. Another localization scheme proposed in [14] in which mobile anchor points are used for localization in wireless sensor network.

Another scheme proposed by Saad Ahmed Munir, Yu Wen Bin and Ma Jian, the approach was based on the communication range of the sensor nodes [15]; and with the help of the motion of a mobile sink in a straight line, the localization of the sensor nodes is achieved. Bin Xiao, Hekang Chen and Shuigeng Zhou presented two distributed range-free localization methods (ADO and RSS) that use only one moving beacon within a sensor network [16].

The remainder of the paper is organized as follows: Section 2 identifies the objectives and requirements of the MOBISPEED system. Section 3 represents the Location Estimation Algorithm using mobile sink. Section 4 presents the Performance analysis and section 5 presents the Conclusion.

2   Objectives and Requirements

An efficient and accurate range-based scheme is proposed here, with the help of a mobile sink. This comes up with the near-accurate co-ordinates of sensor nodes within a wireless sensor network. Simulations are conducted for varying sink velocity and for different packet generation interval. Similarly, the performance of this scheme is demonstrated by varying radio communication range error.

In this section, Mobispeed mechanism for estimating the location of sensor nodes within a wireless sensor network is described.

Assumptions are

1. *The mobile sink moves at a randomized speed initially.*
2. *It changes its speed when any event occurs, according to the position of the information driven sensor node.*
3. *The velocity of the mobile sink does not remain constant while moving through the sensor network.*

2.1   Proposed Scheme

In this paper, a novel range based scheme for efficient localization of sensor nodes within a network is explained in detail. The scheme is based on the mobility of a mobile sink introduced within the network. It is assumed that the mobile sink moves in a randomized fashion initially. With the known communication range of the sensor nodes, the mobile sink is able to estimate the location of each and every node in the geographical field.

2.1.1   Event Detection Mechanism

A randomly moving target is introduced as an event, which has to be detected by the set of sensor nodes in the path of the target. The occurrences of this event must be made known to the mobile sink by the sensor nodes. And this will be achieved by the collaboration among the sensor nodes. Intuitively, by selecting the most informative neighbor, the active sensor is seeking good quality data. The sensor selection criterion is described as

$$K_{IDSQ} = \arg\max_{1 \ldots N} I\left(X^{(t+1)}; Z_1^{(t+1)} \mid Z^t = Z^t\right)$$

Where N is the neighborhood, and $I(.)$ measures the mutual information between a sensor's measurement and the underlying target state. This criterion seeks the best complementary data: i.e., the sensor whose measurement $z_i^{(t+1)}$ combined with the current measurement history z^+ provide the most information about the target location $x^{(t+1)}$.

2.1.2 Varying Speed Mobile Sink Mechanism

The mobile sink speed is not necessarily the same as that of the target speed. It must be lesser than or equal to the speed of the target. Once the event is known to the mobile sink, the varying speed mechanism is adopted. It varies its speed according to the location of the event driven sensor. Mobile sink are assumed to have prior knowledge about the sensor field.

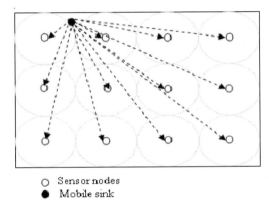

○   Sensor nodes
●   Mobile sink

Fig. 1. Mobile sink broadcasting its IDSQ message when it was introduced in the sensor field

If any node detects the target, it starts sending continuous periodical target information messages to mobile sink. The neighbor nodes within the area of that event driven node will also receive the target information. The neighbor nodes will also start sending the same message. Inter node collaboration is executed. Two possibilities are taken into consideration for analyzing our algorithm. In the first case, if mobile sink is nearer to the event driven node, then it can come close and collect sensor data. In the second case, if the mobile sink is far away from the event driven sensor node, called as source node, then mobile sink gets the notification about the target through the other nodes. To illustrate this concept, in figure 2, the target was detected by the node S_4, and takes a measurement. Now S_4 wants to give notification to mobile sink by acknowledging to its beacon message. The acknowledgement message contains target notification data and its information. It then decides which sensor in its neighborhood is the most informative to handoff the acknowledgement, say S_3. Now S_3 appends its information to the received packet from S_4 and hand off to the next informative neighborhood. This process repeats until it reaches the mobile sink. Once the sink detects the notification, it instantly changes its speed level and move towards the even driven node S_4, since the mobile sink knows the path towards the source node by means of received acknowledgement packet.

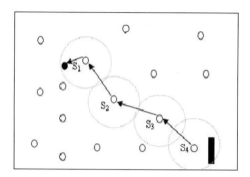

Fig. 2. The event driven node S_4, gives notification about the target to mobile sink, through by deciding which sensor in its neighborhood is the most informative in order to handoff the data

MOBISPEED comes up with area localization within a wireless sensor network and has an advantage of localizing the desired area. The desired region to be localized is traversed by the mobile sink. This scheme also facilitates the location estimation of the places of interest and thereby minimizes the energy and time it takes to localize the whole network.

Assumptions:

• The mobility is controllable and thus predictable,
• The pause time of the mobile sink along its moving trace is negligible.
The new algorithm *MOBISPEED* is introduced, which compensates all the existing problems through the following characteristics:

1. An autonomous speed varying mechanism is introduced in the mobile sink.
2. A variable RF communication range is taken into consideration.
3. The number of beacon points is reduced to two for the mobile sink.
4. The path of the mobile sink is also varied so as to overcome the limitation of the existing localization scheme.
5. Sensor nodes placed farthest from the mobile sink path should not face greater error if they lie within the communication range.
6. Line error should be reduced for the sensor nodes placed on the path of the mobile sink.
7. Only one reference point (Mobile Sink) is introduced which knows the entire heterogeneous network topology.
8. Node mobility is kept uniform.
9. Target speed is not a criterion to collect the optimized information about the target.

3   Location Estimation Algorithm

3.1   Assumptions and System Environments

Fig. 1 and 2 illustrates the system environment where a sensor network consists of sensor nodes and mobile sink. The sensor nodes are distributed randomly in the sensing field. Once the nodes are deployed, they will stay at their locations for sensing tasks. The sensor nodes can receive messages from both other nodes and anchor points. The mobile sink is able to traverse through the sensor field with sufficient energy and broadcast beacon messages during the localization process.

3.2   Location Calculation

As, Mobile Sink knows the entire topology information, based on the entry & exit of the mobile sink over the communication range of the sensor node, it calculates the location of the sensor node based on the simple geometrical equations. Suppose, let (a, b) be the location coordinates of the sensor node to be estimated. Let (x_1, y_1) be the entry location point of the mobile sink and (x_2, y_2) be the exit location point of the mobile sink based on the communication range of the sensor node, whose location (a, b) to be estimated. Then the following equations will help to estimate the (a, b) as follows,

$$(a - x_1)^2 + (b - y_1)^2 = r^2$$

$$(a - x_2)^2 + (b - y_2)^2 = r^2$$

Where r represents the radius, which is communication range of sensor node. Solving the above two equations will give the two possible locations. Sensor node may be resided at either one of the estimated location. The stored information in the mobile sink will gives the sensor location and target estimation.

Corollary:

The most informative sensor node may lie either above or below the chord. To identify the Location of the most informative sensor, the following steps have been executed.

1.   There may be two sensors in two possible locations.
2.   Say S1 is in the upper part and S2 is in the lower part of the chord.
3.   If the target is in the upper part of the sensor, S1 will transmit the signal along with its id and target information to the mobile sink.
4.   Mobile sink receives this information in due course of time as the mobile sink moves in the sensor field with varying speed capability.
5.   As mobile sink captures the information from the sensor nodes directly and it is able to capture the target information from the most informative sensor S1.
6.   Else it has to capture from S2.

Thus the localization algorithm comes up with efficient localization of sensor nodes and our mechanism reduces needed power consumption compared to other schemes This mechanism only requires mobile sink to broadcast beacon messages. The ordinary sensor nodes do not spend energy on neighboring interaction for localization.

3.3 Beacon Points and Information Base in Mobile Sink

This mechanism utilizes mobile sink that move around in the sensing area and periodically broadcast beacon messages, including the current location information. After sensor nodes receive the beacon message, it should give acknowledgement packet containing, its id, location of the mobile sink found in beacon message. The acknowledgement packet is received by the mobile sink when it enters into the communication range of that sensor node.

4 Performance Evaluation

The sensor field for simulation was a square of $100 * 100$ m^2. For simplicity, in the sensing field 12 sensor nodes were placed. In the practical environment, the sensor nodes were deployed randomly in the field. The mobile sink was randomly introduced at any corner of the sensing field at the beginning, as illustrated in figure 3. The mobile sink cannot be placed within the sensing area. Otherwise, the mobile sink will take the first beacon as a beacon point that is, however, not located on the communication circle. The mobile sink has been designed in such a way that it has sufficient energy for moving and broadcasting Information driven sensor query message, otherwise called as beacon messages, during the localization process.

The mobile sink is able to move by themselves or other carriers such as RC plane. It will move through the sensor field with a different speed. The level of speed will change according to the situation in the sensor field. Thus the mobile sink is designed with an autonomous speed varying mechanism. The localization scheme was analyzed with different communication range of the sensor node. The simulations were conducted for our localization scheme in TOSSIM [17] and [18]. A sensor network as shown in figure 4 is implemented wherein a mobile sink was introduced to traverse through the sensor field in a random direction at various levels of speed. For simplicity, the direction of the mobile sink initial movement is shown in the figure.

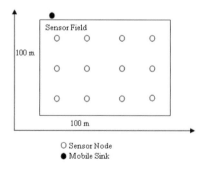

Fig. 3. Simulation Environments

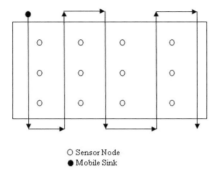

O Sensor Node
● Mobile Sink

Fig. 4. Area localization for sensor nodes with a mobile sink

Performance results are presented for the difference in location estimation based on our implementation and the actual location of the sensor nodes. Simulations were conducted to study the effect of two values, that is, the sink speed and induced radio communication range error. Simulations were conducted for different radio communication range errors are presented. The location estimation error (e) is calculated as follows: Distance between the sensor node's real coordinates (x_0, y_0) and the computed Coordinates (x, y), given by

$$e = \sqrt{(x - x_0)^2 + (y - y_0)^2}.$$

The average location estimation error is calculated as,

$$Average\ location\ error = Sum\ (e)\ /\ number\ of\ nodes.$$

These induced errors correspond to varying degree in communication range error as part of the theoretical known communication range. In our simulation, radio range was set at 10, 20, 25 and 30m. The induced error, of course has some effect on the

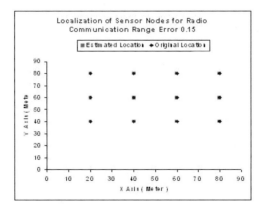

Fig. 5. Localization of sensor nodes for radio communication range error 0.15

performance of the localization of sensor nodes. With an increased induced communication range error, the performance degrades and is worse for the high value of range error as 1.22. For a low value of range error, that is 0.15, the performance of our proposed scheme is greatly better than existing schemes. Finally, communication overhead in MOBISPPEED is only included the broadcasting information driven sensor querying (beacon) message.

5 Conclusion

In this paper we have presented a range based localization scheme, MOBISPEED, without using distance or angle information. The scheme was designed to come with efficient localization of sensor nodes within a sensor network. With the help of mobility of mobile sink presented within the network, location estimation is performed. Based on the location information from mobile sink and the principles of elementary geometry, the mobile sink can compute the sensor nodes position without additional interactions. The localization mechanism that proposed here reduces needed power consumption compared to other schemes. Our mechanism only requires that mobile sink broadcast beacon messages. The ordinary sensor nodes do not spend energy on neighboring interaction for localization. Simulations conducted in TOSSIM verify that MOBISPEED, performs efficiently and is accurate in its functionality. Simulations were conducted with varying mobile sink velocity and for various communication ranges of sensor nodes. The execution time for the localization mechanism can be shortened if the moving speed is increased and by reducing the beacon interval and increasing the number of beacon messages. Our localization scheme comes with an efficient localization with minimum error as compared to other range-based localization schemes.

References

1. Zhao, F., Guibas, L.: Wireless Sensor Networks - an information processing approach. Morgan Kaufmann publishers, San Francisco (2004)
2. Hightower, J., Boriello, G., Want, R.: SpotON: An indoor 3D location sensing technology based on RF signal strength (February 2000)
3. Bahl, P., Padmanabhan, V.N.: RADAR: an in-building RF-based user location and tracking system. In: INFOCOM (March 2000)
4. Klukas, R., Fattouche, M.: Line-of-Sight Angle of Arrival Estimation in the Outdoor Multipath Environment. IEEE Transactions on Vehicular Technology (July 2003)
5. Bulusu, N., Heidemann, J., Estrin, D.: GPS-less low cost outdoor localization for very small devices. IEEE Personal Communication (October 2000)
6. Niculescu, D., Nath, B.: DV based positioning in ad hoc networks. Telecommunication Systems (January 2003)
7. He, T., Huang, C., Blum, B.M., Stankovic, J.A., Abdelzaher, T.: Range-free localization schemes for large scale sensor networks. In: Proc. ACM Int. Conf. Mobile Computing Networking (MOBICOM) (September 2003)
8. Bulusu, N., Heidemann, J., Estrin, D.: GPS-less Low Cost Outdoor Localization for Very Small Devices. IEEE Personal Communications Magazine (October 2000)

9. Nasipuri, A., Li, K.: A directionality based location discovery scheme for wireless sensor networks. In: First ACM International Workshop on Wireless Sensor Networks and Applications (September 2002)
10. Sichitiu, M.L., Ramadurai, V.: Localization of wireless sensor networks with a mobile beacon. Center for Advances Computing Communications (July 2003)
11. Dutta, P., Bergbreiter, S.: MobiLoc: Mobility enhanced localization, http://www-bsac.eecs.berkeley.edu/~sbergbre/publications/CS294.pdf
12. Sun, G.-L., Guo, W.: Comparison of distributed localization algorithms for sensor network with a mobile beacon. Networking, Sensing and Control (March 2004)
13. Galstyan, A., Krishnamachari, B., Lerman, K., Patterm, S.: Distributed online localization in sensor networks using a mobile target. Information Processing in Sensor Networks (2004)
14. Ssu, K.-F., Ou, C.-H., Jiau, H.C.: Localization with Mobile Anchor Points in Wireless Sensor Networks (May 2005)
15. Munir, S.A., Bin, Y.W., Jian, M.: Efficient Minimum Cost Area Localization for Wireless Sensor Network with a Mobile Sink. In: International Conference on Advanced Networking and Applications. IEEE, Los Alamitos (2007)
16. Xiao, B., Chen, H., Zhou, S.: A Walking Beacon-Assisted Localization in Wireless Sensor Networks. In: IEEE Communications Society, ICC 2007 proceedings (2007)
17. Levis, P., Lee, N.: TOSSIM: A Simulator for TinyOS Networks (September 2003)
18. Levis, P., Lee, N., Welsh, M., Culler, D.: TOSSIM: Accurate and Scalable Simulation of Entire TinyOS Applications. In: SenSys 2003, Los Angeles, California, USA, November 5-7 (2003)

Development of Controllability Observability Aided Combinational ATPG with Fault Reduction

Vaishali Dhare and Usha Mehta

Institute of Technology, Nirma University, Ahmedabad, Gujurat, India
{vaishali.dhare,usha.mehta}@nirmauni.ac.in
http://www.nirmauni.ac.in

Abstract. With the increase improvement in VLSI design and progressive complication of circuits, an efficient technique for test pattern generation is necessary with the intension of reducing number of faults and with use of testability measures. Using the fault equivalence method, the number of faults are reduced. The line justification and error propagation is used to find the test vectors for reduced fault set with the aid of controllability and observability. The programs are developed for fault equivalence method, controllability observability and finally for automatic test pattern generation using object oriented language C++. ISCAS 85 C17 circuit is used for analysis purpose. Standard ISCAS (International Symposium on Circuits And Systems) netlist format is used. The stuck at fault model is considered. The complete ATPG based on controllability and observability for reduced fault set is discussed in this paper.

Keywords: ATPG, fault equivalence, controllability, observability.

1 Introduction

ATPG (Automatic Test Pattern Generation) for digital circuits is a major research topic,due to its great economical importance and high theoretical attractiveness [1]. A significant amount of research has been done in the area of gate-level combinational ATPG using the stuck-at-fault model. As the numbers of transistors are increasing on chip, it is becoming difficult to generate the test vectors to test all faults. Conventional external testing involves storing all test vectors and test response on an external tester-that is, ATE. But these testers have limited speed, memory, and I/O channels. The test data bandwidth between the tester and the chip is relatively small; in fact, it is often the bottleneck determining how fast you can test the chip. The objective of testing is filtering defective chips from manufactured ones to reduce the fraction of defective parts those are erroneously sold to customers as defect-free parts [2]. Historically the single stuck-at-fault model has been widely accepted as a standard target model to generate a set of test patterns to detect all the stuck faults in the circuit. A single stuck-at fault represents a line in the circuit that is fixed to logic value 0

N. Meghanathan et al. (Eds.): NeCoM, WiMoN, and WeST 2010, CCIS 90, pp. 682–692, 2010.

or 1. The single-stuck fault model is also referred to as the classical or standard fault model because it has been the first and the most widely studied and used. Although its validity is not universal, its usefulness results from the following attributes:

- It represents many different physical faults
- It is independent of technology, as the concept of a signal line being stuck at a logic value can be applied to any structural model
- Compared to other fault models, the number of SSFs in a circuit is small
- SSFs can be used to model other types of faults

If we consider single stuck at fault then the number of faults is 2n, where n is number of net. In this case we have to find 2n test vectors, for each fault (stuck at 0, stuck at 1) on each net. Size of test vector becomes large for large combinational circuits. ATE (Automatic Test Equipment) bandwidth problem cause to handle these test vectors and testing time may be more in this case. No doubt test vector compression methods are available, prior to that, before test generation the number of faults can be reduced sothat the test vectors. The number of faults can be reduced using fault equivalence method and fault dominance method. In this paper an attempt is made to reduce the fault set using fault equivalence method is developed in C++. The logic and flow chart of the program is given in this paper. The results for ISCAS C17 benchmark circuit are analyzed.

ATPG(Automatic Test Pattern Generation) is generally guided by the testability measures to choose a decision during justification and propagation. These measures serve as heuristics and represent the relative difficulty of justifying a gate value to a control input or propagating a fault effect to an observe point. The testability measures, controllability and observability are developed using C++. The logic and flow chart for testability measures are discussed in this paper. The results for ISCAS C17 benchmark circuit are analyzed. The test patterns are generated for reduced fault set using line justification and error propagation concept. The generated test pattern for ISCAS C17 circuit [8] is discussed in result section. The logic and flow chart is discussed in this paper. The programs for ATPG are developed in C++ language.

2   Reduced Fault Set

We can get the reduced fault directory using fault equivalence method. Two faults f and g are considered functionally equivalent iff $Z_f(x) = Z_g(x)$. There is no test that can distinguish between f and g. i.e. all tests that detect f also detect g [4].

Controlling value (c): Whatever the other input value, the output will not affect is known as controlling value for that gate. For nand gate it is "0" means if one of the inputs of nand gate is "0" and other may be "0" or "1", for both the cases the output will remain always "1".

Inversion Value (i): If the gate has inversion nature than its value is "1" otherwise it is "0".

For a gate with controlling value c and inversion value i, all the input s_a_c faults and output s_a_(c xor i) are functionally equivalent. Consider nand gate, input s_a_c means s_a_0 is equivalent to output s_a_(c xor i) means s_a_1.

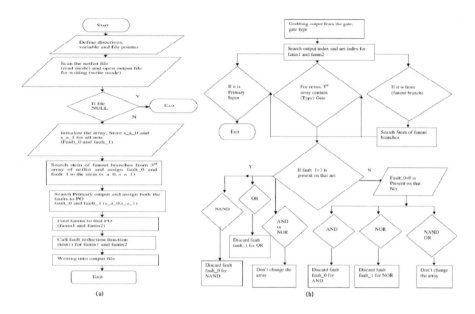

(a)   (b)

Fig. 1. Flow chart for (a) reduced fault set using fault equivalence method (b) Fault reduced function

The flow charts of the fault equivalence and is shown in figure 1 (a). We start from primary output (PO) and reach upto the primary input (PI). ISCAS netlist format for C17 circuit is input to this program. First of all we scan this netlist. Then initialize the output array fault_0 and fault_1 with fault_0=0 and fault_1=1 for every net. After applying equivalence logic if any fault has to be discarded then its corresponding value will be replaced by 8 (i.e. 0 or 1 will be replaced by 8). Then Search the stem of branches, assign both the faults fault_0=0 and fault_1=1 to the stem (netno). For this purpose, if 3rd array of the netlist is "from" then find fanout from 4th array of netlist for total number of rows and assign both the faults to that net number which is stem. Search Primary output (PO) and assign both the faults fault_0=0 and fault_1=1 to the PO (netno). If 4th array of netlist contains "0" then it is PO, assign both the faults to that net number (netno). Starts from Primary output (PO). Find fanins to that PO from 6th and 7th array (fanin1, fanin2). Call fault reduction function (test1) for all fanins. Write the reduced faults into the output text file . If it contains fault_0=0 and 8 means fault_1=1 is discarded and if it contains fault_1=1 and 8 then fault_0=0 is discarded. Only net number (netno) and stuck value 0 or 1 for particular net is printed. The flow chart for fault reduced function (test1) is shown in figure 1 (b). The reduced fault set for ISCAS C17 circuit is shown in figure 10 in results section. Logic is, start from primary output (PO) and reach up to primary input (PI). For all succeeding nets, it may be "from", "gate" or "input". Take action according to the 3rd array of the netlist, discard particular fault means store 8 numeric values for discarded fault (Instead of 8 we can take any integer value but can't take character type since it will differ from integer type and size of array). If it is PI then stop.

3   Controllability Observability

The search process of any Test Generation algorithms involves two important decisions. The first one being to select one of the several unsolved problems existing at a certain stage in the execution of the algorithm, the second type is to select one possible way to solve the selected problem. Selection criteria differ mainly by the cost functions they are used to measure "difficulty". Typically cost functions are of two types [7]:

1. Controllability - For a digital circuit it is defined as the difficulty of setting a particular logic signal to state 0 or 1.
2. Observability - For a digital circuit it is defined as the difficulty of observing the state of a logic signal.

The testability measures combinational controllability 0-CC0, combinational controllability 1-CC1, and combinational observability -CO (Ob) are implemented using C++. The Controllability 0 -CC0 and Controllability1-CC1 value for the fanout branch is same as the value of stem.

   If a and b are inputs of a gate and z is the output then the following are the controllability 0-CC0, controllability 1-CC1 values for input a and b. Values for different gates are given [5]

AND:
$CCO(Z)=min(CC0(a),CC0(b))+1$
$CC1(Z)=CC1(a)+CC1(b)+1$
NAND:
$CC0(Z)=CC1(a)+CC1(b)+1$
$CC1(Z)=min(CC0(a),CC0(b))+1$
EXOR:
$CC0(Z)=min(CC0(a)+CC0(b),CC1(a)+CC1(b))+1$
$CC1(Z)=min(CC1(a)+CC0(b),CC0(a)+CC1(b))+1$
EXNOR:
$CC0(Z)=min(CC1(a)+CC0(b),CC0(a)+CC1(b))+1$
$CC1(Z)=min(CC0(a)+CC0(b),CC1(a)+CC1(b))+1$
NOT: $CC0(Z)=CC1(a)+1$

OR:
$CC0(Z)=CC0(a)+CC0(b)+1$
$CC1(Z)=min(CC1(a),CC1(b))+1$
NOR:
$CC0(Z)=min(CC1(a),CC1(b))+1$
$CC1(Z)=CC0(a)+CC0(b)+1$

$CC1(Z)=CC0(a)+1$

Figure 2 shows the controllability 0-CC0 and controllability 1-CC1 values for ISCAS C17 benchmark circuit.

   The observability value calculation for various gates is as follows, where CO (Z) is the output observability, CC0 (a) and CC0 (b) are controllability 0 values

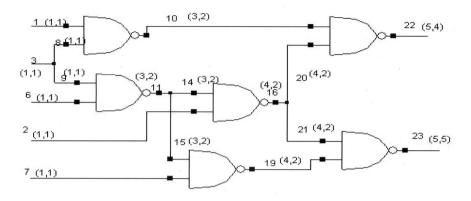

Fig. 2. ISCAS85 C17 benchmark circuit along with CC0 and CC1 values

for a input and b input respectively. CC1 (a) and CC1 (b) are controllability 1 value for a input and b input respectively. CO (a) is observability for input a and CO (b) is observability value for input b.

AND:
CO(a)=CO(Z)+CC1(b)+1
CO(b)=CO(Z)+CC1(a)+1
NAND:
CO(a)=CO(Z)+CC1(b)+1
CO(b)=CO(Z)+CC1(a)+1
EXOR:
CO(a)=CO(Z)+min(CC0(b),CC1(b))+1
CO(b)=CO(Z)+min(CC0(a),CC1(a))+1
EXNOR:
CO(a)=CO(Z)+min(CC0(b),CC1(b))+1
CO(b)=CO(Z)+min(CC0(a),CC1(a))+1
NOT: CO(a)=CO(Z)+1

OR:
CO(a)=CO(Z) +CC0(b)+1
CO(b)=CO(Z)+CC0(a)+1
NOR:
CO(a)=CO(Z)+CC0(b)+1
CO(b)=CO(Z)+CC0(a)+1

If a is stem and having branches Z1, Z2 upto Zn then observability is

CO (a) = min (CO (Z1), CO (Z2), CO (Zn))

The flow chart for testability measures is shown in figure 3 . The controllability function is developed separately shown by part "C"of figure is given in figure (a). The observability function developed separately shown as part "O" in figure 3 is given in figure (b).

Firstly We Initialized the output array which contains netno, controllability 0 (CCO), controllability 1(CC1) and Observability (ob), c_0 (CC0) and c_1 (CC1) to "0" since minimum value of it is "1" and Observability to "-1" since it has minimum value as "0". To find the controllability we proceed from primary input (PI) upto primary output (PO). The value CC0 and CC1 is calculated for different gates as discussed previously. The flow chart for controllability function is shown in figure 4 (a). The observability function is shown in figure 4 (b). Firstly

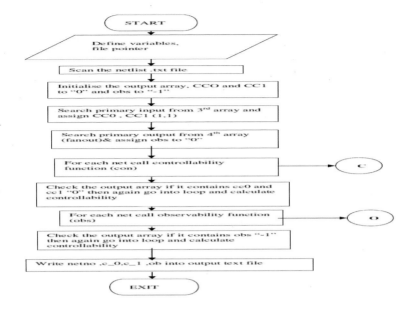

Fig. 3. Flow chart of testability measures

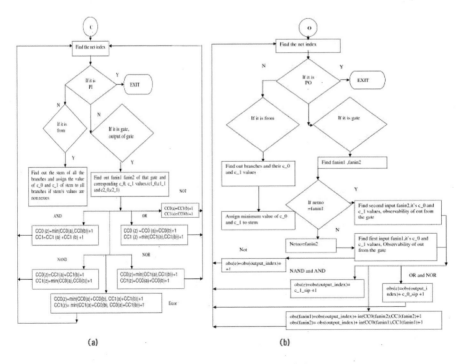

Fig. 4. Flow chart of (a) controllability function (b) Observability function

it finds out the net indices. If that net is primary output then return since we already stored Observability to "0" value. If it not primary output then it may be from or gate. If it is gate then it finds two inputs to that gate.

Then function will calculate the observability for net under consideration using following rules

If gate type is
'and'   :ob (e)= obs(output_index)+ c_1_sip +1
'nand' :obs(e)= obs(output_index)+ c_1_sip +1
'or'   :obs(e)= obs(output_index)+ c_0_sip +1
'nor'   :obs(e)= obs(output_index)+ c_0_sip +1

Where e is net index for the net under consideration, output_index is the index for the net which is gate output.

c_1_sip is the controllability 1 of second input to that gate and c_0_sip is the controllability 0 of the second input to that gate. If net under consideration is stem then assign minimum observability out of the two observabilities for branches to stem. For that purpose we have developed simple minimum function separately to find minimum of among all fanout branches.

4   Controllability Observability Aided ATPG for Reduced Fault Set

ATPG (acronym for both Automatic Test Pattern Generation and Automatic Test Pattern Generator) is an electronic design automation method/technology used to find an input (or test) sequence that, when applied to a digital circuit, enables testers to distinguish between the correct circuit behavior and the faulty circuit behavior caused by defects. The generated patterns are used to test semiconductor devices after manufacture, and in some cases to assist with determining the cause of failure (failure analysis) the effectiveness of ATPG is measured by the amount of modeled defects, or fault models, that are detected and the number of generated patterns.

The ATPG process for a targeted fault consists of two phases: fault activation and fault propagation [6]. Fault activation establishes a signal value at the fault model site that is opposite of the value produced by the fault model. Fault propagation moves the resulting signal value, or fault effect, forward by sensitizing a path from the fault site to a primary output.

Line justification function shown by part "J" in figure 5 is developed separately. Flow chart of Justification function is shown in figure 6 (a). Here the selection of any one input will be done based on controllability 0 and 1 functions. Find the CC0 and CC1 values for both the fanins. Value to justify is 0, compare both the fanins for CC0 and select the fan in with minimum CC0.If value to be justifying 1, compare both the fanins for CC1 and select the fan in with minimum CC1.

Error propagation function is shown in figure 6(b). If given net is not a primary output but it is a stem then propagation can be forwarded to any of its branches.

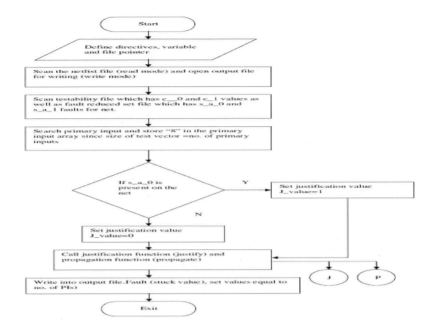

Fig. 5. Flow chart of testability based ATPG for reduced fault set

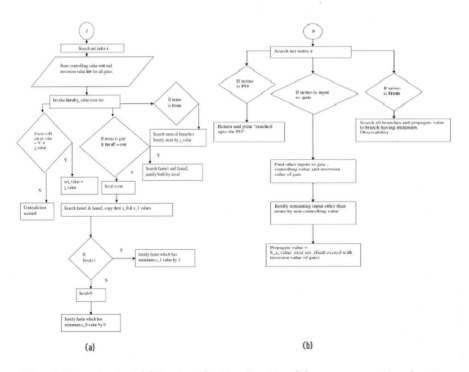

Fig. 6. Flow chart of (a)line justification function (b)error propagation function

Selection of branch will be done here on the basis of observability function. Find out the branches of given stem and index for each branch. Find out the observability for each branch from corresponding element of obs array. Select the branch with minimum observability and call the propagation function for selected branch with value for propagation error value (stuck value).We can use the output of testability measures program to get the values of controllability 0-CC0, Controllability 1-CC1 and observability. Testability measures help us to select a line for justification and to select a path for error propagation. Hence this ATPG is based on controllability and observability. Again we are finding test vectors for reduced fault, generated by fault equivalence method.

5   Results

The programs for all above concepts are developed in C++. The snap shots of output window are shown in results section for all programs. The programs are generic can be used for any combinational circuit but for the result purpose only results for ISCAS85 C17 benchmark circuit are shown. Figure 10 shows the reduced fault list for ISCAS85 C17 benchmark circuit. The first column of the

Fig. 7. Snap shot of output for ISCAS 85 C17 benchmark circuit for reduced fault set

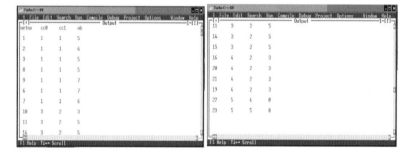

Fig. 8. Snap shot of output for ISCAS 85 C17 benchmark circuit for controllability and observability

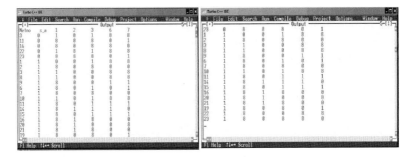

Fig. 9. Snap shot of output for ISCAS 85 C17 benchmark circuit for controllability observability aided ATPG for reduced fault set

output window shows the net number and second column shows the fault present on that corresponding net number. The fault present is either stuck at 0 or stuck at 1. Both the faults are separated and shown in figure 7. Figure 8 shows the output of testability measures controllability and observability. Here first column of output window shows the net number, second column is for controllability 0-CC0, third is controllability 1-CC1 and forth column shows the observability-ob for corresponding net number. Figure 9 shows the output of controllability observability aided ATPG with reduced fault set. In this first column is net number, second column is stuck at fault present on that net either stuck at 0 or stuck at 1. The length of test vector is equal to the number of primary inputs so that the array size is equal to primary inputs. All other columns represents test vector for corresponding fault on net. Here "8" is stored instead of don't care (x) so that array type can't differ.

6   Conclusion

The object oriented generic program is developed to reduce the number of single stuck at faults. For these reduced faults, test vectors are generated based on controllability and observability using line justification and error propagation. The complete ATPG based on controllability and observability for reduced fault set is developed using C++. The results are shown for ISCAS 85 C17 benchmark circuit which matches to manual calculations.

References

1. Lee, S., Cobb, B., Dworak, J., Grimaila, M.R., Ray Mercer, M.: A New ATPG Algorithm to Limit Test Set Size and Achieve Multiple Detections of all Faults. In: Proceedings of the Design Automation and Test in Europe Conference and Exhibition (2002)
2. Srinivasan, S., Swaminathan, G., Aylor, J.H.: Algebraic ATPG of Combinational Circuits Using Binary Decision Diagrams. IEEE Transaction, 240–248 (1993)

3. Abramovici, M., Breuer, M.A., Friedman, A.D.: Digital Systems Testing and Testable Design. IEEE Press, NJ (1990)
4. Abramovici, M., Breuer, M.A., Friedman, A.D.: Digital Systems Testing and Testable Design. Jaico Publication (1997)
5. Bushnell, M., Agrawal, V.: Essentials of Electronic Testing. Springer Publication, Heidelberg (2000)
6. Abramovici, M., Aitken, R.: Error, Fault and Defect Diagnosis: A Detective Story: Tutorial. In: IEEE International Test Conference (1997)
7. Goldstein, L.H.: Controllability/Observability Analysis of digital circuits. IEEE Transactions on Circuits and Systems, 26(1984), 685–693 (1979)
8. Bryan, D.: ISCAS 1985 benchmark circuits and netlist format. North Carolina State University

Implementation of ADPLL with 0.6μm CMOS Process for SOC Applications

V. Leela Rani[1], V. Suma Latha[2], G.T. Rao[1], and D.S. Murty[3]

[1] Associate Professor, ECE, GVPCOE Visakhapatnam, AP, India
[2] Assistant Professor, ECE, GVPCOE Visakhapatnam, AP, India
[3] Professor, GVPCOE Visakhapatnam, AP, India
{lee_rani,suma_vlsi,dsmurty41}@yahoo.co.in,
tirumalagrao@gmail.com

Abstract. In this paper, we propose a new All Digital Phase Locked Loop (ADPLL) for SOC applications. The proposed ADPLL can be designed with any standard cell library. The ADPLL has been implemented using standard cells of 0.6μm CMOS process from CADENCE TOOLS. The designed ADPLL operates in the range between 12.5 MHz to 100MHz with phase error of less than 10ns. Portability over different processes is ensured in the new ADPLL. The complexity in the design process is reduced. The time for redesign considerably decreases making it suitable for SOC applications.

Keywords: All Digital PLL, Phase/Frequency detector, digitally controlled oscillator.

1 Introduction

PLL's are widely used in many communication systems to clock, data recovery and frequency synthesis [1,3,4,5]. Cellular phones, motor speed controllers are some examples based on PLL application [3]. In conventional designs, PLL is often designed by analog approaches. However, analog PLLs have to overcome the digital switch noise coupling with power supply and also are sensitive to process parameters [2,3,4,5]. Advancement in the IC technology has made ADPLL's attractive over their analog counter parts. With the advent of digital implementations such as area of On Chip occupancy, power consumption and higher immunity for switching noise [2,3,4,6,11] PLL designs have improved considerably in performance. This paper presents a new ADPLL for SOC applications. The proposed ADPLL can be designed with any standard cell library. Thus, the portability over different processes is ensured and the time for redesign and complexity can be reduced that makes the proposed system suitable for On Chip applications. Different stages in the architecture are individually designed and integrated for the complete architecture. The proposed design has been implemented using standard cells of 0.6μm CMOS process from Cadence.

This paper is organized as follows. Section 2 describes the architecture of ADPLL. The proposed PFD and DCO are given in section 3. Section 4 shows the experimental results of the ADPLL. Finally, the conclusions are given in section 5.

N. Meghanathan et al. (Eds.): NeCoM, WiMoN, and WeST 2010, CCIS 90, pp. 693–701, 2010.
© Springer-Verlag Berlin Heidelberg 2010

2 Architecture Overview

Fig.1 shows the block diagram of the proposed ADPLL. The major building blocks in the ADPLL are Phase and Frequency Detector (PFD), Digital word Control Oscillator (DCO) and an enable circuit to route the generated synchronous circuit signal.

Phase/frequency detector responds both to phase differences and frequency differences. A PFD has several desirable characteristics. Once the loop is locked it will be highly stable with the reference signals and   has no ripple. The major downside, that limits the highest frequency, is PFD being an edge triggered circuit, is susceptible to noise. As a part of phase and frequency detection, the incoming signal frequency is first determined. Frequency is determined by counting the number of clock pulses between two successive rising edges of the incoming signal. The count so obtained is given to the digital word controlled oscillator. The phase difference between the two signals is determined by counting the number of clock pulses between the rising edge of incoming signal and oscillator signal. This count is the phase error word.

The advantage of a digital oscillator is that it can lock to any frequency over a wide range. According to the frequency word generated a predetermined frequency signal can be routed. PLL locks only to a fixed range of frequencies. Once the signal of the required frequency is generated in the DCO, phase error is measured using phase detector for phase correction. This error word is used to correct the DCO signal so that it locks to the reference signal.

DCO signal is in synchronization with the reference signal by providing a delay using the error word.

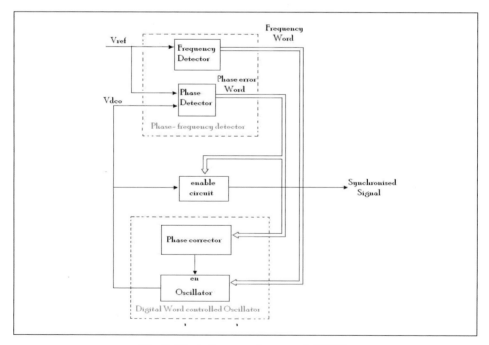

Fig. 1. Block diagram of proposed ADPLL

3   Circuit Design

We proposed a DCO circuit and a PFD circuit to achieve the high performance ADPLL. These essential components of the ADPLL are implemented with cell library without any passive components, so it is easy to integrate ADPLL.

3.1   Phase/Frequency Detector

The block diagram of phase/frequency detector is shown in fig 2. The frequency detector and the phase detector forms the two functional blocks generating the error words.

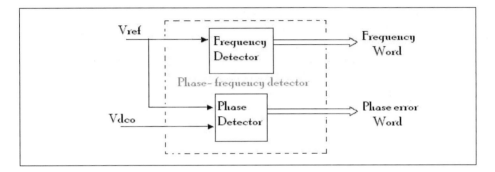

Fig. 2. Block diagram of Phase/Freq. detector

3.1.1   Frequency Detector
An incoming signal is observed at the input of the PLL and the frequency of the signal is determined. This frequency is determined by counting the number of clock pulses between two successive rising edges of the incoming signal. The count so obtained (frequency word) is given to digital word controlled oscillator.

Fig.3 shows the schematic of Frequency detector which consists of a rising edge detector and counter. The rising edge detector is a sequential circuit which provides an output pulse of 1.1 ns on period every time a rising edge is detected. This rising edge detector's output is given as toggle input to a positive edge-sensitive T-flip-flop. Thus, the value of Q remains high between two consecutive rising edges of the incoming signals and during the next cycle remains low. This output Q is used as the enable pulse of the 4-bit counter. When Q is high, the number of clock pulses traversed is counted. The counter is cleared using the inverted form of the pulse generated from the rising edge-detector. The advantage with the digital design is that by increasing the clock frequency and also by improving the resolution of the counter, the precision of the frequency detector can be programmed according to the requirement.

3.1.2   Phase Detector
Fig.4 shows the schematic of Phase detector. Once the oscillator's frequency is matched to that of the incoming signal, the phase error is calculated and corrected. For phase detection, the number of pulses between the rising edges of the incoming

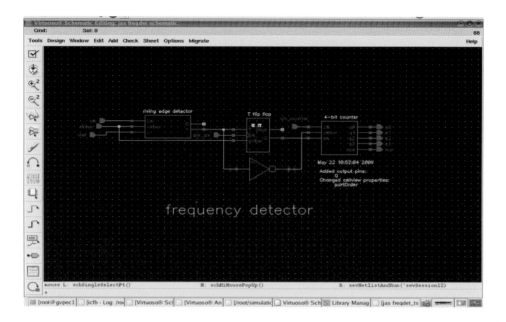

Fig. 3. Schematic of Frequency detector

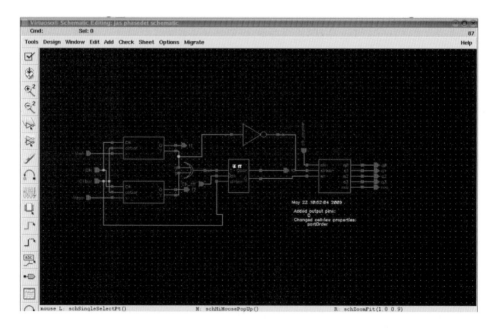

Fig. 4. Schematic of Phase detector

signal and oscillator are counted using a n-bit counter. The clock frequency depends on the designed resolution. Variation in oscillator frequency will appear as phase errors in the system. In the phase detector circuit the phase sensing is at the rising edge of the reference signal or the DCO signal.

When either of the variations occurs, the counter is enabled using the Q output of the T-flip-flop. When the subsequent rising edge is detected the Q output goes low, disabling the counter and holding the value of the error word at the counter outputs.

3.2 Digitally Controlled Oscillator

The block diagram of DCO is shown in fig 5. Phase corrector and frequency corrector are two main blocks of DCO.

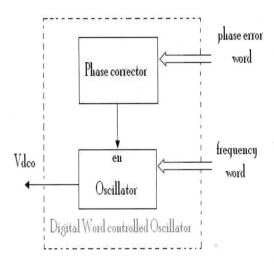

Fig. 5. Block diagram of DCO

3.2.1 Frequency Corrector

Fig.6 shows the schematic of Frequency corrector. The frequency word from the phase/frequency detector is taken as input and according to the digital word obtained a corresponding frequency signal is generated by the DCO. The frequency corrector schematic is similar to a multiplexer. The frequency error word coming from the detector selects the required frequency signal which is the output of the DCO.As the number of bits of the frequency word is increased the locking precision is improved. This functionality can also be realized by using a digital frequency mixer, where the output frequency is the sum of input frequencies.

3.2.2 Phase Corrector

Fig.7. shows the schematic of Phase corrector. The phase corrector block consists of a comparator and a D-flip-flop.

The phase error word obtained from the phase/frequency block is used to correct the phase error between the two signals. The error word from the phase detector is then transferred to a full-subtractor, where it is differenced from the frequency word to generate the delay word. The DCO signal is given as input to the D-flip flop. The clear pulse (active low) of a D-flip flop is held low till the count (count − Delay) is reached. There is an inherent delay in the D-flip flop of 0.5ns designed. Therefore, to produce correctness in the delay provided to the D-flip flop, the subtractor is given '1' as "borrow in".

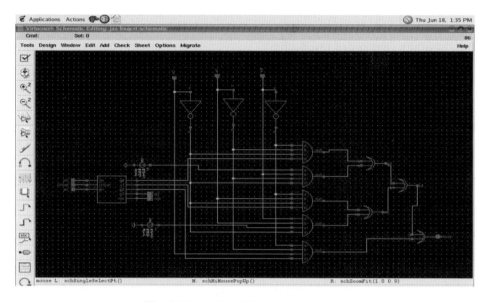

Fig. 6. Schematic of Frequency corrector

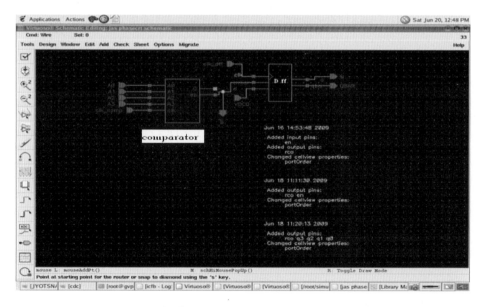

Fig. 7. Schematic of Phase corrector

4   Experimental Results

The ADPLL has been implemented with 0.6μm CMOS standard cell library from CADENCE. The simulation results of various blocks in the proposed ADPLL are given. One of the blocks in the proposed ADPLL is phase/frequency detector, which has individual blocks of frequency detector and phase detector. Fig.8 and Fig.9 shows the simulation results of above mentioned blocks.

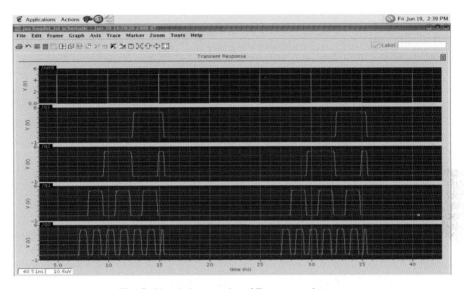

Fig. 8. Simulation results of Frequency detector

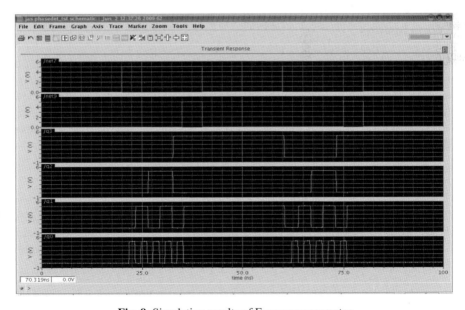

Fig. 9. Simulation results of Frequency corrector

The main block of ADPLL is DCO, consisting of frequency corrector and phase corrector. The simulation results of these two blocks are shown in fig.9 and fig.10.The simulation results shows that proposed ADPLL operates over the range of 12.5MHZ to 100MHz with 5V power supply and phase error of less than 10ns.The simulation of integrated ADPLL has been successfully performed using CADENCE TOOLS.

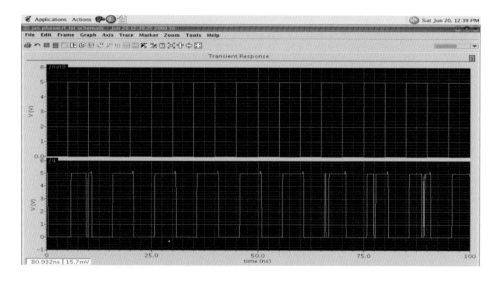

Fig. 10. Simulation results of Phase corrector

5 Conclusions

In this paper, a new ADPLL is presented for SOC applications. The proposed ADPLL can be implemented with standard cell library, and has good portability over different processes. The ADPLL is implemented with 0.6µm CMOS standard cell library and can operate from 12.5 MHz to 100 MHz. Portability over various processes is ensured in the new ADPLL as well as the complexity can be reduced and the time for redesign is considerably decreased.

Acknowledgments

The CADENCE TOOLS were procured for this project under Research Promotion Scheme (RPS) from AICTE. We express our gratitude to AICTE for the RPS funding. Also, we would like to thank all our colleagues for fruitful discussions and suggestions for this paper.

References

[1] Stefo, R., Schreiter, J., Schlubler, J.-U., Schuffny, R.: High Resolution ADPLL Frequency synthesizer for FPGA and ASIC based Applications. In: Field programmable Technology Proc. IEEE international conference, December 2003, pp. 28–34 (2003)

[2] Chiang, J. -S., Chen, K.-y.: A 3.3V All Digital Phase Locked Loop With Small Dco Hardware And Fast Phase Lock. In: Proc. IEEE international conference circuits and systems, May 31- June 3, pp. 554–557 (1998)

[3] Zhao, J., Kim, Y.-B.: A Novel All Digital phase Locked Loop with Ultra Fast Frequency and Phase Acquisition

[4] Wang, C.C., Lee, T.j., Tseng, S.L.: A Low Power All Digital Phase Locked Loop Using Binary Frequency Searching

[5] Chung, C.C., Lee, C.Y.: An All Digital Phase Locked Loop for High Speed Clock generation. IEEE J. Solid State Circuits 38 (February 2003)

[6] Mendel, S., Vogel, C.: A Z- Domain Model and Analysis of Phase-Domain All –Digital Phase-Locked Loops. In: IEEE international conference (2007)

[7] Chen, P.-L., Chung, C.-C., Lee, C.Y.: An ALL Digital PLL with cascaded Dynamic Phase Average Loop for Wide Multiplication Range Applications. In: IEEE international conference (2005)

[8] Mendel, S., Vogel, C.: Improved Lock Time in All-Digital Phase-Locked Loops Due to Binary Search Acquisition. In: IEEE international conference (2008)

[9] Sheng, D., Chung, C.-c., Lee, C.y.: An All-Digital Phase-Locked Loop with High – Resolution for SOC Applications. In: IEEE international conference (2006)

[10] Olsson, T., Nilsson, P.: A Digital PLL made from Standard cells. In: ECCTD 2001- European Conference on Circuit Theory and Design, Espoo, Finland, August 28-31 (2001)

[11] Kratyk, V., Hanumolu, P.K., Mayaram, K., Moon, U.-K.: A 0.6GHz to 2 GHz Digital PLL with Wide Tracking Range. In: IEEE Custom Integrated Circuits conference, CICC (2007)

Fault Diagnosis of Analog Circuits Utilizing Reconfigurable Computing System

P. Poonguzhali and N. Sarat Chandra Babu

Centre for Development of Advanced Computing, Hyderabad
{poonguzhalip,sarat}@cdac.in

Abstract. Advances in the field of Integrated Circuits (ICs) has resulted in high density Very Large Scale Integrated (VLSI) chips comprising of both digital and analog components onto a single chip. Consequently, testing of these ICs with analog and digital components are challenging and time consuming. Moreover, the techniques available for testing analog components when compared to digital are less and also difficult. This paper describes a approach of utilizing Field Programmable Gate Arrays (FPGAs) for fault diagnosis of analog circuits describing the technique of Reconfigurable Computing Systems (RCS). The paper provides a brief about Fault diagnosis, FPGAs and utilization of FPGAs for RCS followed with the approach of the research. In summary the paper provides a brief about utilizing a digital hardware to perform testing of analog cicuits.

Keywords: Analog Circuits, Fault Diagnosis, Reconfigurable Computing System, Field Programmable Gate Arrays.

1   Introduction

> *"Everything is going Digital. Analog design seems obsolete but in fact, Analog ICs are growing almost exactly in same phase of Digital. The digital revolution is constructed on top of an Analog reality."*[1]

Often, analog circuits are employed for high speed, low precision, high complexity functional blocks. It can be obviously understood that both analog and digital share about equal importance and demand in todays IC designs. Designers of digital chips focus on Design-For-Testability(DFT), logic verification and synthesis quality. The main concern would be area, power and timing constraints of the design, obtaining timing closure of the physical design, and other high level issues. But analog design is performed at a very low level of abstraction, traditionally the transistor level and hence are more challenging in terms of fault diagnosis. They often deal with handling unusual voltages and currents that require special consideration. Analog designs are driven from schematics rather than from high level code and are highly dependent on the quality of the simulation models. Literature survey depicts that methodologies for testing analog circuits when compared to digital circuits remain relatively underdeveloped. The

N. Meghanathan et al. (Eds.): NeCoM, WiMoN, and WeST 2010, CCIS 90, pp. 702–711, 2010.
© Springer-Verlag Berlin Heidelberg 2010

reason for the lack of proper fault model of the devices is due to the existence of multiple values (voltage, current, frequency, etc) at each node of the circuit.

Fault diagnosis systems are capable of detecting and isolating faults. Moreover, these systems are capable of identifying their type and characteristics in which detection implies the decision that a fault is present whereas isolation implies the determination of the source of the fault. After a fault is detected and isolated, actions to eliminate the fault should be taken to prevent further damage[2]. In this paper, we propose a technique of diagnosing faults in a analog circuit by adopting RCS. Here the analog circuits are subjected to fault simulation and the values are stored in a fault dictionary. Then, these fault dictionaries are converted into a form that can be stored in the memory of FPGA. FPGA, on reconfiguration loads the fault dictionary corresponding to the analog Circuit Under Test (CUT).

The remainder of the paper is structured as follows. The second section of the paper provides a brief about Fault Diagnosis of Analog circuits, the third section briefs about RCS. The fourth section describes the research approach adopted followed with the system decomposition in the fifth section. The paper concludes with the summary of the research work.

2   Fault Diagnosis of Analog Circuits

Fault diagnosis [3], [4], [5] of analog circuits is one of the most challenging task and is ever-increasingly important owing to the rapidly increasing complexity of ICs. Fault diagnosis as the name depicts means the diagnosis of faults based the circuit parameters. In other words, given the circuit topology and nominal circuit parameter values, fault diagnosis is to obtain the exact information about a faulty circuit based on the analysis of the circuit responses. The bottlenecks of analog fault diagnosis primarily lie in the inherited features of analog circuits which varies frequently in the continuous time domain of analog circuits. There are various techniques proposed for testing analog circuits [6], [7], [8].

The techniques of testing analog circuits can be classified as either specification-driven or fault model driven [9]. In specification-driven technique, the circuit parameter is verified with their associated tolerance values, while in fault model driven, a dictionary of faults is constructed initially and the circuit parameters are subjected to verification with these values. A fault in an analog IC can be either catastrophic or parametric. In most cases, the former is caused by physical defects, which change the topology of the chip while the later is caused by the variations in the device parameters. The level of fault diagnosis of analog circuits and components of mixed-signal electronic systems is still in its infancy inspite of continuous development in this field, especially for circuits with limited measurement accessibility. The calculations or verification are complex even for simple linear circuits, and their complexity grows faster than the number of circuit components [10], [11].

The methods of analog fault diagnosis can be broadly classified into Simulation Before Test (SBT) and Simulation After Test (SAT) [12], [13]. The technique varies in the fact that the simulation is done before or after the test. SBT methods are usually preferred as it cuts down the testing time. But SAT provides the exact solution to the circuit parameters and can be applied to detect large parameter changes when the number of independent measurements are greater than the number of faults in the CUT.

3   Reconfigurable Computing System

Reconfigurable Computing [14], [15] is a technique which involves manipulation of the logic within the FPGA at run-time. These are also termed as Configurable Computing or Custom Computing. This combines the flexibility of software and the speed advantage of hardware. Though general purpose processors are suitable for a wide range of tasks, they cannot handle computationally intensive problems. To address the computation intensive problems, Application Specific Integrated Circuits (ASIC) are designed specifically to perform a computation. Although ASICs are fast and efficient in performing the computation, they cannot be altered after fabrication. Any change in the circuit needs the redesign of the whole hardware [16]. There is always a trade-off between speed and flexibility.

Reconfigurable Computing, a major player in the recent advancements are advantageous to both the user and the designer. One of the key component to perform RCS is FPGA. FPGAs, orginally created to serve as a hybrid device between Programmable Array Logics (PAL) and Mask-Programmable Gate Arrays(MPGA). FPGAs blend both PALs and MPGAs by the characteristic of electrical programmability which can also be customized nearly instantaneously. Also, they can implement very complex computations on a single chip. Because of these features, FPGAs are being considered as a glue-logic replacement and a device for rapid prototyping [17]. FPGAs are advantageous in the factors like flexibility, capacity and performance of the devices, which has formed the basis of reconfigurable computing [18].

3.1   Field Programmable Gate Arrays

FPGA [19], an integrated circuit containing gate matrix designed to be configured by the user in the field. Its a set of programmable logic gates and rich configurable interconnect resources which can be used to implement any logic function. The logic components can be programmed by an end user to describe the functionality of basic logic gates to more complex functions. In other words, FPGAs are an array of uncommitted elements that can be programmed or interconnected according to an user specification. This feature of reprogramming the FPGA devices over and over again along with the flexibility of programmable interconnects makes this an ideal solution for prototyping ASICs.

Now a days, FPGAs are designed to meet most of the performance requirements of ASICs. The configuration of the FPGA is stored on embedded static Random Access Memory (RAM) within the chip, which in turn controls the contents of the Logic Cells and multiplexers that perform routing.

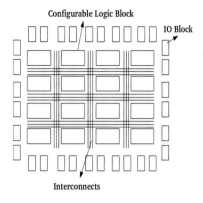

Fig. 1. FPGA Architecture

Architecture of FPGA Figure 1 depicts the general architecture of FPGA. The major components in FPGAs are

1. Configurable Logic Blocks (CLB)
2. Input/Output Blocks (IOB)
3. Programmable interconnects

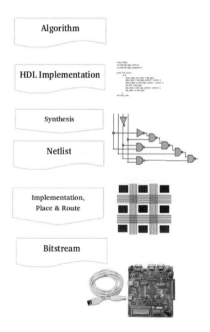

Fig. 2. FPGA Configuration Flow

Configurable Logic Blocks: CLB forms the basic logic unit in an FPGA. FPGAs are built from one basic "logic-cell", duplicated hundreds or thousands of time. A logic-cell is basically a small LookUp Table (LUT), a D-flipflop and a 2-to-1 multiplexer.

Input/Output Blocks: FPGAs provide support for many I/O standards, thus providing the ideal system interface bridge. Inputs and Outputs in FPGA devices are grouped in banks, with each bank independently able to support different I/O standards. The interconnect wires also go to the boundary of the device where I/O cells are implemented and connected to the pins of the FPGAs.

Programmable Interconnects: Each logic-cell can be connected to other logic-cells through interconnect resources. Logic cells connected together are utilized to create complex logic functions.

Figure 2 depicts the design flow of FPGA. The basic design flow of an FPGA comprises of the steps beginning from design entry either by HDL/Schematic, Simulation, Synthesis, Place and Route till the generation of the bitstream. The bitstream is then used to configure the FPGA for realizing simplex to complex logic functions.

4   Approach

Testing of ICs play a major role in the determination of the design cost. Normally, testing of analog circuits in the IC dominates overall testing cost. The techniques available to verify the analog circuits are less which are also challenging and time consuming. To facilitate faster testing of analog circuits, we propose an approach of testing the analog circuits with the help of digital hardware.

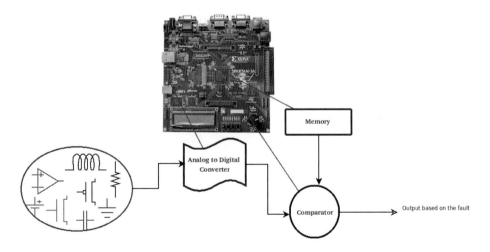

Fig. 3. Block Diagram of the Proposed System

Hardware implementation of the testing process provides the speed flexibility. The cost incurred by the hardware is reduced by implementing a reconfigurable hardware logic, which reconfigures itself based on the analog circuit under test. The system modules of the proposed approach is depicted in Figure 3.

The components on the FPGA includes the interfacing of ADC with the FPGA, memory module to store the fault dictionary values and a comparator to compare the values on the fly.

5   System Modules

The proposed system can be decomposed into the following modules.

1. Analog Circuit Simulation
2. Fault Dictionary Storage
3. Reconfiguration using FPGAs

5.1   Analog Circuit Simulation

The technique opted for fault diagnosis of analog circuit is SBT, which enables to reduce the time incurred in the testing process. The circuit is subjected to fault simulation and the simulation results are stored as a list of faults or dictionary of faults. The fault dictionary is constructed for all the analog circuits of interest. These fault dictionaries are then converted into its binary equivalent, thereby enabling the storage of analog fault dictionaries into the memory.

Quite Universal Circuit Simulator (QUCS) [20], an open source electronics circuit simulator was used to setup the circuit with a graphical user interface (GUI). The circuit was then simulated with faults introduced as represented in the table below (resistors open/short). The resultant values are then stored in a dictionary called the fault dictionary. The values in the fault dictionary are then integer coded by which the values can be represented more efficiently.

The Figure 4 depicts the circuit under test while the table below depicts the sample fault dictionary constructed by simulating the analog circuit.

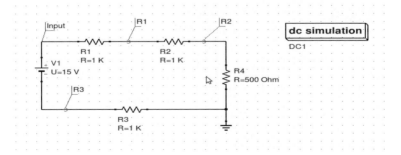

Fig. 4. Analog Circuit Simulation

Fault Dictionary

S.No	Faults	Input Voltage	Node1 Voltage	Node2 Voltage	Node3 Voltage	Binary Equivalent
1	Nominal	15	14.9	14.9	-0.03	11111111
2	R1 Open	15	0	0	0	00000000
3	R2 Open	15	15	0	0	11110000

5.2   Fault Dictionary Storage

The integer coded fault dictionary are then subjected to a process of conversion, where the values are converted into its equivalent binary format, thereby enabling its storage onto the memory. This has been achieved by a Python [21] script which would convert the fault values into its binary format.

Python Code Snippet for Converting Fault Values

```
def appendConvVal(num): # append the array with converted values
        for j in range (16):
                print (faultName[j]+bin(num)[2:])
                finalFaultName.append(faultName[j]+bin(num)[2:])

def readFaultName(): # Fault Names
        for i in range(16):
                faultName.append(f.readline()[2:].rstrip())
```

The python code snippet as shown above was used to convert the fault values into its equivalent binary. In order to store these binary values onto the memory, a Hardware Description Language (HDL) code for Read Only Memory(ROM) was generated with the option of dynamic insertion of fault dictionary values. The same has been achieved with the help of C code which reads the fault dictionary values and creates a ROM HDL code. The code snippet for generating the memory module is given below.

C Code Snippet for generating Read Only Memory HDL

```
fprintf (outfile, "\
\n\
ARCHITECTURE arch OF PROM_MEM IS\n\
  TYPE rom_type IS array (0 TO 2 ** SIZE - 1) OF
                          std_logic_vector(WIDTH - 1 DOWNTO 0);\n\
  SIGNAL rom : rom_type := (", SIZE, argv[3]);
/** Loads the ROM memory with the values from the fault dictionary **/
  while ((fgets (buf, SIZE + 1, infile) != NULL))  {
      fprintf (outfile, "%d => \"%s\"", i, buf);
      fseek (infile, 1L, SEEK_CUR);
      if ((i != ((2*SIZE)-1)) ) {
          fprintf(outfile,",");
      }
```

```
        i++;
    }
/** Loads the rest of ROM memory with the Zero values **/
    program_size = power (2, atoi (argv[3]));
    while (i < program_size) {
        fprintf (outfile, "%d => \"00000000\"", i);
        if (i != (program_size - 1)) {
            fprintf (outfile, ",");
        }
        i++;
    }
```

5.3   Reconfiguration Using FPGAs

Spartan-3A [22] FPGAs are used for the design as they are very cost effective and provides better options in terms of flexibility to design a system. Moreover, it supports all the basic features required for the proposed system at much lower cost. Also, they have a special feature, called MultiBoot that allows the FPGA to selectively reprogram and reload its bitstream from an external memory. The MultiBoot feature allows the FPGA application to load two or more FPGA bitstreams under the control of the FPGA application. The FPGA application triggers a MultiBoot operation, causing the FPGA to reconfigure from a different configuration bitstream. The multiboot feature was utilized to achieve reconfiguration using FPGAs. The FPGA loads the bitstream corresponding to the signal from the user, thus making the hardware to perform multiple operations without changing the logic every time.

6   FPGA Implementation

The overall system functionality is achieved by integrating the above three modules. The process of integration on the FPGA included the following steps:

1. **Interfacing on-board ADC available on Spartan-3A board to the FPGA:**
   This includes the development of HDL code for ADC, simulation and synthesis of the developed module. The input to the ADC interface is from the analog circuit under test. The analog signal is then converted into digital signal of ones and zeros which can be used for the comparison purpose.

2. **Integrating the ROM code generated:**
   This includes the simulation and synthesis of the ROM HDL code generated utilizing the C code.

3. **Development of Comparator logic:**
   A HDL code for comparing the ADC output value with the values stored in ROM. This logic helps in identifying the faults present in the circuit.

4. **Reconfiguration logic on FPGA:**
   The number of ROM files depends on the number of analog circuits under test. Each analog circuit is associated with a specific fault dictionary, thereby requiring separate ROM files for each circuit. These modules are subjected to the normal design flow of FPGA to generate the bitstream. On successful generation of the bitstreams for various circuits, they are pushed into the flash memory of the FPGA. The FPGA would be loaded with one configuration file at a time based on the analog circuit under test. This can be enabled using the multiboot feature of the FPGA.

7   Conclusion

In this paper, we have proposed a new technique for diagnosing faults in analog circuits. This approach reduces the time involved in testing analog circuits. We provided the research approach detailing the system components. We also examined the feasibility of the approach and the results of the experiments conducted were also provided. This approach enables to reduce the testing time involved in the testing of analog circuits. Also the reconfiguration technique provides the flexibility of both the software and hardware. The major advantage of this would be the extensibility of the same hardware to test various other analog circuits.

References

1. Camenzind, H.: Designing Analog Chips. Virtual Bookworm.Com Pub. Inc.
2. Fault Diagnosis Using System Identification Techniques,
   http://www.personal.rdg.ac.uk/~shs99vmb/notes/asi/Lecture8.pdf
3. Lin, P.M., Elcherif, Y.S.: Computational approaches to fault dictionary. In: Ozawa, T. (ed.) Analog methods for computer-aided circuit analysis and diagnosis, pp. 325–364. M. Dekker, New York (1988)
4. Rutkowski, J.: A DC approach for analog fault dictionary determination. In: Dedieu, H. (ed.) Proc. ECCTD, Davos, pp. 877–880. Elsevier, Amsterdam (1993)
5. Hochwald, W., Bastian, J.D.: A DC Approach for Analog Fault Dictionary Determination. IEEE Tr. CAS-26, 7 (July 1979)
6. Pan, C.-Y., Cheng, K.-T.: Implicit functional testing for analog circuits. In: Proceedings of the 14th IEEE VLSI Test Symposium
7. Kabisatpathy, P., Barua, A., Sinha, S.: Fault Detection and Diagnosis in Analog Integrated Circuits Using Artificial Neural Network in a Pseudorandom Testing Scheme. In: 3rd International Conference on Electrical & Computer Engineering, ICECE 2004, Dhaka, Bangladesh, December 28-30 (2004)
8. Lin, D., Starzyk, J.A.: A Generalized Fault Diagnosis in Dynamic Analog Circuits. International Journal of Circuit Theory and Applications 30, 487–510 (2002)
9. Kabisatpathy, P., Barua, A., Sinha, S.: Fault Diagnosis of Analog Integrated Circuits. Springer, The Netherlands
10. Czaja, Z.: A Fault Diagnosis Algorithm of Analog Circuits Based on Node-Voltage Relation. In: 12th IMEKO TC1 and TC7 Joint Symposium on Man Science & Measurement, Annecy, France (September 2008)

11. Liu, R.: Testing and diagnosis of analog circuits and systems. Van Nostrand Reinhold, New York (1991)
12. Bandler, J., Salama, A.: Fault Diagnosis of Analog Circuits. Proc. IEEE 23, 1279 (1985)
13. Prasad, V.C., Babu, N.S.C.: Selection of test nodes for analog fault diagnosis in dictionary approach. IEEE Trans. I&M 49(6), 1289–1297 (2000)
14. Reconfigurable Computing,
    `http://www.netrino.com/Embedded-Systems/How-To/Reconfigurable-Computing`
15. Reconfigurable Computing,
    `http://asic-soc.blogspot.com/2007/11/reconfigurable-computing.html`
16. Compton, K., Hauck, S.: Configurable Computing: A Survey of Systems and Software. Northwestern University, Dept. of ECE Technical Report (1999)
17. Compton, K., Hauck, S., Compton, K.: An Introduction to Reconfigurable Computing. IEEE Computer Journal (2000)
18. Hauck, S.: The Roles of FPGAs in Reprogrammable Systems. Proceedings of the IEEE 86(4), 615–638 (1998)
19. Field Programmable Gate Arrays,
    `http://en.wikipedia.org/wiki/Field-programmable_gate_array`
20. Quite Universal Circuit Simulator, `http://qucs.sourceforge.net/`
21. Python Programming Language, `http://www.python.org`
22. XILINX Documentation on SPARTAN 3A, `http://www.xilinx.com`
23. Hammes, J., Bohm, A.P.W., Ross, C., Chawathe, M., Draper, B., Najjar, W.: High Performance Image Processing on FPGAs. In: Proceedings of the Los Alamos Computer Science Institute Symposium, Santa Fe, NM
24. Radunovic, B.: An Overview of Advances in Reconfigurable Computing Systems. In: Proceedings of the 32nd Hawaii International Conference on System Sciences (1999)
25. Srivastava, A.K., Sharma, A., Raval, T.: Development of Reconfigurable Analog and Digital Circuits for Plasma Diagnostics Measurement Systems. In: 18th International Toki Conference (ITC18), Ceratopia Toki, Toki Gifu Japan, December 9-12 (2008)

A Low Voltage High Performance OTA in 0.18 Micron with High Linearity

Nikhil Raj[1], Ranitesh Gupta[2], and Vikram Chopra[3]

[1] Department of Electronics and Communication Engineering,
[2] Department of Electrical Engineering,
National Institute of Technology, Kurukshetra, Haryana, 136119, India
[3] Department of Electrical and Instrumentation Engineering,
Thapar University, Patiala, Punjab, 147004, India
{nikhilquick,ranitesh01}@gmail.com, vikram.chopra@thapar.edu

Abstract. The increasing demand of personal health monitoring products with long battery life had forced designers to use of those circuits which consumes low power. Operational Transconductance Amplifier (OTA) operating in sub-threshold (weak inversion) region introduces a versatile solution for the realization of low power VLSI building blocks. This paper demonstrates a modified OTA with high linearity and better performance achieved by using High-swing improved-Wilson current mirror for low power and low-frequency applications. The achieved linearity is about $\pm$ 1.9 volt and unity gain bandwidth (UGB) of 342.30 KHz. The OTA is operated at power supply of 0.9 volt and consumes power in range of nanowatts. The OTA simulation has been performed in a standard TSMC 0.18 micrometer technology on BSIM 3v3 model using ELDO Simulator.

Keywords: Bulk-input, Low supply voltage, Linear range, subthreshold OTA, improved Wilson current mirror.

1   Introduction

Today the trend of scaling down channel length in CMOS technology to facilitate submicrometer high density systems on a single integrated circuit (IC) and emergence of portable devices like Ambulatory Brain Computer Interface (ABCI) systems, insulin pumps, hearing aids and mobile communications had led to development of circuits that consumes less power. The rapid increasing use of battery-operated portable equipment in application areas such as telecommunications and medical electronics imposes the use of low-power and small-sized circuits realized with VLSI (very large scale integrated) technologies. As the technology of biomedical instrumentation amplifier is moving towards portability, lower power consumption is highly desirable for devices which monitors patient whole day.

Circuits needed for processing of biological signals are a typical and good example of low-power and small-sized building blocks. The main features of biological signals are their low amplitude and low frequency range. In biomedical instruments to process low frequency signals, low-pass filter circuits with sufficient large time constant

N. Meghanathan et al. (Eds.): NeCoM, WiMoN, and WeST 2010, CCIS 90, pp. 712–721, 2010.
© Springer-Verlag Berlin Heidelberg 2010

are required, typically for a capacitor value of less than 5pF which in turn require very high resistance. For example, in ECG signal detection, low-pass filter required must have cut-off frequency less than 300 Hz for which use of low-power continuous-time OTA-based filters are preferred [1]. However, major limitation of conventional OTAs is its limited linear range. As device sizes are scaling down, traditional saturation-based OTAs are facing design challenges to overcome poor linearity and limited output impedance. Various techniques for extending linear range have been proposed among which one is based on source-degeneration and multitanh principle [2]. An alternative method forces to employ diodes as source degeneration elements to extend the linear range [3], but using stacked diodes in series as degeneration elements increases the need of supply voltage. In [4], the OTA uses 21-transistor operating in subthreshold mode gives a linear range of about 700 mV. The OTA referred in this paper is detailed in [5]. Since the OTA is a current source device, the output impedance of the device must be high.

This paper is focused on use of super-Wilson current mirror as a replacement of simple mirror which not increases the output impedance but improves the performance of OTA. Section 2 covers short review on bulk-driven MOS transistors, followed by basic operation of OTA and its modified architecture is discussed in section 3. In section 4, simulations results are discussed and finally conclusion in section 5.

2   Review on Bulk-Driven MOS

Threshold voltage of future CMOS technologies may not decrease much below than what are available today, creating difficulties for analog designers to design analog circuits with lower supply voltage. To support low threshold voltage devices proper scaling of supply voltage must be done to appropriately bias the device. A promising approach in low voltage analog circuits is "bulk-driven" MOSFET method where the gate-to-source voltage is set to a value sufficient to form inversion layer while the input signal is applied to bulk terminal.

In gate-driven MOS transistor, the gate-to-source voltage controls the drain current of the transistor while for a bulk-driven MOS transistor where threshold voltage is a function of the bulk-to-source voltage, controls the drain current. Using this technique, transistor can remain in active mode even at zero-input bias voltage. However, there are few drawbacks in bulk-driven transistors like one most important drawback is its low dc gain [6].

The current expression for well-input MOS transistor in subthreshold mode is given by

$$I = I_0 e^{-kV_{gs}/V_T} e^{-(1-k)V_{ws}/V_T} \qquad (1)$$

where V_{gs} and V_{ws} is the gate-to-source and well-to-source voltage, k is subthreshold exponential coefficient, I_0 is subthreshold exponential parameter, V_T $(= KT/q)$ is thermal voltage. From (1), it can be observed that dependence of k on gate and $(1-k)$ on well creates the condition that when gate is active, well remains inactive and when well is active gate is inactive.

3 Proposed OTA

3.1 The Amplifier Core

The OTA is a transconductance type device, which means that the input voltage controls an output current by means of the device transconductance, labeled g_m. This makes the OTA a voltage controlled current source (VCCS). In the past few years, engineers have improved the linearity of MOS transconductor circuits. Such improvement has been primarily in the area of above-threshold, high-power, high-frequency, continuous time filters. The architecture of OTA is shown in Fig. 1 which provides a linearity of 1.7 volt by combination of four techniques. Firstly, the well terminals of the differential-pair transistors W_1 and W_2 is used as amplifier inputs. Secondly, feedback techniques like source degeneration via S_1 and S_2 transistors whereas gate degeneration via GM_1 and GM_2 provide further improvement. Finally, B_1 and B_2 used as bump transistors. The bump-linearization technique is used to overcome parasitic effects which occur at low input voltage, generally less than 1 volt.

The P transistor act as bias current source and the remaining transistor M_{p1}, M_{p2}, M_{n3} and M_{n4} are configured as simple current mirrors. Besides, there is an offset voltage adjustment which sets V_{OS} around 5 mV less than V_{DD}. To improve OTA performance, simple current mirror used is replaced by complex mirroring, that is, High-swing improved-Wilson current mirror. This technique not only removes the offset voltage adjustment but increases output resistance compared to case of simple current mirror.

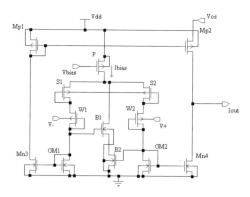

Fig. 1. Basic OTA [5]

Analyzing left half-circuit of OTA, the overall transconductance g is reduced by a feedback factor $\left(1+1/k_p+1/k_n\right)$,

$$g = \frac{1-k}{1+1/k_p + 1/k_n} \tag{2}$$

where $1/k_p$ and $1/k_n$ are the loop gain of S_1 and GM_1 transistor respectively.

From (1)

$$I \alpha\, e^{-(V_s - g V_w)/V_T} \tag{3}$$

$$\frac{I_{OUT}}{I_B} = \frac{I_d}{I_T} = \frac{I^+ - I^-}{I^+ + I^-} = \frac{e^{-(V_{s2} - g V_{w2})/V_T} - e^{-(V_{s1} - g V_{w1})/V_T}}{e^{-(V_{s2} - g V_{w2})/V_T} + e^{-(V_{s1} - g V_{w1})/V_T}} \tag{4}$$

$$\text{Solving} \quad \frac{I_{OUT}}{I_B} = \frac{e^{g V_d/V_T} - 1}{e^{g V_d/V_T} + 1} = \tanh\left(\frac{g V_d}{2 V_T}\right) \tag{5}$$

where $V_d = V_{w2} - V_{w1} = V^+ - V^-$

$$I_{OUT} = I_B \tanh\left(\frac{V_d}{V_L}\right) \tag{6}$$

where I_{out} is the output current, I_B is the bias current of P transistor, V_L is the linear range of OTA expressed as

$$V_L = 2 V_T / g \tag{7}$$

where g is the overall reduced transconductance of OTA. From tanh series expansion $\tanh\dfrac{x}{2} = \dfrac{x}{2} - \dfrac{x^3}{24} + - - -$; it can be observed that if V_L is made sufficiently high then cubic order term in the tanh series expansion can be easily neglected thereby reducing distortions of non-linearity.

3.2 High-Swing Super-Wilson Current Mirror

The current circuit is one of the most important building blocks for analog IC design. Generally, a current mirror is characterized by the current level it produces, the small-signal ac output resistance and voltage drop across it. The simple current mirror uses the principle that if gate-to-source potentials of two identical MOS transistors are equal then their channel currents are equal. In late 1967, George Wilson proposed a modified current mirror just by adding one extra transistor which increases output impedance to appreciable amount and named the circuit as Wilson current mirror. The Wilson current mirror implemented using three nMOS transistors is shown in Fig. 2

(a). The architecture consists of simple current mirror and a current to voltage converter connected in the feedback loop. If there is any increase in output current due to output voltage variation, the simple current mirror transistors senses this variation and feed back the current to input node thereby reducing gate voltage of output transistor followed by reduction in original current increase. But these current mirror suffered systematic gain error along with unequal voltages across input and output transistors. To compensate systematic gain error, Barrie Gilbert; added a fourth transistor in diode connected form in the input branch and later this circuit became famous by name improved Wilson current mirror [7] as shown in Fig. 2 (b). These circuits require an input voltage of two diode drops and output compliance voltage incorporates a diode drop plus saturation voltage. Such diode drop made Wilson mirror unattractive for low-power design units. To overcome this, a new Wilson topology was introduced [8], which sense the output current at low input voltage of a diode drop plus a saturation voltage whereas output senses only two saturation voltage. As seen from architecture, the diode connected transistor on input side biased by current source I_b, causes the input voltage to decrease much lower than gate voltage needed as in case of simple mirrors to sink input current. This makes it a low voltage high-swing improved-Wilson current mirror as shown in Fig. 3. The mirror achieves high output resistance by using negative feedback and is directly proportional to the magnitude of the loop-gain of the feedback action from the output current to the gate of output transistor M_{n3}. The transistor M_{n1} and M_{n2} samples the I_{OUT} and compares it with I_{in}. In combination with current source load I_{in}, transistor M_{n1} act as a common source amplifier used to maintain gate voltage of M_{n3} to avoid mismatching of I_{OUT} to I_{in}. Neglecting 2nd order effects, the output resistance r_{out} is approximated as:

$$r_{out} \approx g_{m1}r_{o1}r_{o3} \tag{8}$$

where, g_{m1} and r_{o1} are transconductance and output resistance of M_{n1} whereas r_{o3} is output resistance of M_{n3}.

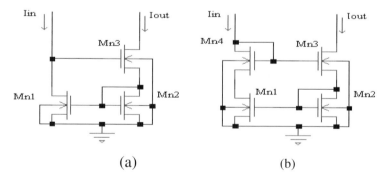

Fig. 2. (a) Wilson current mirror, (b) Modified Wilson current mirror

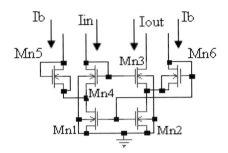

Fig. 3. High-swing improved Wilson current mirror

3.3 Proposed OTA

The proposed architecture of OTA using high-swing improved-Wilson current mirror is shown in Fig. 4. The architecture works on low supply thereby introducing appreciable reduction in power consumption. A bias current generator circuit is attached to OTA which generates current in the range of nanoamperes.

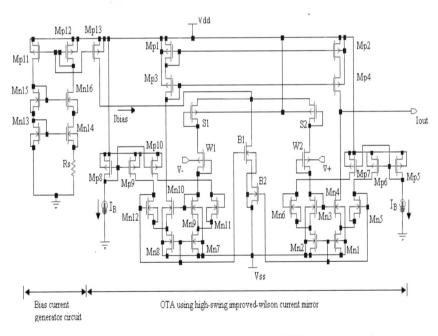

Fig. 4. Proposed OTA using High-swing improved Wilson current mirror

Transistors $M_{n13} - M_{n16}$ and $M_{p11} - M_{p12}$ along with R_s comprises current generator circuit. As the source-to-gate voltage of M_{P11} and M_{P12} are equal their corresponding currents are equal, i.e. $I_{D11} = I_{D12}$ (neglecting channel length modulation). Furthermore, it can be noted that $I_{D13} = I_{D11}$ and $I_{D14} = I_{D13}$.

The equation for drain current of MOS transistor is given by

$$I_D = \frac{1}{2}\mu_n C_{ox}\frac{W}{L}(V_{GS} - V_{Tn})^2 \tag{9}$$

Solving for V_{GS}

$$V_{GS} = \sqrt{\frac{2I_D}{\mu_n C_{ox}(W/L)}} + V_{Tn} \tag{10}$$

In Fig. 3

$$V_{GS,n13} = V_{GS,n14} + I_{D,n14}R_S \tag{11}$$

From (10)

$$\sqrt{\frac{2I_{D,n13}}{\mu_n C_{ox}(W/L)_{Mn13}}} = \sqrt{\frac{2I_{D,n14}}{\mu_n C_{ox}(W/L)_{Mn14}}} + I_{D,n14}R_S \tag{12}$$

Rearranging above expression and solving for $I_{D,p12}$ by equating equivalent currents, the $I_{D,p12}$ is given as

$$I_{D,p12} = \frac{2}{\mu_n C_{ox}(W/L)_{Mn13}}\frac{1}{R_S{}^2}\left(1 - \sqrt{\frac{(W/L)_{Mn13}}{(W/L)_{Mn14}}}\right)^2 \tag{13}$$

The output current I_{bias}, that is, $I_{D,p13}$ is now the function of $I_{D,p12}$. By adjusting the aspect ratio of M_{p13} relative to M_{p12}, desired I_{bias} can be obtained. The W/L ratio of M_{p13} is kept four times lower than M_{p12}, which results in output current $I_{D,p13} = I_{bias} = I_{D,p12}/4$.

4   Simulation Results

The design of low voltage, high performance OTA circuit on TSMC 0.18 micron technology provide low power consumption exhibiting performance levels that satisfy the demands of state-of-art mixed-signal circuits. The simulations were performed under normal condition (room temperature) using ELDO Spice Simulator and BSIM 3v3 model. Current generator circuit generates I_{bias} of 65nA at $R_S = 10K\Omega$. The supply voltage is kept at 0.9 volt. Fig. 5 shows the linear response of OTA. The linearity extends to range about ± 1.9 volt with no offset voltage adjustment. Fig. 6 shows the ac response of OTA under no load condition. The achieved phase margin is

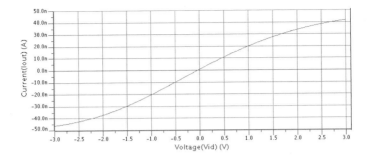

Fig. 5. Linear response of proposed of OTA

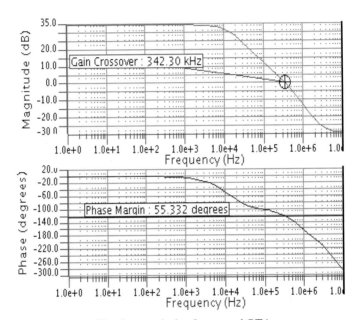

Fig. 6. ac analysis of proposed OTA

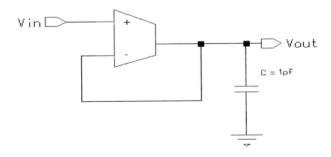

Fig. 7. Follower integrator

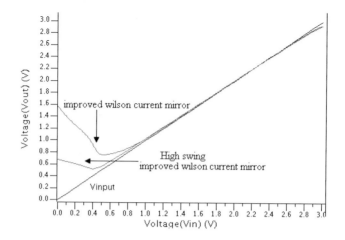

Fig. 8. Follower integrator DC characteristics at 1pF load

5 Conclusion

This paper explored the approach of low-voltage OTA design using the bulk-driven technique and enhancement of output impedance using high-swing improved-Wilson current mirror. The design of such low voltage, high performance OTA circuit on TSMC 0.18 micron technology satisfies the required parameters for its implementation not only in power-saving devices but also in biomedical portable devices like biomedical implantable sensors, disk read channel integrated circuits (ICs), video filters, ADSL front-ends, and RF ICs. However, since several biomedical signals have frequencies much less than 342.30 KHz, so less emphasis has been made on achieving high UGB.

Acknowledgement

The author would like to thank R. Sarpeshkar, R. F. Lyon, and C. A. Mead for the measurement assistance and meaningful discussions on bulk-input OTA.

References

[1] Solis-Bustos, S., Silva-Martínez, J., Maloberti, F., Sánchez-Sinencio, E.: A 60 db dynamic-range CMOS sixth-order 2.4 Hz lowpass filter for medical applications. IEEE Trans. Circuits Syst. II, Analog Digit. Signal Process. Conf. 47, 1391–1398 (2000)

[2] Furth, P.M., Andreou, A.G.: Linearised differential transconductor in subthreshold CMOS. Electron. Lett. 31(7), 547–554 (1995)

[3] Watts, L., Kerns, D.A., Lyon, R.F., Mead, C.A.: Improved implementation of the silicon cochlea. IEEE J. Solid-State Circuits 27(5), 692–700 (1992)

[4] Opris, I.E., Kovacs, G.T.A.: Large-signal subthreshold CMOS transconductance amplifier. Electronics Letters 31(9), 718–720 (1995)

[5] Sarpeshkar, R., Lyon, R.F., Mead, C.A.: A low-power widelinear-range transconductance amplifier. Analog Integrated Circuits Signal Processing 13, 123–151 (1997)

[6] Ferreira, L., Pimenta, T., Moreno, R.: An ultra-low voltage ultra-low-power CMOS miller OTA with rail-to-rail inpu/output swing. IEEE TCAS II 54(10), 843–847 (2007)

[7] Hart, B.L., Barker, R.W.J.: D. C. Matching Errors in the Wilson Current Source. Electronics Letters 12(15), 389–390 (1976)

[8] Minch, B.: Low-Voltage Wilson Current Mirrors in CMOS. In: IEEE ISCAS, New Orleans, LA, USA, pp. 2220–2223 (2007)

Author Index

Printing: Mercedes-Druck, Berlin
Binding: Stein+Lehmann, Berlin